SOURCEBOOK
OF
PLANNING
INFORMATION

'The correction of Textual Errors (Courteous Reader) is a work of time, and that hath taken wing. The more faults thou findest, the larger field is presented to thy humanity to practise in. Be indulgent in thy censure, and remember that error, whether Manual or Mental, is an inheritance, descending upon us, from the first of our Race '—Errata leaf in Francis Bacon's *Of the advancement and proficience of learning* (Oxford, 1640)

SOURCEBOOK OF PLANNING INFORMATION

A discussion of sources of information for use in urban and regional planning, and in allied fields

BRENDA WHITE

ALA

*Research Fellow
Department of Urban Design and
Regional Planning
University of Edinburgh*

CLIVE BINGLEY  LONDON

FIRST PUBLISHED 1971 BY CLIVE BINGLEY LTD
16 PEMBRIDGE ROAD LONDON W11
SET IN 10 ON 12 POINT LINOTYPE TIMES
AND PRINTED IN GREAT BRITAIN BY THE CENTRAL PRESS (ABERDEEN) LTD
COPYRIGHT © BRENDA WHITE 1971
ALL RIGHTS RESERVED
0 85157 121 2

CONTENTS

LIST OF ILLUSTRATIONS

PREFACE

ONE OF THE RECOMMENDATIONS arising out of the survey of information requirements in planning carried out during 1968 and 1969 with the financial support of the Office for Scientific and Technical Information, was that a comprehensive monograph text should be prepared to provide guidance to available sources of information both for planners and for librarians and information specialists. This book is the direct result of that recommendation.

In the course of the text, I have endeavoured to describe the nature and scope of planning and the ways in which it is evolving. It is as well, however, at this preliminary point, to indicate that planning, in the context of this book, is a shorthand word to indicate the very wide range of subjects and activities with which it is concerned, a range which takes in areas of study and practice such as population, regional science, urban studies, the environment generally, traffic and transportation planning, and many others whose interests are so closely involved with the central planning activity that they cannot be divorced—indeed, they are all increasingly viewed as contributory parts of a total process.

The volume is intended for two audiences. Firstly, and I think primarily, it is intended for planners, and the planners of this audience are not only those who are formally qualified in planning but also the growing number of specialists in subjects related to planning, who are now working within the planning field, whether their activity is in practice, in teaching, or in research. I hope that the various chapters of the book will demonstrate to them the great variety of information sources in all categories which are available for exploitation. Secondly, it is intended for librarians and information specialists who may require guidance to the literature of planning, and for them I have tried to set out something of what planning is about so that the sources described can be seen against the background of their use. The number of librarians working specifically in planning in Britain is as yet small, but I am confident that it will grow, because it is an increasingly accepted fact that it is vitally important that planners should be provided with good information.

Despite its size, the book is not, and was not intended to be, comprehensive in its inclusion of material. Its scope is quite clearly defined in a number of ways, and an elucidation of these limits here will perhaps reduce the frustration of readers. In the first place, I have excluded data from the book, except insofar as data management is discussed as a planning technique in chapter 11. Imprecise usage of the words data and information has resulted in confusion between the two: what are excluded from this text are the data which are gathered in the course of surveys and which are used in raw, or nearly raw, form for basic planning purposes; what are included are the various physical presentations of processed information, whether in narrative, tabular, or graphic form. This is not a semantic nicety, it is a functional distinction, and I have tried to adhere to these definitions in my own use of the words as they occur throughout the book.

Secondly, the information sources discussed are largely British in origin, in some chapters exclusively so. There is a tendency to be carried away by the flood of books, reports, and journals with promising titles which emanate from other countries, in particular from the United States, but so often it is the case that behind the title lies a text of very local interest conceived in a peculiarly local context. I have therefore restricted coverage to material which is applicable to British planning and its associated studies, and have included foreign sources only where they seem to be relevant, the main weight of these falling in the chapter on documentary sources.

Institutional sources of information have been omitted. Principally, this was because the forthcoming directory from the Centre for Environmental Studies (see chapter 13) will cover this area fairly fully, although not in great detail; but it was also because to cover such sources adequately would have substantially increased the size of this volume, and would have delayed its compilation still further. This did not seem justified in the light of the anticipated CES publication.

The terminal date for systematic collection of material was December 31 1970, but additional material has been added as it

8

came to hand up to the end of March 1971. Most of the titles mentioned in the text have been examined personally, but where this has not been possible, the references have been checked with reliable sources. Where it has not proved possible to do even this, I have omitted the reference. I hope therefore to have achieved as high a degree of bibliographical accuracy as is humanly possible. The only journal title which is abbreviated is the *Journal of the Town Planning Institute,* which is rendered throughout as *JTPI.* Where the place of publication is London, only publisher and date are indicated; elsewhere the place is given also.

Many changes have taken place while this book has been a-writing, notably in central government organisation. To the best of my ability, the contents are up to date as at March 1971. With regard to the former Ministry of Housing and Local Government, which figures prominently throughout the book, I have retained this name where events or publications before its amalgamation into the Department of the Environment are under discussion; elsewhere, the new form is used. The Town Planning Institute became the Royal Town Planning Institute too late for the necessary amendments to be made.

So many people have contributed to this volume, wittingly and unwittingly, directly and indirectly, that it is impossible to name them all. It is, however, possible, and a pleasure, to acknowledge my debt to those who have read sections of the book in draft and who have offered constructive advice: to Donald Cross, of Manchester University; Mrs Edith Frame and James Milligan of Strathclyde University; George Stewart, of the Ordnance Survey; and in particular to Dr Gordon Collins, of Leeds University, who expanded my draft on air photographs with an authority which I could never hope to achieve. It is hardly necessary to add the rider that the faults of the book are mine, and not theirs. Many people have answered my letters of enquiry, and I thank them collectively. I have received much help from librarians who have allowed me to use their (usually overcrowded) libraries and who have put their resources at my disposal, and I have been most grateful for this to the librarians of the Department of Town and Country Planning of Heriot-Watt University; the University of Edinburgh; the Map Room of the National Library of Scotland; the Fine Art Department of Edinburgh Public Libraries; and the Scottish Office. In particular, I should like to acknowledge the debt which I owe to Wilfred Pearson, Chief Librarian of the Department of the Environment, who has not only allowed me to make full use of his library resources but also given me the benefit of his considerable experience in providing information for planners; I have learned a great deal from him over the last four years. I am most grateful to the Regional Studies Association for an award from the John Madge Memorial Fund, which has helped the compilation of the book in several practical ways. Mrs Peggy McArthur has typed the entire manuscript with an equanimity which has been a continuing source of moral support, particularly through the final test of physical endurance necessary to meet the deadline. My family and friends have provided comfort and hospitality on countless occasions, and I thank them all. But my largest debt of gratitude is to my husband, who has helped me in so many ways, tangible and intangible, over the years; to him and to our small daughter who is not sure what it is all about, but who suffers it with remarkable patience, I dedicate this book.

BRENDA WHITE

Planning Research Unit
Department of Urban Design and Regional Planning
University of Edinburgh
June 1971

1

THE HISTORY OF PLANNING

FROM THE EARLIEST TIMES, wherever men congregated together, there were settlements. As long ago as 2,500 BC there is evidence of an order being imposed on the layout of a settlement; and so the history of the town as artefact stretches back for five thousand years. Its origins lie in Egypt and Asia, in the ancient Maya cities of Central America, in the empires of Greece and of Rome.

The earliest towns planned as new foundations on virgin ground were those of the Greeks. The first known town planner was Hippodamus of Miletus who, in the fifth century BC, laid out Piraeus, Thurii, and perhaps Rhodes; and to whom is generally ascribed the first use in Europe of the gridiron plan, whose criss-cross pattern of straight streets has been a recurring feature in town planning through the centuries, even to the present day. As the Greek empire stretched eastwards, a chain of strategically placed imperial outpost towns was established (Alexander the Great was responsible for the creation of nearly sixty new towns), the focus and strength of the empire gradually shifting from the west towards the east.

In the same way, Rome reached towards the east, and in the second century BC overran Greece and established similar strategic outposts to preserve her empire. Rome also reached to the west, the final expansion of her empire, the conquest of Britain, beginning in 43 AD. The Romans were a thoroughly urbanised society, well aware of the advantages of properly organised towns, and the generals who arrived in Britain ' carried army-issue town-planning schemes in their knapsacks '.[1] The history of British town planning begins with the Romans : before their arrival, there is no evidence to suggest that anything existed except unordered settlements. They stayed a long time, nearly four hundred years, and founded many

11

towns—Caerwent, Silchester, Winchester, Colchester, Cirencester, and of course London, among them—all laid out on the regular grid-iron pattern, all containing forum, amphitheatre, temples, and public baths as standard features.

The focus of the Roman empire moved eastwards, as that of the Greek empire had done, in 326 AD, when a new city was created for the emperor. Constantinople, founded on a promontory on the tip of which was already established the Greek colony of Byzantium, was built at great speed as a matter of political necessity, and while the city was not the artistic marvel which the emperor desired, it nevertheless became, in subsequent rebuilt and expanded forms, the centre of a culture and an empire that was to last for more than a thousand years.

Scarcely a hundred years after the foundation of her eastern capital, the western empire of Rome collapsed, and the occupying legions retired, leaving the countries of western Europe to regress into the Dark Ages.

From an urban viewpoint, Britain was fortunate in her conquerors. The Normans, who invaded in the eleventh century, were, like the Romans, fully versed in urban settlement, bringing experience of town plantation in France into England. The towns of the Middle Ages, from William the Conqueror's first settlement at Hastings, through the great reign of Edward I (1272-1307) to the last example of medieval town-building at Queenborough in 1368, were in many cases established, as were the Greek and the Roman towns, for the strategic purpose of controlling a conquered population—Edward I's chain of castle-towns in Wales, from Caernarvon to Harlech, is the finest example of this—and conformed to the same sort of rigid grid pattern.

As the end of the Middle Ages saw the end (temporarily) of practical town building, so the beginning of the Renaissance saw the emergence of urban theory, urban aesthetics, the hypothetical creation of the ideal city. More's *Utopia* and Bacon's *Bensalem* were products of the Renaissance period in England. On the continent, the discovery in the fifteenth century of the third century manuscripts of Vitruvius, containing his plans for an ideal city, provided a catalyst and a pattern for successive Renaissance planners from Alberti in 1458 to Scamozzi in 1615. It was a characteristic of

12

the Renaissance that new thought preceded new art, which in turn preceded new applied skills such as architecture; and new developments overall came first on the continent and quite considerably later in England. So it was not until the seventeenth century that practical manifestations of a new town planning appeared in England: in Inigo Jones' Covent Garden piazza, in the quadrangles of Oxford and Cambridge, in the large-scale plans of Wren and Evelyn for the rebuilding of London after the Great Fire of 1666. The grand sweep of these two plans, the straight broad avenues, the piazzas, the carefully calculated magnificence of the views down the avenues, broke away from the conventional grid patterns and introduced the new European ideal, the baroque city, into England. The fact that neither of the plans ever became a reality in no way lessens their importance or their influence.

Jones' Covent Garden, the development of the London squares (Bloomsbury was the first), the plans of Wren and Evelyn, were in fact the forerunners of the classical Georgian tradition in town planning and architecture, in which the new freedom of the overall plan was coupled with close attention to classical detail in the manner of its execution. The Georgian period, embracing most of the eighteenth century and several decades of the nineteenth, saw some of the finest statements of the art of town planning and urban architecture: James Craig's new town of Edinburgh; the Bath of John Wood, father and son; John Nash's west end of London; the centre of Newcastle, planned by Dobson and executed by Grainger; and other lesser examples, such as New Brighton and Bournemouth.

Such comprehensive planning or re-planning of towns is rarely met, unless occasioned by disasters such as the Great Fire or, in this century, saturation bombing, being the product of a peculiar combination of circumstances, not the least important of which is finance. As the nineteenth century progressed, town planning and town building acquired an increasingly functional purpose, the clearest evidence of which was the rapid establishment of transport towns—ports for sea transport, the towns which grew with the coming of the canals, finally the railway towns—and the equally rapid growth of existing towns to house industry and its concomitant population. One of the features of British life in the nineteenth

13

century was the enormous difference in living conditions between the rich and the poor, and nothing illustrates more clearly this vast gulf between two strata of society than the physical environment in which they lived: the elegance of Nash and Craig on the one hand, the squalor of the growing slums on the other. For the nineteenth century saw a rapid growth in population, and more particularly, the concentration of an increasing proportion of it into towns which had been designed to accommodate neither the developing industries nor the people. The urgent need in manufacturing towns and the main seaports to pack as many people as possible into the centre of the town, close to their work, resulted in the growth of unplanned, solidly residential areas, the houses seriously overcrowded, open space an unknown commodity.

By the middle of the century, conditions were sufficiently bad—overcrowded, insanitary, ridden with crime and disease—to provoke a series of legislative measures aimed at alleviating them. The Public Health Act of 1848 was followed by the housing acts of Shaftesbury (1851), Torrens (1868), and Cross (1875), and the measures of all these were consolidated in the Public Health Act of 1875; the Housing of the Working Classes Act of 1890 re-enacted with amendments the provisions of Shaftesbury's 1851 Act, reiterating the responsibility of municipal authorities for housing and their role in solving the problem within their own areas, a role which private enterprise had signally failed to fulfil.

Nineteenth century town planning, then, was primarily a matter of public health, of relieving overcrowding, of creating better sanitary conditions. The second half of the century did see an improvement: central urban areas were improved within practical limitations, essential services were provided, streets were improved. But in most cases it was difficult to change the centre of a town whose physical structure was firmly established, and improvements were slow, piecemeal and limited in extent. Frustration with existing conditions certainly contributed to the natural human urge to begin afresh, which resulted in the creation of new model villages and towns to house factory workers: generally these were new communities built round a new factory—Robert Owen's New Lanark, Titus Salt's Saltaire—or built as part of an expansion of an existing business—Cadbury Brothers at Bournville, Lever Brothers at Port

14

Sunlight. This philanthropic urge, the desire to create better living conditions for human beings, culminated in Ebenezer Howard's plans for a self-contained garden city, combining the advantages of the town with those of the country, originally published in 1898 in his book *Tomorrow*, and put into practice (partially, at least) at Letchworth in 1903, and subsequently at Welwyn in 1920.

Even before the first garden city, the development of public transport facilities had encouraged an increasing number of people to migrate from town centres to the outer areas of their towns, thus to live at a distance from their place of work, and this resulted in a corresponding increase in suburban residential development, and the emergence of the garden suburb. The most famous exemplar of the garden suburb was the low-density housing scheme at Hampstead, designed by Raymond Unwin and built in 1907, which achieved wide acclaim and publicity and had considerable influence on subsequent suburban developments. Unwin was an architect, and his garden suburb was an architectural expression of the good environment. Howard's ideals went much wider and deeper, conceiving the garden city as a self contained unit providing not only homes in a pleasant environment but also the jobs and other facilities to go with them; and in fact the garden suburb has been criticised as a degenerate version of a few of Howard's principles.

Finally, out of these sixty years (since the 1848 Public Health Act) of gradual improvement in public health and housing, sparked by practical example at home and abroad[2] and pressurised by the campaigning of such bodies as the Garden City Association and the National Housing Reform Council, came the first statutory encouragement to town planning, the Housing, Town Planning, etc, Act of 1909.

The scope of the Act was limited. It had nothing to offer the existing urban areas. Its emphasis was solely on raising standards of new development. It enabled local authorities (subject to obtaining permission from the Local Government Board) to prepare town planning schemes for controlling the development of new suburban housing areas, thus aiming to control the independent private building of new garden suburbs. Despite the practical limitations of the legislation (and few schemes were actually completed under

15

the 1909 Act) '. . . the importance of a first step often derives from its priority rather than its magnitude, and it may well be judged that this was so in the present instance. Few would be disposed to claim more for the town planning measure of 1909 than that it was a symptom of change in the orientation of policy and outlook in matters of urban improvement.'[3]

Nevertheless a town planning movement had been born, and slowly it began to grow. In 1909, the School of Civic Design was founded at Liverpool University. In 1910, the Royal Institute of British Architects held the first British town planning conference. In 1914, the Town Planning Institute was formed, its members mainly architects, civil engineers, surveyors and lawyers.

Town planning in practice was established as an architectural conception, exemplified in Unwin's low-density residential suburb. In 1911, the Town Planning Committee of the Royal Institute of British Architects (a body of some influence) issued a statement *Suggestions to promoters of town planning schemes,* which asserted that the supreme role of designer of the town plan should be given to the architect. Unwin, himself an architect, firmly endorsed this view in his book *Town planning in practice* (1909). The main critic of architectural supremity was Patrick Geddes, who propounded his comprehensive view of town planning in his books *City development* (1904) and later in *Cities in evolution* (1915). Geddes was an ecologist whose approach to town planning was more sociological than that of any of his contemporaries, and who attached great importance to the influence of the environment on human life. Criticism of the administration of town planning came from J S Nettlefold who, in his *Practical town planning* (1914), proposed the replacement of the Local Government Board by one new comprehensive central authority to govern all aspects of town planning, including the design of new roads, and the application of such planning throughout the town and not only to its suburbs.

The first revision of town planning legislation, the Housing, Town Planning, etc, Act of 1919, did not introduce any new concept of planning itself or of its administration (the Ministry of Health had replaced the Local Government Board as central authority by then). It became obligatory for boroughs and urban districts with populations of over twenty thousand to prepare town

16

planning schemes. A time limit was fixed for preparation of such schemes, but this was subsequently extended and finally repealed (in the Town and Country Planning Act of 1932).

The 1919 Act introduced state subsidies for housing. Thus the 1920's saw the suburban juxtaposition of council housing and private development. The 1920's also saw rapid developments in transportation, which fostered better communications, not only between town centre and suburb but also between town and town. Hand in hand with these developments grew the concept of decentralisation, both of population and of industry, and the realisation that for such a policy to be effective, planning had to be on a regional or even a national scale: no longer could each individual town be considered in isolation.[4] Strong incentive towards national and regional planning was provided by the example of the United States, where master plans had been prepared for several regions. In the United Kingdom, there was the example of the second garden city, Welwyn, planned as a self-contained satellite town to London, in which people would both live *and* work.

Legislation did not keep pace with the new concepts, which were in any case held by only a minority and not reflected in practice. The Town Planning Act of 1925 was a consolidating Act, and the first concerned solely with town planning. The Town and Country Planning Act of 1932 (similar legislation for Scotland was passed in the same year) was the first to refer to country planning, and extended planning powers to almost any type of land, whether built-up or undeveloped; but the administrative machinery for putting a planning scheme into operation was so cumbersome as to be inimical to positive planning. ' The noteworthy characteristic of a planning scheme was its regulatory nature. It did not secure that development would take place: it merely secured that if it did take place in any particular part of the area covered by the scheme it would be controlled in certain ways.'[5]

The 1932 Act also introduced the practice of interim development control. This power was granted to a local authority after it had made a resolution to prepare or adopt a planning scheme for any area under its control; any person then wishing to build in that area must first obtain permission, or else his building was liable to be removed without compensation if it conflicted with the planning

17

scheme. By 1939, more than half the country was subject to interim development control.

Thus at the outbreak of war in 1939, formal planning in Britain had achieved little positive success. There were too many planning authorities and little coordination between them, so that each planning scheme was prepared in isolation. More fundamentally, local authorities were financially hamstrung by having to pay compensation out of their own resources if they refused development.

The war years saw the emergence of more workable administrative machinery in the nature of central control; they saw three significant reports which fostered the concept of wide-scale planning; and finally, through the destruction of so many cities, or areas of cities, they provided the opportunity to start afresh and to introduce new measures.

Administratively, although planning was still the preserve of the local authorities (over 1,400 in 1944) central control was tightened up by the creation, under the Minister of Town and Country Planning Act of 1943, of the Ministry of Town and Country Planning, charged with the responsibility for ' securing consistency and continuity in the framing and execution of a national policy with respect to the use and development of land '. (In Scotland, central responsibility still rested, as before, with the Department of Health for Scotland). But the total planning function was still fragmented, for the Ministry of Health remained the central authority for housing, and the Board of Trade was responsible for the location of industry.

A national policy for the location of industry was one of the many far-seeing recommendations of the Barlow Report (*Report of the Royal Commission on the Distribution of the Industrial Population*, HMSO, 1940, Cmnd 6153). The commission was initially set up before the outbreak of war to study the problem of the depressed areas, a problem which rapidly disappeared in the face of the war effort; but its wide terms of reference—to enquire into the cause of and probable change in the geographical distribution of the industrial population and to propose remedial measures—resulted in a report which ' . . . is of significance not merely because it is an important historical landmark, but also because some of its major policy recommendations have been accepted by all post-war govern-

18

ments as a basis for planning policy. Only recently have these policies been questioned.'[6] This comprehensive national view of planning was reiterated in two subsequent reports of major importance. The Scott Report (*Report of the Committee on Land Utilisation in Rural Areas,* HMSO, 1942, Cmnd 6378) was concerned with preservation rather than with initiation, its recommendations laying the foundation of a national policy of countryside planning. The Uthwatt Report (*Report of the Expert Committee on Compensation and Betterment,* HMSO, 1942, Cmnd 6386) proposed a comprehensive system of national ownership of development rights in all undeveloped land. This was the trilogy of reports on which new planning legislation would be based when times were more propitious.

Other reports of a different kind contributed to the growing receptiveness of the British public to planning for the future. Public interest in planning was already there in any case, arising from a general desire to create out of the devastation of war, something better than what had gone before, and it was fired by practical plans for reconstruction and development presented by leading planners such as Sir Patrick Abercrombie, notably for London itself, but also for many other towns and cities which had been the target of enemy action. And so the stage was set, and the climate created. ' The early post-war years were times of great enthusiasm for ideas. Plans were drawn up for rebuilding our blitzed towns and they incorporated many of the ideas which have since become so commonly accepted as to make repetition now boring and unfruitful . . . Whatever criticisms we may have of some of these schemes today, they were, in fact, immense enterprises from which almost all later ideas in city planning developed.'[7]

The new administrative framework within which planning would function was established in 1947. The Town and Country Planning Act of 1947 (and companion legislation for Scotland) introduced a new concept of planning, a new legal framework at both national and local level. In place of the multitude of local planning authorities, planning powers were vested in counties and county boroughs in England and Wales, in counties and large burghs in Scotland. In England and Wales, most counties operated a system of delegation of some planning powers to county districts within their areas, though in Scotland no such system was practised. The planning

19

scheme of pre-war planning was replaced by the development plan; further, the legislation was no longer permissive, planning authorities being now obliged by law to prepare a development plan for their area. The plan was to show in detail how the area was to be developed, the proposals being based on a survey of existing land use and likely requirements in the future; the area was to be re-surveyed every five years, and necessary modifications incorporated into the original plan. Control over development was achieved by the necessity for obtaining planning permission before any development could take place. The development plan in all its detail was subject to the approval of the Minister, who had the power to stipulate changes before approval was given; the right of appeal to the Minister was available to private developers regarding decisions of the planning authority on development control, and the Minister had power to confirm, modify, or revoke any such decisions.

Thus was set up the framework within which British planning has operated, and still operates over a large area of the country, since World War II. The achievements of British planning in these years have been considerable, and the system has been admired and envied in many countries. Within it, and sometimes despite it, planning in Britain has become a recogisable and recognised force, whose concept and practice have been developed by problems which were largely unforeseen in 1947, until that system, so innovatory in its day, has in turn been outgrown and superseded by another new system introduced in 1968 though not yet fully implemented, within which the new concepts and the new practices will be able to develop to meet the problems and the challenge of the 1970's and beyond.

REFERENCES

1 Colin Bell and Rose Bell *City fathers: the early history of town planning in Britain* (Barrie and Rockliff, 1969) 7.

2 T C Horsfall *The improvement of the dwellings and surroundings of the people: the example of Germany* (Manchester, Manchester UP, 1904). The most influential exposition of the merits of continental methods of housing and planning as opposed to the demerits of the British system.

20

3 William Ashworth *The genesis of modern British town planning* (Routledge and Kegan Paul, 1954) 167.

4 H Warren and W R Davidge (*eds*) *Decentralisation of population and industry: a new principle in town planning* (P S King, 1930). The first major statement of the necessity for a national policy for planned decentralisation, contained in papers given at a London symposium.

5 J B Cullingworth *Town and country planning in England and Wales* (Allen and Unwin, third edition 1970) 24.

6 J B Cullingworth *op cit* 27.

7 Wilfred Burns Presidential address to the Town Planning Institute 1967 *JTPI* 53(8) September/October 1967 329.

2

THE MODERN DEVELOPMENT
OF PLANNING

IT IS NOT THE PURPOSE of this book to discuss in detail the evolution of planning thought and practice from 1947 to the present day—the ramifications are so diverse, and the impetus which has caused planning to develop so rapidly in the last decade has by no means slackened, the subject in sum is so huge that it extends far beyond the confines of this pair of covers. Nevertheless, since it is the purpose of this chapter, and of the preceding chapter, to provide a historical and conceptual background to what follows (particularly for those readers who are not involved in planning) a short and necessarily summary account of the main forces bearing upon planning since 1947 and the developments in which these have resulted is appropriate here.

The two major influences in British planning since the end of World War II have been the colossal and then unanticipated increases in population and in traffic, particularly, in the latter instance, the rise in private car ownership. The planning machinery, as established in 1947, has proved inadequate to cope with these factors, for the principal reason that the legislation called for the preparation of plans for self-contained areas of the country and made no provision for liaison or cooperation between these. The need to cope with them, and the growing recognition that the only measures which would do so were those conceived on a national or at least regional scale, has led to the broadening of the spatial base of planning in the sense that the smallest areal unit which can usefully form a basis for practical planning is now seen to be the sub-region, the town or city within the context of its sphere of influence. The necessity to plan major road networks invalidated the self-contained local plan, as did the necessity to control and manipulate the distribution of population and of industry as part of a national economic plan. It was evident that since Britain was a small island with only a limited amount of land available for each of her vital functions (some of which had already been wasted by suburban sprawl over large areas of mineral wealth and agricultural land), it was essential to her survival that the available land and resources, both natural and human, be apportioned as efficiently as possible.

The roots of British regional planning, in the sense of the allocation of national resources down to regional level, go back to the 1930's, the decade which witnessed the emergence of the depressed regions resulting from the decline of long-established industries, and also the appointment of the Barlow Commission on the Distribution of the Industrial Population specifically to study the problems of these areas (see also chapter 1). The Barlow Report laid the basis of regional planning in Britain. It stressed the economic and social disadvantages of the major urban areas (although it also acknowledged the benefits accruing from them) and forecast that further growth of these areas could constitute a serious handicap to the nation's life and development; in particular, the commissioners were aware of the dangers inherent in the expansion of London and the continuance of migration to the metropolis and the whole south east region, and viewed this growth as a severe disadvantage to the rest of the country and, in particular, to the depressed areas. Their solution, viewing the nation as a whole, was that industrial concentrations and their concomitant population should be decentralised, and that by means of a policy of relocation a balanced distribution of industrial and human resources should be achieved throughout the country, further achieving within each region a sufficient diversification of industry to insure against further depression resulting from the run-down of a single major industry. Since the implementation of such a policy demanded a national overview, the commissioners required that a new central authority be created to carry it through, although they were not unanimous in their definition of the powers to be given to this authority. The Barlow Report's recommendations were finally formulated in the Distribution of Industry Act of 1945, which gave to the Board of Trade the

23

national responsibility for the distribution of industry and the power of maintaining a list of special development areas which were eligible for special economic promotion. Firms moving to these areas were eligible for financial assistance and the board itself could purchase land on which to erect industrial premises as a positive inducement to industry; trading estates also qualified for loans to establish factories. The Town and Country Planning Act 1947 also provided the negative power of the Industrial Development Certificate (IDC) which had to be held before any factory buildings over five thousand square feet (three thousand square feet in London and the congested regions) could be erected, and which would be awarded only if the development was in accordance with national policy on the proper distribution of industry. ' With these two Acts, the board was in a position to promote industrial dispersal to the development areas by the twin policy of industrial control and financial inducement—a system which has remained in operation throughout the post-war period '.[1] But December 1970 saw a relaxation in the IDC controls: exemption limits have been raised from five to ten thousand square feet and from three to five thousand square feet according to region.

Although the Barlow Report and its proposals were born into the atmosphere of post-war enthusiasm described in the previous chapter, the 1950's did not see a continuation of the concept of regional planning into practice, and the twin policy of positive inducement and negative control was not practised with any assiduity. Further Distribution of Industry Acts were passed in 1950 and 1958, but there remained, however, ' growing unease about the adequacy of the government's policy for tackling the location of industry as a national problem and not merely as a development area problem '.[2] Nor was the machinery of town and country planning geared to provide a solution to the problem, for in it there was no bridge between central and local government levels, no provision for regional policy or regional physical planning beyond those embodied in the advisory regional plans of the immediate post-war years. The first signs of change in official thinking on regional policy emerged in the Local Employment Act of 1960, which repealed the previous Distribution of Industry Acts and abolished the development areas in favour of ' a more flexible

24

approach . . . whereby the government could intervene to counteract unemployment wherever it occurred '.[3] The emphasis thus shifted from a concentration on narrowly specified areas to a broader interest in the development of a region as a whole, and in the balance between one region and another within a national framework. The concept of growth points, first introduced in 1952 by the Scottish Council (Development and Industry), was promoted as a positive policy, centres favourable to growth which would form the focus of investment and economic growth within the less prosperous regions.

The re-birth of positive regional planning on this broader scale can be dated from 1963. In this year appeared the National Economic Development Council's manifesto *Conditions favourable to faster growth* (HMSO, 1963) which stated that ' a successful regional development programme would make it easier to achieve a national growth programme '. In the same year, the government issued its White Paper on the London region *London—employment: housing: land* (HMSO, 1963, Cmnd 1952) which stated ' that the need to match jobs, land, transport and housing over the next twenty years in London and south east England calls for a regional plan '. Finally, this year of regional renascence witnessed the first two full-scale regional studies in the form of White Papers, *Central Scotland: a programme for development and growth* (Edinburgh, HMSO, 1963, Cmnd 2188) and *The north-east: a programme for regional development and growth* (HMSO, 1963, Cmnd 2206). In both of these studies the problems of the whole region were surveyed and assessed and projected growth points proposed to stimulate economic growth; though, as J B Cullingworth has pointed out, ' their importance lies not so much in the actual proposals made, but in the advance in thought and policy which they represent '.[4]

The advent of a Labour government in October 1964 set the seal on the revival of regional planning: the Department of Economic Affairs was established in the same month to take over from the Board of Trade the responsibility for regional policy and planning, though the detailed execution of the policy remained with the board. Subsequently eight economic planning regions were delineated in England, with Scotland and Wales constituting a separate region each in addition, and economic planning councils and boards were set up for each. So far as possible, the regional machinery of the DEA existed alongside the regional machinery (newly revived) of the then Ministry of Housing and Local Government, whose regional staffs, particularly the research staffs, have been much involved in the work of the regional economic planning councils. Thus were the strands of economic and physical planning intertwined, and national and local planning brought together, at least in physical contiguity if not always in complete harmony, for, as Peter Hall has indicated, 'there have been cases, quite well-known ones, where the two sets of policies have come into conflict '.[5]

While government sights continued to be set on the development areas—five new ones were established under the Industrial Development Act of 1966—pressure simultaneously increased for a review of the special problems of the ' intermediate ' or ' grey ' areas, those areas which, while not having the severe economic problems of the development areas, nevertheless had a rate of growth giving, or likely to give, cause for alarm. This pressure resulted in the setting up of the Hunt Committee which reported on *The intermediate areas* (HMSO, 1969, Cmnd 3998). Subsequently, though not following the committee's recommendations, the government identified seven intermediate areas into which funds for assistance to industry were to be channelled from development area funds.

In October 1969 the DEA was absorbed into the Ministry of Housing and Local Government under the overlordship of the Secretary of State for Local Government and Regional Planning, the Ministry taking over the economic planning councils and boards. Simultaneously the responsibilities of the Board of Trade with regard to detailed location of industry passed to the Ministry of Technology. This state of affairs, however, was short-lived, for after the advent of a Conservative government in June 1970, further changes were announced in October 1970.[6] Regional policy and planning is now shared between the Department of the Environment, responsible for maintaining the infrastructure for industry in the regions, and the Department of Trade and Industry, responsible for the residue of the industrial location policy by establishing ' a general framework of requirements, incentives and restraints within which firms can operate as freely as possible to their own individual advantage '.[7] Subsequently the government announced the curtail-

26

ment of regional investment grants. As a writer commented in *The guardian* of October 16 1970, ' this deeply Tory philosophy probably spells the end of Labour's regional policy '.

But even in the years of its resurgence, regional planning did not achieve satisfactory results within the framework created for it.[8] A successful liaison between physical and economic planning was not properly established and the many regional studies and feasibility studies which have been produced under the aegis of the DEA have never had any guarantee of implementation. In addition to these studies and reports, most of them economically based, the decade just gone has seen a veritable flood of documentary information relating to the future development of numerous parts of the country, from economic planning regions down to parts of towns. As Harry Gracey wrote in *Town and country planning* in July 1969, ' one cannot observe British planning today without being impressed by the number of studies undertaken to guide future development plans, by the lack of coordination between these studies, both within the same region and between adjacent regions and sub-regions, and by the lack of any imperative connection between these studies' recommendations and the actual planning of local authorities '.

The actual planning of local authorities was, as we have seen, geared by the 1947 Act to individual self-contained units. In the climate of the 1960's, this spatial straitjacket was clearly unrealistic. Not only was the spatial basis of practical planning unsatisfactory, but its machinery had become overburdened and was subject to delays which were equally unrealistic. In short, the provisions of the Act were out of tune with the realities and the requirements of the times. The 1947 Act and subsequent legislation was consolidated in the Town and Country Planning Act of 1962, but even at this stage unease was felt with the system in operation, and in May 1964 a Planning Advisory Group was set up by the Ministry of Housing and Local Government, the Ministry of Transport, and the Scottish Development Department to review the planning system and, in particular, the development plan system. Such a review was felt to be necessary principally because of the long delays resulting from centralised procedures, and because of the less than satisfactory quality of the results. The Planning Advisory Group reported in 1965. *The future of development plans: a report by the Planning*

Advisory Group (HMSO, 1965), summed up the merits and demerits of the development plan system thus :

'The main merits of the present development plans have lain in the basis they have provided for the exercise of development control, and for projecting probable land uses and values, particularly in urban areas . . .' But 'We conclude that the present development plan system is too detailed for some purposes and not detailed enough for other purposes. It brings before the Minister issues of major importance but in a form which may be incomplete and out of context, and also many issues of local interest which have no policy significance requiring the Minister's approval. Yet it does not provide a satisfactory medium for positive environmental planning at the local level.'

The recommendations of the Planning Advisory Group were embodied in the government White Paper *Town and country planning* (HMSO, 1967, Cmnd 3333), in the Town and Country Planning Bill introduced in December 1967, and finally in the Town and Country Planning Act 1968 (comparable legislation followed for Scotland in 1969).

The development plan system—one plan for each area, requiring ministerial approval in all its aspects—has been replaced by the structure plan system. A structure plan showing policy over the whole area of the planning authority, and indicating action areas, that is, areas which are in most urgent need of attention and which require wholesale development (a rather wider interpretation of the former comprehensive development area), is to be prepared, and will be subject to ministerial approval; within this 'broad brush' framework, local plans containing the detail formerly accorded the whole area will be prepared, which are not subject to ministerial approval. Such local plans would be, for example, for action areas, for urban sectors of counties, or for town centre improvements, and would be in line with the policy laid down in the structure plan. Structure plans will indicate the broad pattern of future development, taking into account factors such as transport, population distribution, employment, recreational requirements and communications, but will not include detailed land use allocations. They will be, in effect, the bridge between national and regional policy planning, and local planning. The local plans will include detailed

28

land use allocations; they will provide the basis for development control as well as for more positive action, and will be subject to formal adoption by the planning authority.

The concept of the structure plan clearly has in view its application to areas larger than those at present determined by local government boundaries: it is in fact a sub-regional concept, and will have to wait for full implementation on the reorganisation of local government and the introduction of new and larger units of administration (see chapter 3). Additionally, the work involved in the preparation of structure plans is much greater than the average present planning department can accommodate, particularly with regard to the requirement for continuous monitoring of the plan which replaces the former five-yearly revision, and this is another very practical reason why implementation of the new system must be preceded by local government reorganisation. In the meantime, however, some of the existing planning authorities which do have adequate resources are engaged in the preparation of structure plans with the support and cooperation of central government, and in a few cases groups of contiguous authorities are jointly engaged in similar exercises, again with central government support. In a written answer in the House of Commons on November 10 1970, the Minister for Local Government and Development announced measures to speed up the preparation of development plans by amending the procedure for structure plans in England and Wales and by eliminating the necessity for borough structure plans in London. The Department proposes 'to secure joint preparatory work by local planning authorities for areas of the size which makes sense in strategic planning terms. Such working in groups is already a feature of the structure plans now in preparation. It cannot, however, under existing powers, be taken to the point of a submission to the Minister of a joint structure plan covering such areas, even where the authorities concerned wish it. We propose, therefore, that for England outside Greater London, and for Wales and Monmouthshire, the appropriate secretary of state shall have power to authorise local planning authorities, with their consent, to submit a joint structure plan for the agreed area; and to hold his inquiry into that plan.' In the case of London, the thirty three boroughs will not now have to submit structure plans for ministerial approval but will have the power to prepare local plans for their areas in the context of and conforming to the Greater London Development Plan (in whatever form that finally emerges). Amending legislation will of course be necessary before these measures can come into force.

Within the post-war framework of legislation the character of British planning has in some ways been more negative than positive, and its tangible results have seemed in many cases piecemeal. But there has been one major achievement: the new towns. The first new town was designated in 1946; there are now thirty, at varying stages of creation. 'Few people now dispute that new towns represent the one really solid and successful achievement of the voluminous planning legislation of the last twenty five years. Visitors come from afar to look at and learn from the British new towns, and frequently to admire them. Nothing else that we have done excites this interest, understandably enough. Most town planning has a restrictive image; new towns are positive achievements, the unique flowering of public initiative and enterprise. With all their faults and limitations, the new towns point a finger towards a better environment and society.'[9]

The concept of new towns as a practical solution to overcrowding within existing cities, and as a practical method of dispersing population and employment, was established in Sir Patrick Abercrombie's *Greater London plan* of 1944 (see chapter 9), which proposed the rehousing of half a million people from the metropolitan area in ten new towns in the surrounding counties. A New Towns Committee, under the chairmanship of Lord Reith, was set up in 1945, and produced three reports—*Interim report of the New Towns Committee* (HMSO, 1946, Cmnd 6759), *Second interim report . . .* (HMSO, 1946, Cmnd 6794) and *Final report . . .* (HMSO, 1946, Cmnd 6876)—which underlined the rightness of Abercrombie's principle. Legislation followed soon after, in the form of the New Towns Act 1946 (and a Scottish counterpart in the same year), consolidated in the New Towns Act 1965 and the New Towns (Scotland) Act 1968. Northern Ireland is separately provided for in the New Towns Acts (Northern Ireland) 1965 and 1968.

The first new town to be designated under the new legislation was Stevenage in Hertfordshire in 1946 which, along with others in the home counties designated in the late 1940's, absorbed overspill from London. In the first decade from the passing of the New Towns Act, fourteen new towns were designated and began to take shape. Collectively, these fourteen form the first series of new towns, known as Mark I.[10] Mark II began in 1955 with the designation of Cumbernauld in Scotland; it introduced a significant development into new town planning, in that for the first time the motor vehicle was considered as a vital factor and the implications of existing and increasing car ownership were examined, and the conclusions reached from these deliberations were then translated into a radically different approach to traffic planning. In short, ' Cumbernauld can claim to be the first town in Britain where the road system was designed from the beginning on scientific principles to cater specifically for the motor age '.[11] Mark III and beyond are now developing, in the early stages of creation or on the drawing board. Many of the new towns were designed primarily to take overspill from, and to form a counter-magnet to, the large overcrowded conurbations such as London and Glasgow; other more recent examples, such as Washington in County Durham and Irvine in Ayrshire, have the additional purpose of becoming centres of industrial growth for a whole region.

A second means of relieving overcrowding and encouraging industrial growth is provided by the Town Development Act 1952 and the Housing and Town Development (Scotland) Act 1957, under which large cities with congestion problems can make arrangements with small towns for the latter to accommodate people and jobs from the city. The principal beneficiaries under these Acts have been London and Glasgow; but many of the arrangements have involved very small numbers in terms of the total problem. More recently, the tendency has been to plan for substantial expansions and for such development to be under a partnership arrangement of a new town development corporation and the local planning authorities involved in the area, as at Northampton, Peterborough, and Warrington. There is also a broadening of approach to the planning of both new towns and town expansions, in that they are being considered in relation to their regional context and also in relation to other new towns and expansion schemes; this approach was first practised in Scotland in the planning of the new town of

31

Livingston but is also in evidence in England where, for example, the expanded town of Northampton is being planned as part of a huge city-regional complex taking in expansions of other existing towns in the area and also the new town of Milton Keynes (see chapter 9).

The other decisive factor in post-war planning has been the increase in traffic and transport generally and in particular the spectacular rise in the numbers of private cars. Although it is now recognised both in theory and in practice that transport planning and land use planning are integral parts of the total process of urban and regional planning, this recognition has come about only during the last decade. Transport planning had no equivalent of the Barlow, Scott or Uthwatt Reports to lay its conceptual base in the immediate post-war years; indeed, as Tetlow and Goss observe, ' it is curious that in Britain fifty years of the development of motor vehicles passed by before it began to be realised that here was a new form of transport which would completely upset our towns, creating a town planning revolution.'[12] Not only has it become imperative to consider traffic and transport in a wider context, it has also become imperative to consider the various modes of transport, public and private, as an integrated process, instead of each one in isolation. A policy such as that proposed in the Beeching Report, which considered the railways in isolation from all other forms of transport and whose primary aim was to formulate a policy of making the rail system an economic proposition, is barely conceivable under the conditions of the 1970's; indeed Beeching's insular scheme was immediately challenged by the concepts embodied in the Buchanan Report *Traffic in towns* (HMSO, 1963; shortened version Harmondsworth, Penguin Books, 1964), which recognised the need for cheap efficient public transport systems as a vital factor in containing the growth of private transport in congested areas. *Traffic in towns* was the product of a study group under Colin Buchanan, subsequently a working group of the Ministry of Transport, set up to ' study the long-term development of roads and traffic in urban areas and their influence on the urban environment '. The group's report was such a comprehensive study, and set out basic principles for reconciling the efficient movement of traffic with the preservation of a decent urban environment. One of the clearest

32

lessons to be learned from the Buchanan Report is that traffic planning, and particularly the planning of primary road networks, was no longer a matter of purely local concern, that a city's road network could not be considered in isolation from its surrounding region.

The concepts and proposals of the Buchanan Report were endorsed in the government White Paper *Transport policy* (HMSO, 1966, Cmnd 3057), although it was clear that some of its more ambitious recommendations were beyond the resources of local planning authorities at that time. The integrated preparation of transportation and land use plans called for by Buchanan and confirmed in the Town and Country Planning Act 1968 and the Transport Act of the same year (see below) will await full implementation in the same way as the new planning system *in toto*. That the government of the day were fully aware of the need for comprehensive transport planning was demonstrated in the White Paper *Public transport and traffic* (HMSO, 1967, Cmnd 3481), the forerunner of the Transport Act of 1968. The White Paper put forward five principles on which this comprehensive approach was based: that local authorities should be responsible for public transport; that all matters connected with these transport responsibilities should be coordinated into a transport plan conceived within the framework of the general plan for the area; that central government should subsidise local public transport; that the main public transport network should be publicly owned; and that transport planning should be conceived (as in the case of economic and physical planning) in terms of larger spatial units than had previously been the case. These policies were translated into the Transport Act of 1968, the most comprehensive and far-seeing policy statement on transport planning to date. The need for planning over a wider area than formerly and the urgency for such broader-based planning in certain regions of the country led to the provision within the Act for setting up Passenger Transport Authorities in these regions in order to secure efficient integrated planning. Authorities were set up for Greater Manchester, Merseyside, the West Midlands, and Tyneside; the problems of other regions are considered to be less acute and can be left to await local government reorganisation, though in 1970 the Secretary of State for Scotland announced a PTA for Greater

33

Glasgow (a plan which has met with considerable local opposition). Each authority consists of two bodies, the authority, which is concerned with policy-making over the whole of the area, and the executive, which is responsible for the implementation of the policy and general administration. It is the duty of the latter body to prepare a transport plan for the area, which then has to be approved by the authority. London is the subject of special provisions, stated in the White Paper *Transport in London* (HMSO, 1968, Cmnd 3686) and carried into law by the Transport (London) Act 1969. The Greater London Council is the single authority which coordinates traffic and transport planning and prepares the plans in accordance with their policy. The London Transport Executive, which came into operation in 1970, is the equivalent of the executive bodies of the Passenger Transport Authorities, its members being appointed by the GLC.

Within the administrative machine, also, the trend is towards merging the functions of transport planning and land use planning. The pioneer of such mergers was the Scottish Development Department, which in 1962 took over, and now administers, the responsibilities of the former Scottish Home Department for local government, roads and industry together with those of the former Scottish Department of Health for town and country planning, housing and environment generally. In the same year the Ministries of Housing and Local Government and of Transport set up a Joint Urban Planning Group which was later joined by the Scottish Development Department, composed of both administrative and technical staff; the group has functioned as a study group and also in an advisory capacity to the departments involved, and has been responsible for the preparation of a number of advisory publications of the joint departments including several planning bulletins (see chapter 11). In practical terms, the decade just gone has seen the rapid increase in large-scale land use/transportation studies, of all the major conurbations and a good many large towns, some of them concluded and some still in progress. In October 1969, the Greater London Council combined its Departments of Planning and of Highways and Transportation ' so as to bring together in one department all the strategic planning and transportation activities for which the Greater London Council is responsible '. This merger in particular raised questions

34

of priorities, and was a catalyst for much professional soul-searching, as can be seen in the columns of *JTPI*. In the same month also came the governmental merger of the ministries of Transport and of Housing and Local Government, a merger ratified a year later by the next government. Thus the two branches of planning are welded together in administration, in legislation, and in practice, and within the national/regional framework and the new concept of sub-regional strategic structure plans the unified practice of land use and transport planning is equally insolubly wedded to economic and social planning.

One other major strand in the planning process remains to be discussed in the context of this chapter, its evolution traced from its early post-war legislation to its present position of importance. Legislation central to land use or physical planning has, since 1932, borne the name 'town and country', continuing the notion that town and country are separate entities, to be planned as such. Such a distinction is no longer valid : the towns have encroached upon the country, town-dwellers invade it and are in growing numbers spasmodic country-dwellers, formerly sharp boundaries have blurred into the 'rural-urban fringe ', the extensive personal mobility granted by the motor car and better roads renders even remote parts of the countryside vulnerable to urban influence. Alongside these developments has grown up a distinct practice of countryside planning which is concerned primarily with the proper exploitation and conservation of rural resources for the benefit of both urban and country dwellers.

Countryside planning has its legislative roots in the post-war years, the Scott Report of 1942 providing the basis for the National Parks and Access to the Countryside Act of 1949. The Act provided for a central body, the National Parks Commission, whose functions, though mainly advisory, included the right to designate areas of country as national parks; it also placed the responsibility for the upkeep and administration of these parks firmly with the newly-created local planning authorities. In making these provisions (which met with considerable criticism), the recommendations of two reports emanating from the Ministry of Town and Country Planning and focusing on the same topics, were largely ignored. These were the Dower Report *National parks in England and Wales*

35

(HMSO, 1945, Cmnd 6628) and the Hobhouse Report *Report of the National Parks Committee (England and Wales)* (HMSO, 1947, Cmnd 7121) both of which argued that the cost of national parks, as a national amenity, should be borne by the nation from central resources, and that the management of each park should be the responsibility of a park committee jointly appointed by the National Parks Commission and the local authorities concerned, and run by staff appointed and employed by the commission who would form a local executive body acting on its behalf. The government's conception was totally different from that of Dower and Hobhouse. The Act proposed administration by a joint planning board in cases where the park lay within the areas of more than one planning authority: but in practice only two joint boards have been established, in the Peak and the Lake Districts, elsewhere in similar situations joint advisory committees have been formed with separate park planning committees in each of the local authorities involved; in the remaining cases, the park falls entirely within the area of one local authority and full responsibility for it devolves on that authority, for example, Devon County Council assumes full responsibility for Dartmoor.

Dower and Hobhouse both also recommended, and the Act gave, the power of designation of Areas of Outstanding Natural Beauty to the National Parks Commission. Generally such areas are smaller than the national parks, and each one is solely the responsibility of the planning authority within whose boundaries it lies. Additionally, areas of high landscape, scientific, or historic value are designated by planning authorities in their development plans, on the advice of the Nature Conservancy (a body set up in 1949 and given additional powers under the 1949 Act, since 1965 a part of the Natural Environment Research Council) and developers within these areas are normally required to achieve high standards of design and to have regard to the existing amenities.

During the 1960's a much more positive and constructive attitude towards countryside planning has emerged, largely because the increased amount of leisure time which most people nowadays enjoy, and their ability to travel substantial distances as and when they wish, have resulted in a large proportion of the population regularly invading the countryside, particularly at weekends, for recreational purposes of various kinds. A policy therefore has become an urgent necessity with the twin purpose of conserving those parts of the countryside which ought in the national interest to be conserved, and of developing other parts so as to provide a constructive outlet for outdoor activities. Countryside planning is thus closely involved with recreational planning, with nature conservation, with the problems of access to the countryside generally, with the provision of organised facilities for tourism, with forestry and landscape and many other facets of the outdoor environment. The White Paper *Leisure in the countryside* (HMSO, 1966, Cmnd 2928) embodied proposals for constructive action which were carried into the Countryside Act of 1968. The Act gave to the National Parks Commission a wider range of powers, represented in its change of name to the Countryside Commission (the Countryside (Scotland) Act was passed in 1967 and gave similar powers to the new Country-side Commission for Scotland). In addition to its functions retained from the 1949 Act, the commission is additionally charged to ' review, encourage, assist, concert or promote the provision and improvement of facilities for the enjoyment of the countryside generally, and to conserve and enhance the natural beauty and amenity of the countryside, and to secure public access for the purpose of open air recreation '. The Act proposes the creation of country parks, in addition to national parks and areas of out-standing natural beauty, to provide organised leisure facilities for urban dwellers and to take pressure off existing designated areas and the countryside generally. The Act also gives powers for the organised provision of facilities such as camping sites, a policy which has the dual function of both providing demarcated facilities and protecting the adjacent countryside from unofficial use for similar purposes.

The discussion of the preceding pages has been confined to the major trends and developments in planning over an eventful period of twenty three years. Many of the minor, and often significant themes which make up the total picture have had to be omitted for reasons of space, although most of these are described in the course of chapter 11, in the context of the documentary information which relates to them. The scope of planning can be partially deciphered in the range of legislation with which a planner must be familiar:

not only the Town and Country Acts but also the Transport Act, the Countryside Act, the New Towns Acts, the Civic Amenities Act of 1967, and until recently the Land Commission Act of 1967. A more detailed attempt to find out the subjects which were relevant to planning was made in the course of a survey of information use in planning, financed by the Office for Scientific and Technical Information, and carried out in 1968 and 1969 with a sample of 284 planners (the results of the survey are summarised in chapter 6). Twenty subjects were listed in the questionnaire, and respondents were asked to indicate those which were actually or potentially relevant to their current work; the list was not intended to be a comprehensive one of all subjects relevant to planning, and this was emphasised in the questionnaire. Of the sample, 32% expressed an interest in eleven or more subjects, and a further 51% expressed an interest in between five and ten. Heading the list of relevant subjects is traffic planning, considered relevant by 76% of the sample, followed by sociology (70%), economics (68%), and recreation and statistics, both at 65%. At the lower end of the rating scale come ecology (28%), marketing (21%), and meteorology (11%).[13] Not only is the subject content of planning expanding—and by this is meant the subjects which are relevant to or influenced by planning—but the contribution to the various activities of planning by specialists in other disciplines is growing, concepts and ideas from other disciplines are being introduced—the view of the city or region as a dynamic social system rather than a static state, the introduction of ideas from biology and social physics—and techniques such as mathematical modelling and the methods of regional analysis are being utilised and explored; all these are contributing to planning and causing it to develop and stretch its frontiers both conceptually and methodologically.

It has been the purpose of these two chapters not only to provide a backcloth to the chapters which follow, but also to demonstrate how planning has developed from its original concept of imposing an orderly pattern on a settlement, through an intermediate phase when its primary purpose was the negative one of imposing controls on the development of towns, to the planning of the 1970's and beyond, which has developed into a multi-disciplinary practice whose spatial and ideological base has broadened immeasurably in the space of a decade, whose plans are increasingly flexible to adapt to rapidly changing circumstances, and whose concrete manifestations in terms of total plans committed to the ground or even to paper become fewer and fewer. As Colin Buchanan has expressed it in the report on the South Hampshire sub-regional study, ' planning . . . is becoming less and less a matter of precise propositions committed to paper and more and more a matter of ideas and policies loosely assembled under constant review, within which, every now and then, some project is seen to be as ready for execution as human judgment can pronounce '.[14]

The key point in this assertion is that, in the final resort, human judgment must pronounce. If human judgment is to pronounce with any degree of authority, it must be an informed judgment, and this depends partly on experience and partly on information. Only the individual has control over his own experience; but the provision of information is a matter for wider concern and one which involves all planners. The quality of information directly affects the quality of the judgment: it is therefore vital that every planner should know where and how to find relevant information. It is the primary object of the chapters which follow to bring to the attention of both users and providers of planning information, the very wide range of sources from which they may draw this information.

REFERENCES

1 G C Cameron and B D Clark *Industrial movement and the regional problem* (Edinburgh, Oliver and Boyd, 1966) 8.

2 Derek Lee *Regional planning and the location of industry* (Heinemann, 1969) 24.

3 Derek Lee *op cit* 25.

4 J B Cullingworth *Town and country planning in England and Wales* (Allen and Unwin, third edition 1970) 298.

5 Peter Hall *Theory and practice of regional planning* (Pemberton Books, 1970) 76.

6 *The reorganisation of central government* (HMSO, 1970, Cmnd 4506).

7 *The reorganisation of central government op cit* 8.

8 See, for example, Anthony Goss ' Regional planning and central government ' *Town and country planning* 36(6) June 1968 286-

292; and M A Ash ' Realism—and regionalism ' *Town and country planning* 36(4) April 1968 206-208.

9 Peter Self 'A new vision for new towns ' *Town and country planning* 38(1) January 1970 4.

10. The term Mark I was first applied to new towns by a leader writer in the *Edinburgh evening dispatch* October 25 1946.

11. John Tetlow and Anthony Goss *Homes, towns and traffic* (Faber, second edition 1968) 100.

12 John Tetlow and Anthony Goss *op cit* 68.

13 Brenda White *Planners and information: a report of an investigation into information provision in town and country planning* (Library Association, 1970, Research Publication 3) 91-92.

14 Ministry of Housing and Local Government *South Hampshire study: report on the feasibility of major urban growth* (HMSO, 1966). The quotation is taken from the main volume.

3

THE STRUCTURE OF PLANNING : PRACTICE

IT IS POSSIBLE to define three main areas of planning activity: practice, teaching, and research. Most planners—and under this collective umbrella are included the increasing number of specialists in other disciplines such as economists and sociologists who are involved in planning—fit into one or other of these categories, though not necessarily in the same context. Research, for example, is carried on within central and local government as well as in research organisations. Nor are these activities watertight compartments: planners in practice may be part-time lecturers; lecturers may be engaged in research. But it is the practice of planning that is the core of the subject, to which the other two activities relate: for the purpose of teaching is to produce the practising planners of the future, and the purpose of research (hopefully) is to achieve better planning in practice.

CENTRAL GOVERNMENT

At the apex of the planning pyramid is the Department of the Environment, in which is vested central and ultimate responsibility for ' the whole range of functions which affect people's living environment ', including administration of the Town and Country Planning Act 1968. Comparable central responsibility rests with the Secretary of State for Wales, the Secretary of State for Scotland, and with the Minister of Development in Northern Ireland, for their respective countries.

The Department of the Environment has evolved through a number of transmogrifications from the Local Government Board, which in 1909 brought the first town planning legislation into the

41

light of day. Or, as official terminology has it, 'the responsibilities of the department . . . have from time to time been adjusted in response to changing social needs'. The Local Government Board itself was formed in 1871 through the amalgamation of the Poor Law Board, the Medical Department of the Privy Council, and the Local Government Department of the Home Office.

Eighty years later in 1951, the Ministry of Local Government and Planning, shortly to change its name to the Ministry of Housing and Local Government, was set up, taking over the housing and local government functions of the Ministry of Health and the total functions of the Ministry of Town and Country Planning. The Minister of Housing and Local Government had, as his predecessor had in 1943, the duty of 'securing consistency and continuity in the framing and execution of a national policy with respect to the use and development of land throughout England and Wales'. Responsibility for planning of roads and transport networks remained with the Ministry of Transport, and that for industrial location policy remained with the Board of Trade. In 1964, two new departments were established: the Department of Economic Affairs, together with its regional machinery in the two subsequent years, and the Ministry of Land and Natural Resources. The latter of these was short-lived: it was absorbed into the Ministry of Housing and Local Government in 1967 and is notable mainly as the agent of creation of the Land Commission, now also defunct. The Department of Economic Affairs was eliminated in the major central government reorganisation of October 1969, and its functions absorbed into the Ministry of Housing and Local Government. This reorganisation produced two new super-departments, the Ministry of Technology with responsibility for industry both in the private and the public sectors including the former responsibilities of the Board of Trade and the DEA in the field of regional economic development; and the merged ministries of Housing and Local Government and of Transport under the overlordship of a Secretary of State for Local Government and Regional Planning. The details of this reorganisation are of little more than historical interest: the new departments had little chance to settle into their redefined roles before the general election of June 1970, and the resultant change of government.

In October 1970, the Conservative administration introduced further sweeping changes in the organisation of central government, which (at the time of writing) have had equally little chance to settle down into defined patterns of practice. The ministries of Housing and Local Government and of Transport remain wedded, but are joined now by the Ministry of Public Building and Works in a mammoth Department of the Environment. The Ministry of Technology and the Board of Trade have become similarly married as the Department of Trade and Industry. The Department of the Environment has overall responsibility for land planning, transport planning, and for the construction industries including the housing programme. An official statement from the department on October 26 1970 indicated the pattern of responsibility within the department. The Secretary of State for the Environment holds all the statutory powers previously held by the three separate Ministers of Housing, Transport, and Public Building, and also has control over expenditure. His main concern will be with strategic issues of policy and priority; and with coordinating the fight against environmental pollution. The Minister of Housing and Construction has responsibility for all aspects of the housing programme, and also for relations with the building and civil engineering industry, building research and development, and government accommodation. The Minister for Transport Industries looks after ports, general policy on nationalised transport industries, freight, international aspects of inland transport, road and vehicle safety and licensing, sport and recreation, and the Channel Tunnel. The Minister for Local Government and Development is responsible for transport planning and road passenger transport, regional and land use planning, local government and its reorganisation, water, sewerage and refuse disposal, and the countryside and conservation. A further press release on November 6 1970 indicated the priority objectives of the new department as being a reform of housing finance, local government, planning, and a drive to make the polluter pay for pollution.

The Ministry of Housing and Local Government was set up in 1951 with a network of regional offices; this organisation was dismantled in 1956, with the exception of the Welsh regional office. Regional offices were again opened in Manchester and Newcastle in 1962 and 1963 respectively, primarily to add weight to the redevelopment effort in the north. A full regional network was re-established in 1965, contemporary with the setting up of regional economic machinery by the then Department of Economic Affairs, with offices in Leeds, Nottingham, Birmingham, and Bristol in addition to the three already existing; and this regional network still operates. The regional offices, with the exception of the Welsh unit, had no executive powers, but were ' responsible regionally for the expanding housing programme, for helping local planning authorities in the region in the exercise of their planning functions; for providing the Minister with local advice and information and for the department's share in the work of the regional economic planning boards and councils '.

In Wales, the Welsh Office at Cardiff, the seat of the Secretary of State for Wales, has executive responsibility for town and country planning, including new towns, and for housing, roads, water resources and local government. In Scotland, the comparable unit to the Department of the Environment is the Scottish Development Department in Edinburgh, part of the Scottish Office, the seat of the Secretary of State for Scotland. The department has executive responsibility for town and country planning, housing, and local government services, and also for roads, electricity, water supply, and industrial development. Similar executive responsibilities are vested in the Ministry of Development for Northern Ireland, the seat of the Minister of Development, at Belfast.

The last report of the Ministry of Housing and Local Government covered the years 1967 and 1968 (HMSO, 1969, Cmnd 4009). No subsequent record has been produced. Since 1967 the tables of statistics, previously included in the annual reports, have been produced separately as an annual under the title *Handbook of statistics* (HMSO). The Scottish Development Department also issues an annual report, published by HMSO. Details of the publications of relevant government departments can be found in the sectional lists issued by HMSO, and available free. No 5 covers the Ministry of Housing and Local Government; no 65, the Scottish Development Department; no 22, the Ministry of Transport; no 51, the Board of Trade. All the lists are revised from time to time. There has so far been no indication whether sectional lists will be merged in the same way as their originating departments.

44

The New Whitehall series, published by Allen and Unwin, is a series of monographs by authoritative authors, each one devoted to a government department. *The Ministry of Housing and Local Government,* by Evelyn Sharp, was published in this series in 1969, and describes the situation as it existed in 1968. Overtaken by events as soon as it appeared in print, it is nevertheless a fairly informative —if now historical—account of the workings of a complex department, concentrating on its four main functions of housing, public health, planning, and local government together with general issues such as the relationship with local authorities, finance, staffing and organisation. As Baroness Sharp points out, ' most of the Ministry's work consists . . . in dealings with local authorities, both individually and collectively '. *Central departments and local authorities* by J A G Griffith (Allen and Unwin, 1966) is a detailed study of the ' working relationships between central government departments and local authorities in England and Wales over a number of major services ' including highways, housing, and planning, and remains relevant by virtue of its penetrating analysis of central/local relationships generally.

LOCAL AUTHORITY PLANNING DEPARTMENTS

While central government has ultimate responsibility for planning, and administers the Town and Country Planning Acts over the United Kingdom as a whole, the responsibility for implementing the provisions of the Acts on the ground, as it were, rests with those local authorities which have planning powers vested in them.

In England and Wales, these are the counties and county boroughs. In Scotland, the planning authorities are the counties, the cities, the large burghs, and the small burghs of St Andrews and Thurso. In Northern Ireland, they are the counties and large boroughs. Within England and Wales, London has a unique administrative structure consisting of the Greater London Council, thirty two London boroughs, and the City of London. In some areas, for example the national parks, special arrangements exist (see chapter 2). This is the structure which has gone hand in hand with the provisions of the 1947 Town and Country Planning Act. The provisions of the 1968 Act are inextricably bound up with the reorganisation of local government, and it is clearly difficult to write with any degree of certainty about the formal structure either of planning or of local government. The most recent government statement on local government reorganisation is contained in two White Papers, *Local government in England: government proposals for reorganisation* (HMSO, 1971, Cmnd 4584) and *Reform of local government in Scotland* (Edinburgh, HMSO, 1971, Cmnd 4583). For England, a two-tier structure is proposed, with six new metropolitan counties based on Merseyside, the Selnec area, the west midlands, west Yorkshire, south Yorkshire, and Tyneside/Wearside, included in the new system of county and district authorities. For Scotland, a similar two-tier structure is advocated, with regional and district authorities. The main burden of strategic planning will lie with the county and the regional authorities.

The government's timetable is to bring the new authorities into being at both operational levels throughout England during 1973 and to have them fully operational in 1974. The Scottish timetable envisages the new authorities in operation in 1975. From the planner's point of view, the principal interest lies in the boundaries of the new authorities and their validity in relation to the preparation of structure plans. The proposals for the new county and metropolitan district boundaries throughout England are contained in Circular 8/71 from the Department of the Environment. Proposals for Scotland are contained in the White Paper itself, which incorporates a map showing the proposed boundaries; a more detailed version will eventually be issued separately by HMSO. The proposals for both England and Scotland are offered as a basis for discussion; as the Scottish White Paper states, more explicitly than its English counterpart, ' local authorities ' areas must be delineated by boundaries drawn to accord with travel to work, shopping and education patterns, recreational and leisure movements, and lines of communication '. A substantial amount of research into these patterns of social geography was included in the work of the two royal commissions on local government under Lord Redcliffe-Maud and Lord Wheatley, and failure to apply the results of this to the English boundary proposals is pointed up by Peter Hall in an article ' Commuting across the new boundaries ' in *New society* 17(439) February 25 1971 314.

As the system operates at present, there are huge disparities between the planning departments, and, as a result, the quality of planning varies widely. This is inevitable within a system which contains, on the one hand, planning authorities such as the Greater London Council, the large English boroughs and the highly urbanised counties such as Kent and Essex, which have the resources to support large planning staffs and to promote planning projects capable of attracting the most able professional people; and on the other hand, the small county boroughs of England and Wales and the huge thinly-populated rural counties of Scotland in which hopelessly under-staffed planning departments (if such a separate section exists), sometimes with no qualified planners, can do no more than practise the negative aspects of planning. As J B Cullingworth points out, ' an adequately staffed planning machine cannot be achieved in a small authority ';[1] though equally it is necessary to observe that size alone is not a criterion of quality, and that some small planning authorities are extremely efficient within the limits of their resources. The Town Planning Institute recommended, in a statement of policy put forward in 1967, that separate planning departments should be established in local planning authorities: ' . . . the Town Planning Institute strongly supports the view that both the preparation of the plan and its implementation need to be under the direction of a single chief officer in charge of an adequately staffed planning department '. Most large county authorities and many large boroughs do in fact now have separate planning departments, although there are still plenty of instances where planning remains wedded to its architectural or engineering origins, these latter not necessarily confined to the smallest authorities.

The larger planning authorities usually group their staff according to broad categories of work. The most frequently occurring sections are those dealing with development plan and development control, and even quite small staffs may be demarcated into two such functional groups. It is also quite common to find designated sections dealing with specific problems or a specific type of area: for example, housing, traffic, or central areas. Several of the large boroughs and counties have research sections, either separately established or as part of a policy or development plan section. In addition to such functional groupings of staff, many of the major

47

counties practise decentralisation and have area offices at strategic points, the reason for this being quite simply that the area of planning authority is so immense, and local conditions so varied, that it cannot be administered properly from one central point.

To describe the work which is undertaken by the local planning authorities is much the same as trying to describe the topography of the country in a couple of paragraphs—it is in fact just as varied as the land with which it is concerned. Perhaps the best way to give an indication of its scope is to describe a pair of contrasting departments: neither of them to be taken as typical, because no planning department is typical.

Glasgow is the largest city in Scotland. It has the largest planning department, city or county, in the country, formerly a part of the City Architect's Department but independent since 1967. Of its total of one hundred staff, about one third are qualified planners.[2] The city has a serious planning problem resulting from the existence of around one million population in an area roughly equivalent to that of, say, Leicester (with four hundred thousand population). Glasgow's average housing density is 450 people per acre, compared with an average of fifty to sixty per acre in most other towns. Planning thus involves the necessity to move thirty thousand people out of the city each year: new towns, such as Cumbernauld, are absorbing much of this overspill. Allied to this problem of housing is the problem of industry, which tends to concentrate heavily in small areas, for example, Clyde shipbuilding; and the industry itself tends to be unstable—look, for example, at the recent history of the consortium of Upper Clyde Shipbuilders. Glasgow, with these two main problems, plus a major road-building programme under way, plus twenty nine designated comprehensive development areas, eight of which are under way, is an area of very rapid change, and planning has to work fast to keep up with it, let alone forecast its requirements.

Cambridgeshire is a small to medium sized English county (531,555 acres with 301,470 population) with a separate planning department. Of its total staff of about sixty, just under one quarter are qualified planners. The department has no area offices; but the staff is grouped loosely into a development control section and a design section concerned with village and local plans. There is also a separately established research section. Planning in this county is a business of contrasts: in the north, the fenlands, the population is declining, while in the south, things are booming. There is the problem of Cambridge, which is committed to preserving and enhancing its present character at the expense of industrial expansion.[3] There are further contrasts in some of the specialised planning activities: conserving the wild life of the fen country, on the one hand, preparing for the possibility of a third London airport on the other. While just far enough away from London to be out of its immediate orbit, the county is nevertheless in the line of direct communication between the metropolis and the east coast ports. These are only a few very broadly indicated aspects of planning in Cambridgeshire, but they are enough to demonstrate that while the legal framework of planning is consistent throughout the United Kingdom, and while the techniques for dealing with it are much the same, the content of the planning, the actual problems which arise in each area, varies widely from one authority to the next.

It remains to round off the picture of local authority planning by describing the administrative structure of planning in London, which is unique, as are the range and size of the planning problems which come within its machinery. Under the London Government Act 1963 (operational from April 1 1965) the London County Council ceased to exist, and a new body, the Greater London Council, came into being. The GLC took over most of the functions of the old LCC, plus some of the functions of the Middlesex County Council (which joined the LCC in limbo) and a few functions of those parts of Essex, Kent, Surrey, and Hertfordshire which lie closest to the centre of London. Broadly speaking, the GLC (administrative area over six hundred square miles, population nearly eight million) is responsible for strategic planning over the whole of the London region: roads and transport and traffic management; overall distribution of employment, housing, and other matters normally dealt with on a regional basis. The London boroughs, including the City of London, are responsible for local planning within this framework. Clearly, this is a distinction which looks logical enough on paper, but which in practice encounters many anomalies and problems.

In addition to this administrative structure, each region also has

49

a standing conference of all the local planning authorities. The oldest of these is the Standing Conference on London and South East Regional Planning, established in 1962 (then on London Regional Planning only). Its membership now comprises all the local planning authorities whose areas make up the South East Economic Planning Region. Its functions are

' a to keep under review the principal planning issues affecting its area and to assemble, assess and disseminate planning information for the area;

' b to make recommendations to the constituent authorities with a view to establishing a joint policy;

' c to co-ordinate the subsequent action taken; and

' d for these purposes to consult the appropriate government departments and other authorities and bodies concerned.[4]

The standing conferences have no statutory or executive powers; their value lies in their provision of a coordinating forum for planning authorities within a region.

Documentary information on the organisation of local authority planning departments is virtually non-existent, probably because such departments merge, and separate, and now perhaps merge again; their internal organisations are very much on an *ad hoc* and therefore unstandardised basis, even the labels attached to planning hierarchies are remarkable for their inconsistency. The specific entity is thus difficult to define. A reliable account of the local planning machine is that given by J B Cullingworth in chapter 5 of *Town and country planning in England and Wales;* Lewis Keeble includes a similar account in his *Principles and practice of town and country planning*.[5] Plenty of city and county planning departments issue booklets about their work, but generally these are public relations tools aimed at the ' planned '. A very detailed study, from an operational research point of view, of the work of Coventry's planning department over a two-year period, during which a review of the city's development plan was carried out, is contained in *Local government and strategic choice: an operational research approach to the processes of public planning* by J K Friend and W N Jessop (Tavistock, 1969). In February 1970, the journal *Official architecture and planning* contained the first of a series of profiles of public and private architecture and planning offices; Harrow's Department of

Architecture and Planning was described in *Official architecture and planning* 33(4) April 1970 338-347. In 'Planning department organisation' in *The surveyor* 136(4090) October 30 1970 32-33, 36, R W Batty proposes a form of organisation best suited to the production of development plans under the 1968 Act. As background on local government in general, W E Jackson's *The structure of local government in England and Wales* (Longmans Green, 1966) and W A Robson's *Local government in crisis* (Allen and Unwin, 1966) are excellent sources; on the peculiar circumstances of London there are two complementary texts, *The government of London: the struggle for reform* by Gerald Rhodes (Weidenfeld and Nicolson, 1970) and *The government of Greater London* by S K Ruck and Gerald Rhodes (Allen and Unwin, 1970).

NEW TOWNS

Aside from central and local government, planning is practised in two further types of organisation, the new towns, and private practices (consultants).

The New Towns Act 1946 (companion legislation was passed for Scotland in the same year) permitted the Minister of Housing to designate any area of land as the site of a new town. Such designation would be based on extensive enquiry and survey of the area to ensure that its development was in all respects appropriate, and that the effects of development on other areas would be in no way detrimental. The Minister appoints a development corporation for each new town, to be responsible for its planning and development. The New Towns Act (Northern Ireland) 1965 gives the Minister of Development similar powers, to designate and appoint a development commission.

Under a further New Towns Act in 1959, a Commission for the New Towns in England and Wales was set up to supervise the later stages of a new town's growth and to manage it after completion, responsibility for the town passing then from the development corporation to the commission. To date, Crawley, Hatfield, Hemel Hempstead, and Welwyn Garden City have passed to the commission. Such transference does not apply in Scotland or in Northern Ireland.

A development corporation consists of a chairman, a deputy

51

chairman, and up to seven members. Each corporation has its own staff of professional and administrative officers, ranging in size from around one hundred in the smaller towns to three to four hundred in the larger towns. Planning is not generally considered as a separate function: the chief design executive is normally Chief Architect/Planner (or equivalent) with, in some cases, a Principal Architect (Planning) or a Deputy Chief Planner sharing the second hierarchical level.[6] At Livingston, one of the growth points for central Scotland, a new town designated in 1962 with an area of 6,692 acres, and an original population of two thousand planned to expand to seventy to one hundred thousand, there is a total planning staff of fifteen under the Chief Architect and Planning Officer. There are also three landscape architects who act as consultants to the planners. A high proportion of the staff engaged on planning are architect/planners. In this particular case, the master plan for the new town was prepared by the staff of the development corporation (current practice is for consultants to prepare it—as at Redditch, Washington and, most recently, Milton Keynes).

The practical work of planning in a new town differs from the practical work of planning in an existing county or borough authority in that in the existing authorities there is a high proportion of ' administrative planning ', that is to say, the day to day work of planning applications, implementing the plan, enforcement, and so on; in new towns, particularly in their earlier stages, the emphasis is on ' design planning ', in the sense that the plan is being designed rather than implemented, and administrative work is small because there are few planning applications and no enforcement. This emphasis on design planning undoubtedly explains the higher pro- portion of architect/planners in new town planning teams (this is a general feature, not confined to Livingston) than in local authority planning departments. Although information in book and pamphlet form on the theory and practice of new town planning is not un- plentiful (see chapter 11) from the point of view of the administrative structure and the nature of planning in a new town, there is very little to point to for further reading save the chapter on new and expanding towns in Cullingworth's *Town and country planning in England and Wales,* and this also is written within the wider context.

There are throughout the United Kingdom some three hundred private practices which engage in planning work. These vary in size from a staff of one to a staff of hundreds and several offices. Few of these practices are engaged solely on planning work. To a greater or a lesser degree the majority are also architectural. There are also a small number which engage in specialised aspects of planning, such as economic planning, or in related specialisms such as landscape or transport.

The type of planning work which is done in private practice varies from the administrative and legal work of planning appeals and inquiries and enforcement cases, which forms the staple diet of many small practices, to the large-scale design planning represented by the preparation of a new town master plan or a sub-regional study—both of these frequently government-commissioned —which is the prerequisite of the bigger firms. Each kind of practice is best suited to the kind of planning work which it normally does: the small local practice knows in detail the local circumstances of the area in which it operates, and is well qualified to investigate local planning appeals. The large practice, on the other hand, has continuity of work to attract, and the resources to hold the kind of multi-disciplinary team which is required for a complex planning job.

The firm of Llewelyn-Davies Weeks Forestier-Walker and Bor, to take a random example, is a large London practice with offices overseas, and engages in both architectural and planning work. The architectural work came first, with a strong interest in hospital buildings, now tending towards 'prestige' jobs (the Tate Gallery, the Stock Exchange); the secondary interests of planning and housing have grown rapidly, and now focus on new town master plans and low-cost housing. The main planning interest currently is the work on the master plan for the new town of Milton Keynes, completed and published during 1970 (see chapter 9) on which the practice had a multi-disciplinary team of around ten working full time.

A fairly detailed account of the work undertaken by such a practice in the preparation of such a plan is given by Dr P H Levin in a paper *Toward decision-making rules for urban planners* (Garston, Building Research Station, 1968, Current Paper 41/68) also published in *JTPI* 53(10) December 1967 437-442). The main theme of the paper is Levin's research into the decision-making process in urban design, but the context in which he sets it is a reliable description of the process of work in a large consultants' office. The Town Planning Institute have published a booklet *Employing a chartered town planner: a guide for those requiring planning advice* (TPI, 1969) which, as the title suggests, is aimed at prospective clients: it is basically a list of planning practices, with a useful geographical as well as alphabetical arrangement. A new edition is in preparation. The series of articles in *Official architecture and planning,* mentioned under the heading of local authority planning departments, is also relevant to this section: only one private practice has so far been discussed, the Austin-Smith/Lord Partnership in *Official architecture and planning* 33(2) February 1970 151-162.

REFERENCES

1 J B Cullingworth *Town and country planning in England and Wales* (Allen and Unwin, third edition 1970) 123.

2 Since there are only about one hundred qualified planners working in Scotland, it follows that Glasgow has attracted one third of the country's professional planning manpower.

3 Cambridge: Department of Architecture and Planning *Future shape of Cambridge* (Cambridge, City Council, 1966).

4 Standing Conference on London and South East Regional Planning *Constitution and membership* (Standing Conference, 1967).

5 Lewis B Keeble *Principles and practice of town and country planning* (Estates Gazette, fourth edition 1969) 374-389. A detailed description of the structure and work of a county planning department.

6 Keeble *op cit* comes down hard on this anomaly. 'The general practice has been to appoint a Chief Architect *and* Planner for each new town, thus suggesting . . . that town planning is a kind of extension of architecture. In fact, of course, enormous quantities of work need to be done on the design of a new town before architectural considerations begin to assume appreciable, still less dominant, importance. It is typical of the lack of logic and clarity in evolving planning organisations that this should not have been recognised in setting up new town staffs.'

4

THE STRUCTURE OF PLANNING: EDUCATION

WHEN THE Town Planning Institute was founded in 1914, there were no Chartered Town Planners to make up the membership, no recognised discipline of town and country planning. The founder members of the institute were principally architects, engineers, surveyors, and lawyers: related specialists with an interest in town planning. Forty five years later, the Royal Charter granted to the institute on September 14 1959 acknowledged these origins in one of its main objects, ' the securing of the association of those engaged or interested professionally or otherwise in town planning and the promotion of their general interests '. One of the other main objects, as stated in the institute's charter, is ' the advancement of the study of town planning and of the arts and sciences as applied thereto '; in other words the Town Planning Institute is concerned to promote and to develop formal education in planning. It is in fact the co-ordinating force in planning education, as the system is at present.

The institute's central role in professional education was envisaged in the first document to discuss seriously the whole question of manpower for planning, and its training for the job: another product of the post-war planning interest, the *Report of the Committee on the Qualifications of Planners* (HMSO, 1950, Cmnd 8059) —the Schuster Report. The committee was appointed in May 1948 (following the introduction of the 1947 Town and Country Planning Act) by the then Minister of Town and Country Planning with these terms of reference: ' to take account of the present and prospective scope of town and country planning and to consider and report what qualifications are necessary or desirable for persons engaged in it and to make any recommendations affecting those persons which appear to the Committee to be relevant '.

The resultant report stressed the value of university education, and advocated in particular postgraduate courses for those already qualified in a relevant discipline. It stressed also the need to experiment with planning courses, and to watch carefully the success or otherwise of the newly-instituted five-year undergraduate courses; and it laid emphasis on the advantages to be gained from preceding, or interspersing formal education with practical training.

In nominating the Town Planning Institute as the ' national institution to watch the whole field of planning studies, and to promote liaison between workers in this field ', the Schuster Committee at the same time stipulated that ' the basis of membership must be substantially widened ' and urged that ' the council of the institute should also be changed . . . The council should be empowered to co-opt at least one third of its members and in doing so should bring in persons representing the economic and social sciences . . . Meanwhile the membership should be broadened by admitting persons well qualified by education and experience to practise in planning, notwithstanding that they do not possess one of the existing qualifications necessary for membership.' The theme is still topical.

The way to qualification as a planner is through the intermediate and final examinations of the Town Planning Institute. This can be achieved either by part-time study while working in a planning office (day release or evening classes) or more usually by attendance at a course which qualifies for exemption from the institute's examinations. In all cases, a minimum of two years practical planning work is essential.

The trend in planning, as in other subjects which are establishing themselves as university disciplines—librarianship is a parallel example—is away from on-the-job part-time study. But it is still possible to qualify as a Chartered Town Planner in this way, although the number of centres in which evening or day release classes in the TPI examinations are available, is small. The College of Estate Management (now part of the University of Reading) is the single source of correspondence courses. Qualified legal practitioners with experience of the law of town and country planning may apply for admission as Legal Associate Members of the institute, for which they must pass the legal membership examination.

For the undergraduate, there are a number of full-time courses at university or non-university schools of planning, at the end of which (if the course is officially recognised by the TPI) a degree or diploma is awarded which affords exemption from the institute's final examination. Such courses are either four-year, or five-year sandwich. Planning cannot be studied at all or even most universities or colleges. At the time of writing,[1] the following offer courses which are recognised by the institute: University College, London; the Universities of Manchester, Newcastle upon Tyne and Sheffield; the University of Wales Institute of Science and Technology, Cardiff; the Heriot-Watt University, Edinburgh; Lanchester Polytechnic, Coventry; Duncan of Jordanstone College of Art, Dundee; Glasgow School of Art; Leeds Polytechnic; Trent Polytechnic (formerly Nottingham College of Art and Design); Oxford Polytechnic; and the Polytechnic of the South Bank.

In addition to undergraduate courses, there are also a number of postgraduate courses available. Those holding an approved professional qualification in a related subject—architecture, surveying, civil or municipal engineering—or an approved degree in architecture, civil engineering, estate management, geography, economics, or sociology, are exempt from the TPI intermediate examination, and can further gain exemption from the final examination by taking a part-time or full-time postgraduate course at the end of which a recognised degree or diploma is awarded. Postgraduate courses are either two-year full-time or three-year part-time. As with undergraduate courses, planning cannot be studied at postgraduate level outside of a small number of universities and colleges. The Universities of Strathclyde, Edinburgh, and Liverpool offer postgraduate courses only. Postgraduate courses of either two or three years duration are available at the Universities of London, Manchester, Newcastle upon Tyne and Sheffield; the Heriot-Watt University in Edinburgh; the University of Wales Institute of Science and Technology, Cardiff; Birmingham Polytechnic (now affiliated to the University of Aston); Leeds Polytechnic; Trent Polytechnic; Oxford Polytechnic; Glasgow College of Art; and the Polytechnic of Central London.

The shortage of qualified planners generally is a reflection of the small number of planning courses and the correspondingly small number of places open to those wishing to study. The demand for places on full time courses is constantly and increasingly in excess of their supply: six applications per place in 1965-6 compared with nineteen per place in 1968-9. In answer to a question in the House of Commons in June 1968 as to whether steps were being taken to ensure the recruitment of sufficient planners to meet the requirements of the new planning system, it was stated that the University Grants Committee had made provision for 'a substantial increase in the number of university places for students of planning. They expect to see an extra 250 full-time and 250 part-time places by 1972. Additional places will also be available outside the universities.' To a further question as to whether these measures were sufficient, it was stated that the number of qualified planners in Britain should double by 1974 as a result of the extra places available. 'As for the new planning system, I hope that as a result of it we will make better use of qualified planning staff and reduce the work on detailed matters, because this will tend to alleviate rather than aggravate the shortage of planners.'[2]

Details of recognised schools of planning may be found in the Town Planning Institute's publications *Town planning as a career* (latest edition August 1969) which also contains notes about the practice and profession of planning; and the *Examinations handbook* (latest edition April 1969) which gives the detailed examination syllabi and relevant rules and regulations. Much the same information also appears in the institute's *Yearbook*. The *Journal of the Town Planning Institute* regularly carries notes on the examination syllabus, comments on examination questions from examiners, and details of planning school courses which have been recognised as giving exemption from the institute examinations.

Information about planning courses can be obtained from several other sources. The Careers Research and Advisory Centre at Cambridge issue a booklet *Architecture, town and country planning, landscape architecture: a guide to first degree courses in UK universities and colleges,* which is revised every two years (latest edition July 1969), and which compares university and non-university courses in the three subjects together with short notes on the respective professions, reading lists, and other miscellaneous information. The Advisory Centre for Education performs much the same service in its guide *Architecture and town planning: guide to higher educa-*

tion courses (1969), and also issued in December 1968 the *Where* Supplement 17, *Environmental studies.* Wider coverage, but within the context of the whole range of educational courses, can be found in such publications as *The world of learning* (Europa Publications, annually); the *Commonwealth universities yearbook* (Association of Commonwealth Universities, annually); and the *Year book of technical education and careers in industry* (Black, annually). More specialised, in that it is concerned with a defined region, is the *Handbook of town planning education in Scotland 1967-68,* edited by Anthony S Travis for the Scottish branch of the Town Planning Institute (Edinburgh, Scottish Education Department, 1968) which summarised the position of planning education in Scotland, and gave detailed information about the courses available at that time. As a preliminary to its working party on educational objectives in urban and regional planning (see below) the Centre for Environmental Studies have issued two Information Papers on the present state of planning education. *Facts about planning courses* (CES, 1970, CES-IP-14) contains detailed information about the courses; *The provision of planning education* (CES, 1970, CES-IP-15) presents a summary and analysis of the information. A detailed profile of the organisation and methods of the planning school of the University of Newcastle upon Tyne, edited by Charles F Riley, appeared in *JTPI* 56(6) June 1970 234-241, as the first in a series of articles contributed by planning schools in the United Kingdom. A list of American and Canadian universities offering courses in planning as at 1968 is included in Melville Branch's bibliography *Comprehensive urban planning* 313-323 (discussed in chapter 13).

The Town Planning Institute is not the only professional body concerned with the education of planners; nor are the universities and colleges which operate officially recognised courses the only ones to offer education in planning or a more specific or related aspect of it.

In March 1969, the Regional Studies Association published a document on *The new planning courses,* and followed this up with a conference on the same subject in May of the same year, at the London School of Economics.[3] Under discussion at the conference were the courses newly under way, or in process of being established, within existing university social sciences departments, which offered postgraduate training by non-planners in sociology and its contribution to planning. Such courses, and others of the type of Aberdeen University's course in rural and regional resources planning and Liverpool's in transport design, have a potential contribution to make in providing practising qualified planners with a broader disciplinary base than they derive from the recognised planning courses, although at present they attract principally graduates from related disciplines, such as geographers.

Among other professional bodies with an interest in planning is the Royal Institute of British Architects. In 1965 it published a report by Anthony Goss, *The architect in town planning,* which analysed the role of the architect in town planning chiefly by means of an assessment of planning education and opportunities from the architect's point of view. The report, endorsed by a steering committee and later by the full RIBA Council, affirmed the importance of architects in planning, their supremacy as designers of the built environment, and the fitness of the architect's own professional education to equip him for full participation in the affairs of planning and planners. By a gradual process of evolution, these views have been translated into a proposal for an urban design diploma, first mooted in 1968, to be awarded at the end of a full time course of at least one year to students who are not qualified planners but who wish to specialise in urban planning and design. Discussions are still being carried on between the RIBA Board of Education, the Social Science Research Council, and departments or schools which have suitable facilities for the establishment of such courses. Whether the award of such a diploma will create architect/planners who will wish to participate in the total development process along with, and on equal terms with the other involved professionals, or whether it will produce a new super breed of architects who will wish to dominate the process, remains to be seen.

The new planning system is creating a demand not only for qualified planners but also for planning technicians who equally require a formal and advanced training in the techniques associated with planning. In 1968 the Town Planning Institute with the approval of the Department of Education and Science instigated the establishment of three courses for planning technicians, a number which was expected to increase to fourteen during 1971 with around three hundred technicians in training. The courses lead to the award of Ordinary and Higher National Certificates in surveying, cartography, and planning. The institute has also been engaged, through the agency of a joint working party of planners and technicians, in setting up an organisation to deal with all the issues affecting planning technicians. The Incorporated Association of Architects and Surveyors has also announced that it ' has initiated examinations in town planning leading to technician and to full professional membership . . . The examinations will have a bias towards land use control and are expected to be of particular interest to local government officers concerned with planning who are at present denied ready access to a professional qualification.'[4] But a letter in the *Architects' journal*[5] from Ian Melville (then of Newcastle upon Tyne University's Department of Town and Country Planning) claims in no uncertain terms that these examinations ' have so little to do with physical planning that they could not conceivably be an acceptable test of competence in this respect '.

The activity of teaching in a planning school is an intensive one: ' compared with many university teachers, staff in planning schools have to spend a far greater proportion of their time in teaching (including preparation, assessment and administrative tasks ancillary to teaching) '.[6] In addition to lecturing in a wide range of subjects (see the Town Planning Institute's *Examination handbook* for details) many of which require practical demonstration to become meaningful to students, there is also much emphasis on project work, the mounting of live planning projects involving collection and analysis of data and other time-consuming activities. New techniques which are applicable to planning education are being introduced, for example, the use of gaming and simulation methods,[7] and a lecturer in planning must keep abreast of developments not only in the processes of teaching but also in the subjects which he teaches and in the general trend of planning itself. There are two hundred full-time planning teachers, plus an unknown number of part-time lecturers, and recently the need has been expressed for a forum for discussion of common problems and ideas. The idea of an association of planning teachers was born at a conference held by the Education Committee of the Town Planning Institute in Coventry in April 1970, in the course of which a number of teachers agreed that an effort should be made to form some kind of standing conference to deal with a wide range of matters requiring attention and discussion. An inaugural conference was held at Birmingham University in January 1971 to discuss the proposed association further, and to hear papers on the themes of student selection and teaching methods.

From planning teachers it is only a small step to planning students. What makes a good planning student? Some answers to this intriguing question are provided by R D Savage in 'Factors involved in attainment in university training in town and country planning' in *Planning outlook* new series 8 Spring 1970 40-54. The author presents results of a survey of ninety six undergraduate and postgraduate students in town and country planning in the University of Newcastle upon Tyne in June 1969, and is particularly interested in the personality factors involved in the achievement or non-achievement of a degree; clearly, as he points out, there is a fruitful field of research here. Collectively, planning students are increasingly well-organised and vocal. The Association of Student Planners was formed in 1964.[8] Its functions are both national and regional. At the national level, it is a 'pressure group to ensure consistency and continuity in all matters pertaining to planning education', and its decisions are taken by a national council. There is also a regional organisation, four large regions each with a regional council, which organises regional conferences (in addition to the national conferences) and coordinates planning student activities within each region. It communicates its activities and opinions in a regular feature in *JTPI*.

The association has issued two reports on planning education. The first, issued in 1966 and now out of print, was *Planning education,* whose main recommendation was that sandwich courses should be introduced into planning schools (at that time there were none: now seven schools operate a 'year out' in their courses, although not all in the same way). In December 1969, the association issued a second report, *Aspects of planning education,*[9] which reviews developments since 1966 (it also includes a useful list of references to articles and reports on planning education in its broadest sense) and wrestles with several thorny problems such as the place of research in planning schools—' we consider that the major emphasis

62

of research sponsorship should go to planning schools rather than to institutions concerned solely with research . . . we recommend that all the larger schools should have at least two permanent senior research staff '; the advantages or otherwise of a university base for planning schools—' we can see no case for arguing that basic physical planning courses should exclusively be in universities or in any one institutional type. We would, however, expect courses either to be in universities or polytechnics, because of the need for location within a broadly-based institution, but beyond that we would hope that basic courses (both for undergraduates and for graduates) will develop in both institutions '; and, inevitably, the problem of the definition of planning and the scope and content and purpose of its educational system.

The ASP report provides a good working definition of physical planning in relation to the total development process ' the corporate practice of which might best be termed environmental management '. Within the context of this interdisciplinary process, the report sees two fundamental elements in planning education :

' (a) comprehension of the total development process, to be able to work within it as a member of an interdisciplinary team, to understand the specialist contribution of the physical planner and of other specialists and to be aware of the physical implications of non-physical actions and vice versa. One of the lessons of planning practice appears undoubtedly to be that almost everything affects almost everything else;

' (b) knowledge and understanding in depth of the specialist skill of the physical planner.'

The view of planning as a part of an integrated interdisciplinary process is not new, nor are students the first to think of it. Dr David Eversley, in a paper to the 1966 Town and Country Planning Summer School[10], in which he discussed regional planning and the inadequacy of present education as exemplified by the courses of the TPI-recognised planning schools to equip planners to play an effective part in it, put forward a clear view of a broader-based education. ' Personally, I would wish that there were a still broader approach to the whole question, and that we could blur the lines of professional jealousies and boundary claims by calling the whole thing environmental studies : thus to plant it firmly both within

63

the social and the physical sciences and allow us to introduce wider and less utilitarian notions, such as those concerned with the aesthetics of environment and the sociology of leisure '—a view which was reiterated at the Regional Studies Association Conference in 1969.[11] The trend therefore is towards a broader-based educational process, and official thinking goes along with this, both in the Town Planning Institute—reflected in its revised syllabus—and in universities such as London, where the Chair of Environmental Studies combines planning, architecture and sociology, and the Heriot-Watt in Edinburgh which has created a School of the Built Environment.

The government also endorses this view in its acceptance of Lady Sharp's report for the Ministry of Transport, *Transport planning: the men for the job* (HMSO, 1970). Lady Sharp found that her brief —to investigate the manpower requirements for urban transport planning—was too narrow, and that she could not investigate transport planning in isolation from land use planning: ' I feel sure that the people engaged in transport planning should be interchangeable with those engaged in land use planning; and that what is really at issue is the development of a core of people with a wide variety of education, training and experience to work in the whole spectrum of environmental planning and to be members of a single society in which all can meet to discuss their common problems . . . I believe that unless it is done planning will not be adequately served.' The publication of the report was accompanied on the same day by a statement from the then Secretary of State for Local Government and Regional Planning that an advanced training centre of the type envisaged by Lady Sharp would be established within a university, for high calibre education in transport planning and environmental management. Subsequently the Ministry of Transport asked universities whether they would be interested in setting up such a centre, it being the government's wish that alternative ways of achieving the same objective of a better supply of specially trained people should be explored before any action was taken. A decision is expected in 1971.

Clearly, as these developments indicate, the new concepts and practices of planning in the 1970's and beyond will demand—are demanding now—corresponding developments in planning educa-

64

tion both in its contents and its methods. The nature of these developments is the subject of a working group on 'Educational objectives in urban and regional planning' sponsored by the Centre for Environmental Studies, which held its first meeting in November 1970. The group will examine current theories about the nature and purpose of planning and the character of future planning activities and will attempt to identify educational objectives in accordance with these. It will also examine the extent to which planning schools are fulfilling their objectives at present. The purpose of the group is strategic rather than detailed, and is to outline one or more feasible future frameworks in which planning education can develop.

REFERENCES

1 Winter 1970; but the TPI makes regular assessments of the courses offered by planning schools and awards official recognition as appropriate. Therefore it is probable that this list is already out of date.

2 Parliamentary debates (Hansard) fifth series v766. House of Commons official report session 1967-68 column 901.

3 Regional Studies Association *The new planning courses* (RSA, 1969).

4 From a report in *Architects' journal* 151(13) April 1 1970 795.

5 *Architects' journal* 151(20) May 20 1970 1230-1231.

6 Anthony Goss ' Research in recognised planning schools ' *JTPI* 55(5) May 1969 203-205.

7 Research has been done, principally (in the UK) at Sheffield University, on the benefits and applications of these techniques to planning education. See, for example, John L Taylor and K R Carter ' Some instructional dimensions of urban gaming-simulation ' *Planning outlook* new series 7 Autumn 1969 35-53.

8 A review of the origins and development of the Association of Student Planners is given in *JTPI* 54(9) November 1968 443.

9 Publications of the Association of Student Planners are available from John Perry, City Planning Department, Civic Centre, Newcastle upon Tyne NE1 8PH.

10 D E C Eversley ' The economics of regional planning ' in *Report of the Town and Country Planning Summer School*, Keele, 1966 (TPI, 1966) 16.

11 Regional Studies Association *op cit*.

3

5

THE STRUCTURE OF PLANNING: RESEARCH

THERE IS NO CLEAR-CUT universally accepted definition of planning research. The lack of definition applies not only to the subject or content of the research, but also to the level at which it is carried on, from investigation of basic concepts to straightforward collection of facts. Moreover, this lack of definition is a fact which is very largely accepted by planners as something which is inherent in their research activity, arising from the lack of definition and the diversification of planning itself.

A survey financed by the Office for Scientific and Technical Information (of the Department of Education and Science) of the information use and requirements of planners in all types of activity, experienced this lack of definition in its attempt to draw a sample of research workers from a poorly-defined population, and failed as a result to draw any significant conclusions about planning research as a coherent activity with regard to its pattern of information use. But the report of the survey[1] went on to express the belief that ' some of the research which is now on-going may, on its fruition, provide a stabilising influence and that in perhaps five years' time planning research may have a clearer focus and a more clearly defined population '. Whether this is a pious hope, will be seen in the course of time.

In the meantime, the problem remains; and it is naturally a problem which is insistent in any attempt to erect a framework in which to pigeon-hole the various types of planning research which are being carried on in the UK, and the various types of organisation which house the research activity. The only documentary attempt at such a framework is an Information Paper published by the Centre for Environmental Studies in October 1968, *The structure of urban and regional planning research in Britain* by Cynthia Cockburn (CES-IP-3).[2] Mrs Cockburn also experienced, among other problems, the lack of definition. ' Since the nature of the contributions to this research [ie urban and regional planning research] are in reality greatly varied, ranging in subject matter from geography, through economics and sociology, to construction, and in physical scale from the road intersection to the nation, to have imposed a definition would have been arbitrarily to exclude some field of interest '.

It is possible to identify four[3] levels of planning research:

1) basic conceptual research, which is concerned with the nature of planning and its basic conceptual framework and with building up a body of theory which will substantiate future action;

2) basic applied research, which is concerned with the development of techniques for practical application, for instance model building, or the example mentioned in the previous chapter of educational simulation techniques;

3) planning studies, which investigate in detail the various factors relevant to planning within a designated area, which may be as large as a whole region or as small as a town centre; the purpose of the study is to analyse these factors—social, demographic, industrial, land use, recreational, etc, etc—and to use them as a basis for forecasting the probable requirements of the area, and for the formulation of alternative plans for meeting these requirements;

4) planning surveys, or more accurately, surveys relevant to planning, which are basically exercises in collection and analysis of data reflecting a situation at a given point in time or over a given period, though some of them are on a large scale and employ sophisticated methods of analysis; these are usually confined in their operation within a given area (though the results may be of much wider interest) and are frequently concerned more with a subject approach than with the physical aspects of the area as such, for example, use of public parks or reaction to living in high flats, and range from the land use survey carried out by a local authority planning department to the large scale social surveys undertaken by the Institute of Community Studies.

No one of these categories of research is confined in its furtherance to any one type of organisation. Indeed, the organisations in which planning research is carried on vary widely in all respects, and it is impossible to categorise any of them as being primarily concerned with one or other type of research. Cockburn (see above) identifies eight distinct categories of organisation within which research is regularly carried on which is either directly concerned with planning or potentially relevant to it, plus the Centre for Environmental Studies itself, which occupies a unique position in the structure. She discusses, *inter alia,* the contribution made by industry, and by public authorities, boards and nationalised industries, which is strictly speaking marginal; and is particularly informative on the complex structure (pre-1970) of central government departments which are involved, however slightly, in planning. Here, we examine planning research in three main categories of organisation: those whose primary function is practice, those whose primary function is education, and those whose primary function is research.

Within the first category, research at varying levels is carried on in central government departments, most of it being concentrated in the various sections of the Department of the Environment which were previously part of the Ministry of Housing and Local Government. The Scottish Development Department sponsors, and is itself involved in a number of planning studies, and has cooperated with MOHLG on various projects, for example, the two study teams set up in 1969 (involving local authorities also) one to examine the data requirements of structure, district, and action area plans under the Town and Country Planning Act 1968, the other to develop a national system of terms for classifying land uses. For fuller details of the research programmes of relevant central government departments, the reader is referred to Cockburn.

Research, mainly at the fourth level described above, is carried on in the local authority planning departments, but both quantity and quality are dictated by the resources available, and it is only in the larger county and borough departments that a separately constituted, continuously staffed research section of a size sufficient to pursue a programme of useful research is found. In units of smaller population there is often hardly enough staff to plan, without the additional burden of research. Yet research is basic to the plan: 'if new planning ideas are to be produced and our work of city rebuilding improved, it is essential to have a research section shielded from the day to day pressures of statutory planning and able to devote time to analysis and to thinking things out from first principles.'[4]

The larger private practices, again those with resources and continuity of work to support it, are frequently involved in research at the third level, on planning studies, sometimes independently but often in conjunction with specialist consultants in, perhaps, economic planning or transportation. Such studies may be for developing a whole area, for conserving a historic town centre, for establishing the feasibility of a new town or the expansion of an existing one in relation to its region. The reports of studies of this type, which are usually very detailed, form a category of planning information in themselves, and are discussed in chapter 9.

Within the category of practical planning organisations, the Greater London Council occupies a unique position, not only because of the extent and nature of its planning functions but also because of its huge size and complex administrative structure which embraces a wide range of specialist professional staff. In 1966, a Research and Intelligence Unit was established in the GLC to provide services for both its parent body and the London boroughs. Originally attached to the Director-General's Department, the unit subsequently moved to the combined Planning and Transportation Department as an independent entity with a staff of nearly two hundred, organised into five divisions. Its terms of reference were ' to provide a unified statistical intelligence and research service for all GLC departments and the London boroughs '.[5] The unit was subsequently split up as a result of a further internal reorganisation within the GLC during 1970, and its parts distributed between the various branches of the Strategic Planning Wing of the Planning and Transportation Department. From December 1967, the unit issued a *Quarterly bulletin,* and also produced occasional papers on specialised topics.[6]

The second category of organisation in which planning research is undertaken comprises the planning schools. In this sector, there is less activity than might be expected, or desired. In 1968, the Research Committee of the Town Planning Institute promoted an enquiry into the extent of research in the thirteen planning schools whose courses were at that time recognised by the institute.[7] The conclusion reached was that ' there is a limited tradition of research allied to planning education ', and that if such a tradition is to be nurtured and developed a measure of financial support for that specific purpose will have to be forthcoming. The main obstacles to continuing research programmes in the planning schools have been partly the lack of time on the part of the teaching staff and, mainly, lack of sponsors and finance for research projects. Nevertheless, some worthwhile research has been done, sponsored by central government, by local authorities, or by various independent agencies; from which good examples are provided by the intensive study of containerisation conducted by the Universities of Strathclyde and Glasgow, and the studies of office location carried out for the Location of Offices Bureau at the Leeds School of Town Planning.

In total, then, the contribution to planning research of these two categories is quite small. Naturally enough, the major contribution is that made by the research organisations themselves. These comprise a variety of types including units within planning schools, centres affiliated to universities, government financed organisations and privately financed organisations. Some of these organisations combine research with teaching, some sponsor research as well as maintaining an in-house programme, some concentrate exclusively on research. Most of them have formal or informal links with a university. Any of the four defined levels of research may be found in all of them.

Two factors must be noted with regard to the total activity of planning research. Firstly, that it lacks coordination. There is no central guiding force, and no overall programme. Secondly, that in proportion to the importance of planning now and in the future, and the complexity of the issues involved, the research effort is tiny, and the amount of money available is minimal.[8] One of the leading British research workers in the planning field, Peter Cowan, has summed up the weaknesses in British planning as ' a basic lack of concern with the scientific bases of planning ', and goes on to point out that ' British planners are still working on the assumptions which they inherited from the founders of the movement. Very little research, other than social surveys, has been carried out

70

in Britain, and the little that has been done seems to have left the bulk of British planning practice unaffected ... Gaps in the theoretical basis of a subject become apparent only very slowly, and, as the achievements of British planning today are considerable, the reasons for changing to a more rigorous pattern are difficult to demonstrate. But unless British planning does achieve a more consistent basis for action, and if it continues to operate upon the *idées reçues* of earlier generations the profession will become redundant, and the planning of cities will be taken over by geographers, economists and administrators. The lack of an adequate and growing body of knowledge upon which to base action must lead in the long run to the gradual demise of any profession.'[9]

There is undeniably a need for a central focus of planning research. The body which comes nearest to filling this role is the Centre for Environmental Studies in London, which was established in 1966 with funds from the British government and the American Ford Foundation as an ' independent body with the broad aims of promoting research and education in the planning and design of the physical environment; at the same time it was hoped to provide a forum where practitioners and researchers, both in this country and abroad, could discuss problems of common interest and determine research needs '. The centre was initially guaranteed finance for a five-year period; further funds were made available in 1971 to ensure continuity. The centre sponsors research by awarding grants, usually to individuals or teams working within a university, and maintains its own interdisciplinary research team. The work of the centre is described by David Bayliss, a former member of its research team, in *JTPI* 55(2) February 1969 68-71; by its second (but first full-time) Director, David Donnison, in *New society* 14 (376) December 11 1969 935-937; and also in its annual reports. A *News sheet* which includes notes on staff and visitors, new publications, conferences and meetings organised by the centre, and progress reports on research projects, is circulated in accordance with a mailing list. Publications are in the series of Working Papers and Information Papers, both of which now have a substantial number of titles, and in the more recently instituted University Working Papers. Details of these, and the publications themselves, are available from the centre.

While the Centre for Environmental Studies is one of the main bodies, and perhaps the most obvious one which financially sponsors research in planning, support also comes from the Social Science Research Council, which, while it casts its net throughout the entire range of the social sciences, has granted sums of money for research projects in planning at the discretion of its committee on that subject. Details of these are included in the quarterly *SSRC newsletter*. The committee, originally for human geography and planning, was reconstituted at the end of 1969 into two committees, one dealing specifically with planning. Thus the continuing interest of the council in planning research seems to be assured.

Also in a central position is the research committee of the Town Planning Institute which, owing to its lack of funds, is not able to play a very active role in the furtherance of planning research. Its terms of reference are ' promotion of research; co-ordination of effort; dissemination of information; data classification; studies and and memoranda on behalf of the Council '. One of these studies, on research in planning schools, has been mentioned. One of the most useful functions of the research committee is the publication of the volume *Planning research*,[10] the only comprehensive guide to planning research in progress throughout the UK, whose maintenance is now supported by a grant from the Centre for Environmental Studies.

A body which is not wholly concerned with planning research, and which has no powers of implementation, but which is of some interest in this context by virtue of a memorandum issued at the beginning of 1970, is the Buchanan Report Standing Joint Committee. This is a body which was formed by the Institution of Civil Engineers, the Institution of Municipal Engineers, the Royal Institute of British Architects, the Royal Institution of Chartered Surveyors, and the Town Planning Institute, after the publication of the Buchanan Report, *Traffic in towns,* in 1963, to watch developments in planning and traffic planning. In their memorandum, the committee find that British planning research is fragmented and uncoordinated, and has inadequate funds. It advocates the establishment of a planning research organisation within the (then) Ministry of Housing and Local Government, a central agency which should work in close cooperation with the universities and which might be used for channelling grants and contracts for research. It also comments on priority needs in planning research, and lists five topics requiring attention. The committee further realises that there is a large quantity of information and data accumulating in depositories all over the country, and suggests that this should be made available centrally, envisaging the expansion of the MOHLG Library into a proper storage and retrieval system to cope with the extra volume of information.

A casual glance through the pages of *Planning research* (see above) will give an indication of the range of projects on which work is being done in the UK. It is our purpose now to round off this account of planning research by discussing briefly the work of some of the organisations which are engaged exclusively, or almost exclusively in this activity. These have been selected arbitrarily from a wide range and no evaluation is implied.

At Manchester University the Centre for Urban and Regional Research was established in 1966 to coordinate work which was already being done independently in several departments on urban and regional problems. Three of its major projects are financed by the Social Science Research Council; another has been commissioned by the National House-Builders' Registration Council, who have contracted with the centre for it to provide the council with a statistical service, primarily for demand forecasting. The other major projects are into the development of a comprehensive computer model of a town; the application of cybernetic principles to towns in an attempt to define the control systems which govern urban activity; and into the rationalisation and coordination of regional statistics for planning. A booklet giving information about the centre and its work was issued in September 1969 and is available free from the secretary.

The Planning Research Unit in Edinburgh was established in 1962, one of the earliest such units in the country. It is an integral part of the Department of Urban Design and Regional Planning of the University of Edinburgh, but is an independent unit in that it is financially self-supporting through its own commissions. Its major activity has been in the field of sub-regional planning studies, and between 1962 and 1967 it participated in three of these—of the Lothians, the Grangemouth/Falkirk region, and the Scottish Cen-

73

tral Borders—all commissioned by the Scottish Development Department.[11] The unit has been particularly concerned in recent years with the development of threshold analysis,[12] a technique which was applied for the first time in British planning in the study of the Scottish Borders; several small short term grants have been made available for its development and in 1970 the Scottish Development Department commissioned a full scale project into its development for British planning. The unit has also carried out a survey of the requirements of disabled people in towns for the Central Council for the Disabled. In March 1971 the Office for Scientific and Technical Information awarded a grant to the unit for a three-year project to examine the structure of planning information and to develop methods of organising it, as a follow-up to the survey of information use and requirements mentioned above.

Away from the university environment, the Urban Planning Division of the Building Research Station was set up in 1966. It has a multi-disciplinary in-house research team, and also commissions work externally. It has been particularly active in the area of user studies, many of them in relation to housing; has completed research into various aspects of urban location; and has investigated decision making processes in planning. Currently, the Location Studies Section is engaged on an intensive study of shops and shopping behaviour. The Urban Growth Group is concentrating its attention on new towns, firstly in a retrospective study of Mark I towns and secondly in monitoring the growth of Washington new town in County Durham. There are also on-going projects to develop scales for measuring environmental quality and assessing satisfaction with it, and to develop the use of the computer in evaluating alternative planning proposals. Of particular interest in the context of this book is a project to discover the kind of information which is used on the job by planners in private practices. Results of BRS research, including that in planning, are usually disseminated by means of the regular Current Papers (some of them reprints from journals) which are comprehensively listed and indexed in the station's own publication *Information 70: a select list of publications and films,* issued in 1969, and also in the quarterly *BRS news. BRS news* 12 Summer 1970 contains a list of research projects with the publications that have arisen from them. Current

Paper 46/68 is entitled *Urban planning research at the Building Research Station* and is a reprint of a seminar paper by K Alsop, the Head of the Urban Planning Division. Details of BRS publications, and the publications themselves, are available from the Publications Officer at the station.

It is by no means unique to the planning profession that those engaged in practice are in the main divorced from those engaged in research, and that the results of research are slow to percolate through to the average planning department. In an effort to bridge the gulf, the Centre for Environmental Studies has initiated a scheme of fellowships—the first two were awarded during 1970—whereby planners working in local or central government or in private practice will be enabled to take a period of leave, up to twelve months, to work at one or more research institutions. The main purposes of the scheme are to increase understanding of research and its use in the field, to assist in the development of research in planning departments and agencies, to inform research workers about problems facing planners, and generally to promote collaboration between research workers and planners. The centre's scheme will obviously affect only a few planners directly, but it is a beginning which in the interests of the profession generally, and the validity of its practice, must be followed through.

REFERENCES

1 Brenda White *Planners and information* (Library Association, 1970) 126.

2 A companion paper covering Europe appeared at the same time: Cynthia Cockburn *The organisation of urban and regional planning research in European countries* (Centre for Environmental Studies, 1968, CES-IP-2).

3 This is the author's interpretation. Other writers have identified less or more levels, and have attached different labels to them. David Bayliss, for example, divides into three: planning studies (situation-specific), research (problem-specific), pure research (nonspecific to real life problems). David Bayliss 'Environmental research' *Official architecture and planning* 31(10) October 1968 1329. See also the breakdown adopted for the Town Planning Institute's research register *Planning research*.

4 Wilfred Burns *Newcastle: a study in replanning at Newcastle upon Tyne* (Leonard Hill, 1967) 14. This contains a good description of the work done in the research section of a large city planning office. Research techniques in planning offices were the subject of a discussion group at the 1965 Town and Country Planning Summer School, and a summary of this is contained in *Report of the Town and Country Planning Summer School, St Andrews, 1965* (TPI, 1965) 88-93.

5 An account of the origins of the unit is given in *Quarterly bulletin of the Research and Intelligence Unit* 1 December 1967 5-7. The unit in its reconstituted form (as it existed up to 1970) is described in *Quarterly bulletin of the Research and Intelligence Unit* 8 September 1969 3.

6 Details of GLC publications, including those of the Research and Intelligence Unit, and the publications themselves may be obtained from the Information Centre, County Hall, London SE1.

7 Anthony Goss 'Research in recognised planning schools' *JTPI* 55(5) May 1969 203-205.

8 Lionel March, in a letter to *New Society* 14 (374) November 27 1969 874, quotes comparative figures of expenditure by the government research councils for the academic year 1969-70 ranging from £45.8 million in science down to £2.5 million in social science. The Centre for Environmental Studies at that time had funds to spend on planning research of about £0.15 million annually.

9 Peter Cowan *et al The office: a facet of urban growth* (Heinemann, 1969) 5.

10 *Planning research* is discussed more fully, along with other research registers, in chapter 13.

11 The reports of these studies are discussed, along with other development plans, in chapter 9.

12 Some documentary sources of information on threshold analysis are discussed within the section on 'Planning techniques' in chapter 11.

6

THE PATTERN
OF INFORMATION USAGE

THE NOTION OF each small piece of work having its own special information requirements is not unique to planning; it applies to all fields of work and study. Nevertheless, while it may be true, it is not a helpful basis for systematic attempts to meet information requirements, and for this purpose it is necessary to observe and record the many thousands of requirements which arise, and to endeavour to identify from these some sort of pattern from which it can be deduced that certain types of work require, in basic terms, certain types of information. It is also possible to observe and record the information-seeking habits of information users and to deduce from a synthesis of these that certain types of user employ different approaches in the search for information. Investigations to establish patterns of these types are normally called information use studies or user studies.

User studies in the fields of scientific and technical information are well established and have been in progress in various subject areas for nearly thirty years. Information services of varying degrees of sophistication exist for many subject fields in science and technology, some of them designed on the basis of user studies, some of them arbitrarily developed. In the social sciences—and if it is necessary to categorise planning, it fits more comfortably under this heading than under any other collective umbrella—the scientific study of information requirements and of user habits is much younger. In a mimeographed paper *The flow of behavioral science information: a review of the research literature* (Palo Alto, California, Stanford University Institute for Communication Research, 1965), W J Paisley essayed a review of user studies in the social sciences: his conclusion was that there were none to review. In

1970, J M Brittain asserts, in *Information and its users: a review with special reference to the social sciences* (Bath, Bath University Press, 1970) that ' there are no more than eighteen user studies in the social sciences that have used empirical methods, and not all of these could be called user studies in terms of strict definitions '. Brittain's monograph is an offshoot of the first comprehensive study of the information requirements of the social sciences, completed at Bath University at the end of 1970, and due to report during 1971. It is a valuable review, which draws together a widely scattered literature, and discusses it in terms of user studies generally, and their methodology, and then—the major part—in terms of the various studies which have been carried out in the social sciences generally and in specific disciplines within them, including a short section on urban and regional planning. Brittain also includes a chapter devoted to studies of the literature itself, or the ' artifacts of communication [which] include citations, articles, monographs, and prepublication papers '. The bibliography is full and well-documented.

Brittain's section on urban and regional planning is based to a large extent on the results of the survey of information provision, use, and requirements financed by the Office for Scientific and Technical Information and carried out during 1968 and 1969. The results of this survey are embodied in the report *Planners and information: a report of an investigation into information provision in town and country planning* by Brenda White (Library Association, 1970, Research Publication 3). The survey was different from most other user studies, in whatever subject fields, in that it incorporated a survey of organised library resources which attempted to discover the extent to which planning information was being provided in public libraries, in university and college libraries, and in planning organisations; and then attempted to examine the results of the use study in the light of the standards of provision. The sample for the survey was 450 planners, the majority being qualified planners but including also those qualified in other disciplines and working within the planning field, operating in the three areas of practice, teaching, and research, throughout the United Kingdom. Of these, 284 completed the survey questionnaire, a response rate of 63%. This was a small sample, and the number of basic variables involved

78

—type of organisation and primary qualification, for example, which between them necessitated a high number of categories— inevitably resulted in some categories being numerically under-represented when the data were analysed. Clearly, therefore, the results cannot be regarded as conclusive: as Brittain points out, 'in line with good research methodology, other confirmatory studies are now required'. Nevertheless, they do indicate a pattern, which can usefully be stated here before embarking upon discussion of individual types of information source.

With regard to the provision of information, the survey finds, very briefly, that, compared with other subjects, 'planning is fairly well served in city and county public libraries as regards special services and bibliographical services'; that there is lack of agreement about the provision of specialised departmental collections in university libraries; and that organised libraries are virtually non-existent in local authority planning departments. These conclusions were formed on the basis of data collected in 1968; but the third, pertaining to local authority planning departments, has since been corroborated by a survey of library provision within such planning departments by Nottinghamshire County Planning Department, *Planning department libraries: report of a questionnaire survey* (West Bridgford, Nottingham, 1971), which reports the information gained from a survey of forty five English and Welsh county and borough planning departments, including eight London boroughs and the Greater London Council (a response rate of 87%) carried out during 1970. The report gives information about comparative expenditure on books and journals, the journals taken, the existence of librarians, the methods of arranging information, and the procedures for obtaining new publications; and attempts to compare the efficiency of county departments which do employ a librarian, with those which do not.

The major achievement of the earlier survey of existing use of information by planners is to establish a rank order of importance of fourteen sources of operational information, operational sources being defined as 'those sources of information or of data which are used in the course of planning work, which are in fact tools essential to the job in hand'. These sources are, in order of importance, as follows:

1 data from own survey
2 maps and plans
3 development plans and reports
4 statutory government publications
5 advisory government publications
6 office records
7 journals
8 statistical sources
9 monograph texts
10 data/information from other surveys
11 corporate texts
12 air photographs
13 newspapers
14 theses

The relative ranking of these sources suggested three groups. The first and second emerge fairly clearly as the two really important operational sources. The third to the eighth form a middle range, with very little difference in degree of importance. The ninth to the fourteenth constitute a group which fairly clearly lags behind the second group, and which shows marked differences in importance between the constituent sources. This overall ranking is based on responses from planners in all three areas of activity. Further analysis indicates that the pattern is not consistent within these areas: in practice, the three most important sources are, in order, maps and plans, data from own survey, and office records; in teaching, the important operational sources are monograph texts, journals, and corporate texts; and in research, the pattern varies again, to data from own survey, journals, and data from other surveys.

The report also incorporates a detailed analysis of the methods used by planners in all areas of activity to locate information required to solve problems which arise in the course of their work. The possible methods of approach were categorised into printed, library, and personal sources, and the proportional use of these measured in the search for information on planning, and for information on subjects related to planning. In the former kind of search, the use made of the three categories is roughly equal; but in the search for planning-related information, most planners go through

80

library and personal channels, rather than printed sources. Of the printed sources available, abstracting and indexing services and bibliographies are little used: references in books and, particularly, in journals provide most of the required guidance. Matching this pattern with the provision of formal printed services, it seems reasonable to infer that the small use made of these arises from their general non-availability in planning organisations. Roughly equal use is made of librarians (where one exists within the organisation), of library catalogues, and of browsing along library shelves. From an analysis of the use made of personal contacts for locating information, it emerges that planners make most use of colleagues within their own departments and of known subject experts, with less reliance being placed upon contacts outside the departmental orbit. These indicated patterns beg many questions, and leave many fields unexplored. The habit of browsing, for example, and the wider topic of the accidental discovery of information, which is recognised to play an important part in information-gathering generally, could not be examined in the course of this particular survey. Much more detailed study is also required of the informal personal channels of communication used by planners, and particularly where such channels exist between planners and specialists in other subject fields.

One of the problems facing any subject specialist, whatever his working context, is that of keeping up to date with current thinking and development in his own field and in others closely related to it. It is a little surprising to discover that only 60% of the sample consider that it is very important to keep up to date with current developments in all relevant fields. It is well known, of course, that the range of subjects which are relevant to planning is wide and that the problem of current awareness may loom large if many related subject fields are to be considered over and above the central aspects of planning itself. Traffic planning, sociology, economics, recreation, statistics, architecture, and landscape are all indicated as relevant by more than half the sample of planners, a wide range of subjects in which to be aware of current developments. Journals and personal contacts are the most commonly used methods of keeping up to date. But planners, by and large, do not read widely in the journal literature: it was found that 64% of the sample sees six or less journals regularly. This is significantly lower than the average number of journals scanned by scientists, engineers, and technologists, whose average is ten, and, as the report observes, ' taken in conjunction with the limited and fairly stereotyped journal provision within planning organisations, and with the small use made of abstracts and indexes, it is obvious that the majority of planners are keeping up to date with the same developments in planning through the same small number of journals '.

The overall picture which emerges is of a profession which has at its disposal a wide range of information sources, but which in general fails to exploit any category fully, even those which it ranks most important. Always acknowledging the very real limitations of time and opportunity, it seems fairly clear that if planners were more fully aware of the range of primary and secondary sources which already exist, and which increase with gathering momentum every year, their information usage would improve also, not only in terms of quantity but also in terms of quality. The following chapters give some indication of these sources.

7

MAPS AND PLANS

PART I: MAPS, PLANS, ATLASES

MAPS AND PLANS are the basic working tools of the planner. They are for him in much the same category as is the level for the surveyor, or the musical score for the musician.

Proof of the importance of maps and plans, if such was needed, was obtained from the results of the OSTI-financed survey of information requirements in planning (see chapter 6). But the bald statistics, the unqualified statement that to planners in practice maps take priority over all other sources of operational information, conceal much more than they reveal. They conceal interesting facts such as the types of maps which are used, the scales which are most useful and the scales which are most appropriate to different situations; they conceal also the opinions of planners about the quality of the maps which they use, whether they use them to the best advantage, and, perhaps most importantly, whether their non-use of many map types is due to ignorance of the existence of material outside their own organisation's collection.

In discussion at the Conference on Information and Urban Planning, held by the Centre for Environmental Studies in May 1969, Dr Roger Kirby of the Department of Geography at Edinburgh University, stressed the need for a detailed survey of planners' use of maps.[1] A survey of map use, embracing map users of all types and therefore including planners as a small percentage of the total population, has in fact been carried out by Dr Kirby, financed by the Social Science Research Council, during 1967 and 1968.[2] Among the 1,553 respondents to his questionnaire are 138 members of the Scottish branch of the Royal Institution of Chartered Surveyors, a number which includes thirty eight planners and architects. But

83

this is only 2.4% of the total return, and cannot be considered a representative sample of planners, particularly as the survey as a whole was limited to Scotland and the north of England.

As the principal map-producer in Great Britain, the Ordnance Survey is concerned with ascertaining the requirements of map users, and in particular the requirements of those users who may have special mapping interests, such as planners. The Survey holds five annual consultative meetings, one with government departments and nationalised industries, two with local authorities associations (one in England and one in Scotland) and two with map users (one devoted to large scales mapping and the other to small scales). The purpose of the meetings is not only to ascertain requirements but also to advise users—particularly the specialist groups—of the special services which the Survey has to offer. The need for close liaison has been acknowledged in the appointment of Ordnance Survey liaison officers in nearly all local authorities to provide a recognised channel of communication between the authority concerned and the Survey, operating through its regional offices. Attendance at the Survey's meetings is by invitation, and a summary of the proceedings is circulated to participants only; a report of the map users' meetings appears annually in *JTPI*.

The data on map use from the OSTI survey show that, of the total number of planners who specified their usage, 53% use both topographic and thematic maps, 45% use topographic maps only, while 2% use thematic maps only, topographic maps being defined as those which record the physical features of an area, thematic maps as those which concentrate on a theme (which may be physical, economic, or social) and show its geographical distribution within an area. Combining these percentages, it appears that, of the planners who do use maps, 98% use topographic ones, and a much small percentage—55%—use thematic ones. In the first category, the major use is of the various series of the Ordnance Survey. In the second category, the major use again is of the standard series issued by the Ordnance Survey. It is justifiable to postulate that this pattern of use is dictated by the familiar situation of supply and demand and that it is a reflection of the actual provision of map series within planning organisations (and in particular the local authority planning departments) which is dominated by the

84

Ordnance Survey series. County planning departments in general hold a wider range of maps than do borough departments: a logical corollary of the wider range of land uses and degrees of urbanisation within the boundaries of a county. Public libraries in most cases hold a wider selection of maps than either county or borough planning departments: a fact which few planners seem to appreciate, and even fewer exploit.

This distinction between topographic and thematic maps was used for practical reasons in the survey of information use, and is pursued in several textbooks on maps in their various aspects. It is not, however, a distinction which is recognised by such authoritative sources as the Ordnance Survey, which considers all its standard maps to be topographic in character; and the Map Library of the Department of the Environment, whose specially-devised classification scheme includes topography as only one theme among many. This is a reflection of the wide range of information and data which are now considered to be mappable, for it is increasingly recognised that, particularly with the development of computer mapping techniques (see below), a map is a convenient and easily-assimilated graphic means of presenting information which would be much more indigestible in its original form.

This chapter falls into two parts: the first embraces the maps themselves, and the second sets out the associated literature. The aim of this first part is to discuss a full range of single maps, map series, and atlases relating to the whole or parts of the United Kingdom; it is divided into sections, the first and second of which discuss comprehensive map series and atlases of national, regional, and local coverage, and the subsequent sections deal with single maps, map series and atlases which concentrate on specific themes. The only criterion of inclusion is that of potential usefulness to planners.

COMPREHENSIVE ATLASES AND MAP SERIES: NATIONAL

In this first section we shall discuss those atlases and map series which deal with the whole country in all its aspects, and which are illustrative of topography, of land use, population, industry, social areas, and many more variables which can usefully be shown in map form. It is not reasonable to suppose that the section which follows (or any of the sections which follow it) are comprehensive in the sense that they contain details or mention of all the atlases and maps which could be of use to planners. There is clearly a great deal of mapping activity going on—in university departments, in government departments, in local authorities, in specialised organisations throughout the country, and the bulk of this remains unpublished, and certainly unpublicised. Some of the map output, particularly that emanating from central and local government departments, is produced for a specific purpose and has little relevance beyond that purpose. Much of the output on the other hand, has a wider relevance, were its originators but aware of this. But a veil of secrecy is drawn over a large proportion of it, even in the face of serious enquiries—and this is a pity, for it results in the exclusion, through ignorance, of much (how much?) potentially valuable material. The problem of unpublished information is a large one in planning; and as an increasing amount of information is regarded as mappable this problem increasingly concerns unpublished maps. There is clearly a need for cooperation, coordination, and improved communications in this sphere of activity : journals, such as the *Geographical journal,* perform a valuable service by listing, and reviewing, new maps and atlases, but they are dependent on the producers of the maps and atlases informing them of their existence and therefore their service is by no means comprehensive, even for published material.

The Ordnance Survey is the official mapping agency for England, Scotland, and Wales. (Northern Ireland has its own Ordnance Survey, see below.) Ordnance Survey maps fall into two groups: large scales and small scales.[3] The large scales comprise three series, at 1:1,250 (approximately fifty inches to one mile), 1:2,500 (approximately twenty five inches to one mile), and 1:10,560 (six inches to one mile), now being superseded by the series at 1:10,000. Small scales comprise all series at 1:25,000 (approximately $2\frac{1}{2}$ inches to one mile) and smaller. Within the small scales group is the series of maps at the scale of 1:625,000 (approximately one inch to 9.7 miles), known as the ten-mile series. This is a comprehensive range of maps depicting topographic, geological and other themes, produced as a result of close collaboration between various government departments with the Ordnance Survey as publisher for the whole series; some are productions of the Ordnance Survey alone, but the majority are from the Department of the Environment working in conjunction with the Scottish Development Department. The maps cover Great Britain (not Northern Ireland) in two sheets, North and South, which together form a map of 42 inches by 64 inches. The sheets join at a line through Kendal, in Westmorland. Most of the themes illustrated are covered by both North and South sheets; but Gravel and Associated Sands is represented only on a South sheet, and the sheet entitled Vegetation: Reconnaissance Survey of Scotland, is quite obviously confined to the north. The manuscript maps, which are compiled at large scale from a wide range of data ranging from the census returns to unpublished material, are maintained in a state of continuous revision at the Department of the Environment and the Scottish Development Department, and are available for official consultation.

The first in the series is a topographic base map, an outline version of the Route Planning map (see below) in black only on white, on which all the other maps in the series, with the single exception of the physical sheets, can be superimposed. The Physical map shows the land formation by relief and drainage systems, and names mountains, hills, rivers, and all other important physical features. It differs from the other maps in that it does not have a standard topographic background. Relief is shown by layer tints at 200, 400, 600, 800, 1,000, 1,400, 2,000 and 3,000 feet, with spot heights indicated; and inland water is represented in blue.

The Route Planning maps, which form a part of the ten-mile series but which are also known independently as motorists' maps, have been designed with the requirements of the long distance road user in mind. These two sheets are revised annually: the 1971 edition, published late 1970, has major roads revised to July 1970. The map is useful, not only to the motorist, but also as an annual record of the development of road communications in Britain. It shows all classes of roads, from motorways down, and those with dual carriageways are thus indicated; motorways under construction are shown, but not dual carriageways under construction. Sea, rail, and air ferries are also shown, and there are inset maps of the larger conurbations.

The Ordnance Survey has a statutory obligation to publish maps showing the position of administrative boundaries; these boundaries are shown on all standard series, and also on the map of Administrative Areas forming part of the ten-mile series. This map shows in colour, on an outline base, the areas of all local authorities from counties and county boroughs down to urban and rural districts in England and Wales and the corresponding authorities in Scotland. A new edition is published annually.

There are two types of maps showing population: that of Population Change, 1951-61, and of Population Density, 1951. The first was compiled from data from the 1961 census and shows the net changes resulting from births, deaths, and migration. Symbols of proportionate size show the number of persons by which the population of each administrative area changed over the period covered by the map. The map of Population Density, which is based on data from the 1951 census, shows seven gradations of population density ranging from dense urban to virtually uninhabited.

The two maps concerned with land and its use were both compiled from information collected in surveys by the (first) Land Utilisation Survey. The map of Land Classification, based on information collected in 1939-42, shows ten categories of land utilisation from good quality agricultural land down to the poorest (sand, shingle, etc). The map of Land Utilisation, based on information collected in 1931-39, shows six categories of use: woods and forests; heath, moor, and rough pasture; permanent grass and meadow; arable land; nursery gardens and orchards; urban areas.

The map of Solid Geology has been drawn by the Geological Survey. It is available in the standard edition; in an outline edition; and in an edition overprinted with the sheet lines of the one-inch Geological Series. Also in the series is a map showing the incidence of limestone throughout the country: the Limestone sheets, which show the situation as it was in 1949, indicate the geological horizons of economic limestone, limestone quality and utilisation, and the output of mines and quarries. One sheet only, the South one, shows the distribution of Gravel and Associated Sands as it was in 1959: all deposits of economic significance are realised, distinction being made between shingles, valley gravels, high level gravels, pebble beds, and 'estuarine' alluvium. Wet and dry workings are classified according to their output in 1959.

The map of Local Accessibility draws its information from the 1951 census and from winter bus services in 1949-50 (for Scotland) and in 1947-48 (for England and Wales). It shows by means of coloured circles of proportionate size, the populations and hinterlands of main urban areas.

The most recent edition of the rainfall map is that showing Rainfall: Annual Average, 1916-1950, compiled from information and data in the Meteorological Office. It shows the annual average rainfall over a standard thirty five-year period (the previous edition covered 1881-1915). Dispersion graphs show the monthly expectation of rain throughout the year for a number of representative stations throughout the country.

The last map which is currently available is the North sheet for Vegetation: Reconnaissance Survey of Scotland. The data relate to 1940, and the north of England is included through a special survey for the purpose. The map shows the fundamental boundaries and regional divisions of Scotland according to their prevailing vegetation types and plant communities.

These maps described above form the current published output of the national ten-mile series, in print and available. They do not represent the total original published content of the series, however: as from the beginning of 1970, a number of sheets have been withdrawn from sale by the Ordnance Survey although some of these are still available from the Department of the Environment. The withdrawn sheets are those on Coal and Iron (South sheet only); Iron and Steel (South sheet only); Population: Total Changes, covering 1921-1931, 1931-1938/39, and 1938/39-1947 (the last a South sheet only); Population: Changes by Migration, covering the same three periods; Electricity: Statutory Supply Areas (1946), Gas and Coke (Areas of Supply); the earlier Rainfall: Annual Average sheet, covering 1881-1915; and the Vegetation: Grasslands of England and Wales, South sheet only.

All the maps in circulation carry clear and informative keys to their contents. Despite this, some of the subjects represented are fairly technical to the layman, and need further explanation. To this end, the Department of the Environment and the Scottish Development Department have prepared a series of explanatory texts, published by the Ordnance Survey, to accompany the following maps: Land Classification; Average Annual Rainfall; Population (covering both types of population maps); Local Accessibility; and Vegetation: Reconnaissance Survey of Scotland. The text on the Vegetation map of England and Wales has been withdrawn with the map itself; a text on Limestone also appears to be no longer available.

A full account of this series, its origins, and detailed descriptions of the individual maps together with a complete list of the maps available and in preparation at the time of writing (now, inevitably, out of date, as are the prices quoted) is included in *Government information and the research worker* edited by Ronald Staveley and Mary Piggott (London, Library Association, second revised edition 1965), as an appendix to the section on the Ministry of Housing and Local Government.

The Department of the Environment are responsible for the *Desk atlas of planning maps* which is issued on a limited circulation basis. First issued in 1953, the component map sheets fit into large loose-leaf binders and are up-dated as appropriate: there are now (at time of writing) 111 sheets in two volumes. The coverage is restricted to England and Wales, as the cover-title, *Planning maps of England and Wales,* indicates. The maps, with two exceptions, cover the whole area in a single sheet at a scale of about one inch to thirty miles. The data are drawn largely from the 1961 census, but also from a large number of other sources, for example, the *Digest of port statistics 1966,* the *Census of distribution 1961,* and Ministry of Power data.

The first map is an outline base map showing economic planning regions as at April 1969, and administrative counties, county boroughs and Greater London at the same date. The second map, Land Classification (published in 1965) is generalised from the 1:625,000 (ten-mile) map compiled by the Land Utilisation Survey of Britain in 1943 and published by the Ordnance Survey; as is the third map, Types of Farming, generalised from the ten-mile map compiled by the Ministry of Agriculture and Fisheries in 1939, also published by the Ordnance Survey. In the remainder of the maps, population is depicted in detail, from a group showing Total population changes, Changes by migration, Persistent decrease, and Persistent increase all for 1921-1947, through to a group showing

Changes 1951-1965, then Annual changes, Total change, Natural change, and Balance, mainly migration, all covering 1961-1965, and a sheet showing Duration of residence at 1961 address. Housing is also treated in detail, the maps based in the main on data from the 1961 census; also included are geology, employment, industry (compiled from the industry tables of the 1951 census), rateable values, institutions of higher education 1963-1964, derelict land at 1964, commuting to conurbations in 1961, and energy in the UK.

There are two exceptions to the standard presentation of a single map per sheet. The section of sheets representing Regional immigrant population, which shows origin by geographical counties, has ten maps, each one showing one region, at a much reduced scale; and Dwellings in conurbations lacking a fixed bath are shown on a folded sheet with one map per conurbation at a larger scale.

Colour is used throughout the series, and a variety of cartographic techniques are employed to present the statistical data.

The two series of maps which have been outlined in the preceding pages are national series, published by national agencies with the cooperation and approval of interested government departments. An atlas which is national in every sense of the word except in so far as it is not published by a national agency, received no official financial support and therefore does not carry the official imprimatur, is the *Atlas of Britain and Northern Ireland* (Oxford, Clarendon Press, 1963), planned and directed for the Press by David P Bickmore and M A Shaw. The *Atlas,* which has been widely acclaimed not only for the range of its thematic coverage but also for its cartographic techniques, has some advantages over the Ordnance Survey series. Its spatial coverage is wider, in that it includes Northern Ireland; its subject coverage is very much wider; and it is more up to date than most of the maps in the official series. The 234 pages of the *Atlas* are made up of twelve pages of introduction in which the authors state their aims and their methods; two hundred pages of maps; and twenty two pages of gazetteer. The scale adopted for the majority of the maps is 1:2,000,000 (2M), which allows the whole of the country to be represented on a single page. Larger scales, at 1:1,000,000 (1M) and 1:500,000, are used for regional representations, and for some general thematic maps.

91

There are four main series of maps. The first contains about fifty pages of maps, mainly at 2M scale, devoted to aspects of physical geography such as geology, surrounding sea areas, coastal geomorphology, climate, soil, and vegetation, which are then summarised in a series of eight regional sets at 1M scale displaying vegetation, superficial deposits, solid geology, and relief. The second main series, at 2M scale, begins with agriculture and fisheries, and then goes on to a detailed treatment of industry, showing for each industry represented its distribution in terms of employment. This section is also concluded by a series of regional sets at 1M scale showing total employment, fuel consumption, industrial employment, and new factory buildings. The third section is concerned with demographic characteristics, housing, administrative boundaries, communications, and trade, which are mapped at 2M scale. A summary again follows in the form of a set of maps at 1M scale depicting population, roads, airports, railways, and waterborne freight. Finally, there is a series of general reference maps, at 1 : 500,000 scale, which present in considerable detail a complex and varied quantity of data ranging from elevations to land uses, from communications to boundaries.

The larger scale maps are printed with the National Grid; for the basic maps at 2M scale, an inserted transparent overlay, printed with the National Grid, must be used. The gazetteer refers to locations by means of National Grid references. A folded section at the back of the *Atlas,* which can be opened out for use with the maps, carries details of authorities and sources of data: the 1951 census was a fruitful source, but many data were derived from unpublished sources and from *ad hoc* collection.

COMPREHENSIVE ATLASES AND MAP SERIES: REGIONAL AND LOCAL

In the field of comprehensive regional atlases, the most interesting work is being done in the geography departments of various universities. Although it has not yet become a reality, the National Atlas of Wales is more than just a possibility. The project was first mooted in 1951; currently it is in the charge of Professor Harold Carter, of the Department of Geography in the University College of Wales, Aberystwyth, on behalf of the Social Sciences Committee of the Board of Celtic Studies (University of Wales). Although it will be some time before any maps appear, there is a firm intention of developing the project in the next few years.[4]

In the University of Aberdeen, the staff of the Department of Geography are working on a large-scale project for an Atlas of Northeast Scotland. This will contain about sixty maps at scales ranging from 1 : 4,000,000 to 1 : 500,000, and will cover physical and human geographical topics both for the north east of Scotland as a whole and for selected sub-regional examples. Planning of this atlas is at an advanced stage, and compilation has already begun. It is hoped that a provisional selection of these maps will be published by January 1972.[5]

A product of the University of Liverpool is the sixty four-page atlas *Merseyside in maps* edited by J A Patmore and A G Hodgkiss (Longman, 1970). There are some thirty pages of maps, drawn in the university's Cartographic Department, each map accompanied by a corresponding page of text explaining and analysing it. The first part of the atlas provides a rather cursory treatment of the physical background of the area, which takes in Merseyside and its hinterland, and goes on to a series of historical maps showing the evolution of the region from 1800. The second part considers present-day Merseyside, and comprises a set of maps depicting various themes, for example, housing, social structure, journey to work, communications, the Mersey crossing, air pollution, and recreation.

Cities are also becoming a focus of attention for comprehensive thematic mapping. One of the most ambitious projects is the *Atlas of London and the London region,* prepared under the direction of Emrys Jones and D J Sinclair (Oxford, Pergamon Press, 1968-70).[6] The *Atlas* consists of seventy sheets containing 120 maps of London and the south east region, with short explanatory comments on each. Each map, or sheet of maps, represents one of five areas ranging in size from the smallest area, comprising central London, to the largest, comprising the whole south east region. The scales used range from 1 : 50,000 for the smaller areas, to 1 : 1,000,000 for the south east region. The first eight sheets form an introduction, covering physical features, climate, historical development, and administrative boundaries. The remainder of the *Atlas* is in two main sections, the first dealing with a wide variety of social factors, the second dealing with a comprehensive range of economic factors. Data, which are drawn from the 1966 census and many other sources, some of them unpublished, are mapped in areal units expressing various levels of generalisation; local authority areas, wards and civil parishes, enumeration districts, kilometre grid squares, 500 metre grid squares, and employment exchange areas.

The Scottish capital city is also the subject of an atlas published by the Edinburgh Branch of the Geographical Association, *An atlas of Edinburgh* (Edinburgh, 1965). This is a smaller and much less ambitious project than the *Atlas of London and the London region;* it was aimed primarily at the senior forms of secondary schools, but its excellent conception and execution illustrate so clearly the stages of the city's growth and its present day setting within its sub-region that its appeal is a great deal wider than originally envisaged and it is of particular interest to urban geographers. Throughout its thirty nine pages, the maps, at scales of 1 : 1M upwards, are interspersed with photographs, diagrams, graphs, and drawings, all of them annotated. The data mapped cover a wide range of social and economic factors, for example, house types, land use and distribution of industries, as well as a full coverage of physical features and climate.

In the same tradition is *An atlas of Durham City,* edited by Professor H Bowen-Jones, and produced by the Department of Geography of the University of Durham as number four in its series of Occasional Papers. A third edition of the *Atlas* was published in 1970. It is in two sections, the first showing the city in its sub-regional setting, the second depicting the local pattern. Maps at different scales, plans, graphs, and diagrams illustrate a variety of features from population, sphere of influence, and journey to work, through geology, morphology, soils and climate, to detailed descriptions of the central area, the cathedral and the castle. Each section has an accompanying text.

Although the purview of this chapter is limited to maps and atlases, the field is not so rich with examples relating to cities and regions that it can afford to ignore a series of publications each devoted to a town or city within the context of its sub-region exploring, in words, the same fields of activity as an atlas depicts graphically. It would seem unduly myopic in these circumstances to omit the annual publications of the British Association for the Advancement of Science, particularly as the texts of these are supported by maps. The books are issued to coincide with the annual meetings of the association, and are basically concerned with the description and analysis of the town or city in which the meeting takes place and its setting within its surrounding region. The handbooks are made up of specialist contributions by experts, who are largely, though not exclusively, selected from the academic staff of the civic university. The editorial committee is often headed by the Professor of Geography. Each handbook is produced by the local executive committee for that meeting, which is usually also the publisher, although sometimes the university press may publish for the local committee. Collectively, the handbooks form a growing library of the urban geography of British provincial cities. Meetings were held in 1970 in Durham, in 1969 in Exeter, in 1968 in Dundee, and so on back.

THEMATIC MAPS AND ATLASES : TOPOGRAPHY (GENERAL)
The major part of the map output of the Ordnance Survey is topographic in character, and maps representing the topography of England, Scotland and Wales are available at scales from 1 : 1,250 down to 1 : 1,000,000. These are the maps which are used by 98% of planners (see above). As a generalisation, large scale plans are used mainly by planners working in, or concerned with urban planning : a city or borough planning department will have complete coverage of its area of authority at 1 : 1,250, or 1 : 2,500 or both, similarly a firm of consultants engaged on a town expansion scheme requires large-scale coverage of the town in question. The smaller scales are chiefly used in county planning departments for the non-urban areas of their counties : in addition to complete coverage of the area of its authority at 1 : 10,000 or 1 : 10,560 and at 1 : 25,000, the county department must also hold large-scale coverage of its urban areas.

Maps at the scale of 1 : 1,250 now cover all towns and urban areas with a population of about 20,000 and over. The re-survey of these urban areas was the first major post-war task of the Ordnance Survey, and it was completed early in 1970. Each map represents an area 500 metres square, there are about fifty thousand maps in the series, and they are being kept up to date by a system of continuous revision.[7] The maps show a great deal of detail in the built-up areas, including the numbering of individual properties along each road. Spot heights are given along some roads, and the positions of bench marks are indicated; administrative and parliamentary boundaries are shown. Conversion of the 1:1,250 series to metric measurements is now under way, and all new or revised sheets are now issued in metric style. All the Ordnance Survey map series have for many years carried a metric grid and the sizes of the map sheets have been based on this grid. Heights of bench marks are given to two decimal places of a metre, and spot heights to one decimal place. Some administrative boundary information is also given in metres.

Maps at the scale of 1:2,500 cover the whole of England, Scotland and Wales except for areas of mountain and moorland. In urban areas which have been mapped at the basic scale of 1:1,250, the 1:2,500 maps are derived from the larger scale maps by combining photographic reductions of the component 1:1,250 sheets. The original coverage of 1:2,500 maps known as the County Series, was published before World War II. A programme of revision and resurvey has been under way for some years, resulting in the production of a new National Grid Series. Most of the minor towns and many rural areas have now been mapped at this scale, and the counties of Renfrewshire, West Lothian, and Dunbartonshire are completely covered by the National Grid Series. The entire project is not expected to reach completion until about 1980; until it is complete, it is worth remembering that in many parts of the country the largest scale map available—the original 1:2,500 County Series —is anything up to half a century out of date. Each map represents an area of one square kilometre, but most sheets are published in pairs covering an area of two square kilometres. When completed, the National Grid Series will contain about ninety thousand maps, all subject to continuous revision. The 1:2,500 maps, in addition to showing much urban detail, are the fullest topographic record available, delineating the landscape in great detail: roads, fields, hedges, streams, varying categories of non-agricultural land and much more. Spot heights and bench marks are given as in the 1:1,250 series, and in addition parcels of land are indicated and their areas given.

Metrication is proceeding in this scale of maps as in the 1 : 1,250, and the same comments apply with the additional conversion of the area of parcels to three decimal places of hectares, given alongside the original figure in acres.

Planners clearly have an interest in knowing the state of publication of large-scale maps relating to their own area. In February, May, August, and November of each year, the Ordnance Survey produces an index which shows, by means of symbols, the 1 : 1,250 and 1 : 2,500 scale maps that have been published to date, though neither the date of publication nor the edition of the plans is indicated. The index is in looseleaf form, each page covering an area 50 kilometres square (one quarter of the 100 kilometre national grid square). Individual pages are self-contained, and users of the maps can specify to the Ordnance Survey which areas they are interested in and can be supplied with the pages which cover these areas.

The main users of these two series of large scale maps are professional people, rather than the general public, and planners form a high proportion of the professional users. With such professional users in mind, the Ordnance Survey offers various special services in connection with large scale maps which are of considerable value to planners. The most valuable of the services are those which aim to provide information relating to an area which is more up to date than that which appears on the published map. The larger the scale of the map, and the more detail which it shows, the more subject it is to change within its area and it becomes rapidly out of date. This applies in particular to urban areas, which can change in small detail almost from week to week, and in overall shape almost from year to year. Surveyors are continuously at work in the field keeping large scale maps up to date, and through its advance information service the Ordnance Survey will supply to users, on demand, copies of surveyors' up to date field sheets in advance of publication as revised editions.

It has already been mentioned that in areas which are mapped at the basic scale of 1 : 1,250, the derived 1 : 2,500 maps are made by combining photographic reductions of the component 1 : 1,250 sheets. The component sheets are revised independently as changes occur on the ground, but the Ordnance Survey have for some time

97

taken steps to avoid any lack of sympathy across internal plan lines. This is done by incorporating revision material into the derived 1:2,500 which has not yet been published at the larger scale. The Ordnance Survey also offer a reduction service, by which reductions (to 1:2,500) of revised 1:1,250 sheets are supplied so that users can up-date their own 1:2,500 sheets. Such reductions are only supplied to order, and only if an up to date edition of the derived 1:2,500 map does not exist.

In addition to these two advance services, the Ordnance Survey will also supply enlargements: of the 1:1,250 scale maps at 1:500,[8] and of the 1:2,500 scale maps at 1:1,250 scale. Transparencies to scale of most Ordnance Survey maps can be supplied against specific orders. At the end of 1970, a 35mm microfilm service was introduced through which plans at 1:1,250 and 1:2,500 can be supplied in the form of 35mm diazo negative microfilms mounted in aperture cards. Details of these and other services are obtained very easily by writing to the Director General of the Ordnance Survey.

The largest scale at which the entire country (that is, England, Scotland, and Wales) is mapped is 1:10,560, known more familiarly as the six-inch series. It is the first edition of this series, the prewar County Series, which covers the entire country. For all parts of the country except the mountainous areas of Scotland and the islands, the County Series has been replaced by the National Grid sheets each covering an area five kilometres square. The six-inch maps are also undergoing metrication, and the maps at the present scale of 1:10,560 will be replaced by maps at 1:10,000 with metric measurements. Heights above sea level are given in metres; contours have been surveyed at 25 feet vertical interval but values are given to the nearest metre. The first of these metric sheets were introduced in 1969, but it will be some years before the new series is complete. A start was made in 1970 of the resurvey at the new scale of 1:10,000 of the mountainous areas of Scotland which were still covered only by the old County Series. The six-inch scale is the smallest at which individual buildings can be adequately represented, although in closely built-up areas they are blocked in rather than showing individual properties. It also provides a very adequate representation of the landscape, omitting only minor details. The numbers and areas of land parcels are not shown.

The Ordnance Survey offers a special enlargement and reduction service in connection with the six-inch and 1 : 10,000 map series. The service is intended to minimise the inconvenience caused by using maps along the junctions between six-inch and 1 : 10,000 mapping. For limited areas, and again to order only, enlargements of the six-inch map to 1 : 10,000 or reductions from 1 : 10,000 to six-inch will be supplied to enable a proper match to be achieved along the boundaries. As with the other services described above, enlargements and reductions are supplied either on film or on electro-photographic paper.

The largest of the small-scale series is that at 1 : 25,000 popularly known as the $2\frac{1}{2}$-inch series. The first provisional series at this scale covers the whole of England, Wales, and Scotland except for the Highlands and the islands, and is based on pre-war surveys at six-inch scale, with post-war and more recent changes incorporated into revised sheets. The series comprises about two thousand sheets, each covering an area ten kilometres square. More recently, production of a second series of maps at 1 : 25,000 scale has begun. Initially, these are being issued only for areas which have been fully re-surveyed at larger scales (six-inch, 1 : 2,500 and 1 : 1,250), such areas being chiefly in the south west and in the Scottish Highlands beyond the area covered by the first series; but eventually the second series will replace the first series. About seventy sheets have so far been issued, and the corresponding first series sheets withdrawn. The sheets of the second series cover twice the area of the first series sheets: twenty kilometres east to west by ten kilometres north to south, and each sheet carries an explanation of the symbols used. The 1 : 25,000 scale maps are good working field maps, carrying nearly all the detail of the six-inch maps in a more compact form. The process of metrication has not yet affected this series.

The other two major small-scale series are those at 1 : 63,360, the popular one-inch series, and 1 : 250,000, the quarter-inch series. The one-inch series, which covers the whole of Great Britain, is the country's most authentic, accurate, and informative small-scale map. There are 189 sheets in the series, most of which cover an area of 1,800 square kilometres. The current edition, the seventh series, was begun in 1952. The sheets are revised as regularly as is

99

necessary, sheets covering heavily urban areas of rapid change naturally requiring more frequent up-dating than those which cover largely rural areas. About twelve revised sheets are issued each year. Special surveys are carried out on motorways and similarly significant additions or changes, and the new or amended features are incorporated when the relevant sheet is reprinted. Rights of way are added to the England and Wales sheets if information about them is to hand when a new edition is being prepared.[9] The maps incorporate a wealth of detail, with a wide range of symbols indicating features such as National Trust properties, bus stations, AA and RAC telephone boxes, and town halls. Relief is shown by means of spot heights and contours at fifty feet intervals. The one-inch series of maps is virtually a household commodity by now, easily read and understood and manageable for a variety of purposes; for professional use, it offers a compact but still detailed view of a large area of land, laying out in easily recognisable form the pattern of settlement within an area, the density and extent of urban areas, the main lines of communication, and much more.[10]

The quarter-inch series was started in 1859, maps being produced at the true quarter-inch scale of 1:253,440; replacement by the 1:250,000 started in 1957. There are seventeen sheets in the series, and in addition a special map covering the whole of Wales and the Marches is published which differs slightly from the main series in that a green tint is used for land up to 200 feet above sea level and shading for land above that line. The quarter-inch maps are derived from the one-inch series. They are revised from small scales revision material, but not on the same cycle as the one-inch maps; revision of dense sheets may be as frequent as every three years. Detail for inclusion in the quarter-inch maps is selected from the larger scale sheets and generalised to help reduction; the series is mainly of use in motoring and route planning for which purpose motorways, classified roads (with dual carriageways indicated) and other motorable roads are clearly shown. The seventeen sheets of the quarter-inch series are also available in a hard covered loose-leaf binder under the collective title of the *Quarter-inch atlas of Great Britain,* together with an introduction, map sheet index, and gazetteer. The maps are folded for insertion, and may be easily pulled out flat for reference. Users of the *Atlas* may place a stand-

100

ing order for the annual supply of all new editions of the quarter-inch maps which are published during the previous year; the sheets being provided trimmed, folded and punched ready for insertion into the *Atlas*. A companion to the quarter-inch map series is its gazetteer which lists the 33,000 towns and villages and other named features which appear on the seventeen sheets, and gives for each both the sheet number of the map on which it appears and its National Grid reference to the nearest kilometre.

The Ordnance Survey also produces and publishes the two Great Britain sheets in the International Map of the World series at a scale of 1 : 1,000,000. These sheets are produced in accordance with the United Nations ' Bonn specification '; their appearance is thus quite different from the normal ranges of Ordnance Survey maps, and they have in addition a light grey border instead of the usual white one. The maps show communications, centres of population classified according to size and importance, geographical features, and international boundaries.

The use of colour in some of the map series described above has been mentioned, and this is one of the attractive features of the maps on which it is used. But for planning purposes, colour on a map is not necessarily desirable. In preparing a plan, the planner starts from a base map, which is an outline map showing only the existing physical features of the land, on which information gathered from surveys relating to (for example) demographic or industrial characteristics of the area may be superimposed. The success or failure of a set of planning maps depends to a large extent upon the suitability of the base maps used : they should give just enough detail to make the information superimposed on it fully compre-hensible, but no more. The large-scale series of the Ordnance Survey —the 1 : 1,250, 1 : 2,500, and the 1 : 10,560 (1 : 10,000)—are in any case outline maps, being depicted in black and white only. In addition the Ordnance Survey produce outline maps at various other scales printed in black or grey with all colour (for example, road fillings) omitted, and intended specifically for planning or re-cording purposes. These are at scales of 1 : 25,000, showing the same information as the coloured maps at the same scale except for contours; 1 : 63,360, also showing much the same information as the coloured one-inch series with the exception of the contours;

101

a series at 1:100,000 covering England and Wales only, showing a single county on one or more sheets; 1:250,000, the outline equivalent of the coloured quarter-inch maps showing the same information except for contours and relief; and finally, an outline map of England, Wales, and Scotland at 1:1,250,000 printed in black on one sheet, and showing main towns, county boundaries and names with the National Grid overprinted.

The Ordnance Survey is by no means the only producer of maps relating to the United Kingdom, although, as one would expect from the national mapping agency, its range is the most comprehensive. The firm of John Bartholomew and Son Ltd, of Edinburgh, also publish a wide range of maps and atlases. Their fullest series is that which covers England, Scotland, and Wales in sixty two sheets at a scale of 1:126,720 (one inch to two miles) known as the 'half-inch' scale. This series was first published in 1875, and preceded the Ordnance Survey half-inch series, which was authorised in 1902, reached an unfinished fourth edition and was finally abandoned as a national series in 1962. The Bartholomew series is thus the only set of maps covering the country at this scale. Relief is shown by means of layer colouring[11] (this was the first series of maps to use this technique, now an accepted practice), there is detailed information about roads from motorways down to tracks, and a full range of other information is depicted by means of special symbols. The series is primarily aimed at the motorist, and outdoor travellers such as cyclists, climbers and walkers. The sheets are regularly revised and updated.

Northern Ireland: The standard topographic map series described in the foregoing pages do not cover Northern Ireland. The Ordnance Survey has no responsibility for the province, nor for Eire. Both Northern Ireland and the Republic have their official Ordnance Survey. The latter does not come within the scope of this book; but the various map series relating to the North do, and are discussed now. Some of them cover Northern Ireland and Eire as a single unit, and these are also included.

The Ordnance Survey of Northern Ireland was formed as a separate institution in 1921,[12] when it took over the map series which until that time had been the responsibility of the Ordnance Survey (UK).

After World War II some replanning and reorganisation took place, including a retriangulation to provide a basis for a new Irish Grid, and the introduction of the 1:1,250 scale for major urban areas. Now, large-scale maps at 1:1,250 and 1:2,500 are available which are comparable to those covering the rest of the United Kingdom. A new detailed survey is in progress at 1:1,250 scale covering those towns with a population of more than 10,000, plus some smaller towns. For those towns which are not yet published, enlargements of the 1:2,500 sheets can be provided. The total of 412 plans in the series were expected to be completed in 1970.

The 1:2,500 series in its original form, the County Series, covers the whole of Northern Ireland except for the mountainous and moorland areas. The County Series is gradually being replaced by a new Irish Grid series, on different sheet lines (the new 1:1,250 maps are also on the Irish Grid), which will total three thousand plans when complete.

The whole of the country, including the barren areas, is covered by the six-inch series at 1:10,560. As with the 1:2,500 series, the original County Series of six-inch maps is being replaced by a new series on the Irish Grid. A special six-inch map was prepared for Belfast, dating from 1938, which is in four sheets showing land features and contours in black, water in blue, parks in green, roads in orange, and buildings in red. A single sheet direct photographic reduction, printed in black, at a scale of three inches to one mile, is also available.

At small scales, there is an Ordnance Survey series of one-inch maps covering Northern Ireland in nine sheets. These are contour-coloured maps showing main and secondary roads, footpaths, railways, spot heights in feet, and so on. Outline editions are available for use as base maps. A quarter-inch topographic map also covers the same area in a single sheet, available in colour or in outline. A first series of half-inch maps covered the whole of Ireland in twenty five sheets, of which eight gave cover for Northern Ireland. Only the sheet covering Belfast is published by the Ordnance Survey of Northern Ireland, which is now producing a second series at half-inch scale covering Northern Ireland and adjoining parts of the Republic in four sheets. These also are available either in colour or in outline. All small-scale maps carry the Irish Grid.

The Ordnance Survey of Northern Ireland provides special services in much the same way as does its counterpart in Southampton. The continuous revision of 1:1,250 and selected 1:2,500 Irish Grid plans is recorded on transparent plastic field documents, and copies of these (there are four to each plan) can be made available on paper or as transparencies. Copies of large-scale plans, from fair drawn manuscripts, can be obtained in advance of publication. Transparencies of the 1:1,250, 1:2,500 and six-inch series can be ordered; 1:500 enlargements of 1:1,250 plans can be made, and also enlargements at 1:1,250 of 1:2,500 plans.

The Isle of Man is included in the standard Ordnance Survey (GB) series at scales of one-inch and smaller. Geographia Ltd also issue a map of the island, at a scale of 1:45,000 ($\frac{3}{4}$ inch to one mile) which shows all classes of roads, island railways, steamer routes, and the TT course and Clypse circuit, and includes a plan of Douglas.

The Channel Islands: Of the six islands, only Guernsey is covered by the Ordnance Survey, which produces a map at a scale of 1:21,120 (three inches to one mile) showing the whole of the island in great detail. Bartholomew and Son Ltd issue a single sheet containing road maps of all six islands, the scales varying between one inch and two inches to the mile; the maps are contour coloured.

London: 'The first problem with London is to define it', observed Peter Hall.[13] It is a problem which the map-makers have not solved. There are many maps and atlases relating to London, and each one has its own definition. It is inevitable that most of these maps are aimed at the tourist, and that they should feature tourist facilities fairly prominently. An atlas of long-standing reputation, now in its thirteenth edition (1968), is the *Reference atlas of Greater London* published by Bartholomew and Son Ltd. The coverage, of 1,700 square miles, extends from Windsor to Gravesend and from St Albans to Reigate. This edition includes, for the first time, plans of nine dormitory towns. The maps, which are coloured, are at scales of two inches to one mile for the outer area; four inches to one mile for the Greater London area; and ten inches to one mile for the central area from Westminster to the City. There are also seven general and administrative maps, an introduction, and an index of over 62,000 names.

Geographer's Map Co's *Master atlas of Greater London* can be used independently or in conjunction with the same publishers' series, the *Master map of Greater London*. Both cover the same area, roughly from Hillingdon to Grays and from Potters Bar to Caterham. The atlas contains in 160 pages of sectional maps the same coverage as does the map in nine large (40″ × 30″) sheets, both at a scale of three inches to one mile. Both atlas and map use the same index references.

The Ordnance Survey publish a one-inch map of Greater London, based on the standard maps of the seventh series, and comprising the metropolitan areas of sheets 160, 161, 170, and 171, together covering the whole of Greater London. Detail shown is the same as in the standard maps in this series.

THEMATIC MAPS AND ATLASES : GEOLOGY

The main producer of geological maps covering Great Britain is the Geological Survey which, with the Geological Museum, now forms part of the Institute of Geological Sciences in London. Geological Survey maps are published by the Ordnance Survey, and are available through the same channels as Ordnance Survey maps, and also from the Geological Museum bookstall.

At a very small scale, to cover the whole country in a single sheet, is the map at 1:1,584,000 (one inch to twenty five miles) of the British Islands, the fifth edition of which was issued in 1969. This is available in colour or in an outline edition. The Survey is also responsible for the two maps which make up the contribution on Solid Geology to the Ordnance Survey series of ten-mile maps (see above).

There are three small scale series of geological maps, at 1:25,000 (2½-inch), at 1:63,360 (one-inch), and at 1:253,440 (quarter-inch). At 1:25,000 scale, a series devoted to ' Classical areas in British geology' is in progress, of which ten sheets are available for areas of England. A map of Edinburgh District at the same scale is in preparation. Explanatory handbooks are available for the sheets covering Craven Arms, Church Stretton, and Wenlock Edge. Northern Ireland has no comparable series at this scale; but at 1:21,120

105

(three inches to one mile) is the Map of Northern Ireland, of which a Special Engineering Geology Sheet covering Belfast is in preparation.

The one-inch series covers England and Wales, from Norham to the Lizard, in 360 sheets although the set is not yet complete. These are a new series of coloured sheets with the National Grid overprinted, showing either solid or drift geology or a combination of both according to the region covered. In a few areas, where a new resurvey is unlikely to be practical for some years, provisional colour-printed geological maps are being issued to meet demand: the maps are compilations based on the old series one-inch sheets and on published material from non-Institute sources wherever available, but as no recent geological surveying has been done in these areas it is likely that the superficial deposits are inadequately represented. In addition to the standard one-inch new series, there are also one-inch special sheets of England and Wales in a new series, covering the Isle of Man, the Isle of Wight, Anglesey, and Bristol.

A revised edition of Sheet 339 (Teignmouth) of the one-inch series is being prepared by the Department of Geology at Exeter University under contract to the Natural Environment Research Council. The map will conform to established practice as regards colours and symbols. The work of mapping is not yet completed, and it will be some years before the actual one-inch map is published.

Scotland is covered by its own series of one-inch geological maps, in 122 sheets, though some gaps in the sequence still remain to be filled. The note about provisional editions of the English sheets, above, applies also to a few Scottish areas. The Scottish sheets similarly show solid or drift geology, or a combination of both on the same sheet, according to the characteristics of the area. Special sheets cover Glasgow District, Assynt District, Arran, Northern Skye, Northern Shetland, and Western Shetland.

A series of Memoirs runs parallel with the one-inch sheets of England and Wales, and Scotland, having the same numbering, each Memoir being an explanatory text covering the area of the corresponding sheet. Memoirs are not available for all, or even most, of the published sheets.

106

The one-inch geological maps of Northern Ireland, overprinted with the Irish Grid, will eventually form a series of thirty six sheets, of which only five pairs of solid and drift maps have been published: those for Giants Causeway, Ballycastle, Carrickfergus, Dungannon, and Belfast. Provisional dyeline editions of the Enniskillen and Clogher sheets are available direct from the Geological Survey of Northern Ireland.

Quarter-inch geological maps cover England and Wales in a series of twenty four sheets, still in progress. Scotland is covered by a similar series of seventeen sheets. Northern Ireland is represented by only two sheets at this scale which form a part of a series of sixteen sheets covering the whole of Ireland: these were the original geological survey of Ireland, dating from the early years of this century, and the two sheets relating to the north are reprints from this edition (two of the original sheets relating to parts of Eire are still in print, dated 1913 and 1921). In addition a quarter-inch map of mineral deposits, was issued in a provisional dyeline edition in 1970.

Geological maps at 1:10,560 scale (six-inch) have also been prepared for the coalfields and other important areas. These were originally in a County Series of quarter sheets which is now being replaced by larger-size[14] National Grid sheets, uncoloured in either case. Coloured quarter sheets cover the London District. Also at this scale, the counties of Tyrone and Antrim are covered by uncoloured geological sheets.

In addition to the published map series, manuscript copies of six-inch geological maps covering a large part of Great Britain, and also copies of out of print one-inch geological maps are available for inspection by the public in the libraries of the Geological Survey offices of the Institute. British maps are available at the Institute's offices in London, Leeds, and Edinburgh; those for Northern Ireland can be seen in Belfast. Dyeline or photographic copies of unpublished six-inch National Grid geological maps can be purchased from the relevant office, where available. Photographic copies of unpublished six-inch County Series can also be ordered.

Geological maps illustrative of texts are to be found in two valuable series. The Institute of Geological Sciences issue the *British regional geology handbooks,* covering England and Wales and Scotland, each volume of which describes the characteristics of each geological system represented, including notes on the economic minerals of the region, illustrated with maps and sketches, documented with a bibliography of maps and publications. The regions discussed are fairly broad ones: *Northern England; Bristol and Gloucester district; The midland valley of Scotland,* for examples. The other series is formed by the guides produced and published by the Geologists' Association,[15] which cover Northern Ireland in addition to England, Wales and Scotland. Thirty seven guides have been published to date. In general they discuss smaller areas than do the *British regional geology handbooks*: there are several under the generic title *Geology around the university towns,* for example Liverpool, the Durham area, Swansea; and independent titles such as *Geology of the Cotswold Hills. Geology of the Weald,* and *Geological itineraries in South Shropshire.*

An atlas, so-called, which is in fact more of a text with illustrative maps, is *Stanford's geological atlas of Great Britain,* published most recently in 1964 in an edition entirely re-written and re-drawn by T Eastwood. England, Wales, and Scotland, including the Isle of Man, are covered. There is an introduction on what geology is about, with notes on Geological Survey maps, followed by chapters on stratigraphy and economic products. The country is then divided into twenty nine sections—for example, south east England, north Wales, Galloway—each one beginning with a black and white sheet at a scale of one inch to twelve miles indicating by means of a notation (which is explained on the back endpapers) the geology of the area. Each map is followed by pages of explanatory text, with diagrams.

THEMATIC MAPS AND ATLASES: GEOMORPHOLOGY
The whole of England, Wales, and Scotland is to be covered by the Geomorphological map at 1:625,000, currently being prepared by the British Geomorphological Research Group within the Department of Geography, University College of Swansea. The project is under the direction of Professor D L Linton, with five regional editors supervising the work on Scotland, Wales, north, south west, and south east England. The map shows the surface forms of the three countries as they are usually classified by British geomorphologists.

Geomorphological maps are frequently published as part of articles or reports which concentrate on small areas of the country. For example, two productions of the Department of Geography of the University of Aberdeen may be mentioned: *The beaches of Sutherland* by W Ritchie and A Mather, commissioned by the Countryside Commission for Scotland in 1969, contains a series of geomorphological maps of the beaches of the county of Sutherland at various scales; and in *The coastal geomorphology of North Uist* by W Ritchie (Aberdeen University, 1968, O'Dell Memorial Monograph 1) is a series of maps of the same type also at various scales, covering the island of North Uist in the Hebrides.

THEMATIC MAPS AND ATLASES : SOIL

Soil Survey maps are published by the Ordnance Survey in the same way as the Geological Survey maps are published. Soil maps are published for the Soil Survey of England and Wales, and for the Soil Survey of Scotland at the Macaulay Institute for Soil Research. The maps themselves are available through the normal Ordnance Survey channels, but the accompanying Memoirs and Bulletins are available only from the respective Surveys, or from Edward Stanford Ltd in London.

Soil Survey maps come at two scales, 1:63,360 (one inch) and 1:25,000 (2½-inch), both for England and Wales and for Scotland. None of these countries is by any means comprehensively covered at either scale. The one-inch series potentially covers England and Wales in 360 sheets, of which only a small fraction have been published (twenty at the time of writing) plus large composite sheets covering Anglesey and Pwllheli. Scotland is potentially covered in 122 sheets, of which again only a small fraction have been published (nineteen at the time of writing). The one-inch series is accompanied by Memoirs, which offer explanatory texts for use with certain of the maps; in many cases folded copies of the maps are included in the Memoirs.

In the series at 1:25,000 scale five sheets have been published : Romney Marsh, Selsey Bill, Chichester, Bognor Regis, and Worthing, along with three sheets of the Breckland Forest. Only one sheet has been published to represent Scotland: that taking in Candacraig and Glenbuchat, and the Island of Rhum.

The Soil Survey is also responsible for, in addition to the Memoirs, a series of Bulletins, of which four have so far been published. The Bulletins are accompanied by maps, sometimes more than one: these are either from the 1 : 25,000 scale series, or specially drawn as in the case of the Bulletin on *The Soils of the west midlands* (number two, 1964) which has a map at 1 : 625,000 scale. The Bulletins achieve a high standard of authority, as do the maps. The latest in the series, number four *Soils of Romney Marsh* by R D Green (1968), an account of the development of the Marsh accompanied by a composite map at 1 : 25,000 scale showing the distribution of soil over the whole area, is described by Professor J A Steers of Cambridge University as ' the best example in this country of a map relating recent, often very recent, deposits to drainage, inning and to agricultural and pastoral uses '.[16] The Bulletin also contains several smaller maps illustrating the geology and drainage of the Marsh.

Soil maps can sometimes be traced down as supplements to journals, or in books. A notable instance of the latter is *The agrarian history of England and Wales* edited by H P R Finberg (Cambridge, Cambridge UP, in progress) which, when complete, will be a prolific source of soil maps. In the journal literature, another prolific source of information which from time to time focuses on soil, is the annual journal of the Field Studies Council, *Field studies*. The issue of September 1969, 3(1), includes a paper on ' Soils of Snowdon ' by D F Ball, G Mew and W S G Macphee which is available as an offprint accompanied by two folded maps at 1 : 10,560 scale, based on the Ordnance Survey map of the area, one showing parent materials of Snowdon soils by means of choropleth shading in black and white and the other showing in colour the distribution of the soils themselves.

THEMATIC MAPS AND ATLASES : LAND USE

The first Land Utilisation Survey of Great Britain was initiated by Sir L Dudley Stamp, and carried out, largely by teams of voluntary workers, in the early years of the 1930's. The work, carried out at a scale of six inches to one mile on Ordnance Survey base maps, was reduced and published at one-inch scale in a series of 150 sheets covering England, Wales, and large parts of Scotland.

The maps depicted fourteen categories of land use in colour, including forest and woodland, arable, heathland, market gardening, and unproductive land. The findings of the Survey were coordinated and published in a series of county reports,[17] each one being a detailed survey of the agriculture and land use of the county illustrated with sketch plans and statistical tables.

Only a very few of the original sheets, and of the county reports, are still in print and available. Edward Stanford Ltd, of London, hold all remaining stocks, and for some items only a few copies remain. When the existing stocks have been exhausted they will not be reprinted. No useful purpose would be served by listing here the numbers which are still available: such a list would be out of date within a few months. The findings of the Survey are, of course, embodied in the two land maps of the Ordnance Survey ten-mile series, discussed above.

A significant by-product and parallel activity of the first Land Utilisation Survey was the grassland survey of England and Wales; an individual reconnaissance survey was also carried out in Wales and the results of this, mapped at quarter-inch scale, are contained in *A survey of the agricultural wastelands of Wales* by R G Stapledon and W Davies (Faber, 1936).

The Second Land Utilisation Survey of Great Britain began in 1960 under the direction of Alice Coleman for the Isle of Thanet Geographical Association, and is based on King's College, London. The maps were conceived as ' a graphical data storage bank—a factual record of the use being made of British land during the 1960s '.[18] As in the case of the first Land Utilisation Survey, the field work is being done by voluntary workers, using Ordnance Survey 1:25,000 maps as the base. The land use maps are prepared and published at the same scale. The 1:25,000 scale was chosen because ' it can portray regional contrast without generalising local detail too severely. No field is too small to be legible yet the total sheet area of seventy eight square miles can embrace several types of terrain . . . The only real limitation of the 1:25,000 scale is that it cannot accommodate every conceivable subdivision of urban use.'[18] Changes which the Ordnance Survey have introduced into the second series of maps at 1:25,000 scale are incorporated into the land use maps through the basic transparencies, for example,

111

the replacement of grey by black for field boundaries and buildings, the black hatch now being used for buildings instead of solid grey. The Ordnance Survey maps and the land use maps both use the same sheet lines: the Ordnance Survey changed their sheet size to seventy eight square miles (two hundred square kilometres) while the Land Utilisation Survey adjusted the position of their north to south sheet lines in order to coordinate the two series at the same scale. Only four land use maps were produced on the old sheet line grid: those for Princes Risborough, Crowland Fens, Nuneaton, and Downham Market. Each map consists of two ten kilometre squares placed side by side, as do the maps of the Ordnance Survey second series at 1:25,000 scale. The maps identify sixty four categories of land use, including fourteen classifications of industry, and are printed in eleven colours. Major classes are represented by separate colours which are instantly recognisable at first glance; minor classes are represented by subdued tints of the major colours or as overprinted symbols, and require closer scrutiny for identification.

More than one hundred sheets have now been published. Sheet number s138 covers Dunfermline in Scotland; the rest cover parts of England and Wales. Unpublished maps, which afford a much more extensive coverage of all three countries, can be consulted at the headquarters of the Survey at King's College, London. A list of available maps is obtainable from the same source, as are the Index Sheet showing sheet names, main towns etc., and the *Land Use Survey handbook: an explanation of the second Land Use Survey* . . . (fifth edition 1968). The maps themselves are not published by the Ordnance Survey, but are retailed through Edward Stanford Ltd. A research team is now at work at the Survey's headquarters analysing the information contained in the maps, with a view to producing a series of county reports (as Stamp did from the first Land Utilisation Survey). One of the features of these reports will be sets of comprehensive statistics for the various types of land use.

In addition to its coverage by the Second Land Utilisation Survey, Wales alone has been the subject of an independent land use survey carried out from the University College of Wales, Aberystwyth. The whole of Wales is covered by the maps from this survey, which are at a scale of six inches to one mile. The survey was carried out

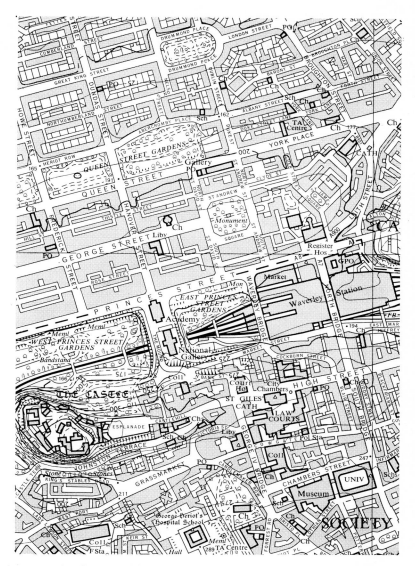

FIGURE 1: Central Edinburgh at 1:10,560 scale. Reproduced from the Ordnance Survey map with the sanction of the Controller of HM Stationery Office, Crown copyright reserved.

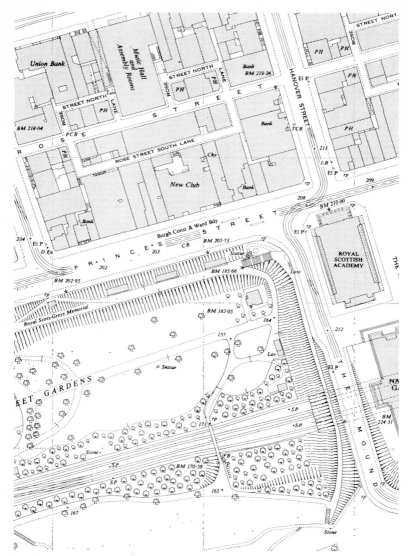

FIGURE 2: Central Edinburgh at 1:2,500 scale. Reproduced from the Ordnance Survey map with the sanction of the Controller of HM Stationery Office, Crown copyright reserved.

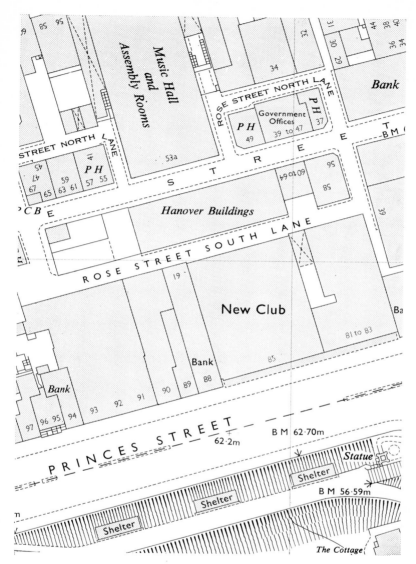

FIGURE 3: Central Edinburgh at 1:1,250 scale. Reproduced from the Ordnance Survey map with the sanction of the Controller of HM Stationery Office, Crown copyright reserved.

between 1961 and 1966, and the maps refer to these years. The maps are not published in the commercial sense, but are available to *bona fide* enquirers provided full acknowledgement is given to the surveys. The supervisor of the survey was J A Taylor of the Department of Geography in the University College of Wales.

Northern Ireland is not being covered by the Second Land Utilisation Survey. The Ordnance Survey of Northern Ireland were responsible for the production of maps from the Land Utilisation Survey of Northern Ireland, which was carried out in 1937 and 1938 by the Geographical Association, Northern Ireland. In this series, eleven maps at a scale of one inch to one mile cover the province, showing land use classified under six headings. There was a very long delay between the publication of these maps and the production of the report, *Land use in Northern Ireland: the general report of the Land Utilisation Survey of Northern Ireland,* edited by L Symons (University of London Press, 1963)—the equivalent of Stamp's county reports for Northern Ireland. Mainly a product of the Department of Geography at Queen's University, Belfast, the volume contains a detailed analysis of land use in Ulster, fully illustrated by maps and photographs. The final section is an analysis by county.

The series of land use maps described above are concerned with all kinds of use, from dense urban to uninhabited moorland and many categories in between. Other projects have been concerned with mapping the distribution of one particular kind of land use, usually in considerably more detail than is possible in a general land use map. One of the most notable projects of this type is Professor J T Coppock's *An agricultural atlas of England and Wales* (Faber, 1964), which contains 205 maps showing the distribution throughout England and Wales of most types of farming land, and a text which explains and amplifies the maps. The maps, which are at various scales according to the area covered, are in black and white, most of them choropleth, but with some dot maps. Most of the maps are based on data from the agricultural census of June 4 1958; the topics represented depend on the mappable data available, and are therefore dictated by the questions asked in the census. Following an introduction dealing with sources and methods, the topics covered are the physical basis of farming, tillage crops, grasslands, horticultural crops, livestock, and intensiveness of farming. Also included are pointers to areas of profitable future research in agricultural land use; and appendices on the production of maps by computer, and selected statistics. There is a select bibliography; and the atlas is indexed. Professor Coppock is also preparing a similar atlas for Scotland, on which work began in October 1966.[19]

The Ministry of Agriculture, Fisheries and Food is responsible for a series of agricultural land classification maps of England and Wales, based on the seventh series of Ordnance Survey one-inch maps. The maps classify land into five qualitative grades on a national basis; the major non-agricultural areas are also shown, existing and scheduled urban areas coloured red, other areas primarily in non-agricultural use, such as woodlands, coloured orange. The maps are all labelled 'provisional': this is because of some unevenness in the exactitude of the survey due to variations in the amount of basic information available for different parts of the country. It is intended to revise them in the light of experience and new information, after coverage of England and Wales has been completed. The maps are available only from the Ministry, who also issue an *Explanatory note* on the maps; *Agricultural land classification* (MOAFF, 1966, Agricultural Land Service Technical Report 11) discusses the evolution of the classification.

At a more local level is a map produced from the Department of Geography of the University of Glasgow on residential land use in Glasgow in 1965, at 1:50,000 scale, which formed part of an article on 'Visual perception and map design' by M Wood, in *Cartographic journal* 5(1) June 1968 54-64. The source material for the map came from a survey carried out by students of the Department of Geography, and the object was to illustrate two selected aspects of residential housing—types of houses, and age of houses.

THEMATIC MAPS AND ATLASES: VEGETATION
As well as mapping the use of land, the Second Land Utilisation Survey of Britain has also incorporated a complete field survey of vegetation, in which all plant communities occupying over five acres have been recorded at six-inch scale. It is proposed to publish the results of this survey for the whole of England and Wales in the form of a *Wildscape atlas,* in two volumes, the first of which

114

is due in August 1971. The atlas will use a specially reduced 1:100,000 scale Ordnance Survey base map as a guide to location. Farmland and settlement will be left in monochrome, while a full range of colours will be used to portray the distinctive subdivisions of vegetation and habitat type in mountain, moorland, heath, marsh, woodland and roughland environments. The data will fall into fifty categories and will be represented on 160 coloured pages, together with about fifty pages of explanatory and interpretative text. When it is completed, the *Wildscape atlas* will form the most comprehensive and detailed source of information on the distribution of British vegetation.[20]

Detailed studies of the vegetation of small local areas of the country, illustrated with textual maps, are to be found in relevant subject journals. As an example of this type of study, G F Peterken's study of the ' Development of vegetation in Staverton Park, Suffolk ' in the journal *Field studies* 3(1) September 1969 may be cited. *Field studies,* which has already been mentioned in connection with information on soil, is a journal which repays investigation and is frequently a fruitful source of detailed information on aspects of land use, geology, botany, geography and other topics. Peterken's paper, which is available as an offprint, comprises thirty nine pages of text discussing the existing vegetation and its development to its present state against a short background introduction dealing with climate, geology and soil, illustrated with twenty one black and white textual maps, diagrams, and plates.

University departments are also active in the mapping of vegetation, one of the most prominent being the Department of Geography at the University College of Wales, Aberystwyth. This was the base for the Vegetation Survey of the Welsh Uplands, directed by James A Taylor, and financed by grants from the Nature Conservancy and other bodies. All land above the moorland edge has been surveyed, an area of some 2,700 square miles forming about one third of the whole country, field mapping being done at a scale of six inches to one mile. The aim of the Survey was both geographical and botanical, in that the vegetation pattern has been recorded as a basis for land use studies.[21] The department has also produced a map of the vegetation of Skomer Island, at 1:5,000 scale (March 1969), and also maps at 1:63,360 and 1:10,560 scales of the vegetation of Dartmoor (June 1969) covering all the unenclosed land of the moor. These maps are available for consultation within the department, although with certain limitations as to use.

From detailed studies of small areas, to the other extreme of fairly generalised surveys of one type of vegetation throughout the whole country. Into the latter category come the maps (sketch maps almost, although drawn to scale) produced by the Forestry Commission to show the incidence of their forests throughout England, Wales, and Scotland. The commission's annual report contains the set of maps relating to all three countries: the most recent (at time of writing) is the *Forty-ninth annual report and accounts 1967-69* (HMSO, 1970) which contains, as an appendix to the report itself, six maps at a scale of approximately one inch to thirty miles showing by symbols the situation of the commission forests and the boundaries of the conservancies as at March 31 1969; county boundaries, major towns, and the location of conservancy or deputy surveyors' offices are also shown. The same information is mapped, though using slightly different symbols in the cases of England and Wales, in the individual booklets *Forestry in England, Forestry in Scotland* and *Forestry in Wales,* all published in 1969 by the Commission in London, Edinburgh, and Cardiff respectively.

THEMATIC MAPS AND ATLASES : CLIMATE

The principal survey of the British weather in map form is the *Climatological atlas of the British Isles* prepared by the Meteorological Office (HMSO, 1952) which is now out of print but available in many libraries. The atlas was begun in 1938, although progress on it was suspended during World War II, and most of its maps show the average conditions for the period 1901-1930, this being the standard period selected by the International Meteorological Organisation for climatological averages for all meteorological services throughout the world. As comparable observations for some elements, such as visibility and cloud, had not begun as early as 1901, data for later periods covering as many years as possible have been substituted. The atlas has 220 maps altogether, and is divided into ten sections, each one dealing with one of the climatological elements, for example, snow, sunshine, and cloud. Each section is complete in itself, with an introduction in which are briefly described the methods of making observations and correcting the data when necessary for the preparation of the plates, concluded with some bibliographical references, and followed by the maps themselves. The whole-page maps are at 1:4.13M scale along parallel 54°, along a meridian the scale is 1:4.24M. Where there are four maps per page, these are scaled down accordingly. Most of the maps are coloured, and the majority of these employ tints of the one colour over the whole map. The whole atlas is prefaced by an introduction, and a list of references to the principal publications in which weather data for the British Isles appear.

THEMATIC MAPS AND ATLASES : MISCELLANEOUS PHYSICAL FEATURES
Under this heading are assembled some maps which have been produced with the primary purpose of depicting the distribution or the characteristics of a feature which is basically physical in character.

A good example of this somewhat ill-defined genre is the *Green belt map of the west midlands* compiled by G T Warwick (Birmingham, Midlands New Towns Society, 1966), drawn at a scale of one inch to one mile, and printed in a transparent green superimposed on a monochrome base of Ordnance Survey data on streams, woodlands, buildings, and communications. The map shows the composite green belt around the main urban nucleus of the region, and also the separate centre of Coventry and a number of smaller towns and villages.

The Water Resources Board issue maps of hydrometric areas and river authority areas at various scales. At 1:625,000 scale are two sheets covering England and Wales showing hydrometric areas and river authority areas overprinted on the Ordnance Survey base; at the same scale are two maps also on the Ordnance Survey base covering England and Wales and Scotland and showing the same information as the first two sheets mentioned plus the river purification board areas in Scotland. Hydrometric areas are shown on sheets at 1:2,500,000 scale (approximately one inch to forty miles) covering England, Wales and Scotland which also indicate the river authority areas of England and Wales. The Ordnance Survey quarter-inch series at 1:250,000 scale is used as base for a series of sheets covering England and Wales only, which show rivers and watercourses overprinted in blue on the grey base.

117

A specialised, and probably unique, example of a survey carried out over a specialised area for the end purpose of its preservation, is the survey sponsored by the National Trust in connection with Enterprise Neptune, of the coastal areas of England, Wales, and Northern Ireland. Enterprise Neptune was established in 1963 primarily to raise funds to buy land or obtain covenants over land on the English, Welsh and Northern Irish coasts in order to preserve it from spoliation and keep it for the benefit and use of everyone. In addition to raising the money, Enterprise Neptune needed also as much information as could be obtained about the ownership, control and land use of the coasts to a depth of about half a mile hinterland. The first part of the survey therefore mapped onto the outline edition of the Ordnance Survey one-inch maps, the position and extent of existing and designated National Trust coastlands and also lands in other public ownership. These maps are revised as land comes into the possession of the National Trust, and can be seen in the trust's offices.

The second part of the survey involved the detailed mapping of the coastal areas, and for this, student field workers were made available under the direction of Dr J B Whittow of Reading University. Information from the coastal areas of the maps of the Second Land Utilisation Survey was made available to Reading University, and, after a pilot project, the survey started in earnest with thirty two students in July 1965. In September of the same year, the first four sheets, covering coastal areas of Merioneth, Norfolk, Llandudno, and Anglesey, with accompanying preliminary notes, were submitted to the National Trust. It was agreed that, as the maps were flimsy and mounting would be too expensive, they should be retained at the trust headquarters in London together with the accompanying written reports, and it is there that the maps, a detailed record of the coasts of Britain, may be consulted.

THEMATIC MAPS AND ATLASES : ADMINISTRATIVE BOUNDARIES
The Ordnance Survey has a statutory obligation to publish maps showing the positions of administrative boundaries. This it does by showing the boundaries on the standard series of maps, and also by producing special maps. The Administrative Areas map in two sheets at 1 : 625,000 scale forms part of the national ten-mile series,

118

and is revised annually. It shows the areas of all local authorities from counties and county boroughs down to urban and rural districts in England and Wales and the corresponding authorities in Scotland, in colour on an outline base. The counties of England are covered by separate administrative areas maps at 1:100,000 scale, which show the boundaries of parliamentary constituencies, administrative counties, county boroughs, municipal boroughs, urban and rural districts, and civil parishes. The maps are in colour and are on a base reduced from the one-inch series, carrying the National Grid. Outline editions of the maps are also available, showing the base detail only. Similar coverage of the Welsh counties is in progress, to replace the present coverage at a scale of half an inch to one mile. The half-inch maps are in two styles: style A, showing in colour the same information as appears on the 1:100,000 scale series of English counties, and style B, showing the same information except for parliamentary constituencies. The Greater London Council is covered by administrative areas maps at one-inch and 1:25,000 scales. The one-inch map shows parliamentary constituency boundaries, and boundaries of the GLC, the City of London, and the London boroughs, in colour on an outline base. At 1:25,000 scale there are twenty five sheets showing all administrative boundaries, from the GLC down to London borough wards, overprinted in red on grey outline base maps.

Scotland is covered by nine sheets at 1:250,000 scale, which show the boundaries of parliamentary constituencies, counties, counties of cities, burghs, districts and civil parishes overprinted on a base map compiled from the quarter-inch series. A separate map at a scale of one inch to one mile is produced for Glasgow and district, which shows on a one-inch base the same information as appears on the nine Scottish sheets with the addition of electoral divisions.

The Ordnance Survey of Northern Ireland publish a Parliamentary Constituency Map of Northern Ireland at quarter-inch scale, which shows district electoral divisions and Northern Ireland and UK parliamentary constituency boundaries on a grey base; the map carries an inset showing the parliamentary constituencies within the county borough of Belfast. An Administrative Map of Northern Ireland, at the same scale, is a grey base map carrying district electoral divisions in black and rural districts, urban districts, municipal boroughs, and county boroughs in red. Insets show the Belfast wards and a list of the remaining wards in the other urban areas. Belfast and district is also separately covered by a map at 1:21,120 scale showing administrative boundaries in colour on a grey base.

Related to administrative boundaries are the estate boundaries in Highland Scotland, and a map of these at 1:625,000 scale, prepared by R Millman of the Department of Geography in the University of Aberdeen, was issued as a supplement by the *Scottish geographical magazine* in December 1969. The map is available from the Royal Scottish Geographical Society.

THEMATIC MAPS AND ATLASES : TRANSPORT AND COMMUNICATIONS
Maps showing transport routes and channels of communication are usually aimed at those who travel, or transport, or communicate, and do not thereby necessarily contain much information of value to planners. Road maps, in particular, are aimed primarily at the private motorist wishing to travel between two points by the most direct route or, increasingly, to recognise which minor roads to take to avoid the bottlenecks on the most direct routes. Nevertheless, the best specimens of this genre give an indispensable overall picture of the network of communications which covers the country.

Of road maps, the Route Planning map forming a part of the Ordnance Survey ten-mile maps has already been mentioned. At larger scales, Geographia Ltd publish two series of maps which show the road system and a wide range of ancillary information. At 1:316,000 scale (one inch to five miles) there is a series of primary routes maps, covering England, Wales and Scotland in six sheets, and displaying existing and projected motorways and by-passes, primary and class 1 and 2 roads, minor roads, service areas, airfields (commercial, county and national), canals, and rivers. At 1:190,080 scale (one inch to three miles) comes the series of 'new super detailed motorists' maps ', which covers the three countries in twenty seven sheets, some of them overlapping. A wide range of information is incorporated, including all roads from motorway to minor status, including projected motorways, toll points, steep hills, car ferries, National Trust properties and national parks, airports, canals, wireless/tv masts, and railways; town areas are shaded grey, and all villages are shown.

120

Railway maps tend to become out of date almost as quickly as road maps, particularly in the remoter areas of the country. The most recent map showing the current British Rail system is the *British rail system map* published in 1969 by Geographia Ltd. Three maps at 1:475,000 scale, contained in a card sleeve, illustrate the railway system on a plain white base, indicating freight, passenger and shipping services, and including also a range of associated information such as collieries, generating stations, cement works, docks, gas and steel works and oil refineries.

Waterways are mapped on a national basis in the *Waterways atlas of the British Isles* by John Cranfield and Michael Bonfiel (Cranfield and Bonfiel Books, 1966). The atlas is designed to cater for the historian on the one hand, and for those engaged in cruising and commercial carrying on the other, by including in addition to waterways currently in use, all those known to have been built and used but which are now derelict. The authors have a crusading purpose also: ' it is to be hoped that this atlas may show the usefulness of present transport routes that are under utilised, and also the possibilities of extension to give nationwide transport that cannot be beaten for economy '. There are forty maps altogether, of which the first is a key map to England and Wales, the twenty sixth is a key map to Scotland, and the thirtieth is a key map to Ireland (including Eire). The main maps, which are at 1:506,880 scale (one inch to eight miles), show, by means of coloured lines, navigable canals, derelict canals, navigable rivers, derelict river navigations, other rivers. County boundaries and towns are indicated, and there is a gazetteer for each country. A loose insert with the atlas gives additions and corrections up to October 1968.

Individual canals within a specified region are the subject of a series of books published by the firm of David and Charles, of Newton Abbot in Devon, under the generic title ' Canals of the British Isles ', and these volumes all contain useful maps. Edward Standard Ltd produce waterways maps, with recreation as their primary purpose: these include a map at a scale of $1\frac{1}{4}$ inches to one mile of Norfolk Broads and rivers; one at a scale of $1\frac{1}{2}$ inches to one mile of the River Thames from Richmond to Lechlade showing, *inter alia,* weirs, locks, and maximum draught for all reaches of the river; and another at a scale of one inch to eight miles under the title 'Inland cruising—map of England' showing all navigable waterways, with locks, tidal limits, and mileages.

Subsidiary companies of the National Bus Company throughout England and Wales, subsidiaries of the Scottish Bus Group, and the independent companies—Lancashire United Transport Ltd, Sheffield Joint Omnibus Committee, Barton Transport Ltd, the London Transport Board—produce maps of their services as a feature of their time-table booklets. These maps are frequently issued separately, folded inside a card cover. The map issued by the Bristol Omnibus Company Limited, for example, covers at 1:250,000 scale the area of the company, and indicates the routes of its own services and those of associated companies. No indication of frequency is given.

One feature of bus services which is of interest in particular to planners (rather than the bus travellers, who are the main audience for the simple route maps issued by the bus companies) is their capability of analysis to provide an indication of local accessibility and the extent of urban hinterlands. The map of local accessibility in the Ordnance Survey ten-mile series, which has been mentioned already, showed a pattern based on analysis of winter bus services in 1947-48 in England and Wales and in 1949-50 in Scotland. This analysis was the subject of an article by F H W Green, 'Urban hinterlands in England and Wales: an analysis of bus services' in *Geographical journal* 116(1) March 1950 64-88. Sixteen years later, the same author brought the subject up to date in another article 'Urban hinterlands: fifteen years on' in *Geographical journal* 132(2) June 1966 263-266, in which he reviews the most recent production in this field of activity, the British bus services map compiled and drawn by J C Gillham (Shepperton, Locomotive Publishing Co and Ian Allan, 1965). The five sheets, mapped at a scale of approximately one inch to 3.4 miles, cover a continuous strip of country from Cornwall to Kent, and are based on winter bus services in 1964-65. Green discusses each sheet in turn, in some detail, and estimates that bus routes still provide a good index of local accessibility.

THEMATIC MAPS AND ATLASES: INDUSTRY

The principal publisher of industrial maps relating to Great Britain is Geographia Ltd. Their maps are aimed primarily at a marketing and commercial audience, but nevertheless contain information not readily to be found elsewhere in map form about the distribution of industry, retail and service outlets, and other factors of relevance.

Their most ambitious publication is the *Survey of manufacturing industry,* an undated, spiral-bound volume whose information is based on Board of Trade statistics, mainly from the *Census of production 1961.* The *Survey* has a full introduction containing geographical notes, sources of statistics, and definitions of terms used including a definition of the Standard Industrial Classification, an abridged form of which is used for the headings to the maps and tables. Also included in the introduction are national and regional summaries of the numbers of all industrial establishments together with a key map showing regional code numbers. Part I contains twenty eight fold-out maps showing the national distribution of twenty eight categories of manufacturing industry; distribution is shown by the number of establishments in each category and on the reverse side of each map a graph presents by means of actual numbers and by percentages of the national total, the regional distribution of all establishments in that category. Part II of the survey illustrates the regional distribution of manufacturing industry, and groups seventy one regions into eleven groupings approximating to the geographical coverage of ITV areas. Eleven fold-out maps show the boundaries of the regions in the groups, and each one carries on the reverse side graphs and tables showing for all twenty eight industrial categories the number of establishments within each region. Where more than thirty establishments in any one category are located in a single region, an additional analysis by size of establishment based on the number of employees is provided.

Complementary to the *Survey of manufacturing industry* is Geographia Ltd's *Marketing and media survey,* also spiral-bound and undated but based on data from the 1961 census. The introduction follows the same pattern, containing geographical notes, sources of statistics, and definitions of terms. National summaries of population, and a national map showing the code numbers allocated to marketing regions precede the main part of the volume, which is based on the same eleven regions as the regional section of the

Survey of manufacturing industry. Eleven fold-out maps distinguish sixty five marketing regions, and each map is accompanied by tables of population and households, retail outlets, service trades, and other information mainly concerned with advertising media. For each of the eleven groupings of regions, ITV audience data is analysed by numbers of households, ITV households, social class, age of housewife, and so on.

Similar in scope and purpose to the *Marketing and media survey* is the *Marketing manual of the United Kingdom* issued by the British Bureau of Television Advertising (1967), which uses a breakdown into thirteen ITV areas, interpreted in terms of local authority administrative areas.

Geographia Ltd also publish, in association with the London Press Exchange, a series of *Conurbation marketing maps,* of which three have so far appeared: covering the west midlands, at a scale of $1\frac{3}{4}$ inches to one mile; Liverpool and Merseyside, at a scale of $4\frac{1}{2}$ inches to one mile; and Glasgow and Clydeside, at a scale of $1\frac{3}{4}$ inches to one mile. Each map indicates the layout of the main retail, industrial, and residential districts in the area. Shopping centres are classified in three grades according to the facilities provided and the approximate number of shops in the centre; residential areas are classified in three categories of density; industrial areas show five categories of industry and indicate the location of factories employing more than a specified number of employees. Each map is accompanied by an explanatory booklet.

The Central Electricity Generating Board produce a map, published by George Philip, showing at a scale of one inch to ten miles, the location of generating stations (including those under construction), transforming stations, switching stations, transmission lines and cables throughout England and Wales and part of Scotland, as at April 1 1969. Symbols are used on a black and white base, and the boundaries of the regional boards are shown prominently in red.

The inclusion of industry in comprehensive atlases and map series has already been noted, but it is worth reiterating in this context that the *Atlas of Britain and Northern Ireland* contains detailed treatment of industry at national and regional level showing distribution in terms of employment for each industry considered. The

Atlas of London and the London region also contains detailed treatment of industry. Finally, stepping outside the limits of the atlas, J E Martin's *Greater London: an industrial geography* (G Bell, 1966) is worth investigating for its graphic presentation of a mass of data relating to the contemporary location of major industries in the metropolis, in the form of maps of employment densities.

THEMATIC MAPS AND ATLASES : POPULATION

Within the last decade, there has been an increase in interest in the mapping of social data of various kinds : of these, population, and aspects of population, have received perhaps the greatest attention. Logically, since population is one of the basic factors in planning and in the country's economy generally, there is considerable advantage to be gained from a knowledge of its composition, movement, rates of increase and decrease according to area, and other aspects, and a graphical presentation of such data can often be more easily assimilated than pages of statistical tables. Several techniques have been developed, and are still developing for the graphic presentation of demographic statistics, and some interesting series of maps have resulted.

Population maps figure prominently both in the *Atlas of Britain and Northern Ireland* and in the *Atlas of London and the London region,* particularly in the latter. Two population maps also form a part of the Ordnance Survey ten-mile series. These are all discussed above.

Population itself, aside from the mapping of it, is the subject of serious study, and is the focus of interest of the Population Studies Group of the Institute of British Geographers (since January 1968 the Institute of British Geographers Study Group in Population Geography). The group was formed at the annual conference of the institute in 1963, with the broad aim of promoting population studies within the institute, and the specific aim of producing a pilot atlas supplement to the 1961 census, for which latter purpose a working party was formed within the new group. Maps were compiled for eight aspects of the distribution of population in the British Isles, including the Republic of Ireland, and were completed in 1965. Lack of funds to meet the cost of drawing over two hundred plates prevented publication of the proposed census atlas in the form originally envisaged. However, twelve of the maps were subsequently redrawn at a reduced scale so that each one covered the British Isles on a single sheet, and compilers of the maps were invited to write an account of their compilation and purpose. The maps and papers, which together form a pilot survey of selected aspects of the distribution of population in 1961, were published by the institute as a special number of their Transactions. 'Special number on population maps of the British Isles, 1961' edited for the Population Studies Group by A J Hunt *Institute of British Geographers transactions* 43 1968 is in the form of a carton containing the twelve maps and an explanatory booklet of forty five pages. The maps, all except one of which are choropleth, are at approximately 1:2,300,000 scale, and are in black and white. They show the distribution of five aspects of the population as recorded in the 1961 census: age structure, overcrowding, household tenure, housing quality, and overseas-born population. The supporting documentation is full and detailed, beginning with an introduction by the editor on problems of population mapping, and closing with a list of census volumes consulted.

The main purpose in producing a pilot atlas, as the Population Studies Group initially conceived it, was to suggest to the Registrar General that the publication of an atlas supplement to the decennial census tables might be considered as a normal part of standard census procedure. The end purpose is by no means lost, but, as Hunt points out in his introduction to the explanatory booklet, 'since the census atlas project was adopted, the circumstances which prompted it have changed significantly. Recommendations for improving census procedure have been accepted . . . by the Registrar General. Further recommendations are under consideration at the time of going to press. The reform and rationalisation of local government areas is under review. Experiments have been made in the use of grid squares as areal units for census purposes . . . It is to be hoped that all data for future censuses will be recorded on magnetic tape, related to permanent statistical units independent of changing administrative boundaries, and stored so as to be more readily available for research . . . Meanwhile, it remains to be seen whether changing circumstances will justify or eliminate the need for a census atlas on traditional lines in 1971.'

A similar range of maps, also based on the 1961 census, were produced for the city of Glasgow, not as a separately published entity but as part of an article entitled 'A cartographic analysis of the Glasgow 1961 census ' by Mary Jelliman in *Cartographic journal* 4(1) June 1967 44-49. The maps, at 1 : 100,000 scale, cover land use and house types, household tenure, sex ratio, fertility ratio, population, population density, household amenities, and households without fixed baths. The whole of Scotland is the subject of *A map of the distribution of population in Scotland on census night, April 23rd, 1961* (Glasgow, Collins, 1966), produced at 1 : 500,000 scale from Glasgow University's Department of Geography, and edited by J B Caird and D R Diamond.

University geography departments are also producers of population maps and atlases, and are responsible for two separate atlases of population change. The Department of Geography at Nottingham University has published the *Atlas of population change in the east midland counties, 1951-1961* by Professor R H Osborne (1966) with thirty four pages of text, twelve maps at a scale of about one inch to six miles, and tables. This is a cartographic record of population change in the east midland counties of England during the intercensal period 1951-1961. Each county is illustrated by two black and white maps, one showing absolute and relative change by urban administrative areas and individual civil parishes, and the other showing the structure of change (natural change and net migration) by urban areas and rural districts. There is a general introduction explaining the cartographic methods and discussing the data. In addition there are short commentaries for each county, with summary tables. The counties illustrated are Derbyshire, Leicestershire with Rutland, Lincolnshire-Lindsey, Lincolnshire-Holland with Kesteven, Northamptonshire, including Soke of Peterborough, and Nottinghamshire.

From the University of Hull's Department of Geography, D G Symes and E G Thomas produced, in 1968, *The Yorkshire and Humberside planning region: an atlas of population change 1951-66* (Department of Geography, University of Hull, Miscellaneous Series 8). The maps began as an experimental exercise in mapping characteristics of population change, and resulted in the present atlas of sixteen maps, each with an opposing page of interpretative notes,

127

six pages of introductory text discussing the data and the content and presentation of the maps, a list of sources used, and two appendices which give graphs of crude birth and death rates for the period covered, and a summary of the statistical data used. The maps are all at approximately 1:565,000 scale; all are in black, white, and red. Three maps show population size and absolute change by the use of proportionate spheres; the rest, showing total percentage change, percentage change by natural increase and by migration, birth rate, death rate, fertility rate, natural increase rate, and net migration rate, use the ' standard score ' method with choropleth shading. The area covered is that of the economic planning region, taking in the East and West Ridings of Yorkshire together with Lincolnshire-Lindsey (except for Lincoln county borough).

One of the advantages of the mapping techniques developed in the atlas for showing characteristics of population change, as the compilers point out in the preface, is that they can easily be adapted to represent other types of social data. Such advantage is being utilised in the preparation of a social area atlas of Hull and Haltemprice by Professor H R Wilkinson, Head of the Department of Geography, and Dr R N Davidson, which will include at least ten maps, using choropleth shading of component scores for enumeration districts. The atlas will be in two parts, the first, the atlas itself, and the second containing the text, both to be published in the University's miscellaneous series in 1970 or 1971.

The University of Newcastle upon Tyne is also active in the cartographic field. The Department of Geography has issued a series of planning reports under the programme of research into migration and mobility in northern England sponsored by the then Ministry of Labour of which number four is *Northern region and nation: a short migration atlas, 1960-61* by J W House and K G Willis, published in 1967. The atlas is concerned with the spatial representation and structural analysis of patterns of migration within the northern region, and between the northern region and other parts of Great Britain, during the year 1960-1961. The data used have been taken, in the main, from the 1961 census, and in particular from the migration tables for England and Wales, published in 1966. The data are presented in a series of twenty two maps at various scales, all in black and white, and employing a variety of techniques such as proportionate circles and bar graphs. The maps are preceded by an introductory section containing a note on the methods used, the limitations of the data, and a set of definitions of terms used; and they are followed by a section containing the conclusions which have been drawn from the data, and an annotated bibliography.

THEMATIC MAPS AND ATLASES : DISEASE

In 1959 the Royal Geographical Society set up a Medical Geography Committee, whose first practical project was the preparation of an atlas of disease mortality. The *National atlas of disease mortality in the United Kingdom* prepared for them by G Melvyn Howe (Nelson, 1963) is a pioneer of its type, and so far the only example in this area of investigation. Its purpose, as stated by its compiler, is to display the facts, but in no way to interpret them (although the interpretation is clear enough in many cases even to the layman). The maps, which are at the scale of 1 : 3M, illustrate general mortality from all causes, and then proceed to a breakdown of mortality from cancer, diseases of the circulatory system, diseases of the respiratory system, diseases of the digestive system, and miscellaneous causes including infant mortality. This first edition covers the years 1954 to 1958. A revised and enlarged edition published in 1970 repeats these data in its first half, and in its second half adds data for a further five year period, 1959 to 1963. The second part of this edition, in addition to giving more up to date information, also represents a new method of plotting the information so that statistical errors can be avoided and so that the statistical significance of the data can be seen as well as its geographical distribution. The accompanying text also includes some interpretation of the distribution.

HISTORICAL MAPS AND ATLASES

These fall into two distinct categories. First, there are the maps which reconstruct from modern evidence a situation which existed sometime in the past. Second, there are facsimile reproductions of old maps.

Into the first category come most of the Ordnance Survey's historical maps, some of which are primarily of archaeological interest.

There are now several of these, including Ancient Britain and Southern Britain in the Iron Age, both at 1 : 625,000 scale; Roman Britain and Britain in the Dark Ages, both at 1 : 1M scale; a series of strip maps covering the entire length of the Antonine Wall at 1 : 25,000 scale; and the entire length of Hadrian's Wall in a similar format at 1 : 126,720 scale.

Also in this category are historical atlases, which trace the development of a town or a country from evidence uncovered in the course of modern research into contemporary sources and modern archaeological excavation. William Rees' *An historical atlas of Wales from early to modern times* (Faber, new edition 1959) is a scholarly example of this type. It traces the development of Wales from the Bronze Age to the end of the nineteenth century in a series of seventy maps and plans accompanied by seventy one pages of explanatory text.

The doyen of historical atlases, in scope, scholarship, and standard of production is *Historic towns: maps and plans of towns and cities in the British Isles, with historical commentaries from earliest times to 1800* (Lovell Johns—Cook, Hammond and Kell Organisation, v 1 1969). This is the British section of the *Historical atlas of town plans for Western Europe*. The project originated in the International Commission for the History of Towns (itself a group of the International Congress of Historians) and a British Committee of Historical Towns, based on Oxford, guides the work of the British section. The general editor is Mrs M D Lobel, who explains the purpose of the project in her introduction to the first volume. ' The main task set by the commission was to produce a large-scale plan (1 : 5,000) of each selected town, as it was in the first quarter of the nineteenth century before it had been much affected by the Industrial Revolution and the accompanying rise in population. The principal late medieval features and the medieval street pattern were to be incorporated, so that the reader might see at a glance the main differences in plan between the two periods. We decided, in order to meet this condition and at the same time preserve our national scale, to produce two main plans—one at 1 : 2,500 scale as a working tool, and the other at 1 : 5,000 scale which was derived directly from the larger scale plan.' The first volume was published in 1969, covering the towns of Banbury, Caernarvon, Glasgow,

Gloucester, Hereford, Nottingham, Reading, and Salisbury. The second volume, comprising Bristol, Cambridge, Coventry, Winchester, and Windsor, will be published in 1971. The third volume will include Bury St Edmunds, Colchester, Lincoln, and Norwich, and is scheduled to appear in 1972/73, and the final volume, which will be devoted to London, is scheduled for 1974. Some towns are also being published as separate facsimiles: Nottingham and Reading are the first to appear in this form.

The first volume is a superb production and, like all top quality atlases, is a pleasure to handle and to use. The section devoted to each town is the work of a specialist, and has a text introduction tracing the development of the town followed by the set of maps relating to it. The subject matter of both text and maps is similar for all the towns, and the arrangement of each section follows a similar pattern. The section on Banbury, for example, which is the work of P D A Harvey, has an introduction which discusses the site and situation of the town, the new (ie twelfth century) borough, the topography of the medieval town, the economy of the medieval town, from the Reformation to the early nineteenth century. References are given in footnotes. Then come the maps: the situation of Banbury, showing at 1:250,000 scale the setting of the town in its region; the site c1800, at 1:5,000 scale; medieval street names at 1:5,000 scale; the large scale plan of Banbury c1800, (1:2,500) covering two pages; the borough boundary c1800, at 1:5,000 scale; finally, the derived 1:5,000 scale plan of the town. The main town plans are in full colour: an explanation of the colours and conventions used is carried on the back endpaper.

In the second category, that of facsimile reproductions of historic maps and plans, there are several productions which are worthy of attention. In collaboration with the Ordnance Survey, the firm of David and Charles, of Newton Abbot, are publishing a reprint, edited by J B Harley, of the first edition of the Ordnance Survey one inch to one mile series covering England and Wales. Publication began in 1969 and is expected to be completed in 1971, after which the reprint will be extended to Scotland. The maps of the first edition were published between 1805 and 1873, and were revised from time to time until about 1890, the most important change being the addition of the railway network. The reprint is made up of facsimiles of the later, revised printings; the number of sheets has been reduced to ninety seven by transferring small sections of coastline which were the subject of complete sheets in the original into spare space on adjoining maps. Each sheet carries introductory notes, designed to assist in the dating and interpretation of the maps.

It is surprising to find how few British towns are represented by collections of plans illustrating their development. Southampton Corporation published in 1964 a collection, *Southampton maps from Elizabethan times,* consisting of twenty four facsimiles with a text introduction, which was a model of what such a collection should, and could, be. More recently, the printing firm of Silk and Terry Ltd, of Birmingham, have produced two slim volumes in collaboration with public libraries: *Birmingham before 1800: six maps in the Local Studies Library, Birmingham Reference Library* (1968), comprising maps dating from 1553 to 1795; and *Maps of Manchester 1650-1848* (1969), also containing six facsimiles. These are nicely produced sheets, but could do with some descriptive notes to supplement the brief captions on the reverse of each sheet. Other city libraries are ideally situated to follow suit with similar collections.

PART 2: GUIDES TO MAPS AND MAPPING

It is possible to classify or categorise the literature relating to maps and mapping to the stage where each category contains only one item: this is just another way of saying that no two writers have the same approach to maps and that even when the basic aspect of the subject is the same—map interpretation, for example—very different treatments can emerge. This apart, some form of categorisation is helpful, and has therefore been attempted, with the qualification that it is sometimes difficult to ascertain the author's basic premise and that it is consequently doubly difficult to interpret the results to fit into one category or another, and the further qualification that inevitably some books would fit into several categories.

The nature of this book dictates that the primary concern shall be with guides to maps and atlases, and these are discussed first.

Following these, the following broad categories have been identified and are discussed in order:

the history of maps

the interpretation of maps

the presentation and content of maps, both topographic and thematic

the techniques of map-making, which is principally concerned with automatic cartography.

GUIDES TO MAPS AND ATLASES

Under this heading it is possible to identify several different categories, the first of which can conveniently be labelled 'publishers' catalogues', although the services and catalogues which are issued in connection with maps are in general much more informative and factual than publishers' catalogues promoting their books. The catalogue produced, and regularly up-dated, by Edward Stanford Ltd, publishers of maps and atlases but more noteworthy as the major retailer of maps and related material in the UK, is a mine of factual information about a wide range of maps, including those of the Ordnance Survey, the Soil Survey and other important series. The complete catalogue covers the whole world, but separate sections are included (and can be obtained independently) relating to the UK. Geographia Ltd produce a handsome catalogue, annually revised; the world catalogue of John Bartholomew and Son Ltd is also annually revised, and the firm maintains a mailing list so that new editions are automatically supplied.

The Ordnance Survey issue an annual *Map catalogue,* an informative illustrated booklet containing details of the various series published by the Survey. This is supplemented by the monthly *Publication report* whose main function is to report new and revised sheets issued in all series during the month, but which also regularly contains notes on matters of interest to map-users such as prices of maps and of services, details of the services available, and lists of bench marks. Separate leaflets giving prices, and a list of agents in England, Wales, and Scotland are also available. The *Map catalogue* is available free, and it is possible to receive the monthly *Publication report* regularly for a nominal annual charge, both direct from the Ordnance Survey. The Ordnance Survey of Northern

Ireland issues the catalogue of its own maps. The current issue is the *Map catalogue 1968*, published in June of that year; it is not an annually revised publication, but is kept up to date by *Map publication reports*. A separate leaflet gives prices of maps and of services. These publications are available direct from the Ordnance Survey of Northern Ireland: a small charge is made for the *Map catalogue 1968*, subsequently the supplements are sent regularly and without charge if this requirement is notified.

Every quarter, in March, June, September, and December, the Ordnance Survey *Publication report* includes, as an insert, a *Geological report* covering the preceding quarter, issued by the Ordnance Survey on behalf of the Geological Survey, which gives details of new and revised geological sheets in all series, also of new Memoirs. The Geological Survey issues in its own right, a twice-yearly (June and November) *List of geological maps* which lists all available maps in all series (including those relating to Northern Ireland), also the Survey's geophysical, aeromagnetic, and hydrogeological maps. The *List* indicates, by symbols, those sheets which are accompanied by Memoirs or other explanatory texts; details of these are to be found in the *Government publications sectional list 45: Institute of Geological Sciences,* which is periodically revised.

As well as catalogues and lists put out by publishers to publicise their own productions, there are also a number of continuing services which include details of recently published maps and atlases in the context of geographical literature in general. Prominent among these is *New geographical literature and maps,* issued twice a year (June and December) by the Royal Geographical Society, each issue providing bibliographical details of new additions to the society's Library and Map Room during the six month period ending March 15 and September 15 respectively. All important new books, atlases, and current maps are included, together with all articles in twenty of the principal British and foreign geographical journals, and a selection from others; the coverage is world wide. The lack of a proper index is a disadvantage. Maps and atlases are also represented in *Geographical abstracts* series D covering 'Social geography and cartography'. Cartography is treated as a separate category within this context, and maps and atlases are listed as a sub-category of it. *Geographical abstracts* is published six times a year from the University of East Anglia. British maps and atlases are included also in the Department of the Environment Library's bi-monthly *Classified accessions list;* and journal articles relating to them and to cartography in general are abstracted in the same Library's monthly *Index to periodical articles* (these last three publications are discussed fully in chapter 13). Reviews and notices appear selectively (inclusion being dependent on donation) in journals such as *Geographical journal, Geography, Scottish geographical magazine* and *Cartographic journal.* The latter is the most systematic in its coverage and has a section ' Recent maps and atlases ' in each bi-annual issue which includes Ordnance Survey issues, maps and atlases for all parts of the world, and map catalogues.

Next for consideration is a group of single publications which discuss maps and atlases either within a geographical context or as the sole topic. In the former category, is the *Concise guide to the literature of geography* edited by Jack Burkett (Ealing Technical College, 1967, Occasional Paper 1) which includes a section on maps and atlases with annotated entries; C S Minto's *How to find out in geography* (Oxford, Pergamon Press, 1966) is arranged by classes according to the Decimal Classification and accords only cursory treatment to maps and atlases; and on the periphery of usefulness in this context is *Geography: a reference handbook* by C B Muriel Lock (Bingley, 1968) which is an alphabetical arrangement of the ' main focal points of geographical study ' including notes on important atlases and map series among those relating to cartographic publishers, journals, institutions and so on.

Within the second category of descriptive works having maps and atlases as their sole subject matter, by far the most comprehensive work is C B Muriel Lock's *Modern maps and atlases: an outline guide to twentieth century production* (Bingley, 1969) a large book (619 pages, over one hundred of them occupied by a monumental index) of close-packed text covering the whole world. The British Isles are dealt with on pages 122-176 under the heading ' National and regional maps and atlases ', and also throughout the section on ' Thematic maps and atlases '. Unfortunately the book suffers from all the sins—of omission, inconsistency, inaccuracy, indeed of including whole chunks of information which are completely erroneous—which render a text of this nature, comprehensive as it is, unreliable and dangerous in inexperienced hands.[22] The book has value as a guide to what is available over a wide field, but users should check any items which they wish to follow up from more reliable sources.

Part of the trouble with Lock's book probably arises from the huge amount of detail which has had to be marshalled and constantly up-dated. Texts which have set their sights a little lower and which describe only a few series in detail are, in general, both more reliable and more readable. The Ordnance Survey was responsible for excellent examples of this with its three booklets *A description of Ordnance Survey large scale plans* (1947), *A description of Ordnance Survey medium scale maps* (1949), and *A description of Ordnance Survey small scale maps* (1947), dealing with the twenty five-inch maps, the six-inch and 2½-inch maps, and the one-inch maps respectively. These concise, illustrated booklets were all reprinted at various later dates but are now out of print. A new guide to all scales of topographic maps which will be contained in one volume, is in preparation by the Ordnance Survey but publication is not expected for some time.[23] Also out of print, but still of interest, is a fuller account of the six-inch and twenty five-inch series in *The national plans* by H StJ L Winterbotham (Ordnance Survey, 1934, Professional Papers new series 16).

In 1962 and 1963, three articles by J B Harley, of the Department of Geography in the University of Liverpool, were printed in the journal *Amateur historian* (now *Local historian*) discussing the Ordnance Survey large, medium and small scale maps from the point of view of historical interpretation, followed by an article by C W Phillips on ' The period maps of the Ordnance Survey '. These four articles are collected together with a section on the Ordnance Survey maps of Scotland, to form a booklet, *The historian's guide to Ordnance Survey maps* (London, National Council of Social Service for the Standing Conference for Local History, 1964). The three major sections of the booklet trace the development of the one-inch series, the six-inch, twenty five-inch, and 2½-inch series, and the town plans and series at scales smaller than one-inch, from their original printings to contemporary coverage. Index maps in the text summarise the main patterns of publication for all the series discussed.

J B Harley is also responsible for a further series of articles in the same journal under the collective title 'Maps for the local historian: a guide to British sources'. There are six articles in the series, as follows: 'Maps and plans of towns' (*Amateur historian,* 7(6) 1967 196-208); 'Estate maps' (7(7) 1967 223-231); 'Enclosure and tithe maps' (7(8) 1967 265-274); 'Maps of communications' (*Local historian,* 8(2) 1968 61-71); 'Marine charts' (8(3) 1968 86-97); 'County maps' (8(5) 1969 167-179). The articles follow a basic standard pattern, with variations according to the type of maps under consideration. Each article begins with a guide to bibliographic sources, and goes on to outline the development and content of the maps and, as relevant, specialised types within the main class. The articles are to be reprinted in booklet form by the National Council of Social Service (the publishers of the journal), with an introduction, classified bibliographies and a note on the main map repositories in Britain.

Maps relating solely to Wales are the subject of an article by G Walters (of the National Library of Wales) entitled 'Themes in the large scale mapping of Wales in the eighteenth century' in *Cartographic journal* 5(2) December 1968 135-146, which is illustrated with facsimile reproductions and includes a bibliography of sixty nine items plus a check list of the printed maps discussed. Ireland is covered most fully by *Ireland in maps . . . with a catalogue of an exhibition* edited by John Andrews (Dublin, Trinity College, 1961).

The two series by Harley were primarily, though by no means exclusively of interest to those whose study is the history and development of urban and rural Britain. The same applies to some of the publications in the final category of this section of guides. In this are included straight bibliographies (as opposed to the descriptive reviews discussed above) and catalogues whose contents may be circumscribed in one of three ways: by concentrating on one type of map only; by concentrating on maps relating to one place; or by concentrating on the maps in one collection.

The first of these is a rare breed. The single subject candidate for inclusion is the three-volume *International bibliography of vegetation maps* edited by A W Küchler (Lawrence, University of

137

Kansas Libraries, 1965-1968). The second volume covers Europe. The published title of each map is given, together with the colours used and the features distinguished.

A very different project which nevertheless falls within the definition of bibliographies limited to one type of production, is the series *County atlases of the British Isles 1579-1850* compiled by R A Skelton and members of the staff of the British Museum Map Room, produced in instalments by the Map Collectors' Circle. The years 1579 to 1703 have now been produced in a single volume *County atlases of the British Isles 1579-1703* (Carta Press, 1970) which now forms the definitive source of reference on the county cartography of the British Isles, prior to the expansion of official surveys, for the years covered, superseding Thomas Chubb's standard work *The printed maps in the atlases of Great Britain and Ireland: a bibliography, 1579-1870* (The Homeland Association Ltd, 1927; facsimile reprint, Dawsons Pall Mall, 1966). Another publication covering much the same ground is Elizabeth M Rodger's *The large scale county maps of the British Isles 1596-1850: a union list* (Oxford, Bodleian Library, 1960) which is based on the collections of seven major libraries. A revision is in progress. A much slighter volume, which nevertheless offers some account of the development of British town plans, is the twenty second volume in the Map Collectors' Circle series, *Town plans of the British Isles: series appearing in atlases from 1580-1850* by Angela Fordham (1965). It has an introductory note, followed by descriptive notes on the atlases from which the following forty facsimile maps are taken.

Bibliographies of maps relating to one geographical area are in the main concerned with historic printed or manuscript maps. Scotland is particularly well served in this respect. The Royal Scottish Geographical Society has two titles to its credit: *Early maps of Scotland* (Edinburgh, RSGS, second edition 1936—and a further edition in progress) and *The early views and maps of Edinburgh, 1544-1852* (Edinburgh, RSGS, 1919). Also devoted to Edinburgh is William Cowan's *The maps of Edinburgh 1544-1929; second edition, revised with census of copies in Edinburgh libraries by Charles B Boog Watson* (Edinburgh, Edinburgh Public Libraries, 1932). Cowan's original work extended to 1851, and was brought up to 1929 by Boog Watson. A list of libraries in which the plans are located is included. Scotland has also set a noteworthy precedent in the establishment of the *Union catalogue of large scale ms maps of Scotland*. The master catalogue, in the National Library of Scotland, in Edinburgh, now contains about 2,500-3,000 main entries.

Moving southwards, a notable publication of recent years was *Printed maps of London circa 1553-1850* by Ida Darlington and James Howgego (George Philip, 1964), a catalogue of maps relating to London and to London and environs, culled from many collections but primarily from those at the (then) London County Council, the Guildhall, and the British Museum. Another well-regarded work, whose entries provided a model of form and content for Darlington and Howgego, is *The printed maps of Warwickshire 1576-1900* by P D A Harvey and Harry Thorpe (Warwick, Warwickshire County Council, 1959) which takes in the early Ordnance Survey series from 1828. Also of note is *Printed maps and plans of Leeds, 1711-1900* by Kenneth J Bonser and Harold Nichols (Leeds, Thoresby Society, 1960) which covers both general and specialised town plans.

The largest catalogue of a single map collection is that of the British Museum: the photolithographic edition of *The British Museum catalogue of printed maps, charts and plans* was issued in fifteen volumes in 1967 and is a major source of reference. For the many towns which have not been the subject of separate treatment, it offers the most useful general listing of the range of available plans.

Among government departments, the Department of the Environment has an extensive map library, but no catalogue is issued. The Scottish Development Department produce a *Catalogue of map library*, most recently revised in January 1970, which is chiefly concerned with maps relating to Scotland, many of them the work of the departments of the Scottish Office. The *Catalogue* is available free on request.

In recent years, the collections of the Public Record Office and the Scottish Record Office have been made known to a wider public through the publication of one volume for each, with more to come. These are valuable collections, and the volumes are welcome. The first volume of *Maps and plans in the Public Record Office* (HMSO, 1967) covers the British Isles from c1410 to 1860, and contains over four thousand entries. The classes of records consisting of, or containing maps which are included, are listed in detail in the introduction. Most of the maps described are manuscript, although there remain a good proportion of printed ones. The Scottish Record Office collection is in two main series: Register House Plans, which form a general series drawn from a variety of sources, and Sheriff Court Plans, which relate mainly to railways and other nineteenth century public utilities. The first volume of its *Descriptive list of plans* (Edinburgh, HMSO, 1966) is concerned with the former series only, and contains references to 1,200 items, many of them manuscript maps, and most of them executed between 1750 and 1850.

In England and Wales, county record offices are the municipal repositories of early maps, and increasingly they are making their collections known through the publication of catalogues. Essex was one of the first in the field, and published a *Catalogue of maps in the Essex Record Office 1566-1855* (Chelmsford, Essex County Council, 1947, with supplements in 1952 and 1964 and 1968). Smaller catalogues have come from, for example, Huntingdon: *Maps in the County Record Office, Huntingdon,* compiled by P G M Dickinson (Huntingdon, Imray Laurie Norie and Wilson Ltd, 1968), a seventy two-page booklet which is somewhat sparse on detail about maps.

THE HISTORY OF MAPS
The most concise short history of cartography is *Maps and their makers: an introduction to the history of cartography* by G R Crone, formerly Librarian and Map Curator at the Royal Geographical Society (Hutchinson University Library, fourth revised edition 1968). This is a very readable illustrated survey of the main stages of cartographic development up to the mid-1960's, with a tentative look into the future. Mapping activity in individual countries is not considered although a chapter on ' The British contribution to 1800 ' forms a part of the overall world picture. Chapters also deal with ' National surveys and modern atlases ' and ' Contemporary cartography ', both on a world basis. Chapter references are supplemented by an appendix listing general works on cartography; a second appendix refers to reproductions of early maps and charts. There is a short note on the principal map collections and bibliographies.

140

A fuller account is given in Leo Bagrow's *History of cartography* (C A Watts, 1964). The original German edition of Bagrow's *History* was published in 1944, and first translated in 1960 by D L Paisley; subsequently, for its most recent edition, the work was revised and augmented by R A Skelton, Map Curator of the British Museum. There are many illustrations, some in colour; bibliographies; and an alphabetical list of cartographers at work up to 1750. Physically larger, and lavishly illustrated with fourteen facsimile maps and over three hundred illustrations, is *A history of cartography* by R V Tooley and Charles Bricker (Thames and Hudson, 1969). This is a handsome book, perhaps more at home on the coffee table than in the planning office, but textually it offers nothing that cannot be found in Bagrow's *History* and other sources.

Tooley alone is responsible for *Maps and map-makers* (Batsford, second edition 1952), which surveys the whole world from earliest times to the nineteenth century, arranged by schools of geography, and ' combining an application of the popular decorative side of early maps with historical and bibliographical notes '. Plenty of illustrations, some in colour, and chapter references, support this statement. British activity is discussed in three chapters: on English map-makers, including marine atlases; on county maps of England and Wales; and on Scotland and Ireland. The text includes many chronological lists, for instance, of English marine atlases. There are also lists of county maps of England, arranged by counties, and English county atlases, arranged by authors.

Narrowing the spatial sights to Great Britain, the instinctive assumption that the history of the Ordnance Survey must be fully documented is unfounded. An official history is currently in progress, but is unlikely to be published by the time this book appears. The only partial record in book form is Sir Charles Close's *The early years of the Ordnance Survey* (Newton Abbot, David and Charles Reprints, 1969). Originally a series of articles in the *Royal Engineers journal,* and subsequently published in book form by the Institution of Royal Engineers in 1916, this new edition has an introduction by J B Harley, and a new index. The period covered is 1746-1846: the Ordnance Survey did not formally exist until 1791, but Close discusses its origins and the events which led up to its establishment. The text is well substantiated from contemporary sources.

From Elizabethan times to as recently as mid-Victorian, the county was the basic unit of regional mapping in Britain, and so the history of British maps is inextricably tied to the county region, which can thus form a logical focus for the local history of mapping. An example of local cartographic history is Arthur Raistrick's *Yorkshire maps and map-makers* (Clapham, Yorks, Dalesman Publishing Co Ltd, 1969) an attractively-produced booklet, illustrated principally with facsimile maps.

THE INTERPRETATION OF MAPS
Texts on the interpretation of maps in the main deal with topographic maps and the majority of them are directed at students who require such competence for fieldwork studies.

Two which fit into this category in both respects are *Map reading and interpretation* by P Speak and A H C Carter (Longmans Green, 1964), aimed at o and a level students, with an exposition based on extracts from Ordnance Survey maps of the British Isles; and T W Birch's *Map and photo reading* (Edward Arnold, second edition 1968) which, as its title indicates, takes in the interpretation of photographs also. An older book, now out of print but still available in libraries, which is of interest for its individual approach based on the author's experience of teaching in the Universities of Durham and Manchester, is Dorothy Sylvester's *Map and landscape* (George Philip, 1952). Primarily intended for students, it discusses topographic maps and the representation of features on them, then deals with the features in detail—physiographical regions, lines of communication, settlement patterns; and finally expounds the three-dimensional study of landscape, first from the point of view of looking at it, and then of representing it, discussing such matters as the horizon and the field of vision, selection of viewpoint for studying landscape and region, correlation of landscape photographs with maps, and methods of representation from field sketching to panorama drawing. Users should bear in mind that references to maps (in particular the first chapter of Section II on choice of topographic maps) are in most cases now out of date.

The most useful up to date text, which offers a systematic evaluation of the various principles of map interpretation, is G H Dury's

Map interpretation (Pitman, third edition 1967) which is aimed not so much at students' fieldwork but more at the geographer or planner who wishes to interpret maps in order to gain information with which to substantiate his work. Dury treats the interpretation of physical features in detail—eroded folds, unglaciated upland, coasts and shorelines, for example—and then moves on to an equally detailed study of 'features of occupance' which covers the interpretation of land use, settlement studies, the form of towns of all types, and the interpretation of prehistoric features. Each physical feature, each example of settlement or town is illustrated by reference to a map showing that feature, which is then discussed in detail, making it essential that the relevant map should be used with the book. There are two special chapters, on morphometric analysis and on cartographical appreciation; text diagrams and maps plus some photographs; and an extensive, carefully selected bibliography giving references to journal articles and books which, inexcusably, gives no dates of publication for the books (journals are fully documented).

Examples of map interpretation in practice are contained in the Geographical Association's series 'British landscape through maps'; each booklet treats an area as it is represented on the Ordnance Survey one-inch map series, and is intended to be read in conjunction with the specified sheet. To take an example, number six in the series, *Merseyside* by R Kay Gresswell and Richard Lawton (Sheffield, Geographical Association, 1965) is a description of the one-inch sheet no 100 covering Liverpool, and any reference in the text to any place at all is immediately followed by the grid reference to the map. The thirty six large pages of text are supplemented by illustrative half-tone plates and detailed sketch maps. Geology, evolution of the coastline, land use and development, and human habitation from prehistoric times to the 1961 census are all discussed, and despite the essential conciseness of the text a surprising amount of detail is packed in. This is an interesting and well-executed series of booklets.

THE PRESENTATION AND CONTENT OF MAPS
This is a fairly heterogeneous section containing books on the presentation and content of maps and also books describing how

143

existing maps are presented and what to look for in them, and combinations of and permutations on all these themes.

Two titles are concerned almost exclusively with the presentation of maps as a means of graphic illustration. *Maps for books and theses* by A G Hodgkiss (Newton Abbot, David and Charles, 1970) is a fairly basic text, aimed at beginners, students, and interested laymen, which progresses from the principles of illustration, drawing instruments and equipment and lettering through the visual presentation of statistical data and map design and layout, to specialised types of maps. The scope and audience of Arthur Lockwood's *Diagrams: a visual survey of graphs, maps, charts and diagrams for the graphic designer* (Studio Vista, 1969) are indicated adequately in the sub-title. The book is a collection of samples of graphic material, with a minimum of text which serves primarily to emphasise good points or to suggest where improvement could be made. Graphs, maps, charts and diagrams are chosen from a wide variety of modern sources, including the daily press and television. The chief advantage of this book over other, more basic teaching texts, is its up to dateness.

T W Birch's *Maps, topographical and statistical* (Oxford, Clarendon Press, second edition 1964) is descriptive in that it describes existing maps, how they are made and presented and the information which is contained in them and comprehensive in that it includes thematic maps of all kinds. The first part of the book deals with topographic maps: Birch surveys modern (at 1964) maps of Britain and overseas countries, discusses the technical aspects of surveying and the equipment used, outlines methods of representing relief (hachuring, hill shading, etc) explains the various projections and grid referencing systems, and devotes the remainder of this part to 'the outstanding aspects of maps, a knowledge of which is necessary for sound map-reading, and . . . the broad geographical interpretation of landscape as depicted on topographical maps' including a chapter on the interpretation of air photographs. The second part of the book deals with thematic or statistical maps, and these are discussed according to the method of representation employed: thus there are chapters on dot maps, density maps, isoline maps, graphs (including bar charts, line graphs, and pie charts) and diagrams and diagram maps. The text is supplemented by a section

144

of questions and answers, and details of sources of information. The index is very sketchy.

A book which is descriptive, but which concentrates on topographic maps is G C Dickinson's *Maps and air photographs* (Edward Arnold, 1969). The author employs an individual approach to the subject: his treatment of maps (air photographs are very much the minor part of the book) falls into three sections, ' Thinking about maps ', ' Working with maps ', and ' Looking at maps '. The first of these describes the evolution of maps and map-making throughout the world and the institution of national map series, with chapters on the content of the maps, and on map printing and reproduction; the second section is concerned with ' the practical side of maps and the day-to-day routine tasks which they are called upon to perform ', expounding upon scale, how to determine position and measure area, enlarging or reducing or straight copying of maps, how to see in three dimensions, with a final chapter on the map as an historical record; the third section is an attempt to show what the map-user can gain by looking beyond the straightforward fact as represented on the map, in other words by creative analysis rather than just reading, and applies the technique to the physical landscape and then to the human, social, and economic landscape. The book suffers from a certain lack of balance in that it treats some aspects in great detail and others rather superficially. There is no bibliography, and documentary footnotes are not greatly in evidence.

The same author produced an earlier, companion volume on *Statistical mapping and the presentation of statistics* (Edward Arnold, 1963), a useful commentary on the subject which benefits from a clearer, more logical presentation than his *Maps and air photographs*. The earlier work discusses simple techniques of diagrammatic presentation of statistics and deals extensively with statistical maps, including organisation of the data and methods of presenting them. There is a short chapter on sources of statistics.

The most comprehensive text on the presentation of thematic maps is *Maps and diagrams: their compilation and construction* by F J Monkhouse and H R Wilkinson (Methuen, third edition 1971) which incorporates an appendix by R G Barry, 'An introduction to numerical and mechanical techniques '. In a review of the second edition in *Scottish geographical magazine* 80(3) December 1964 194, Ian Mumford goes so far as to claim that ' there is little doubt that *Maps and diagrams* played a large part in making British geographers aware of the possibilities and pitfalls of thematic mapping over the last ten years '. After a lengthy section on materials required and techniques used in cartographic work, the authors discuss in full the representation in graphic form of relief, climate, economic factors, population, and settlements. Each section deals first with the data and the sources from which they are obtained (content is not confined to British sources), and then goes on to examine the various forms of maps and diagrams most appropriate to the type of data to be represented. The treatment is full throughout, there are many textual maps, diagrams and tables, and the text is fully supported by documentary references. The new edition brings the work up to date mainly as regards the techniques of cartography and the use of statistical methods to cope with increasing quantities of data.

An interesting and significant contribution to the literature of thematic mapping is contained in a set of papers given at a symposium organised by the Cartography Subcommittee of the Royal Society's British National Committee for Geography under the title *Experimental cartography: report on the Oxford Symposium, October 1963* (Oxford UP, 1964). The symposium had two objects: firstly, to examine the art of cartography as a research tool and for communicating scientific ideas; secondly, ' to consider whether the cartographic analysis of different subjects, eg vegetation, has anything to contribute to topographic maps in the sense that such maps are inevitably concerned to synthesise from a wider range of subjects '. The contributions are divided up according to themes, each section being concerned with the problems and techniques of mapping that particular theme: industry; geology; demographic distributions; climate; transport; vegetation, flora and fauna; history and archaeology; hydrography and oceanography, are the themes covered.

Specialised contributions on the mapping of one particular theme are mainly, though not exclusively, the province of the journal literature. Alice Coleman, Director of the Second Land Utilisation Survey, is an authority on land use mapping and she has made several contributions to journals on various aspects of the Survey. A progress

146

report, illustrated with photographs and colour reproductions of the first maps, was given in ' The use of Britain's land ' in *Geographical magazine* 36(12) April 1964 687-697. ' Some cartographic aspects of the Second Series Land Use maps ' were discussed in *Geographical journal* 130(1) March 1964 167-170. A full account of the work of the Survey and the problems and practice of mapping is in ' Land use survey and regional planning ' in *Planning outlook* new series 4 Spring 1968 30-36, and future work is assessed in ' Land use survey: the next step ' *Geographical magazine* 42(1) October 1969 39-42. A specialised aspect of land use is discussed by Professor J T Coppock in ' The cartographic representation of British agricultural statistics ' in *Geography* 50(2) April 1965 101-114, illustrated with line maps and documented with references to associated literature.

Geological maps are more fully documented from the point of view of their interpretation. A R Dwerryhouse's old standard work, *Geological and topographical maps—their interpretation and use* (Edward Arnold, second edition 1924) has been joined in recent years by *Geological maps and their interpretation* by F G H Blyth (Edward Arnold, 1965) and *Geological maps* by Brian Simpson (Oxford, Pergamon Press, 1968). An exhibition of geological maps at the University of Reading in 1967, in honour of the eightieth birthday of Emeritus Professor H L Hawkins, gave rise to a slim pamphlet by N E Butcher, *The history and development of geological cartography* (Reading University, 1967) which contains notes on the maps in the exhibition and an introduction on the subject.

Vegetation maps are the subject not only of the *International bibliography* mentioned above but also of a comprehensive treatise by A W Küchler (editor of the bibliography) in *Vegetation mapping* (New York, Ronald Press, 1967), which contains an extensive bibliography. Küchler is Professor of Geography in the University of Kansas and is a member of, *inter alia,* the Unesco Working Group on Vegetation Mapping. Chapter VI of *Geography at Aberystwyth: essays written on the occasion of the departmental jubilee 1917-18— 1967-68* edited by E G Bowen and others (Cardiff, University of Wales Press, 1968) is a contribution by James A Taylor on ' Reconnaissance vegetation surveys and maps (including a preliminary report of the Vegetation Survey of Wales, 1961-6) '.

The same volume from Aberystwyth includes, as chapter IV, a contribution by G Melvyn Howe on 'Climatology and the geographer', which discusses classifications of climate and their application to climatic patterns in Wales and elsewhere, illustrated with maps and diagrams. A comprehensive text dealing with climatological maps is *British weather in maps* by James A Taylor and R A Yates (Macmillan, second edition 1967). The authors present ' a method of geographical analysis and interpretation of the " primary documents " of British weather, viz, the British Daily Weather Reports'. The book consists basically of examples of weather elements taken from the Weather Reports: the distribution of each element is examined by means of maps and explanatory text. The second edition incorporates revised and additional material throughout, and has a new chapter on classifications of British weather and climate in general and comparative terms. A Meteorological Office publication, now out of print, is the *Weather map* (HMSO), first published in 1915 and most recently in a fourth edition in 1956. It traces the development of weather maps, and describes how they are constructed, with illustrative examples of weather maps.

G Melvyn Howe is also the editor of the *National atlas of disease mortality in the United Kingdom,* discussed earlier in this chapter, and this formed the subject of his article of the same title in *Geographical journal* 130(1) March 1964 15-31. The atlas was the subject of a lengthy review by A Leslie Banks under the title ' The geography of disease ' in *Geographical magazine* 37(3) July 1964 175-183, which includes reproductions of several of the maps. The geographical distribution of disease and mortality was also expounded by Sir L Dudley Stamp in the University of London Heath Clark lectures in 1962, collected in book form as *Some aspects of medical geography* (Oxford UP, 1964); Stamp covered much the same ground, but presented for the layman, in *The geography of life and death* (Collins, 1964, Fontana Library).

Quite different, but equally specialised, is a booklet issued by the Commons, Open Spaces and Footpaths Preservation Society in 1970, *A guide to definitive maps of public paths* by Mary McArevey, which is not as its title might suggest, a guide to existing maps, but is in fact a guide to the preparation of draft, provisional and definitive maps of public paths, revised maps and details of public rights of representation and objection, as laid down in the National Parks and Access to the Countryside Act 1949 and the Countryside Act 1968.

Finally, this part rounds off, as did its counterpart in the first section of the chapter, with historic maps and plans and the interpretation of historic events from modern plans. Historic plans and their literature are a little difficult to sort out: the maps and plans themselves (or their facsimile reproductions) were discussed in the first part of this chapter; guides, both descriptive and non-descriptive, to historical material were listed in the first section of this second part; and at this point, in the fourth section of the second part, the focus is on the description of the content and interpretation of maps and plans to establish past events. One of the principal British authorities on this subject is M R G Conzen, Professor of Human Geography at the University of Newcastle upon Tyne, who asserts that ' existing and old town plans can shed much light on the history of urban communities, their size and structure at different periods, their phases of development, their institutions and the relation between them and the urban community which they serve.'[24] This is demonstrated in his own work in *Alnwick, Northumberland: a study in town plan analysis* (Institute of British Geographers, 1960, Publication 27). More examples are offered in his paper ' The use of town plans in the study of urban history ', included in *The study of urban history* edited by H J Dyos (Edward Arnold, 1968), which contains preliminary interpretation of the medieval layout of Ludlow and Conway; and Whithorn and Frodsham are added to the collection in his contribution ' Historical townscapes in Britain: a problem in applied geography ' in *Northern geographical essays in honour of G H J Daysh* edited by J W House for the Department of Geography at the University of Newcastle upon Tyne (Newcastle, Oriel Press, 1966). All these discuss the types of plan available, their content and use, illustrated with practical examples. On the evidence of the examples indicated here, this use of maps and plans may seem limited, yet, as Conzen points out, ' in the majority of cases the kernels of our towns show in fact an historical townscape in the sense that existing town plan and building fabric are dominated more or less by traditional forms ranging from the medieval or even Roman era to the late Georgian or Regency period '.[25]

149

The chapter concludes with a short and selective review of the techniques associated with map-making. The scope is limited to topics which are relevant in the context of planning, and which are of interest to planners in two ways: firstly, that they add to an understanding of the content of maps, secondly, that they are techniques which the planner may have occasion to use himself, or at least be associated with their use. Techniques which are primarily relevant to cartography, such as trend surface mapping, are not included here; photomaps and orthophotomaps are discussed with air photographs, from which they are derived (chapter 8).

A knowledge of the practical methods used by the Ordnance Survey can aid the interpretation of its map series. In this connection, the Survey itself has provided several publications. The most substantial of these is its *History of the retriangulation of Great Britain* (HMSO, 1967, 2v) which describes the primary triangulation of Great Britain in 1935-1952, together with associated work which has been completed since, the object being to give a complete record of the methods used and of the results obtained. Information on the National Grid, which is carried by all modern Ordnance Survey maps, is contained in the booklet *An introduction to the projection for Ordnance Survey maps and plans and the national reference system* (HMSO, 1968). Levelling information is available for most parts of the country in the form of Bench Mark Lists, which contain the latest available values. The same values may appear on the current map or plan, though in many areas the Bench Mark Lists will show more recent levelling. The lists, which may consist of more than one sheet, are compiled by kilometre squares, each bearing the same reference number as the corresponding 1:2,500 scale map on National Grid sheet lines. Bench Mark Lists are available direct from the Ordnance Survey.

Metrication of Ordnance Survey maps is now well under way, the first maps based completely on metric measurements having been published in the autumn of 1969. An article on 'The adoption of the metric system in the Ordnance Survey' by F M Sexton, Director of the Small Scales Division of the survey, appeared in *Geographical journal* 134(3) September 1968 328-342, discussing the problems involved and the ways in which they are being overcome. A further paper by Sexton is reprinted in *Advancement of science* 26(4) June 1970 364-366, under the title ' Metric maps '; and a note on progress to date was included in the monthly *Publication report* for May 1970. Specimen sets of metric maps can be obtained direct from the Publications Division of the Survey. Progress on development in all aspects of the Survey's work, including metrication, and the current state of mapping at various scales, is reported in the annual reports, published by HMSO; also in a paper by A Walmesley White on ' The mapping programme of the Ordnance Survey ' in *Advancement of science* 26(4) June 1970 361-364.

The Ordnance Survey being the major mapping agency in Britain, it is obviously interested in developing and adapting the most up to date techniques in modern cartography : its annual reports provide a regular reflection of cartographic practice, including the use of computers in automatic cartography. Computers are by now well established in map-making, although it would not be true to claim that their possibilities had been either fully developed or even fully explored. A special issue of *Geographical magazine* 42(1) October 1969 looks ahead to the vast possibilities opening up in mapping, and under the collective title of ' Cartography for the 1970's ' includes much of interest to planners, for example, the article on 'Automated urban planning ' by K E Rosing and P A Wood (pages 60-64). There are two aspects of automation in cartography which particularly concern the planner : one is the prospect of the cartographic data bank, and the other is its application in the graphic presentation of data (statistical mapping).

Production of thematic maps by computer is of quite recent origin, the first experimental maps having been produced in 1962 at the University of Washington, Seattle, where a statistical mapping technique was developed. Harvard University followed, with the development of the SYMAP system (SYnagraphic MAPping) which is still being extended and improved. These systems have been used by planners in many countries, and offer great scope for the automatic presentation of large quantities of statistical data in map form. An article by Jean C M Marshall appeared in *Official architecture and planning* 32(10) October 1969 1221-1229 on ' Synagraphy : computer map-making for planners '. In recent years, the Urban Planning Directorate of the Department of the Environment have been working on a computer mapping system called LINMAP I (LINe printer MAPping). For some years, the Urban Planning Directorate have been studying the development and use of a national locational referencing system, based on the National Grid as a universal location code, which will facilitate the geographical location of data; LINMAP was developed to illustrate the use and facility of the co-ordinate referencing system for such location. Subsequently, LINMAP II, a very much extended version of the original system, is being developed, together with COLMAP (COLour MAPping). All these systems and their development are fully described, with text maps and diagrams for elucidation, by G M Gaits (of the Urban Planning Directorate) in an article ' Thematic mapping by computer ' in *Cartographic journal* 6(1) June 1969 50-68, which includes references to other work.

In the forefront of pioneer work in automatic cartography and its associated possibilities is the Experimental Cartography Unit, under the direction of David P Bickmore, at the Royal College of Art in London, together with the College's Cartographic Laboratory at Oxford. The unit was established in 1967 with funds from the Natural Environment Research Council, and became operational in 1968; its purpose is to study methods of computer mapping and the feasibility of cartographic data banks, and much of the data used for experimental purposes relate to the enviromental sciences, although the unit's interests do range widely, from astronomy to crystallography. An article by Sandra Howard on the data banking aspect, under the title 'A cartographic data bank for Ordnance Survey maps ', appeared in *Cartographic journal* 5(1) June 1968 48-53. Papers on the work of the unit have been delivered from time to time at conferences and meetings, and articles have appeared on the general subject of computer mapping as a result of its activities, for example, ' Maps for the computer age ' by David P Bickmore in *Geographical magazine* 41(3) December 1968 221-227. Most recently, a full-length book has been published under the title *Automatic cartography and planning* (Architectural Press, 1971) which embodies the fruits of the unit's work using the results of a complementary project, funded by the then Department of Economic Affairs, which was concerned with the availability of planning data in the East Anglian region and the feasibility of their incorporation into a data bank. The text discusses in detail the application of automatic cartography to data for planning, including the problems and possibilities of geographic referencing, and incorporates sample maps produced by automatic methods. Techniques under development at the unit, together with other research and development in the field, are described and assessed. Two valuable appendices provide a descriptive catalogue of UK statistical data available for mapping purposes, and a proposed standard format for the exchange of cartographic data. The book constitutes a valuable statement of the present development, and the future potential, of the new cartographic techniques in the service of planning.

REFERENCES
1 Centre for Environmental Studies *Proceedings of the conference on information and urban planning* (CES, 1969, CES-IP-8, two vols) vl 114-115.

2 Gerald McGrath and R P Kirby ' Survey methods in the use of maps and atlases ' *Canadian cartographer* 6(2) December 1969 132-148, includes a description of the conduct of the survey; R P Kirby 'A survey of map user practices and requirements ' *Cartographic journal* 7(1) June 1970 31-39, describes and analyses the results of the survey.

3 Formerly the maps were divided into three groups: large, medium, and small scales, the medium scales being those at 1 : 10,560 (1 : 10,000) and 1 : 25,000. The term ' medium scales ' is no longer used by the Ordnance Survey.

4 Personal communication from Professor Harold Carter.

5 Personal communication from Professor R E H Mellor.

6 Emrys Jones ' The London atlas ' *Geographical journal* 131(3) September 1965 330-343; Emrys Jones ' London life in maps ' *Geographical magazine* 41(1) October 1968 62-66.

7 W A Seymour and B StG Irwin ' Continuous revision of Ordnance Survey plans ' *Geographical journal* 131(1) March 1965 76-85.

8 Brief details of this and other services are included from time to time in the monthly *Ordnance Survey publication report.*

9 The *Publication report* of May 1970 incorporates a map showing those areas for which public rights of way information has been published in the one-inch series, as at March 1970.

10 A press announcement in March 1971 indicated that the one-inch series is likely to undergo metrication beginning in 1971. It seems likely that the scale will convert from the present 1:63,360 to 1:50,000; contours will be at twenty metre intervals, with spot heights indicated in metres. But a subsequent statement from the Ordnance Survey denied that a decision had been taken, nor would be taken before the end of 1971, and that in any case it would be at least three years before any new maps were on sale.

11 'Layer colouring is the overlapping of graded colours to emphasise the altitudinal belts which contouring has already marked out. The conventional range of colour upward is from dark to light greens then through light buffs to middle and darker browns . . . The great advantage of layer colouring is that it shows absolute height [*ie* height above mean sea level] with great clarity over the whole map.' Sylvester *op cit* 23-24.

12 W R Taylor ' The Ordnance Survey of Northern Ireland : an outline of its history and present mapping tasks ' *Cartographic journal* 6(2) December 1969 87-91.

13 Peter Hall *London 2000* (Faber, second edition 1969) 19.

14 Quarter sheets size $22\frac{1}{2}'' \times 17''$ (57×43 cms); National Grid sheets size $30\frac{1}{2}'' \times 27''$ (77×69 cms).

15 All publications of the Geologists' Association are obtainable from Benham and Co Ltd, Sheepen Road, Colchester, Essex.

16 *Geographical journal* 136(1) March 1970 112-113 (review).

17 L Dudley Stamp (*ed*) *The land of Britain: the report of the Land Utilisation Survey* (Ordnance Survey, 1936-1946, ninety two parts).

18 Alice Coleman ' Land use survey and regional planning ' *Planning outlook* new series 4 Spring 1968 30-36.

19 J T Coppock 'An agricultural atlas of Scotland ' *Cartographic journal* 6(1) June 1969 36-46.

20 Alice Coleman 'A wildscape atlas for England and Wales ' *Geographical magazine* 43(1) October 1970 19-26, with colour illustrations and specimen page.

21 James A Taylor ' Reconnaissance vegetation surveys and maps (including a preliminary report of the Vegetation Survey of Wales, 1961-6) ' in *Geography at Aberystwyth* edited by E G Bowen and others (Cardiff, University of Wales Press, 1968) 87-110.

22 See, for instance, Edith Frame's review in *Library review* 22(4) Winter 1969 201-203.

23 In June 1970, it was not expected to be available within the next two years.

24 H J Dyos (*ed*) *The study of urban history* (Edward Arnold, 1968) 115.

25 J W House (*ed*) *Northern geographical essays in honour of G H J Daysh* (Newcastle, Oriel Press, 1966) 57.

8

AERIAL PHOTOGRAPHS

AERIAL PHOTOGRAPHS ARE one of the true primary sources of planning information in the sense that facts are recorded direct from the ground. In *this sense* they are roughly equivalent to the large scale plans produced in earlier years by the Ordnance Survey, for which field surveyors recorded in detail, and without generalisation, the physical features of the area which they were mapping; and to the maps currently being produced by the Second Land Utilisation Survey of Great Britain for which, as the survey's director has explained, ' the data are recorded directly, field by field and building by building. They are not plotted at second hand from statistics and they are not generalised in any way that obscures the true shape of any area.'[1]

There are, however, some advantages inherent in aerial photographs which make them superior to maps in terms of their potential as sources of information. They are firstly a faithful record of virtually all that can be seen from the air: they thus contain a vast quantity of information, which makes them more difficult to interpret than a map but which equally gives them a greater information potential—both quantitative and qualitative. Air survey allows extensive areas to be recorded within a very short space of time: it therefore not only reduces the man hours necessary for detailed field survey, it also guarantees that over the entire area the record applies to the same point in time (maps are frequently compiled over a long period of time up to their date of publication). Air survey can record areas of land which may not be directly accessible from the ground, and can see into areas to which ground surveyors may be specifically denied access; in addition, information may be recorded by air photography which is not visible on the ground, for example, the routes of underground waterways such as pipelines

156

or old streams, and archaeological remains. In some instances the air photo may be used to record and monitor certain elements of the landscape which are not shown on maps, for example, the traffic flow in a city, or the extent of damage caused by flooding, or gale force winds.

The scale of an aerial photograph depends upon the height of the aircraft above the land and the focal length of the camera lens used. Particularly in built-up areas, aircraft may not descend below a specified height; such restrictions do not normally apply in rural areas. Dr W G Collins of the Air Photo Unit at Leeds University has stated that a camera 'using the standard six inch lens, and flying about 1,250 feet gives a photo scale of around 1 : 2,500 '.[2] The scales most commonly used for air photographs in the United Kingdom are approximately 1 : 10,500 and 1 : 25,000.

Aerial photographs may be taken using one or more of several different types of emulsion/filter combinations, and there have been some significant developments of these over the last few years. The most common type of emulsions are black and white panchromatic, and standard colour, both designed to record that part of the visible optical spectrum (see figure 4) which coincides approximately with normal vision. More recent developments include black and white infra-red film which is capable of optically recording heat differences; 'false' colour film, which is basically a combination of infra-red and colour emulsion; and 'multispectral' film which records usually only part (ie a narrow band) within the visible spectrum. The two standard types of photograph are the vertical (figures, 8, 9, 11), which is taken with the camera lens pointing straight down upon the object being photographed, and the oblique (figure 13), which is taken with the camera lens at an angle to the vertical. Composite photographs, normally made up of one vertical and several obliques, may be obtained either by the simultaneous use of several cameras or by the use of a camera with several lenses. Vertical aerial photographs are usually taken by flying 'strips' in which the successive photographs 'overlap' by about 60% along the flight line. This enables adjacent photographs to be observed as a three-dimensional model, when viewed under a stereoscope. An air photo mosaic, or photo map, is made by joining together a number of vertical photographs along their common boundaries to

157

produce a representation of a large area. Care has to be exercised in the use of photo maps: ' the mosaic will represent *an accurate map* only if the photographs taken to form it are perfectly vertical, if they are all taken at precisely the same height above the ground to give the same scale and if the ground is perfectly flat '.[3] A combination of conditions which in practice is unlikely ever to occur. Photo mosaics may be uncontrolled or they may be controlled. In the former case, the photos are assembled by matching the detail of one to the detail of the next, and in this way a certain amount of error will accumulate. In the latter case, the area covered by the photos is plotted on a base and the photo detail is matched up with this before being assembled, the result frequently being overdrawn with a map grid to form a photo map. The introduction of automatic techniques into photogrammetry and cartography generally has resulted in the commercially produced ' orthophoto ', which is essentially a true controlled photo map, combining the detail of the air photograph and the geometrical characteristics of the orthogonal map. Dr Collins ' can foresee that within the next ten years this may well become as important a source of information to planners as maps and plans are now '.[4]

The documentation of photogrammetry is quite extensive, but that which concentrates on the use of aerial photographs in planning is sparse in the extreme. Roughly, it is possible to identify three categories: the literature which is concerned with the techniques of aerial photography and photogrammetry in general (photogrammetry being defined as the science of making maps from aerial photographs); that which is concerned with special uses and applications of aerial photographs; and that which is concerned with its potential for urban and regional planning and its use in the practical processes of planning in the UK. None of these compartments is watertight; many texts deal with both the techniques of air survey and the uses to which it can be put.

There are a number of standard textbooks devoted exclusively, or almost exclusively, to photogrammetry, including the *Manual of photogrammetry* published by the American Society of Photogrammetry (Washington, third edition 1966, 2 vols). The principal sources of information on the uses and applications of aerial photography include two volumes also published by the American Society

158

of Photogrammetry, the *Manual of photo-interpretation* (Washington, 1960) and the *Manual of color aerial photography* (Washington, 1968); also the *International bibliography of photogrammetry* and the various publications of the International Training Centre at Delft, in the Netherlands, and the professional journals associated with several national societies of photogrammetry, for example, *Photogrammetric record* and *Photogrammetric engineering*, the journals of the (British) Photogrammetric Society and the American Society of Photogrammetry respectively.

In addition, there is *Air photography applied to surveying* by C A Hart (Longmans Green, 1963) first published in 1940, a book which, although it is mainly concerned with map making as it was in 1939, also has some useful comments on the interpretation of aerial photographs. Aerial photographs from the more general point of view of use and interpretation form a section of G C Dickinson's *Maps and air photographs* (Edward Arnold, 1969) and of T W Birch's *Map and photo reading* (Edward Arnold, second edition 1968).

Two books which are essentially picture books show the results which can be achieved by air photography: these are *Our world from the air* by Erwin A Gutkind (Chatto and Windus, 1952) an exemplary series of photographs showing development patterns of all kinds, and *Europe from the air* by Emil Egli and Hans Richard Müller (New York, Wilfred Funk, 1960) consisting of a short textual introduction followed by a series of annotated photographs.

Air photography has been successfully used to illustrate the evolution of the English landscape and the form of medieval settlements and towns, indeed, J K S St Joseph has remarked that ' the varied pattern of the English landscape with its towns and villages is a subject that lends itself particularly well to air photography '.[5] One of the best examples of this is the combination of photographs, original plans and textual explanation which makes up *Medieval England: an aerial survey* by M W Beresford and J K S St Joseph (Cambridge, Cambridge UP, 1958, Cambridge Air Surveys 2). Earlier demonstrations of the use of air photography to reveal ancient, and now obscured, outlines of fields, footpaths and similar features, are E C Curwin's *Air photography and the evolution of the cornfield* (A and C Black, 1938) and W G Hoskins' *The making of the English landscape* (Hodder and Stoughton, 1955). The wide range of practical uses to which air photography can be put is demonstrated in *The uses of air photography: nature and man in a new perspective* edited by J K S St Joseph (John Barker, 1966), a collection of contributions by members of the Cambridge Committee for Aerial Photography illustrated by photographs from the committee's collection. Applications discussed include cartography, geology, plant ecology, zoological studies, and the final chapter by Lord Esher is on ' air photographs and contemporary planning '. Other uses are proposed by J P Shercz in 'Aerial photography: a promising tool for pollution control ' *Safety maintenance* 135 March 1968 33-36; and in the Countryside Commission's *Recreation news* 3 January 1968 2, where a study to discover the value of air survey in recreation planning is described. In Canada, where the use and exploitation of aerial photographs is much greater than in the UK, *The Canadian surveyor* 22(1) was published as a special photo and orthophotomap issue, edited by L A Gale (Ottawa, Canadian Institute of Surveying, 1968)—a substantial volume in itself with numerous illustrations and a loose insert orthomap at a scale of 1 : 10,000. This volume constitutes a valuable collection of state of the art reports, with W A Radlinski's article ' Orthophoto maps versus conventional maps ' serving to indicate the complementary nature of the two types. Exploitation of natural resources in Canada demands up to date large scale maps at a rate that exceeds the capabilities of traditional methods of map production. L M Sebert's ' Photo maps for resource development in Canada ' in *The Canadian cartographer* 5(1) June 1968 50-53 describes five types of photomaps being produced by the Canadian government's Survey and Mapping Branch in Ottawa. Their use in the British Ordnance Survey programme is discussed by B St G Irwin in ' Photomaps ' *Advancement of science* 26(4) June 1970 369-371.

One of the earliest books dealing with the use of air photography specifically for planning purposes was *Aerial photography in urban planning and research* by Melville C Branch (Cambridge, Mass, Harvard UP, 1948). As a single comprehensive text on the potentialities of this subject it has not been superseded. It has been supplemented, however, in certain directions by more recent journal articles and conference papers. M G Burry, for example, writes on

160

'Air survey methods: their application to physical planning' in *Town planning review* 38(2) July 1967 135-150. The first part of the paper (which is based on a thesis submitted for the Diploma in Town and Country Planning at the Birmingham School of Planning) describes the use of air photographs and the methods of obtaining good quality photographs—this includes instructions to planners on how to draw up contracts with survey firms—and the second part describes the potential uses of air survey in planning practice. These uses include regional surveys, traffic, housing, industry, and recreation: as Burry observes, 'there is hardly a single facet of planning in which air survey cannot play a valuable part'.

The use of air survey as part of an integrated information process for planning purposes is discussed by Derek Rigby Childs in 'Our changing world: an introduction to a combined exercise in planning' *JTPI* 52(9) November 1966 367-380; the integration of air survey, census data, and Ordnance Survey maps on an experimental basis in Hertfordshire is outlined. A subsequent exhibition to demonstrate the approach is described by Rigby Childs in 'Planning information for planners' *JTPI* 53(9) November 1967 416-418. The scheme is also described by P G Mott (of Hunting Surveys Ltd) as 'Air photography as an aid to environmental planning' in the proceedings of the Symposium on Methods of Landscape Analysis held by the Landscape Research Group in May 1967 (LRG, 1967).

The principal sources of aerial photography of the UK are the four commercial air survey companies: Fairey Surveys Ltd, Maidenhead; Hunting Surveys and Consultants, Elstree; Meridian Airmaps Ltd, Lancing; and BKS Surveys Ltd, Leatherhead, all of which maintain substantial photographic libraries of the air cover they have flown. The other two principal agencies are the Royal Air Force, who fly for government departments, and the Ordnance Survey, who commission photography for the national map making programme.

Although the four commercial air survey companies started off as purely map making agencies, most of them have developed and recruited considerable expertise in the applications of remote sensing systems.

Hunting have a technical service section which provides a highly efficient service in a very wide range of disciplines, many of which

161

overlap into various aspects of planning. Fairey Surveys are also continuing to develop and extend their ' multi-disciplinary ' activities, and are increasingly becoming involved in those aspects of environmental monitoring and control which relate to planning. Meridian Airmaps are offering ' package deals ' in which they will not only take the photography, but they will carry out specific air photo interpretation studies according to the requirements of the client.

The principal collections of air photographs in the UK are those at the Department of the Environment in Whitehall, London, the Scottish Development Department in Edinburgh, and the Public Record Office in Belfast; at Cambridge University, under the aegis of the Cambridge Committee on Aerial Photography; and that maintained on a commercial basis by Aerofilms Limited in London. Newspaper offices also frequently maintain collections of air photographs, and are a possible source for local cover.

The collection maintained by Aerofilms Limited (which incorporates Aero Pictorial) is based on the firm's headquarters in London and can be consulted in person or enquiries made by telephone or letter. The library is a huge collection increasing by about 12,000 items every year, covering all parts of the UK in addition to overseas countries, its coverage going back to the early days of air photography. Most of the collection has been flown in response to specific orders for clients. Photos comprise both black and white and colour, verticals and obliques. The periodically revised *Aerofilms book of aerial photographs* is not intended as a complete catalogue, but rather as a sampler; an up to date index is maintained in the library.

The Air Photographs Library of the Department of the Environment, in Whitehall, is the largest non-commercial library of its kind in the UK, containing over two million photographs of England and Wales flown since 1945. The department has the services of the Royal Air Force, and is in fact the only source of supply for RAF photographs. The library exists primarily to serve its own department, and other government departments, but private individuals may, by appointment, examine photographs on the premises provided that prior enquiry has enabled the relevant items to be searched out. A preprinted form for requesting a cover search is

162

available from the library. Prints may also be purchased, but they cannot be borrowed. The collections in the Scottish and Northern Irish departments are restricted to cover for their respective countries, and are similar in function and facilities to the Library of the Department of the Environment. The collection in Cambridge also exists primarily for the use of the members of the committee. These resources, however, are not widely known to planners, and are certainly not widely used.

At the University of Leeds, Dr W Gordon Collins has, over the past ten years, developed an air photo unit which has a particular interest in the application of remote sensing in general, and aerial photography in particular, to the fields of ecology and planning.

Three symposia have been held at Leeds: the *Proceedings of the Derelict Land Symposium, September 1969* was published by Iliffe Science and Technology Publications Ltd, and the proceedings of the more recent symposium held in April 1971 on ' The application of aerial photography (remote sensing) to planning ' are now being prepared for press.

A number of research projects have been completed, and more are currently in progress. Three of the main areas of study, relevant to planning, are concerned with urban land use, derelict land, and population, and a very brief review of these follows.

Urban land use: An initial study of urban land use mapping from aerial photographs of the city of Leeds, showed that by using an existing set of 1:10,500 scale black and white verticals (figure 9) and preparing annotated trace overlays (figure 10) according to the classification used (figure 5), it was possible to identify nearly 90% of the nine major land use categories (figure 6) in a sample area of ten square miles.[6] The same photography was used to compile maps showing the extent, location and distribution of back to back and terraced houses, and also to map the type and location of industry, over an area of about seventy square miles, covering both the city and the suburban fringes. This initial work is now being further developed by a comparative study of Cumbernauld and York, using better quality photography at the slightly larger scale of 1:7,500.[7]

From these, and other urban projects carried out, it is considered that the optimum scale of photography for most needs, is about

1 : 2,500, and the additional cost of acquiring this larger scale cover is more than offset by the additional advantages which can be derived—assuming, of course, that full use is made of the photography.

Derelict land: The first phase of a derelict land study has now been completed.[8, 9, 10] In this phase, a set of 1966, black and white vertical aerial photographs at a scale of approximately 1 : 10,500 was used to identify, locate and map about thirty different types of dereliction in an area of two hundred square kilometres. Figure 8 shows an annotated aerial photograph of the key area, and figure 7 is the index to the air photo compiled for this study.

Photography at this scale proved to be ideally suitable as a source of both quantitative and qualitative information relating to derelict land. The required information was obtained in greater detail, and with greater accuracy and speed than would have been the case using the traditional field survey methods. Furthermore, by using a landscape definition—as opposed to the Department of the Environment's ' grant aid ' definition—of derelict land it was found that the former revealed about four times more dereliction than the latter. Another set of 1 : 10,000 scale air cover is currently (May 1971) being obtained of the West Riding of Yorkshire to coincide with the census of population, and the two sets of photography (1966 and 1971) will be used to determine both the current derelict land situation and also to determine, locate, map and analyse the changing patterns of dereliction during this five year period, in the entire West Riding of Yorkshire.

Population: Following on from the urban land use study, and because of the relationship of population densities with housing types and location, an experiment was carried out to assess to what extent photography at a scale of approximately 1 : 10,500 was of value in determining population patterns.[11] This 1963 photography (figure 11) was used in conjunction with the 1961 census enumeration district maps (figure 12), and the 1961 census data.

The aerial photographs were used to determine the type and quantity of housing stock, and the census data to calculate the population densities of the various housing types, in a number of sample areas. These ' density per housing type ' values were then applied to three sets of housing stock—again derived from the photographs —and the population figures were calculated. These calculated values were then compared with the true values recorded in the census, and the errors were determined.

Taking each of the three major housing groups of enumeration districts, the *total* population estimates showed the following errors:

back to back	+0·32%
terraced	+0·87%
semi detached	−6·40%

but within each group the errors for individual enumeration districts showed considerable variation, and these areas were subject to a careful analysis so that the system could be refined.

Some of the errors were caused by the fact that although the census data were collected in 1961, the aerial photography was flown in 1963, furthermore the scale of the photographs was barely adequate to abstract the required detail. Another study is now being planned to develop this project and 1 : 3,000 scale air cover of Leeds has just been flown coincident with the 1971 census week. The combination of larger scale photography, flown at the same time as the census, should, in this second phase of the study, lead to considerable improvements in the accuracy.

An additional advantage in using aerial photographs is that, with the aid of a co-ordinate digitiser, such as the d-mac, the photo co-ordinates can be computer transformed to the national grid. This is significant because the current and future censuses are to be based on the national grid system rather than the existing unstable and irregular enumeration district units.

A number of other air photo studies are in progress at the University of Leeds: these include the monitoring of traffic flow in the city centre,[12] and a detailed investigation into how people are using their gardens in Reading, Berkshire.[13] Completed studies include a survey of rural land use of five hundred square miles of Jamaica[14] in which all the under-utilised land of the area was identified, located and mapped to aid a land development programme; and a study of spoiled land in West Cornwall.[15]

Some of these air photo based studies are making use of d-mac digitisers, computers and automatic drafting equipment in an attempt to reduce the manpower requirements still further. One particularly significant study which has just been initiated by Dr Gordon Collins is an attempt to completely automate the system, using multispectral photography and a high speed digital densito-meter. The object of this study is to machine-identify various aspects of the landscape direct from the aerial photograph, and to obtain computer compatible tape from which a programmed output could provide statistical or mapped information at any desired scale—all based on the national grid system. This will enable other data—educational, medical, occupational, etc—to be fed into the same system so that a regional data bank may be established which would be of value to the planner.

During the last few years, not only have more sophisticated types of aerial photographs been produced, but—even more significant— new types of remote sensing systems have been developed which record parts of the electromagnetic spectrum outside visible light.

Figure 4 shows just how narrow is the visible light band with respect to the entire electromagnetic spectrum. Bearing in mind what can be achieved with normal photography, the potentialities of exploiting the whole range of the spectrum appear particularly fruitful. Many of these new systems, which include thermal line scanning, radar and spectrometry, have taken place on the infra red side of visible light.

Current trends clearly indicate that new types of information and data are being, and will be, provided for the planner. Atmospheric and hydrological pollution will, in the near future, be accurately monitored, physically, and probably even chemically, by airborne remote sensing. These new systems will provide types of information which, although highly desired by those working in the ecological and planning fields, were formerly thought to be unobtainable.

With the urgent need to both exploit and conserve the human and natural resources of the earth, the American Space Agency is, for the first time, turning its attention from space to the earth. A major programme has been initiated in which a series of satellites will obtain cyclical information about the earth, and transmit this information to ground stations. Earth Resource Technical Satellites (ERTS) A and B are two unmanned rockets, and ERTS A is to be launched in April 1972. For its life period of one year it will orbit the earth every ninety minutes, and will give repeated cover every eighteen days.

Another 'earth study' exercise is Skylab, where an orbiting laboratory will be visited by several sets of astronauts for periods up to fifty six days to conduct a series of experiments, including photographing selected areas of the earth. Some of the material from these experiments should be of value in macro regional planning.

Despite their potential as sources of information, aerial photographs are under-utilised by planners. The OSTI-financed survey of information use (see chapter 6) found that planners ranked air photographs twelfth in order of importance out of fourteen sources of operational information. More specifically, the survey found that planners engaged in practice use air photographs more than those engaged in research or teaching, but that only a small proportion of the research and practice samples rate the source as an important one and none at all in the teaching sample do so. Their use and importance appears to be higher in county planning offices than in those based in towns, probably because of the greater areas involved. The survey found that not only was the extent of use small, but also where photographs were being used they were not being used fully. The report states that 'the extent of the use of air photographs is at present limited mainly for two reasons: firstly, the cost of having air cover flown; secondly, the necessity of training in the proper interpretation of air photographs. The quality of use is poor in many cases, because the full potential of air photographs as a source of information is not realised and it is frequently the case that, where air photographs are available, they are being used in a very limited way ... There are solutions to all these problems.'[16]

The OSTI survey was further concerned to ascertain the uses to which air photographs were actually being put, and the potential uses to which they might be put. The major actual uses—based on the responses of twenty six percent of the sample who claim 'considerable' experience of air photographs, and a further fifty three percent with 'small' experience—are for land use surveys, revision of Ordnance Survey maps, and landscape interpretation, with other applications such as development control and traffic surveys well down the list. Of the respondents to these questions, eighty one

167

percent thought that air photographs could be exploited further as a source of information, and offered as examples of such exploitation, the revision of Ordnance Survey maps, regular surveys to provide continuing data, and land use surveys, with other applications again well down the list. The similarity between the actual and potential uses is noticeable, and also the overlap between these uses, for example, photographs used to up-date Ordnance Survey maps could subsequently be used for a whole range of land use surveys.

One development which should help to stimulate the use of aerial photographs in planning is the proposed establishment by the Department of the Environment, in conjunction with other interested government departments, of a central registry of aerial photographs, which will act, not as a provider of actual prints, but as a clearing-house of information about the location and availability of prints. There is a Canadian precedent for this venture, and it is anticipated that such a central service in the UK will not only meet a major information need in planning but will also encourage the greater exploitation of existing air cover, as has been the case in Canada.

In the final analysis, though, whether or not the planning profession will realise the full potential of aerial photographs as a source of information depends to a large extent on its readiness to be convinced by the small number of experts who constantly both demonstrate and advocate, verbally and in print, their use. As Dr Collins has pointed out, ' there is a technological revolution taking place in the acquisition of information by airborne methods, and if the planner is to remain professionally competent to tackle some of the new and complex problems which exist then he must be aware of the various sources of information that are, or could be, available to assist him in his work '.[17]

REFERENCES
1 Alice Coleman ' Land use survey and regional planning' *Planning outlook* new series 4 Spring 1968 30-36.

2 W Gordon Collins ' The aerial photograph—an alternative to field survey?' in *Proceedings of the derelict land symposium, Leeds, 1969* (Iliffe, 1970) 43.

3 M G Burry 'Air survey methods: their application to physical planning' *Town planning review* 38(2) July 1967 135-150.

4 W Gordon Collins *op cit* 43.

5 Preface to *Medieval England: an aerial survey*.

6 W Gordon Collins and Aly H A El-Beik 'The acquisition of urban land use information from aerial photographs of the city of Leeds (Great Britain)' *Photogrammetria* 27 1971 71-92.

7 Paul I McDonald 'The aerial photograph as a source of urban land use information' in *Proceedings of the symposium on the application of aerial photography (remote sensing) to planning, Leeds, 1971* (in press).

8 W Gordon Collins and Peter W Bush 'The definition and classification of derelict land' *JTPI* 55(3) March 1969 111-115.

9 W Gordon Collins and Peter W Bush 'An airphoto key for studies of derelict land' *JTPI* 55(6) June 1969 248-255.

10 W Gordon Collins and Peter W Bush 'The use of aerial photographs for the study of spoiled lands in Yorkshire' *JTPI* 57(3) March 1971 103-110.

11 W Gordon Collins and Aly H A El-Beik 'Population census with the aid of aerial photographs: an experiment in the city of Leeds' *Photogrammetric record* 7(37) April 1971 16-26.

12 John B Garner 'Traffic studies from oblique time lapse photography' in *Proceedings of the symposium on the application of aerial photography (remote sensing) to planning, Leeds, 1971* (in press).

13 Rowan MacTaggart and W Houghton-Evans 'The micro land use of residential private open space' in *Proceedings of the symposium on the application of aerial photography (remote sensing) to planning, Leeds, 1971* (in press).

14 W Gordon Collins 'Aerial photography applied to tropical land use' *Chartered surveyor* 99(5) November 1966 253-259.

15 W Neil James 'Spoiled land in west Cornwall: an assessment, using aerial photographs, of its suitability for development' in *Proceedings of the symposium on the application of aerial photography (remote sensing) to planning, Leeds, 1971* (in press).

16 Brenda White *Planners and information* (Library Association, 1970, Research Publication 3) 62.

17 W Gordon Collins 'The aerial photograph—an alternative to field survey?' in *Proceedings of the derelict land symposium, Leeds, 1969* (Iliffe, 1970) 50.

169

9

DEVELOPMENT PLANS AND REPORTS

OVER THE LAST DECADE the gradual official recognition of national policy and regional planning has resulted in a substantial and very valuable literature in the form of commissioned development plans and reports covering varying sizes of areal unit from the region downwards. These are sometimes referred to by planners as the real ' textbooks ' of the subject, being in the main examples of practical forward planning of a constructive nature and often containing detailed descriptions of the techniques employed, the studies carried out, and the guidelines adopted in the solution of problems arising from different sets of circumstances. Particularly in recent years, the major development plans have shown how the twin concepts of systemic planning and of structure plans for areas of sub-regional character can be put into practice under present conditions.

There are two major constraints upon the contents of this chapter. The first relates to the type of plan, and the second to the date of its production. It is possible to identify two broad categories of plan: those which were produced by local authority planning departments as statutory undertakings within the framework of the Town and Country Planning Act 1947, largely in the decade 1950 to 1960, and the subsequent quinquennial reviews and detailed plans for parts of the authority area which have been produced as a result of the original plan; and those which have been produced outwith the legal framework, largely within the decade 1960 to 1970, and largely by consultants, sometimes working in conjunction with universities or central and local government. It is the second category which forms the subject matter of this chapter. Statutory development plans and their offshoots are not included, for three reasons: the existence of a plan for any local authority area can be safely assumed, and therefore guidance to what is available is not necessary; the plans are based on patterns of activity and land use

170

which no longer apply in the majority of cases, and were conceived in accordance with a concept of planning which equally no longer applies; and they are not widely accessible.

To this second category, a date limit has been applied. The periods of highest productivity of advisory plans have been the years immediately following the end of World War II, and the 1960's (though there is no reason to suggest that productivity will decline in the present decade). The years 1943 to 1950 saw the production of many notable plans: Abercrombie's for London and the Clyde Valley, Thomas Sharp's for Oxford, Durham, Salisbury and other cities, Max Lock's for Middlesbrough and the Hartle-pools, Holford's for Cambridge, Nicholas' for Manchester, and many others. Guidance to these is provided in three sources which conveniently supplement each other. The first is an article by L Dudley Stamp on 'British town planning schemes' *Geographical review* 36(4) October 1946 609-612, which contains a list of the town and regional plans which apeared from 1940 to 1946. The second is the report of the Ministry of Local Government and Planning *Town and country planning 1943-1951* (HMSO, 1951, Cmnd 8204) which contains a select bibliography of the major reports, surveys, outline and advisory plans published during the period indicated. The third source is the Library Bibliography 45 of the Department of the Environment Library, which constitutes a complete list of plans and surveys other than development plans published between 1939 and 1950. This chapter therefore concentrates, in the main, on providing guidance to the development plan literature of 1960 onwards (the 1950's were fallow years) with the exception that some earlier plans are included which have influenced subsequent developments in their area (London, the Clyde Valley) or have introduced new concepts whose influence has extended into the 1960's (Cumbernauld new town).

Within these specified limits, then, the question arises, what constitutes a development plan? Other writers have encountered a similar problem: Gavin McCrone, for example, though discussing regional economic planning, has observed that 'it is a rather fruitless exercise to debate what constitutes a "plan" and what does not. At one extreme, obviously, there is the report or survey which analyses the problems of an area and may make recommendations

171

without there necessarily being any official government commitment to implement them . . . At the other end of the scale is a document setting out a programmed development of the economy complete with target figures for industrial output and public expenditure to which the government commits itself . . . In between one may find a range of documents which are part plan and part survey . . ."[1]

The plans which will be discussed within this chapter are concerned with economics also, and many of them derive from the base of an economic study of a region or sub-region, but they are concerned also with physical planning and, to a lesser extent, with social planning, and in the final analysis they must indicate a broad pattern of land use allocations for further development. It is possible to identify three basic types: the survey or study, mentioned by McCrone, which analyses the various factors at work in an area and which makes recommendations for solving the problems involved; the feasibility study, which starts from a similar analysis but predicts whether development within the area is feasible and the most likely form it should take; and the plan, which makes firm recommendations for development, although in recent years there is an increasing tendency to indicate only a broad strategy and to formulate goals and policies rather than to make specific recommendations about detailed physical layouts and buildings (see the quotation from Colin Buchanan's *South Hampshire study* at the end of chapter 2). No attempt has been made to differentiate between these three types in the course of this chapter: most plans contain an element of all three. Instead a geographical arrangement has been adopted, with the principal aim of showing how the development planning of the various regions has evolved during the last decade, as demonstrated in its literature.

The base for many of the development plans has been the regional studies produced initially by government departments and subsequently by the regional economic planning councils. In describing the evolution of regional planning in chapter 2, it was pointed out that one of the catalytic events in the rebirth of positive regional thinking was the publication of the government White Papers on London, central Scotland, and north east England (discussed below within the respective sections of this chapter). These studies were the first of many, the beginning of a veritable flood

172

of documentation relating to the regions of Britain. The Scottish and north east studies in particular were notable because, as J B Cullingworth has indicated ' they involved a degree of government commitment which is notably absent from their successors, even when they have been prepared by central government '.[2] Exceptions to this dictum are provided by the subsequent Welsh and Scottish studies (see below) but with other studies it was made increasingly clear that these were to be regarded as bases for discussion and that they involved no commitment to action. McCrone has summed up the salient characteristics of the basic regional studies nicely: ' the reports for the English regions are similar in character: they provide a mine of information about their regions, they analyse its problems, its economic structure and its future prospects; they also put forward a great number of recommendations for policy. Essentially they try to provide the analysis on which a discussion of the regions' future can be based. There is a tendency for the prosperous regions to be concerned with the physical problems of accommodating their expansion, while giving insufficient weight to economic projects and assessments; the problem regions, such as the north, are much more concerned with the economic problems of stimulating expansion. Such an emphasis is perhaps natural. But the reports are not and are not intended to be regional plans. Detailed forecasts and targets are not given—could not be in the absence of greatly improved statistical data. Neither do the recommendations involve any government commitments.'[3]

The premise of the Scottish and north east studies is very similar: an assessment of problems and potential and a proposal of solutions. For Scotland, several growth points were proposed; for the north east, a single growth zone taking in Tyneside, Teesside and part of County Durham to the east of the Great North Road. In each case, a massive increase in public investment was required to carry through the programme. These studies of ' depressed ' areas were followed, in March 1964, by the *South east study* from the Ministry of Housing and Local Government, which tackled a very different problem—that of restraining growth—and which postulated as its main principle the decentralisation of population and employment, the creation of three new cities and the expansion of several others as growth points in the outer part of the region to act as counter-magnets to the metropolis and to accommodate its over-spill. Two further reports emanated from central government, from the Department of Economic Affairs, before the work was taken over by the regional economic planning councils. These are *The north west: a regional study* (HMSO, 1965) and *The west midlands: a regional study* (HMSO, 1965); both of these are discussed, along with *The Scottish economy, 1965 to 1970: a plan for expansion* (Edinburgh, HMSO, 1966, Cmnd 2864) produced from the Scottish Office, by P M Smith in a review article 'What kind of regional planning?' in *Urban studies* 3(3) November 1966 250-257. An appendix to the north west study was published later in the same year, *The problems of Merseyside: an appendix to the north west study* (HMSO, 1965).

From 1966, with the exception of the Scottish study of 1966 (see above) and the Welsh study of 1967 (see below) the regional studies emanate from the economic planning councils. First came the *Challenge of the changing north* (1966), calling for an influx of technology and research into the area, modernisation of the areas of population concentration, and recognition of Teesside as a national growth point. In the following month came *A review of Yorkshire and Humberside* (1966) urging priority for increased housing, reclamation of derelict land, and a motorway network and proposing two growth points. At the end of the year *The east midlands study* joined the growing library, pointing up the principal regional problems of the declining Nottinghamshire/Derbyshire coalfield, poor east-west communications, and the inadequate provision of drinking water.

1967 began with *The west midlands: patterns of growth* (1967) which highlights the problem of Birmingham, the necessity of containing the conurbation within its present limits and the equal necessity for an integrated, comprehensive overspill policy. *A region with a future: a draft strategy for the south west* (1967) followed, proposing Plymouth as a growth point to attract industry, supporting the government's proposal for the large-scale expansion of Swindon, and calling attention to the poor road system and to the need to develop the port of Bristol. *A strategy for the south east* (1967) puts forward the idea of development in the form of 'corridors' following major lines of transportation from London to the provinces, giving easy access to the major expansion schemes previously proposed. Country zones are proposed, countryside which is to be strictly preserved from any form of development. *Wales: the way ahead* (HMSO, 1967, Cmnd 3334) proposes a development programme which has inspired much of Welsh planning in the last five years. The last basic study to be completed was *East Anglia: a study* (1968).

Further regional studies produced by the economic planning councils were follow up studies to the basic exercises. Thus, *The north west of the 1970s* appeared in 1968; and *Opportunity in the east midlands* in 1969. Other studies were of small parts of regions, or sub-regions, sparked off by the earlier full-scale surveys. For example, the 1966 *Review of Yorkshire and Humberside* specified areas within the region which could profitably bear further examination, and this recommendation resulted in three area studies: of *Halifax and Calder Valley: an area study* (HMSO, 1968), *Doncaster: an area study* (HMSO, 1969), on which the planning departments of the West Riding County Council and the County Borough of Doncaster cooperated with the Economic Planning Council and Board, and of *Huddersfield and Colne Valley: an area study* (HMSO, 1969). The South West Economic Planning Council produced the *Plymouth area study* in 1969; and in the same year came the *South east Kent study*. Most recently the Yorkshire and Humberside Council have issued *Yorkshire and Humberside: regional strategy* (HMSO, 1970) which assumes a growth of 3% per annum compound in public investment in the region up to 1981; unhappily, this assumption was made public only two days after the government had announced cuts in regional investment grants, and therefore the schemes of the council for rapid completion of major road projects, enlarged slum clearance programmes, more reclamation, faster urban renewal, and an upgrading of what is now often a depressing environment, must hang—like those of other regions—very much in the balance.

ENGLAND

The most planned part of the country is surely the London and south east region of England, both in terms of actual activity and of

175

resultant documentation. The starting point of comprehensive planning for London was the Barlow Report of 1940, which has been discussed fully in chapter 2. The broad principles of the report found expression in the advisory plans for London prepared in 1943 and in 1944, the *County of London plan* by J H Forshaw and Patrick Abercrombie (Macmillan, 1943) and the *Greater London plan 1944* by Sir Patrick Abercrombie (HMSO, 1945). The *County of London plan* is an attempt to 'retain the old structure, where discernible, and make it workable under modern conditions'. Prepared in two years, under great pressure and in difficult wartime conditions, it provides for short-term needs in the urgent work of rebuilding and rehousing, within the framework of an overall concept for the next fifty years. The major part of the report is taken up with the results of a detailed study of all aspects of the city, for, ' if a plan is to be authoritative, the planners must first make a profound study of existing conditions by means of a civic survey of the most detailed character; secondly, they must familiarise themselves with the wishes of the people . . .'. The plan, as produced, provided a tremendous stimulus to positive planning: ' here is the chance to show London on a grand scale what her reconstruction really means. In three directions there are immediate opportunities, corresponding to the three major aspects : the provision of new housing and open spaces in the damaged industrial boroughs: the creation of the southern embankment and cultural centre; and the construction of new roads '. Half way through the preparation of the advisory plan, Abercrombie was also appointed by the Minister of Works and Planning to prepare a comprehensive plan for the development of Greater London, taking in 143 local authorities and 2,599 square miles outside the administrative county of London, an area containing a population of ten million. The key factors in the *Greater London plan* were the principles of restraining London's growth by the maintenance of a green belt around it, and the large-scale decentralisation of population and employment to new towns planned beyond the green belt. The green belt was proposed as a five miles deep ring around the built up area of London between thirteen and sixteen miles from the centre. The plan proposed also to decant 400,000 population into eight new towns, each new town to have a maximum size of 60,000 population and to be constrained, like London itself, by a

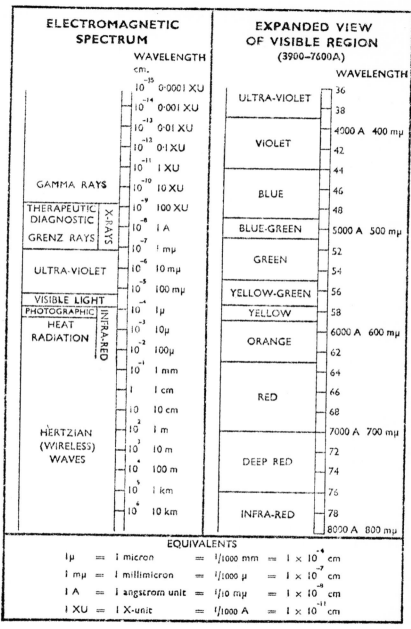

FIGURE 4 : The electromagnetic spectrum.

facing p 176

1	Commercial		C
	(a)	offices	C_1
	(b)	shops	C_2

2	Industrial		I
	(a)	offices	I_1
	(b)	factories	I_2
	(c)	petrol storage tanks	I_3
	(d)	gas storage tanks	I_4
	(e)	power stations	I_5

3	Residential		R
	(a)	detached houses	R_1
	(b)	semi-detached houses	R_2
	(c)	terraced houses	R_3
	(d)	back to back houses	R_{3b}
	(e)	single storey houses	R_4
	(f)	block of flats	R_5

4	Bodies of water		W
	(a)	streams and rivers	W_1
	(b)	lakes	W_2
	(c)	reservoirs and water works	W_3

5	Transportation		T
	(a)	railways	T_1
	(b)	roadways	T_2
	(c)	waterways ·	T_3

6	Public buildings		B
	(a)	educational	B_1
	(b)	hospitals	B_2
	(c)	churches	B_3

7	Open improved land		P
	(a)	parks	P_1
	(b)	cemeteries	P_2
	(c)	sports	P_3
	(d)	parking place (vehicles)	P_4
	(e)	allotments	P_5

8	Open unimproved land		V

FIGURE 5 : Key to urban land use.

Type of urban land use	A	F	C	C (%)	$\frac{(A-F)}{F}$ %
Commercial	48	39	33	84.5	+ 23.0
Industrial	173	184	159	86.5	− 6.0
Residential	222	235	216	92.0	− 5.0
Bodies of water	3	3	3	100.0	0
Transportation	11	9	9	100.0	+ 22.0
Public building	152	159	145	91.0	− 4.4
Open improved land	70	70	69	99.0	0
Open unimproved land	23	24	23	96.0	− 4.0
Complex urban land use	20	33	12	36.4	− 39.4
Total no. of areas	722	756	669	88.5	− 5.2

Explanation of vertical column headings: A = number of units recorded from aerial photographs; F = number of units recorded from field investigations; C = number of units correctly identified; C % = percentage of correctly identified units; and $(A-F)/F \times 100$ = percentage over or under estimated derived from the aerial photographs.

FIGURE 6: Urban land use: accuracy check of air photo identification.

local green belt. The new towns were proposed on the principles of Ebenezer Howard, each town and its surrounding zone of agricultural land conceived as a unit, with provision of employment sufficient for the population, and a full range of service and cultural facilities; commuting between the new town and London was to be discouraged. In addition, a selected number of existing communities in the outer portions of the London region were designated for planned growth. 'Such communities had already received heavy inflows of evacuees during the war and social ties between some residents of central areas and particular peripheral communities had thus been established.'[4] These twin concepts of green belt and new towns have formed the basis of a 'coherent strategy for the future physical development of the metropolitan region'.[5] As an American observer has pointed out, the *Greater London plan* and the earlier complementary *County of London plan* 'contained an adroit mixture respecting the traditional and taming the unwanted. They reemphasised the singular and dominant importance of the great center of London with its traditional functional precincts. The plans maintained the main transportation lines feeding into this center, and preserved the pyramid of residential densities stressing the distinct centrality of it all. On top of this traditionally monolithic and unitary pattern was added the reinforcing character of a circular green belt designed to offer contrast and to assure containment. By these plans, British citizens were offered the reassuring impression that the best features of London as they knew them could be maintained while forces at work to change the London they revered could be brought under control. This was a welcome and hopeful message.'[6]

Another product of the war years was an ambitious and revolutionary plan for London conceived by the Modern Architectural Research Group, known as the MARS plan, published as 'A master plan for London' by Arthur Korn and Felix J Samuely in *Architectural review* 91 (546) June 1942 143-150. The MARS plan 'is particularly notable because it boldly faced the traffic problem and based its proposals on a logical transport system'.[7] The proposals took the form of a linear plan, with a main railway route running parallel with the Thames and a ring of long-distance railway lines, and a road system consisting of a north to south spine road through the

177

centre of the city with parallel routes for public transport. Residential development was to be in the form of units, combining to form neighbourhood units; these in turn combining to form borough units of which twelve would make up a district. This residential development would be placed in a band up to half a mile wide on either side of the traffic routes. Future expansion could be accommodated by lengthening the main spine and creating more sub-spines. ' The MARS plan contained the only important alternative ideas as to how a metropolitan area might be spatially organised . . . It provided for a number of advantages that deserved serious consideration, but because it so ruthlessly disrespected London's existing features, most Londoners, and political leaders, could not take it very seriously. Thus, although it provided a stimulating exercise in the design of a metropolis, in completely failing to recognise and to build from the here-and-now it also failed to serve as a responsible alternative for dealing with tradition-rich London '.[8]

Although Abercrombie's detailed proposals for siting new towns were not in all cases adhered to in subsequent practice, the principle was established and has continued in practice. The metropolitan green belt also became established in reality in 1959 when the last of the home counties' development plans under the 1947 Town and Country Planning Act was approved by the Minister of Housing and Local Government. Abercrombie's assumptions have been falsified mainly by events which were unforeseen at the time he was preparing his plans for London and other parts of the country. These events have been the growth of population in the south east region generally, both from natural causes and as a result of immigrants from overseas, and the expansion in manufacturing and service industries in London, and particularly the growth of office employment and development. Pressures inevitably arose for development within and beyond the green belt and the problems of congestion and poor quality housing continued in the city. An isolated, and abortive, attempt to provide some relief to these problems was made by the London County Council in its plan for a new town at Hook, in Hampshire, some forty miles from London. Its report on the project *The planning of a new town: data and design based on a study for a new town of 100,000 at Hook, Hampshire* (LCC, 1961) contains detailed studies laying the basis for a plan for a compact

178

linear town, with residential areas in the form of 'concentric rings increasing in density, height and concentration of building towards the centre', and dispersed industrial estates. The plan follows that for Cumbernauld in Scotland (see below) in its rejection of the traditional neighbourhood planning common to the earlier new towns, and is usually bracketed with the Scottish town as the first Mark II new towns. The Hook plan also allows for full car ownership with consonant parking facilities, and at the same time for 'the highest practicable degree of pedestrian and vehicular separation, with precedence given to the pedestrian'. In the event the project was laid aside in favour of cooperation between the LCC and Hampshire County Council for major expansions at Andover, Basingstoke and Tadley to accommodate London overspill, which could be provided more rapidly than a completely new town. But the document is a valid contribution to the literature, both in the nature of its planning proposals and in its detailed studies. The Hook exercise only served to emphasise the clear need for cooperation between planning authorities, and in 1962, the local planning authorities in London and the home counties set up a Standing Conference on London Regional Planning, to provide a forum through which they could work together on planning issues over the whole region. Subsequently, membership was extended to take in the entire south east region, and the name changed to the Standing Conference on London and South East Regional Planning. At the same time, the government examined the situation and produced a White Paper *London—employment: housing: land* (HMSO, 1963, Cmnd 1952) which recognised the need for a regional plan. The result was *The south east study 1961-1981* (HMSO, 1964) commissioned by the Ministry of Housing and Local Government and carried out by a team from that Ministry.

The study considers the south east region from the Wash to Dorset. The main problems to be considered were the growth and movement of population, and its concomitant industry and employment, and transport questions. The need for a second generation of new towns was to be examined. The team was further charged to provide a regional framework into which local authorities could fit their development plans. 'There are expected to be at least $3\frac{1}{2}$ million more people living in south east England by 1981; it might prove to be more. Such an increase will present formidable problems for what is already the most rapidly growing part of the United Kingdom. This report explains why such a large increase should be planned for and suggests the various ways in which the planning of it could most effectively be done.' Plans are proposed for an overspill of about one million people; about 400,000 of these would move to the outer metropolitan region within commuting distance of the city, and the remainder would have homes and jobs well outside the green belt. The report confirms the policy of retaining the green belt. A second generation of new and expanded towns is proposed, on a larger scale than those currently being built. Major urban development is projected in the Southampton/Portsmouth area, the Bletchley area, and the Newbury area, together with new towns at Ashford and Stansted. Large scale town expansion schemes are put forward based on Ipswich, Northampton, Peterborough, and Swindon. The report stresses the vital need for regular and frequent reviews of the proposed policies.

Reviews and revised proposals have certainly been forthcoming. Late in 1964 the government (Labour had just replaced Conservative) instituted a review of the *South east study* and in 1966 published a *Review of the south east study* (HMSO, 1966) which incorporated revised proposals resulting from revised policy ideas, changed thinking on planning generally, and new information which had become available in the interim period. While the study and its review were significant documents in the planning of the south east region, their focus was primarily physical: economic and social considerations were largely ignored, as were the effects of the regional plan on other regions and the effects of other regions on it. The purely regional outlook ignores the effects of creating new urban growth areas which will, in practice, compete with the growth areas established in depressed areas in the competition for industry. ' Indeed, the result of the policy could well be to accelerate the drift from other regions to the south east rather than solve London's problems.'[9]

The economic element was added by the South East Economic Planning Council in its first report on the region for the Department of Economic Affairs, *A strategy for the south east* (HMSO, 1967). This study is based on the population projections produced in 1966 by the General Register Office which predict an increase in the region of 2·14 million by 1981; most of this will be natural increase, immigration from abroad being estimated as of little significance. The report supports the development of major urban expansion schemes at a distance from London, as put forward in the *South east study*, but also makes proposals for development within the outer metropolitan area in the form of 'corridors' following major lines of transportation from London to the provinces, and suggests feasibility studies of various sub-regions as bases for growth. The continuance of the green belt is strongly advocated, and in addition country zones are proposed within which major development should not take place. Various suggestions for further study and for continuous review of progress in planning throughout the region are incorporated.

Most recently there has been the *Strategic plan for the south east* (HMSO, 1970) carried out for the Ministry of Housing and Local Government by its South East Joint Planning Team. The study was commissioned in 1968, and was designed to 'consider and report with recommendations on patterns of development for the south east, taking as a starting point the strategy proposals of the South East Economic Planning Council, but also taking account of the planning work of the Standing Conference on London and South East Regional Planning and having regard to government policies, with the object of producing a regional framework—a) for the local planning authorities to carry out their planning responsibilities including, as appropriate, the preparation of structure plans under the Town and Country Planning Act, 1968, and b) for government decisions on investment, and economic and social policies relating to the region's future development'.

The base for the study was the *Strategy for the south east* (see above) and also the document *The south east: a framework for regional planning* produced by the Standing Conference on London and South East Regional Planning together with the conference's series of reports *The conference area in the long term* (Standing Conference, 1968, and 1966-). The report consists of studies of the major aspects of the regional situation—employment, housing, town and country, public utilities, traffic and transport—and from these a summary of the likely position at 1981 is given, and two alternative hypotheses at 1991 described, based on two strategic concepts.

These are evaluated, and a recommended strategy proposed. The uncertainty of population projections, evidenced in earlier studies, is expressed candidly: 'the recommended strategy is designed to accommodate different levels of population since no one can be sure what population levels will, in the event, need to be catered for '. For design purposes, however, a growth of $4\frac{1}{2}$ million between 1966 and 2000 was adopted, and to accommodate this increase a limited number of major growth areas at varying distances from London are postulated, using existing or planned urban settlements as bases for growth: these are in the south Hampshire area; the Milton Keynes/Northampton/Wellingborough area; the Reading/Workingham/Aldershot/Basingstoke area; south Essex; and the Crawley area. In addition, medium growth areas are proposed at the Maidstone/Medway area; Ashford; Eastbourne/Hastings area; the Bournemouth/Poole area; Aylesbury; Bishop's Stortford/Harlow; and Chelmsford. Expansion of medium-sized employment centres which have potential for growth, is proposed, together with relatively small scale development in other parts of the region; the green belt is again upheld, together with a policy of preservation of extensive areas of open country. Once again, a comprehensive road and rail network is planned, both for inter-regional and intra-regional use. The main difference between this plan and its predecessors is that it does give a reasonably firm indication of where the main weight of development should fall within the area within a fifty mile radius of London, over the next thirty years. The plans of 1964 and 1966 avoided this issue; the Economic Planning Council plan of 1967 did give a general indication, but lacked official status. The supporting studies which formed the basis of the *Strategic plan* are to be separately published in five volumes, of which the first appeared in March 1971.

The *South east study* of 1964 has had a considerable amount of spin-off in the form of documentary studies and plans of the various areas within the region which were designated as locations for expansion. The study proposed major urban development in three areas: Southampton/Portsmouth, the Bletchley area of Buckinghamshire, and the Newbury area of Berkshire. All of these projected growth areas have been the subject of study and of planning proposals. The basic documents for these three areas are, respectively, the *South Hampshire study: report on the feasibility of major urban growth* (HMSO, 1966, with two supplementary volumes); *Northampton, Bedford and north Bucks study: an assessment of inter-related growth* (HMSO, 1965); and *A new city: a study of urban development in an area including Newbury, Swindon and Didcot* (HMSO, 1966). The first and third of these are out of print. These are all sub-regional studies of importance, particularly that of the south Hampshire area which constitutes a major statement of planning in practice. The *New city study* differs from the other two, however, in that the latter consider the physical form which expansion might take, whereas the former considers only the feasibility of accommodating an increased population within the area and recommends the general location for the development.

The *South Hampshire study* was prepared by Colin Buchanan and Partners in association with Economic Consultants Ltd, for the Ministry of Housing and Local Government, Hampshire County Council, and the county borough councils of Portsmouth and Southampton. The *South east study* indicated that south Hampshire should accommodate a planned intake of 250,000 population, of which 150,000 should be accommodated by 1981, representing a total increase by 1981 of about 300,000. The study area is bounded to the south by the coastline, to the east by the county boundary of Hampshire, to the north by the boundaries of Petersfield, Winchester, and Romsey and Stockbridge rural districts, to the west by the county boundary with Wiltshire and the western boundary of the New Forest rural district. The sub-region centres on Southampton and goes east to Chichester, north to Andover, west to Salisbury and Weymouth. The terms of reference laid down to the consultants were to study, report and recommend on the physical suitability of the Southampton/Portsmouth sub-region for development, the feasibility of accommodating the specified population increase, the form such development would take, and the effects on areas of high amenity value such as the New Forest and on major centres of employment, and the provision of an adequate system of transport and communications.

As a result of their study, the consultants conclude that the sub-region is suitable for development, and that it would be feasible to accommodate population growth of this order. A corridor of growth

183

is proposed, some twenty five miles long and ten to twelve miles wide, with Portsmouth and Southampton at either end, as the main location for new development, to be expanded as one urban unit. The main initial concentration would be on Southampton. The existing industry of the area offers a firm base for such expansion. Design for a flexible transport system is incorporated. The main volume contains the report of the study and the proposals for growth; two supplementary volumes deal with particular aspects of urban expansion in greater depth and detail than is possible in the main volume. In 1969 the South Hampshire Plan Advisory Committee was set up to oversee the work of a technical team, the South Hampshire Plan Technical Unit, which is considering, and planning for the future of, the sub-region. The advisory committee is an experiment in local authority cooperation, fostered by the Ministry of Housing and Local Government, to demonstrate that effective city region planning is possible in advance of local government reorganisation. *The First interim report on the South Hampshire plan* (Winchester, Advisory Committee, 1970) is a progress report on the first year's work on the plan. Involving the public in the plans for the area is an important feature of the work of the committee and the unit, and this report is published so that organisations and individuals can consider and discuss the progress thus far. It discusses the purpose of the south Hampshire plan, outlines the next stages of work, summarises the findings of the surveys which formed a major part of the first year's work, and includes suggestions for the future of the sub-region. Subsequently, a final report was issued, *South Hampshire plan: four possibilities for the future* (Winchester, Technical Unit, 1970) which narrows down the possibilities to four alternative future patterns of development, from which a preferred pattern will be finally selected, perhaps taking features from all four schemes. The technical unit is also publishing a series of technical documents in the course of its work, intended for planners rather than for the public. Twenty nine of these reports are envisaged, grouped under the headings of rural conservation; urban services; urban form; people, activities and housing; transportation; finance; trends and changes in society; and two summary reports of problems and opportunities. Two already published are D2 on employment, and D3 on shopping, both of which describe in some detail the methodologies employed and the problems involved. Details of the reports, and the documents themselves, are obtainable from the technical unit.

The first proposals for a new city in north Buckinghamshire came from Buckinghamshire County Council in 1962, when a development area was proposed in the north of the county as a reception point for overspill from towns in the south of the county and also from London, and a study was made of possible ways to develop a city for 250,000 population. The study was reported in *North Bucks new city* (Aylesbury, County Council, 1966) but the county council did not proceed with the proposal. The potential of this area for development was affirmed in the *South east study,* which proposed Bletchley (already undergoing expansion by agreement with London under the Town Development Act 1952) as a suitable location for a new town to accommodate London overspill. A regional feasibility study was commissioned and in October 1965 the Ministry of Housing and Local Government published the *Northampton, Bedford and north Bucks study.* The *South east study* had recommended not only a new town in the Bletchley area, but also a planned increase of 100,000 in the population of Northampton and an increase of at least 30,000 at Bedford, as overspill points for the south east.

Consultants Hugh Wilson and Lewis Womersley were commissioned to study, report and make recommendations on a) the inter-relationships of development of this order within the area roughly within fifteen miles of any one of these three towns; b) the merits and demerits of a closer and more integrated grouping of the planned developments; c) the possible site or sites for closer development; d) the problems of providing an adequate system of transport and communication allowing free movement between the separate parts of the development. The study area lies at a central point on the London-Birmingham axis, and forms a triangle, with the three main towns at the points, within the counties of Northamtonshire, Bedfordshire, and Buckinghamshire. As a result of their studies, the consultants propose that Northampton is suitable for expansion, to about 100,000 by the year 2000, and that planning proposals should involve replanning the central area of the town and the dispersal of employment to allow an adequate transport

185

system. Bedford should be expanded to at least 70,000 population, the development to take place to the west of the town; redevelopment proposals for the town's central area should be reconsidered, and a comprehensive plan for communications will be required. Two possible sites are considered for development of a new city of about 200,000: one near Wolverton, and one near Bletchley; the latter is recommended. The need for maximum flexibility of design is stressed, and particular attention paid to the role of public transport in the large settlements. An appendix to the body of the report contains details of statistical data, an example of development, and theoretical considerations for coordinated linear growth. Subsequently a draft designation order was made for an area of 25,000 acres, and following a public inquiry in 1966 an order was made under the New Towns Act designating nearly 22,000 acres in north Buckinghamshire as the site of a new town for 250,000 people, to include the existing towns of Bletchley, Wolverton, and Stony Stratford, and to be called Milton Keynes (after a small village in the area). A development corporation was established in May 1967, and in December of the same year the consultants Llewelyn-Davies Weeks Forestier-Walker and Bor began work on the preparation of a plan for the new city.

At the end of 1968 the consultants published *Milton Keynes plan: interim report*. The report represents ' the strategic approach of the corporation towards the new city at this half way stage of the planning process . . . it has two purposes: first it is to enable us to start development work on a limited scale in advance of the plan. Secondly it is to enable—indeed to encourage—the ideas which we are developing for the new city to be discussed and considered, at an early stage, by the public and organisations and authorities concerned.' One of the conditions of the consultants' brief was that there should be a thorough examination of the goals on which the development of the city should be based. This examination has taken place largely in discussions and seminars with experienced and interested people on topics such as education, leisure, and transport. As a result of these discussions, general and particular goals have been established. The interim report is concerned mainly with discussion of these goals and how they can be achieved under various broad headings. In March 1970 the development corporation pub-

186

lished *The plan for Milton Keynes* in two volumes, the first volume containing the corporation's submission to the Minister of Housing and Local Government and describing the proposals in summary form, the second containing in detail the evidence and reasoning behind the plan. Ten technical supplements are also available containing reports of studies carried out by the main consultants and by their various specialist associates; a list of these is given on page xii of the second volume. The main feature of the plan is its flexibility and its hospitality, within its proposed framework, to individual initiative and design. Much of the content is concerned with broad policy rather than with precise blueprints for development. The plan ' provides a starting point. It does not attempt to lay down in detail the ultimate structure of the new city. Many of the proposals contained in the plan are for social and institutional initiative. But it also contains proposals for meeting the physical needs of a large city . . . The central aim of the plan is to arrange these necessarily fixed elements in the new city so as to allow the greatest possible scope for freedom and change as it is built. They have also been planned as far as possible to allow wide variety in patterns of life and the greatest possible choice for the future inhabitants.' The basic framework of the city is based on two concepts: that of a kilometre grid network of primary roads, and the dispersal of traffic-generating land uses throughout the area of the city. There are no detailed plans for layout or for the physical appearance of buildings. A sketch of a typical kilometre unit is included, but there are no plans for residential area layout; there is also a sketch model of the city centre, proposed as a basis for discussion. The emphasis throughout is on active public participation, fully reported in the second volume and in two of the technical supplements, and on the necessity for continuous monitoring and evaluation. Of considerable interest are the proposals for a social development programme to progress alongside the physical and economic plans. But the volumes are a mine of information on all aspects of urban development and incorporate many ideas which are not common to the published plans for new towns.

The third area of major urban growth proposed in the *South east study,* the sub-region containing Newbury and Swindon, was studied by consultants Llewelyn-Davies Weeks and Partners (as the

187

firm was then) and their report was published by the Ministry of Housing and Local Government as *A new city* in 1966. The *South east study* had recommended Newbury as the centre of an area of major urban growth and Swindon as the focus of large scale town expansion. The area of expansion studied was bounded by Hungerford, Thatcham, Didcot and Swindon, and the actual study area extends beyond this boundary to include much of Berkshire and parts of Hampshire, Wiltshire, Gloucestershire, and Oxfordshire. The terms of reference laid down for the consultants were to investigate the feasibility of planning a major development within this area to accommodate some 300,000 additional population, and to recommend the location and form of such development. In their report, the consultants recommend that ' planned development should take place in the Swindon area in preference to Newbury to absorb an increased population of 125,000 by 1981, rising to about 300,000 by the end of the century. Taking into account the present population of Swindon, and the immediate surrounding area, this will result in a total population in the new city of about 250,000 by 1981, and perhaps over 400,000 by the end of the century.' The consultants recommend that a study should be commissioned for the planning of a new city to include Swindon. This recommendation was accepted in principle by the Minister of Housing and Local Government, who decreed, however, that the pressures generated on the surrounding countryside and villages by growth to an extent suggested in *A new city* might be harmful and that it would be more realistic to limit the numbers from London to 75,000 by 1981. This would result in a town of about 200,000 by 1981 expanding to about 250,000 by the end of the century. He therefore suggested that the councils of Wiltshire, Swindon and Greater London consult together with a view to carrying out an expansion of Swindon under the Town Development Act 1952. This revised strategy was supported in the South West Economic Planning Council report *A region with a future: draft strategy for the south west* in 1967 and again in the South East Economic Planning Council report *Strategy for the south east* which followed later in 1967. *Swindon: a study for further expansion* (Swindon, Borough Council, 1968) is the report of a feasibility study carried out by a joint team from the borough, Wiltshire County Council and the Greater London Council in

188

response to the Minister's proposal. The area studied was Swindon and its sub-region: the latter was assessed by determining the influence of the town as a shopping, service and employment centre, and extends to a radius of about twelve miles from the town centre. The sub-region is predominantly rural, and includes areas of the Cotswolds and the Downs. The report is not a master plan for development, but a basic policy statement from which a master plan can be evolved. It proposes that the intake of 75,000 should be phased to 1986 instead of 1981 because of the technical and economic problems which are likely to be created by more rapid growth. A population increase of 48,000 outside the new city area (which is limited to about 21,000 acres including the existing town) is expected by 1986, and this is to be accommodated by infilling, by limited expansion of some existing settlements and villages, and by limited development at specified places. An overall strategy for all types of development in the countryside will have to be implemented or expansion will have undesirable effects on the sub-region. Detailed proposals for landscape and open space, shopping and service centres, employment, transportation, housing, engineering services, and the social framework of the new community, are incorporated.

Further spin-off from the *South east study* has come in the plans for large-scale town expansions proposed at Ipswich, Northampton, and Peterborough; the expansion proposed at Swindon has been discussed in the context of the Newbury sub-regional study. The volumes relating to the expansion of Ipswich form a more detailed and comprehensive study than those for Northampton or Peterborough in that the expansion of the town has been considered within a long term regional strategy and the latter is discussed in some detail as well as the possible forms of physical development. Peterborough and Northampton have both been designated as new towns under the New Towns Act, both of them being (like Warrington in Lancashire) partnership towns in which development is to be undertaken jointly by a development corporation and the local authorities concerned. The draft basic plan for Ipswich bears the prefatory epitaph: 'In June 1969, after a public local inquiry had been held into objections to a draft designation order, the Minister of Housing and Local Government announced that he had decided not to proceed with the designation of Ipswich under the New Towns Act 1965. The draft basic plan is however now published as a contribution to the literature of town planning.'

In 1962 several firms of planning consultants were instructed by the Ministry of Housing and Local Government to examine and report on the practical and financial implications of expanding certain towns by 50% and 100%. These town development studies were to be part of an examination by the Ministry of the problems connected with overspill population from the south east region. Consultants Leonard G Vincent and Raymond Gorbing were commissioned to carry out such an examination of Ipswich, and to investigate the feasibility of expanding the town to 180,000 and 240,000 making allowance for the natural increase in the current population of 120,000 The consultants reported in *Ipswich: a study in town development* (MOHLG, 1964) that it was technically feasible to expand to either of the population targets, and that expansion to the larger figure would be more economical in terms of cost per unit. A completely new water supply system would be required in the event of any major expansion; it would also be necessary to replan the town centre and to acquire substantial areas for reconstruction. The report contains the results of tests on two schemes for 50% expansion and on two schemes for 100% expansion, one of them concentric and the other linear in form; also tested was a scheme for the development of a linear town incorporating an expanded Felixstowe. Acceptance of these results was indicated by the citing of the town as the site of major expansion in the *South east study* and subsequently the consultants Shankland, Cox and Associates were commissioned to carry out a two-part study: firstly, to consider the implications of absorbing 70,000 overspill population from London by 1981, the designation of an area under the New Towns Act 1965, and the possible development in the rest of the sub-region; secondly, to prepare a draft basic plan for the expansion of the town. The Ipswich sub-region is an area of about 289 square miles falling in the counties of East and West Suffolk, mainly within ten miles of Ipswich itself. 'The area has no sharp geographical boundaries—except the coastline on the east—or distinct economic character. Its unity is derived entirely from the influence of Ipswich as a major shopping and service centre.' In their report

190

Expansion of Ipswich designation proposals: consultants' study of the town in its sub-region (HMSO, 1966), the consultants estimate that the sub-region could accommodate an eventual population of half a million. Major development should be concentrated along a band of communications running south west and north west from Ipswich, with two new settlements at Belstead and Bramford to take the bulk of the Ipswich expansion, together with an extension of the built-up area of Ipswich itself and smaller scale development of other existing towns. A total area of 22,900 acres, including Ipswich county borough, is proposed for designation. Extensive provision of recreational facilities and an improved road system are among other features of the plan. Shankland, Cox and Associates then went on to fulfil the second stage of their commission in *Ipswich draft basic plan: consultants' proposals for the expanded town* (HMSO, 1968). The draft plan is based on the sub-regional strategy contained in the earlier report (and summarised in the present volume, pp 2-3) and is for an expanded town of about 273,000 population. The plan proposes a grid of primary roads, starting in the new districts and extending into the existing town, with the new A45 urban motorway as the spine. The new districts are to have their own shopping and service centres, and the use of public transport from new districts to district centres and the town centre is to be encouraged. A separate report on the economics of expansion was issued as *Expansion of Ipswich: comparative costs, a supplementary report* (HMSO, 1968).

A feasibility study of the expansion of the city of Peterborough was carried out in 1963 for the Ministry of Housing and Local Government by Henry Wells, and reported in *Peterborough: an expansion study* (MOHLG, 1965). Acceptance of Wells' affirmative report was indicated by the *South east study's* proposal to expand, and in 1965 Tom Hancock was commissioned by the Ministry to prepare a report defining a suitable area for designation under the New Towns Act, and, following on this, to prepare a master plan for expansion. In *Expansion of Peterborough: consultant's proposals for designation* (HMSO, 1966) Hancock reports his study of an area including the city of Peterborough and the urban district of Old Fletton, together forming an urban complex with a population at 1965 of 78,000 and, assuming a total population for this complex of 172,000 by 1981, proposes the designation of an area of 15,500 acres including the existing built-up area of Peterborough and land to the west of it taking in several villages, with additional peripheral expansion to the north east and the east of the city. After 1981, expansion would be to the south west. The report proposes the initiation of complementary policies at an early stage in development to cover the sub-region around the designation area. An area of 15,940 acres was subsequently designated in July 1967, and in February 1968 a development corporation was set up to carry out the expansion in partnership with Huntingdon and Peterborough City Council. The consultants, now Hancock and Hawkes, were retained to carry out the second stage of their commission, the preparation of a master plan. *Greater Peterborough: draft basic plan* (HMSO, 1968) became the target for public objections which led to the amendment of the road network; these amendments, together with an exposition of the principles on which development should be carried out, were incorporated into *Draft master plan: interim policy report* (Peterborough, Development Corporation, 1969), and finally into the *Greater Peterborough master plan* (Peterborough, Development Corporation, 1970). A summary booklet and a structure map are available with the main volume. The plan is designed to accommodate a total population of 100,000 by 1985, thereby creating a ' new regional city of high quality '. To achieve this, large and rapid improvements in the existing city structure and its facilities will be necessary.

The expansion of Northampton is closely linked with the creation of the new city of Milton Keynes and the development of the whole sub-region containing these two towns. Expansion was proposed in the *South east study* and affirmed in the subsequent sub-regional feasibility study *Northampton, Bedford and north Bucks study* (see above). Consultants Hugh Wilson and Lewis Womersley were commissioned by the Ministry of Housing and Local Government to study an area including Northampton county borough and its vicinity comprising a rough circle from seven to ten miles in radius entirely within the county of Northamptonshire, with a current population of 121,410; and to recommend the area to be designated for expansion, and the location and form of large-scale development to accommodate an intake of 70,000 population by 1981 in addition to natural increase. *Expansion of Northampton: consultants' proposals for designation* (HMSO, 1966) recommends designation of an area of 23,615 acres including 10,241 acres which form the existing county borough, and including parts of Brixworth, Wellingborough and Northampton rural districts. The form of the growth is to be a linear development to the east and the south of the city. After objections raised at the public inquiry into the designation order, the proposed area for designation was reduced, and finally in February 1968 an area of 19,952 acres was designated and a development corporation set up to carry out the expansion in partnership with the county borough.

Expanding Northampton (Northampton, Development Corporation, 1968) contains the consultants' proposals for expanding the town to an expected population of 300,000 by the end of the century. The linear town will have a primary spine road for public transport running along the middle of the existing and new development, with secondary spines into the new residential areas. The proposals for redevelopment of the central area have the core of the centre circled by a road reserved for buses, within which only essential service traffic would be allowed. Outside the bus ring are short-stay car parks, primary roads to the centre, and, further out, long-stay car parks. The master plan is contained in the two volumes of *Expansion of Northampton: planning proposals* (Northampton, Development Corporation, 1969), the first of which contains the plan and the second, technical appendices. This is a valuable report in respect of its detailed discussion of the methods used in evolving the plan, and of the reports of the specialised surveys which were carried out, such as the social surveys done by the Institute of Community Studies and a special study of the Nene Valley as part of the assessment of land required for recreation.

The remaining plan directly inspired by the *South east study* is that for Ashford in Kent, where a new town was proposed. Consultants Colin Buchanan and Partners were commissioned by the Ministry of Housing and Local Government to recommend an appropriate area for designation under the New Towns Act to take a planned increase in population of 150,000 over the next twenty five years, as overspill from London. Their conclusions, based on a study of an area of ten mile radius around Ashford, are contained

193

in *Ashford study: consultants' proposals for designation* (HMSO, 1967). The consultants point out that one of the problems of a designation study is that it must be sufficiently detailed to be a reliable basis for the choice of site and yet the boundary must be drawn wide enough to allow flexibility in the design of the master plan. The report makes recommendations on the space required for various land uses, based on a low-density development with the motor vehicle as the main form of transport. Possible urban structures are examined, though not in great detail, a square form emerging as the favoured one. As background to Buchanan's study, Kent County Planning Department produced their own report *Expansion at Ashford: an appraisal of its impact on east Kent* (Maidstone, Kent County Council, 1967). The east Kent sub-region itself is expected to absorb a population increase of between 93,000 and 157,000 by 1981, quite apart from additional increase at Ashford. The county council also intend to promote growth of employment and population at Sheppey, based on its port facilities. In view of major developments such as these within the sub-region, the council produced their sub-regional study so that the creation of a major new city at Ashford could be seen in context. In the event, the Minister decided not to act upon the recommendations of Buchanan's report, and therefore the *Ashford study* is of academic interest only; but it remains a good example of the systematic preparation of a designation study.

The problems of the west midlands were surveyed in *The west midlands: a regional study* by the Department of Economic Affairs (HMSO, 1965), which proposed the overspill of 530,000 people from the Birmingham conurbation between 1964 and 1981 into three major growth areas at Dawley, Worcester, and Stafford/Stoke on Trent. John H D Madin and Partners, together with other consultants in specialised aspects of planning, were commissioned by the Ministry of Housing and Local Government to study the area round the new town of Dawley, taking in the towns of Wellington and Oakengates also, and to prepare a plan for the development of the area to accommodate a planned intake of 100,000 population by 1981 (half of these from the conurbation, the other half planned to move into the new town) which, with natural increase, would expand the population of the area to about 200,000 by 1981. The three named towns are the main centres of a scattered urban complex based on the Coalbrookdale coalfield in east Shropshire (the seat of the industrial revolution, for the world's first iron bridge was cast and erected at Ironbridge over the River Severn) and lying thirty miles west of Birmingham and ten miles from the edge of the conurbation. The consultants in their report *Dawley, Wellington, Oakengates: consultants' proposals for development* (HMSO, 1966) recommend an area for development of approximately 21,700 acres including the new town of Dawley (designated in 1963 with 9,100 acres). Some 4,900 acres are affected by shallow mining or other geological restraints, and therefore some reclamation of affected land is involved. Housing of 100,000 immigrants is considered to be physically feasible, rather more than half to be in Dawley, the rest in Wellington and Oakengates. Establishment of joint planning machinery with authorities in surrounding areas should be considered to regulate the effects of expansion. Urban development should be arranged along the major transportation corridors, with residential areas and employment zones interspersed.

The same consultants were retained to complete the second stage of their commission, to prepare a basic plan for the enlarged new town, whose area of 19,243 acres was formally designated in October 1968, and whose name by this time had been changed to Telford. The terms of reference were to provide a flexible plan to accommodate a population of about 220,000 by the mid or late 1980's; the consultants have taken 1988 as the end of the intake period and projections have been made on this basis. The overall plan was to incorporate a plan for an urban transport system covering the whole area. The *Telford development proposals* (Birmingham, John Madin Design Group, 1969, two volumes) is not a master plan but a basis for detailed consultation and for public participation. The objective at this stage was the preparation of a draft structure plan: ' our aim is not to produce detailed and fixed land use allocations, but to examine and recommend goals, policies and standards and to establish the broad structure of a new city. The structure plan will form the basis for more precise and detailed local plans. However, it is recognised that the structure plan will require constant revision and adaptation as circumstances and requirements change.' The plan is based on an extendible primary grid with a

195

distribution of attraction and generation uses to obtain a balanced and economic transport system. A major element of this structure is an extendible central band containing centralised activities following the major east/west transport axis. The road pattern is based on a hierarchy of primary, district and local distributors with local access roads to individual properties. A three-tier commercial and retail structure is proposed, with a main centre, district centres, and local centres. Residential planning is based on local clusters of between two hundred and four hundred dwellings, a community unit of 8,000 people, and the district of 24,000 to 30,000 people, with shared education and recreation facilities mainly at district level. The first volume of the plan contains the results of studies and the reasoning which have led to the development of policies; the second volume contains technical details of the studies and projections involved, the models and methods used, and additional technical information to further understanding of the component elements.

The other new town designated in April 1964 to take overspill from the Birmingham conurbation is Redditch in Worcestershire. The designated area of nearly 7,200 acres based on the existing town of Redditch lies fourteen miles south of Birmingham in a rural area on the border between Worcestershire and Warwickshire, and is only one of several growth areas in a broad band south of the projected Birmingham green belt. Consultants Hugh Wilson and Lewis Womersley were engaged to plan for an increase in population from the existing 29,000 to about 70,000 over fifteen years, the new town to be self-contained with employment to match population, and able to accommodate an eventual population of about 90,000 by the end of the century. Redditch, the consultants point out in their report *Redditch new town: report on planning proposals* (Redditch, Development Corporation, 1966) is really the forerunner of a series of expanded towns ' and many new and difficult problems arise which are not present when towns are planned on more or less clear sites. It will be necessary to achieve a considerable measure of integration between the old and the new; the introduction of the new town concept must not result in two competing towns on the site with all the complications of differing standards and problems of assimilation of the incoming population.' The proposals con-

196

tained in the plan are in effect a development of the consultants' concepts stated in their *Northampton, Bedford and north Bucks study:* a cellular approach to urban structure, the plan form being a series of districts on a public transport route—like beads strung on a necklace. For Redditch this concept has been interpreted as four linear urban areas radiating from the town centre with additional public transport cross links between them. This open ended form allows for further growth. Industrial areas are dispersed so far as site conditions allow; though the new industrial areas are small units and are located with residential areas within the basic district. An open ended plan form of this nature allows for further growth as and when necessary. The plan makes no provision for a town centre: this omission is rectified by a small booklet *Redditch town centre* (Redditch, Development Corporation, 1968) published for public discussion, with plans and drawings and a minimum of text. The proposals are to increase the town centre's 120,000 square feet of retail floor space to 500,000 by 1981, with a system of link roads giving access to the centre from the primary road system incorporating a central area ring road.

The problems of the south east Lancashire/north east Cheshire (SELNEC) conurbation were apparent before they were formally identified by the North West Economic Planning Council. In particular, the problems of overcrowding were acute in Liverpool and Merseyside, and in October 1961 an area of 4,029 acres was designated at Skelmersdale in Lancashire to assist in the relief of overcrowding on north Merseyside, the principal exporting authority being Liverpool itself. This was the first new town to be designated in England after a gap of eleven years (the previous one being Corby, designated in 1950). Its designer was Sir Hugh Wilson, also the designer of Cumbernauld in Scotland (see below), designated in 1955; and the approach to urban structure in Skelmersdale is closely related to that adopted in Cumbernauld and in its closer contemporary (and abortive) project at Hook in Hampshire (see above). Wilson's proposals for the new town are embodied in his *Interim report on planning proposals* and *Skelmersdale new town planning proposals: report on basic plan* (Skelmersdale, Development Corporation, 1963 and 1964 respectively). The basic plan is in two volumes, the second containing maps and plans. Wilson used

197

in this report the term 'basic' plan instead of 'master' plan; the two are more or less equivalent, but 'basic' implies more flexibility. The designated area is situated between Ormskirk Plain and the western edge of the south Lancashire coalfield, and shares a boundary in the south with that of the proposed North Merseyside Green Belt. The town of Wigan lies six miles to the east, Liverpool is twelve miles to the south west; and the new town is less than two miles east of the M6 motorway to which it is being directly linked. A compact development is proposed, with fairly high density housing development linked to the town centre by a system of footpaths: a high proportion of the residents will be able to walk to the town centre, where all service facilities will be concentrated. The pedestrian system of footpaths is separate from the network of main roads and distributor roads. Unrestricted use of the private car is envisaged, but a rapid public transport system is also incorporated in the plan. The old towns of Up Holland and Skelmersdale will be redeveloped and integrated into the new development. Industrial areas are dispersed.

Further relief for Liverpool was planned with the designation in April 1964 of the new town of Runcorn in Cheshire, an area of nearly 7,250 acres on the south bank of the Mersey and itself lying on the outer fringe of the Merseyside conurbation. Professor Arthur Ling was engaged to prepare a plan for the new town to accommodate an eventual population of 90,000. His *Runcorn new town master plan* (Runcorn, Development Corporation, 1967) in fact caters for possible expansion to 100,000 by the year 2000. The plan is for a linear development, the spine formed by a public transport route in the form of a figure eight with the town centre at its central point, with residential development in the form of neighbourhood communities of about 8,000 population with shops and other services. Open space, parks and recreational land flank the residential areas. Communities are planned so that everyone is within five minutes walking distance of local social and shopping centres, where rapid transit stops are located. A balance between private and public transport is the aim: full use of the private car is not allowed for. The renewal of existing Runcorn is an integral part of the development, which disperses industry to the outer areas. This is a closed development, because the consultants do not consider that further

198

physical growth will be desirable in view of the high landscape value of the surrounding countryside.

The first new town designated to relieve overcrowding in the Manchester conurbation was Warrington in Lancashire, as proposed in *The north west: a regional study* (HMSO, 1965). The Austin-Smith/Salmon/Lord partnership was commissioned by the Ministry of Housing and Local Government to recommend an area for designation under the New Towns Act 1965 and to determine the regional effects of developing Warrington and Risley under an integrated plan. Both towns lie in the urbanised belt midway between Manchester and Liverpool. The proposals are contained in *Expansion of Warrington: consultants' proposals for designation* (HMSO, 1966). A designated area of 22,340 acres is proposed to allow for an expansion in population to 205,000 by 1991 (the population at 1965 was 126,800) the major part of the increase to be accommodated by development of large tracts of derelict land to the north of Warrington, with a small development to the south east in Cheshire. An important element in the strategy is the rehabilitation of many obsolete areas and the improvement of the environment generally. Subsequently, a formal designation order was made in April 1968 for an area of 18,650 acres; and in the same year the development was proposed as a regional growth point in the North West Economic Planning Council's *The north west of the 1970's: strategy II* (HMSO, 1968). Substantial revision to the strategy has not been necessary in the light of this reduction in area, and the consultants went on to prepare a master plan for the town which is presented in *Warrington new town: consultants' proposals for the draft master plan* (Warrington, Development Corporation, 1969). This is not so much a detailed physical plan as a flexible framework within which decisions will be taken in accordance with specific long term goals. Five development areas are proposed, ranging in size from Risley at 22,000 population to Warrington at 75,000, their physical limits defined by a 'continuous web of open space', and three of the five integrated with existing suburban development. The transportation system is based on three primary distributors linking with national and regional motorways on the edge of the town, with district distributors and local distributor roads to access roads. A linear park system is projected along the waterways in the new town area. The consultants have also prepared, at the request of the county borough council (with whom they are to cooperate in the work of rehabilitation and improvement) schemes for a new housing area of 7,500 people—*An action area plan: Padgate*—for central area redevelopment—*Primary core area proposals*—and for a renewal exercise—*Whitecross renewal proposals*—all published in 1969 by the county borough council.

In north west England, a major new town expansion is planned in the north east Lancashire sub-region, based on the existing towns of Preston, Leyland and Chorley. The expansion of population in Leyland and Chorley was originally proposed in the county development plan and in other county reports. In 1965 a government policy statement on the housing problems of the north west region put forward a similar proposal, but added to the functions of the new town that of reception of overspill from Manchester, and also of contributing to the industrial revival of the whole region and forming a focus for urban renewal. In 1966, the Ministry of Housing and Local Government asked consultants Robert Matthew, Johnson-Marshall and Partners to test the feasibility of a new town and to make proposals for the area to be designated under the New Towns Act. The study area was defined as a broad band of land taking in Preston, Leyland, Chorley and several smaller settlements, whose limits were defined by the agricultural belts on the north and west, the hills and moors on the east, and the Wigan coalfield in the south. The consultants' proposals are contained in *Central Lancashire: study for a city—consultants' proposals for designation* (HMSO, 1967). In July 1967, the Ministry requested the consultants to carry out further study to determine the effects of the new town development on north east Lancashire as a whole, and the results of this further exercise are reported in *Central Lancashire new town proposal: impact on north east Lancashire* (HMSO, 1968). The north east Lancashire sub-region contains twenty two local authorities in the Blackburn, Burnley and Rossendale areas, covers some 269 square miles and had in 1966 a total population of 472,770. The report considers the present condition of the study area and its future if a new town is *not* established. It then summarises the new town proposal, and estimates what the region's future will be with it. Appendices to the report contain data and information gathered for the study, and describe the method of approach to the project as a whole and to specific aspects of it such as migration. The report, as a commentator pointed out in *JTPI* 54(10) December 1968 491, ' is essential reading for anyone who claims an interest in the large scale issues of urban and regional planning. It is a useful reference on a whole range of techniques—social and industrial questionnaires; the Lakshmanan and Hansen retail potential model; the application of gravity model techniques to both journey to work and migration.' Subsequently an area of 41,045 acres was designated in March 1969, and a public inquiry was held in May 1969 as a result of which the proposed area was reduced quite substantially. Early in 1971, the Secretary of State for the Environment announced that the new town was to go ahead.

The problems of the north east region of England are quite different from those of the north west region, being associated with the rundown of major industries and migration of population. The White Paper *The north east: a programme for regional development and growth* (HMSO, 1963, Cmnd 2206) stimulated two major development plans, those for Washington new town in County Durham, and for the Teesside conurbation. In its plan for stimulating the growth and economy of the region, the White Paper included a specific proposal for a new town at Washington, and another for a comprehensive survey and plan of Teesside. The strategy was supported by the Northern Economic Planning Council report *Challenge of the changing north* (HMSO, 1966).

Washington new town was designated in July 1964, an area of 5,300 acres occupying most of the urban district of Washington and parts of Houghton-le-Spring and Chester-le-Street rural districts and lying between the large urban areas of Tyneside and Wearside, with an existing population of 20,000. In February 1965, the firm of Llewelyn-Davies Weeks and Partners were appointed consultants to survey the area and to prepare a master plan and report for the development corporation. In September 1965 an interim plan and report was submitted—*Washington new town: report of survey and interim proposals* (Llewelyn-Davies Weeks and Partners, 1965)—containing most of the survey material in complete and final form, and setting out the general principles on which the master plan would be based, together with interim proposals regarding the way in which these principles could be applied in detail. The target population of 80,000 was to be achieved by the end of the century, with between 60,000 and 65,000 accommodated by 1981. *The Washington new town master plan and report* (Washington, Development Corporation, 1966) comprises ' a physical plan for the new town, supplemented by a proposed set of principles which may be used to govern the development of the town in practice '. There are two main components in the physical plan: the transportation network and the land use plan, which are closely interconnected. The primary transportation network is a grid of roads at approximately one mile spacing, with a secondary network connecting the main shopping centre, local centres and village centres, and a pedestrian network planned on a half mile grid. The basic residential unit will be a village of 1,350 to 1,400 dwellings and a population of around 4,500, planned around a centre. The main shopping centre will have a wide range of services and facilities. Six industrial estates are projected, all connected to the A1 road and the freightliner rail service terminal at Follingsby.

The survey of Teesside was commissioned from two firms of consultants, Hugh Wilson and Lewis Womersley, and the engineering firm of Scott Wilson Kirkpatrick and Partners, by the Ministries of Transport and of Housing and Local Government. The study area was defined as 360 square miles at the mouth of the River Tees, its population in 1966 being 479,000, its economy dominated by heavy industry. ' In geographical location, physical appearance, social relationships and economy, Teesside is set apart from the rest of north east England.' The Economic Planning Council's report (see above) laid great stress on the need for technological change in the area, and on the urgent need for a new technological university. The council's policy was for Teesside to increase its population both absolutely and in relation to other sub-regions, rising to about 726,500 in 1981. To meet the needs of such expansion, official policy recognised the need for modernisation of the sub-regional infrastructure and for attraction to the area of employment sufficient to meet the needs of the increased population. The consultants were requested, in the light of this policy, to prepare a unitary plan showing the disposition of the main land uses and transport requirements, the general planning proposals to be based on the principles of the Buchanan Report, and the transport survey to cover road planning and the transport system generally. They were further required to estimate the cost and feasibility of implementation, and the time scale involved. The first volume of the *Teesside survey and plan: final report to the Steering Committee* (HMSO, 1969) contains the policies and proposals (the second volume will contain technical reports on the methods employed, and results of the surveys, analyses and forecasts). The proposals are based on extensive survey and analysis within the area and 'pragmatic testing of the alternative opportunities for its future urban structure'. The main policy objectives are for diversification of the employment structure and the creation of 60,000 new jobs mainly in light manufacturing industry which will have to be attracted to the area; conservation of existing natural resources such as the use of the river for navigation; proper development of the surrounding countryside, with four country parks proposed; further urban development to be located close to the existing built up area and not in a new town, though jobs should be dispersed among a number of centres; development of four areas of both residential and light industrial growth plus one area of light industrial growth only. The transportation system is to provide for a high level of car ownership and for a heavy use of private cars for trips. A new high capacity primary road network is planned carrying most of the Teesside traffic with existing roads operating as a secondary system for local access and distribution; public transport will be mainly bus operated. The quality of the environment is to be improved by redevelopment and the rehabilitation of old housing, by the elevation of Middlesbrough central area to regional status with improved service facilities, by attention to landscaping throughout, and by the reclamation of derelict land. The Teesside plan has particular significance because it is the first comprehensive land use and transportation study of an English conurbation, initiated as a direct result of the recommendations of the Buchanan Report *Traffic in towns* (see chapter 11, section on traffic and transport).

It has been mentioned at the beginning of the chapter that, with the exception of those plans which have proved over the course of the years to be truly seminal, 1960 was the starting point for inclusion in this survey. This of course excludes a number of new towns which were designated, planned and built soon after the end of World War II: these are Stevenage (designated November 1946), Crawley (January 1947), Hemel Hempstead (February 1947), Harlow (March 1947), Newton Aycliffe (April 1947), Peterlee (March 1948), Hatfield (May 1948), Welwyn Garden City (May 1948), Basildon (January 1949), Bracknell (June 1949), and Corby (April 1950). Many of the original master plans for these towns have been revised, some more than once, to accommodate populations which have increased beyond their envisaged limits or to adapt to changing functions. In some cases, the revised master plans have not involved anything much more than modifications and additions to the original concept; but in others, major revisions have been necessary and studies have been carried out on which to base the new plans.

One such study was carried out by a study group in the School of Social Studies of the University of Sussex for West Sussex County Council and is reported in *Crawley expansion study* (Chichester, West Sussex County Council, 1969). The original target population of Crawley was 60,000 ; projections made by the study group indicate that by 1991 it will have reached between 118,000 and 218,000. The present study concentrates on identifying the growth pressures on the town and on methods of coping with them. The town centre, it is estimated, could just accommodate the lower population figure, but above that, it would have to be expanded or surrounding centres expanded in conjunction with it. The present allocation of land for housing will not be sufficient: the second half of the study is devoted to the selection and evaluation of sites for an extra 14,000 dwellings, the selection process being done by sieve map and the evaluation being mainly in terms of site features. A variety of projection methods are used for forecasting variables such as population and employment.

Basildon is another town whose population has increased far beyond the original target of 50,000. The target was increased in 1960 to 106,000, and subsequently to 133,000. In 1965 the development corporation produced its *Basildon master plan for 140,000 population*. A feature of the new plan is that the expanded town has been studied in its regional context and the plan takes into account its effect on the surrounding area. The purpose of the plan is to set out methods of achieving the new target population and to draw up plans for coping with the resultant expansion in terms of land, traffic, employment, and recreation. It proposes to gain land for building by absorbing areas within the town which were originally to have been restored to farmland, a process which has not proved viable. Some decentralisation from the town centre is proposed, together with the rerouting of through traffic and a revised internal road network; on a regional basis, the planning of employment and recreation is projected as part of the surrounding sub-region rather than for the town in isolation, and the town centre is to be extended to serve as a regional centre. Also published by the development corporation is a second volume by Carole Bryan entitled *Basildon: shopping, work for women, leisure* (1967) which contains the results of surveys of these three factors carried out in three residential districts of the town.

The first new town, Stevenage, has also been subjected to a revised population target, from the original of 60,000 to a later figure of 105,000. Following *The expansion of Stevenage: a technical appraisal* (Stevenage, Development Corporation, 1963) an increase to 150,000 population was suggested; but this plan was rejected by the Minister of Housing and Local Government, who nevertheless accepted a revised figure of 105,000. The *Stevenage master plan 1966* was subsequently produced (Development Corporation, 1966) in accordance with the lower figure. The first volume contains the planning proposals by Leonard G Vincent, the town's chief architect, and there are also three further volumes containing the results of traffic studies. Two new neighbourhoods are projected to accommodate extra population, and the town centre is to be doubled in size to incorporate an ambitious range of facilities. The report is of interest primarily for its assessment of the successes and failures of the original master plan.

The new town of Corby in Northamptonshire was built to serve the steelworks of Stewarts and Lloyds Ltd. Expansion of the steelworks has meant expansion of population and therefore expansion of the town itself, whose designated area has been increased by 1,602 acres to accommodate a population which is anticipated to reach about 75,000 by 1999. John Madin and Partners were commissioned by the development corporation to prepare a second master plan for the increased area of the town, including necessary modifi-

205

cations to the original plan; also to make a detailed study of the town centre and to recommend ways of extending it to meet increased demands, and to make two detailed local studies. Corby and its steelworks are interdependent—over half of the occupied population of the town work in steel or in immediately associated industries: the new plan proposes to diversify industry so that the proportion is reduced to about one third, and to introduce new industry and service facilities to achieve this. The plan has to surmount various obstacles: development of the original designated area is now almost complete, and further development is hindered by quarrying within the extended area and also by the desirability of retaining the area of Great Oakley as one of amenity and natural beauty. Such obstacles will impede the achievement of a housing rate sufficient to meet needs by limiting the amount of land presently available for housing development. The plan is based on the principle of residential areas linked to each other by a chain of walkways, or town greenways, 'which will take full advantage of existing woodland features'. There is a phased plan for extension of the town centre to provide services and facilities and car parking for people from the town and its hinterland.

One of the major deficiencies in British planning pointed up by the regional studies produced by the Department of Economic Affairs and the regional economic planning councils was the lack of a series of comprehensive studies of the sub-regions of which the major regions were composed. Such a series would provide the detailed knowledge of local issues which would be vital to long-term regional planning. The impetus for a series of sub-regional studies came from Richard Crossman, when Minister of Housing and Local Government. He believed that city regions (defined as towns and their immediate hinterlands) based on towns such as Plymouth, Coventry, and Leicester, had problems of a type similar to those of the major conurbations, if not of similar magnitude, and that cooperative planning ventures between such towns and their surrounding authorities could and should begin in advance of local government reorganisation and its concomitant alterations of boundaries. Crossman's 'initial aim was to persuade the authorities in a small number of selected areas to come together and set up *ad hoc* teams to prepare long-term " broad brush " plans for land uses and transportation. These were to be called " sub-regional planning studies ".[10] A lead had already been given to such cooperative ventures by the Bedfordshire authorities; no formal published development plan has been produced as a result of this cooperation, though several articles by Eric L Cripps have appeared in the professional press (see within chapter 11) mainly concerned with the application of a systemic approach to sub-regional planning and the various techniques associated with this. The first ' Crossman-type ' study to be set up was that by Leicester City Council and its county authority: the study team was formed late in 1966 and the project began in January 1967. It is reported in *Leicester and Leicestershire sub-regional planning study* (Leicester, City and County Councils, 1969, two volumes). It was followed in early 1968 by a study sponsored by the city councils of Nottingham and Derby together with the respective counties, which is reported in *Nottinghamshire and Derbyshire sub-regional study* (West Bridgford, Nottinghamshire County Council, 1969). Later in 1968, Coventry, Solihull, and Warwickshire joined forces in a similar venture; no full report has been published of this study (at the time of writing) but a very useful internal memorandum has been published describing the data file which has been built up in the course of the study, including the procedures and problems involved, as *Data for sub-regional planning* (Coventry, Coventry Solihull and Warwickshire Sub-regional Planning Study, 1970, Memo 32). The studies so far set up have similar terms of reference, all of them having been based on a model produced by the Ministry of Housing and Local Government.

The Leicester study has been carried out by a team under the direction of J Brian McLoughlin, and the exercise, and therefore its report, is of particular interest for its application of the systems approach to sub-regional planning (McLoughlin's book *Urban and regional planning: a systems approach* is discussed in chapter 11) in which field it is a pioneer. The sub-region for this study is roughly the same as the geographical county of Leicestershire. The main objective of the study ' is to take a broad strategic look at an area which is roughly the geographical county *as one composite unit,* and in accordance with specified terms of reference to recommend an overall land-use and transportation framework for the future which is consistent with regional considerations and within which the respective local planning authorities can develop and extend their planning policies for the common good'. The detailed terms of reference are set out in the second chapter, together with a discussion of the way in which these terms were interpreted and the basic techniques developed. The first volume contains the report of the study and the recommendations resulting from it. The national and regional contexts are established, and then the sub-region is examined in detail through the results of surveys of population, employment, housing, traffic and transport, shopping centres, and personal spending power. Using existing and purpose-collected data, the development of the sub-region was simulated and six alternative patterns of growth from 1971 to 1981 produced and tested; as a result of the tests, four were selected for simulation to 1991, and evaluated. Finally, a recommended strategy was selected incorporating three main elements: concentration of the expected sub-regional growth in and around Greater Leicester, but in suburban rather than central locations; the building up of new forms of employment in the northwestern parts of the sub-region to rejuvenate the local economies; and the progressive development of two ' growth corridors ' outwards from Leicester, one to the north west and one to the south west, with emphasis on the former. The second volume of the report contains very detailed discussion of the technical methods used, the reasoning behind them, and the significance of the results. The whole report is very well laid out and extremely clearly written.

The Notts/Derbys Sub-regional Planning Unit, under the direction of Andrew Thorburn, has studied an area comprising the county boroughs of Derby and Nottingham, the whole county of Nottinghamshire and those parts of Derbyshire lying east and south of the Peak District National Park. Like the Leicester study, it is of interest for the methodologies employed: some details of these are contained in appendices to the main report, but full details are available only on application to the unit. The objectives of the study were to examine the needs and the potential for development of the sub-region, to define proposals for the location of major land uses including population, industry and employment, shopping, and recreation, and to consider the relationships between these components and transport. The first part of the report discusses ' eco-

facing p 208

No in air-photo key	Code in derelict land key	Brief description of derelict item	Photo used as example
1r	A1ia	ridge tip	10/49
1f	A1ia	low flat tip	10/46
1c	A1ia	conical coal tip	9/193
2	A1ib	coal dump	10/46; 10/49
3	A1if	degraded land above ground level associated with coal mining	10/49
4	A1ig	degraded land above ground level peripheral to a coal mine	9/185
5	A1ij	coal sludge above ground level	10/44
6	A2ia	a tip of domestic refuse	9/193
7	B1ic	open cast coal workings	9/185
8	B1ih	open cast coal workings not yet ' excavations '	10/49
9	B1iic	a dry brick clay quarry	10/44
10	B1iid	a wet brick clay quarry	10/44
11	B1viic	a dry sand and gravel excavation	9/193
12	B1viid	a wet sand and gravel excavation	9/193
13	B1viie	degraded land below ground level, resulting from sand and gravel workings, but partially restored	9/193
14	B1viih	sand and gravel workings not yet ' pits '	10/46
15	C1ib	coal dump site at ground level	10/49
16	C1ie	degraded land at ground level, resulting from coal workings	9/185
17	C1if	degraded land at ground level, associated with coal mining	9/185; 10/49
18	C1ig	degraded land at ground level, peripheral to a coal mine	9/193
19	C1ij	coal sludge at ground level	10/49
20	C1viif	degraded land at ground level, associated with sand and gravel workings	9/193
21	C1viij	sand and gravel sludge at ground level	9/193
22	C3if	degraded land at ground level, associated with a brick works	10/44
23	C3vj	power station waste at ground level	9/195
23a	B1i/3v	power station waste used to fill a coal excavation	9/185
23b	B1vii/3v	power station waste used to fill a sand and gravel excavation	9/193
24	C3vij	sewage sludge at ground level	10/49
25	C4iiie	railway dereliction at ground level	9/193
26	D3i	a disused brickworks	10/49
27	I1i	a coal mine	10/49
28	I1vii	a sand and gravel works	9/193
29	I3i	a brickworks	10/44
30	I3v	a power station	9/195
31	I3vi	a sewage works	10/49

FIGURE 7: Air photo key to figure 8, opposite.

FIGURE 8: Annotated aerial photograph of area of derelict land. Courtesy of Meridian Airmaps Limited.

FIGURE 9: Urban land use: industrial area of Leeds.

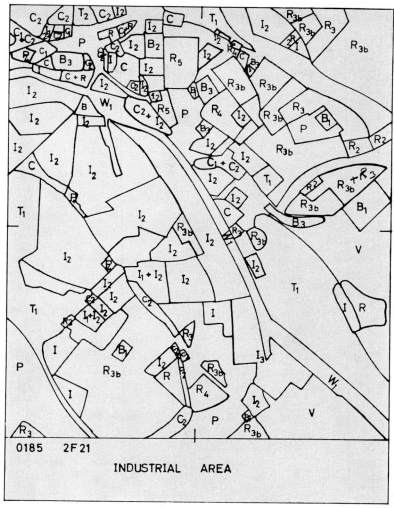

FIGURE 10: Trace overlay for aerial photograph in figure 9, opposite.

FIGURE 11: Aerial photograph showing enumeration districts in Leeds, as in figure 12, opposite. Courtesy of Meridian Airmaps Limited.

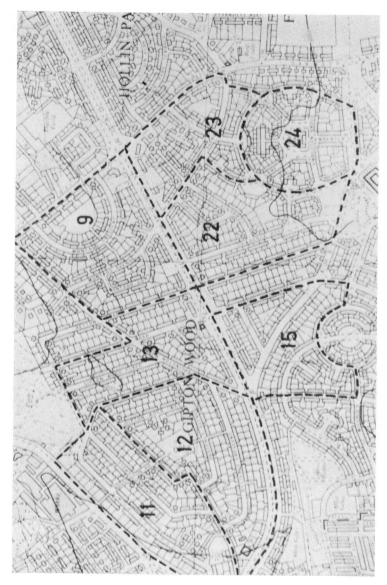

FIGURE 12: Enumeration district map (1961 census) of part of Leeds, based upon the Ordnance Survey map with the sanction of the Controller of HM Stationery Office, Crown copyright reserved.

FIGURE 13: Oblique aerial photograph: Edinburgh new town. Courtesy of John Dewar Studios, Edinburgh.

nomic potential and social needs', the second part deals with 'environment and physical potential' and the third contains the recommended strategy. The main element of this strategy is the development of a major growth zone stretching from Mansfield to Alfreton, with a population of at least 260,000 in 1986 and perhaps 300,000 by 2000. Nottingham is to be expanded as a regional capital and office centre, while Derby is to become a major centre of industrial technology and services (presumably the model failed to forecast the demise of a large part of the town's industry). Three regional parks are designated for outdoor recreation purposes, and a major programme of environmental improvement is proposed in the Erewash valley including reclamation of derelict land and rehabilitation of town fabric. Further proposals are included for additional growth points, the transport infrastructure, and countryside planning. The report also recommends the institution of new administrative agencies to implement and monitor the major development proposals over a long period. Compared with the report of the Leicester study, the report of this later exercise is not easy to understand, principally because of its presentation: the results of the studies are divided into several sections, each one dealing with the same subject matter from a different angle, and at a different degree of depth.

More recently, Gloucester county and city planning departments have collaborated on a sub-regional study of the northern part of their county, following the model of the Leicester and Leicestershire study, and the report of this is available as *North Gloucestershire sub-regional study* (Gloucester, County Planning Department, 1970). The sub-region, which includes the towns of Gloucester, Cheltenham, and Stroud, is one of industrial expansion and increasing population, and a continuing trend in this direction is assumed. After a consideration of the various factors at work in the area, such as transportation, agricultural quality land, mineral deposits, and landscape value, the study results favour limited development between Cheltenham and Gloucester, with development at Eastington to draw industry westwards from the Stroud area, within the framework of a preferred strategy projected up to the end of the century.

A different type of sub-regional study is reported by Nottingham-shire County Planning Department in the *Trent Valley study* (West Bridgford, 1970). The study examined the existing and future resources and potential of the River Trent and its valley and associated towns and villages. The premise is that the basic agricultural economy of the valley will remain and should be conserved. The report also discusses the many other competing demands on the valley resources, such as water cooling, transport, drainage, leisure and recreation. The report formulates a strategy to conserve and improve the valley environment, with provision for both basic functions and emerging public demands.

Following a national review of population trends and settlement patterns made in 1966, the government of the day decided that new areas suitable for large-scale development ought to be examined in an effort to formulate a long-term national strategy for the location of population. Three feasibility studies were therefore planned, of the Humberside, Severnside, and Tayside regions; the first and the third of these have (at the time of writing) reported.

The first study to be initiated, that of Humberside, was the first major work of the Central Unit for Environmental Planning, a research team set up in July 1966 within the Department of Economic Affairs, and staffed from that department, drawing also on the staffs of the Board of Trade, the Ministry of Housing and Local Government, the Ministry of Transport, and the Department of Employment and Productivity. For the exercise, a Physical Planning Unit was set up at Barton on Humber, made up of staff seconded from the local planning authorities within the area, to assist the CUEP. The area studied was north and south Humberside, forming a part of the Yorkshire and Humberside economic planning region. Precise boundaries were not defined for the purpose of the study: the area extends about fifty miles from east to west, and about forty miles north to south. Its essential elements are the three main towns of Hull-Haltemprice, Grimsby-Cleethorpes, and Scunthorpe, and the areas centring on them. The terms of reference were to make a detailed economic and physical study of the area and to assess the feasibility of a large influx of population into it. The results are embodied in *Humberside: a feasibility study* (HMSO, 1969). The study assesses the probable development of the area up to 1981 to find out the physical and economic base it would provide for major expansion. The effects of a major expansion are then examined in the light of the area's ability to cope with them; costs and administrative aspects of such development are also considered. The main recommendations are that major growth should not take place before 1980, and that a decision on whether or not it should take place at all ought to be delayed until 1972. Nevertheless, the area should in the meantime be prepared for the possibility of major development by improvements in roads, an increase in the rate of replacement of sub-standard housing, a Humber bridge to be in use by 1976, and the ' maintenance of economic growth prospects '. The study, like so many others, is published without government commitment, ' in order to give the local planning authorities, as well as the regional economic planning councils concerned, the opportunity to express their views and to encourage public participation in the process of planning '.

WALES

Wales is a region unified by its culture and its history rather than by its economic coherence. In the latter respect, the south is more a part of the Severnside sub-region than of its own country, while north Wales looks to Merseyside. The country as a whole suffers from depopulation and the decline of its basic industries of coal and steel.

Modern planning in Wales rests on the foundation of an economic survey and plan prepared by the Welsh Office and published as *Wales: the way ahead* (HMSO, 1967, Cmnd 3334). This is a study which, like its Scottish counterpart (see below), implies some degree of central government commitment since the work was carried out by a team from the Welsh Office and since the Secretary of State is the chairman of the Economic Planning Council which, along with the other regional councils, were the initiators of the regional studies. The White Paper forecasts extensive unemployment if present policies are pursued. Further efforts to attract new industry are urged, by the building of eight advance factories. Growth points are identified in the south east sub-region, where office development is to be dispersed from congested areas, and in the north east,

211

where a barrage across the Dee estuary is under consideration to improve communications with Merseyside (see below). Major urban growth is projected for Llantrisant, in conjunction with the establishment there of the Royal Mint, and at Newtown in mid-Wales under the New Towns Act. Development at the latter site was also recommended in an earlier study of *Depopulation in mid-Wales* (HMSO, 1964) which was the report of a committee set up in agreement with the Minister of Housing and Local Government and the Minister for Welsh Affairs.

Wales already had one new town before the White Paper proposed two more. Cwmbran in Monmouthshire was designated in November 1949, with an area of 3,157 acres, its current population of 12,000 being planned to expand to 35,000, and its function being to serve industry in the East Monmouth Valley. The *Master plan* was produced by consultants Minoprio, Spenceley and Macfarlane (Cwmbran, Development Corporation, 1951) and was in the then traditional form of a town centre surrounded by neighbourhood units each with its own local facilities and small shopping centre. Industry was already in the valley, but the plan made provision for accommodating more. In 1962 the planned population was increased to 55,000, and the master plan was revised in the light of this.

Proposals for a new town in mid-Wales were made by consultants Economic Associates Ltd in *A new town in mid-Wales: consultants' proposals* (HMSO, 1966) to the Secretary of State for Wales. Its starting point was the study *Depopulation in mid-Wales* (1964) reinforced by *The west midlands: a regional study* by the Department of Economic Affairs (HMSO, 1965), from which latter study the data were used, although different conclusions were reached on the basis of them. The area studied was that of the middle sub-region of Wales comprising the counties of Cardigan, Merioneth, Montgomery, Radnor, and parts of Brecon. The objective set before the consultants was to examine possible locations and alternative forms of development of ' an economically viable urban centre in mid-Wales which, by making available new opportunities for employment, and by offering up-to-date shopping services and cultural and other facilities, including facilities for tourists, will arrest and possibly reverse the depopulation of the area and strengthen its economy ', and to investigate the capability of the region to support it.

212

The consultants consider that if mid-Wales is considered in association with the west midlands region and its overspill problem, then
the case for major development in the former is strong. The viability of the new town, therefore, would depend on its being
primarily an overspill outlet, and only secondarily a solution to the
Welsh problem. Assuming this context, the consultants propose a
linear town fourteen miles long centred on Caersws, to accommodate a target population of 70,000 over a period of twenty years,
combining traditional manufacturing functions with resort and recreational facilities, and acting as a service centre for the greater
part of mid-Wales. Development of the town should be closely
associated with the opening up of the Plynlimon area immediately
to the west as a new national park. The report is not in fact a
master plan for such a development, but rather constitutes the
results of an exercise amounting to a new economic survey of mid-
Wales, taking into account the likely impact on the sub-region of
the growth of the west midlands. The proposals have not been fully
implemented: considerable opposition was aroused to the conception of an overspill town for the west midlands. However, a Mid-
Wales Development Corporation was appointed in 1967 to carry
through a first stage of the proposal, the doubling in size of the old
town of Newtown to a planned population of 11,000, and an area
of 1,497 acres was designated in December 1967 for this purpose.
Draft planning proposals (Newtown, Development Corporation,
1968) and *Amendments to draft planning proposals* (Newtown,
Development Corporation, 1969) have been prepared with the object
of providing 2,300 jobs by 1977. In the light of the success or otherwise of this venture, the wider proposals of Economic Associates
Ltd will be reconsidered; the corporation will also be available to
undertake other development projects in the area, should the need
arise.

The as yet undesignated development at Llantrisant in Glamorgan has been planned in conjunction with a government decision to
move the Royal Mint to the area. *Glamorgan: a planning study*
(Cardiff, Glamorgan County Council, 1964) recommended the establishment of a new town at Llantrisant to accommodate a population
of over 100,000: further details were put forward in *Feasibility
study for a new town* (Cardiff, Glamorgan cc, 1967). In 1966 Gordon

213

Cullen was appointed townscape consultant to prepare a plan for conserving the old town of Llantrisant, which would be submerged if development took place; his report *Llantrisant: a Welsh hill town* is discussed in chapter 11 under the section heading ' Environment '. The full report by Colin Buchanan and Partners is contained in *Llantrisant: prospects for urban growth* (Buchanan and Partners, 1969, two vols).

In the north east of the country, the Dee river estuary has been the focus of planning attention. Interest in estuary development and the possibility of a crossing was expressed as early as the 1950's by the local authorities concerned, the counties of Cheshire and Flintshire. In 1965 a Dee Crossing Steering Committee and Technical Working Party were formed, and phase one of a feasibility study started in June 1966 under an agreement with the then Ministry of Land and Natural Resources, which financed the work jointly with the two county councils and the river authority. The first phase was a study of the engineering aspects, and for this a firm of consulting engineers, Binnie and Partners, were commissioned. Their terms of reference were to carry out an appraisal of the practicability of the crossing from the engineering and hydrographical aspects, the form a crossing should take, and its probable optimum siting, taking into account such factors as land reclamation, communications, land use and traffic flows on each side of the estuary. The resultant report *Dee crossing study, phase one: a report to the technical working party* (HMSO, 1967)—and by this time the Ministry of Housing and Local Government had absorbed the Ministry of Land and Natural Resources—embodies the main conclusion that a middle to inner zone, staged multi-purpose scheme would be the most satisfactory and viable development of the estuary, and the recommendation that the second phase of the study should proceed accordingly. The engineers propose that the best form of water conservation would be pumped-storage reservoirs rather than a true barrage retaining a gravity fed lake. Reclaimed land could be confined to marginal areas, although there would be some flexibility as to its extent and location. The engineering studies are continuing, with the aim of producing the best scheme for the estuary development, with proposals for its staged implementation. The second phase of the study has been undertaken by Shankland Cox and Associates for the

Secretary of State for Wales and the Ministry of Housing and Local Government, and their report published as *Deeside planning study* (Shankland Cox and Associates, 1970). The Welsh Office commissioned the study to ' assess the potential for growth, natural or induced, on the Flintshire side of the Dee, and to establish the best planning strategy for the area. The study was to have regard not only to the physical potential for integrated development but also the interests of north Wales, Lancashire, and Cheshire in the development . . . A major object of the study is to enable the costs and benefits which may be attributable to development to be taken into account together with those attributable to other elements in the crossing proposals.' Work on the study started in December 1968, assuming a potential population growth within the study area of up to 250,000 by the year 2000, the majority coming from adjoining areas. The principal area for study is Flintshire, but to assess the effects of the crossing properly the study area was extended west to Llandudno, taking in the Vale of Clwyd and Denbigh Moors, the areas surrounding Wrexham and Chester, and the Wirral including south Merseyside. Since the new Dee crossing may not be completed before 1981, the strategy produced by the consultants looks forward to the end of the century with the major development occurring in the last two decades of it. The crossing would provide an opportunity for a major urban growth area in north east Wales near the end of the crossing, with a high level of service provision; this would contribute to the Welsh economy generally and the north east region in particular. For this purpose, the consultants see a crossing entering Wales near Flint as the best basis for urban growth, and propose an urban complex of 280,000 population by the year 2000 in east Flintshire in a triangle between Holywell, Mold, and Queensferry. The new town centre would be on reclaimed land, and would have a catchment of some 450,000 people. A new college and a district general hospital are envisaged as part of the expansion. East Flintshire is ' almost certainly the only place in Wales outside Glamorgan and Monmouth where a new urban complex of city scale would be viable ', and therefore the consultants propose a government move to establish a growth area, and the setting up of a new town development corporation or another agency with similar functions. The problems of development arise mainly from the long time scale, the uncertainty of the engineering proposals, and the application by the Central Electricity Generating Board to build a nuclear power station on Deeside—a move which the consultants regard as incompatible with major urban growth. The body of this report is taken up with the detailed results of the survey, while appendices contain the more technical aspects of population, employment, and service centre studies.

The other sub-region identified in the 1967 White Paper as a potential growth area, the south east, is the subject of a study in the context of the whole Severnside region which, at the time of writing, has not yet been reported. This is the companion study to those of Humberside, discussed above under England, and of Tayside, discussed below under Scotland. The principal city in the sub-region, Cardiff, has however been the subject of studies conducted by Colin Buchanan and Partners, although not in any sub-regional context. Consultants were appointed by the city council in 1964 after ministerial rejection of the proposals in the city's development plan for the central area, in 1959; Colin Buchanan and Partners were appointed to act as advisers on the development of the centre and on the improvement of traffic circulation. Later the Ministry of Transport offered a financial grant to the projected study on condition that its scope be enlarged to include transportation aspects for the whole city. A probe study was therefore initiated as a rapid exploratory measure to set the central area into the context of a provisional highway network system for the city as a whole. The practical objectives of the probe study, whose resultant recommendations are contained in *Cardiff development and transportation study: report of the probe study* (Cardiff, City Council, 1966) were threefold: to prepare interim recommendations for a primary highway network and environmental area system as it may affect the central area; for the future development of the central area and Cathays Park; and for public transport policy. These recommendations were accepted and adopted as the basis of development control policy within the city. The consultants were retained to continue from this base and to predict the probable growth and change in Cardiff up to 2000, preparing stage plans for 1975, 1985, and 2000 (as in the south Hampshire study discussed above). The brief was subsequently revised in the light of high costs, and this report is the end

216

result. It evolves a design plan for the whole city consisting of a land use plan for 2001 incorporating the recommendations of the probe study, a forecast of the movement pattern, and the design and testing of the communications network preparatory to finalising the land use plan; it proposes major population expansion beyond the city boundary only, and restriction and control of existing and new employment areas as part of a plan to disperse traffic, together with a new highway network. Three supplementary technical volumes explaining the plan-making process in greater detail: on surveys and projections, movement surveys, and development and movement studies.

SCOTLAND

Scotland has a longer and stronger tradition of regional planning than the other countries of the United Kingdom, going back in theory to the exhortations to national and regional planning of the Edinburgh-based Patrick Geddes and in actual plan-making to the early post-war years.

The year 1949 saw the publication of three large-scale and significant regional reports which together covered most of the populous parts of Scotland. These were *A regional survey and plan for central and south east Scotland* prepared by Sir Frank Mears for the Central and South East Scotland Regional Planning Advisory Committee (Edinburgh, Advisory Committee, 1949); *The Tay Valley plan: a physical, social and economic survey and plan for the future development of east central Scotland* prepared by Gordon E Payne for the East Central (Scotland) Regional Planning Advisory Committee (Dundee, Advisory Committee, 1949) in two volumes, the first containing the survey and the second, the plan; and *The Clyde Valley regional plan 1946* prepared by Sir Patrick Abercrombie and Robert H Matthew for the Clyde Valley Regional Planning Committee (Edinburgh, HMSO, 1949).

The area studied in the first of these plans is an awkwardly shaped region taking in Edinburgh and the Lothians and the Border counties on the south side of the River Forth together with the counties bordering it on the north side, and Stirlingshire at its western end. The western end of the region is thus almost into the Glasgow conurbation. The total population at the time of the plan was

1,250,000. The main problem to be solved is that of the rural areas, specifically the depopulation and rundown of the Borders. Two other problems also arise: the necessary diversification of industry, and the accommodation of an assumed influx of 200,000 population over the next thirty years emanating from the opening up of the Forth basin coalfields. The proposals include the idea of urban 'constellations' to accommodate the increased population of the central belt, rather than new towns or the expansion of existing ones, each constellation being a union of existing small towns and villages capable of development under the New Towns Act 1946. But the main burden of the report is its study of the Borders region and its plan for rural rehabilitation, and here firmer proposals are put forward for the whole of the Tweed Valley than for the rest of the area studied including the rural equivalent of the urban constellations in the proposals for integration of the small tweed-making towns with the smaller valley units.

The area covered by the Tay Valley plan comprises the whole area of the river valley taking in the county of Angus and most of Perthshire, its population being 400,000. There are several problems: the drift of population away from the rural and glen communities to the large burghs, especially to Dundee; the extreme concentration of industry in the eastern part of Perth and Angus, in Dundee and the surrounding towns; the lack of employment in the non-industrialised areas, apart from that provided by agriculture and seasonal tourism; overcrowded housing in the urban areas; and poor road communications with Dundee and poor public transport facilities in the rural areas. The proposals are made in the expectation of an increase in population of about 40,000 over the whole region, about half of this suggested as coming from Clyde Valley overspill (see below). A limited dispersal of population and industry from Dundee is proposed, partly to neighbouring satellite settlements and partly to settlements further away; a partial result of this policy should be the expansion of selected small towns to take overspill, the expansion of rural settlements and glen communities and the regrouping of isolated hamlets. The hierarchy is viewed with Dundee and Perth as regional centres and Arbroath as a sub-regional centre, followed by district centres with populations of 10,000-12,000, urban villages with populations up to 2,000, and glen centres with populations of less than 2,000. A strong case is put forward for a road bridge across the Tay River to link Dundee with the expanding industrial areas to the south.

The area of the Clyde Valley takes in the counties of Dunbartonshire, Renfrewshire, Lanarkshire, and Ayrshire, and includes the city of Glasgow. The population of 1,800,000 represents one third of the total population of Scotland. The main problems of the region are the concentration on only a few major industries; the severe overcrowding of people and buildings in parts of the area, notably in the centre of Glasgow; the lack of green belt country and the encroachment of urban building into agricultural land; and the lack of recreational facilities in both town and country. One of the most basic proposals made in the report is that for a single regional administrative authority to handle future development of the region. This future development will include the attraction of new industries. It will also include the creation of new towns within the region to take overspill from overcrowded areas, in addition to the decanting of 100,000 population outside the region altogether. Further proposals are made for the establishment of a green belt policy to safeguard agricultural land, the coordination of transport, the creation of national and regional recreation centres, and the provision of adequate open space and amenities in the towns.

When the Conservative government of the early 1960's became alive to the regional economic problems of the country its first step, after the creation of the National Economic Development Council, was to consider as a matter of urgency the deteriorating situations in Scotland and in north east England, where unemployment had risen to crisis proportions during the recession of 1962 and 1963. The two White Papers resulting from these considerations were 'the first large steps towards regional economic planning'.[11] *Central Scotland: a programme for development and growth* (Edinburgh, HMSO, 1963, Cmnd 2188) prepared by the Scottish Office for the Secretary of State for Scotland, is based on an earlier inquiry into Scotland's economy by the Scottish Council (Development and Industry) *Report of the committee of inquiry into the Scottish economy* (Edinburgh, the Council, 1961), known as the Toothill Report after the chairman of the committee. The White Paper sets out no precise targets for expansion, but it does indicate a commit-

219

ment of public investment expenditure of eleven per cent of the national total to sustain the courses of action proposed for a ' comprehensive and sustained programme for the modernisation of the economy of central Scotland '. Major growth areas are identified at East Kilbride, Cumbernauld, Livingston, Glenrothes, Irvine, and the Grangemouth/Falkirk area. Lesser growth areas were pinpointed in north Lanarkshire, central Fife, the Lothians, and the Vale of Leven district of Dunbartonshire.

One of the weaknesses of the growth area proposals was that there seemed to be no consistent basis of selection of such areas: some were clearly capable of growth but others were simply areas of depression. Designation alone could make no practical difference: only if the potential of the area were surveyed and active steps for development pursued would the concept of growth areas become meaningful in practical terms. For two of the areas, this policy was carried out: Livingston new town and its surrounding area, and the Grangemouth/Falkirk sub-region. Teams of independent consultants were commissioned to study these areas and to prepare proposals for development. These studies, notable for their introduction of multi-disciplinary teams into regional planning and their fusion of economic and physical planning, are reported in *The Lothians regional survey and plan* (Edinburgh, HMSO, 1966, two volumes), and in *The Grangemouth/Falkirk regional survey and plan* (Edinburgh, HMSO, 1968, two volumes).

The Lothians survey was carried out by teams from Glasgow University's Department of Social and Economic Research, under Professor D J Robertson, and from Edinburgh University's Department of Architecture, under Professor Robert H Matthew (joint author of the Clyde Valley plan), for the Scottish Development Department and a Joint Advisory Planning Committee consisting of representatives of the county councils of Midlothian and West Lothian, and Livingston Development Corporation. The area studied is that round the new town of Livingston in the eastern half of the central lowland belt of Scotland. The original decision to set up a new town at Livingston (it was designated in April 1962) was taken at almost the same time as the decision was made to survey the whole region: the White Paper on the designation of the new town carried a proposal that a comprehensive regional scheme

220

should be prepared. Instead of the survey preceding the decisions about the town, as is now the norm, in the case of Livingston the active development of the town proceeded alongside the regional survey. The consultants were charged with three main tasks: an examination of the physical possibilities of the area; an evaluation of the economic potential of the area, to include an estimate of prospects for future economic expansion; based on these, the preparation of a scheme of development and rehabilitation in the form of an advisory plan covering both physical and economic planning aspects, including proposals for capital investment and methods of stimulating economic growth. The main conclusions reached as a result of these studies are that the area is suitable for growth although continuing government assistance will be required to sustain it, and that economic growth should be focused on Livingston and its surrounding region (an area of derelict mining land and declining settlements) which should become Greater Livingston with a target population of 185,000 by 1986 and serve as the main shopping and service centre of the area. The employment to support the increased population may come from Edinburgh, but not from Glasgow, and it may also be imported from outside the area: to facilitate this, communications with Edinburgh should be developed and commuting be accepted as normal. To achieve these proposals, a planned programme of rehabilitation and rapid development is seen as essential. The *Livingston new town master plan* (Livingston, Development Corporation, 1963) alongside which the regional proposals were to co-exist was prepared by Peter G Daniel, Chief Architect and Planning Officer to the corporation. This is a very flexible plan for a town of existing population of 2,000 envisaged as expanding to over 100,000, the bulk of the influx coming from Glasgow. The town is viewed as a new focus of industrial activity in Scotland's central belt, a regional employment and service centre. The amended basic plan of 1966 contains modifications of the road system and of the detailed land use allocations, although the original concept is retained; that of a cellular urban structure, with the central area planned as a number of related units built within the landscaped central valley which divides the site and which is designed as a linear core providing the main open space reservation, with dispersed industry, and an emphasis on use of the private car.

The Grangemouth/Falkirk study was carried out by teams from Glasgow University's Department of Economic and Social Research, again under Professor D J Robertson, and Edinburgh University's Planning Research Unit under Professors Matthew and Percy Johnson-Marshall, for the Scottish Development Department and the Stirlingshire, West Lothian and Falkirk Growth Area Joint Planning Advisory Committee. The study had no relation with any other development, as was the case with the Lothians study, but was inspired solely by the White Paper of 1963 which had identified the sub-region as a major growth area and proposed specifically that ' subject to discussions with the local authorities, the assistance of the Universities of Glasgow and Edinburgh will be sought in the preparation of a comprehensive economic and physical expansion scheme designed to increase population in the area by about 50,000 '. The area comprises about eighty two square miles lying along the southern shore of the River Forth on the eastern side of central Scotland: Falkirk, in the centre of the area, is roughly half way between Glasgow and Edinburgh. The terms of reference were similar to those for the Lothians study. The consultants were charged to carry out a survey and prepare a development plan for the area, the latter to be in the form of an advisory plan covering the physical and economic aspects of the area, including proposals for capital investment and measures to stimulate economic growth. Naturally, the experience of the earlier survey is drawn on where appropriate: some of the relevant features are stated on pages three to five of the present report. The consultants propose that the population of the area should be expanded to 230,000 by 1985/1986, and further suggest that the area could contain 300,000 by the year 2000. Redevelopment of existing communities should be incorporated into the plan, and the process of development and redevelopment together would result in the creation of a large urban complex including both Falkirk and Grangemouth, to be developed as one integral unit. Falkirk would serve as the shopping and service centre of the sub-region, and the new community should be constituted as a new large burgh, or a city.

Livingston and Grangemouth/Falkirk apart, of the four other growth areas identified in the 1963 White Paper, three were existing new towns and the fourth was subsequently designated a new town.

Designation as a major growth area clearly had the effect of causing existing towns to review plans and to reappraise factors such as roads and transport. East Kilbride, the first Scottish new town, designated in May 1947, has had its population target increased but a revised master plan has not been published. The second new town, Glenrothes, has produced several documents relating to its expanding status. Originally designated in 1948 to house 3,500 miners from the declining Lanarkshire coalfields, with a population target of 32,000, its role was redefined as a result of changing circumstances, and in 1962 its target population was raised to 95,000 to accommodate overspill from Glasgow. The original outline plan for the town was based on a structure of neighbourhood units, with precincts of 1,150 dwellings grouped around a primary school, each unit being formed of two or more precincts. In 1963 a review of the outline plan was called for together with a reappraisal of the transport system owing to the rapid growth in road traffic. A Road Pattern Group was set up by the corporation to produce a revised road structure, and their proposals are contained in *A transport plan for Glenrothes: report of the Road Pattern Group* (GDC, 1966); this was followed by *Glenrothes new town: interim planning proposals phase 2* (GDC, 1966), and finally by *Glenrothes new town: master plan report* (GDC, 1970). To date, development of the town has been linear in form; two of an envisaged three neighbourhood units have been almost completed, comprising seven residential precincts, the first phase of the central town centre is complete, as are three dispersed industrial estates. The main feature of the new plan is the superimposition of a more sophisticated road network onto this existing structure, consisting of a hierarchy of roads from freeways down to serviceways, a system which defines natural localities or ' areas of containment ', each one visually self-contained with its own micro climate and local characteristics. Residential areas will be composed of dwelling clusters within containment areas, and industrial estates will be dispersed throughout the town. Shopping provision is through a hierarchy of town centre, neighbourhood centres, and corner shops. Linked green wedges will form the basis of the open space system connecting the major recreational areas.

Cumbernauld, the most controversial of British new towns and a focus of world-wide planning interest, was designated in December 1955, and with its radical breakaway from traditional garden city and neighbourhood unit concepts it introduced the Mark II new town. The original plan by Hugh Wilson, then Chief Architect and Planning Officer to the Development Corporation, was contained in *Cumbernauld new town: preliminary planning proposals* (Cumbernauld, Development Corporation, 1958) and has been revised in two subsequent addenda in 1959 and 1962. The principal features of the plan are the multi-level town centre which stretches along the crest of the hill which divides and dominates the site of 4,150 acres, which contains all the town's major facilities and which is easily accessible to all inhibitants; the housing development with increasing densities towards the town centre, with a general minimum of seventy persons per acre and a maximum of 120; and a road system which gives total pedestrian/vehicle separation.

The newest new town in Scotland is at Irvine in Ayrshire, designated in November 1966 as an industrial growth centre and a reception point for Glasgow overspill. The consultant planners are Hugh Wilson and Lewis Womersley who prepared *Irvine new town: final report on planning proposals* (Edinburgh, HMSO, 1967) proposing a flexible plan for the site of some 12,440 acres with development in a linear band. The plan for linked district centres on a communications spine is directly derived from the concepts developed by Wilson and Womersley in their *Northampton, Bedford and north Bucks study*. Subsequently the consultants were required to revise the plan substantially in the light of new information, and their *Irvine new town: revised outline plan* (Irvine, Development Corporation, 1969) abandons the original linear concept in favour of expansion to north and east and the closer integration of the existing towns of Irvine and Kilwinning, with tourist and recreational development at the coast. The plan allows for the accommodation of an eventual population of 200,000 in the area including the neighbouring town of Kilmarnock.

The next stimulus to planning in Scotland, the inspiration of several planning studies, was the White Paper *The Scottish economy: 1965-70* (Edinburgh, HMSO, 1966, Cmnd 2864). This is the equivalent, for Scotland, of the regional studies produced for the various regions of England by the economic planning councils between 1965 and 1967, and the companion to the Welsh White Paper *Wales: the way ahead* (see above). This was the first regional report to be produced under the Labour government, and it is both a survey and a plan. 'As a survey the document is good. It analyses in an interesting way the problems of the Scottish sub-regions, the Highlands, the North-East, the Borders and the South-West, and the proposals it puts forward to build up centres of growth are well conceived . . . As a plan, however, it is poor. Before the 1964 election the Labour Party had virtually committed themselves to producing an economic plan for Scotland, just as they were committed to a National Plan. The techniques of planning, however, take time to build up and the rudimentary state of Scottish statistics only permitted a crude attempt.'[12] The concept of growth areas, propounded in the earlier White Paper, has been abandoned, although proposals are incorporated for development of likely areas; the plan lays stress on the relations between the various regions of Scotland and the contributions that may be expected from each to the overall development of the Scottish economy. The White Paper has been the base for several studies of regions of Scotland, notably *The Central Borders: a plan for expansion* (Edinburgh, HMSO, 1968) by the Planning Research Unit and the Department of Economics of Edinburgh University under Professors Percy Johnson-Marshall and J H Wolfe for the Scottish Development Department; *North east Scotland: a survey of its development potential* (Edinburgh, HMSO, 1969) by a group from the University of Aberdeen under Professor Maxwell Gaskin for the Scottish Development Department; and *A strategy for south west Scotland* (Edinburgh, HMSO, 1970) by a team from the Scottish Development Department.

The White Paper of 1966 decreed that, within the (Scottish) national context, the way in which the Borders should make a more effective contribution to the Scottish economy and offer better prospects for the residents in the area was to receive about 25,000 people into the region by 1980. The area of study is the upper parts of the valleys of the Tweed and Teviot, rural countryside with a number of small towns. The study team was charged to produce short, medium, and long term proposals: first, for the extension of Galashiels southwards by 1,000 new houses; second, for the

225

accommodation of the stated 25,000 extra population by 1980; and third, for broad guidelines for long term expansion. This volume is concerned mainly with phase two of these proposals. Three solutions to the population expansion were investigated and a combination of town expansion plus new community was selected. A new community of 10,000 in the St Boswells area is therefore proposed, in conjunction with a fairly even distribution of the balance of the influx over existing towns. The report is notable for its description of the application of threshold analysis (see chapter 11, planning techniques) for the first time in British planning practice.

The starting point for the survey of north east Scotland is likewise the White Paper of 1966, and more specifically the short study of the north east region which was included in it. The area considered in the White Paper was the north east region as defined for census purposes; that taken as the study area of the present report is rather smaller, and is the north east planning region comprising the counties of Aberdeen, Banff, Kincardine, Moray and Nairn, and the city of Aberdeen. The region is predominantly rural in character with many small towns and villages, and much of the population of just under 450,000 is concentrated in Aberdeen city. The study team was required to survey the current economic and demographic trends and their likely course up to 1975, to examine the methods of achieving expansion of the population in Aberdeen city and other selected centres, and to suggest methods of providing industry and infrastructure to support this population growth. The bulk of the Gaskin Report, as it has become known, is taken up with the survey of the region, in sections on settlement patterns; population and employment; the primary industries of agriculture, fishing and forestry; manufacturing industry; service industries; the construction industry; transport; and power. The survey finds a population declining, albeit slowly, a decline which would have adverse effects on the population structure by 1975; it further finds high unemployment, and an imbalance between expanding and contracting industries. The main policy objective stated in the report is to stabilise the total population of the region by the mid 1970's, and this is to be achieved by the provision of eight thousand jobs over and above those likely to be created by forseeable trends. There should be growth areas centred on Aberdeen and Elgin, with concentration

226

of housing development and new industry into these two areas. In the rural hinterlands a stronger policy should be pursued of concentrating population into fewer and larger villages: to this end, the report recommends further study of the desirable degree of concentration in sparsely populated areas.

The White Paper of 1966 reviewed the south west of Scotland in broad terms and identified those places which seem to offer the best prospects for further development both in terms of local needs, and of the general aim ' to create more employment opportunities so as to take up, in the widest national interest, the available reserves of labour and to reduce immigration '. Further study along these lines was suggested by the South West Economic Planning Consultative Group, which is concerned with the economic problems of the region, so that these latter could be viewed in the light of developments since publication of the White Paper and so that a fuller assessment of future prospects could be made and a regional strategy formulated up to 1976 and beyond to 1986. The study area consists of the south west planning region, population 150,000 at mid 1968, together with the Langholm area, population 4,500: the total population forming about three percent of the national total. Within the region there is considerable contrast in terms of population change and distribution owing to the varying nature of the economy in different parts of the region, though in overall terms the population is declining. The document is not a plan, but rather a background against which planning authorities in the region can develop their own plans. Much of it is taken up with the results of the survey, in chapters on regional trends and prospects; population and employment of catchment areas; potential for physical development; transport and roads; agriculture, fishing and forestry; and tourism and recreation. The main proposal advanced is that the rate of creation of male jobs in manufacturing industry should be increased, with the aim of reducing unemployment and checking outward migration. Various measures are proposed to attract new industry, including the establishment of a regional planning and industrial promotion organisation; the introduction of special measures for rural areas; a review of development plans throughout the region and their amendment to include provision for attracting new industry and assuming an increase in population over the region of some five thousand; the effects of the M6-A74 motorways should be kept under close review and opportunities created by them taken into account and exploited; and finally cooperation between local authorities in preparing proposals for tourism and recreation throughout the region in consultation with the regional tourist association. Appendices to the report contain details of population and employment forecasts, and various specialised surveys.

Among the other areas recommended in the 1966 White Paper as being suitable for development was the south east environs of Edinburgh, in the county of Midlothian, and acting upon this information the county identified the Esk Valley as the area which required intensive study in anticipation of such development. The county council therefore commissioned the Departments of Economics and Town and Country Planning of the Heriot-Watt University, in Edinburgh, to carry out such a study, which is reported in *The Esk Valley: a sub-regional study of eastern Midlothian* (Edinburgh, Heriot-Watt University, 1969). The terms of reference laid down for the study team were to evaluate the economic potential of the region, including future prospects for expansion; to examine the future composition and distribution of the population and labour force; to examine the relationships between industrial growth and local and central government capital investment; and to examine transport and communications facilities. The area studied is in fact a sub-region of the Edinburgh city region, comprising about 150 square miles lying to the south and east of the city. The population in this sub-region is expected to increase by about 19,000 up to 1986, and the demand for labour is calculated to increase by about one percent per annum. The team considers that the supporting resources of land for economic growth is in adequate supply without significant encroachment on good quality agricultural land. An identified need to improve the quality of occupational choice for young people has implications for industrial location policy, and also for educational policy. Major proposals are incorporated in the report for treatment of derelict areas, and for selective development of specified settlements together with their inter-related facilities.

If the White Paper failed to mention the previously identified growth areas of central Scotland, the *First Report of the Highlands and Islands Development Board* (Inverness, the Board, 1967) demonstrated that in that particular region the concept was not dead and that a definite policy was being pursued to establish growth areas in the Moray Firth area and at Thurso and Wick. The Board was established in 1965 to assist the people of the Scottish Highlands and Islands to improve their social and economic conditions and to enable the region to play a more effective part in the growth of the nation as a whole. Their first report stresses the importance of the Moray Firth development, in particular, in their overall policy towards these ends; and subsequently they commissioned the Jack Holmes Planning Group of Glasgow to carry out a study and prepare a plan for the area, the results of which are contained in *The Moray Firth: a plan for growth in a sub-region of the Scottish Highlands* (Glasgow, Jack Holmes Planning Group, 1968). The area studied is that around the Moray Firth in north east Scotland. The consultants were asked to prepare a sub-regional plan which would demonstrate the development potential and population capacity of the area, and illustrate the areas within the sub-region which were suitable for development and the circulation pattern which should link them to each other and to the region in general. They were further requested to prepare a master plan for the development of a town of about 15,000 population in the Alness area. The study demonstrates that the sub-region has a population capacity of between 250,000 and 300,000. Its main strategy is based on the establishment of 'major capital intensive industries' at Invergordon (where a large aluminium smelter plant has been established) and at other sites in the region. Three existing towns and several villages are designated for expansion, to varying population levels, and three new towns of between 16,000 and 20,000 population are proposed. The report calls for further study of particular problems and localities within the sub-region.

The other major study of a Scottish sub-region is *Tayside: potential for development* (Edinburgh, HMSO, 1970) carried out by a joint team from Dundee University and the Scottish Development Department, for the Secretary of State for Scotland. Tayside was one of three parts of the United Kingdom which the Labour government decided to have studied in an examination of long term population distribution needs: the overall UK increase was expected to be

229

about seventeen million by the year 2000 and that for Scotland up to one and a half million. This is the companion study to those of Humberside and Severnside (see above). The study of Tayside was also seen as a stage in the implementation of the White Paper of 1966, which suggested that considerable expansion of Dundee was both possible and desirable and that there was potential for development as a modern city region forming part of the central belt complex. The area studied is that of the fourth Scottish economic planning region, comprising some two million acres with a present population of 450,000, and taking in the counties of Angus and Perth and Fife (the area studied in the Tay Valley plan of 1949 had similar boundaries in Angus and Perthshire, but excluded Fife). The purpose of the present study is to examine the economic preconditions and requirements for a population increase in the region of between 175,000 and 300,000 by the year 2000, and to devise a flexible physical planning and investment programme which would allow a modern city region to develop without the constraints imposed by the congestion that is experienced in existing conurbations. The report discusses these objectives in the light of the proposals embodied in the 1949 report, and points out that the earlier plan's ' proposals for population targets, social policies and the redevelopment of Dundee have had little apparent effect. The total population in the smaller region remained virtually static between 1947 and 1966, and it has, contrary to the plan's recommendations, tended to concentrate in the large towns and migrate from the smaller towns and rural areas.' The main conclusions of the study team are that Tayside is suitable for development on a scale sufficient to accommodate the population increase envisaged and to contribute significantly to the growth of the Scottish economy as a whole, and, more specifically, that Tayside could develop over the next thirty years into a modern city region accommodating 300,000 extra people with high living standards and environmental quality. The present physical and economic structure is suitable as a base for development, providing a wide variety of sites for residential, industrial, commercial, and recreational uses, but increased capital investment will be necessary to sustain the vigorous programme of rehabilitation and growth which is envisaged over the next ten years. As regards the administrative machinery

230

necessary to carry through such a programme, the consultants recommend that, in advance of local government reorganisation, 'immediate joint action should be taken by the local authorities on a first phase programme . . . For this they should agree a joint programme of planning, land assembly and promotion, and use appropriate agencies.' In addition to these main conclusions, the report also contains various supplementary proposals concerning industry, shopping centres, housing, education, water, roads and transport.

NORTHERN IRELAND

Systematic guidance of the economic and physical development of Northern Ireland has been in operation only since the early 1960's. In October 1960, Sir Robert H Matthew was commissioned by the government of the province to prepare an advisory outline plan for the Belfast region, to be completed within two years. He was required 'to relate the survey and plan in the broadest terms to the geographical, economic and cultural pattern of Northern Ireland as a whole'. As a result of one of the recommendations contained in Matthew's report, the Ministry of Development was established to centralise throughout the province planning functions hitherto exercised by local authorities: its responsibilities are for planning generally, roads, housing, transport, water and sewerage, and local government. The plan itself, *Belfast regional survey and plan 1962* (Belfast, HMSO, 1964, in two volumes, one comprising the text and the other being a case of maps) has formed the basis of planning in the region throughout the decade since its production.

The area studied in the survey is that around Belfast roughly bounded by Larne, Ballymena, Portadown, and Downpatrick; though it is stated in the preamble to the report that 'no exact boundaries are defined, and indeed do not exist'. The main objectives of the regional plan were to correct the unbalanced growth of the Belfast urban area in relation to the remainder of Northern Ireland, and to provide a more satisfactory basis for future planning. These objectives are to be met by the designation of growth centres, with defined population targets, and to increase the rate of growth in these centres by the provision of housing and jobs to attract new industry and population. In the rest of the province outside the

Belfast region, industry is to be concentrated into a number of key centres in an effort to arrest the drift from the rural areas to Belfast and further afield. A new regional centre based on the existing towns of Lurgan and Portadown is to be developed, with a target population of 100,000. The spread of development of Belfast itself is to be physically limited by means of a development stop-line. The proposal for centralisation of planning powers has been mentioned above, and the report also recommended that arrangement should be made for the extension and continuing review of the regional plan. The conclusions and recommendations of the regional plan were also presented separately in *Belfast regional survey and plan: recommendations and conclusions* (Belfast, HMSO, 1963, Cmnd 451).

The regional plan was followed at the beginning of 1965 by the comprehensive economic plan for the whole province, commissioned in 1963 from an independent consultant, Professor Thomas Wilson, presented in December 1964 and published as *Economic development in Northern Ireland* (including the report of the consultant Professor Thomas Wilson) (Belfast, HMSO, 1965, Cmnd 479). The plan was adopted by the government as the basis of economic planning for the period 1964 to 1970. Its object is to put forward remedial measures for the main problem of unemployment, and to propose methods of increasing public investment. The report constitutes a detailed examination of the restraints on growth in Northern Ireland, and puts forward a detailed programme of action covering the establishment of growth centres, amenity, expanded road and housing programmes, industrial training facilities, and schemes of inducements to industry. The Wilson Report affirms the choice of Lurgan/Portadown and Antrim/Ballymena as growth centres, made in the Matthew plan, and adds another major area of expansion at Londonderry. The Wilson and Matthew documents together have thus formed the basis of physical and economic planning within Northern Ireland since 1965: the need for a comprehensive economic and physical plan for the province was recognised by the appointment of Professors Wilson, Matthew, and Jack Parkinson to undertake a survey and prepare a plan on such comprehensive lines in conjunction with the Northern Ireland Economic Council. Their joint report and proposals for a further programme

232

of development are contained in *Northern Ireland development programme 1970-75* (Belfast, HMSO, 1970), and confirmed in the government statement *Northern Ireland development programme 1970-75* (Belfast, HMSO, 1970, Cmnd 547). This is a plan for integrated economic, physical and social development. Outside of the Belfast area, Londonderry and Ballymena are designated as centres of accelerated industrial growth together with eight key centres of growth at Larne, Newry, the Coleraine triangle, Dungannon, Omagh, Enniskillen, Strabane, and Downpatrick. In the Greater Belfast area, urgent acceleration of housing redevelopment is stressed, and specific outward adjustment of the Belfast stopline to accommodate public authority housing and industry is advocated, together with overspill arrangements to facilitate movement to Craigavon, Antrim, and the inner growth centres of Bangor, Newtownards, and Carrickfergus.

The two major growth areas recommended in the Belfast regional plan have by now achieved documentary record, as has the third growth area recommended in the economic plan, at Londonderry. The expansion based on Lurgan and Portadown is detailed in *New city Northern Ireland: first report on the proposed new city, Co Armagh* (Belfast, HMSO, 1964) and subsequently in *Craigavon new city: second report on the plan* (Belfast, HMSO, 1967). The expansion of Antrim and Ballymena is described in *Antrim new town: outline plan* (Belfast, HMSO, 1965) and in *Ballymena area plan* (Belfast, HMSO, 1966). All of these reports are by planning teams from the Ministry of Development. The *Londonderry area plan* (Belfast, HMSO, 1968) is the work of consultants, the James Munce Partnership, for the Ministry of Development.

Following the submission of Matthew's regional plan for Belfast, the Northern Ireland government set up a design office for the Lurgan/Portadown new town project on the site, and by the end of 1963 a comprehensive survey and research programme had been inaugurated. The first report, of 1964, is 'an outline plan or preliminary statement of principles and objectives; it will be apparent that it does not constitute a physical plan in any detailed sense but it does mark a stage on the road to the master plan'. The team distinguish three interdependent functions for the new city: as a new base for industry; as a new residential area to relieve Belfast;

233

and as a new service centre to contribute to the regeneration of the south and west of the province. The town was designated in July 1965 as an area of one hundred square miles including the towns of Lurgan and Portadown and the rural districts of Lurgan and Moira: the name Craigavon (after the first Prime Minister of Northern Ireland) was adopted in October of the same year. The target population is 180,000. The second report, of 1967, presents more detailed plans for development up to 1981, and looks beyond that to the year 2000, but its main concern is with the programme for the next five years. It develops the concept of Craigavon as a rural city, with a linear core formed by the existing towns of Lurgan and Portadown, each with a present population of 22,000, linked over their five-mile intervening distance by two new residential sectors, each with a proposed population of 20,000, and a new city centre which will be developed as the focal service centre in the sub-region. Two further residential sectors of similar size are projected for the future at the outer boundaries of the existing towns. Industry is dispersed at five industrial estates and at other smaller areas in the rural area, and an eventual total of 21,000 jobs is envisaged. Tourism is provided for by the provision of a large-scale marina on the shore of Lough Neagh. Particular emphasis is laid on landscaping and tree-planting to preserve the image of a rural city.

Development of Antrim and Ballymena presents a special case in that their expansion is viewed as a joint development, and they are in the charge of a single development commission: the area of four hundred square miles designated for the joint development includes both towns and the ten-mile stretch of land in between, but it is not intended that the two towns should merge, rather that they should retain their individual characters and play a complementary role in the area. Antrim was designated in July 1966, and its population of 7,000 planned to increase to 30,000. The outline plan of 1965 envisages the eventual development of the town as a holiday and tourist centre, to which the good countryside will contribute along with park and recreational facilities in the town and on the north shore of Lough Neagh. The plan also proposes a new road system, neighbourhood development with local shopping centres, the zoning of extra industrial land, and, at a later stage of development, a pedestrianised shopping centre on the site of the present central area. Ballymena was designated in August 1967, and its population of 22,000 planned to increase to 70,000. The area plan of 1966 includes schemes for the expansion of four villages in the area. For the town itself, 12,000 new homes are planned, together with a new road system with pedestrian ways, four new industrial estates, and the comprehensive redevelopment of much of the existing town with open space and sports and recreational facilities included.

Londonderry was one of the points outside the Belfast region which was identified for concentration of industry in the Belfast regional plan of 1962. Professor Wilson reinforced this by designating the town as a growth centre, and proposed that a development plan for the area should be commissioned. In February 1968, therefore, the James Munce Partnership was commissioned by the Ministry of Development and the Londonderry Area Steering Committee to prepare an outline development plan for the area comprising Londonderry county borough and Londonderry rural district, a triangle of about 134 square miles occupying the western quarter of County Londonderry, for the period up to 1981, the area to be considered in the context of adjoining areas and Northern Ireland as a whole. The area itself is predominantly rural, with Londonderry the only urban unit of any size, its population being 56,000. ' The study was to consider main communications, land use requirements for housing, education, industry and commerce, open space and recreation, other types of development and finally the architectural character and general appearance of the area. The type of plan envisaged was a " broad brush " one generally in accord with the aims laid down in the report of the Planning Advisory Group.' The consultants propose that large areas of land should be designated to form an industrial land bank as part of a growth area stretching from Londonderry to Coleraine and Strabane, with improved communications with Belfast and the south; the provision of 12,000 new jobs by 1981 is envisaged. Residential growth will be associated with industrial expansion, including a major new residential development for 18,000 people. Major redevelopment of the city centre is proposed, together with the renewal of areas of unfit or obsolete housing. The report is to some extent a precis of nine detailed reports submitted to the steering committee, and the following supplementary reports are available from the consultants:

235

no 2 on population, no 3 on hinterland, no 4 on industry, no 6 on shopping, no 7 on rural settlements, no 8 on communications, and no 9 on landscape, recreation and tourism (nos 1 and 5 are superseded by the final report).

The plan for the Coleraine area is also the work of consultants, Robert Matthew, Johnson-Marshall and Partners in association with Percy Johnson-Marshall and Associates, whose report is published as *Coleraine, Portrush, Portstewart area plan* (Belfast, HMSO, 1968). The need for a plan for Coleraine—designated as a growth point in the Belfast regional plan and in the Wilson Report on economic development—was reinforced by the recommendation of the Lockwood Report on higher education that a new university should be established in Northern Ireland on a site north of Coleraine, to accommodate 7,000 students in the long term. The consultants were commissioned to prepare an area plan which would coordinate the growth of the university and the development of the region; the terms of reference required that the three towns forming the Coleraine triangle should ' be developed in a manner reflecting the influence of the university in the stepping-up of their existing functions as ports and centres of commerce, culture and recreation, with special emphasis on the promotion of tourist trade in the area '. The study area covers about ninety square miles, with the sea as its northern boundary; Coleraine is the main service centre of the sub-region. The report proposes a linear development lying along the main transportation routes, linking Portstewart initially with Coleraine and subsequently with Portrush. New residential zones are projected in seven community groups, each group having about 5,000 people served by a local centre with primary schools and shops. Coleraine should continue as the main centre, with Portrush and Portstewart as district centres. The tourist potential of the coast and along the River Bann, which flows northwards through the area, should be developed, with accommodation for an extra 1,500 caravans over the next fifteen years. A multiple land use plan is recommended to fully exploit the countryside for both recreational and agricultural uses. Recommendations are included for the implementation and programming of the plan, with the preparation of fourteen action area plans for different parts of the sub-region seen as the most urgent planning problem.

236

In December 1966 the Building Design Partnership were commissioned by the Ministry of Development to prepare an area plan for the whole of the area referred to by Professor Matthew in the Belfast regional plan as the Belfast Urban Area, and to examine the effects of development on the surrounding region and on regional strategy. This was an extension of an original brief to the consultants from Belfast Corporation, which had required them to prepare a comprehensive development plan for the area within the city boundary, and to advise on more detailed matters mainly relating to redevelopment areas, and to relate these studies closely with those of the consultants R Travers Morgan and Partners who were engaged on the Belfast transportation study. The plan is published in two volumes as *Belfast urban area plan* (Building Design Partnership, 1969) together with a set of eight plans. The first volume deals with the urban area as a whole, with an account of public participation and its effect on the work; this is followed by eighteen brief subject studies of, for example, sectors of Belfast, Lisburn, and Newtownabbey; and concluded with a summary of recommendations. The second volume contains ten detailed subject studies covering subjects of particular importance such as population, housing, harbour development, and shopping. The plan was prepared within the context of the 1962 regional plan and of subsequently accepted regional planning policy. The consultants recommend urgent acceleration of the development of growth centres, and control of the growth of the urban area; in the latter connection, they call upon the government to produce a revised guideline for the accommodation of the urban area population, and propose the establishment of overspill targets for movement of population from the urban area to the growth centres and phased overspill agreements between the urban area local authorities and the growth centres. Recommendations are included for restructuring the urban area by the provision of new district centres, and the strengthening of existing centres, which will be capable of growth and change. Housing redevelopment should be accelerated to a clearance rate of 1,500 dwellings by 1970, and completion of currently designated redevelopment areas should be aimed at by 1985. The report stresses the need for better data and the desirability of implementing ways

237

of obtaining these. Further detailed recommendations are contained within the detailed subject studies of the second volume, as are recommendations for further work and research.

There are no specifically-compiled guides to development plan literature *per se*. It is included, along with other categories of material, in the daily, weekly and cumulative lists of government publications; in the Department of the Environment *Classified accessions list;* and in the sectional lists of publications issued by the various government departments. These guides are discussed in chapter 13. Regular discussion of development plan literature of all types can be found in the planning journals and in some geographical journals also: particularly fruitful in this connection are the monthly *Town and country planning,* and *JTPI* which includes comment on the major productions in its ' Current practice and research ' section. Occasionally, articles appear which offer comparative analyses and evaluations of several examples of a similar type of plan: one such by P M Smith was cited in this chapter in connection with the regional economic studies. Also of interest are three articles under the collective title ' New town and town expansion schemes ' comparing plans for new towns or town expansions: two by D A Bull in *Town planning review* 38(2) July 1967 103-114 and 38(3) October 1967 165-186; and one by D Field in 39(3) October 1968 196-216. The purpose of these three articles is to review current planning policies and ideas embodied in recent reports, with particular reference to urban form and structure. The first two articles, by Bull, discuss ten plans for development of existing towns or sub-regions; two of these—Washington, and the mid-Wales new town—are plans for promoting economic development and improving the social infrastructure of a sub-region; the others are plans for accommodating population increase and overspill—north Buckinghamshire, south Hampshire, Swindon/Newbury, and the expansions of Northampton, Peterborough and Ipswich (arising from the south east study), the Dawley/Wellington/Oakengates area (arising from the west midlands study) and the expansion of Warrington (arising from the north west study). The third article, by Field, examines the plans for Skelmersdale, Runcorn, Redditch,

Livingston, and Irvine. Sub-regional plans are the subject of Ian Masser's article 'Methods of sub-regional analysis: a review of four recent studies' *Town planning review* 41(2) April 1970 148-160, in which the studies of Teesside, Humberside, Leicestershire and Notts/Derbys are examined and compared.

REFERENCES

1 Gavin McCrone *Regional policy in Britain* (Allen and Unwin, 1969, University of Glasgow Social and Economic Studies) 225.

2 J B Cullingworth *Town and country planning in England and Wales* (Allen and Unwin, third edition 1970) 298.

3 Gavin McCrone *op cit* 231.

4 Donald L Foley *Controlling London's growth: planning the great wen 1940-1960* (Berkeley, University of California Press, 1963) 42.

5. Ministry of Housing and Local Government *Strategic plan for the south east* (HMSO, 1970) 2.

6 Donald L Foley *op cit* 45.

7 John Tetlow and Anthony Goss *Homes, towns and traffic* (Faber, second edition 1968) 62.

8 Donald L Foley *op cit* 47-48.

9 Gavin McCrone *op cit* 227.

10 *Leicester and Leicestershire sub-regional planning study* (Leicester, City and County Councils, 1969) volume one 1.11.

11 Gavin McCrone *op cit* 224.

12 Gavin McCrone *op cit* 232.

10

STATISTICAL SOURCES

IT IS IN THIS CHAPTER that we collide most directly with the distinction, proposed in the preface, between data and information, and that it becomes increasingly clear that it may not be a useful or a meaningful distinction when applied to statistics in planning. In a paper on ' The future of national information systems ' to the conference on information and urban planning held by the Centre for Environmental Studies in May 1969, F J M Laver stressed the distinction. ' The vocabulary of computer terms produced by the International Federation for Information Processing distinguishes usefully between data and information. Data are representations of facts or ideas in a formalised manner; whereas information is the meaning which some man or woman assigns to those representations.'

This distinction has nothing to do with the raw state of data as opposed to the processed state of information. Taken to its logical conclusion, it can mean that a library of books, or an individual book in itself, is a collection of data awaiting the interpretation of a reader. It is only necessary to read several reviews of the same book to realise the different styles of mental processing which produce the frequently conflicting interpretations, and to realise the confusion which can arise. But this, in fact, is a second-hand re-interpretation of the author's interpretation of the facts at his disposal, and many factors at work in the author's interpretation cannot be known: there is, for example, a world of difference between ' only 25% do ' and ' as many as 75% do not ', although they represent identical facts.

From the planner's point of view, since much of the information which he has to use is processed for purposes other than planning, the nearer he can get to its raw state the better, so that it can be re-interpreted for a specifically planning objective. Thus the extra meaning has come into the definitions of data and information, which implies that for planning purposes the data must be as raw as possible or, if processed at all, then only in accordance with the particular requirements of planning; and that information represents processed data. The basic data on which planners rely cover a wide range of subjects, including population, migration, employment, transport, housing, and recreation, and many of them are available only in published series emanating from government sources. And here the distinction begins to break down, because many of these sources present statistics which have been heavily processed and which are several stages removed from raw data; but yet, in the absence of alternatives, they must be used by planners in conjunction with the true raw data which frequently is collected on an *ad hoc* basis by the planners themselves.

There is thus a conflict between the planner's requirement for basic data relating to his area of interest, and his enforced reliance on centrally produced, processed statistical information which in many instances can offer nothing less than national figures. The principal problem is one of spatial aggregation: the planner's requirement is for data relating to very small areas—the one hundred metre square is usually taken to be the smallest useful unit of aggregation in considering urban areas—but published sources in general can offer no aggregations lower than the local authority area. Closely related is the other major problem of incompatibility between the units of aggregation used by the various published sources: for example, the employment exchange unit used by the Department of Employment and the enumeration district unit used for the census of population are totally incompatible. Other problems of incompatibility arise in the use of official statistical series, of which differing time bases, different definitions of topics, different breakdowns of, for example, occupations and industries, and different amounts of information per spatial unit, are the most significant and the most difficult to overcome. In short, while central sources are producing a great deal of statistical information, its value to planners is limited by these various factors.

There is another problem here in that, while central sources are producing a large amount of published statistical information, they are also not publishing a great deal more. Partly, this is because most of the surveys carried out by central organisations involve the collection of large quantities of raw data, and these cannot be exploited to the full within the confines of a published volume; an increasing number of official statistical series include an introductory note to the effect that the data are capable of much more detailed analysis and that such detailed information may be obtained on request, sometimes on payment of a fee. The addresses of organisations which will co-operate in this way are included in the appendix, and most of the series described in the following pages fall into this category. But there is in addition a quantity of data which are gathered and held by central government departments and other bodies to which planners (and others) are denied access on grounds of confidentiality, and a great deal more which are collected and stored and whose existence is rarely known except by accident. While clearly scrupulous attention has to be paid to the preservation of individual confidentiality, there is a considerable feeling among planners that the policies of confidentiality which cause so much data to be withheld should be reviewed, and that it should be possible to release data for planning purposes so long as they are sufficiently highly aggregated to preserve individual privacy.

The whole problem of data for planning purposes is a complex one, and a very basic and important one, since good quality data are a fundamental prerequisite of the structure plans prescribed in the 1968 Town and Country Planning Act, and since also the lack of such data is the principal deterrent to the development of efficient simulation and modelling techniques. Discussions of the requirement for data and the most useful way of organising it are available in several articles in the British and American press, of which 'Data requirements for urban land use models' by Tim Rhodes in *JTPI* 54(6) June 1968 281-283, 'Planning and information' by Nigel Moor in *Architectural Association quarterly* 2(2) April 1970 56-61 and 'Primary materials in urban and regional planning' by Brenda White in *Aslib proceedings* 23(4) April 1971 187-198, offer concise statements of the various factors involved; if an antidote is required, it is provided in Bernard Benjamin's paper 'Statistics in town planning' in *Journal of the Royal Statistical Society* series A 132(1)

242

1969 1-15, in which the author stresses the need to define precise objectives before collecting a mass of data which may or may not be relevant. A much fuller discussion of the planning process and the data requirements which it begets is contained in a working paper from the Urban Systems Research Unit at the University of Reading, where an extensive inquiry has been undertaken into the rationalisation of centralised data collection and processing, as the first stage of a wider research project. *Information needs of planners: a survey* by Erlet A Cater (Reading University, Urban Systems Research Unit, 1970, USRU-WP-4) examines the sources of data used by planning authorities and their methods of organising them, and indicates where the gaps in provision exist. While the planning authorities surveyed use published statistical sources to a considerable extent, there is yet, the report indicates, 'a lack of information of data which is in fact available to planners.'

The statistical sources discussed in the following pages largely emanate from central government departments or from government sponsored organisations, and most of them are published by HMSO. The publisher is indicated, therefore, only in those cases where it is other than HMSO. These are not sources of raw data, but of processed statistical information. Wherever relevant and possible, the scope of the publication is described both in terms of subjects and the area covered (Great Britain being England, Wales and Scotland together, the United Kingdom being Great Britain and Northern Ireland), the level of aggregation of the data, and the times series included. For further, more detailed guidance to statistical sources, and some of the ways in which they may be exploited, the last section of this chapter should be consulted.

Since 1967, a process of streamlining has been going on in the government statistical services with the aim of establishing a more centrally managed system and of achieving closer integration of government statistics. The main coordinating role is played by the Central Statistical Office, through a system of committees and informal consultations. Apart from its coordinating role, the main function of the CSO is to produce from the data collected by other departments the main economic analyses required for economic policy and management. Further steps towards streamlining have been taken more recently with the creation of the Business Statistics

Office at the Department of Trade and Industry which will undertake the collection and storage of most business statistics on behalf
of other departments (see the section on Production); and the amalgamation of the General Register Office for England and Wales
with the Government Social Survey to form the new Office of Population Censuses and Surveys. It is likely, therefore, that the overall
pattern of official statistics may change fundamentally in the next
decade, with, it is to be hoped, advantage to planning.

GENERAL STATISTICAL SOURCES

General statistical compilations have their main value in their
presentation, in summary form, of a wide range of statistics from
a variety of sources covering many subjects, usually giving a run
of retrospective figures over several years, which allows comparisons
to be made and trends observed. Occasionally the statistics in such
compilations are the only published ones available on their subject,
but in most cases more detailed information is available in the
original source.

The Central Statistical Office prepare the two principal general
statistical series relating to the United Kingdom of Great Britain
and Northern Ireland. The *Annual abstract of statistics* is the suc-
cessor to the *Statistical abstract* prepared by the Board of Trade
which ceased publication at the beginning of World War II. The
Annual abstract presents summarised statistics under these headings:
area and climate; population and vital statistics; social conditions;
education; labour; production; retail distribution and miscellaneous
services; transport and communications; external trade; overseas
finance; national income and expenditure; home finance; banking
and insurance; and prices. The volume for 1970 contains a total
of 395 tables in these various categories. Each table indicates the
source, documentary or institutional, of the statistics presented in
it, and a full list of sources is given at the end of the volume. In the
majority of cases, the figures given are annual totals, but in a few
cases quarterly or monthly figures are given as being more suitable
to the type of series: the tables for registered unemployed, for
example, show monthly totals. Most of the tables give figures for
each of the previous ten years, the volume for 1970 including 1959

to 1969, although those relating to population and vital statistics (births, deaths and marriages) go further back in time. Most of the sections have an explanatory preface pointing out the basis of compilation, deficiencies of data, and other relevant points, and footnotes appear liberally to explain the individual tables. The content of the volume is not static from year to year: revisions are made to incorporate new information, resulting either in new tables or in extensions to existing ones, and others may be omitted. Each annual volume carries a subject index.

The *Annual abstract* is supplemented by the *Monthly digest of statistics* which incorporates only those tables for which monthly or quarterly figures are produced. The number of tables included is therefore smaller than that of the *Annual abstract*—the 1971 issues have a total of 169—but the subject range is similar, the main sections being devoted to national income and expenditure; population and vital statistics; labour; social services; agriculture and food; production, output and costs; fuel and power; chemicals; metals, engineering and vehicles; textiles and other manufactures; construction; retailing and catering; transport; external trade; overseas finance; home finance; wages and prices; entertainment; and weather. Most of the tables present figures for the previous five or six years, yearly totals being given for the earlier years with monthly or quarterly figures for the last eighteen months to two years. Explanatory notes are used throughout, and the sources used are indicated at the foot of each table; there is no comprehensive listing of sources but a subject index is incorporated. The January issue of each year is accompanied by a supplement of definitions and explanatory notes, revised annually, which relates to both the *Monthly digest* and the *Annual abstract*. This is laid out in the same arrangement of sections as the *Monthly digest* itself, and explains in detail the meaning of the terms used, and the coverage and composition of the sources from which the statistics were abstracted.

The *Annual abstract* and the *Monthly digest* both use, in the majority of their tables, a breakdown by the component countries of the United Kingdom. For many purposes, however, a finer breakdown to at least regions is desirable, and to serve this purpose the Central Statistical Office issue the *Abstract of regional statistics* which presents, currently in seventy six tables (in the 1970 volume),

245

a wide range of summarised statistics relating to the whole of the United Kingdom, broken down by new standard regions. An appendix gives detailed descriptions of these regions including breakdowns of the seven conurbations; a second appendix gives descriptions of the sub-divisions of the standard regions of England and Wales and of the planning regions in Scotland, and a few tables include series analysed by these sub-divisions. Figures are given, in general, for five to ten years preceding the date of compilation. Subject coverage is similar to that of the two titles discussed above, the sections being on area and climate; population (without vital statistics); social services; education; employment; fuel and power; production; construction and investment; distribution; transport; and incomes and expenditure. Some of the sections carry more tables than others, depending upon the availability of regional analyses. There is an index of sources, but no subject index; the contents of the supplement to the *Monthly digest* apply also to this series. Also available is *An analysis of regional economic and social statistics* by Edwin Hammond (Durham University, Rowntree Research Unit, 1968). This is a compilation of regional information drawn from official publications, local authority sources, original tabulations, and unpublished government sources, and presented in summary form with analysis by the new standard regions of England, Wales and Scotland. Northern Ireland is not included. The terminal date for inclusion of information was September 1967. A total of 178 tables are grouped into sections on population; employment; housing; education; health; environment; and social factors. The data as presented are highly processed with concentration on percentages and index numbers, and, although figures are given over a sufficiently long period of time to indicate trends, key years only are used rather than every year. The tables are preceded by an explanatory text, commenting on the features of each section. The value of this compilation is not as a source book (which it is not) but as a synthesis of information from scattered sources and as a means of juxtaposition of regional information which is not easily comparable.

The Welsh Office produce an annual *Digest of Welsh statistics*, which presents summarised statistical information for Wales and Monmouthshire. The 1969 volume, published in 1970, contains 131 tables grouped into sections on population and vital statistics; social conditions; education; labour; production; transport and communications; finance; and area and climate; and supported by a subject index. An appendix describes the sub-divisions of Wales used for statistical purposes; some of the tables are analysed in accordance with these, though many give national figures only. In most tables, yearly totals are given, figures going back on average five to ten years before the date of compilation, although in several cases they go back much further; monthly figures are given occasionally, where these are available and appropriate. Sources of information are indicated at the foot of each table.

The *Digest of Scottish statistics* is prepared twice a year in April and October by the Economics and Statistics Unit of the Scottish Office, the issue of October 1970 including seventy six tables in sections headed industrial activity; transport and communication; trade through Scottish ports (sea and air); labour; population and vital statistics; social services; finance; and miscellaneous. Yearly totals are given in all tables except those relating to unemployment, which provide a monthly breakdown, and the figures refer to between five and ten years previous to the date of compilation according to the subject of the table, although some in the population and social service sections go further back. National totals are given in the majority of cases, with analyses in some tables by the Scottish planning regions and in others (for example, trade through Scottish ports) by more appropriate units. A subject index is provided, and the sources are indicated at individual tables.

The Economic Section of the Northern Ireland Ministry of Finance issue twice a year, in March and September, a *Digest of statistics* which relates solely to Northern Ireland. This is a more comprehensive compilation than its Scottish and Welsh counterparts for the reason that more statistical information is collected for the province separately. The issue of March 1971 is made up of 151 tables covering population and vital statistics; labour; education; social conditions and services; fuel and power; production; construction; agriculture, forestry and fishing; transport; post office; tourism; imports and exports; national income and expenditure; home finance; banking and insurance; wages, prices and retail

247

sales; and weather. Figures are largely national totals with occasional finer breakdown where national figures are not appropriate; the majority of tables have yearly totals, going back five to ten years or further when necessary, but a number also show monthly or quarterly figures over the previous eighteen months to two years when these are available. Sources are acknowledged at individual tables; there is no subject index. The inside back cover carries a listing of other government publications which contain social and economic statistics relating to Northern Ireland.

A further source of statistical information on a wide range of topics relating to Northern Ireland is *The Ulster year book: the official handbook of Northern Ireland* prepared by the Northern Ireland Information Service. The sections, on the land and the people; government; justice; protective services; social welfare; education; housing and planning; industry and trade; transport and communication; agriculture; labour; public finance; local government finance; private finance; the arts and sciences; broadcasting and the press; and sport; all contain descriptive narrative text supported by statistical tables, giving the main yearly totals for the province as a whole, going back up to ten years.

The major local statistical abstract is that compiled by the Research and Intelligence Unit of the Greater London Council in conjunction with the London boroughs, and published as the *Annual abstract of Greater London statistics* (GLC). The volume for 1968, published in 1970, contains 260 tables sectionalised under headings for elections; population and vital statistics; employment; transport and communications; social services; education; planning; public services; finance; and weather. For the most part, data relate to the calendar year of the volume (not to the year of publication) except where they are collected for a different period: in such cases the table is annotated to that effect; figures for 1966 and 1967 are shown for comparative purposes in the 1968 volume. Sources are also indicated at each table. The area covered is that of the thirty two London borough councils and of the City of London. Appendices list the constitution of public authorities in Greater London with details of boundary and ward changes 1965 to 1968, employment exchange areas, and the sources used. There is an index.

POPULATION AND VITAL STATISTICS

The census of population which is taken at regular intervals in Great Britain is the primary source of data about the population, its characteristics and vital statistics. The first official census was carried out in 1801, and, apart from the year 1941, censuses have been taken every ten years ever since. Up to and including 1851, the census covered England, Wales and Scotland; from 1861, however, Scotland has been statistically separate and is subject to an independent census. A separate census was taken for Ireland every ten years from 1801 to 1911, following which a census was taken in both the north and the south in 1926; Northern Ireland has subsequently been counted independently in 1937, 1951 and 1961. Up to and including the sample census of 1966, the conduct of the census for England and Wales has been the responsibility of the Registrar General and the General Register Office; in May 1970 that office was merged with the Government Social Survey Department to form the Office of Population Censuses and Surveys which has conduct now of all census and other survey operations. Responsibility for the census operation in Scotland and Northern Ireland rests respectively with the Registrar General for Scotland and the General Register Office, Northern Ireland. An account of the development of the census and its present administration and methods is given by Bernard Benjamin in a Social Science Research Council review *The population census* (Heinemann Educational, 1970).

The most recent full census of England and Wales is that of 1961, and the results of this are published by HMSO in a series of volumes between 1961 and 1966. These published volumes are as follows:

The census 1961, England and Wales: preliminary report (1961) contains only general notes, preliminary statistical commentary, and provisional figures of the population, private households and private dwellings for all local authority areas, regions, conurbations, and new towns.

Scientific and technological qualifications (1962) represents a 10% sample of Great Britain as a whole, and gives statistics of persons with these qualifications and the occupations and industries in which they work.

Report on Welsh speaking population (1962) is a full representation of Wales and Monmouthshire.

249

Usual residence tables (1964) compare the enumerated census population in local areas with the population usually resident in those areas.

Age, marital condition and general tables (1964) comprise summaries of the information given in the county reports (see below) on local population, age and marital condition, with the various categories of non-private population.

Birthplace and nationality tables (1964) are similarly summaries of the information in the county reports on these subjects.

Housing tables (1964-5) in three parts, contain summaries from the county volumes together with more extensive tabulations for England and Wales, dealing with buildings, dwellings and households, tenure and household arrangements, and summary local housing indices.

Household composition tables (1966) are a 10% sample representation of composition of households and families and their socio-economic characteristics.

Migration tables (1966), also a 10% sample, give detailed information on the numbers and characteristics of people who changed their usual residence in the year before Census Day 1961, and compare these with similar information about the rest of the population. Numbers of people moving are also given, mainly for local areas.

Workplace tables (1966) present a 10% sample survey of people who live in one area and work in another, areal units being boroughs, urban and rural districts and new towns.

Occupation tables (1966), on a 10% sample basis, give statistics of the occupied population based on their personal occupation (classified according to the 1960 classification of occupations) including figures for usually resident populations of the larger areas, with analysis by age, marital condition, employment status and socio-economic group.

Industry tables (1966) are in two parts, each on a 10% basis; the first part analyses the employed population by the branches of industry in which they are employed, using the Standard Industrial Classification, and the second analyses each important industry or group of industries by the principal occupations which contribute to them.

250

Education tables (1966) give details of the terminal education age of persons resident in local areas, and, for England and Wales and the regions and conurbations, classifications by age and by occupation, of a 10% sample.

Fertility tables (1966) are a full coverage of the population at risk, based on date of marriage and number of children born to women who had ever been married.

Commonwealth immigrants in the conurbations (1965) gives statistics of the demographic, social, and economic characteristics of a 10% sample of commonwealth immigrants in the six conurbations.

Socio-economic group tables (1966) on a 10% sample basis, analyse economically active males and economically inactive males in terms of socio-economic groups, for all types of areas and aggregates of areas down to local authority areas.

Great Britain summary tables (1966) collate statistics on all the subjects detailed above for Great Britain as a whole.

Census 1961 Great Britain: general report (1968) deals with the organisation of the census mainly for England and Wales, discussing the analysis of data, and containing a statistical assessment of the results. The principal procedural differences between England and Wales, and Scotland, are also described.

In addition to the tables detailed above, which relate to the country as a whole, a series of county reports were published between 1963 and 1964 presenting statistics which were collected on a full 100% basis. Each report covers one county, and comprises tables presenting details of various factors grouped into sections on population; boundary changes and detached parts; sex, age and marital condition; birthplace and nationality; housing and households; household arrangements; non-private households; and old people. Also published is a report *Greater London tables* (1966) which gives information under the same grouped headings for the area of the Greater London Council; a *Report on Jersey, Guernsey and adjacent islands* (1966) giving a full range of census information; and a two-part *Report on Isle of Man* (1965-6), part one dealing with population and housing, part two with migration, economic activity and other topics. In conjunction with the census as a whole there are two volumes comprising an *Index of place names* (1965) covering England and Wales and constituting a complete alphabetical index to all areas forming the census enumeration districts and giving for each one its enumerated population, plus other places for which populations have not been ascertained.

The full census of Scotland taken in 1961 is published in ten volumes. The first volume comprises separate reports for the four cities of Edinburgh, Glasgow, Aberdeen and Dundee and for each of the Scottish counties, thirty five parts in all, issued between 1963 and 1964, the remainder being as follows:

V2   *Usual residence* (1965)

V3   *Age, marital condition and general tables* (1965)

V4   *Housing and households,* in two parts (1966), the second, the household composition tables, being a 10% sample.

V5   *Birthplace and nationality* (1966)

V6   *Occupation, industry and workplace,* in three parts (1966) all of them on a 10% sample basis.

V7   *Gaelic* (1966) giving details by age and sex of the Gaelic speaking population.

V8   *Internal migration* (1966) another 10% sample.

V9   *Terminal education age* (1966) a 10% sample.

V10   *Fertility* (1966).

A series of leaflets was also published through 1966 containing data on occupation and industry for individual counties, cities, and local authority areas, grouped into regions, for example, Edinburgh and the Lothians, and the Border counties. These leaflets contain tables showing the distribution of the resident economically active population within the area covered, by occupation, status and sex, and the distribution of the people in employment by industry and sex. An alphabetical list of 'populated places' is also published as *Place names and population, Scotland* (1967).

The results of the 1961 census of Northern Ireland are published in seven regional parts, published between 1963 and 1964, covering Belfast county borough, County of Down, County of Armagh, County of Antrim, County of Fermanagh, County and county borough of Londonderry, and County of Tyrone; plus a *General report* and a *Report on the fertility of marriage* (1965). A *Topographical index* was issued in 1963.

In 1966, 10% sample censuses were taken in England and Wales and in Scotland, and the published results of these are also available (1967-). A series of county reports, covering each one independently, has been published for England and Wales, and there is also a set of reports relating to Scotland which groups cities and counties together so that each report focuses on a single region. These county reports give statistics for administrative counties, county boroughs, local authority areas with population over 15,000, and county aggregates; the Scottish region reports cover cities, counties and large burghs, and small burghs and districts of counties with over 15,000 population, with summary statistics only for those with less than 15,000 population. The subjects covered in these reports are population and acreage; sex, age and marital condition; birthplace; private households, dwellings, tenure and household amenities; private motor cars and garaging; economically active and retired males and their socio-economic groups. In addition to these reports, some areas of Scotland which were enumerated on a 100% basis are covered in a separate volume *Census 1966 Scotland. Report on the special study areas* (1968). The areas selected are Roxburgh, Sutherland and Shetland counties, Lewis and Harris, Livingston new town and surroundings, and Fort William and surroundings. The subjects and tables for these areas correspond to those contained in the region reports, except that, being derived from a full census, the figures are not sample figures and the tables are more comprehensive. *Summary tables* (1967) cover Great Britain as a whole.

Economic activity tables (1968-9) are in four parts and refer to Great Britain as a whole. They provide statistics of the occupied population based on their personal occupations, classified in accordance with the *Classification of occupations 1966* (1966)[1], and the employed population classified into the branches of industry in which they are employed, according to the Standard Industrial Classification, with breakdowns by age, marital state, employment status, socio-economic group, and other variables. Industries are analysed by contributory occupations, occupations are analysed by the principal industries in which people are employed. A series of *Economic activity county leaflets* gives tables for counties and large local authority areas in England, Wales and Scotland, presenting statistics for the county and, within it, for county boroughs, urban areas over 50,000 population, new towns and conurbation centres, and down to local authority areas in addition in the table of economically active males by area of residence and socio-economic group. *General explanatory notes* to this series are published separately. Most recently, a volume of *Economic activity sub-regional tables* has been published (1970) which has five tables—economically active persons by area of residence: occupation and status by sex; persons in employment by area of workplace: occupation by sex; persons in employment by area of workplace: industry and status by sex; economically active males by area of residence and socio-economic group; economic activity: males by age, females by age, married females by age—analysed by sub-divisions of regions of England and Wales and economic planning sub-regions of Scotland.

Statistics of migration are presented for England and Wales in two main volumes, the first *Migration summary tables* (1968) and the second *Migration tables* (1969), and in a set of nine *Migration regional reports* (1968) each one covering an economic planning region, including Wales. The statistics are analysed from national units down to local authorities of 15,000 or more population. Tables for Scotland are published separately in two parts (1968-9) relating to the whole country; no regional reports are issued. Analysis is by national totals down to small burghs and districts of counties over 15,000 population, according to the table.

The Workplace/transport tables are issued in two volumes for England and Wales and one for Scotland (1968) and give details of the resident population and the population employed in each area and of the main workplace movements from one area to another, the main means of transport to work used for making these movements, and the characteristics of the people making them.

Household composition tables and *Housing tables* are published separately for England and Wales and for Scotland, the first in one volume each, the second in two and one volumes respectively (1968). The *Usual residence tables* for England and Wales (1969) are also published separately from the *Usual residence and birthplace tables* for Scotland (1969). The *Commonwealth immigrant tables* (1969) cover the whole of Great Britain. Results from the 100% census of

Northern Ireland taken in October 1966 are incorporated into the volume of *United Kingdom general and parliamentary constituency tables* (1969), though difficulties are noted in achieving comparability of data. The volume has some summary tables relating to the UK as a whole, and then for each constituency are tabulated details of population, dwellings, households, tenure, amenities, cars and transport to work. Yet to be published are the *Education tables* which will cover Great Britain as a whole, and an administrative report on the census in general and a statistical report on its methodology. No preliminary report was issued for the 1966 census.[2]

The foregoing discussion relates to the published information produced as a result of the census. It is possible also to obtain unpublished data and information, both for variables which are not published at all and also at lower aggregations for variables which are published but only analysed for large areas. Computer print-out is available giving general information for each census enumeration district (in the 1971 census these units are being replaced by kilometre grid squares[3]). Tabulations are also available covering a standard range of census variables for individual local authority areas and subdivisions of these, and for census enumeration districts.

Basic continuing demographic information is contained in the annual *Registrar General's statistical review of England and Wales.* This is in three parts. *Part 1, tables, medical* is concerned principally with mortality, and analyses serial mortality records, vital statistics by local areas, causes of death, stillbirths and infant mortality, and infectious diseases. *Part 2, tables, population* gives detailed analyses of present and projected population numbers, marriages and live and stillbirths, vital statistics by local areas, marriage rates, divorces, natural increase and migration, births and adoptions, commonwealth and foreign population, and fertility. In many of the tables, comparative figures are given for preceding years. *Part 3, commentary* is mainly textual and comments on parts one and two. More detail than is possible in the *Statistical review* is provided in the *Registrar General's decennial supplement, England and Wales,* dealing with area mortality tables. The most recent edition covers the years 1959-63 (1967, with amendments 1970), being the latest in a series of decennial area mortality analyses which cover periods from 1851-60 onwards. Deaths from all causes of males and females

255

are analysed by areal units from England and Wales together down to local authorities, as are stillbirths and infant mortality expressed in proportion to live births.

The *Statistical review* is supplemented in some of its tables by the *Registrar General's quarterly return for England and Wales* which contains figures which are provisional until confirmed in the annual volumes. The scope of the quarterly parts is narrower, being limited to births, deaths, marriages and infectious diseases, with population estimates. More up to date, but even more limited in scope and containing little detail is the *Registrar General's weekly return for England and Wales* which contains figures of births, deaths, infectious diseases, and national insurance claims. Roughly comparable to the *Statistical review* is the *Annual Report of the Registrar General for Scotland,* also in two parts, the first on mortality statistics, the second covering population and vital statistics. This is selectively supplemented by the *Quarterly return of the Registrar General, Scotland* reporting births, deaths and marriages registered in the previous quarter, and by weekly returns also. Similar annual, quarterly and weekly statements are made by the Registrar General for Northern Ireland.

Estimates of population are produced annually both for England and Wales and for Scotland. *The Registrar General's annual estimates of the population of England and Wales and of local authority areas* contains the estimated home population figures for the middle of the current year broken down by local authority areas; figures are also given for the standard regions, the conurbations, and urban and rural aggregates. A breakdown by sex and age is given for the two countries as a whole. The 1970 *Annual estimates* contain also the revised figures for mid-1967, 'for the guidance of those concerned with town and country planning'. Similar information is produced for Scotland in the *Annual estimates of the population of Scotland.*

Figures of estimated future total population of the UK (population projections) are published annually in the *Monthly digest of statistics* as well as later in the *Annual abstract.* The projections are prepared in the Government Actuary's Department in consultation with the Registrar General, using the latest mid-year estimates. In 1968 and 1969 the projections were included in the tables of the

April issue; in 1970 they appeared as a supplementary table in the May issue, the table giving mid-year estimates from 1970 to 1976 and then for 1981, 1991, and 2001, with breakdown by age and sex. The assumptions on which the projections are based are explained in a note. The Department of the Environment's quarterly *Housing statistics Great Britain* includes from time to time (issues of August 1969 and February 1970) projections of numbers of potential households; the projection in the February 1970 issue being based on the 1968-based population projections published in the *Registrar General's quarterly return* for the first quarter of 1969, giving a regional breakdown covering England and Wales and projecting to 1976 and 1981. The *Statistics for town and country planning*, prepared by the Department of the Environment, recently added a third occasional series on population and households, of which the first issue has appeared, containing two papers, *Statistics for town and country planning, series III Population and households: No 1 Projecting growth patterns in regions* (DOE, 1970). The first paper, *Population projections within regions 1968-1991* discusses, from a planning viewpoint, the Registrar General's 1968-based population projections for the subdivisions of the standard regions of England and Wales, and presents, in tabulated form, the projections in more detail than was previously published together with various analyses including comparison with past trends. Also included is a discussion of the rationale behind the migration assumptions incorporated into these projections. The second paper, *The projection of households,* describes in great detail the techniques and definitions used in the department for calculating household projections; observed and projected regional headship rates are set out, and variations between areas discussed. Also set out and discussed are the sub-divisional household projections derived from the population projections described in the first paper.

Statistics of internal migration are included in the main census of population reports, in some detail, as are statistics of commonwealth immigrants. These are supplemented by two annual Home Office publications, both issued as Command Papers, *Statistics of foreigners entering and leaving the United Kingdom* and *Control of immigration: statistics,* the latter of which gives numbers admitted, embarked and refused admission. Retrospective data is

9

contained in the Jones Report, *The brain drain: report of the working group on migration* (1967) which estimated the in and out migration of scientists and technologists between 1961 and 1966.

ECONOMIC CONDITIONS

The principal vehicle of continuing economic information relating to the United Kingdom is the monthly *Economic trends* prepared by the Central Statistical Office. Each issue contains articles on current economic topics, followed by charts and statistics presenting trends in the economy of the United Kingdom as a whole (breakdowns by country are not provided). The prefatory note to each issue stresses that ' the purpose of the charts and tables is to provide the broad background to the trends of the economy rather than to give detailed information about particular series (for which the *Monthly digest of statistics* and other publications may be consulted)'. The trends are presented in sections which cover income and expenditure; investment; production; employment; output and prices; home finance; and external trade. Most of the charts and tables cover a long period of time, so that trends can be observed. Figures given are, in the main, monthly or quarterly totals. Each issue carries a list of sources. The more important articles contributed to *Economic trends* are collected separately and published every two to three years as *New contributions to economic statistics*. Each monthly issue of *Economic trends* carries as its first contribution a survey of ' The economic situation ' prepared by the Treasury, which replaces the former annual Treasury *Economic report*. The issues of January, April, July, and October carry the tabulated quarterly estimates of national income and expenditure prepared by the Central Statistical Office, together with a commentary (the tables without commentary are also published in the *Monthly digest*), the October issue carrying a longer run of quarterly figures which is consistent with the annual publication, *National income and expenditure* (see below).

Further continuing information on a full range of economic factors is processed through the quarterly *National Institute economic review* published by the National Institute of Economic and Social Research in February, May, August and November. The

Review is 'intended to be of service to those, in business or else-where, who need to take a view of the general economic situation and prospects.' Each issue comprises a short survey of the economic situation in the UK and abroad, which in the February issue of each year expands into a full-length survey of several chapters; followed by articles of topical economic interest, and concluded with a statistical appendix incoporating tables presenting yearly totals for the UK as a whole over a ten-year period, and also tables relating to overseas countries in comparison with the UK covering a similar period, over a range of economic factors. *Trade and industry* is the weekly journal which has evolved from the former *Board of Trade journal*. It is the official publication of the Department of Trade and Industry and its contents reflect the departmental range of interests. It incorporates a statistical section of varying length and content each week, and being a weekly production is an ideal vehicle for up to date figures. Much more statistical information is disseminated through the department's series of 'Business monitors', which are compiled from original data collected by the department's Business Statistics Office. There are four series of 'Business monitors': the production series, which carries up to date output figures on a variety of manufactured products together with data on exports, consumption of raw materials, stocks and prices, each 'Monitor' being devoted to an individual product; the civil aviation series, in which each part deals with a separate part of the business and gives the movement of aircraft, passengers and freight at reporting airports in the UK, passenger flows on the main domestic and international routes and traffic carried by UK airlines; the service and distributive series showing the latest movement of turnover in various sectors of the retail and service trades; and the miscellaneous series, giving detailed statistics on a variety of subjects, for example, motor vehicle registrations, and cinemas. Most of the 'Business monitors' are revised monthly, or quarterly, and a few annually. The most recent complete list of titles (at time of writing) was given in *Trade and industry* 2(10) March 10 1971 507. Details of new inquiries being set up for additional industries are given from time to time in *Trade and industry*, for example 3(1) April 7 1971 37-39.

259

FINANCE: INCOME AND EXPENDITURE

The principal source of data on financial income and expenditure in all sectors is the monthly *Financial statistics* compiled by the Central Statistical Office, in collaboration with other government departments and the Bank of England. The statistics relate to the United Kingdom and are national totals throughout. Figures given are mainly totals for calendar months, with time series data in most tables going back seven to ten years. The sources from which the data have been derived are indicated at the foot of each table. The issue of March 1971 contains 111 tables grouped into sections on summarised financial accounts; public sector accounts; central government; local authorities; public corporations; the banking sector; money supply and domestic credit expansion; other financial institutions; the company sector; the personal sector; overseas finance; capital issues and stock exchange transactions; and exchange rates, interest rates and security prices. There is an alphabetical subject index.

Further information is presented in *National income and expenditure*. Each annual volume (known as the ' blue book ') contains estimates of the national product, income, and expenditure of the UK for the previous ten calendar years, the volume for 1970 covering 1959 to 1969, with a few tables extending back for a further ten years. The volume for 1970 is made up of seventy six tables, the first thirteen of which are summary tables presenting, in aggregated form, figures which are given in more detail, or in a different way, in the following tables. The tables are in sections dealing with expenditure and output; industrial input and output; the personal sector; companies; public corporations; central government; local authorities; combined public authorities; the public sector; capital formation; and financial accounts. Yearly totals for the UK as a whole are given throughout. The 1970 volume contains no input-output tables, as previous volumes had done up to that of 1968, in deference to the detailed study *Input-output tables for the United Kingdom 1963* (see below). Another useful source is the Bank of England *Quarterly bulletin,* which contains articles on aspects of banking and finance, and a statistical annexe containing tables on central government finance; detailed banking analyses; the capital markets; external finance; and yields, rates and prices. Figures are given up to three years back in some tables, and refer to the UK as a whole. In 1971, the Bank produced a *Statistical abstract* covering most of the financial series which appear regularly in the *Quarterly bulletin*, but presenting figures over a much longer period than is possible in the latter publication, in the main from 1945 to 1969 or March 1970. The thirty one tables are grouped into sections which correspond to those of the *Quarterly bulletin*.

Details of government income and expenditure are to be found in various publications issued throughout the year, in greater or lesser amount of detail. The most detailed source is the annual *Finance accounts* which set out the main trends of revenue and expenditure of the Exchequer in the preceding year.

Local authority finance is detailed in the annual summary *Local government financial statistics England and Wales* produced by the Department of the Environment and the Welsh Office, with a substantial time-lag, the returns for 1968-69 being published in 1971. The figures for England and for Wales are presented separately, although tables of combined statistics are included. The returns include those from local authorities and also from a range of other local bodies such as drainage and river authorities, water boards, harbour boards, and the trustees of certain London squares. National totals appear throughout. The Scottish Development Department present similar information in their annual *Local financial returns Scotland* (with an equivalent time-lag) as do the Ministry of Health and Local Government, Northern Ireland, in *Local authority financial returns*. The Society of County Treasurers issue two annuals, *Financial and general statistics of county councils* and *Capital expenditure of county councils*, both based on information supplied by the authorities themselves, which give details of income and expenditure on all services for all English and Welsh counties. Analyses of local authority income from rates are provided in the annual *Rates and rateable values in England and Wales* compiled by the Department of the Environment and the Welsh Office. The return gives particulars of the rates levied for the financial year under consideration and the rateable values in force at the beginning of that year, for all rating authorities throughout the two countries. Similar information relating to Scotland is compiled in

261

Rates and rateable values in Scotland; and to Northern Ireland in
Local authority rate statistics, Northern Ireland.

Inland revenue statistics is an annual compilation from the Inland
Revenue, first published in 1970, containing most of the statistical
information which previously appeared in the annual reports of the
Commissioners of Inland Revenue. The statistics relate to the UK,
and are grouped into sections on taxation, incomes, personal
incomes, capital, and valuation. The main weight of tables is in the
section ' survey of personal incomes ' which analyses by income
groups, family circumstances, and type of income, and then goes
on to a regional breakdown of incomes. Much more detailed information on earnings is presented in the *New earnings survey 1968*
(1970) compiled by the Department of Employment from a sample
survey of earnings of employees in Great Britain in September 1968.
The 149 tables are mainly concerned with analyses by occupation
or industry, age, sex, and region, and other factors as relevant,
of the gross weekly and hourly earnings of full-time adults and
full-time employees. The ten major groupings and sixty three sub-
groupings of occupations are not compatible with the standard
occupation units used in the census of population. The tables presented in the published volume represent only a part of the information collected, and further unpublished analyses are available on
request. The department propose an annual survey, each April
from 1970; the preliminary results of the 1970 survey are contained
in four consecutive issues of the *Department of Employment gazette*
from November 1970 to February 1971, and will be published in
volume form in due course.

The principal source of data on personal, consumer expenditure
is the annual *Family expenditure survey report,* also compiled by
the Department of Employment. The survey collects, in addition to
data on the expenditure of private households, a great deal of data
also about the characteristics of each household in the sample and
the income of its members. ' In consequence ', as the introduction
to the 1969 report points out, ' it has become a multi-purpose survey
and provides a unique fund of important economic and social data.'
The area covered is that of the United Kingdom. Quarterly analyses
at national level are made in advance of the annual volume and are
published in the *Department of Employment gazette*. The tables of

262

the annual volume contain detailed analyses, by a wide range of factors, of household income and expenditure; distribution of households by income; sources of income; characteristics of individuals in households; and distributions of weekly earnings of individuals. There is also a set of regional tables covering much the same headings. Northern Ireland is included in these regional tables, but the main tables relating to the province are compiled separately by the Ministry of Finance and published most recently in *Family expenditure survey 1968 and 1969 (Northern Ireland)* (1970). The tables give details of household income and expenditure in each of the years 1968 and 1969, with comparisons for 1967, the expenditure analysis covering ninety four categories. The *Surveys* give details of family expenditure in all categories. Detailed information about private expenditure on food only is given in the annual reports prepared by the National Food Survey Committee of the Ministry of Agriculture. The most recent (at time of writing) is *Household food consumption and expenditure 1968* (1970) which includes a supplement giving preliminary estimates for 1969. The report contains detailed tabulations of average household food consumption, expenditure, and prices paid by housewives throughout Great Britain for each of some 150 categories of food in each quarter of 1968, with further breakdowns for Scotland, Wales, and the standard regions of England, and in various categories of urban and rural areas. Details of average expenditure and consumption for each of about forty five broader categories of food are presented for households in various income groups and for various sizes of family. Unpublished data from the survey are available for some detailed analyses.

A detailed analysis of income and expenditure in the agricultural industry is presented in *Farm incomes in England and Wales 1969-70*, a report based on the farm management survey which compares the physical and financial results in 1968/69 and 1969/70 in farms throughout England and Wales. The survey is operated by university departments of agricultural economics and issued from the Ministry of Agriculture. Its object is ' to maintain by means of records from a sample of farms a body of economic and financial information about farming at the farm level '.

263

It was mentioned above that the provisional input-output estimates included in the annual *National income and expenditure* up to and including 1968 were discontinued after that volume. The provisional tables printed in the 1968 volume, and also in the August 1968 issue of *Economic trends* related to 1963, and are now replaced by a detailed study prepared by the Central Statistical Office, *Input-output tables for the United Kingdom 1963* (1970, Studies in Official Statistics 16). The tables are based largely on the results of the census of production for 1963, the last year for which detailed data on manufacturing industry are available. Seventy separate industries are distinguished and presented in matrix form, with the sources of each industry's purchases (or 'inputs') in a column and the destination of its output in a row. A wide variety of relationships can be derived from the various tables, for example, the extent to which each industry is dependent for its purchases on other industries and on imports, and the extent to which each one is dependent for its sales both directly and indirectly on other industries, on personal and public consumption, and on investment.

PRODUCTION

Statistics of production by industry, or industrial statistics, are currently being streamlined by the government statistical service. The principal source of industrial statistics has been, and still is, the large-scale censuses of production which have been taken at regular intervals in Great Britain since 1907, most recently in 1968. This undertaking is to be replaced by the creation of a central register of business establishments and other units such as companies, business units, and enterprises, which will be used for all industrial statistics and which, when fully set up, will allow results from different enquiries to be related, and thus to form an integrated system of data. In conjunction with the register, a comprehensive system of current data collection over the entire industrial field would replace the former large-scale and irregular surveys. The major feature of the current statistics programme will be a series of quarterly enquiries to collect data on the sales of each industry's products, and publication of these figures will be coordinated with the production series of the existing ' Business monitors '. The main burden of organisation and data collection will be carried by the Business Statistics Office of the Department of Trade and Industry. In addition, an annual census is to be taken, starting in 1970, covering all mining, manufacturing, and public service industries, but excluding construction; businesses employing less than twenty five persons will not be included except in certain industries.

Publication of the results of the 1963 census of production is now complete, in 133 parts. The first part is an introduction explaining methods, terminology and contents. This is followed by 128 reports, each containing a stardardised set of tables relating to one industry. Part 130 is an index of products. The three final parts contain summary tables presenting analyses by industry, enterprises, and regions respectively. The last part was published in 1970. The census covers the four countries of the United Kingdom, and embraces the whole of mining, manufacturing, gas, water, electricity and construction. The standardised tables for each industry in the report of the 1963 census are as follows (those marked with an asterisk only apply to certain industries):

1 Industry summary: estimates for all firms, 1958 and 1963.

2 Analysis of larger firms (ie those employing twenty five or more persons) by sub-divisions within the industry, 1958 and 1963.

3 Analysis of larger firms by size of enterprise within the industry, 1963.

4 Percentage analysis of employees, by age and sex, all firms, 1963.

5 Sales of principal products of the industry by larger firms, 1958 and 1963.

6 Sales of principal products of the industry by establishments classified to other industries, 1958 and 1963.

7 Sales of other than principal products by larger firms in the industry, 1958 and 1963.

*8 Production of certain principal products of the industry by larger firms, including production by establishments classified to other industries, 1958 and 1963.

*9 Purchases of selected principal products of the industry by larger firms, 1963.

10 Purchases by larger firms in the industry, 1958 and 1963.

9*

11 Transport costs and employment of larger firms, 1963.

12 Payments for services, etc, by larger firms, 1963.

13 Percentage analysis of twelve-month periods covered by returns from larger firms, 1963.

*14 Sales of all parts of machinery and plant by larger firms, 1958 and 1963.

Very limited censuses were taken in the years 1964 to 1967, relating only to the value of the stocks and capital expenditure of industrial business units, and the results for all of these are published in *The report on the censuses of production for 1964, 1965, 1966 and 1967* (1971). Results from the 1968 census are not yet available in full published form, though provisional results have appeared in *Board of trade journal* 197(3798) December 31 1969 1758-1769.

In addition to being included in the census of production reports covering the UK, Northern Ireland is also covered separately in the *Report on the census of production of Northern Ireland* (1966). The report on the 1963 census is published in four parts: a general report and summary tables; textiles and clothing; engineering, food, drink and tobacco, paper, printing and publishing; and a fourth part embracing timber and furniture, mineral products, other manufacturing trades, construction, gas, electricity and water. Between 1964 and 1967, limited censuses were taken in which firms employing less than twenty five persons were not included and less detail was required from larger firms than in the 1963 census. The results of these annual censuses were prepared by the Ministry of Commerce and published in single volumes, the most recent, 1967, appearing in 1969.

The annual census of agriculture began in 1866. *A century of agricultural statistics: Great Britain 1866-1966* (1968) contains comparative tables presenting the main time series over the hundred year period, and illustrates the most striking changes in charts and maps, most of the latter referring to the three dates, 1875, 1938, and 1966. The record is continued in the annual *Agricultural statistics England and Wales* prepared by the Ministry of Agriculture, Fisheries and Food (1968/69 published 1971). The report is in three sections, on agriculture, horticulture, and prices: the section on agriculture is the major one and contains detailed analyses, with

266

comparative data over a ten-year period in some cases and break-downs to county level, of acreages; livestock; production of crops; yield; agricultural holdings; frequency distribution of crops and livestock; agricultural workers; and agricultural machinery. Comparable information is given in *Agricultural statistics Scotland* prepared by the Department of Agriculture and Fisheries for Scotland; and in the annual report of the Ministry of Agriculture, Northern Ireland. The three departments jointly produce nationally aggregated statistics in the annual *Agricultural statistics United Kingdom* (1967/68, published 1971). A booklet from the Ministry of Agriculture, *Output and utilisation of farm produce in the United Kingdom—1964/65 to 1968/69* (MOAFF, 1970) is the second in an annual series of statistical tables showing the production and utilisation in the UK of all the principal agricultural and horticultural crops, and livestock and livestock products, which replaces the less regular series of the same title published by HMSO. Two volumes under the title *Horticulture in Britain,* the first, dealing with vegetables, published in 1967 and the second, on fruit and flowers, published in 1971, jointly provide a comprehensive background of comparative statistics over a period of some twenty years, relating to the most important horticultural crops grown in the UK.

The former annual *Statistical digest* produced by the Ministry of Power has now given way to the annual *Digest of energy statistics* prepared by the Department of Trade and Industry. The main emphasis is on annual statistics, although quarterly figures are included in some tables; the whole of the UK is covered. The first section of tables is devoted to energy consumption generally, with a regional breakdown; thereafter, sections deal with coal; petroleum; natural gas; gas; electricity; and coke and manufactured fuel. Other sections include prices and values, consumption by large industrial users, and production of minerals other than coal. Sources of data and information in individual parts of the power industry are in the second volume of the National Coal Board annual *Report and accounts,* containing financial tables and national and area statistical tables; the *Annual report and accounts* of the Gas Council and the twelve *Area gas board annual reports and accounts;* and the *Electricity supply handbook* (Electrical Times Ltd, 1970), the *CEGB statistical yearbook* (Central Electricity Generating Board, annual), and the *Handbook of electricity supply statistics* and *Domestic surveys* prepared and published by the Electricity Council.

The construction industry is covered in the *Monthly bulletin of construction statistics* from the Department of the Environment (DOE, Statistics Construction Division), which covers Great Britain. National totals, with some regional breakdown, are given in the tables, which are grouped into sections dealing with value of output and new orders; employment in the construction industry; housing; production of materials and components; exports; industrial building; local authority design work; three tables relating to Northern Ireland separately; and value of work done and operatives employed by local authorities. The same department issues an annual statistical account of *Sand and gravel production* covering England, Wales and Scotland, which provides analyses by counties and by gravel regions.

DISTRIBUTION

Distribution statistics are concerned with the retail distribution of consumer goods and closely related service trades such as hairdressing and boot and shoe repairs. The statistics are collected by the Department of Trade and Industry through the censuses of distribution, and the results of these form the primary source of statistical information in this field. The first full census of distribution related to 1950, the second and most recent one was taken in 1962 relating to 1961; sample censuses were taken for 1957 and 1966. The purpose of the census of distribution is ' to provide a detailed analysis of the structure of retail trade and a fresh basis for the monthly or quarterly statistics relating to retail sales and stocks; hire purchase transactions; and capital expenditure. The census is one of the basic statistical sources used in compiling the official accounts of national income and expenditure.'

The results of the 1950 census were published in four volumes as *Census of distribution and other services 1950*. The first volume contains area tables of retail and service trades; the second volume contains general tables of retail and service trades; and the third volume relates to wholesale trades. These are preceded by a preliminary volume constituting a report on the retail trade. The 1950

268

census was the only one to include the wholesale trade as well as the retail and service trades. The full results of the census for 1961 are published in fourteen separate parts as *Report on the census of distribution and other services 1961* (1963-64). The first of the fourteen parts contains a general analysis of retail establishments in terms of their numbers, turnover, number of branches, persons engaged, and types of commodities; the last of the fourteen parts contains estimates for retail trade as a whole based on the information about various financial items obtained from all large retail organisations and from a sample of smaller ones. The intervening parts are devoted to areas of Great Britain, the second part containing summary figures for all areas, the third dealing with the northern region, through to the thirteenth part which deals with Scotland. Northern Ireland, the Isle of Man, and the Channel Islands are not included. The area reports contain tables giving analyses by region and then by towns of varying sizes within the region, of the numbers of retail establishments, turnover, and persons engaged, the first table giving also comparative figures for 1957.

Preliminary results of the sample census for 1966 were published in the (then) *Board of Trade Journal* 194(3701) February 23 1968 582-589. Radio and television relay services were included for the first time in this census, which also included, for the first time, questions about the floor space of shops in main shopping centres and about transport costs. The first of two volumes containing the results of the census has been published as *Report on the census of distribution and other services 1966* (1970). The tables here are in three main sections. The first provides information on retail establishments and gives estimates of the number of establishments in the twenty two identified kinds of business, the total turnover in each kind of business and the number of persons engaged, with further analyses by form of organisation and by area (the ten standard regions of Great Britain). The second section gives information for retail organisations as a whole by classifying them into three groups, of cooperative societies, multiple organisations with ten or more branches, and independent organisations. The third section relates to the service trades, hairdressing, boot and shoe repairing, and laundering. The second volume will incorporate tables on transport costs and floor space data for retail trade together with tables on special forms of trading and sampling errors for some of the main estimates. A further census of distribution relating to 1971 is now in preparation, and will be conducted in 1972.

Northern Ireland had a separate census of distribution for 1965. The *Report of the Northern Ireland census of retail distribution and other services 1965* is similar in scope and presentation to the reports of the censuses for Great Britain, and includes also an extensive geographical section giving data for each local authority area and for over thirty towns.

Aside from this basic source of information, the most fruitful source of continuing information on distribution is the journal *Trade and industry.* Up to the end of 1969, detailed index numbers of retail sales compiled by the Department of Employment were reported in the journal; starting with the figures for January 1970, these numbers are being published monthly in the ' Business monitor ' service and distributive series. Four series have been introduced for the retail trade, each one relating to a group of shops: food shops, clothing and footwear shops, durable goods shops, and miscellaneous non-food shops. Each of the 'Monitors' contains monthly and quarterly index numbers covering at least two years.

Summarised statistical information on the trade of the UK with other countries, prepared by the Department of Trade and Industry, was published monthly in its *Report on overseas trade,* but this stopped publication with the issue of February 1971. The principal remaining source, apart from *Trade and industry,* is the same department's monthly *Overseas trade statistics of the United Kingdom,* which gives statistics of imports and exports for the current month and the cumulative total for the year to date, and detailed analyses by commodities and countries. Even more detailed information is available for years up to 1969 in the *Annual statement of the trade of the United Kingdom with commonwealth countries and foreign countries* published since 1963 in five volumes. The first volume contains information relating to the annual trade in each of the items listed in the Statistical Classification for Imported Goods and for Re-exported Goods and in the Export List. The second and third volumes contain particulars of the trade in these items with the principal countries from and to which they are consigned. The

270

fourth and fifth volumes contain for each country and each port respectively, particulars of the principal commodities imported into and exported from the UK.

EMPLOYMENT

The major source of continuing information on labour and employment in the UK is the monthly *Department of Employment gazette,* formerly the *Ministry of Labour gazette,* which contains in each issue a quantity of current statistics on manpower, employment and unemployment, training for employment, industrial organisation, wage rates, earnings, labour costs, and other relevant factors, expressed in up to date annual, quarterly, and monthly statistics as they become available from surveys carried out by the Department of Employment and other agencies. The section of ' monthly statistics ' in each issue gives in tabulated form, or in charts, the principal statistics compiled by the department in the form of time series, including the latest available figures together with comparable figures for preceding dates and years. They are grouped into sections on the working population, employment, unemployment, unfilled vacancies, hours worked, earnings, wage rates and hours of work, retail prices, and stoppages of work resulting from industrial disputes. National totals are given in some tables, which may relate to either Great Britain or the United Kingdom; in other cases, regional breakdown is provided, usually in accordance with the standard regions for statistical purposes.

Each year, the *Gazette* carries national and regional summaries of the Employment Return II (ERII), the survey carried out annually based on the 25% of national insurance cards due for exchange each June. Data on the number of cards held, by sex and exchange date, are collected by the local employment exchange from all employers of five or more persons within the exchange area, all persons being allocated to their actual place of work if this differs from the location at which their cards are held. National figures from the June 1970 ERII were given in *Department of Employment gazette* 79(2) February 1971 157-164; the following issue 79(3) March 1971 252-263 carries tables giving corresponding regional analyses and estimates of regional changes in the total

271

civilian labour force between June 1969 and June 1970. Up to June 1969, the *Department of Employment gazette* was supplemented by the same Department's quarterly *Statistics on incomes, prices, employment and production*, in which month the latter ceased publication. Current statistics continue to be carried in the *Gazette*, but the quarterly is to be replaced by a new annual, the *Yearbook of labour statistics*, which will bring together in a single volume all the main statistics relating to a calendar year. The first yearbook will cover 1969, but at the time of writing it has not yet appeared. It is being preceded by a historical abstract of the statistics produced up to and during 1968, under the title *British labour statistics: historical abstract 1886-1968*.

Various surveys have been carried out, and their results published, of manpower in specialised sectors of industry and the professions. Some of these survey existing supply, others attempt to forecast demand. From the Department of Employment comes the series of 'Manpower studies', each one devoted to a separate industry, which report on a detailed examination of the industry concerned and its likely occupational trends in the light of developments and technological change. A detailed short-term forecast of occupational requirements is provided, with a broader assessment of longer-term needs. The information presented is partly original and partly derived from existing sources. Reports so far have dealt with the metal industries, the construction industry, electronics, food retailing, and printing and publishing, and also with more general topics such as the growth of office employment, computers in offices, and occupational changes between 1951 and 1961.

The Department of Trade and Industry have issued three titles in the series 'Studies in technological manpower'. The first is *The survey of professional engineers 1968* (1970), containing the results of a second survey of the engineer and his work (the first was carried out in 1966 and reported in *The survey of professional engineers 1966* (1967)), which form a statistical profile of the characteristics of the professional engineer—age, income, work, responsibility, training, and other factors—both in summary and in detailed tabular form. Comparable data on scientists are contained in the second title in the series *The survey of professional scientists 1968* (1970). The third in the series, *Persons with qualifications in engineering, technology and science 1959 to 1968* (1971), draws data from the Department of Employment manpower surveys and from the 1961 and 1966 censuses of population, and constructs from these a coherent picture of the changes and trends in the professionally qualified population. The annual *Statistics of science and technology* includes analyses of expenditure on research and development, and of scientific and technological manpower, including stock and deployment, new supply, and students and staff in educational institutions.

Civil service statistics 1970 (1971), compiled in the Civil Service Department, presents a ' broad statistical picture of the civil service on January 1 1970 '. The tables are grouped into three sections, one of historical data, and two giving analyses of non-industrial staff in post, and of movements of non-industrial staff during 1969.

SOCIAL FACTORS

' The growing realisation in Parliament, the press and elsewhere, that economic progress must be measured, in part at least, in terms of social benefits makes it more important that the available key figures about our society should be readily accessible.' This statement ushers in the first issue of *Social trends* (1970) prepared by the Central Statistical Office to meet this requirement, and to be published, initially at least, on an annual basis. The great merit of this publication is that it draws together statistics relating to a variety of social factors from a number of sources and presents them in juxtaposition in tabular and diagrammatic form so that trends and developments may be seen. The tables in this first issue are grouped into sections showing public expenditure on social services; population and environment; employment; leisure; personal income and expenditure; social security; welfare services; health; education; housing; justice and law. Appendices set out statistical notes, definitions and terms, and sources and further references. The figures relate to the UK where possible, and otherwise to Great Britain. National totals are given in the majority of cases, with a limited number of regional tables.

Social statistics are scattered through a number of sources in addition to the published volumes of the population census and

273

the annual and monthly digests of the Central Statistical Office. The *Annual report of the Department of Health and Social Security* and the Scottish Home and Health Department's annual *Health and welfare services in Scotland* both contain a large quantity of statistical information in addition to narrative discussion. The English report is the sole published source of detailed statistics on the numbers receiving supplementary benefit. It is supplemented by the annual report of the chief medical officer of the department, *On the state of public health,* which gives detailed statistics of the incidence of various types of disease and of general public health factors.

The Department of Health and Social Security have prepared since 1969 an annual *Digest of health statistics for England and Wales* which presents ten year trends (usually) in health and welfare services, under the headings population and vital statistics; finance; manpower; hospital administrative statistics; executive council services; local health authority domiciliary services; services for the elderly and disabled; maternity and child welfare services; health services for school children; psychiatric services; preventive medicine; and morbidity. Most of the figures are national totals, but there are some breakdowns in the sections on manpower and executive council services. The sources used are mainly the returns made to the department by the various authorities, and also health statistics collected by other government departments. Selected detailed statistics are published in the department's *Statistical report* series, which has included three reports, numbers four, five and eleven, under the title *Psychiatric hospitals and units in England and Wales: in-patient statistics from the mental health enquiry,* the most recent covering the year 1968 (1970); no 7, *A pilot survey of patients attending day hospitals* (1969); and no 10 *The facilities and services of psychiatric hospitals in England and Wales 1969* (1970).

The department issues an annual abstract of statistics on *Retirement pensions and widows' benefits* which amplifies the tables given in the department's *Annual report* and shows the numbers of retirement pensioners and widow beneficiaries under the National Insurance Acts. Totals throughout are national figures. Also available is a series of *Digests of statistics analysing certificates of incapacity* (DHSS) which contain tables analysing incapacity for work recorded in respect of men and women of working age in connection

274

with claims for sickness and injury benefits under the National Insurance Acts. The most recent issue covers the period June 1964 to May 1967. There are detailed analyses by age, sex, period of incapacity, and the industries involved, and regional breakdowns and time series data are also included.

The Scottish Home and Health Department issue an annual digest of *Scottish health statistics* which presents its information in sections devoted to population and vital statistics; two sections on morbidity including mortality; maternity services; infant and child health; general medical services; hospital and specialist services; dental services; general ophthalmic services; cost of the health services; food and drugs administration; and mental health. National totals for the whole of Scotland are given in the main, but there are a few regional breakdowns; time series data are given in a number of tables. Another annual publication brings together *Scottish hospital in-patient statistics* which relates to patients discharged from hospitals in Scotland during the calendar year under consideration, except those discharged from mental or maternity hospitals. There are detailed analyses by age, sex, diagnosis, length of stay, and other variables, with some regional breakdowns and some by area of residence. In the series 'Scottish health service studies' is *Infant mortality in Scotland* by I D Gerald Richards (SHHD, 1971, no 16), which contains a high proportion of tables, maps and graphs presenting detailed statistical information.

A series of annual statistical returns is published jointly by the Institute of Municipal Treasurers and Accountants (IMTA) and the Society of County Treasurers (SCT) which includes *Local health service statistics, Children services statistics* and *Welfare services statistics*. These returns are for England and Wales only. They provide breakdowns for county boroughs, London boroughs, and counties, of expenditure in the various categories of each service, and in some categories give the numbers being catered for. The IMTA and SCT also publish statistical returns, primarily concerned with local authority expenditure, on *Fire services statistics, Police force statistics,* and *Public library statistics*.

The principal continuing source of statistical information on housing is *Housing statistics: Great Britain,* a quarterly publication compiled by the department of the Environment in collaboration

275

with the housing departments of the Scottish Development Department and the Welsh Office. The figures, which relate to England, Wales, and Scotland, are presented in tabular form in sections on new construction; improvement grants; slum clearance; housing loans; and miscellaneous tables. The section on new construction is grouped into summaries of progress; types of housing; areas and costs; housing densities; and scheme size and type of contract. The tables are followed by a comprehensive section of notes on the tables and definitions of the terms used. Time series data are given in many of the tables, and aggregations are in the main national, with regional figures under some headings. A finer breakdown into local authority areas is provided by the quarterly *Local housing statistics* compiled by the Department of the Environment and the Welsh Office, relating to England and Wales only. The major table presents statistics of housing progress and unfit houses by regions, counties, and local authority areas, and shows annual cumulative figures. Supplementary tables are included as data become available. Since 1965, the statistical content of the annual reports of the former Ministry of Housing and Local Government has been presented separately in the form of a *Handbook of statistics* which covers housing in addition to the other departmental interests (at the time of writing, a *Handbook* has not been published under the imprint of the Department of the Environment). Figures relate to England and Wales only, and national totals only are given in the tables, which cover a range of topics similar to those of *Housing statistics: Great Britain,* though in very summary form. The IMTA publish annually *Housing statistics* and *Housing maintenance and management statistics,* both compiled from information supplied by local authorities. Housing statistics in summary form relating to Scotland are to be found in the annual reports of the Scottish Development Department, and in fuller form in the same Department's quarterly *Housing return for Scotland,* which indicates, with time series data, the progress of public and private house building in Scotland, with figures of slum clearance and house improvements. An analysis by local authorities is included. The Ministry of Development, Northern Ireland, publish a *Quarterly housing return for Northern Ireland* which includes figures of dwellings completed, under construction, approved, demolished, converted and improved,

276

information as to the type of dwellings being built and the number of contracts and tenders being submitted, as well as details of new housing, broken down by local authorities.

Education statistics are comprehensively supplied for all countries of the United Kingdom. Overall UK statistics are presented in the annual *Education statistics for the United Kingdom* (1968 publ 1970) compiled jointly by the Department of Education and Science, the Scottish Education Department, the Northern Ireland Ministry of Education, and the University Grants Committee. More detailed statistics for the component countries appear in the annual publications *Statistics of education* from the Department of Education and Science; *Scottish educational statistics* from the Scottish Education Department; and *Northern Ireland education statistics* from the Northern Ireland Ministry of Education. *Statistics of education*, relating to England and Wales, now appears in six volumes, on schools; school leavers; further education; teachers; finance and awards; and universities; the latter being produced in conjunction with the University Grants Committee. *Scottish educational statistics* covers, in one volume, primary and secondary education; further education; universities; training of teachers and teachers in service; awards; building; and finance; giving, in the main, national totals, but including also a short section of tables by local education authority areas. *Northern Ireland education statistics* gives mainly national figures, with a few breakdowns by local education authority areas, under headings for schools, from nursery through to special; scholarships and awards; teachers; and building. A further source of information relating to England and Wales is the annual *Education statistics* published jointly by the IMTA and the SCT, which gives figures, mainly relating to income and expenditure, for all local education authorities. *Education statistics for the United Kingdom 1968* (1970) contains a description of 'sources of United Kingdom education statistics', which gives pointers to statistical information in publications which are not primarily statistical in content.

The principal source of statistical information on the processes of town and country planning is the Department of the Environment, although their publications relate only to England and Wales. The first series of *Statistics for town and country planning* is concerned with *Planning decisions* and has so far been confined to the

277

annual issue of *Statistics of decisions on planning applications in England and Wales.* This is concerned with applications which are determined by local planning authorities, and categorises the applications into two classes, of building, engineering and other operations; and changes of use. Statistics of appeals are included in the annual *Handbook of statistics,* which contains a variety of summary tables on aspects of planning practice. The second series of *Statistics for town and country planning* is concerned with floor space, and the first issue deals with *Floor space in industrial, shopping and office use: changes April 1964 to March 1967, England and Wales* (1969). The data used are those obtained by the Inland Revenue in the preparation of valuation lists. There are summary tables, for additions, reductions and net increases over the three-year period, regional breakdowns for the same factors in a yearly analysis, and an analysis of net increases 1964 to 1967 by planning authorities. Annual *County planning statistics* are compiled by the County Planning Officers' Society and the Society of County Treasurers, and present figures, mainly on income and expenditure, for various aspects of planning in county planning authorities in England and Wales.

TOURISM AND RECREATION

The British Tourist Authority (formerly the British Travel Association) have issued a *Digest of tourist statistics* (BTA, 1969) relating to the UK as a whole, and presenting analyses of income from tourism, UK tourists abroad, and overseas visitors in Britain; the primary concern is with visitor figures in terms of numbers and expenditure, and there is also a detailed breakdown of overseas motorist traffic to Britain. The BTA also commission an annual sample survey of British holidaymakers and the nature of their holidays, but the results of these surveys are not generally available (see chapter 11, the section on recreation, for details of this and other publications which contain statistical information).

Recreation statistics are scattered over a range of sources, and the Countryside Commission have performed a valuable function in drawing some of them together into a *Digest of countryside recreation statistics 1969,* which they issue free of charge. The *Digest* is to be reviewed and revised from time to time. There are three sections. The first, on population characteristics, has tables on population change, age structure, leisure time, income and expenditure, and use of a car; the second, on countryside recreation activities, carries tables analysing holidaymaking and outdoor recreation; the third section contains tables on land resources and water resources, both analysed by regions.

TRANSPORT

The principal continuing source of information on all forms of transport of people in Great Britain is the annual *Passenger transport in Great Britain* from the Department of the Environment. The tables, which present national totals in most cases over a ten-year period, are in five sections: the first contains summary tables of all forms of passenger transport, the following sections deal separately with passenger transport by rail, public service road vehicles, private road vehicles, and domestic scheduled air services.

Road transport is covered in more detail in the annual *Highway statistics* from the Department of the Environment, which presents information on public and private road vehicles carrying both passengers and goods, throughout Great Britain. Northern Ireland is included in some tables. The tables are in four sections, the first containing information on the total road vehicle fleet, with analyses of vehicles currently licensed by type of vehicle and by planning regions and licensing authorities, and of those newly registered during the year. The second set of tables gives analyses of road traffic, its distribution, and trends over a three-year period. The third set of tables gives details of the roads themselves and expenditure on them, and the final set gives estimates of the use made of the road system for the carriage of passengers and goods, and of the taxation paid and amounts spent on road transport by all road users. The *Annual report of the licensing authorities,* which consists of sectional reports from each of the authorities, followed by summary tables, contains figures showing the number of applications for each type of licence within the area, vehicle examinations, objections to applications and other related information. Monthly figures of new vehicle registrations are provided in the monthly ' Business monitor '

M1 *Motor vehicle registrations* published by the Department of Trade and Industry, which has summary tables for the UK and Great Britain followed by a breakdown for Great Britain by type of vehicle.

The fullest annual source of data about the motor industry generally is *The motor industry of Great Britain* issued every year by the Society of Motor Manufacturers and Traders Ltd, and containing a wealth of tables detailing production, new and current registrations, and overseas trade. Coverage includes Northern Ireland. Yearly, quarterly or monthly figures are given according to subject, and most tables present time series data. Breakdown by licensing authorities is given in the major tables. The society also issue a *Monthly statistical review* which contains tables under the same headings as those of the annual volume, giving the monthly figures, with quarterly summaries. The British Road Federation issue an annual booklet of *Basic road statistics* covering Great Britain with a separate section on Northern Ireland. It gives long runs of figures, in some cases over fifty years, in the major categories of motor vehicles; traffic and accidents; the transport industry; roads; motor taxation; and road transport legislation. Since the information is very summarised, it is only of use for very general enquiries. Statistics of road accidents are prepared jointly by the Department of the Environment, the Scottish Development Department and the Welsh Office, and published annually as *Road accidents*. This contains a narrative review of road accidents, followed by tables showing trends over a number of years in various categories, and going on to detailed tables for the year under review, specifying types of accidents, types of casualties, vehicles and drivers involved. There are no sub-national figures.

The principal source of systematic statistical information on air transport is the Department of Trade and Industry's 'Business monitors' in the civil aviation series. There are eight titles in this series. CA1 on airport activity is issued monthly, and presents figures of air transport movement at UK airports; CA2 is a monthly sheet analysing air passenger traffic at UK airports; CA3 incorporates monthly figures of air freight and mail; CA4 and CA5 both deal with airline operations on scheduled and non-scheduled services, the first being produced on a monthly frequency, the second being issued quarterly; CA6 is a quarterly analysis of domestic passenger traffic, and CA7 performs a similar function for international and cabotage passengers; CA8 is an annual analysis of the financial returns of UK airlines. Annual summaries are also produced in series CA1 to CA7. CA1 to CA4 include time series data for about five years. The annual reports and accounts of the British Airports Authority and the individual airlines also contain statistical tables. Detailed analysis of passenger movements at the London airports of Gatwick, Heathrow, Luton, Southend, Manston, and Southampton was carried out as a preliminary to the enquiries of the Roskill Commission into a third major London airport, by the then Board of Trade, and the results are published as *Passengers at London's airports: origin and destination survey 15 August-14 November 1968* (1970).

On rail transport, the principal source is the British Railways Board, whose *Annual report and accounts* contains a section of statistical information on all aspects of rail services, including ships, hovercraft, and harbours. It is published as a House of Commons paper.

On shipping, the principal sources of information are the annual reports of the Chamber of Shipping of the United Kingdom, from which the statistical tables and diagrams are presented separately as *British shipping statistics,* grouped into sections which detail world and UK tonnage; shipbuilding; UK seaborne trade; shipping movement; freight; world and UK trade; and costs. Runs of annual figures are given in most tables, going back five to ten years in the majority of cases. The National Ports Council publish an annual comprehensive review, *Digest of port statistics,* which presents data from a variety of sources on all aspects of all ports in the UK, including organisation; expenditure; labour; goods and passenger traffic; and shipping movements. Time series data are included in the general tables, and analyses by planning regions and by individual ports are included in all sections. The council also prepares a small annual booklet, *Port unit transport statistics Great Britain,* based on information supplied by forty ports with facilities for unit transport traffic. Generalised statistical information on inland waterways is contained in the annual reports of the British Waterways Board.

GUIDES TO STATISTICAL SOURCES, AND THEIR USE

There is no shortage of guidance to statistical sources, but there is no publication which discusses them from the point of view of their use in planning. Over the whole field in which statistics are collected, the most up to date narrative guide is Joan M Harvey's *Sources of statistics* (Bingley, second edition 1971). Harvey describes American as well as British statistical series, and the amount of detail is small, but the details given are accurate and the view is wide-ranging; the discussion is in chapters on general sources; population; social; education; labour; production; trade; finance; prices; transport; tourism; justice; public administration; and advertising.

Very much fuller, but well out of date for current series, is *The sources and nature of the statistics of the United Kingdom* edited for the Royal Statistical Society by Maurice G Kendall and A Bradford Hill (Oliver and Boyd, two vols 1952 and 1957). Each volume is divided into sections containing specialist contributions on the statistics of a specific field. The first volume covers production and distribution; oversea trade; agriculture; labour; statistics of particular commodities, for example, coal mining, iron and steel, electricity and gas, the motor industry; transport; and a miscellaneous section taking in housing, cooperative trading and publishing. The second volume covers population and vital statistics; land use; national income; regional economic statistics; local government statistics; banking; financial investment; medicine and medical services; education; commodities, taking in clothing, food, petroleum, timber, and the Scotch whisky industry; transport and communications, taking in international air transport statistics; telecommunications; and a miscellaneous section covering advertising, British insurance, and criminal statistics. These volumes are now being up-dated by a new series sponsored by the Royal Statistical Society in conjunction with the Social Science Research Council, and the first batch of contributions have been commissioned, on social services; tourism; housing; construction; engineering; and crime. It is proposed to issue the new series as individual booklets, or, perhaps, small collections of related topics, with a cumulative index. The editor of the new series is Dr W F Maunder of the Department of Statistics at the London School of Economics.

Continuing information about British official statistics is disseminated in the quarterly *Statistical news,* a service prepared by the Central Statistical Office and begun in May 1968. Each issue contains several articles on aspects of British official statistics, and a news section describing developments, mainly related to published items, in the various subject fields covered by the government statistical service. Details are given of the preceding quarter's new publications, and of developments in the statistical service itself. This is an invaluable source of reference for current published statistics.

The series 'Guides to official sources' includes several items which discuss the statistical output in a specific subject field, most of them prepared by the Interdepartmental Committee on Social and Economic Research, but some by an appropriate government department. Again, some of the titles are very out of date. The first of the series was *Labour statistics,* revised in 1958, followed by *Census reports of Great Britain* (1951), *Local government statistics* (1953), *Agricultural and food statistics* (1958), *Social security statistics* (1961), and *Census of production reports* (1961), the last of which traces the development of the census between 1907 and 1961. The series title has now given way to 'Studies in official statistics'. The eleventh in this series is the *List of principal statistical series available* (1965) compiled by the Central Statistical Office, which lists the official series in which various categories of economic, financial, and regional information may be found. The thirteenth in the series is *National accounts statistics: sources and methods* (1968), and the fourteenth is *Agricultural and food statistics: a guide to official sources* (1969) compiled by the Ministry of Agriculture, which supersedes no 4 in the earlier series. The *Directory of construction statistics* (1968), from the Ministry of Public Building and Works, describes existing sources of statistical information relating to the construction industry. The National Economic Development Office published *Food statistics: a guide to the major official and unofficial United Kingdom sources* (1969) which focuses on the food manufacturing industry, and complements 'Studies in official statistics' 14. Various economic development committees concerned with specific areas of industry have compiled guides to statistical sources, which are published by NEDO: for example, the

283

Economic Development Committee for Electronics prepared *Electronics industry statistics and their sources,* which consists partly of original statistical information and partly of guidance to sources; and the Distributive Trades Economic Development Committee was responsible for *Distributive trades statistics: a guide to official sources* (1970) which includes discussion of the census of distribution.

In 1968, a joint working party was set up from the Library Association and the Royal Statistical Society to enquire into the provision of sources of economic statistics throughout the UK. One of its first tasks was to prepare a list of the basic sources which should be available for use in all public libraries; a second edition of this was issued by the Library Association in December 1970 under the title *Recommended basic statistical sources for community use,* consisting of a basic list of key sources plus a more detailed extended list for inclusion in larger libraries and organisations. The working party, which is now styled the Committee of Librarians and Statisticians of the Library Association and the Royal Statistical Society, have also produced the first volume of a projected Library Association series under the collective title *Resources in economic statistics* which will constitute an inventory of statistical series held in organistations throughout the country. The first volume is *Economic statistics collections* (1970) and is a directory of the sources held in business firms, trade unions, and trade and other associations. The main part is a geographical listing of collections, with details of their location, organisation, composition, and accessibility. Subsequent volumes in the series will cover libraries.

None of these guides is intended for planners. They do provide guidance to a wide range of available sources over a wide subject field, but in no case is there any indication of the information which would be useful for planning purposes within this range. There is a great need for evaluative, analytical guidance to the content of British statistical series, comparable to two excellent American publications: *Land use information: a critical survey of United States statistics, including possibilities for greater uniformity* by Marion Clawson and Charles L Stewart (Oxford UP, 1965) and *Social and economic information for urban planning* by Doris B Holleb (Chicago, Chicago University Center for Urban Studies, 1969, two vols). The latter in particular is a most comprehensive and constructive piece of work, setting out the information available against a detailed contextual discussion of the work for which it would be required. The nearest approach to this covering British statistics is Working Paper 6 from the Urban Systems Research Unit at Reading University, *Statistics for planning, 2, A review of government statistics* (1970) by Alison Cheshire, which reviews, under detailed subject headings, the information available (or not available) to meet the requirements dictated by the 1968 Town and Country Planning Act, and takes into account the full range of official sources excluding the census of population, which is discussed in detail in the preceding Working Paper 5 *Statistics for planning, 1, The census of population* (1970) by Alison Cheshire.

Studies in the practical use of various types of data are useful to planners. The Research and Intelligence Unit of the GLC, for example, issued an Occasional Paper 2 on *The census of population as a source of information for local authority planning departments* (1969) which is the proceedings of a seminar held by the London boroughs in March 1969; and their *Quarterly bulletin* has on several occasions included reports on the use of published data or on the collection of data to supplement published sources. These reports apply to the London boroughs, but the experience is of much wider interest. The book *Population growth and planning policy* by David E C Eversley and others (Frank Cass, 1965) includes a systematic attempt to evaluate population data for regional planning. In ' Population studies' *Official architecture and planning* 33(7) July 1970 621-624, Margaret A Roberts reviews sources of data and information on population and discusses methods of forecasting based on these, with a note on the factors such as fertility and migration which influence forecasting and may render it unreliable. David Jordan gives a commentary on the workplace tables of the 1966 census of population in ' Commuting into London' *JTPI* 55(2) February 1969 72-73.

The interest of the Centre for Environmental Studies in forecasting and modelling has inevitably led to a parallel interest in the data available for these purposes. CES-IP-17 consists of *Papers from the seminar on the use of census data in the estimation of income distributions for small areas* (1970); in CES-WP-49 on *Occupa-*

285

tional earnings (1970), M J H Mogridge sets out a detailed analysis of the distribution of occupational earnings in Britain using the data collected in the Survey of earnings, and published in the *Department of Employment gazette* of May 1969 (see above). Mogridge is also the author of CES-WP-48 on *An analysis of household income in Great Britain and its relationship with employment income* (1970) using data from the Ministry of Social Security and from the *Family expenditure survey report*.

Manpower statistics, and in particular the need for data on labour supply and demand in occupational terms, are discussed by J R Crossley in a contribution 'Essential statistics for manpower forecasting' in *Manpower policy and employment trends* edited by B C Roberts and J H Smith (G Bell, 1966). The difficulties in regional and sub-regional planning of basing manpower forecasts on data expressed in industrial, rather than occupational terms, are set out by P E Lloyd and P Dicken in 'The data bank in regional studies in industry' *Town planning review* 38(4) January 1968 304-316. An attempt to overcome this lack of a satisfactory occupational classification and of suitable statistics published in accordance with it, is described by F Livesey in 'The uses of occupational data in regional planning' *Urban studies* 7(2) June 1970 137-152, drawing on the results of a study undertaken in connection with the projected new town in central Lancashire.

R Wilkinson reviews 'Building society statistics' in *Urban studies* 2(2) November 1965 186-192, which constitutes a comparison of two surveys carried out by the Building Societies Association in October 1964 and the Cooperative Permanent Building Society in November 1963.

P R Smethurst discusses 'The national travel surveys: a source of data for planners' in *Town planning review* 38(1) April 1967 43-63, which includes description of the data to be derived from a number of additional sources such as the surveys carried out by the Government Social Survey for the Ministry of Transport, and land use/transportation studies.

REFERENCES
1 This is now superseded by the *Classification of occupations 1970* (HMSO, 1971) prepared for use with the 1971 census, though there are only slight differences in detail.

2 Percy Gray and Frances Gee 'The 1966 ten per cent sample census—why there was no preliminary report' *Statistical news* 10 August 1970 9-10.

3 Nigel Moor 'Planning and information' *Architectural Association quarterly* 2(2) April 1970 56-61.

11

DOCUMENTARY SOURCES

THIS CHAPTER IS CONCERNED with documentary sources, and within this wide range it focuses on books, pamphlets, reports, government publications, excluding those which are primarily statistical sources, special issues of journals, and articles from journals. This wide range of formats has been included because many aspects of planning have not been documented in book form; to restrict the coverage to books alone would have been arbitrarily to exclude these aspects—the recent techniques associated with planning, such as model-building and gaming, are clear examples of this. The aim has been to include as many as possible of the subjects central or related to planning and to review the documentary information associated with each one. These subjects have been dictated by the information available rather than by any preconceived notions of what should or should not be included; similarly the arrangement of subject sections within the chapter was suggested by the composition of the sections themselves rather than by any classification scheme, and there is no implication that this is the only possible sequence. Inevitably many items could be included in more than one subject section: and while duplication has been kept to a minimum for obvious reasons, some of the legitimate cases have in fact been discussed at more than one place so that each section may be as self-contained as possible.

PLANNING: HISTORY

It seems appropriate to begin with a review of the history of planning. The history of planning is very much the history of town planning (country planning, as we remarked in chapter 2, only entered into it at a comparatively recent date), and so, in this section, the focus is almost exclusively on the development and planning of towns and cities. The documentary record is by no means complete, although of recent years some gaps have been worthily filled and the overall situation is considerably improved.

It is possible to distinguish three broad general approaches to the documentation of the history of town planning. There are the comprehensive approaches, whether in a single volume or a series of volumes, embracing city planning in all countries at all times; there are the approaches to a specific period in time, which attempt to discern features of planning which are generic to that period irrespective of country, although—and this applies particularly to the earlier periods—such temporal approaches may be of necessity limited to only a few countries in which planning activity was evident; finally there are the approaches to a specific country, which record the development of planning within that country through one or more periods in time.

There is no work available in the English language which gives a full treatment of the history of planning from the earliest times to the most recent, as it developed throughout the world. In French, there is Pierre Lavedan's *Histoire de l'urbanisme,* published by Henri Laurens in Paris in three volumes between 1926 and 1952, a classic monumental study from antiquity to the twentieth century which has never achieved translation into English. In English, there are two multi-volume projects in progress which aim at a comprehensive coverage of planning history. The more substantial of these is Erwin A Gutkind's *International history of city development* (Collier-Macmillan, 1964-) of which four volumes have been published at the time of writing: v 1, *Urban development in Central Europe* (1964); v 2, *Urban development in the Alpine and Scandinavian countries* (1965); v 3, *Urban development in Southern Europe, Spain and Portugal* (1967); v 4, *Urban development in Southern Europe, Italy and Greece* (1969). The series represents ' an attempt to present a world-wide survey of the origin and growth of urban civilization '. Each volume brings the respective story up to the mid-nineteenth century; the comparative analysis of town planning from that time to the present is to be contained within one final volume. The work is scholarly, well produced and well illustrated, and each volume has a selective bibliography. Dr Gutkind died during 1970, but the continuing production of the work is being carried on by his daughter. The other series is that published by Studio Vista under the collective title *Planning and cities*. Twelve volumes have been published in 1969 and 1970 and together form a conspectus of city planning from the earliest to the comparatively recent. Inevitably, they suffer from the inherent disadvantages of such a series, the individual approaches of individual authors and the omissions caused by compartmentalisation, leading to a lack of homogeneity; but they are nicely produced, albeit slim volumes, predominantly illustrations with supporting text, and all of them decently documented.

Of the single volume views of city development, probably the best known is Lewis Mumford's *The city in history: its origins, its transformations, and its prospects* (Secker & Warburg, 1961). This large book, the product of a lifelong passion and absorption with the city, examines the cities of the western world from their fore-shadowings to their futures. It is a stimulating exposition, which must surely fall between two stools: too long-winded for the general reader, and yet too personal and too persuasive of causes for the student or the professional.

Such works always have their critics and their detractors: for example, H J Dyos in *The study of urban history* observes that ' it strikes me as a little fatuous to attempt too much and, in effect, to take on the whole history of cities at once . . . At worst, it leads rapidly to " the city in history ", to unhistorical and even apocalyptic visions which, like Mumford's, conveys all the images and excitement of a fireworks display that fizzles out in chilling caricature of itself!' Yet it is a unique work and it should be read, not so much for the facts which it processes but for the thoughts which it provokes. Similar in scope and firmly rooted in fact is Frederick Hiorns' *Town-building in history: an outline review of conditions, influences, ideas, and methods affecting ' planned' towns through five thousand years* (Harrap, 1956) a detailed, copiously illustrated account of planning throughout the world from its origins to the industrial age and its effects, with an epilogue on the culture of cities. Arthur Korn's *History builds the town* (Lund Humphries, 1953) is a perceptive review, but constitutes no more than a summary of city development. *The urban pattern: city planning and design* by Arthur B

Gallion and Simon Eisner (Princeton, NJ, Van Nostrand, second edition 1963) is a good textbook examining the links between urban morphology and the history of planning, from ancient cities to the present. A different approach is adopted by Cecil Stewart in *A prospect of cities, being studies towards a history of town planning* (Longmans, 1952), which makes no pretence to being a comprehensive history but comprises a series of essays, studies of cities from the Greek city state to British new towns, the garden city movement and the first post-war new towns, with essay-interludes giving contextual glimpses of the wider world beyond; this is an attractive, easily-read book, perhaps aimed more at the layman than at the professional planner. An individualistic view is that of Leonardo Benevolo as propounded in *The origins of modern town planning* translated by Judith Landry (Routledge and Kegan Paul, 1967) which can be most succinctly classified as fascist in outlook, and in sum adds little to the existing store of knowledge. Helen Rosenau's *The ideal city in its architectural evolution* (Routledge and Kegan Paul, 1959) is concerned with a special aspect of the general history of city development. Dr Rosenau's thesis is that the ideal city, normally associated primarily with the Italian Renaissance, is in fact encountered throughout history, and that it is one of the basic recurrent themes of European art and philosophy. The idea of the ideal city is traced from its biblical origins through to the eighteenth century, with particular attention paid to French and English eighteenth century development, finally moving on to the theories and theorists of the nineteenth and twentieth centuries which, however, are rather sketchily treated. The text is well illustrated and documented, but translations of the quotations from foreign writers would have helped those not blessed with linguistic ability. Another specialised aspect of city development forms the theme of *European cities and society: a study of the influence of political climate on town design* by James Stevens Curl (Leonard Hill, 1970), in which the author's thesis that political climate—defined as ' the prevailing mood of a society as determined by its ruling elements, *ie* the groups holding political power '—has always influenced the design of major urban settlements, is demonstrated in discussion of European cities from ancient to modern times. Finally in this line-up of ' apocalyptic visions ', comes Sybil Moholy-Nagy's *Matrix of man:*

an illustrated history of urban environment (Pall Mall Press, 1968) an attractively produced book with many excellent illustrations and a stimulating text which inclines more to Mumford than to Hiorns; approached in a spirit of critical enquiry, the book is both informative and entertaining, and is also well-documented.

In the approaches to the history of planning by periods of history, it is noticeable that distance lends enchantment, for the earlier periods are more fully documented than are the more recent times. The record of ancient town planning begins with Aristotle who earns his place in the literature of planning by being the earliest extant chronicler, in his *Politics,* of the achievements of the first town planner, Hippodamus of Miletus '. . . a man who loved the limelight, which led him into eccentric habits. The result was that some looked upon him as a crank, with his flowing hair . . .'[1] The authoritative source on ancient Greek city planning is R E Wycherley, whose *How the Greeks built cities* (Macmillan, second edition 1962, reprinted with minor amendments 1967) is an eminently readable and detailed review of the development of Greek city planning, the form of the classical Greek city, and the principal architectural elements of which it was composed. There are useful annotated guides to further sources of information. F Haverfield's *Ancient town-planning* (Oxford, Clarendon Press, 1913) is still an interesting short introduction to both Greek and Roman town building activity (including an appendix on China) but, according to Wycherley, is now out of date. It is an enlargement of a paper read to the University of London as the Creighton Lecture for 1910, which was also submitted in part to the seminal London Conference on Town Planning in the same year. Sadly enough, Rome is yet without a Wycherley. There are, however, an abundance of titles on various aspects of Roman urban settlement in Britain, from which the following are selected as being the most appropriate to the present purpose (many are primarily of archaeological interest): *Roman Britain and the English settlements* by R G Collingwood and J N L Myres (Oxford, Clarendon Press, 1936); Ian A Richmond's *Roman Britain* (Cape, 1963; first published by Penguin Books 1955) which contains chapters on ' Towns and urban centres ' and ' The countryside '; and George C Boon's *Roman Silchester: the archaeology of a Romano-British town* (Max Parrish, 1957) which, although its principal interest is archaeological and the author writes from first-hand experience of the site excavations, does contain a full account of all aspects of the ancient town of Calleva near Silchester.

The chronicle lapses during the Dark Ages, as did town building itself, and takes up again in the Middle Ages. Until quite recently, the only source of information on this period of town planning was T F Tout's lecture delivered in 1916 on *Mediaeval town planning*, originally published in the *Bulletin of the John Rylands Library* 4(1) May/August 1917 26-58, and republished with corrections in 1934 by Manchester University Press. This is a classic concise account but, as befits its original form, is no more than an outline. The full authoritative source on the period is now *New towns of the middle ages: town plantation in England, Wales and Gascony* (Lutterworth Press, 1967) by Maurice Beresford. The interest of the author in the subject was first aroused by reading Tout's essay, and he was subsequently ' seduced from agricultural history ' to carry out the research on which his scholarly treatise is based. He considers the town planting activity of the English kings of the Middle Ages and their subjects in England and Wales, and in south west France, and his coverage is limited to towns planted *de novo,* where no settlement previously existed. The volume includes gazetteers of plantations or probable plantations for England, Wales, and Gascony; and the appendices include one on medieval town plantation outside of these countries, containing mainly references to documentary sources. After the Middle Ages, the period approach is the province of the *Planning and cities* series mentioned above but these volumes in no way approach the scope and authority of Wycherley and Beresford.

Finally we come to the country approach, and inevitably, since we are concerned primarily with works in English, the main interest is in the history of town planning in Britain. One of the earliest books to record this is *Towns and town-planning, ancient and modern* by T Harold Hughes and E H G Lamborn (Oxford, Clarendon Press, 1923), a brief historical sketch which devotes most attention to the development of towns and villages in Britain, from the first Roman layouts to the advent of the industrial revolution, followed by an examination of the (then) modern movement in

Britain and in other countries as well, with the customary, almost obligatory, 'look to the future'. Hughes and Lamborn have now been supplemented by *City fathers: the early history of town planning in Britain* by Colin and Rose Bell (Barrie & Rockliff, 1969), which surveys town development from Roman Britain to the late nineteenth century, stopping at the garden city movement, and covering England, Wales and Scotland; like Beresford, the Bells are concerned only with town plantation *de novo*. The account is written with the minimum of technical detail and, being fully illustrated, has an obvious readership among interested laymen; though information is not lacking for interested planners. A very useful volume from the United States is *Town origins: the evidence from medieval England* by John F Benton (Boston, D C Heath, 1968), which takes the form of an anthology of basic factual information about English medieval towns, drawn from a variety of sources. An important and authoritative survey of the birth and development of the town planning movement as it is recognised today is given in William Ashworth's *The genesis of modern British town planning* (Routledge and Kegan Paul, 1954, International Library of Sociology and Social Reconstruction). Sub-titled ' a study in economic and social history of the nineteenth and twentieth centuries ', the book is a thorough and well documented (particularly with regard to contemporary sources) examination of the origins of planning in the social and housing reforms of the nineteenth century and its development to its first legislative measure of 1909, taking in its physical manifestations and economic implications at the same time. The main thesis of the book ends at 1909, but a further chapter of nearly forty pages looks at 'Approaches to town planning 1909-1947'. As a record of planning in all its aspects through a critical phase in its evolution, Ashworth's is unlikely to be superseded. It has not been brought up to date; but it seems that this omission will be rectified, for on December 18 1969, the Prime Minister announced in the House of Commons that ' environmental planning' will be the subject of one of three official histories commissioned by the government as part of a new series on peacetime episodes. The history is to be written by Professor J B Cullingworth in collaboration with Gordon E Cherry (Director and Deputy Director respectively of the

Centre for Urban and Regional Studies, Birmingham University) and will cover the period 1938-1968.

In a consideration of the history of planning and the literature which documents the development of cities it is inevitable that at some stage an effort has to be made to disentangle planning and architecture. This problem is particularly acute in the period of the grand designs of British town planning, the Georgian era which gave us some of the finest examples of civic design in the world. Such examples do not lack for printed chronicle, and the bulk of this chronicle falls firmly within the scope of architecture. Of the contribution which seems particularly relevant to the planning literature, Donald Olsen's *Town planning in London: the eighteenth and nineteenth centuries* (New Haven, Yale UP, 1964) is a sumptuous production which looks searchingly at success and failure in the planned development and maintenance of two central London estates during the period; and which can be regarded as an extension of Sir John Summerson's classic *Georgian London* (Barrie and Jenkins, second revised edition 1970) which covers in full detail the Georgian period alone. Two more authoritative volumes, selected at random, on classical planning in cities other than London, are A J Youngson's *The making of classical Edinburgh 1750-1840* (Edinburgh, Edinburgh UP, 1966) and *Tyneside classical: the Newcastle of Grainger, Dobson and Clayton* by Lyall Wilkes and Gordon Dodds (John Murray, 1964). Asa Briggs' remark to the effect that ' there is no good general history of nineteenth century London ' is still applicable, but there are several authoritative accounts of other periods. An early stage in the planning of London is chronicled in T F Reddaway's definitive study *The rebuilding of London after the Fire* (Cape, 1940). Fairly recent history is documented in Donald L Foley's *Controlling London's growth: planning the great wen 1940-1960* (Berkeley, University of California Press, 1963), one of the objective transatlantic studies of British planning which form such a valuable contribution to the literature. Foley examines the plans for London's post-war development and the ideas contained in them; he then looks at the machinery and policies through which the plans were put into action and the ways in which they were modified; and finally at the implications and future of the policies involved. A comprehensive review from the earliest to the comparatively recent is to be found in *London, the unique city* by Steen Eiler Rasmussen (Cape, revised edition 1948) a perceptive analysis by a Danish architect tracing the development of what he calls the 'scattered city' (as distinguished from the 'concentrated city' of which Paris and Vienna were the prototypes).

Across the Atlantic the history of American planning—which is in effect the history of city planning—has only recently been creditably documented. *The making of urban America: a history of city planning in the United States* by John W Reps (Princeton, NJ, Princeton UP, 1965) is a comprehensive, fully documented description and assessment of the towns and cities founded from the time of colonial settlement to the beginning of World War II, copiously illustrated with photographs and plans. Reps' smaller work *Town planning in frontier America* (Princeton, NJ, Princeton UP, 1969) is based closely on the earlier title, and represents an attempt to make available to a wider audience the material first presented in that volume. The smaller work is limited to an examination of city plans prepared before the middle of the nineteenth century beginning with the first permanent European settlement in 1565 at St Augustine; it incorporates some new material discovered since publication of the parent volume. Christopher Tunnard's *The modern American city* (Princeton, NJ, Van Nostrand, 1968) outlines the development of American cities from the mid-nineteenth century to the mid-twentieth; the second part of the book consists of a series of readings from the works of a wide variety of authors which illuminate the themes discussed in the first part. Individual cities have merited description and analysis also. In *Streetcar suburbs: the process of growth in Boston, 1870-1900* (Cambridge, Mass, Harvard UP, 1962) Sam B Warner traces the growth of the city through a period of dynamic expansion and examines in detail the various factors at work. Los Angeles has always been taken as 'the archetype, for better or worse, of the contemporary American metropolis'. In *The fragmented metropolis: Los Angeles 1850-1930* (Cambridge, Mass, Harvard UP, 1967) Robert M Fogelson examines the 'extraordinary expansion' of the city during the period of eighty years when it developed from a Mexican village into an American town, and investigates the factors which have resulted in its fragmentation. John W Reps has also provided a scholarly and well

296

illustrated record of the capital city in *Monumental Washington: the planning and development of the capital center* (Princeton, NJ, Princeton UP, 1967). ' The chief theme of this study is the plan prepared for the central portion of Washington in 1901 and the fate of its proposals ... That plan, prepared by the Senate Park Commission, may be regarded as the country's first modern city planning report '. Washington is also the subject of two meticulously researched volumes by Constance McLaughlin Green, *Washington: village and capital 1800-1878* (Princeton, NJ, Princeton UP, 1962) and *Washington: capital city 1879-1950* (Princeton, NJ, Princeton UP, 1963). These are classics of urban history.

Planning the Canadian environment edited by L O Gertler (Montreal, Harvest House, 1968) is a collection of papers from the first five years of *PLAN, Canada* (the journal of the Town Planning Institute of Canada) from the end of 1959 to the first quarter of 1965, chosen to illustrate the evolution of planning in Canada. The papers are grouped to show the origins of planning in Canada, the background ideas, land resources, and regional planning.

France's great period of town rebuilding as exemplified in its capital city is examined by D H Pinkney in *Napoleon III and the rebuilding of Paris* (Princeton, NJ, Princeton UP, 1958) and by J M and Brian Chapman in *The life and times of Baron Haussmann: Paris in the second empire* (Weidenfeld and Nicolson, 1957). The record is brought up to date in the first volume of a new series edited by H J Dyos under the title ' Studies in urban history ', *The autumn of central Paris: the defeat of town planning 1850-1970* by Anthony Sutcliffe (Edward Arnold, 1970). This is a study of the central business district of Paris and the reasons why (unlike that of London) it has survived so long without being rebuilt. Haussmann's work in Paris (1853-1870) is the starting point, and his achievements are assessed in the light of the work of his successors: Sutcliffe suggests that Haussmann's influence lasted too long and that his methods continued to be copied even when they were no longer applicable. He examines the interplay of changing urban functions, municipal responsibilities, planning decisions, demands for preservation, and shifting economic pressures throughout the period under review.

Finally, Holland, the subject of an authoritative text by Gerald

297

L Burke *The making of Dutch towns: a study in urban development from the tenth to the seventeenth centuries* (Cleaver-Hume Press, 1956) which, in the words of the author, is ' a brief account of urban and rural evolution in a country which, endowed initially with the poorest of natural resources, stood in constant danger, throughout the ages, of losing most of them to the depredations of the North Sea '.

PLANNING IN PRACTICE

In this section we are concerned with what might be called the core of our subject: the principles and the practice of town and country planning. Although when the various texts which purport to embrace this subject are examined and compared, the variety of approaches to the core and the disparity of the contents of the various volumes are adequate evidence that there is little agreement about even the central theme of planning, never mind the periphery. Nevertheless, in this section are collected those titles which focus on the comprehensive practical process of planning in one of three broad ways: firstly, introductions to or expositions of the practical methods of town and country planning, in other words ' how to plan ' (but expositions which relate primarily or solely to towns are discussed below at urban planning); secondly, expositions, aimed at either the layman or the professional, of how planning works in practice; finally, what can only be called ' general special ', being examples of a specialised subject or conceptual approach to the general theme of planning.

Planning is not well endowed with general statements of its principles and practice. Reasons can be advanced for this lack: principally the one that planning is not a subject which is susceptible to textbook analysis on account of its rapid development, the constant disagreement over its content and the redefining of boundaries, and the variations in local practice which go to make up the complete picture. The lack of conventional textbook material and the need or otherwise for it are discussed elsewhere by the present author.[2]

The term ' planning ' has been used throughout this book for reasons which are stated in the preface. But planning, as many people have remarked, can mean many things to many men, and in its broadest sense goes much wider than the allocation of land and

298

the regional manipulation of population and industry. These wider applications are discussed by Melville C Branch in *Planning: aspects and applications* (New York, John Wiley, 1966) which is an attempt to relate planning in its widest sense and planning in its specific applications. After an overview, the applications discussed are project planning, city planning, corporate planning, and military planning. The contents are more in the nature of a set of essays on each topic than a connected text, and, while the chapters are well-documented, would be of more interest to the layman than to any of the professionals whose interests are represented.

Turning to the specific application of city planning or, in Britain, town and country planning, it is possible to trace a long line of 'statements' of the principles of planning starting appropriately with Sir Patrick Abercrombie, a planner of both town—eg London —and country, or region—eg the Clyde Valley. His book *Town and country planning* was first published in 1933, and most recently in a third edition which has been revised and brought up to date by Derek Rigby Childs (Oxford UP, 1959). Abercrombie's own text is in three sections: the first, on the origin of planning, shows its history and development; the second deals with the practice of planning, the objects, the survey, the plan, the legal framework; the third discusses country planning and preservation. To the third edition, Rigby Childs has added a review of 'the first half-century of planning'.

The first (and the only?) volume to actually call itself a textbook was the *Town and country planning textbook* compiled under the auspices of the Association for Planning and Regional Reconstruction (Architectural Press, 1950). At a time when planning education was developing into a recognisable discipline it was logical that a textbook should appear with the needs of students particularly in mind. 'This book aims at providing the student with as complete a course of study in the theory and practice of town and country planning as is possible within the compass of a single volume. It endeavours particularly to meet the needs of those students who are unable to attend a school of planning . . .' It is of interest to examine the contents of this self-confessed 'indispensable book for town planners, architects, and students'. An impressive line-up of contributors, from Mark Abrams to Jack Whittle, is responsible for the constituent parts of six sections: on geography, planning survey, social survey, transport, industry and power, law and economics. There is a concluding section, 'The realization of a development plan: an introduction to planning practice' by Jack Whittle and J M Hirsh, with a note on the Report for the Reconstruction of the City of London by Holden and Holford. Appendices are as follows: the preparation of planning maps; the use of air photographs; Board of Trade Distribution of Industry Act 1945; Town Planning Joint Examination Board; details of the Final Examination. There is a substantial bibliography, arranged by a special AAPR subject classification.

Contemporary with the AAPR *Textbook* were M P Fogarty's *Town and country planning* (Hutchinson, 1948); James W R Adams' *Modern town and country planning* (Churchill, 1952); and the first edition of Lewis Keeble's *Principles and practice of town and county planning* (Estates Gazette, 1952, fourth edition 1969). The latter title, in its latest edition, represents the only up to date statement, taking into account the most recent planning legislation, of the general principles of practical British town and country planning. It includes a historical review of the development plan system; expositions of town and regional planning, and the conduct of surveys for both; space standards and detailed planning design for specialist aspects such as transport, residential areas, and industry; and an analysis of the processes of development control and of the administration of planning at central and local levels. There are many references throughout the text, and a full, sectionalised bibliography. That said, it must also be pointed out that a certain amount of bias is present, that there are many statements which are statements of opinion (albeit based on long experience) rather than of concrete fact—'. . . some inspectors are simply not sufficiently intelligent or sufficiently well trained to perform their very important duties adequately '—and that Keeble's thinking is not in line with that of a substantial section of the profession. The personal bias comes out in his opposition (quite well-aired elsewhere) to the Planning Advisory Group report *The future of development plans* and to the new structure plan system. His view of planning is one which is at variance with the more recent inter-disciplinary view of planning which sees its concern as being the total environment and

300

not only the physical one;[3] he also pays scant attention to the systems view of planning—' *deliberate control of the man-environment relationship must be firmly based on a systems view* '[4]—the single entry in the index referring to a small section of text which is mainly a quotation from a paper written in 1966, and a further footnote which again is largely composed of a quotation. Thus although Keeble's is a central statement, it is by no means a full one, since it is concerned almost exclusively with physical planning; but within this view it still brings together in convenient form far more information on the physical standards of planning than any other work.

The fullest statement of American practice is contained in *Principles and practice of urban planning* edited by William I Goodman and Eric C Freund (Washington, DC, International City Managers' Association, fourth edition 1968). The three previous editions were published under the title *Local planning administration;* this fourth edition has been widened in scope and completely rewritten, containing contributions by more than twenty authorities. All books which attempt such a comprehensive coverage as the entire theory and practice of planning are bound to have congenital defects, but despite a share of these this is a valuable reference book on American planning, with an extensive bibliography. There are six parts. ' The context of urban planning ' gives a short account of the development of planning in the United States. Part two is concerned with planning techniques and studies, including population, transportation planning, economic and land use studies. Part three on ' special approaches to planning ' consists of chapters on city design, on quantitative methods and data processing, and on social welfare planning. ' Implementation ' occupies parts four and five, and covers the plan-making process, zoning, and urban renewal. Finally, part six is a discussion of the planning agency, including the role of public participation. An American compilation which approaches planning practice in a completely different way from Goodman and Freund is *Planning design criteria* by Joseph DeChiara and Lee Koppelman (New York, Van Nostrand/Reinhold, 1969), a compendium of data and information selected by the authors as reference for a variety of ' professionals interested in physical aspects of current urbanisation '. There are nineteen sections on topics such as vehicular circulation, educational facilities, parks and recreation: the coverage is extensive, from climate to kerbstones; but the lack of definition of the rationale for selection of material detracts from the authority of the book, which is further undermined by the absence of any guide to further sources of information.

The Australian approach is displayed in *An introduction to town and country planning* by A J Brown and H M Sherrard (Sydney, Angus & Robertson, second edition 1969), which has a prominent slant towards practice in that continent. The authors' standpoint is revealed in their statement that ' town and country planning is the direction of the development and use of land to serve the economic and social welfare of a community in respect of convenience, health and amenity '. There is a world-wide historical background preceding the body of the text which is concerned with the components of planning—roads, parks, landscape design, surveys and maps; and urban, national and regional planning, location of industry, legislation and finance. A bibliography is included. British practice is considered, but very sketchily and only up to 1959.

Distinct from the books discussed above is Kevin Lynch's statement on *Site planning* (Cambridge, Mass, MIT Press, 1962). ' Between site planning and town planning there is no line of demarcation, and the main principles which govern the one would also apply to the other ', observed Sir Raymond Unwin; ' but there is none the less a considerable difference between the two, and it is convenient to treat them separately, because in site planning the first consideration will be the arrangement of the buildings and the development of the site to the best advantage, whereas in town planning the first consideration must be the general convenience of the town, and the arrangement of the main roads.'[5] Lynch himself defines site planning as the art of arranging an external physical environment in complete detail, and the scope of the site ranges from a few houses to a complete new town. Site matters, such as drainage and services, are included, as well as soil, plants and climate, and various types of buildings and special types of site planning, also the spaces in between them. The text relates to American standards, but the thesis is relevant anywhere, as are the copious marginal sketches.

Turning to overviews of the planning system and how it works in practice, there are three titles which aim to explain planning

302

to the general public: D W Riley's *The citizen's guide to town and country planning* (Town and Country Planning Association, 1966), a concise and clear account of how planning works (as at 1966) with a short resumé of how it arrived at its present state and a brief discussion of the most obvious problems such as urban renewal and conservation of the countryside. In very much the same vein is *Town and country planning in Britain* issued by the Central Office of Information (HMSO, 1968). *Town planning: the consumers' environment* by David Woolley and John Bolt (Research Institute for Consumer Affairs, 1965) is angled more specifically towards the rights of the ' planned ' in the planning process.

The most comprehensive account of the machinery of British planning and the major issues with which it has to contend is J B Cullingworth's *Town and country planning in England and Wales* (Allen and Unwin, third edition 1970). Not for nothing is this new edition sub-titled ' the changing scene ': although completely revised and incorporating the government reorganisation of October 1969, it nevertheless appeared almost simultaneously with the general election of 1970 and was in some respects out of date on publication. But books cannot be held back in anticipation of coming events, and, this minor reservation aside, Cullingworth's monograph is a full descriptive survey of the framework of planning in England and Wales (Scotland and Northern Ireland are not included) its evolution and the current legislative system, taking in the most recent planning legislation, going on to a full treatment of the administrative structure, both central and local, and then discussing at length selected topics—amenity, leisure, and public participation—which ' have been largely ignored in previous works ' and, more cursorily, the better-documented topics of land values, derelict land, new and expanding towns, urban renewal, and regional planning. Each chapter has a list of selected references to further reading.

A study in depth of the detailed functioning of the process of planning at local level is provided in *Local government and strategic choice* by J K Friend and W N Jessop (Tavistock Publications, 1969). This is a difficult book to categorise. Its vision is the whole area of British local government, relevant enough to the work of a planning department, but particularly so in this case since the authors' study is based on their close observation of the working of

Coventry City Planning Department during the period of the review of the city's development plan. The authors had access to all departmental facilities, and their descriptions of the complex workings and inter-relationships of the local government machine are excellent, their discussion of decision-making, information (and the lack of it) and uncertainty in the context of urban planning most illuminating. They also consider the organisation of local government and put forward proposals (based on those of the Maud Commission) for restructuring. This is a well-written, thoroughly worked out, empirically based British study of an important subject of considerable relevance to planning.

Other accounts of British planning in action are now out of date in many respects, although this is not to say that their interest is dead. Lewis Keeble's *Town planning at the crossroads* (Estates Gazette, 1961) is a reflection of the prevalent climate of opinion at the time of its writing: it observes the growth of planning legislation and the development of the machinery for translating it into action, offers an estimate of the current state of British planning and comments on the problems then uppermost. A more useful British view in that it is contributed by a team of authorities and therefore is broader in outlook is *Land use in an urban environment: a general view of town and country planning* (Liverpool, Liverpool UP, 1961). This was also published as two consecutive issues of *Town planning review* 32(3,4) October, January 1961-2, and the team of contributors is F J McCulloch, Paul Brenikov, G P Wibberley, Charles M Haar, H M Parker, Josephine P Reynolds, D H Crompton, William Holford, and Myles Wright. An objective transatlantic view is provided by D R Mandelker in *Green belts and urban growth: English town and country planning in action* (Madison, Wisconsin UP, 1962).

An early view of American planning, by a British author, was provided as part of *Outline of town and city planning: a review of past efforts and modern aims* by Thomas Adams (J & A Churchill, 1935), which reviews the history of city planning before moving on to a survey of modern phases of urban growth and planning the bulk of which is occupied with the development and current state of city planning in the United States. Mel Scott's *American city*

304

planning (Berkeley, University of California Press, 1969) was commissioned by the American Institute of Planners, and describes the political events, persons, institutions, and legislation which comprise the story of American planning since 1890. The theme of Henry W Maier's *Challenge to the cities: an approach to a theory of urban leadership* (New York, Random House, 1966) is the theory and practice of city government in the United States, based on the author's practical experience as Mayor of Milwaukee. Of special interest to planners are the sections on policy formulation, the establishment of the Milwaukee Department of City Development, decision-making, and expenditure planning, all of which have a message for British planners even though the local circumstances differ. The most penetrating and comprehensive analysis of American planning is that provided by Alan Altshuler in *The city planning process: a political analysis* (New York, Cornell UP, 1965) which is a case study in depth of the process of city planning. Professor Altshuler is a political scientist on the staff of the Government Department at Cornell University, and his book, while not so easy to read as that of Friend and Jessop, is yet like theirs an important contribution to the growing literature on planning observed from outside the profession. Basically, Altshuler is concerned with the political and social problems of the planning process, and he illustrates these by means of four case studies of planning decisions in the 'twin' American cities of Minneapolis and St Paul: decisions concerned with the siting of an urban motorway, with a hospital site, with a land use map, and with a central area plan. These detailed studies form the first part of the book; the second is a commentary on the literature of the political aspects of planning.

It is of course of interest, and relevant for purposes of comparison, to know how planning functions in theory and in practice in other countries. Apart from these studies of American practice, planning in overseas countries is sparsely documented in the English language. Poland is adequately treated in *City and regional planning in Poland* edited by Jack C Fisher (New York, Cornell UP, 1966) a collection of contributions by a group of Polish scholars on urban, regional and national planning in their own country, covering a wide range of Polish planning activity both theoretical and practical. This title is the first of a series, in which further titles are to come.

305

Kell Astrom's *City planning in Sweden* (Stockholm, A B Byggmas-
tarens Forlag, 1967) is a fully illustrated account of the development
and present state of city planning in Sweden. The planning structure
and process in West Germany is described by Norman Perry in ' The
Federal planning framework in West Germany ' *JTPI* 52(3) March
1966 91-93; and by William Solesbury in ' Local planning and the
German Bebauungsplan ' in *JTPI* 54(3) March 1968 117-122. The
Spanish Ministerio de la Vivienda is responsible for the preparation
of *Architecture, housing and urbanisation in Spain* (Madrid, Minis-
erio de la Vivienda, 1963) which is principally concerned with
housing but contains also synopses of official policy in architecture
and town and country planning. Maurice F Parkins surveys the
development of city planning in Russia in *City planning in Soviet
Russia* (Chicago, Chicago UP. 1953) from its initial stage 1922-31,
through the transitional stage of 1931-44 culminating in the General
Plan for Moscow, to the third, reconstruction stage. The body of
the text takes the account up to 1950, material up to 1952 is added
in an appendix. A review of planning structure and its processes is
included. Nearly half of the book is occupied by an annotated
bibliography of available Russian and non-Russian sources, containing over eight hundred titles. An indication of how planning
works in New Zealand is obtained from *Town and country planning principles in New Zealand* prepared by the Town and Country
Planning Branch of the Ministry of Works (Wellington, Government
Printer, 1963). The Town and Country Planning Act of 1953 gave
planning functions to local authorities throughout New Zealand,
and this publication is a digest of extracts from decisions made
under the Act, arranged alphabetically by topic. More material on
aspects of planning in overseas countries will be found in the
appropiate following sections of this chapter.

In this general section on planning we have looked at the principles
and practice of the subject, and at what may broadly be called its
administration; it now remains to examine the concept of planning,
a concept which, as we have already seen, is still subject to fluctua-
tion and redefinition. In this context we are concerned not with the
range of subjects which may be relevant to planning but rather

with its ideology, that is to say the body of ideas which together make up the central concept of planning.

In 1960, Donald L Foley published a seminal article under the title 'British town planning: one ideology or three' in *British journal of sociology* 11(3) September 1960 211-231. In it, he argued in stages from the basic function of planning to achieve a useful and consistent allocation of land uses, through its intermediate function of providing a decent physical environment, to his final premise that the provision of such a physical environment is only the basis on which a programme of social goals, providing a better community life, may be founded. The early 1960's saw a new approach to planning, consistent with Foley's thesis, gradually taking effect; they saw the introduction of multi-disciplinary teams into practical planning studies at regional level, and an increasing awareness of the potential contribution of social scientists to planning. So far the major contribution has been from economics, with a smaller one from sociology. 'Attention has been focused on the economist because it is economics which has had most to offer to the recent debate, and economic forces have played a major part in the change of attitude. It is economic planning which has provided the link between national and regional policy, and the social well-being of a community is ultimately dependent on its economic health.'[5] And indeed, regional physical and regional economic planning are now inextricably interwoven, and the evidence of this may be seen in the section of this chapter on regional planning. The contribution of the sociologists has so far been on a smaller scale. 'The sociologist in this country is still more interested in the family and the neighbourhood group, and thus has more to offer to planning at the micro level . . . Apart from the findings of an all too small number of social surveys, sociology has as yet little to offer to the larger issues of modern urban and regional policy.'[6] There is, however, an alternative proposition that the real contribution to planning by sociologists may be in a different direction. 'Sociologists could perhaps make their own contribution to social policy connected with the built environment, not by market research into activity patterns, but by the analysis of planners' goals and values and by the sociological analysis of the process of planning itself.'[7]

The contribution of economics to planning is discussed in broad terms in a number of papers, of which two given at Town and Country Planning Summer Schools are both readable and informative: D J Robertson's 'The relationship between physical and economic planning' in *Report of the Town and Country Planning Summer School*, St Andrews, 1965 (TPI, 1965); and 'The economics of regional planning: the example of the west midlands' by D E C Eversley, in *Report of the Town and Country Planning Summer School*, Keele, 1966 (TPI, 1966). The very useful volume *Regional and urban studies: a social science approach* edited by J B Cullingworth and S C Orr (Allen and Unwin, 1969, University of Glasgow Social and Economic Studies) is a collection of papers which demonstrates the practical approach to specific aspects of planning by social scientists, mainly, in this context, economists. All of the papers are based on practical experience of the problems discussed and set out the techniques which have been applied. Two essays which blend the economic and sociological approaches to planning, although in very different ways, are John Rex's 'Economic growth and decline: their consequences for the sociology of planning' and R A Bird's 'The relationship of economic and physical planning', both in *Report of the Town and Country Planning Summer School*, Manchester, 1968 (TPI, 1968).

The sociological contribution to planning and the social ideology of planning are discussed in *Planning for people: essays on the social context of planning* by Maurice Broady (National Council of Social Service, 1968); and in a collection edited by R E Pahl, *Whose city? and other essays on sociology and planning* (Longman, 1970). Eric Reade, in a paper 'Some notes toward a sociology of planning: the case for self-awareness' *JTPI* 54(5) May 1968 214-218, put forward the case, later reinforced by Pahl, for sociology and sociological analysis to be applied to planning itself rather than to the effects of the physical environment. The social ideology of British planning is most fully stated in Gordon E Cherry's *Town planning in its social context* (Leonard Hill, 1970). Cherry puts forward a case for the identification of a distinct area of concern, social planning, within the broader field of town planning, for a flexible, adaptive approach to the making of plans and the formulating of goals based on a view of the city as a dynamic, constantly-changing social system, and for the preparation of a social plan to complement the physical development plan. 'In the twentieth century, planning has struggled without great success to embody its social idea within a largely physical planning system. The time is now right for a reappraisal of both concept and practice, and we are helped to this end by reverting to seeing the " community " not as the end product of planning but as the starting point.' The main social concerns of current American planning are discussed in the thirty four short essays which make up *Urban planning and social policy* edited by Bernard J Frieden and Robert Morris (New York, Basic Books, 1968). The six parts of the book are indicative of the areas of these concerns: approaches to social planning; housing and urban renewal; racial bias and segregation; citizen organisation and participation; urban poverty; guidelines of social policy.

Recognition of the city as an evolving system is the fundamental tenet of the ' systems ' approach to planning, or systemic planning. Such a view derives basically from the large-scale land use/transportation studies initiated in the United States in the early 1950's but it is only in the last decade that the implications of the idea applied to urban planning have been fully considered. Much of the thinking has been done in America—Professor Britton Harris was, and is, a leading figure—and it was not until 1967 that the systems view of planning was well aired in Britain. In that year, J B McLoughlin expounded it in detail at the Town and Country Planning Summer School in a paper 'A systems approach to planning ' in *Report of the Town and Country Planning Summer School, Belfast, 1967* (TPI, 1967); an earlier paper by George Chadwick, 'A systems view of planning ' in *JTPI* 52(5) May 1966, 184-186, was to some extent anticipatory, and should not be overlooked. Basically the approach involves simulating the complete city system, in all its many interrelationships, in mathematical terms, using a computer, and testing it to ascertain the effects on the total system of changes in any one or more of the factors involved. As McLoughlin explains, in his 1967 paper, ' we know that the city is comprised of a myriad relationships, but if we have the vision to identify and describe these in the right way they can be expressed in mathematical terms. The way changes occur through time can be built in to the equations, and the computer, handling the instructions provided, can in a

309

matter of minutes enable us to observe decades of growth in a large city. In effect, changes in the location of many kinds of activity in the city, the flows along roads and railway lines, the accompanying shift in land values, clearance and renewal operations, the growth, change and shifting of manufacturing and commercial enterprises, the evolving life of the city in outline is mirrored in the model or " family " of models. We can experiment, we can test, we can observe, we can learn . . . The extent to which we have a correct and appropriate method of forecasting the city's future depends on how clearly we have been able to describe the system we are simulating in the models . . . Simulation exercises have the very salutary effect of forcing us to find out how the real world actually works.' The full statement of systemic planning is contained in J B McLoughlin's *Urban and regional planning: a systems approach* (Faber, 1969) which has been widely acclaimed as one of the significant planning texts of recent years. The great merit of McLoughlin's work is that it is not only an exposition of a new approach to planning, it is also a drawing together of existing knowledge on the wider issue of cybernetics generally and a review of work done on the application of cybernetic and other techniques to planning. The first two chapters are a review in general terms of ' man in his ecological setting ' and the effect on him and his actions of environmental factors; from this, McLoughlin moves to a concise chronological review of location theory and its associated literature. Using this as a base, McLoughlin moves on to devote the remainder of the book to an examination and exposition of ' the environment as a system and its control by the application of cybernetic principles ', viewing this approach as a framework within which the locational behaviour of human beings can be explored and perhaps finally understood, and explaining the practical requirements and processes involved in applying systems planning to practical situations. He concludes with a review of the implications of systems planning not only for planning in practice but also for education and research. The bibliography refers to a full and representative coverage of further reading, both British and American. An exposition of how systemic planning can work in a local authority planning department is given by Eric L Cripps in 'A management system for planning: a review of the application of a systems approach to

310

planning' *JTPI* 55(5) May 1969 187-195, in which he discusses the development of a computer-aided systems approach to planning in Bedfordshire, the technology required, and the information system necessary to support it. The systems approach was applied in the Leicester and Leicestershire sub-regional planning study, of which McLoughlin was director (see chapter 9).

PLANNING LAW AND PROCEDURES
However widely the debate may range as to the scope and content of planning, however wide the range of its socio-economic affiliations, it is nevertheless a process which in its day to day practice is carried on within a legal framework, and which is therefore subject to formalities of procedure. In this section we shall review the available information on planning law and procedures: under this umbrella are the associated processes of development plan making, development control, the machinery of applications and appeals and inquiries, and public participation in planning, as they relate to British planning practice, with a look also at American practice.

The principal legislation affecting planners is the Town and Country Planning Act 1968 in England and Wales, the Town and Country Planning (Scotland) Act 1969 in Scotland. As we indicated in chaper 2, practical implementation of the provisions of the 1968 Act must, in the majority of cases, wait on the reorganisation of local government and the introduction of larger administrative units with larger planning staffs; and therefore, the provisions of the Town and Country Planning Act 1947 are still relevant. Cognate legislation which is of direct concern to planners, such as the Countryside Act 1968, is discussed within the appropriate sections of this chapter. In conjunction with the Town and Country Planning Act 1968 are the Statutory Instruments and the Circulars which are issued under it. Statutory Instruments, which are numbered consecutively throughout each calendar year, contain orders and regulations made under the provisions of the Act. Circulars, which are also numbered consecutively throughout each year, are issued by the Minister to explain the policy which he is following within the terms of the Act, and are not in themselves statutory.

The most comprehensive and up to date guide to planning law is the *Encyclopedia of the law of town and country planning*, edited by Desmond Heap and published by Sweet and Maxwell Ltd. Commenced in 1959, the *Encyclopedia* is in loose-leaf format and has now expanded into three volumes, being regularly up-dated by means of additions and amendments which are sent to subscribers for incorporation. It refers only to England and Wales; there is no equivalent publication for Scotland. Desmond Heap is the foremost authority on planning law: his well-known manual *An outline of planning law* (Sweet and Maxwell, fifth edition 1969) has been a standard since its first appearance in 1949, and has now been revised to incorporate the changes effected by the 1968 Act. This is the most readable and the most intelligible guide to current planning law, reducing the mass of detail effectively to pocket-size. Heap was also the author of *The new town planning procedures* (Sweet and Maxwell, 1968), an easily read outline of the 1968 Act: with its publication only a month after the Act received the royal assent this was the first guide to appear in print, but suffers from its speed of preparation in that it includes no cognisance of the Regulations and Directions made under the Act. A E Telling's *Planning law and procedure* (Butterworths, 1970) is another well-known guide, now in its third edition incorporating the new legislation and procedures arising from it. The familiar presentation of annotated legal text is available from two writers: H H Karslake in *An annotated text of the Town and Country Planning Act 1968* (Rating and Valuation Association, 1968) and C H Beaumont in *The Town and Country Planning Act 1968* (Butterworths, 1969). Lewis F Sturge throws in a bonus in *The Town and Country Planning Act 1968 and the Civic Amenities Act 1967* (Estates Gazette, 1969), which includes the texts of both Acts in full together with Commencement Orders and Statutory Instruments made under them, also the Acquisition of Land (Authorization Procedure) Act 1946 as currently amended and a synopsis of the Town and Country Planning Act 1962 with notes showing the effects on it of the most recent legislation. Now out of date, in that it does not take into account legislation beyond its date of publication, but still worth mentioning, is John J Clarke's *The gist of planning law* (Macmillan, 1964). This was in its day an excellent and very readable concise guide to the legislation; a new edition was expected in 1970 but the author's death at the beginning of that year appears to have delayed, or perhaps stopped altogether, this publication. Should it appear in the interim, it would be recommended along with Heap's *Outline*. Historical accounts of legislation are often valuable, and in this context W Wood's *Planning and the law* (Percival Marshall, 1949) is a clear and readable exposition of early post-war planning legislation. American planning law is also of interest for comparative purposes, although it is very different in many respects. A useful set of papers from a 1960 seminar in comparative planning law are collected together in *Law and land: Anglo-American planning practice* edited by Charles M Haar (Cambridge, Mass, Harvard UP, 1966). In sections on the theory and framework of planning, on the making of plans, on the place of the individual in the planning process, and on the financial aspects of planning, the papers compare, contrast and evaluate the British and American approaches to similar problems. Haar is also the author of *Land planning law in a free society: a study of the British Town and Country Planning Act* (Cambridge, Mass, Harvard UP, 1951), an observation, intended primarily for the American reader, of how the 1947 Act works in practice.

The crux of the 1947 Town and Country Planning Act was the development plan system. An explanation of the system was contained in an advisory booklet issued by the Ministry of Housing and Local Government, *Development plans explained* by B J Collins (HMSO, 1951, now out of print). Guidance on the actual preparation of development plan maps was also provided by the Ministry in Planning Bulletin no 6, *Town and Country Planning Act 1962. Development plan maps, Part 1, Continuous revision. Part 2, The addition of colour* (HMSO, 1964). A brief review of the development plan system and its working in practice begins the report of the Planning Advisory Group of the Ministry of Housing and Local Government, the Ministry of Transport, and the Scottish Development Department, *The future of development plans* (HMSO, 1965). This report sounded the death knell of the old system, for its recommendations for a new system based on structure plans (see chapter 2) were incorporated into the Act of 1968 and now form the letter of the law. The Ministry of Housing and Local

Government have issued a new advisory manual, *Development plans: a manual on form and content* (HMSO, 1970), giving information about the nature, range and content of structure and local plans under the new system. A MOHLG press release indicates that the manual will be supplemented from time to time, as more experience is gained of the new planning system in operation and to reflect developments of planning thought, particularly as regards resources and investment and the social aspects of planning. It is also intended to issue other advisory publications on various aspects of planning under the new system. A separate booklet *Development plans: characteristic notations* (HMSO, 1970) sets out the notations suggested for diagrams and maps. A companion manual for Scotland is expected during 1971.

Development control is exercised by local planning authorities in accordance with their development plans. The system of development control, as set out in the Town and Country Planning Act 1947, was also examined by the Planning Advisory Group, which found that it had worked, and was still working quite satisfactorily. 'As regards procedures, our general conclusion is that the present system of development control is basically sound and can work efficiently. But we have found wide variations in the performance of local planning authorities, in terms of the time taken to deal with planning applications. This raises questions of management rather than policy.' The group recommended the commissioning of a management study of planning administration at the local level ' concerned primarily with the way in which development control is operated and ways in which it could be improved and expedited '. Such a study was carried out by consultants appointed by the Minister of Housing and Local Government and the Local Authorities Association, and their findings and recommendations are embodied in a report *Management study on development control* (HMSO, 1967). The Ministry of Housing and Local Government have also issued a series of *Development control policy notes* (HMSO, 1969) as follows : —

1 General principles
2 Development in residential areas
3 Industrial and commercial development
4 Development in rural areas

These *Notes* have replaced the *Bulletin of selected appeals decisions,* later the *Selected planning appeals, second series,* which have been discontinued. In February 1970 the Town Planning Institute and the Royal Institute of British Architects agreed to set up a joint working group to examine the existing system of development control, taking into account the new framework introduced by the Town and Country Planning Act 1968, and to make recommendations for its improvement. An interim report setting out the main issues for examination was discussed in October 1970, and is to be used as a basis for constructive discussion with the Department of the Environment.

Development control necessitates a system for its enforcement, and the procedures involved are the subject of several treatises. They clearly do not inspire any originality in the way of titles. In chronological order we have *The enforcement of planning control* by Douglas Frank and Guy Seward (Estates Gazette, 1958); *The enforcement of planning control* by Harold J J Brown (Sweet and Maxwell, 1961); and, the most up to date, *The enforcement of planning control* by A J Little (Shaw and Sons, second edition 1970) which brings the law up to date with the provisions of the 1968 Act and new decisions of the courts. This latter text is well-informed, clear and concise, and deals not only with ordinary enforcement notices but with such notices in relation to buildings of special architectural or historic interest, tree preservation, advertisements, and waste land. Wider in scope is R N D Hamilton's *A guide to development and planning* (Solictors' Law Stationery Society, fifth edition 1970), a revised version of a clear, concise text, fully supported by case references, which embraces not only the whole field of control including chapters on compulsory purchase and betterment levy but also deals very comprehensively with the fundamental matters of development plans, the nature of development,

315

and planning permissions. An insight into the day to day working of the development control system is provided in the booklet issued by Essex County Planning Department, *Development control procedures* (Chelmsford, Essex CPO, 1963).

In the furtherance of its development plan, and also as a means of controlling development, a local planning authority is empowered to compulsorily acquire land. These powers are fairly wide under the terms of the 1968 Act. Procedures associated with compulsory purchase and with compensation are discussed in the general guides to planning law (see above) but are also treated independently in another of Sweet and Maxwell's loose-leaf up-dated guides, the *Encyclopedia of the law of compulsory purchase and compensation* edited by R D Stewart-Brown; who is also the author of *A guide to compulsory purchase and compensation* (Sweet and Maxwell, fifth edition 1961).

A developer wishing to develop land must make application for planning permission to the local planning authority within whose development plan area the land falls; the authority may grant or refuse permission, and if the latter, then there is the right of appeal against the decision to the central authority. Subsequent to an appeal being made, where necessary, an inquiry may be held. The whole business of these various procedures is discussed fully in *Planning applications, appeals and inquiries* by A E Telling and F H B Layfield (Butterworths, 1953); and in *Planning appeals and inquiries* by L Blundell and G Dobry, now brought up to date in a second edition by Paul L Rose and Michael Barnes (Sweet and Maxwell, 1970) which brings the original up to date with current legislation. This is a practical guide, concise but at the same time full, to all matters concerned with the making of appeals; it is particularly well laid out, with a very comprehensive table of contents facilitating easy access to the text. *Planning procedure tables* by R N D Hamilton (Oyez Publications, 1968) is a clear explanation of the procedures to be followed in all normal planning matters, for example, planning appeals, building regulations and applications for office development.

In many respects, American and British land use control methods represent opposite extremes of approach; for example, the American system depends on the establishment of formal and consistent

316

standards and the avoidance of discretionary power in the hands of the planning authority. Although it is thus different and naturally geared to American conditions and American notions of democracy, it is not irrelevant to British planning in the sense that it is one of the few alternatives available to the British system. John Delafons' *Land use controls in the United States* (Cambridge, Mass, MIT Press, second edition 1969) is an excellent exposition of the system, and is particularly useful in that it is written by a British author for a British audience. The second edition incorporates a review of the main changes which have taken place in the 1960's, with some reference to parallel developments in Britain. Within the framework of land control, zoning is the American practice of allocating land for specific purposes. The most readable account of the system of zoning is Richard F Babcock's *The zoning game: municipal practices and policies* (Madison, Wisconsin UP, 1966), in which the theory and practice, merits and demerits are discussed and liberally illustrated with examples from the author's experience as a lawyer specialising in land use. *The structure of urban zoning: its dynamics in urban planning and development* by Norman Williams (New York, Buttenheim Publ Corp, 1966) is primarily a collection of case studies of judicial proceedings which illustrates how they are interpreted legally, based on a series of monthly articles ' Zoning and planning notes ' in the journal *The American city*. Also available are S J Marielski's *The politics of zoning: the New York experience* (New York, Columbia UP, 1966) which is aimed at a political science audience rather than a planning one; and Herbert H Smith's *The citizen's guide to zoning* (New York, Chandler-Davis, 1965) which is .a thorough treatment intended for the ' planned ' rather than the ' planner '.

Mention of the ' planned ' leads to a topic which could hardly be called a planning procedure in the strict sense of the term but which, with the stimulus of the 1968 Act, has become a central and important issue in the planning process—public participation, or citizen participation. As J B Cullingworth has observed, ' the 1968 Planning Act is a legislative landmark in the development of a new framework of planning designed to bring about a greater degree of citizen participation '.[8] Furthermore, ' citizen participation is more than a desirable adjunct: it is an essential basis. If citizen participation

317

does not work, the system [*ie* the new development plan system laid down in the Act] will collapse '.[9] Experience of citizen participation in Britain being small, a Committee on Public Participation in Planning under the chairmanship of Arthur Skeffington was set up in March 1968 ' to consider and report on the best methods, including publicity, of securing the participation of the public at the formative stage in the making of development plans for their area '. The committee's report, *People and planning* (HMSO, 1969) is a joint publication of the Ministry of Housing and Local Government, the Scottish Development Department, and the Welsh Office. The recommendations contained in it are fairly obvious, commonsense ones concerned rather with the desirability of participation than with the critical means of implementing it; to quote Cullingworth again, ' the mundane nature of many of the recommendations is testimony to the distance which British local government has to go in making citizen participation a reality '.[10] Many bodies submitted evidence to the Skeffington Committee, among them the Town Planning Institute. The institute's memorandum is reproduced in *JTPI* 54(7) July/August 1968 343-344.

Public participation does not figure prominently in the British planning literature : the concept is young, and experience small. One of the most substantial contributions to the debate is contained in ' Public participation in planning ' edited by Josephine P Reynolds in *Town planning review* 40(2) July 1969 131-148. This is a report by a group of postgraduate students in the Department of Civic Design at Liverpool University which examines the concept of participation from first principles : it attempts to define the aims of involving the public in the planning process and the extent to which the present system succeeds in achieving them, and then goes on to examine the underlying social theories, the communicative and the educational aspects of the problem. The specific difficulties of participation at the regional level are reviewed together with some discussion of the position in the United States and its relevance to the British situation. Also worth reading is Graham Ashworth's article ' Planning with the public ' in *Architectural Association quarterly* 1(2) April 1969, 75-79. Ashworth was a member of the Skeffington Committee, and in this article, written before publication of its report, he sets out what he sees as the major issues involved in planning with the public and relates these issues to the changes in planning procedures effected by the Act of 1968. David Hall is the author of ' The participation " experiment " ' in *Town and country planning* 37(9) September 1969, 390-391. Ditchley Paper no 21, *Public participation in urban planning* (Enstone, Oxon, Ditchley Foundation, 1969) contains a report by Peter Robshaw on an Anglo-American conference held by the foundation in association with the Civic Trust in June 1969 which compares British and American experience.

Experience of public participation in North America is greater, and as a result the documentation is quantitatively more substantial. A special issue of the *Journal of the American Institute of Planners* 35(4) July 1969 was devoted to the theme of citizen participation, the papers all referring to American experience with one exception, which discusses the emergence of participation in a new community in Sweden under the title ' Politics and planning in a Swedish suburb '. Hans Spiegel is the editor of two volumes under the title *Citizen participation in urban development* (Washington, DC, Center for Community Affairs of the NTL Institute for Applied Behavioral Science, 1968), the first volume dealing with ' Concepts and issues ' and the second with ' Cases and programs '. The first volume includes a useful overview of the subject in the form of a literature review. In 1968 the US Department of Housing and Urban Development held a staff conference on citizen participation, and the proceedings of this are contained in *Citizen participation today: proceedings of a staff conference, June 3-4, 1968* (Chicago, HUD, 1968). Two early works in the field were *Community organization for citizen participation in urban renewal* by William C Loring and others (Cambridge, Mass, Cambridge Press Inc, 1957) and *Citizen participation in urban renewal* by William B Nixon and Joseph M Boyd (Nashville, Tennessee State Planning Commission, 1957). A description of an actual large-scale exercise in citizen participation is given in *The politics of urban renewal: the Chicago findings* (New York, Free Press of Glencoe, 1961) by Peter H Rossi and Robert A Dentler, which describes how residents in the deteriorating Chicago suburb of Hyde Park-Kenwood contributed to a plan to conserve and revitalise their area. Three separate areas of Boston are the setting of Langley Carleton Keyes ' *The rehabilitation planning game: a study in the diversity of neighbourhood* (Cambridge, Mass, MIT Press, 1969), inner city areas in process of rehabilitation in which citizens were drawn into the planning effort.

Canadian experience, in particular experiments in Montreal and Toronto, is discussed by N H Richardson in ' Participatory democracy and planning: the Canadian experience' in *JTPI* 56(2) February 1970, 52-55. Richardson sums up the essence of the problem: ' the professional planner tends to work from the top down . . . his view is synoptic and long-range. But the average citizen is concerned with what is going to happen across the street next week. Both these perspectives are legitimate and indeed essential. The problem of how to bring them together in a constructive way, however, is an extremely difficult one.'

PLANNING METHODOLOGIES AND TECHNIQUES

The survey is basic to the planning process and has been so for many years, a fact which has been rehearsed several times in the preceding chapters. This being so, and since, as John N Jackson points out, ' a survey does not just start of its own accord; it has to be organised with meticulous care from beginning to end ', it is surprising that there is only one book on the subject and even that is nearly ten years out of date. John N Jackson's *Surveys for town and country planning* (Hutchinson, 1963) is a practical manual. It defines the place of the survey in the planning process, reviews the sources from which information and data can be obtained, and the various methods used in carrying out a survey; and then goes on to discuss surveys according to type—physical and land resource, land use and building, communication, traffic and parking, industrial, population and social. There are full references to other sources at the end of each chapter.

The growing number of activities which concern the planner mean that very often surveys have to be specially designed and operated in order to obtain information on very specific matters over a wide range of subjects, and these are normally carried out on an *ad hoc* basis to fit the particular situation. A note on some wider based texts may therefore be appropriate within this section. C A Moser's *Survey methods in social investigation* (Heinemann, 1958) is a very full, authoritative treatment of the survey from its inception to its processing and presentation, with thorough treatment of sampling, methods of collecting the information such as interviewing and questionnaire design, and other relevant topics. There is a very full bibliography covering a wide range of sources. A more recent text is Margaret Stacey's *Methods of social research* (Oxford, Pergamon Press, 1969). On specific aspects of the survey, there are many useful texts, such as Frank Yates' *Sampling methods for censuses and surveys* (Griffin, third edition 1960) and *Questionnaire design and attitude measurement* by A N Oppenheim (Heinemann, 1966). The Government Social Survey has issued a *Handbook for interviewers* prepared by J Atkinson (HMSO, 1967) which is a practical manual with a wider range than the title indicates. Another practical manual is the *Classification manual for household interview surveys in Great Britain* by G Hoinville and R Jowell (Social and Community Planning Research, 1969) which is intended as a working document for those who use survey data; bearing in mind the need for comparability between survey data, the manual proposes a classification of socio-economic variables into thirty two categories. G Kalton's *Introduction to statistical ideas for social scientists* (Chapman and Hall, 1966) is a very good short introduction to this aspect of the survey. *Statistics in the making: a primer in statistical survey method* by M L Mark (Columbus, Ohio State University, 1958) is also a useful text with a good exposition of tabulation procedures. A comprehensive text on graphic methods of presenting survey information is C F Schmid's *Handbook of graphic presentation* (New York, Ronald Press, 1954) and the narrative presentation is treated in the United Nations Statistical Office *Recommendations for the preparation of sample survey reports* (New York, UN, 1964, Statistical Papers Series C, no 1 Rev 2). Practical demonstration of how surveys are carried out in a county planning department is provided by three technical memoranda issued by East Sussex County Planning Department: *Survey manual* (Tech Memo CP 58/1), *Coding manual* (Tech Memo CP 61/1), and *Analysis manual* (Tech Memo CP 61/3) (Lewes, County Planning Department, 1965).

Surveys of all kinds, from centralised operations such as the national population census down to small-scale specialised exercises planned and operated by local planning departments for specific purposes, provide the data which in raw or semi-processed state, form the basis of planning: the survey as a source of such data is ranked the most important single operational source by planners, as was demonstrated in chapter 6. We have explained the distinction between data and information in the preface to this book, and have intimated the exclusion of data from its contents. The discussion at this point, therefore, is confined to the theoretical and methodological aspects of data organisation insofar as they may be construed as planning techniques.

The need for data, and not only for more data but most significantly for better data, increases as planning becomes more sophisticated in its processes: the advent of modelling, for example, has stimulated a voracious appetite for data, and, as many planners have observed, the development of techniques such as this is more likely to be hindered by the lack of suitable data than by the competence of the planners and the capability of the machines. The need for data in planning, particularly in the light of new concepts and techniques, is discussed fairly widely in the professional press on both sides of the Atlantic. Tim Rhodes discusses data specifically in relation to the use of models in 'Data requirements for urban land use models' JTPI 54(6) June 1968 281-283. A more general discussion is offered by Nigel Moor in 'Planning and information' Architectural Association quarterly 2(2) April 1970 56-61. Data as a primary source in planning was examined by Brenda White in a paper to the first conference of the Aslib Social Sciences Group in January 1971, Aslib proceedings 23(4) April 1971 187-198. Similar problems exist in the United States and are discussed by William Alonso in 'Predicting best with imperfect data' Journal of the American Institute of Planners 34(4) July 1968 248-255.

Two major projects are concerned with the data requirements of planning as it has emerged under the 1968 Act, since structure planning and the requirement for continuous monitoring of plans (replacing the former quinquennial review stipulated by the 1947 Act) demand that a more systematic approach to the collection and management of data be evolved and practised. Since March 1969 a team has been working in London, based on the Department of the Environment, to examine the information (ie data) requirements of the new planning system. The team is composed of representatives from central and local government, working under the direction of a similarly-constituted steering group. The approach of the team was to attempt to isolate the decisions which have to be taken at various levels by local planning authorities under the Town and Country Planning Act 1968 and other related Acts, and to identify the information which can help in reaching these decisions. Five levels were identified: national, regional, structure, district, and action area. In addition the team were charged to develop the structure of a comprehensive planning information system for each level of plan including methods of geographic referencing. A draft report on the team's work and its proposals was produced at the end of 1970; no final document has been issued as yet. Some overlap is apparent between the work of this team and the work of the Urban Systems Research Unit at Reading University: the first stage of the latter project has been to investigate the information (again, read data) requirements of structure planning particularly with respect to sub-regional modelling, to survey the present availability and quality of data and to propose methods for rationalising processing procedures to produce data of the required standard. The ultimate objective of the Reading project is to develop an operational sub-regional land use model which will be capable of more than local application. The first stage of the research was concluded at the end of 1970, and several papers have been issued, all of them informative and useful. The first major statement of progress was contained in a paper delivered by Peter Hall and Eric Cripps, Director and Associate Director respectively of the unit, at the conference on information and urban planning held by the Centre for Environmental Studies in May 1969 and published in the proceedings (CES, 1969, CES-IP-8 volume 1) under the title 'An introduction to the study of information for urban and regional planning'. Also available are the following: *Spatial theory and information systems* by Michael Batty (USRU WP 3/0); *Information needs of planners—a survey* by Erlet Cater (USRU WP 4/0); *Statistics for planning, 1, the Census of Population* by Alison Cheshire (USRU WP 5/0); *Statistics for planning, 2, a review of government statistics* by Alison Cheshire (USRU WP 6/0); and *A comparative study of information systems for urban and regional planning, 1, Scandinavia* by Eric L Cripps (USRU WP 7/0) all published by the University of Reading Department of

323

Geography. A comprehensive report on the first part of the project was expected at the end of 1970, which would formulate a conceptual framework for an information system for urban structure planning.

There is no doubt that the advent of the computer has created a revolution in planning thought and practice. As Britton Harris observed in 1967, 'during the next ten years, hundreds of planning offices throughout the United States [and of course in Britain also] are going to begin working with computers. Some planners will approach this novel experience like shy virgins, others like vinegary spinsters, and still others with soft cries of joy. None of them will ever be the same again.'[11] Much cerebral activity has been channelled into formulating the role which computers can most profitably play in the planning process. Their functions so far have been in two main directions: in data management, which includes the organisation of data for storage and retrieval and the devising of information systems for planning; and in simulation processes including the various types of modelling discussed below. Discussion of the use of computers in planning in the main focuses on or around either or both of these areas. An early critical appraisal of their potential was made by Anthony James Catanese in 'Automation in town planning: problems and potentials of the coming revolution' *JTPI* 53(10) December 1967 448-451. Britton Harris reveals ' How to succeed with computers without really trying' in *Journal of the American Institute of Planners* 33(1) January 1967 11-17: he sees the advent of the computer as inevitable and suggests that the most productive way to approach it is by starting with relatively straightforward operations such as automation of data files and progressing gradually to more complex exercises such as simulation. Subsequently, however, he warns that ' Computation is not enough', in an address to the Association for Computing Machinery in 1968 in which he states that ' we cannot successfully exploit the very considerable capabilities of computers until we greatly increase our understanding of the world with which we are dealing and the means with which we will represent it and manipulate it inside the computer'. A special issue of the journal *Socioeconomic planning sciences* 1(3) July 1968 was devoted to 'Application of computers to the problems of urban society' and consisted of papers presented at the Annual Symposium for Computing Machinery, including contributions by Britton Harris (see above) and T R Lakshmanan. The Computer Group of the Town Planning Institute Research Committee produced in 1968 a report on *The use of the computer in planning* (TPI, 1968) which concentrated primarily on the organisation of data for data banking and included a detailed land use classification for this purpose; the various suggestions put forward have not, however, been followed up. Subsequent to the publication of the report, the Computer Group held a conference at Birmingham in April 1969 on 'The computer in planning' at which papers were presented detailing some current computer applications. The papers were published (TPI, 1969).

Problems of data management are not unique to planning, and there is a strong case for the total local authority data bank as opposed to one set up for purely planning purposes, although as a practical proposition this ideal is still distant. Central to the process of organising data is a classification system, and in this respect it is clearly disadvantageous to have a situation where each planning authority uses a different system and equally clearly advantageous to have a national standardised system to ensure compatibility. Much thought has been given to the matter of classification. A team at the Department of the Environment, working in tandem with the team investigating information needs, has been engaged for the past two years on the development of a national system of land use classification, although (at time of writing) no concrete results have been produced in documentary form. Much work has been done also within the Department of the Environment on the development of a coordinate referencing system to be used in conjunction with the National Grid. In 1967 the Regional Studies Association held a conference on *Grid squares for planning: possibilities and prospects* (RSA, 1967) which included three papers by planners from the Department under the session heading of 'A coordinate referencing system for planners': G M Gaits' 'The general concept of a coordinate referencing system for land use planning', G M Stubbs' 'Point data and its use', and G P Woodford's 'The use of metric grid for town study'. Data banking and its place within the total information system has exercised planning minds on both sides of the Atlantic to a considerable extent, and a substantial volume of literature has resulted. There is a problem here to distinguish between descriptions of systems which are (and may well remain) hypothetical concepts, and those which have actually been put into practice and their performance evaluated. Leslie S Jay provides a realistic assessment of the potential of data systems in a small booklet *The development of an integrated data system* (TPI, 1966) in which he describes the methods developed in East Sussex County Planning Department for the collection, storage and analysis of data. Procedures are explained in simple terms and applications for development control are mentioned. The application to development control is taken further by J A Zetter of West Sussex in 'Development control and the integrated data system' *JTPI* 54(10) December 1968 473-476. An authoritative collection of statements on American thought and practice in the design and operation of information systems is contained in *Threshold of planning information systems* (Chicago, American Society of Planning Officials, 1967), reviewed in some detail by Adrian S Pope in *JTPI* 53(10) December 1967 459-460. These are selected papers from the adp workshops conducted at the ASPO national planning conference at Houston in April 1967, and their usefulness lies, at least in part, in their criticisms of current practice and their discussion of the problems involved. A useful short comment on information systems, based on one of the papers included in the ASPO collection, and on the implications of American experience for British practice, together with a review of four American systems, is given by R E Fry in 'Urban information systems in the United States: a review and commentary' *Quarterly bulletin of the Research and Intelligence Unit of the Greater London Council* 3 July 1968 3-7. The American literature on planning information systems is fairly extensive, much of it being of little more than local interest apart, perhaps, from methodological considerations: one of the best examples is *A recommendation for a state planning information system* being a report to the Bureau of State Planning of the State of Wisconsin by Kenneth J Dueker (Madison, Wisconsin Bureau of State Planning, 1967). The first collective statement of British thought and experiment, mainly on data banking rather than on the comprehensive information system, was contained in the proceedings of the conference *Urban data management* held in London in 1968 by the Planning and Transport Research and Computation Co Ltd (PTRC, 1968), though as a collective statement this lacks the clarity of thought and the critical attitude of its American counterpart. A second set of proceedings from the second conference of the same title was published in 1970.

The planning technique which has attracted the largest quantity of documentation is that of mathematical modelling. Models were introduced into planning from the transportation studies carried out in the United States from the 1950's onwards; their application to the processes of city and regional planning (the American equivalent of British town and country planning) was developed by planners in the US adapting to American conditions and utilising American data types. In the mid-1960's the technique began to be seriously considered in Britain, and since then theoretical research and empirical development have proceeded apace. The growing acceptance of models as a potentially valuable tool in planning has been fostered by the contemporary increasing incidence of computers of sufficient power to handle the large volume of data required for even the most simple model; and by the emergence of the structure plan system which sees the sub-region as the smallest viable spatial unit of practical planning and that sub-region as a constantly evolving system of complex interacting components. As Cripps and Foot express it in their discussion of 'A land-use model for sub-regional planning' *Regional studies* 3(3) December 1969 243-268, ' the structure plan is to be regarded as a depiction of the state of the urban system at a particular point in a given trajectory through time. The plan (a broad statement of urban structure) is flexible to the extent that it should be modified to account for the dynamics of cities and city-regions . . . This approach to urban and regional planning implies two things for the planner. Firstly, he needs an adequate understanding of urban structure and an ability to describe it; secondly, he needs an ability to monitor change in the urban system in response to the goals set for it by the plan.'

The literature of models is notable for its lack of hard covers— much of it is in the form of journal articles or papers. One exception to this is a work which covers a field much wider than that of planning alone, a germane classic of statistical geography *Models in geography* edited by Richard J Chorley and Peter Haggett (Methuen, 1967). This is a monumental, heavily-documented (over two thousand references) exposition of all kinds and applications of models, by seventeen authors, in which there is much of value to planners both in practical application and in the provocation of ideas and thoughts: Haggett's chapter on 'Network models', Garner's on 'Urban geography and settlement location', and Board's on 'Maps as models' for instance.

Three special journal issues, each one presenting a state of the art survey and contributions from experts on both theory and practice of modelling, are notable. The earliest is *Journal of the American Institute of Planners* 25(2) May 1959, edited by Allan M Voorhees: practice in 1959, even in the United States, was not far advanced, but there are excellent literature reviews and examples of then current thinking. The rapid development in modelling techniques, aided by the growth of the computer industry, can be seen from a comparison of this issue and another exactly six years later, *Journal of the American Institute of Planners* 31(2) May 1965 entitled 'Urban development models: new tools for planning' edited by Britton Harris. This issue has achieved a remarkable status within the planning profession, being much sought after (and frequently missing from libraries) and regarded as the basic seminal source on this subject. It includes a pertinent introduction by Britton Harris on the state of modelling; contributions on practical work by a variety of authoritative American planners and other specialists; and an exceptionally lucid 'short course in model design' by Ira S Lowry (whose own *Model of metropolis* is reviewed later in the issue). The whole constitutes a constructive and yet coolly evaluative view of a technique recognised as still very much in its rudimentary stages of development for planning purposes. The most recent special issue is a British one, *Regional studies* 3(3) December 1969, entitled 'Urban and regional models in British planning research' and edited by Roy Drewett. This is clearly intended as the British counterpart of the American issue; indeed, the papers contained in it are those delivered at a series of seminars held by the Quantitative Methods Study Group of the Regional Studies

Association during 1969 and directly stimulated by that 1965 issue which is referred to by the editor as 'probably the learned journal most consulted in urban and regional research in recent years'. The papers, by a group of British planners and other specialists who have been in the forefront of modelling experiments, discuss various types of models in a variety of working contexts. What is notably lacking—and which distinguished the American issue—is a critical and evaluative content.

Critical evaluation at all stages is clearly necessary. As Lowry observed in 1965 'the growing enthusiasm for the use of computer models as aids to urban planning and administration derives less from the proven adequacy of such models than from the increasing sophistication of professional planners and a consequent awareness of the inadequacy of traditional techniques.' More recently a warning was given by C Lee in ' Models in planning—some observations and reservations ' *Planning outlook* new series 8 Spring 1970 9-15, who stresses the need to adapt, rather than adopt, techniques, and indicates some of the limitations of models and some of the unresolved issues which must be investigated and solved before constructive development can be achieved. There are several articles and papers in the British literature (and of course a vast quantity in the American) which discuss models in a general way, and whose content is more descriptive than evaluative. One of the earliest is Louis K Loewenstein's ' On the nature of analytical models ' in *Urban studies* 3(2) June 1966 112-119, which categorises the types of model which planners can use for various purposes. Alan G Wilson (until 1970 Assistant Director of the Centre for Environmental Studies, where the main impetus towards modelling research has been located) has provided an overview in 'Models in urban planning: a synoptic review of recent literature ' in *Urban studies* 5(3) November 1968 249-276, also issued separately as CES-WP-3 (1968). He covers ' model development for spatially aggregated population and economic systems, urban structure, transport, and, more briefly, social systems ', reviews its literature, and proposes its application in planning. The literature reviewed includes books, reports, conference proceedings and journal articles, much of it emanating from the United States and published in the 1960's mainly from 1965 onwards. Wilson is also the author of one of the numerous papers published by the Centre for Environmental Studies (too numerous to be detailed here) on the subject of models of various types, *On some problems in urban and regional modelling* (CES, 1970, CES-WP-59) which discusses the state of the art and some possible developments. *Towards operational urban development models* by Martyn Cordey Hayes and others (CES, 1970, CES-WP-60) examines the need for, and the use of, planning models within the structure plan system of the Town and Country Planning Act 1968.

If the literature is a reflection of activity, then the major activity has been the development of models of urban development. The pioneer of this genre, which has proved an inspiration and a practical basis for much subsequent work, was *A model of metropolis* by Ira S Lowry (Santa Monica, Rand Corporation, 1964, Memorandum RM-4035-RC), in which is described a procedure for locating functions in the metropolis, in this case Pittsburgh, given the total population, the location of basic employment, and the constraints imposed on the use of land by legal and physical circumstances. A state of the art survey of urban development models was reported by Ira S Lowry in *Seven models of urban development: a structural comparison* (Santa Monica, Rand Corporation, 1967); a report which is included in *Urban development models* (Washington, DC, Highway Research Board, 1968, Special Report 97) as part of the proceedings of a conference in June 1967 at Dartmouth College, New Hampshire, the whole constituting a review of a decade of progress in the construction of models that attempt to simulate urban physical development in terms of its spatial distribution. The results of a survey of the use of urban development models are reported by George C Hemmens in ' Planning agency experience with urban development models and data processing' *Journal of the American Institute of Planners* 34(5) September 1968 323-327. The most common problems experienced in twenty five large urban areas in the United States in the development and use of such models have been inadequate staff for computer operations, and inadequate communications between planner and programmer.

The most notable refinement of Lowry's model was expounded by Robert A Garin in 'A matrix formulation of the Lowry model for intrametropolitan activity allocation' *Journal of the American*

Institute of Planners 32(6) November 1966 361-364, a simplification which has been incorporated into much of the work subsequently done to the extent that the model is referred to as the Garin-Lowry model. Garin's article was immediately followed by 'A note on the Garin-Lowry model' by Andrei Rogers *Journal of the American Institute of Planners* 32(6) November 1966 364-366. This version of the model has been used, for example, to assess the effects of the location of a quarter of a million people in the Ribble-Calder sub-region of Lancashire, in other words the impact on the sub-region of the new town of Leyland-Chorley, and the use of the model is discussed by Michael Batty in ' The impact of a new town —an application of the Garin-Lowry model ' *JTPI* 55(10) December 1969 428-435. Further work on the use of the model in Lancashire and in the Nottinghamshire/Derbyshire sub-region is described by Michael Batty in ' Some problems of calibrating the Lowry model ' *Environment and planning* 2(1) 1970 95-114. A general discussion is offered by Alan G Wilson in *Generalising the Lowry model* (CES, 1970, CES-WP-56), setting out some of the issues associated with building a general urban model based on Lowry's work. A model of a different kind is described by Jay W Forrester in *Urban dynamics* (Cambridge, Mass, MIT Press, 1969). This is a theoretical model which simulates the life cycle of a hypothetical urban system through a period of 250 years, and therefore represents a new approach in that it is based on the dimension of time (instead of space or topic) although its validity has not been tested in a real life situation. Edgar S Dunn, in a review of the work in *Urban studies* 7(2) June 1970 215-217, claims that ' the principal value of this work lies in describing and illustrating the use of a methodology that may in time become a useful tool in guiding and monitoring the evolutionary experimentation of social systems '.

The major research effort in modelling in Britain is located at Cambridge University, where the Centre for Land Use and Built Form Studies is within the Department of Architecture, and at Reading University, where the Urban Systems Research Unit is within the Department of Geography. Both projects are financed by grants from the Centre for Environmental Studies. At Cambridge, research, both theoretical and empirical, is being undertaken into the development of a spatial model of a town, based on Lowry's

Metropolis. A progress report on the development of a general urban model is given by Marcial Echenique in *Urban systems: towards an explorative model* (CES, 1969, CES-UWP-2). A series of working papers have been produced by the unit at Cambridge. *Model of a town: Reading* by Marcial Echenique and others (Cambridge, LUBFS, 1969, WP 12) describes the theory of the model and its calibration to the town of Reading. *A structural comparison of three generations of new towns* by Marcial Echenique and others (Cambridge, LUBFS, 1969, WP 25) describes how the model can be fitted also to Stevenage, Hook, and Milton Keynes. A more detailed account of the theory behind the model is provided in *Development of a model of a town* by Marcial Echenique and others (Cambridge, LUBFS, 1969, WP 26). At Reading, the unit was set up to study the information needs of urban and regional planning, within the context of the current proposals for structure planning in Britain, and to develop operational land use models for application in the sub-regional structure planning process. Papers by the members of the unit include the two by Michael Batty mentioned above, and those by Eric L Cripps, either independently or in association with D H S Foot, discussed in the course of this chapter. Working papers issued by the unit so far have concentrated on the results of the first stage of the project (see above).

The other area into which a considerable amount of effort has been concentrated is that of forecasting demand for shopping facilities and the prediction of the location of such facilities. Partly this derives from central place theories concerned with a classification of service centres, but mainly it derives from the principles of retail location expounded by William Reilly in *The law of retail gravitation* (New York, W J Reilly Co, 1931) which first advanced the explanation of the gravity model for retail location behaviour, to the effect that where two towns compete for customers in a hinterland these two towns attract trade from an intermediate point in direct proportion to their population size (later development substituted a quantified measure of their attractiveness as shopping or service centres for population) and in inverse proportion to the square of the distance between the town and the intermediate point. A gravity model developed out of Reilly's law and applied to Baltimore by T R Lakshmanan and Walter G Hansen was described in 'A retail market potential model' in *Journal of the American Institute of Planners* 31(2) May 1965 134-143, and has achieved a seminal and pioneering status in its field similar to Lowry's Metropolis in the field of urban development models. A survey of the evolution of shopping models begins B Mottershaw's article 'Estimating shopping potential' *Planning outlook* new series 5 Autumn 1968 40-68, though the main concern of the author is to consider 'the methods of calibrating the [Lakshmanan and Hansen] model for use in simulating British shopping conditions in the light of available published data, and likely available labour resources'. A British study using the Lakshmanan model as a base is reported in the second volume of the Haydock study *Regional shopping centres: a planning report on north west England, part two, a retail shopping model* (Manchester, Manchester University Department of Town and Country Planning, 1966). Some of the methodology of this modelling exercise was included in tests carried out by the Research Group of the West Midlands Branch of the Town Planning Institute and reported in *Predicting shopping requirements* (Birmingham, 1967). This latter report is concerned primarily with the distribution of available expenditure between competing centres, and develops a model which can be worked manually or used with a computer, for which instructions are included. Examples in map form show the results of the use of the model at regional, sub-regional, and local level. Several surveys are available of developments in the prediction of shopping requirements. In 'The assessment of shopping potential and the demand for shops' *Town planning review* 38(4) January 1968 317-326, J Parry Lewis and A L Traill review analytical techniques for forecasting the demand for shops; they discuss gravity models and an opportunity-claimant variation of the gravity model, and the problems associated with them. The Centre for Environmental Studies has also contributed a paper by Martyn Cordey Hayes, *Retail location models* (CES, 1968, CES-WP-16). An exemplary review of both theory and practice is produced by the National Economic Development Office under the title *Urban models in shopping studies* (NEDO, 1970). This is a report by a working group to the Shopping Capacity Sub-committee of the Economic Development Committee for the Distributive Trades and is based on both an appraisal of the literature of

333

shopping models and a series of interviews with people who have had experience of their building and use; it is clearly and coolly written, with a useful glossary and a good bibliography.

A residential location model, based on gravity principles, is being investigated by the Urban Systems Research Unit at Reading University as a component of the general land use model being developed for sub-regional planning. The empirical work on the sub-model is described by Eric L Cripps and D H S Foot in ' The empirical development of an elementary residential location model for use in sub-regional planning' *Environment and planning* 1(1) 1969 81-90. The concept of opportunity was introduced into the model, and this is one of the concepts discussed also by Alan G Wilson in *Developments of some elementary residential location models* (Centre for Environmental Studies, 1968, CES-WP-22). Wilson has also written *Disaggregating elementary residential location models* (CES, 1969, CES-WP-37). Results of American research are contained in Edward J Kaiser's *A producer model for residential growth* (Chapel Hill, North Carolina UP, 1968) which discusses a model for forecasting the location of single family residential development, from the particular angle of the developer, the purpose being to identify the decision making processes of the developer and the factors which affect them. The study areas were in Greensboro and Winston-Salem in North Carolina, and although the variables arising from the American context are incompatible with those which would arise from a British situation, the methodology is nevertheless of universal interest.

Two further surveys from the Centre for Environmental Studies on specialised models are useful state of the art summaries of techniques and have the additional advantage of giving guidance to the literature. Doreen Massey's *Some simple models for distributing changes in employment within regions* (CES, 1969, CES-WP-24) is a short but fairly intelligible paper on spatial employment models considered in two categories, allocation models and location models. Several operational models are described in each category. *Population growth and movement* by Jeffrey Willis (CES, 1968, CES-WP-12) is a useful summary of techniques in population forecasting. A statement of methods of analysing population growth and movement leads to a discussion of models, from basic statistical types to complex ones using a probablistic approach, and finally to an assessment of current methods of forecasting population at national and regional levels in the United Kingdom. A specialised application of modelling techniques has been recorded by H R Hamilton and others in *Systems simulation for regional analysis: an application to river-basin planning* (Cambridge, Mass, MIT Press, 1969). This incorporates the results of a research project carried on between 1962 and 1967 by a team from the Battelle Memorial Institute, who were commissioned to study and analyse the economy of the Susquehanna River basin in the north west of the US with a view to defining the role of the basin's water resources in the future development of the region. Additionally the team was charged with developing a methodology for such analysis, combining the usual regional economic factors and those specifically relating to regional water resources. The book is mainly a very clear and well illustrated account of the development of the mathematical model to meet these requirements, preceded by useful chapters on models in general, regional economic analysis and river basin planning, a documented comparison of the Susquehanna model with six earlier regional river basin models, and a guide to simulation theory and model building.

Planning models, otherwise termed plan-design or prescriptive models or sometimes optimising models, are the most complex type of simulation and are not far advanced in development. 'Plan-design models are designed to provide the best answer. The planner specifies goals, limiting conditions and criteria for judgment and a plan (defined as the best way of attaining certain goals) is generated within the model'. Margaret M Camina reviews American examples of the techniques of plan-design models in 'Plan-design models: a review' *Town planning review* 40(2) July 1969 119-130, including references to the available literature, and discusses their potential application to British planning practice.

There are several techniques associated with modelling which have been imported from other disciplines, notably mathematics, statistics, and econometrics. The use of some of these is criticised by J Parry Lewis in 'The invasion of planning' *JTPI* 56(3) March 1970 100-103, with replies to the criticism following. The concept of simulation is basic to modelling, but it is sometimes argued that it should be applied only to the replication of those processes in which random events, brought about by chance and unspecified causes, are of interest. Such stochastic events can be generated within the computer by means of Monte Carlo simulation. The impetus towards such simulation studies in the United States came from a small knowledge of the pioneering work in this field of Torsten Hagerstrand in Sweden. Hagerstrand's monograph was published in Sweden fifteen years before it achieved translation in the United States as *Innovation diffusion as a spatial process* translated by Allen Pred (Chicago, Chicago UP, 1967). The main contribution of the study is the development of a process model which allows analysis of changes over time in space; it is still readable (though the style is heavy) as a manual for the Monte Carlo method, its difficulties and problems and the strategy of its use. One of the reasons for the limited use of planning models so far is that the techniques on which they depend—linear or dynamic programming —are sophisticated mathematical procedures which may not be fully comprehended by non-mathematicians. ' The important issue seems to be that there are doubts about the extent to which programming methods can be validly used within the planning process. This is not a question that a planner without mathematical skills can answer, nor is it a question that a mathematician without a knowledge of planning can answer. The problem is not just that most planners do not comprehend the mathematical sophistication (and limitations) of the technique. There is an equal danger that the mathematician, because of the great success of linear programming in other areas, may be carried away by enthusiasm into believing that the technique can be equally well applied in planning, when in fact the environment and the structure of the problems with which we are concerned are very different and much more complex.'[12] Some of the pitfalls of linear programming are expounded by J Parry Lewis in *Misused techniques in planning: linear programming* (Manchester, Centre for Urban and Regional Research of Manchester University, 1969, Occasional Paper 1); and also, in a wider context in his article ' The invasion of planning ' *JTPI* 56(3) March 1970 100-103. One of the concepts which has been introduced into modelling for planning is that of entropy, imported from statistical mechanics and developed by Alan G Wilson at the Centre for Environmental Studies. 'Information on average behaviour over the city as a whole can be converted into probable individual behaviour by defining the entropy of the system and maximising this subject to a number of constraints . . . One can envisage a situation where the " most probable " state—the maximum entropy solution—might correspond to planning goals and thus that the technique could be used in prescriptive modelling.'[13] The concept of entropy is explained in general terms by Alan G Wilson in *Entropy in urban and regional modelling* (CES, 1969, CES-WP-26), and with specific applications in *The use of entropy maximising models in the theory of trip distribution, mode split and route split* (CES, 1968, CES-WP-1) and in *Interregional commodity flows: entropy maximising approaches* (CES, 1969, CES-WP-19).

The use of gaming simulation in planning education was noted in chapter 4. This is a very new technique, new to education generally and not only to planning in particular, although the use of war games in military operations has a long history. Some development has been carried out both in the United States and in Britain, and the methods are clearly of considerable interest and potential value to planners. A conspectus of its use in education generally is provided by P J Tansey and Derick Unwin in *Simulation and gaming in education* (Methuen, 1969). Early development in the United States is reported by Richard L Meier and Richard D Duke in ' Gaming simulation for urban planning' *Journal of the American Institute of Planners* 32(1) January 1966 3-17 and by Allan G Feldt in ' Operational gaming in planning education' *Journal of the American Institute of Planners* 32(1) January 1966 17-23 which describes a land use game developed at Cornell University, New York, and interprets its use by student, faculty and professional groups. A much fuller description of the game is given by Feldt in *The Community Land Use Game* (Ithaca, NY, Cornell UP, 1966, Center for Housing and Environmental Studies, Division of Urban Studies Miscellaneous Papers 5), which explains basic components and rules of play. In *Gaming simulation in urban research* (East Lansing, Michigan State UP, 1965) Richard D Duke describes the conception and development of a model called ' Metropolis '. His book also includes a historical account of the uses of games and an extensive bibliography on gaming techniques. These two American pioneers inspired British planners to begin experiments, and in 1966 work began using the Community Land Use Game as a basis, at Sheffield University and at Lanchester College of Technology in Coventry. The first results are reported by John L Taylor and K R Carter in ' Instructional simulation of urban development: a preliminary report ' *JTPI* 53(10) December 1967 443-447. Sufficient interest was stimulated to mount a symposium on educational simulation at Birmingham University in January 1969; and the proceedings of this are published as *Instructional simulation systems in higher education* edited by R H R Armstrong and John L Taylor (Cambridge, Cambridge Institute of Education, 1970. Cambridge Monographs on Teaching Methods 2). Of particular interest to planners in this volume is the paper by Taylor and Carter 'A decade of instructional simulation research in urban and regional studies ', a good summary of the state of the art at that point in time; the paper by R H R Armstrong on ' The use of operational gaming in the field of local government ' is also relevant to planning, although the terminology is fairly technical. Taylor and Carter's paper is supplemented by a further article ' Some instructional dimensions of urban gaming-simulation ' in *Planning outlook* new series 7 Autumn 1969 35-53 in which the expressed intent is ' to go beyond the authors' earlier pronouncement on this subject [as listed above] and, from the point of view of the land use planner, discuss several, seemingly, neglected aspects of this simulation technique '.

Two analytical techniques which are being developed for planning purposes in Britain, although their application in practical work is as yet limited, are those of threshold analysis and optimisation. Threshold analysis originated in Poland in 1961, and has since become an important factor in Polish town planning. It has been applied in research on the central economic region of the USSR and was first introduced into British practice in the preparation of the sub-regional plan for the Grangemouth/Falkirk area of Scotland by a team from the Planning Research Unit of Edinburgh University. The fundamental tenet of threshold theory is that at certain points towns encounter major limitations to their growth (thresholds) and at these points a sharp rise in cost is necessary to overcome the problems imposed by the limitations; the objective of the analysis is to define these thresholds and to demonstrate the extent of the problems involved.

The principal research worker on the development of threshold analysis in Britain has been J Kozlowski at the Planning Research Unit in Edinburgh. He has documented his progress in several articles in the professional press, from which a reasonable conspectus of the technique may be gleaned. J Kozlowski and J T Hughes are the authors of ' Urban threshold theory and analysis ' in *JTPI* 53(2) February 1967 55-60; and the same two writers produced ' Threshold analysis: an economic tool for town and regional planning ' in *Urban studies* 5(2) June 1968 132-143. Kozlowski himself described the use of the technique in ' Threshold theory and the sub-regional plan ' *Town planning review* 39(2) July 1968 99-116, which is an illustrated review of the method used in the Grangemouth/Falkirk study for determining the availability of land for development. Another contribution on the subject is by the Polish expert Boleslaw Malisz in ' Implications of threshold theory for urban and regional planning ' *JTPI* 55(3) March 1969 108-110; this is reprinted in *Regional economics: a reader* edited by Harry W Richardson (Macmillan/St Martin's Press, 1970). Optimisation method is another Polish development and is based to some extent on the formulation of threshold theory, but, unlike the latter, it ' is not oriented toward defining major limitations (or thresholds) but to finding out how the elements of the programme could be distributed in an " optimised " way within those limitations '. The method is expounded by J Kozlowski in ' Optimisation method: a case for research ' *JTPI* 56(4) April 1970 134-137. The Planning Research Unit of Edinburgh University are the producers of a volume entitled *Analytical techniques in the urban and regional planning process: threshold analysis, optimisation method* (Edinburgh, PRU, 1970) which consists of three papers discussing in turn the development of optimisation, the integration of both techniques into an integrated planning process, and threshold analysis in regional planning.

Planning by its nature is concerned with the future, with the making of strategies which will control the shape of future development. Clearly a plan cannot be made without some basis of knowledge about the future state of a variety of factors, such as the size and composition of population, the extent of car ownership, the increase in leisure time. Systematic forecasting is not a new activity, and short term economic forecasting, for example, is a well-established activity. But within the last decade there has emerged a growing need for forecasts reaching further into the future and covering a wider range of disciplines, and for the development of more systematic methods of anticipating probable future technological and social developments which may affect seemingly established trends. International activity in forecasting and its development is now widespread: in the United States there are the Commission for the Year 2000 and the Institute for the Future at Wesley University; in Europe the Council of Europe coordinates the activities of various agencies such as Futuribles; and in Britain, the Social Science Research Council set up in 1966 a Next Thirty Years Committee to advise the council on how far it was possible to anticipate long-term research needs, followed soon afterwards by the foundation of the Society for Long Range Planning whose primary aim is to improve the quantity and quality of long term planning in industry and in central and local government. The Council of Europe has published a series of volumes which will eventually form a single volume constituting an inventory of activity in the area of long-term forecasting, of which the eighth covers the United Kingdom (this is discussed in more detail in chapter 13).

Some of the papers prepared by the SSRC committee as initial exploratory exercises into methods and problems were collected together under the title *Forecasting and the social sciences* edited by Michael Young (Heinemann Educational for the SSRC, 1968), from which planners will find fruitful material in David Grove's paper 'Physical planning and social change', Christopher Foster's 'Future research needs of transport planners' and Peter Hall's 'Land use—the spread of towns into the country'. A paper from the Centre for Environmental Studies by David Bayliss on *Some recent trends in forecasting* (CES, 1968, CES-WP-17) is an authoritative state of the art survey of techniques embracing a wide range of studies. The first European conference on technological forecasting —also known as total systems analysis or long range economic planning—was held in Glasgow in June 1968, organised by the Centre for Industrial Innovation of Strathclyde University: the proceedings are edited by R V Arnfield as *Technological forecasting* (Edinburgh, Edinburgh UP, 1969). About half of the twenty nine papers included are of interest to planners, in particular the case studies illustrating standard techniques in practice. Two examples of long range forecasting are the volumes *Developing patterns of urbanisation* edited by Peter Cowan (see the section on urban studies) and *The British economy in 1975* by W Beckerman and others (see the section on land economics and economics of planning).

There is an increasing awareness among planners, stimulated by a few recent notable books, that planning as a process is susceptible to analysis using concepts imported from areas such as operational research and management. The principal documentary instrument of this awareness has been the book *Local government and strategic choice* by J K Friend and W N Jessop (Tavistock Publications, 1969) which reports in detail the findings of a four-year project from the Institute of Operational Research to analyse the processes of policy making in Coventry, and is mainly concerned with the work of the planning department in its quinquennial review of the development plan. One of the most interesting features of the book is its examination of the processes of decision-making and their attendant uncertainties. Earlier research into decision-making in planning was carried out by P H Levin from the Building Research Station, and reported by him in *Decision-making in urban design* (Garston, Herts, Building Research Station, 1966, Current Paper Design Series 49) and subsequently in ' Toward decision-making rules for urban planners ' *JPTI* 53(10) December 1967 437-442. These are interim reports, and describe the ' decisions of various kinds made in producing plans for large-scale new urban developments ' and the ' effects on decision-making behaviour of factors such as statutory and administrative procedures, the discretion content of information, the procedure used for reaching design decisions, and attributes of the individual and the organisation '. Levin proposed, and Friend and Jessop confirmed (and described in full detail) the method of Analysis of Interconnected Decison Areas—AIDA—first propounded in 1965 by F Harary and others in 'Analysis of interconnected decision areas ' *Nature* 206(4979) April 3 1965 118. ' AIDA starts by breaking down complex problems into component decision areas. It then makes clear what options are possible within each decision area, and spells out their intercommunications—in particular, which combinations are impossible. The aim is to proceed finally to an evaluation procedure, a form of cost benefit analysis, but specifically related to the complexities of the situation. This stresses not so much sophisticated measurement as getting workable criteria for preferring or trading off one criterion against another.'[14] In the light of the interest aroused by Friend and Jessop's book, and in particular by the method of AIDA, the Centre for Environmental Studies made a grant in 1970 to the Institute of Operational Research to carry out a practical exercise in its application to some real planning problems. The institute has therefore cooperated with six local authorities in applying AIDA to problems as diverse as the development of a bus station and the use of a piece of green belt, with the objective of obtaining feedback on the success or otherwise of the method. Results were considered at a CES seminar and the deliberations reported in *The LOGIMP experiment: a collaborative exercise in the application of a new approach to local planning problems* (CES, 1970, CES-IP-25) in which the six projects are written up in some detail.

Another analytical technique currently under development, notably in the central government sector, is that of Planning, Programming, Budgeting Systems (PPBS, or PPB for short). PPBS is primarily a planning and policy tool which sets out to establish objectives or goals, to analyse programmes in relation to these, to consider the use of available resources to these ends and alternative ways of achieving the same ends. Implicit in this process is the assumption that the use of PPBS will provide in a systematic way information and analysis which will enable better decisions to be made than would have been made without it. Early development of PPBS took place in the United States: an early text is that edited by David Novick *Programme budgeting* (Cambridge, Mass, Harvard UP, 1965), while a more recent account with case studies is provided by Harley Hinriche and Graeme M Taylor in *Programme budgeting and benefit cost analysis* (California, Goodyear Publishing Co, 1969). In Britain the pioneering work in the field was done by the Ministry of Defence, and subsequently carried on by the Home

Office and the Department of Education and Science. Its application in the local government context is outlined in *Starting PPB and strategic planning in a local authority* by R A Ward (Metra Consulting Group Ltd, 1970), in itself a useful introduction to the system. Further information on British application is contained in two articles by J M Bridgeman under the title 'Planning, Programming, Budgeting Systems' in *O & M bulletin* 24(4) November 1969 167-177 and *O & M bulletin* 25(1) February 1970 16-27. Discussion of PPBS in a specifically planning context is contained in the papers presented at a short course on the system held during the 1969 national planning conference of the American Society of Planning Officials, published as *Planning-Programming-Budgeting-Systems* edited by V Curtis (Chicago, ASPO, 1969). The report considers the success of a New York State system, the future of PPBS in evaluating federal programmes, and its implementation on a local level.

DEMOGRAPHY AND POPULATION

Population and the composition of the population is basic to planning, at national, regional, and urban levels. Schnore points out that 'perhaps the most fundamental aspect of the urban community involves human numbers'[15] but the significance of population in the formulation of planning policies goes much wider than the purely quantitative aspect. Its age structure, for example, its rate of increase or decrease, its movement, are clearly of vital importance to the planner; but also of significance are the socio-economic factors of population which are increasingly being correlated with such other factors as juvenile delinquency, infant mortality, social malaise and a wide range of social variables to provide a basis for social planning.[16]

Demography is the study of population; more explicitly, it is 'the study by statistical methods of human populations, involving primarily the measurement of the size, growth and diminution of the numbers of people, the proportions living, being born or dying within some area or region and the related functions of fertility, mortality and marriage'.[17] The standard British text on the subject is Peter Cox's *Demography* (Cambridge, Cambridge UP, fourth edition 1970). Cox starts with an explanation of the basic facts of human life—birth, childhood, marriage, etc—which are significant in the study of population, and the reasons for their significance, and then sets out the basic statistical concepts, these forming a background to his exposition of the characteristics of demographic data, and discussion of British and foreign sources of demographic statistics. Fuller treatment is accorded to the major concepts of fertility, mortality, and migration. Methods of summarisation are discussed in three chapters, and a further five are concerned with mathematical methods and their use mainly in circumstances of deficient or non-existent data—projections, models, and computer techniques are included. Cox then goes back to trace the development of modern demography and the history of population itself, and finally relates population to the wider contexts of world resources, and government population policies. References and examples throughout are to foreign as well as British events and practices. There are bibliographical references at chapter ends.

The standard American textbook on the subject is William Petersen's *Population* (Collier-Macmillan, second edition 1969). An earlier, seminal collection of writings is *The study of population: an inventory and appraisal* edited by Philip M Hauser and Otis D Duncan (Chicago, Chicago UP, 1959). More recently, another American collection has appeared: *Readings on population* edited by David M Heer (Englewood Cliffs, NJ, Prentice-Hall, 1968), consisting of fifteen well-documented essays on various aspects of population size and structure grouped under the six headings of history of population growth, population distribution and density, mortality, fertility, migration, and population policy. None of the titles mentioned above is aimed at a planning audience, although they are all comprehensible to the non-demographer.

In the last two decades historical demography has become a focus of study, in Britain concentrated mainly in Cambridge, where the Cambridge Group for the History of Population and Social Structure is based. Historical demography is ' the study of the ebb and flow of the numbers of mankind in time and space by a combination of geography and history using statistics, and the main concern is to achieve accurate estimates of human numbers '.[18] The first publication of the Cambridge Group was *An introduction to English*

344

historical demography from the sixteenth to the nineteenth century
edited by E A Wrigley (Weidenfeld and Nicolson, 1966). The chapters written by Wrigley, D E C Eversley and Peter Laslett, are concerned primarily with sources of information and the ways in which
these are being exploited; there is a full annotated bibliography, principally concerned with journal articles. The publications of the
Cambridge Group are intended to foster interest in the subject,
rather than to be definitive works. A title which conforms more
readily to the idea of ' definitive ' is T H Hollingsworth's *Historical
demography* (Hodder and Stoughton, 1969, in association with The
Sources of History Limited; Studies in the Use of Historical Evidence). The author describes the nature of demography in general
and historical demography in particular, the techniques of demography, and (the main part of the text) the various historical sources
of information. There is also a discussion of work done and work
which could profitably be done in the future. A full bibliography is
appended. *Population in history* edited by D V Glass and D E C
Eversley (Chicago, Chicago UP, 1965) is a collection of twenty seven
assorted articles giving a general impression of where the current
interest in historical demography lies. In this context, the interest
of historical demography is clearly for the urban sociologist and
the urban historian, rather than for the planner in practice.

Coming back to the present, the populations of individual countries, of continents, and of the world have been the subject of
description and analysis and of trend forecasting. A useful short
introductory account of Britain's present and future population
position is given in *Population* by R K Kelsall (Longmans, 1967;
The Social Structure of Modern Britain). The text begins with
explanatory definitions of terms and concepts used in the study of
population, passes to types of population data, and goes on to an
analysis of Britain's population: general trends, patterns of fertility,
mortality, migration, social class variations and social implications
generally, population and manpower forecasting; with a postscript
on population theories, mainly Malthusian, and a possible national
population policy. Lists of official published sources of British data
are included, and bibliographical references laid out by chapter.
The various international organisations are deeply interested in the

population policies and trends of the world and its individual countries. The Committee on Population and Refugees of the Consultative Assembly of the Council of Europe, for example, prepared and issued a *Report on the problems raised by population trends in Europe* (Strasbourg, Council of Europe, 1963, Document 1689). On world scale, the United Nations produced a *Provisional report on world population prospects in 1963* (Geneva, United Nations, 1964, Document ST/SOA/SER.R7); and continues in the field with its invaluable annual production, the *Yearbook of demographic data*. The standard work on world population in the inter-war years was Sir Alexander Carr-Saunders' *World population: past growth and present trends* (Oxford UP, 1936; reprinted by Frank Cass, 1964), now recognised as a fine demonstration of how wrong the experts can be, in their forecasts of declining populations.

Forecasts of future trends are based on analysis of present situations. ' The purpose of analysis in demographic work is to identify and measure as precisely as possible the influences that underlie population changes. By so doing it is possible to deepen one's understanding of the variations observed in past experience, and also perhaps to arrive at a basis for the prediction of future trends.'[19] The most recent British text on the science of demographic analysis is that by Bernard Benjamin, *Demographic analysis* (Allen and Unwin, 1968, Studies in Sociology 3), which begins with a discussion of demographic techniques and sources of population data as a preliminary to the main text dealing with the scope, content and use of the population census, including chapters on fertility measurement, marriage rates, mortality measurement, migration, population estimation and projection, and sickness measurement. A final chapter discusses manpower statistics for the benefit of economists. An excellent and comprehensive collection of sixty three papers forms the content of *Demographic analysis: selected readings* edited by Joseph J Spengler and Otis D Duncan (Glencoe, Ill, Free Press, 1956), grouped into sections on the themes of past and prospective growth of world population; mortality; fertility; international distribution of population and migration; internal distribution and migration; population composition and utilisation of human resources; and selective regional studies. There is an extensive bibliography.

346

It is now realised that populations are increasing on a world scale, and consequently the implications of population growth attract wide attention. *The population dilemma* [edited by Philip M Hauser] (Englewood Cliffs, NJ, Prentice-Hall, second edition 1969) was first published in 1963 as a collection of papers for background reading for the twenty third American Assembly in New York, meeting to discuss the implications for national and international policy of rapid population growth. In the event, the compilation reached a much wider audience than the one for which it was designed, and therefore a second edition was prepared, the contributions being revised in the light of new knowledge. In the words of the editor (who is Director of the Population Research Center at the University of Chicago) ' it continues to set forth the key population facts, the major problems being generated by accelerating growth, the basic policy issues, and the more important policy and action alternatives '. It becomes increasingly necessary in forward planning to essay estimates and projections of the size of the population at a given date. In a chapter on ' Population ' in *Regional and urban studies* edited by J B Cullingworth and S C Orr (Allen and Unwin, 1969), T H Hollingsworth expounds the details of population projection and the assumptions which underlie projections, and stresses that a population projection must be made in conjunction with an economic projection, the two being interdependent. *Population growth and movement* by Jeffrey Willis (Centre for Environmental Studies, 1968, CES-WP-12) is a sound and detailed review, with references to the literature, of the various aspects of population and methods of estimating and projecting them, paying particular attention to models and their application in planning. *Population growth and movement* (Centre for Environmental Studies, 1969, CES-IP-7) is a report of a CES seminar held with the aim of improving the understanding of the factors behind long and short distance population migration, in order to make a contribution to the science of forecasting and to the evaluation of alternative regional strategies. The three papers deal with migration; with various population projections for the south east region; and with a model simulating migration in East Anglia. Colin Clark's *Population growth and land use* (Macmillan, 1967) is a vast compendium of information culled from a wide range of disciplines—biology, medicine, mathematics,

347

archaeology, to name but a few—and compressed into a book which is more for reference than for continuous reading, on nine different aspects of population growth and its implications. Despite the profusion of facts and figures, there are no bibliographies or guides to sources, and references are frequently incomplete. *Population growth and the brain drain* edited by F Bechhofer (Edinburgh, Edinburgh UP, 1969) is a record of papers given at a seminar held in Edinburgh University in May 1967 discussing current work in demography in Britain and abroad. Topics covered are migration and the brain drain; techniques and methods of study; population forecasts and planning—containing one paper, on ' The contribution of demography to physical and spatial planning ' by W Steigenga; current approaches to world population problems; and historical demography.

National population policies are, or can be, a fraught subject, being concerned with such personal and emotive issues as birth control and family allowances. In *Population policies and movements in Europe* (Frank Cass, 1967—reprint of the 1940 edition, with a new introduction) D V Glass examines the features and implications of governmental policy in England and Wales, France and Belgium, Italy, Germany, and Scandinavia, with a review of the nature and consequences of population trends. A feature of population policy is the concept of optimum population, which stems from a need to judge, in economic terms, whether a country is over or under populated. It was suggested that ' the most advantageous size of population for any country was that which produced the maximum return per head, both larger and smaller numbers being likely to produce a smaller *per capita* return, and to be evidence of over- and under-population respectively . . . In the event, the " optimum " concept has not been widely adopted as a guide to population policy, partly because of the difficulty that, by the time it was realised that the optimum point had been either reached or passed, technological change might well have altered the whole future situation.'[20] In 1969 the Institute of Biology held a symposium in London, the papers from which are collected under the title *The optimum population for Britain* edited by L R Taylor (Academic Press, 1969). In the opinion of ninety percent of the contributors, the optimum has already been passed. However, comfort can be derived from the view of such an eminent authority as David Eversley, who stated that there is no such thing as an optimum population for Britain (or anywhere).

Perhaps the most interesting factor of population from the planning point of view is that of migration, involving the concepts of immigration, emigration and net migration. Migration within and between regions, for example, is clearly crucial in regional and subregional planning. The most comprehensive source of information on migration is a volume called simply *Migration* edited by J A Jackson (Cambridge, Cambridge UP, 1969, Sociological Studies 2), which is a collection of papers, all except one of them original, covering several aspects of the study of migration and suggesting developments and refinements of many of the concepts available for analysis. The approach has been kept as broad as possible: as well as sociological viewpoints, those of demography, economics and history are also included. Scottish patterns are examined in depth by T H Hollingsworth in *Migration: a study based on Scottish experience between 1939 and 1964* (Edinburgh, Oliver and Boyd, 1970, University of Glasgow Social and Economic Studies Occasional Paper 12). There have been two separate empirical investigations into migration within the UK. The wider of the two was that carried out by the Scottish Council (Development and Industry) published as *Survey of migration, emigration and immigration* (Edinburgh, Scottish Council, 1966), which studied inter-regional migration throughout the country and by analysis related emigration, immigration and net migration to social and economic factors. The findings of the survey are examined by A B Jack in ' The Scottish Council study of migration within the United Kingdom— some comments ' in *Regional studies* 2(1) September 1968, 21-26. The University of Newcastle upon Tyne is the base for a programme of research into migration and mobility in northern England sponsored by the then Ministry of Labour, and a series of reports have been issued by the University's Department of Geography incorporating the continuing results of the research; for example, Report no 8 on *Mobility of the northern business manager* by J W House and others (Newcastle University, Department of Geography, 1968) incorporates the results of a study carried out in 1966/1967 which was concerned with business managers in manufacturing industry

349

at the level of decision-taking and decision-implementing ('a key group in the process of regional economic growth') and their changes of job or residence. Migration can be taken as a factor influencing regional development; but it can equally be influenced by regional development, and this latter relationship is discussed, in theory and practice, by A J Fielding in 'Internal migration and regional economic growth: a case study of France' in *Urban studies* 3(3) November 1966, 200-214.

LAND ECONOMICS AND ECONOMICS OF PLANNING

The relationship between land use planning and land economics or land values is a close one. 'In the absence of physical planning, economic forces, defined as the actions of persons and organisations (including public bodies) in using resources under their control to produce, consume or distribute goods and services, will determine the patterns of land use. With physical planning, economic forces must adapt themselves to the patterns of land use laid down, and this may result in a more or less efficient use of the resources of an area than would take place without the planning.'[21] Planning has a direct effect on the value of land over which it exercises control: it may have the effect of considerably increasing the value of a piece of land or it may on the other hand drastically reduce it, according to expressed intentions as to the future use of that piece of land or property. Closely involved with this are the problems of compensation, where value depreciates, and betterment, where value increases. Classical economics, and the tradition still persists into the present century, was primarily interested in agricutural land values, urban problems remaining largely ignored. 'This unconcern for urban land continued until late in the nineteenth century, and even now [1959] the subject is still a neglected one in spite of the enormous importance that cities have attained. The formal analysis of the problems of urban land is more difficult than that for agriculture.'[22]

Land economics is defined as 'the progeny of a cross between economics, commonsense valuation, and estate management' in a book which is the main reference source in the subject, *Aspects of land economics* by William Lean and B Goodall (Estates Gazette,

1966). It cannot fairly be said to be a textbook, for it does indeed only cover aspects of the subject. It is relatively elementary in level, and therefore easy to read; but it is unfortunate that in a subject which is not extensively represented in the literature, a book such as this should be so lacking in documentation and guidance to sources.

Within the parental discipline of economics, the interest of this section centres more specifically on economic planning at national level and the economics of planning and of development at regional or local level. A review of recent economic planning in Britain is provided by George Polanyi in *Planning in Britain: the experience of the 1960s* (Institute for Economic Affairs, 1967, Research Monographs 11) which is further sub-titled ' the theory and practice of planning in Britain and the lessons of failure '. The growth of economic planning is traced from the Council on Prices and Productivity of the early 1960's through NEDC, the DEA, the National Plan, the Industrial Reorganisation Corporation, selective employment tax, up to the situation which obtained at the time of writing. The review is concerned with both theory and practice, but despite the mention of the ' lessons of failure ' there are no solutions proposed to the problems involved. A forecast for the future in Britain is given in *The British economy in 1975* by W Beckerman and Associates (Cambridge, Cambridge UP, 1965), a massive study promoted by the National Institute for Economic and Social Research of what the British economy could look like in 1975 given an increase in total output of 3.8% per annum. The third part of the volume concentrates on energy, transport, housing, health and welfare, and education, and proposes the policies required to accommodate needs in these sectors. Jan Tinbergen's *Development planning* (Weidenfeld and Nicolson, 1967) is a readable introduction to economic planning for the layman, and discusses its development and operation particularly in the context of underdeveloped countries.

In the more circumscribed field of the economics of town planing and development, the pioneering work on the subject was, and it still retains its importance, Nathaniel Lichfield's *Economics of planned development* (Estates Gazette, 1956). Lichfield is one of the foremost experts on the economic aspects of planning in

351

Britain, and has had considerable experience in the application of the technique of cost benefit analysis (see below). Peter A Stone is also prominent in the study of economic problems. His first book on this subject was *Housing, town development, land and costs* (Estates Gazette, 1963). The first volume resulting from Dr Stone's research project at the National Institute of Economic and Social Research to study the economic implications of future urban growth in Britain up to the year 2000, is considered within the section on housing in this chapter.

We turn now to land values (Lean and Goodall's ' commonsense valuation ') as they relate to urban planning and development. At the beginning of this century, when interest was first aroused in urban land values, activity was concentrated in the United States, and it was there that a classic of land economics first appeared— Richard M Hurd's *Principles of city land values* (1903; reprinted from 1924 edition, Washington, Homer Hoyt Associates, 1968). Hurd is essentially concerned with the changing structure of cities and patterns of land values, and gathered his material for study from a wide variety of sources. His text is of interest both to urban historians and to those concerned with contemporary issues of city land values. The American tradition of urban economics has continued strong, with Richard U Ratcliff's *Urban land economics* (New York, McGraw-Hill, 1949) through to William Alonso's *Location and land use: towards a general theory of land rent* (Cambridge, Mass, Harvard UP, 1964), which is concerned with the relation of land values to land uses within the city and focuses primarily on residential land. Alonso considers three components of the demand for urban land: the demand of householders, of urban firms, and (on the periphery) of farmers, and proceeds to analyse each and to erect a structure of land prices. The first chapter of his book is a review of the development of thinking on land economics with references to the literature (further discussion of Alonso's theories follows in the section on regional planning). A British contribution to the debate is Ralph Turvey's *The economics of real property: an analysis of property values and patterns of use* (Allen and Unwin, 1957).

In Britain, much of the debate about land values has centred on the problems of compensation and betterment: compensation to landowners whose land value falls as a result of proposed development of it, and a levy on landowners whose land increases in value for the same reason. The whole matter is highly complex and its ramifications have direct consequences for planning, for example, in central area redevelopment schemes where shifting land values can form a key issue. The first British attempt to achieve order in the matter of development values and land ownership was the setting up of the Uthwatt Committee on Compensation and Betterment whose *Report* (HMSO, 1942, Cmnd 6386) forms, with those of Barlow and Scott, the trilogy on which the 1947 Town and Country Planning Act was based (see chapter 1). The Uthwatt Committee proposed a comprehensive system of nationalisation, not of land itself, but of all development rights in undeveloped land. ' Essentially, this is precisely what the 1947 Town and Country Planning Act did. Effectively, development rights and their associated values were nationalised. No development was to take place without permission from the local planning authority. If permission was refused, no compensation would be paid (except in a limited range of special cases). If permission were granted, any resulting increase in land value was to be subject to a development charge.'[23] The system was subsequently dismantled in the Town and Country Planning Acts of 1953 and 1954, partially restored in the Town and Country Planning Act of 1959, and then, following many years of unsatisfactory working, became the subject of major legislation under a Labour government which introduced a new capital gains tax under the 1967 Finance Act and a new betterment levy under the 1967 Land Commission Act. The objectives behind the establishment of the Land Commission were ' to secure that the right land is available at the right time for the implementation of national, regional and local plans; to secure that a substantial part of the development value created by the community returns to the community and that the burden of the cost of land for essential purposes is reduced '.[24] Under the terms of the 1967 Act the commission can acquire land, compulsorily if necessary, and make it available to public authorities or private developers; and can assess and collect a levy on development value. The land legislation is highly complex, but an excellent introduction to it is provided by Desmond Heap in *Introducing the Land Commission Act 1967*

(Sweet and Maxwell, 1967), a short book based on a series of lectures which explains the Act in outline and gives examples of how it works in practice. Heap is also the editor of Sweet and Maxwell's loose-leaf *Encyclopedia of betterment levy and Land Commission law and practice* (1967-), which is the usual comprehensive regularly up-dated product of this publishing firm. Detailed guides come in standard format: two which were early in the field are *The Land Commission Act* by G Seward and R Stewart Smith (Charles Knight, 1967) and *Betterment levy and the Land Commission* by B Harris and W G Nutley (Butterworths, 1967). These are both detailed guides, setting out the Act in full together with the Schedules; but both were published before all the statutory regulations arising from the Act were available; Harris and Nutley include most of them, though not all. Each book has an introductory background chapter and detailed notes, section by section, on the Act itself. Harris and Nutley include a commentary on the effect of each clause, which makes their book twice the size (and twice the cost) of that of Seward and Stewart Smith, and also the text of parts of the other relevant statutes. Rather more specialised is a short booklet *Land Commission definitions* by R W Suddards and Clifford Joseph (Estates Gazette, 1970). ' The complex nature of the Land Commission Act 1967 may be gleaned from the fact that it contains so many words and expressions which are given specialised, and sometimes quite extended, definition and meaning for the purposes of the Act or, sometimes, for the purposes of that particular part of the Act in which the words or the expressions appear.'[25] The booklet contains over 250 definitions of words and phrases so used, definitions being quoted direct from the Act and other associated Acts. The object of the exercise is merely to list the definitions, not to explain them; as a reviewer pointed out, ' the booklet thus serves to illustrate the complexity of the Act without necessarily making it easier to follow '. The Land Commission is by now under sentence of death, a Bill to abolish it having been published on December 2 1970. It is, however, still sufficiently in evidence to warrant discussion of its theory and practice in these pages.

Rather broader discussion of the Commission is contained in a Hobart Paper by F G Pennance on *Housing, town planning and the Land Commission* (Hobart Paper 40, 1967). General discussion of the problem of betterment and compensation and land values generally, before the advent of the Land Commission, is found in a paper by Nathaniel Lichfield 'Compensation and betterment— what next?' in *Report of the Town and Country Planning Summer School, Exeter, 1964,* (TPI, 1964) which examines the evolution of the practice from the Uthwatt Report to 1964; and *Land values* edited by Peter Hall (Sweet and Maxwell, 1965) based on a colloquium organised by the Acton Society Trust with the object of examining the nature of betterment and evaluating the various schemes for its collection, so that some generally accepted solution might be forthcoming. The papers are excellent: starting with the historical treatment from 1900, going on to the factual, which deal with the causes of increase in land values, and following through to the solutions such as site value rating, nationalisation, and taxation. The whole constitutes an important statement in the betterment debate.

The third progenitor of land economics, estate management, is not generously provided with sources of information. The publishers, Estates Gazette Ltd, who produce the weekly journal of the same name, are the main producers of relevant literature, and are responsible for the two main texts on the subject: R C Walmsley's *Rural estate management* (Estates Gazette, 1960) and W A Leach's *Urban estate management* (Estates Gazette, 1957). The Estates Branch of the former Ministry of Housing and Local Government issued in 1970 three papers on estate management and development which record the practices evolved in various aspects of management involved in the development of the new towns over the past twenty years. Paper 1 *Use of the leasehold system in development* discusses the advantages of leaseholds and the uniformity of control which they may permit in the context of various aspects of new town development such as industrial and commercial estates, shops, offices and residential development; Paper 2 *Use of freehold disposal in the development of new towns* describes the advantages of selling land to local authorities and central government departments, and sets out details of concessionary terms and restrictive covenants used to preserve amenities and values; Paper 3 considers the *Rise in land values* and ways in which development corporations have benefited from such improvement. These papers are not published by HMSO, but are available from the Clerk of Stationery, Department of the Environment.

Finally, within this section, we consider a narrower aspect of the whole. 'Economics of land use planning is a part of the general study of land economics,'[26] and William Lean, co-author of the main text on the wider subject, has produced a slim, surprisingly readable text on this topic, *Economics of land use planning: urban and regional* (Estates Gazette, 1969) which discusses, in parts rather superficially, the application of economic analysis to urban and regional planning. The economics of land use planning, is, Lean emphasises, 'a new subject [and] the ideas put forward in this book are tentative . . . all the ideas in this book are meant to form the basis for discussion out of which a better understanding of the relationship between land use planning and economics will emerge '.[26] Final mention must be made of a technique which is examined by Lean in his book, and which has been applied in several ' live ' planning situations mainly by Nathaniel Lichfield, the technique of cost benefit analysis. A lengthy survey of cost benefit analysis by A R Prest and Ralph Turvey has appeared in *Economic journal* 75(300) December 1965 683-735, under the title 'Cost benefit analysis: a survey'. Discussion of the method as applied in planning projects is readily available: for example, Lichfield's 'Cost benefit analysis in urban redevelopment: a case study, Swanley ' in *Urban studies* 3(3) November 1966, 215-249; 'Cost benefit analysis and road proposals for a shopping centre: a case study, Edgware ' by Lichfield and Honor Chapman in *Journal of transport economics and policy* 2(3) September 1968 280-320; *Cost benefit analysis in town planning: a case study of Cambridge* by Lichfield alone (Cambridge and Isle of Ely County Council, 1968); finally ' Cost benefit analysis in urban expansion: a case study, Ipswich ' by Lichfield and Honor Chapman in *Urban studies* 7(2) June 1970, 153-188. The use of cost benefit analysis in planning is criticised, in company with other imported techniques, by J Parry Lewis in ' The invasion of planning ' *JTPI* 56(3) March 1970 100-103, and at greater length in his *Mis-used techniques in planning, 2, cost benefit analysis* (Manchester, Centre for Urban and Regional Research of Manchester University, 1969).

356

HOUSING

The housing and rehousing of people has always been an integral part of planning, and still in some areas forms the nub of the planning problem. Like planning itself, it is closely involved with, and influenced by, the prevailing political and economic climate, and a study of it cannot be divorced from these two factors; in addition, it is constantly selected as a focus of sociological studies, and a search of recent literature readily produces several articles and books which bear the title ' the sociology of housing ' or a permutation thereof. In effect, as Professor David Donnison has observed, ' to study housing is to explore a cross section of a whole society and its affairs.'[27]

In this section, we are concerned with government and administration of housing, with housing policies, and with the economic aspects of their implementation; with the ' housing situation ', the condition of houses, their description and analysis; with the problems of rehabilitation versus redevelopment; and with studies, primarily from the sociological viewpoint, of the effects of housing and rehousing. We are not concerned with the design or construction of individual dwellings—these aspects are outside the scope of this book, unless they are treated as part of a study of a wider context. Planning and layout of whole residential areas is considered within the section of this chapter on urban planning.

For comparative purposes, information on housing problems and policies in overseas countries can be found in an Economic Commission for Europe report *Major long term problems of government housing and related policies* (New York, United Nations, 1966), which is a detailed factual and descriptive account, including much statistical information, of conditions in European countries; and in Paul F Wendt's *Housing policy, the search for solutions: a comparison of the United Kingdom, Sweden, West Germany and the United States since World War II* (Berkeley, California UP, 1962). In *Housing in the modern world* (Faber, 1966), Charles Abrams focuses his attention on the poorer, but rapidly developing countries of the world in which he had personal experience as a United Nations housing consultant, and discusses critically a number of themes central or related to housing which are common to most of the countries discussed, from the USSR to Ghana to Latin America.

Marian Bowley traces the development of British housing policy up to the end of World War II in *Housing and the state 1919-1944* (Allen and Unwin, 1945) and the story is continued by David Donnison in *Housing policy since the war* (Welwyn, Codicote Press, 1960), the first in a series of Occasional Papers in Social Administration, now published by G Bell and Sons of London. Donnison has a further title in the same series, *Housing since the Rent Act* (no 3, 1961). The two most recent, and the most full accounts of modern British housing policy are *Housing and local government in England and Wales* by J B Cullingworth (Allen and Unwin, 1966) and *The government of housing* by David V Donnison (Harmondsworth, Penguin Books, 1967). The first contains a long historical introduction tracing the development of housing policy over the last hundred years, setting the scene for chapters on the administrative framework, the powers of local housing authorities, the characteristics of council houses and their occupants, housing standards, finance, slum clearance, improvement, the social aspects of housing, and so on, the whole forming a thorough and well-documented source. Cullingworth, one of the main authorities on housing in Britain, is also the author of the earlier *Housing needs and planning policy* (Routledge and Kegan Paul, 1960). Donnison's book divides into two parts: the first, on the political economy of housing, examines the various components which together form the 'housing problem', and against this background the second, larger part looks at housing policy in Britain, tracing its development from the end of World War II and going on to a thorough analysis of the British housing situation, ending with a case study of London and a look at the research and information services required by government. A shorter and more provocative account of British housing problems and policies is given by Stanley Alderson in *Britain in the sixties: housing* (Harmondsworth, Penguin Books, 1962). The Central Office of Information issue a regularly revised pamphlet entitled *Housing in Britain* (COI, 1970, Reference Pamphlet 41), a factual account of all aspects of housing.

Central government has naturally always had a clear interest in housing, and over the years a fairly constant flow of policy statements, legislation, and sponsored reports have emanated from central sources, much of it from the Ministry of Housing and Local

Government and its various predecessors, and in particular from the Ministry's Central Housing Advisory Committee. The committee was originally appointed by the Ministry of Health, and has been responsible for the production of a long series of reports on various aspects of housing policy, management and standards, including the first post-war housing standards postulated in the well-known Dudley Report, *Design of dwellings* (HMSO, 1944), whose findings were confirmed in the subsequent Ministry of Health official *Housing manual* (HMSO, 1944)—which also conferred official blessing on the idea of neighbourhood planning. Five years later, a second *Housing manual* was issued jointly by the Ministry of Works and the Ministry of Local Government and Planning (HMSO, 1949). Both *Manuals* are long out of print, as are the *Technical appendices* and *Supplements* to the 1949 version. The modern equivalent of the Dudley Report is *Homes for today and tomorrow* (HMSO, 1961), the report of a sub-committee of the Ministry of Housing and Local Government's Central Housing Advisory Committee, widely known after its chairman as the Parker Morris report. The sub-committee was appointed ' to consider the standards of design and equipment applicable to family dwellings and other forms of residential accommodation, whether provided by public authorities or by private enterprise, and to make recommendations '. This was interpreted as meaning primarily standards of internal design, but the recommendations are made not only for a general improvement in house design, more generous living space and better heating, but also on such wider aspects of housing as better planning for the conflicting needs of traffic and children at play. The report relates only to England and Wales. The Parker Morris standards were eventually accepted by the Ministry of Housing in 1967: MOHLG Circular 36/67 states that ' it is the Minister's intention that all housing schemes to be designed from now on [April 1967] shall as a minimum incorporate the space and heating standards recommended by the Parker Morris Committee ', and goes on to propose subsidies for houses built in accordance with a new cost yardstick. MOHLG Circular 52/70 incorporates in one document the housing yardsticks given in imperial measure in Circular 31/69 and in metric measure in Circular 56/69.

In recent years, the attention of both central and local government has been bearing upon the problem of the respective advantages, in economic and human terms, of comprehensive redevelopment of areas made up of, or including, unfit housing, and of rehabilitation to bring them up to acceptable standard.[28] This has inevitably posed the problem of definitions and of standards. As Cullingworth points out, 'there is no objective criterion of slum conditions. The legislation—which refers to houses "unfit for human habitation"—certainly does not provide a definition: it merely lists a number of matters which should be *taken into consideration*. Furthermore, a house is deemed unfit only "if it is so far defective in one or more of the said matters that it is not reasonably suitable for occupation in that condition". This can only be a matter of judgment.'[29] Having regard to these matters, in February 1965 the Central Housing Advisory Committee appointed a sub-committee, the chairman of which was Mrs Evelyn Denington and having among its members Professors J B Cullingworth and D V Donnison, the purpose of the sub-committee being ' to consider the practicability of specifying objective criteria for the purposes of slum clearance, rectification of disrepair and other housing powers relating to minimum tolerable standards of housing accommodation; and to make recommendations '. The sub-committee was requested to confine its considerations to the fabric, equipment and services of the house, but it has also taken into account the environment of the house. Problems such as overcrowding were, however, outside the terms of reference. The members based their deliberations upon the ' good foundation ' of the fitness standard postulated by the Miles Mitchell Sub-Committee on Standards of Fitness for Habitation in 1946,[30] subsequently incorporated into the 1957 Housing Act, and produced a list of twenty conclusions and recommendations as a guide for action, which are embodied in their report *Our older homes: a call for action, report of the Sub-Committee on Standards of Housing Fitness* (HMSO, 1966). Subsequent upon the Denington report, the Ministry of Housing and Local Government carried out its own sample survey in 1967 of the condition of houses in England and Wales (see below) which revealed more unfit and sub-standard houses, more widely dispersed, than had been realised, and on the basis of this advice and evidence, supplemented by the

360

Ministry's own improvement feasibility study at Deeplish (see below), a White Paper was issued in 1968 under the title *Old houses into new homes* (HMSO, 1968, Cmnd 3602) calling for a change of emphasis in local authority housing programmes, and a greater share of the available funds to be spent on improving existing housing stock.

Such change of policy is incorporated in the most recent legislation on the central subject of housing, the Housing Act 1969, and this exhortation to restore older houses and areas instead of demolishing and rebuilding them, is in fact its most significant legislative change. The 1969 Act is not a complete code in itself: the principal Act remains that of 1957. C H Beaumont has written a guide to the new legislation, *The Housing Act 1969* (Butterworths, 1970) which consists of an introductory text, a compressed outline of the terms of the Act, an annotated full text of the Act, and a list of the Circulars and Statutory Instruments arising from the Act. Appendix 1 of the Milner Holland report (see below) contains a useful summary of much of the legislation affecting England and Wales. The most comprehensive guide to housing legislation *in toto* is the loose-leaf, regularly up-dated *Encyclopedia of housing law and practice* edited by Percy Lamb and others (Sweet and Maxwell, 1963-), in two volumes.

The housing situation in Scotland differs markedly from that which obtains south of the border, most particularly in the considerably larger proportion of council house tenants and the correspondingly smaller proportion of owner-occupiers; overcrowding is higher, and the privately-owned houses are generally smaller and poorer than their English counterparts, although Scottish averages tend to be depressed by the poor conditions in Glasgow and the remote rural areas. An analysis of the development of Scottish housing policy is contained in R D Cramond's *Housing policy in Scotland 1919-1964: a study in state assistance* (Edinburgh, Oliver & Boyd, 1966, Glasgow University Social and Economic Studies Research Papers 1). Nevertheless, Scottish central policy has followed that of England fairly closely in recent years, working through the agency of the Scottish Housing Advisory Committee. In 1965, the committee appointed a Sub-Committee on Unfit Housing under the chairmanship of J B Cullingworth ' to examine the present

361

statutory provisions relating to the determination of unfitness for human habitation and to make recommendations for amendments '. Not only had the sub-committee to establish a definition, it further had to assess the scale and distribution of the problem and its implications. In this task, the members had the advantage of being able to study the corresponding English report *Our older homes: a call for action* (see above) and were 'impressed by the very real differences which exist between the problems in Scotland and England '. The report—*Scotland's older houses: report of the Sub-Committee on Unfit Housing* (Edinburgh, HMSO, 1967)—finds that some half a million houses will require to be replaced or rehabilitated in the near future, and makes detailed recommendations for dealing with the situation, together with pointers to the most important areas of further study. In the following year, again following the English pattern, a White Paper entitled *The older houses in Scotland: a plan for action* (Edinburgh, HMSO, 1968, Cmnd 3598) was issued by the Scottish Development Department containing proposals for legislation based on the findings of the Cullingworth Report, supplemented by two further surveys, one of Scottish housing and one of Glasgow housing, both carried out in 1965 (see below). The parallel with England was concluded in the resulting legislation, the Housing (Scotland) Act 1969.

The preponderance of council house tenants in Scotland has been mentioned. and it is natural that Scottish central policy should be mindful of the management and the particular problems of local authority housing. The Scottish Housing Advisory Committee has tackled exactly this sphere of operations in two separate inquiries. In 1965, a Sub-Committee on Housing Management was appointed under the Scottish Housing Advisory Committee to 'consider the general question of the management of houses provided by local authorities and to advise on what further guidance should be given on the subject '. The sub-committee conducted a thorough survey of the policies and practice of eighty eight local authorities; their report *Housing management in Scotland* (Edinburgh, HMSO, 1967) criticises the majority of the authorities for building new houses in large numbers, overlooking 'the fact that the end product of their efforts is not merely another unit to be added to the year's statistics, but a home for a family . . .', and warns of the danger of demolishing 'old slums only to replace them with houses which will eventually become new slums, no better than the old'. *Council house communities: a policy for progress* (Edinburgh, HMSO, 1970) is the report of a Sub-Committee on Amenity and Social Character of Local Authority Housing Schemes, set up in 1967 under the chairmanship of Sir James M Miller ' to examine the amenity and social character of existing Scottish local authority housing schemes, including the extent to which these provide a satisfactory environment in modern conditions; and to make recommendations regarding the action which might be taken both to reduce environmental deficiencies in existing schemes and to prevent such deficiencies in future housing developments '. Council houses in fact account for nearly half (at 1969) the total Scottish housing stock of around 1,800,000 houses; and the sub-committee found that ' a substantial number of local authority housing schemes in Scotland have been, or are being reduced to a condition which is not far removed from the slums which they are designed to replace. This situation has grave social and economic consequences and we are convinced that urgent action by local authorities is necessary to correct it.' The report contains detailed recommendations to this end.

While the particular problems associated with council housing do not assume similar proportions in England and Wales, nevertheless local authority housing constitutes one quarter of the available housing stock in these two countries and is a significant factor in any consideration of housing policy and management. In 1968 the Central Housing Advisory Committee appointed a Housing Management Sub-Committee under the chairmanship of J B Cullingworth ' to review the practice of housing authorities in allocating tenancies and rehousing and to suggest rules or principles to be followed in these matters '. The report of the sub-committee's inquiry into local authority housing, with their recommendations for policy, is contained in a joint publication of the Ministry of Housing and Local Government and the Welsh Office, *Council housing purposes, procedures and priorities: ninth report of the Housing Management Sub-Committee of the Central Housing Advisory Committee* (HMSO, 1969).

The economics of housing is balanced between many factors: government policy on rent control and regulation, subsidies, taxa-

363

tion and tax reliefs; central and local government funds; not to mention the personal finances of millions of people and the credit facilities available to them, for, as Cullingworth points out, 'the need for houses can be transformed into demand only if there is some mechanism for long-term credit'.[31] In *Housing finance and development* (Longmans, 1965), A J Merrett and Allen Sykes offer a concise examination of the subject, including the feasibility of bringing the price of good housing within the reach of a larger proportion of potential house-buyers; A A Nevitt examines the same topics within a wider general and historical framework in *Housing, taxation and subsidies* (Nelson, 1966) which demonstrates the effects of the British system of taxation and subsidies and the mechanics of the housing market upon investment in housing, and postulates new policies for the future. An empirical survey which examines the economic aspects of home ownership versus tenancy is *Home ownership in England and Wales* (Housing Research Foundation, 1970) in which the percentage of home owners in each of 789 authority areas is calculated. Lionel Needleman's *The economics of housing* (Staples Press, 1965) is a wide-ranging book offering a descriptive economic analysis of many aspects of the British housing situation. In just over two hundred pages it takes into its orbit the house-building industry, productivity, costs and finance, improvement of quality and much more, and inevitably the treatment is somewhat superficial without any suggestions for future policy. Housing finance came under the microscope of the International Economic Association at a conference at Ditchley Park in 1965: *The economic problems of housing: proceedings of a conference* . . . edited by A A Nevitt (Macmillan, 1967) contains papers by British and overseas speakers including Donnison (The political economy of housing) and Cullingworth (Housing and the state: the responsibilities of government). Looking to the future, Dr Peter A Stone's *Urban development in Britain: standards, costs, and resources 1964-2004* is the result of a major research project at the National Institute of Economic and Social Research and centres on the economic implications of future urban growth in Britain up to the end of the present century. The first volume, *Population and housing* (Cambridge, Cambridge UP, 1970) concentrates on estimates of housing need over this period, and focuses on the policy

364

clash between building new houses and keeping up the condition of the older houses which remain. Stone's conclusion is clear enough: it will be better to switch resources, in part at least, from new construction to maintenance and rehabilitation.

That rehabilitation is a practical proposition can be learnt from publications giving detailed accounts of rehabilitation ' on the ground '. One such is the Ministry of Housing and Local Government publication *The Deeplish study: improvement possibilities in a district of Rochdale* (HMSO, 1966). Deeplish is a mixed, but mainly residential area, a neighbourhood of nineteenth century small terrace houses. It was selected for this feasibility study because ' it seemed to be fairly typical of older urban neighbourhoods which are not slums '. A Ministry team of architects, planners, traffic engineers, sociologists, quantity surveyors and estates officers was brought together to study the whole question of rehabilitation in the area. Their report contains detailed results of their survey, illustrated with photographs, drawings, plans, tables and verbatim comments from residents; draws conclusions on the basis of the results, and examines the implications of these. One of the recommendations was for a pilot scheme for a part of Deeplish to ' show what rehabilitation can achieve on the ground, to gain experience of the management of a concerted effort of rehabilitation and of the means to secure the cooperation of residents and owners '; this was subsequently put into action. *The Halliwell report: Bolton, a study for the redevelopment of an urban twilight area* (Hallmark Securities Limited, 1966) is a comprehensive study of a typical twilight area carried out at the invitation of MOHLG ' to investigate its needs on the widest basis, to propound an acceptable solution, and to discover the nature and scale of the economic problem '. The area selected, Halliwell, was 326 acres in extent and contained 16,500 population. It was thought that the results of such a study would provide useful information for the similar appraisal of other areas, both in the same town and in other towns in the area. Another account of a scheme in action is *Environmental recovery: Skelmersdale* (Manchester, Civic Trust for the North West, 1969), a full illustrated report on the trust's scheme for the rehabilitation of an older housing area, which involved the restoring of twenty two houses, landscaping, and pedestrianisation of the street concerned.

A summary is given under the same title by Graham Ashworth in *Town planning review* 41(3) July 1970 263-292.

It is clear that before any policy can be formulated with regard to housing provision or management, either at national or local level, a detailed knowledge of the existing housing situation must be available. Geddes' dictum of survey, analysis, plan, applies equally to housing. Methods of carrying out a survey of housing are described in a publication of the Economic Commission for Europe, *Techniques of surveying a country's housing situation, including estimating current and future housing requirements* (New York, United Nations, 1962); and to *Regional and urban studies: a social science approach* edited by J B Cullingworth and S C Orr (Allen and Unwin, 1969) Cullingworth has contributed a chapter on ' Housing analysis ', a lucid, documented review, admittedly selective, of ' the main concepts and problems involved in the studies so far undertaken in Britain '. The first national housing survey in Britain was undertaken by the Social Survey for the Ministry of Housing and Local Government in 1960, and the data emanating from it, based on a sample of local authorities and relating to present and future housing condition in terms of present fitness and anticipated life, are contained in *The housing situation in 1960: an inquiry covering England and Wales carried out for the Ministry of Housing and Local Government* by P G Gray and R Russell (Social Survey, 1962, SS 319). Also active in the housing arena was the Joseph Rowntree Memorial Trust, which financed several studies. J B Cullingworth's report *English housing trends: a report on the Rowntree Trust housing study* (G Bell, 1965, Occasional Papers on Social Administration 13) is one of a series arising from these housing studies, and deals with the final national housing survey carried out for the trust by the British Market Research Bureau in 1962. It gives a concise description of the housing conditions prevailing in England at the time of the survey and the main changes then under way. Two years later, the Social Survey conducted a follow-up national survey, again for the Ministry of Housing and Local Government, to obtain current data about the housing situation and full details of the changes which had taken place in the intervening period. The results of this second survey are presented in *The housing survey in England and Wales 1964* by Myra Woolf

(Social Survey, 1967, ss 372). Most recently the Ministry of Housing and Local Government carried out its own sample survey in 1967 of the condition of houses in England and Wales to supplement the findings of the Denington Committee on Standards of Housing Fitness (see above), and these findings were published in *Economic trends* 175 May 1968, xxiv-xxxvi. The first comprehensive survey of housing conditions in Scotland was carried out by Cullingworth for the Social Survey, and the results were published for the Scottish Development Department as *Scottish housing in 1965* (Edinburgh, HMSO, 1967; also Social Survey ss 375).

Apart from the national data-gathering exercises, several studies have been made of housing conditions in individual towns and cities. J B Cullingworth (again) has been responsible for two of the best-known of these: *Housing in transition: a case study in the city of Lancaster, 1958-1962* (Heinemann, 1963); and *A profile of Glasgow housing 1965* (Edinburgh, Oliver and Boyd, 1967, University of Glasgow Social and Economic Studies Occasional Papers 8), both of these valuable sources of data. London has naturally been a focus of attention for housing studies, many of them concentrating on the ' rats in the stew and snakes in the bath ' aspects; more balanced surveys have been conducted by the Milner Holland Committee, appointed by the government to inquire into London's housing problems after the public uproar over Rachmanism in 1963, which—as Donnison puts it—' proceeded to make a more thorough investigation than may have been expected '.[32] *The Report of the Committee on Housing in Greater London* (HMSO, 1965, Cmnd 2605) is a vast compendium of data and information based on massive case study exercises throughout the city into all aspects of its housing. One of the bodies which contributed case study material to the Milner Holland Report was the Centre for Urban Studies, whose evidence is reprinted in *London's housing needs* by Ruth Glass and John Westergaard (University College London, 1965, CUS Reports 5). A more recent estimate, taking April 1966 as the base date for projections, is made by the Standing Working Party on London Housing of the Ministry of Housing and Local Government in *London's housing needs up to 1974*, Report no 3, with an interim report by the Sub-Group on Statistics, *London's housing needs: a quantitative assessment* (MOHLG, 1970). The quantitative assessment occupies the main part of the report. On a more local scale, the Centre for Urban Studies also conducted a survey of housing in Camden, a full-scale operation to provide data to form the basis for a review of housing policy made necessary by the unification of the boroughs of St Pancras, Holborn, and Hampstead: the report was published in 1969 by the London Borough of Camden as *Housing in Camden* in three volumes, a preliminary volume reporting Camden Council's conclusions and subsequent actions and two main volumes containing the research results; and is summarised by Ruth Glass under the same title in *Town planning review* 41(1) January 1970 15-40. The Ministry of Housing and Local Government has produced a series of *Housing survey reports* containing Ministry: no 1, *West Midlands conurbation house condition survey 1967;* no 2, *South East Lancashire conurbation house condition survey 1967;* no 3, *Merseyside conurbation house condition survey 1968;* no 4, *Tyneside conurbation house condition survey 1968* (all HMSO, 1969); no 5, *West Yorkshire conurbation house condition survey 1969* (HMSO, 1970).

A review, now out-dated but still of interest, of the public housing sector is provided by A W Cleeve Barr in *Public authority housing* (Batsford, 1958). The book is first of all a comprehensive factual account of developments in British housing policy and practice since World War II, drawing on government reports and recommendations, on studies by various specialists, and on the author's own experience at the (then) London County Council; and secondly an illustrated review of fifty six of the best post-war layouts built in Britain, about half of them being LCC schemes. Another sector of housing interest is discussed in the Ministry of Housing and Local Government report *The ownership and management of housing in the new towns* by J B Cullingworth and Valerie A Karn (HMSO, 1968), the result of a study commissioned in 1966 by the Minister and the Secretaries of State for Scotland and Wales to provide a better factual basis for the formulation of policy on new town housing. The major part of the study consisted of a social survey of Crawley, Stevenage, Aycliffe, and East Kilbride, and the report incorporates data from these surveys to focus attention onto the main issues involved. The detailed surveys, by Valerie Karn, are published separately as Occasional Papers 8, 9, 10, and 11 of the

Centre for Urban and Regional Studies at Birmingham University (Birmingham, 1970).

The application of sociological survey methods to housing results in one of two studies: user studies, which are concerned with the reactions of tenants to various aspects of the houses they currently live in; and studies of the social effects of rehousing or of living in a particular type of area. Within the category of user studies, the Building Research Station produced a well-documented survey of family activities and the way in which the rooms and the space in the home are used in *Houses and people: a review of user studies* by W V Hole and J J Attenburrow (HMSO, 1966), in which the information relates mainly to dwellings built by local authorities and new towns since World War II, principally in London and the south east. In the private sector, Wates Ltd, the builders, recently commissioned Shankland, Cox and Associates to carry out a study of user reaction to their own homes with a view to using the information thus obtained to shape criteria for better design and layout for their houses. The survey was carried out by teams of sociologists and architects paying personal visits to more than one hundred Wates houses. Their report *Private housing in London* (Wates Ltd, 1969) contains the findings of the survey together with the criteria arrived at; also incorporated are the questionnaire used, and a detailed explanation of the mechanics of the operation. *New housing in SE England* was the focus of a survey carried out by National Opinion Polls for the Housing Research Foundation (HRF, 1970) in which the purchasers are identified, the types of houses they bought analysed, and their attitudes towards house and builder examined. The Ministry of Housing and Local Government, mainly through the agency of their Sociological Research Unit, have also been active in the field of user surveys, and some of their findings are incorporated into their series of Design Bulletins. Design Bulletin 15, *Family houses at West Ham: an account of the project with an appraisal* (HMSO, 1969) describes a project of thirty nine houses designed by the Ministry's Development Group for West Ham Borough Council to Parker Morris standards, with a variety of house types at a high density. An appraisal survey was carried out after the houses had been occupied for over a year, and the findings are contained in the Bulletin, together with the main lessons to be learnt

369

from them. Design Bulletin 17 *The family at home* (HMSO, 1970), is the first of a series of three dealing with a housing project designed by the Ministry's Development Group for Sheffield City Council, and describes a 1962 social study of council tenants in four recent house types with the object of determining the extent to which modern design was meeting the requirements of different types of family. The design implications for the project are enumerated, with a discussion of factors both external and internal to the house.

Planners and sociologists have been much preoccupied with the human effects on people, in terms of family and social life, of re-housing as a result of redevelopment, and with attitudes towards moving out of a familiar locality and towards different types of housing such as high flats. Clearly, while slum clearance and renewal must go on, information on the attitudes of those involved in it is of great benefit in the management of these projects, and can in many cases lessen the often traumatic experiences suffered by many people who find themselves suddenly forced out of a known environment into an alien one. The problem has been recognised for years: for instance, in January 1956 a Housing Management Sub-Committee of the Central Housing Advisory Committee, under the chairmanship of Professor J M Mackintosh, was charged 'to examine problems of housing management arising from the rehousing of families from unfit houses, and to make recommendations '. Their report *Moving from the slums: seventh report of the Housing Management Sub-Committee* (HMSO, 1956) stresses the importance of housing management and the work of the local authority housing department in the smooth running of slum clearance projects. The Ministry of Housing and Local Government is also producing feedback from its own involvement in slum clearance: Design Bulletin 19, *Living in a slum: a study of St Mary's, Oldham* (HMSO, 1970) and Design Bulletin 20, *Moving out of a slum: a study of people moving from St Mary's, Oldham* (HMSO, 1970) are the first two in a series of four Design Bulletins dealing with a slum clearance project designed for Oldham Corporation by the Ministry's Development Group. Design Bulletin 19 describes a preliminary social survey of the redevelopment area carried out in 1962, in which residents' attitudes towards their homes, environment, social life, moving, and preferred new dwellings were examined. Design Bulletin 20 is the report of a

370

second social study, made in 1964/65, covering the period of leaving the slum and settling in to new homes. Aspects discussed include compulsory purchase, compensation, rents, and attitudes towards the new environment. The whole problem is viewed objectively by Alvin L Schorr in *Slums and social insecurity* (Nelson, 1964), a critical review of slum existence and government efforts towards amelioration, including comparisons of British and American experience. *Slum clearance and improvements* is the subject of Bulletin no 2 of the Scottish Development Department's *New Scottish housing handbook* (Edinburgh, HMSO, 1970).

There have been several worthwhile studies of redevelopment incorporating 'before and after' studies, which have provided valuable feedback on which to plan. One of the earliest was *Human aspects of redevelopment* by June Norris (Birmingham, Midlands New Towns Society, 1960), a study of the movement of tenants from clearance areas in Birmingham to the suburbs, basically a feedback survey of reactions to the new environment, satisfaction with new houses, costs, contacts with kin, and so on. A notable piece of work was reported by C Vereker and J B Mays in *Urban redevelopment and social change: a study of social conditions in central Liverpool 1955-56* (Liverpool, Liverpool UP, 1961), the results of a sample survey among households in an inner area of Liverpool. The authors found that family and kinship networks are not so overwhelmingly important as had previously been supposed, and that ' the warm contact emanating from the intimate social groups and from the extended family in particular is clearly deemed by many families to be less important than the opportunity to enjoy the advantages of better physical and social conditions '. The book provides a good solid basis of sociological fact for use in the consideration of what to do with the people involved in redevelopment areas. Another minor classic is *The sociology of housing: studies at Berinsfield* by R N Morris and John Mogey (Routledge and Kegan Paul, 1965, International Library of Sociology and Social Reconstruction), a study of the effects of rehousing of a number of families living in ex-service huts in south Oxfordshire into a new village on the same site. Data were collected from interviews before, during, and after rehousing, and the whole constitutes a fully documented example of sociological research and analysis. A further study of Liverpool's

371

urban renewal programme, partly from the human point of view but mainly from the political is contained in David M Muchnick's *Urban renewal in Liverpool: a study of the politics of redevelopment* (G Bell, 1970, Occasional Papers on Social Administration 33); while Sunderland comes under the microscope in Norman Dennis' *People and planning: the sociology of housing in Sunderland* (Faber, 1970). The thesis of the latter book is that the Corporation of Sunderland, having over-estimated the town's increase in population, embarked on a large-scale housing programme, and subsequently, finding itself short of occupants for its new houses, pulled down more old houses than was strictly necessary in order to provide tenants for the new dwellings; the treatment tends to be emotive and is by no means impartial.

The social needs of new communities have long been recognised and have been the subject of study and recommendation. As long ago as 1935, the National Council of Social Service published *New housing estates and their social problems* (NCSS, 1935) and then *Community or chaos: new housing estates and their social problems* by L E White (NCSS, 1950). More recently, the Central Housing Advisory Committee has attacked the issue in *First hundred families: community facilities for first arrivals in expanding towns* (HMSO, 1964), followed by *The needs of new communities: a report on social provision in new and expanding communities* (HMSO, 1967). Social studies of new communities also form a significant part of the literature. An early example, and a ' classic study of the formation of new secondary groups in response to a new urban situation . . . a forerunner of numerous other studies which have appeared in the last thirty years '[33] is Ruth Durant's study *Watling: a survey of social life on a new housing estate* (P S King, 1939), long out of print, but an extract from it is now available under the title ' Community and association in a London housing estate ' in *Readings in urban sociology* edited by R E Pahl (Oxford, Pergamon Press, 1968). It is not possible to detail the ' numerous other studies ' but is perhaps permissible to point to two as being worthy of study, both because of their workmanship and the interest of their findings. Neither is recent: one is *Neighbourhood and community: an enquiry into social relationships on housing estates in Liverpool and Sheffield* by G D Mitchell *et al* (Liverpool, Liverpool UP, 1954); and the

372

other is *Family and neighbourhood: two studies in Oxford* by J M Mogey—of Morris and Mogey—(Oxford UP, 1956). Further essays in urban sociology are discussed in the section on urban studies.

SPECIAL LAND USES

The importance of industry in the country's economy is clear, and the close involvement of industrial planning and location with regional planning is stressed elsewhere. The distribution of industry is also closely related to the distribution of population: where population is, so must there be the employment which industry provides. Location of industry (and of retail services, outlined below) is discussed in the context of this section with regard to the practical factors, such as government policy or transport facilities, which influence industry in its own choice of location, and to the resulting structure of industrial distribution. It is discussed later in this chapter in the section on regional planning and regional science in the context of studies which attempt to establish a theory of location with a general application.

The national/regional policy of regional planning and distribution of industry through the agency of central government has been outlined in chapter 2. A broad discussion of this policy and practice together with its implications in employment terms, taking the Barlow Report as its starting point, is given by W F Luttrell in a paper ' Industrial location and employment policy ' in *Report of the Town and Country Planning Summer School,* Exeter, 1964 (TPI, 1964). A general text on the subject of industry and employment is Peter Self's early *The planning of industrial location* (University of London Press, 1953). *Industry in towns* is the specific concern of Gordon Logie (Allen and Unwin, 1952) which first examines the problem of urban industry in general and the contemporary state of industrial location together with discussion of industrial density, human relations, industrial nuisance, industrial architecture and layout, before going on to consider the separate cases of sixteen individual categories of industries and their particular problems. In *British industry and town planning* (Fountain Press, 1962) Anthony Goss deals with the overall picture of industrial location, and with some of industry's detailed problems, its siting and relationships with towns and with the countryside. H E Bracey is concerned with *Industry and the countryside: the impact of industry on amenities in the countryside* (Faber for the Acton Society Trust, 1963), which forms the report of a preliminary inquiry for the Royal Society of Arts and administered by the Acton Society Trust. The inquiry was directed mainly at three industries: electricity supply and distribution, the UKAEA, and oil refining and distribution; with special attention paid to their effects in the southern parts of Hampshire and Dorset. Bracey examines the special problems and requirements of each industry and the ways in which these can be met or countered; and then the effects of these industries on, for example, employment, housing, education, social organisations and amenity.

One of the main factors influencing the location and movement of industry since World War II has been the government policy to move it out of the prosperous congested regions into the less well nourished regions, the development areas. Several studies have been carried out of the movement of industry, from national scale down to that of a single urban area. The first national study, carried out in the years immediately after the end of World War II was *Factory location and industrial movement: a study of recent experience in Great Britain* by W F Luttrell (National Institute for Economic and Social Research, 1962, two volumes). The first volume examines the circumstances in which firms, after the close of hostilities, set up factories in new locations in the development areas and elsewhere, most of them branch factories but some being complete moves. The reasons for the choice of location are discussed, and the firms' experiences in establishing and operating the new factories scrutinised; the cost per unit of output in each of the early years is compared wherever possible with the cost of similar work in a parent or older-established factory of the same firm in the same period. The second volume presents a nearly complete set of the case studies on which the discussions and conclusions of the first volume were based, covering eighty nine of the ninety eight cases involved, and taking in the shoe, hosiery, clothing, textiles, engineering, electrical goods, and metal goods industries. More up to date information is provided in a Board of Trade survey of *Movement of manufacturing industry in the United Kingdom 1945-65* (HMSO, 1968) known as the Howard Report after its author, R S Howard.

374

The report analyses the movement (that is, the opening of a new establishment) taking place between fifty designated areas, or from overseas into these areas, in terms of the number of establishments moving and still in operation in 1966, and of the employment provided at November 1966. The findings of the Howard Report are reviewed and interpreted ' with particular reference to the effectiveness of government policies designed to promote movement from the congested areas of the south-east and west midlands to the development areas ' in ' The movement of manufacturing industry ' by A Beacham and W T Osborn in *Regional studies* 4(1) May 1970 41-47. The Howard Report is the most complete national survey of moves ever made; it is supplemented by another study from a rather different viewpoint, *Industrial movement and the regional problem* by G C Cameron and B D Clark (Edinburgh, Oliver and Boyd, 1966, University of Glasgow Social and Economic Studies Occasional Papers 5) which takes the form of an examination of the bases of industrial mobility by means of an analysis of seventy nine firms which set up new plant of dimensions coming within the IDC control net in areas eligible for government assistance, between 1958 and 1963. The result of the study is a realistic assessment of the motivation of firms. These studies are all macrostudies on national scale, and while the fullest of them, the Howard Report, is a very complete survey it nevertheless lacks the depth which is possible within the confines of an exercise limited to a smaller spatial area. Such an exercise is exemplified by D E Keeble's microstudies of north west London, reported in ' Industrial decentralisation and the metropolis: the north west London case ' in *Transactions of the Institute of British Geographers* 44 May 1968 1-54, and earlier in ' Industrial migration from north west London 1940-1964 ' *Urban studies* 2(1) May 1965 15-32. A study on a regional scale is Barbara M D Smith's case study of the west midlands ' Industrial overspill in theory and practice ' in *Urban studies* 7(2) June 1970 189-204, which examines the difficulties which have been experienced in obtaining the movement of industry necessary to hold down the size of the Birmingham conurbation through the implementation of new town and town development schemes.

Given that an industrial firm must move, there are several factors and conditions which may influence its choice of location. A useful study drawing on theoretical and empirical work and on the experience of locational policies in eleven countries, has been prepared by the Economic Commission for Europe as *Criteria for location of industrial plants* (New York, United Nations, 1967) which combines a consideration of the decision-taking units with the programming requirements for policy. *Industrial activity and economic geography* by R C Estall and R O Buchanan (Hutchinson University Library, second edition 1966) is a very clearly written introductory survey, incorporating an extensive literature review, of the conditions and factors which affect the location of manufacturing industry and which therefore determine the pattern and structure of industrial distribution throughout the country, illustrated by studies of the location requirements of the iron and steel, motor vehicle, and oil refining industries. Complementary to this is *A geography of manufacturing* by H R Jarrett (Macdonald and Evans, 1969) a text with world wide coverage, containing much factual information. The major part of Gerald Manners' *The geography of energy* (Hutchinson University Library, 1964) discusses the effects of facilities and costs of transport on the spatial distribution of energy resources—coal, oil, gas, and electricity. 'Locational choice and the individual firm' by P M Townroe in *Regional studies* 3(1) April 1969 15-24, is an analysis of the range of internal and external factors bearing upon the decision makers of an individual firm in their choice of location. Townroe's discussion relates to manufacturing firms but clearly has wider implications.

The constant movement of industrial firms, based on locational decisions, results in patterns or structures of industry within the various spatial units of the country, whether region or urban district. London has been the focus of some analytical studies in this respect: Peter Hall's *The industries of London since 1861* (Hutchinson, 1962) examines the changing pattern of industry in the metropolis over a long period of time, while J E Martin's *Greater London: an industrial geography* (G Bell, 1966) concentrates on the present pattern. The latter volume is a detailed statistical analysis of the industrial structure of the city. The main part is an analysis of contemporary locations of major industrial groups, the mass of detail made intelligible by its presentation in the form of maps of employment densities, and supported by examples from case study investiga-

376

tions. The book also has a guest chapter on the industries of the London region new towns, their origins, and the effects of their movement to the new location. A detailed study of the location and structure of manufacturing industry in the Bristol region since World War II is provided in *Regional analysis and economic geography: a case study of manufacturing in the Bristol region* by John N H Britton (G Bell, 1967). A report emanating from a local planning department is *Industry and wholesale distribution in Manchester* (Manchester, City Planning Department, 1970) which is an analysis of information derived from a questionnaire survey between 1966 and 1969, primarily in three main categories: the location, size and type of firms together with the problems they face in operating within the city, their existing and future land requirements, and the effects of redevelopment on industry and warehousing. The salient points from the survey are reported by John Millar and Tom Mellon in ' Manchester: survey of a city's industry ' *JTPI* 56(9) November 1970 384-388. A microstudy of industrial structure is 'Local industrial linkage and manufacturing growth in outer London ' by D E Keeble in *Town planning review* 40(2) July 1969 163-188. Here, industrial linkage is defined, following Estall and Buchanan, as ' the grouping together in space of a number of separate plants each specialising in a limited contribution to the final product(s) of the area ', local linkages being those which involve short-distance flows. Such linkages are examined in north-west London using the results of a detailed survey of manufacturing firms in 1963, and this is followed by a detailed analysis of the engineering industries in the area.

The shop has progressed over a period of years from being a part of the local community and a part of local planning, through the wider implications of the shopping centre often forming a part of central area development, to its present status where it may be considered not only from local and central urban viewpoints but also as a regional service centre. In its latter role it comes within the purview of regional science, following on the development of central place theory; and demand for retail services and outlets at all levels has been the focus of considerable experimentation in the field of forecasting and model-building (models of shopping potential have been discussed in the section on planning techniques).

A wide-ranging text is provided by Peter Scott in *Geography and retailing* (Hutchinson, 1970) which reviews existing work, mainly of Anglo-American origin, by means of its literature, economic, social and geographical, and also incorporates original results where necessary to substantiate an argument hitherto undocumented. This is a solid state of the art survey of interest both to geographers and to planners whose concern is with the spatial organisation of retail services and outlets. Scott's text provides a general overview of the spatial structure of retailing; more detailed studies have also been carried out in various regions and towns of Britain, such studies being reported almost exclusively in the journal literature, and having a varying degree of bias towards regional science as opposed to practical shopping requirements. An early analysis, wider in scope than shopping centres alone, was that of Ian Carruthers, 'A classification of service centres in England and Wales ' in *Geographical journal* 123(3) September 1957 371-385 where service centres are defined as 'centres where shopping, entertainment, cultural, professional and similar services are sought by people from the surrounding areas '; followed by the same writer's 'Major shopping centres in England and Wales, 1961 ' in *Regional studies* 1(1) May 1967 65-81. Regional studies are provided by G M Lomas in 'Retail trade centres in the midlands' *JTPI* 50(3) March 1964 104-119; and by D Thorpe and T Rhodes in 'The shopping centres of the Tyneside urban region and large scale grocery retailing' in *Economic geography* 42(1) January 1966 52-73. Greater London comes under the microscope in 'Shopping centres in the Greater London area ' by A E Smailes and G Hartley in *Transactions of the Institute of British Geographers* 29 1961 201-213; and in 'Service centres in Greater London ' by W Ian Carruthers in *Town planning review* 33(1) April 1962 5-31. The movement patterns set up within a town by the provision of shopping facilities are analysed by P J Ambrose in 'An analysis of intra-urban shopping patterns ' in *Town planning review* 38(4) January 1968 327-334.

Shopping centres throughout the world are examined in a number of volumes. Wilfred Burns gives a full and authoritative treatment in *British shopping centres: new trends in layout and distribution* (Leonard Hill, 1957). The major part of *Shopping centres: design and operation* by Geoffrey Baker and Bruno Funaro (New York, Reinhold, 1951) contains descriptions of sixty three shopping centres, each with plans and photographs. The Multiple Shops Federation provide information about *Shopping centres in North West Europe* (MSF, 1967) drawn from visits to centres in Sweden, Denmark, West Germany and Holland in 1966 by the Federation's planning advice sub-committee. Valuable surveys of North American practice and experience are contained in *Shopping for pleasure* (Capital and Counties Property Company, 1969) which covers shopping centres in the United States and Canada; and in *Design for shopping* by the same company (1970) which incorporates information from a further visit to North America and study of six more centres.

The operational requirements of shops, and the necessity to take these into account at an early stage in planning, are emphasised by Gillian M Pain in *Planning and the shopkeeper* (Barrie and Rockliff, 1967). The author has brought together a large amount of information from a variety of sources on these requirements, for example, off-loading space, parking space, and generation of traffic. Three case studies are included which demonstrate the difficulties involved; there is a good bibliography. In her conclusions, the author calls for a regional hierarchy of shopping centres to be established on a sound economic basis. Colin S Jones sets out a useful exposition of the theory and practice of this subject in *Regional shopping centres: their location, planning and design* (Business Books, 1969) which also has an extensive bibliography. The book is a solitary British contribution to the American-dominated subject of ' out-of-town ' centres: it reviews the development of such centres in Britain and the US, examines the various factors associated with their location, and discusses in detail the many practical aspects of planning and building shopping centres. Probably the fullest exercise reported in print on the planning of a regional shopping centre in Britain is *Regional shopping centres: a planning report* from the Department of Town and Country Planning of the University of Manchester (Manchester, 1964). In 1963, the Metropolitan Railway Surplus Lands Company was refused permission to develop a large regional shopping centre in the green belt between Liverpool and Manchester. Subsequently the company asked Manchester University's Department of Town and Country Planning to carry out an independent investigation into the planning implications of the development, and this objective and well-documented report is the result. The study forecasts population and employment and shopping for the area in 1971, and studies the effects of a shopping centre at regional level in this context. ' In its degree of sophistication, particularly in assessing the effect of one centre on the sales peformance of other centres, [the report] may be regarded as the most advanced of the " centres and hinterlands " approach to the analysis of shopping provisions.'[34] The study was followed up by the development of a retail shopping model, and the report of this part is discussed along with other shopping models in the section on planning techniques within this chapter.

Office development in Britain is controlled in much the same way as is industrial development, under the Control of Office and Industrial Development Act 1965, ultimate authority resting with the Department of the Environment. New office building was subject under this Act to the granting of an Office Development Certificate; initially the controls applied only in the metropolitan area of London, where they have been operated with considerable stringency, but subsequently they were extended to large parts of the east and west midlands and southern England. In December 1970, however, the controls for London were relaxed to bring the city into line with the rest of the south east region, while in the east and west midlands controls were removed altogether. It has been government policy for many years to aid in the relief of congestion in London by dispersing as many of their own offices to other parts of the country as was feasible; in addition, a special agency, the Location of Offices Bureau, exists, firstly within the Ministry of Housing and Local Government, passing in 1969 to the Board of Trade and now within the Department of Trade and Industry, specifically to encourage the decentralisation of office employment from central London, primarily by providing an information service to firms.

The many aspects of office development were the subject of a major research project of the Joint Unit for Planning Research of

University College, London, and the London School of Economics, the results of which are contained in *The office: a facet of urban growth* by Peter Cowan and others (Heinemann, 1969). An introductory summary on the state of urban studies in Britain stresses the need for a base of theory on which to base practical planning: the body of the text provides a detailed theory and practice of the office, taking in a review of the evolution of the office function, case studies of four large office organisations, two studies of the way in which London's office space is occupied, and discussions of provision of office space, legislative control of office development, office provision in relation to London's growth, the rising number of office workers, and finally some models of office construction, one of which has been built and tested. As the authors point out ' a particular feature of our work has been the attempt to combine mathematical models of urban growth and change with more empirical and descriptive studies '.

As there are distinct factors and conditions which influence industry's choice of location and thereby the structure of industrial distribution, so there are factors at work also in the location of offices. ' It has become a fundamental law of urban location that firms choose sites for their establishments with an eye to minimising the cost of communication imposed by distance on the maintenance of economic linkages, whether these be with customers, suppliers or other establishments within the same organisation. In the case of the office, linkages give rise to the movement of persons and information rather than goods.'[35] Empirical work has further shown that London's central area has functional sub-areas, and that certain types of office tend to cluster in particular localities. In 1964, before government controls came into operation, the Economist Intelligence Unit carried out a survey for the Location of Offices Bureau, who published the results as *Survey of the factors governing the location of offices in the London area* (LOB, 1964). Two years later another study was sponsored by the South East Economic Planning Council's Committee on Research into the office pattern in central London with particular attention being paid to the notion of clustering. The results of this study, which involved tracing the changing location of several different office activities within the central area

381

from 1918 to 1966, are described in 'Changing office location patterns within central London' by John Goddard in *Urban studies* 4(3) November 1967 276-285. A more sophisticated analysis is described by the same writer in 'Multivariate analysis of office location patterns in the city centre: a London example' in *Regional studies* 2(1) September 1968 69-85.

The studies above have focused exclusively on London. Indeed, as Maurice Wright points out, 'public concern with the economic and social problems created by the huge volume of London's new office building has tended to obscure the growth in commercial property development which has taken place elsewhere during the past ten years. While there exists some information about the distribution and growth of offices in London, almost nothing is known about office development in the main provincial office centres.'[36] Wright's own survey of 'Provincial office development' in *Urban studies* 4(3) November 1967 218-257, is a detailed comparative study of the major office centres outside London, based on an earlier study for the Department of Economic Affairs published as *Office development outside the south east* (DEA, 1965), of which it is a revised version. Office building in the new towns is reviewed annually in the January issue of the journal *Town and country planning*. The most detailed study so far produced of offices in a provincial city is contained in three reports prepared for the Location of Offices Bureau by the Leeds School of Town Planning, and published as *Offices in a regional centre: a study of office location in Leeds* by M V Facey and G B Smith (LOB, 1968), *Offices in a regional centre: a follow-up study of infrastructure and linkages* by M J Croft (LOB, 1969), followed by *Offices in a regional centre: follow-up studies* (LOB, 1970), based on Croft's report.

One of the major themes in office location has been that of dispersal or decentralisation, primarily from London. An early examination was that by J S Wabe, 'Office decentralisation: an empirical study' in *Urban studies* 3(1) February 1966 35-55, which points up the fact, *inter alia,* that the ten largest firms of 114 which moved out, accounted for over 50% of the total number of jobs moved. A more recent general view is given by P W Daniels in 'Office decentralisation from London: policy and practice' in *Regional studies* 3(2) September 1969 171-178, while Edwin Hammond's survey of ' Dispersal of government offices ' in *Urban studies* 4(3) November 1967 258-275 is confined largely to the non-industrial Civil Service and assesses the value of the current programme of dispersal from London in relation to the problems of central London and to regional policies. Two detailed case studies of particular exercises in decentralisation are of interest: *Relocation of office staff: a study of the reactions of office staff decentralised to Ashford* by S J Carey for the Location of Offices Bureau (LOB, 1969, Research Papers 4); and Edwin Hammond's *London to Durham: a study of the transfer of the Post Office Savings Certificate Division* (Durham, Rowntree Research Unit of Durham University, 1969). The latter is a detailed study of relocation, examining mainly the social effects of the first part of the transfer, from 1963 to 1965, but including a short account of expected developments during the latter part of the move, 1966 to 1969. The transfer is studied from two points of view: the reactions of the London ' transferees ' (which can be usefully compared with the LOB research paper) and the impact on new recruits from the host town of Durham. The annual reports of the Location of Offices Bureau, published by HMSO, are a further source of information on office relocation.

REGIONAL PLANNING AND REGIONAL SCIENCE

In this section the interest centres on the policies and practice of planning at regional level; with descriptive studies of individual regions; and with the methods of regional science which consists in its most basic terms of the analysis of the structure of the region and the relation of the parts to the whole and to each other. Regional development plans, and surveys and feasibility studies carried out as bases for development planning are discussed in chapter 9.

In a series of lectures delivered at Oxford in January to March 1969, Professor Peter Hall devoted one entire lecture to defining the term ' planning ' and a further entire lecture to defining the term ' regional '. There is clearly some confusion of concepts. In the most generally accepted sense, regional planning is the apportionment of national resources between one region and another involving boosting the economic growth of some underdeveloped regions and dampening down or holding steady the growth of regions of maximum development. In these terms, regional planning is concerned with economics and is dictated by central government policy. Hall labels this 'national/regional' planning, 'a level that allocates national investments down to an aggregate regional level'.[37] The other type of regional planning, which Hall labels 'regional/local' planning,[38] is concerned with the spatial allocation of resources within the region and since this process involves allocating land for the uses demanded by the resources, the accent is on physical rather than economic planning. In theory at least, regional planning forms the bridge between national and local planning, between economic and physical. 'It is a simple matter to say that these two aspects [ie the physical and the economic] of planning should be more closely integrated. It is ferociously difficult to make them even meet. One of the reasons for this difficulty is that economic planning has reached its most refined development at the national level, whereas physical planning in this country has been a local matter for much too long. It is at the regional level that there is the greatest need for them to meet, but as they tend to approach the regional planners from opposite directions, there is bound to be some groping and confusion for a while.'[39]

Broadly speaking, this dual concept of national/regional and regional/local planning applies in most countries of the world where planning is practised in a formal way. Central policies for regional planning and development in countries other than Britain are reasonably well documented for the British planner. Three comparative studies are of note. The International Information Centre for Local Credit, situated in The Hague, published *Government measures for the promotion of regional economic development* (The Hague, Nijhoff, 1964) which contains the results of a study carried out in various countries: the report begins with a discussion of the theoretical background to regional development, then goes on to examine the situations obtaining in Austria, Belgium, Canada, Denmark, France, the German Federal Republic, Great Britain, Italy, the Netherlands, Norway, Portugal, Spain, Switzerland, and the United States. The Organisation for Economic Cooperation and Development was responsible for *Multidisciplinary aspects of regional development* (Paris, OECD, 1968) being the report of the

1968 meeting of directors of development training and research: papers cover various countries including France, Mexico, Argentina, Israel, and Iran. Finally, the Council of Europe produced *Regional planning: a European problem* (Strasbourg, C of E, 1968) containing the results of a three year study by a working party of the Consultative Assembly into the possibilities of a European regional planning policy: the report incorporates a comparative study of the national planning policies of the council's member states.

In *Regional economic policies in Canada* (Toronto, Macmillan of Canada, 1969) T N Brewis provides a useful introduction to Canadian federal and provincial policies. Canadian policy is also discussed and compared with British policy in *Policies for regional development* by Thomas Wilson (Edinburgh, Oliver and Boyd, 1964, University of Glasgow Social and Economic Studies, Occasional Papers 3), in which particular attention is paid to the use of tax incentives and other budgetary inducements to economic growth. The most comprehensive post-war national system of regional planning is that which operates in France, and a clear exposition of the theory and practice of French regional economic planning is available in *French regional planning* by Niles M Hansen (Bloomington, Indiana UP, 1968). Hansen traces the evolution of French policy and critically analyses its main features, and attempts to apply the French experience to the broad issues of the United States. France is coupled with Italy in *Regional problems and policies: Italy and France* by K Allen and M C Maclennan (Allen and Unwin, 1970, University of Glasgow Social and Economic Studies). A short review, ' Regional planning in France ' by Michel Piquard, is in *Report of the Town and Country Planning Summer School*, Belfast, 1967 (TPI, 1967). French regional planning and in particular the Fourth French Economic Plan (1962 to 1965) are examined in the two concluding chapters of J R Boudeville's *Problems of regional economic planning* (Edinburgh, Edinburgh UP, 1966), though the book as a whole is primarily concerned with methods of regional analysis (see below). France, along with the German Federal Republic, forms the focus of the final lecture of Peter Hall's *Theory and practice of regional planning* (Pemberton Books, 1970) in which both national/regional and regional/local levels are explained. West Germany alone is considered in ' Regional planning and the development areas in

West Germany ' by A Mayhew in *Regional studies* 3(1) April 1969 73-79, which is an investigation and assessment of that part of the federal planning framework which is relevant to planning for the depressed rural areas. Italy has peculiar regional problems arising from the existence of its southern region with markedly different characteristics from the rest of the country. The problems are analysed and policies reviewed in *Regional economic development in Italy* by Lloyd Saville (Edinburgh, Edinburgh UP, 1968). A complete issue of the journal *Urbanistica* 49 1967 was devoted to regional planning in Italy, fully illustrated with colour maps and diagrams, and with English language summaries. The Netherlands also have unique planning problems, and arising from the nature of the country much of its planning is of a regional nature. Three large regional projects—the Zuyderzee, the Deltaplan, and the Waddenzee—and their relationship to national planning are examined by G J van den Berg in a paper ' Changing regional planning goals in a changing country ' in *Report of the Town and Country Planning Summer School,* Keele, 1966 (TPI, 1966). W Steigenga looks at ' Recent planning problems of the Netherlands ' in *Regional studies* 2(1) September 1968 105-113; and D Burtenshaw provides similar treatment of Switzerland in ' Switzerland's planning priorities ' in *Planning outlook* new series 8 Spring 1970 55-68. Japan is the main focus of attention in the *Papers and proceedings of the International Symposium on Regional Development* held by the Japan Center for Area Development Research in Itakone in April 1967 (Tokyo, Japan Center, 1967). Papers are included by American and European speakers—Gottmann, Hauser, and J R James—but the main contribution comes from Japanese authorities and is concerned with Japanese problems and practice. Latin America is discussed by W Stöhr in ' The role of regions for development in Latin America ' in *Regional studies* 3(1) April 1969 81-90; and Venezuela is the focus of John Friedmann's *Regional development policy: a case study of Venezuela* (Cambridge, Mass, MIT Press, 1966) which also has wider implications of regional development in developing countries as its conceptual context.

The development of regional planning in Britain has been outlined in chapter 2 in the context of planning generally. As an activity which is controlled in the main by central government policy a certain proportion of its documentation is made up of government pronouncements, and the more important of these were mentioned in the earlier chapter. There is no reason to excuse a further mention of the Barlow Report as the basis of national/regional planning; as Peter Hall has pointed out, ' one simply cannot over-estimate the importance of the Barlow Report on the whole structure of post-war British planning, and indeed on the whole structure of post-war British society '.[40] Most of the documentation, though, has been produced within the last ten years, largely by the Labour government which took office in 1964. The machinery which it established to promote regional economic planning is described in a booklet prepared by the Department of Economic Affairs and the Central Office of Information *Economic planning in the regions* (DEA, second edition 1968). The first major pronouncement of policy was contained in the White Paper *Investment incentives* (HMSO, 1966, Cmnd 2874) which led to the Industrial Development Act of 1966 and the creation of ' a more positive system of investment incentives to improve the efficiency of those parts of the economy which contribute most directly to economic growth and the balance of payments and to encourage development in the parts of the country where it is most needed '. Additional inducement to locate in the development areas was proposed in *The development areas: a proposal for a regional employment premium* (HMSO, 1967), a Treasury scheme which caused some controversy,[41] but was corroborated in a White Paper *The development areas: regional employment premium* (HMSO, 1967, Cmnd 3310). These statements of policy relate to the promotion of the designated development areas. The problems of the intermediate or grey areas were examined in the Hunt Report (see chapter 2) which was simultaneously praised for its breadth of approach and criticised for being inconclusive. If it did nothing else, the report stimulated considerable discussion about the meaning and purpose of regional planning, for example in *JTPI* 55(9) November 1969 392-394; in ' The Hunt Report: a geographer-planner's view ' by G M Lomas *Area* 1969 (3) 14; in ' The Hunt Report ' by C F Carter *Scottish journal of political economy* 16(3) November 1969 248-255; and in ' Policy after Hunt ' by A J Odber *Urban studies* 7(2) June 1970 205-208. The uncertainty was evidenced in Whitehall by the termination of the existence of the

Department of Economic Affairs; its last publication was *The task ahead: economic assessment to 1972* (HMSO, 1969). One of its main legacies is the substantial library of regional studies and reports prepared and produced under its aegis: these are discussed in chapter 9. At the time of writing, two White Papers have been issued by the Conservative government which took office in 1970 which contain proposals of direct relevance to regional planning. *New policies for public spending* (HMSO, 1970, Cmnd 4515) summarises the effects these policies will have on public expenditure programmes; it includes the ending of the regional employment premium in September 1974, the discontinuance of investment grants, and the introduction of new measures to encourage the location and expansion of manufacturing industry in the development areas. *Investment incentives* (HMSO, 1970, Cmnd 4516) issued on the same day (October 27) sets out a new system to encourage investment through tax allowances for expenditure on machinery and plant with preferential treatment for the development areas. In essence the Conservative measures are new in detail but not in principle.

The most comprehensive account of the theory and practice of regional economic planning in Britain from its inception in the 1930's up to the late 1960's is to be found in Gavin McCrone's *Regional policy in Britain* (Allen and Unwin, 1969, University of Glasgow Social and Economic Studies New Series 15) a very readable text which is evaluative as well as descriptive of the policies involved. The Central Office of Information produced a review, *Regional development in Britain* (HMSO, 1968, Reference Pamphlet 86) which offers a concise account of the development of the regional problem, national policy for regional development, and progress in different regions of Britain. Peter Hall's *Theory and practice of regional planning* (Pemberton Books, 1970) is not a comprehensive textbook on the subject but a series of lectures delivered at Ruskin College, Oxford, between January and March 1969. Within this limitation, the text forms an exceptionally lucid exposition of the basic concepts of planning and of regions, of techniques of economic analysis as applied to the regional economy as a whole and of geographical analysis as applied to the internal structure of a region, including model-building, and finally of the experience of regional planning in Britain, and in Europe as typified by France and West

Germany. Coinciding roughly with the renaissance of regional thinking came three publications from the Acton Society Trust under the collective title *Regionalism in England*. The author of all three was Brian C Smith. The first, *Regional institutions: a guide* appeared in 1964; the second, *Its nature and purpose 1905-1965*, and third, *The new regional machinery,* followed in 1965. By the time the Town and Country Planning Association (a body always keenly interested in regional planning) came to hold their conference on the subject in 1968 it was time to take stock and to assess the achievements or otherwise of regional planning. Their *Papers on regional planning* [given at a conference in London in 1968] (TCPA, 1968) collectively provide such an assessment of achievements and of objectives, and definition of the local and central government framework in which regional planning can best operate; the speakers included Rt Hon Peter Shore, Peter Self, Maurice Ash, T Dan Smith, and Nathaniel Lichfield.

Since the early 1960's, economists, planners and others have debated the meaning and the purpose and the methods of regional planning, and as a good deal of the debate has taken place in public there is no shortage of print on the subject. One of the earliest papers to examine the concepts of regional development was that by D J Robertson, 'A nation of regions?' in *Urban studies* 2(2) November 1965 121-136, which gives primary attention to the economic issues involved. This can be contrasted with H Myles Wright's paper 'Regional development' in *Town planning review* 36(3) October 1965 147-164 which discusses the different sorts of regional planning from the physical planning point of view and distinguishes several basic types of regional plan. 'What kind of regional planning' by P M Smith in *Urban studies* 3(3) November 1966 250-257 further examines the 'rather nebulous activity which we call regional planning' against the context of a review of three recently-published regional studies, of the north west, the west midlands, and the Scottish economy. Concluding his review, Smith asserts that 'regional planning in this new phase in Britain is very much on trial at this stage. Results will be evident only in the medium and long term. We must therefore be prepared to look hard and continuously at what is going on . . .' Peter Self takes such a hard look in 'Regional planning in Britain: analysis and evaluation' *Regional studies* 1(1) May 1967 3-10, in which he examines *inter alia* the dichotomy between national/regional and regional/local planning which also concerns Peter Hall (see above). More recently, the debate in print has focused not so much on the search for concepts as on the examination and assessment of work done and its message for the future. In ' Regional economic development—progress in Scotland' *JTPI* 54(3) March 1968 103-112, J H McGuinness provides a conspectus of the origin and development of regional planning in Scotland, the work currently being undertaken, and the influence which the various factors of this work may have on a future pattern of regionalism within the country. In ' Regional planning in practice ' in *Planning outlook* new series 2 Spring 1967 7-18, Paul Brenikov reviews the origins of regional planning in Britain as a whole, and then examines in some detail a practical example in the making of the plan for the Dublin region, drawing from this some assumptions for general principles applying to the whole country. More recently, regional planning in practice in Scotland, Wales, and the south east region is examined by Derek Lyddon, Colin Cooper and Brandon Howell respectively in a joint paper entitled ' Regional planning and implementation ' in *JTPI* 56(8) September/October 1970 325-331.

The location of industry is a crucial factor in regional planning, and necessarily any statement on the wider topic must take it into account to a greater or a lesser degree depending upon the emphasis of the content. One of the seminal statements on regional planning with specific regard to location of industry was a paper under the title ' Regional problems and location of industry policy in Britain ' by L Needleman and B Scott in *Urban studies* 1(2) November 1964 153-173. A more recent analysis of the problems involved is given by Sarah C Orr in a paper ' Regional economic planning and location of industry ' in *Regional and urban studies: a social science approach* edited by J B Cullingworth and S C Orr (Allen and Unwin, 1969). A useful short review of the development of economic planning in general and of governmental efforts to manipulate the distribution of industry is available in Derek Lee's *Regional planning and location of industry* (Heinemann Educational, 1969, Studies in the British Economy 2). The specific problems of the west midlands and the conflict between national and regional policies in a region which contains both economic prosperity and economic depression are analysed in detail in *Employment location in regional economic planning* by G M Lomas and P A Wood (Frank Cass, 1970), a product of the West Midlands Social and Political Research Unit of Birmingham University.

The regional studies produced for the Department of Economic Affairs have been mentioned, and referred to another chapter. But in this context it is worth noting several independent descriptive studies of individual regions. In 1966 the Regional Studies Association formed from within its membership a group of about thirty people interested in different aspects of regional studies in the East Anglia region, known as the East Anglia Group. *Regional planning and East Anglia* (Norwich, 1967) is a report of proceedings of the first conference organised by the group, and includes papers by Peter Hall, David Grove and others on regional and sub-regional planning in general and as it affects the region in particular. The same region was the subject of a pamphlet *East Anglia: a regional appraisal* prepared by the East Anglia Consultative Committee (Bury St Edmunds, the Committee, 1969). The east midlands is the subject of a study by Patrick McCullagh, *The east midlands: a regional study* (Oxford UP, 1969), and the west midlands is discussed by D E C Eversley in a paper ' The economics of regional planning: the example of the west midlands ' in *Report of the Town and Country Planning Summer School, Keele, 1966* (TPI, 1966), though with a rather different emphasis, being a general thesis on the need for better regional data, for national coordination and forecasting of regional requirements and for broad education of future regional planners, with illustration from the one specific region. Rather different, but valuable as source books, are the titles in a new series published by David and Charles of Newton Abbot under the generic title *Industrial Britain*. The volume dealing with the north east, by John W House (Newton Abbot, David and Charles, 1969), for example, concentrates in very readable form a mass of information about the development of the north east region and analyses and compares the growth and problems of its three main centres—Tyneside, Tees-side, and Sunderland. The south west of England is authoritatively and comprehensively described by A H Shorter and others in *Southwest England* (Nelson, 1969).

Regional science, from which 'regional planning derives its basic orientation' is concerned with the spatial aspects of the region and with the location and inter-relationships of the service centres and the units of production within the region. The term was first used by Walter Isard in the early 1950's, and was promoted by the foundation of the Regional Science Association. There has been a continuing debate about the methods, the functions and the content of regional science. In a paper entitled 'Regional science—*quo vadis*?' in *Papers and proceedings of the Regional Science Association* 5 1959 3-21, Lloyd Rodwin asks 'is regional science a new discipline or just a high falutin name either for regional studies or for older fields such as geography and economics?' Rodwin presents an analysis of the papers contained in the first five volumes of the *Papers and proceedings* and finds greatest emphasis on economics. More recently, J N H Britton has put forward the view that 'regional science may be regarded as a disciplinary hybrid (or at least association) that incorporates concepts from a number of fields. It is characterised not only by a collection of various location theories, and an impressive array of quantitative techniques (especially from econometrics and mathematics), but also by an interest in areal units of less than national size—that is in spatial aspects of the economy.'[42]

'A knowledge of the theories and principles of economic location must underlie sound regional planning.'[43] Such knowledge is the basis of location theory, or location analysis, 'one of the most fruitful approaches to the study of regional economic development'.[44] Classical location theory is concerned with the location of the individual unit of production within an otherwise static system; developments in the last two decades have been concentrated more on establishing theories of location within dynamic spatial systems and on developing mathematical methods of simulating such systems.

In classical location theory there was a traditional division between the study of the agricultural unit of production and that of the industrial unit. The agricultural school came first chronologically, and derived from the work in Germany of Heinrich von Thünen, one of the founders, with Alfred Weber (see below), of location analysis; although, as Michael Chisholm emphasises, it is important to recognise that von Thünen's ideas 'do *not* constitute a theory of location. They amount to a method of analysis which may be applied to any situation in any time or place . . .'[45] Von Thünen's major work is *Der isolierte Staat in Beziehung auf Landwirt schaft und Nationalökonomie* (Rostock, 1826). It is available in an English translation by Carla M Wartenberg as *Von Thünen's isolated state* edited with an introduction by Peter Hall (Oxford, Pergamon Press, 1966); and a useful summary of his ideas forms the second chapter of Michael Chisholm's *Rural settlement and land use* (see below).

The classic statement on the location of the firm was Alfred Weber's *Theory of the location of industries* translated with an introduction and notes by C J Friedrich (Chicago, Chicago UP, 1929), first published in Germany in 1909. It is worth mentioning that the classic status of Weber's thesis was questioned recently by Peter Wood in 'Industrial location and linkage' *Area* 1969 (2) 32-39, and that Wood's views were in turn challenged by D M Smith in 'On throwing out Weber with the bath water: a note on industrial location and linkage' *Area* 1970 (1) 15-18.

The classic statement on the wider theory of location applied to a spatial system is that of August Lösch, whose *Die raumliche Ordnung der Wirtschaft* was published in Jena in 1944, the year before his death. A translation was made from the second revised edition by William H Woglom under the title *The economics of location* (New Haven, Yale UP, 1954). A brief statement of his ideas entitled 'The nature of economic regions' is included in *Regional development and planning* edited by John Friedmann and William Alonso (see below). Martin J Beckmann has produced 'Some reflections on Lösch's theory of location' in *Papers and proceedings of the Regional Science Association* 1 1955 N1-N9. The translation of Lösch's work was preceded by the original publication of Edgar M Hoover's *The location of economic activity* (New York, McGraw-Hill, 1948) which provides a thorough basic view over the whole range of location theory.

The dichotomy between agriculture and industry has continued to be observed. On agricultural location, Michael Chisholm's *Rural settlement and land use: an essay in location* (Hutchinson University Library, 1962) forms a good basic introduction. In *The location of*

393

agricultural production (Gainesville, Florida UP, 1954) Edgar S Dunn studies the application of location theory to agriculture in the United States. A more advanced text, but essential reading, is William Alonso's *Location and land use: toward a general theory of land rent* (Cambridge, Mass, Harvard UP, 1964), a theoretical treatise on the relation of land values to land uses within the city, focusing primarily on residential land, but bringing the theory into line with that of agricultural land uses so that ' urban and agricultural theory will form a unified theory of land uses and land values '.[46]

On industrial location, a basic introduction is provided in *Industrial activity and economic geography* by R C Estall and R O Buchanan (Hutchinson University Library, second edition 1966). Melvin L Greenhut's *Plant location in theory and practise: the economics of space* (Chapel Hill, University of North Carolina Press, 1956) is a more advanced text which examines the development of location theory from a base of Von Thünen, Weber and Hoover, and the factors of location (transportation, processing, etc), and progresses through a set of case studies of firms in Alabama to a general theory of plant location. An early essay was the National Institute for Economic and Social Research study by P Sargant Florence *Investment, location and size of plant: a realistic inquiry into the structure of British and American industries* (Cambridge, Cambridge UP, 1948) which develops the hypothesis that there is a significant relationship between the size of an industry's plant and its location pattern.

The first serious attempt to integrate the agricultural and the industrial approaches was made by Walter Isard in what is ' probably the best advanced textbook in the field ',[47] *Location and space economy: a general theory relating to industrial location, market areas, land use, trade, and urban structure* (New York, MIT Technology Press, 1956) in which the author summarises the early thinking in location analysis and greatly extends and develops it into one of the ' great landmarks in the development of regional science '.[48] A shorter text, but one which covers a wide range of theory, is Martin Beckmann's *Location theory* (New York, Random House, 1968). Many of the partial observations of location theorists were drawn together and reformulated by William Alonso in 'A

394

reformulation of classical location theory and its relation to rent theory' in *Papers and proceedings of the Regional Science Association* 19 1967 23-44. In the light of this new framework, Alonso then examines location policies for developing countries in *Industrial location and regional policy in economic development* (Berkeley, University of California Center for Planning and Development Research, 1968, Working Paper 74). 'The strongest development of locational theory has come from one of the social sciences, economics, rather than from within human geography . . . Nevertheless the excellent reviews of economic location literature . . . have served as spurs to the application, development, and refinement of spatial concepts by geographers.'[49] An excellent introduction to, and exposition of, these concepts is contained in Peter Haggett's *Locational analysis in human geography* (Edward Arnold, 1965) which contains a general introduction on systems theory and models, a full treatment of the concept of the region as an open system, and an equally full treatment of methods of collecting information and of measuring, classifying and describing it. A further conceptual approach is presented by Allan Pred in 'Behavior and location: foundations for a geographic and dynamic location theory' *Lund studies in geography*, series B *Human geography* 27 1967 and 28 1969.

Study of the distribution and functional structure of service centres[50] within a region and of the spatial behaviour associated with service provision is known as central place theory. The theory is the best known interpretation of the ordering and spacing of towns and depends on the assumption that there is a correlation between the populations of towns and their hinterlands, and between population and the number of functions a town performs. The theory was first propounded by Walter Christaller in *Die zentralen Orte in Süddeutschland* published in Jena in 1933. An English translation by Carlisle W Baskin is now available under the title *Central places in southern Germany* (Englewood Cliffs, NJ, Prentice-Hall, 1966). A long abstract of Christaller's theories is included in *Central place studies: a bibliography of theory and applications* by Brian J L Berry and Allan Pred (see chapter 13) which also contains a review of the development and present state of the theory. The idea of central places was first presented to the North American audience by Edward L Ullman in a paper entitled 'A theory of location for cities' in *American journal of sociology* 46 1940-41 853-864, Ullman in turn having been introduced to them by August Lösch when the latter was a visiting professor in the United States before World War II. Although Christaller's work is the classic exposition of central place theory, it does draw on the ideas of earlier theorists, a fact which he acknowledged himself: his precursors are discussed by John A Dawson in 'Some early theories of settlement location and size' *JTPI* 55(10) December 1969 444-448. The major development of central place theory has been by a geographer, Brian Berry: in addition to his standard bibliography, his papers 'Cities as systems within systems of cities' and 'City size distributions and economic development', both reprinted in *Regional development and planning* edited by Friedmann and Alonso (see below) are authoritative statements, as are his joint papers with William Garrison, 'The functional bases of the central place hierarchy', reprinted in *Readings in urban geography* edited by Mayer and Kohn (see the section on urban studies) and 'Recent developments in central place theory' in *Papers and proceedings of the Regional Science Association* 4 1958 107-121. Another significant development is contained in 'City hierarchies and the distribution of city size' by Martin J Beckmann in *Economic development and cultural change* 6(3) April 1958 243-248. Brian Berry was further responsible, with Chauncy D Harris, for an appreciation of Christaller's work and its effect on geography throughout the world, after his death in 1969, in *Geographical review* 60(1) January 1970 116-119, reprinted in *Ekistics* 29(175) June 1970 477-479. Two case studies in the application of central place theory are Allan Pred's *The external relations of cities during industrial revolution, with a case study of Goteborg, Sweden, 1868-1890* (Chicago, Chicago UP, 1962, Department of Geography Research Paper 76), a study which attempts to define and interpret, both theoretically and empirically, 'some of the major adjustments in the external relations of cities during periods of industrial revolution, particularly as these alterations relate to the changing role of the city as a focal point in the regional and interregional space economy'; and Harold Carter's 'Functions of Welsh towns: implications for central place notions' in *Economic geography* 46(1) January 1970 25-38.

Location theory, while based in economics, is concerned primarily with spatial organisation and spatial analysis. Regional analysis, or regional science, has a broader total concern than this and includes also the techniques of economic analysis in its purview. The major textbook on this whole field is Walter Isard's *Methods of regional analysis: an introduction to regional science* (New York, MIT Technology Press, 1960) which, as its title indicates, is primarily concerned with methodologies. Also concerned with methodology, and in particular with models, is J R Boudeville's *Problems of regional economic planning* (Edinburgh, Edinburgh UP, 1966), a revised and enlarged version of six lectures delivered at Edinburgh University. A comprehensive collection of papers on the economic aspects of regional science and in particular the techniques of regional economic analysis is contained in *Regional analysis: selected readings* edited by L Needleman (Harmondsworth, Penguin Books, 1968). *Regional economics: a reader* edited by Harry W Richardson (Macmillan/St Martin's Press, 1970) covers a similar subject range in sixteen mainly recent articles from a wide range of journals, nine of them American. Two papers in *Regional and urban studies* edited by Cullingworth and Orr (see the section on planning in practice) are also worth noting: K J Allen's ' The regional multiplier—some problems in estimation ' and E M F Thorne's ' Regional input-output analysis '. A detailed case study in regional economic analysis is provided by Joseph Airov in *The location of the synthetic-fiber industry: a case study in regional analysis* (Cambridge, Mass, MIT Press, 1959, Regional Science Studies Series 2), which develops the approach of interregional comparative cost analysis.

Isard's *Methods of regional analysis* in 1960 contained about one thousand bibliographical references, an indication of the volume of literature inspired by the subject in the comparatively short time of its development. As Needleman points out in his introduction to *Regional analysis,* ' there has been such a proliferation of articles of such diversity of subject matter and treatment that survey articles and books of readings have become not only possible but necessary . . .' The most comprehensive reader on the subject is *Regional development and planning* edited by John Friedmann and William Alonso (Cambridge, Mass, MIT Press, 1964) an extensive work containing thirty five reprinted articles and papers related to the central theme of regional development, drawn almost entirely from North American sources published after 1955. The contents, organised into sections on space and planning, location and spatial organisation, theory of regional development, and national policy for regional development, eschew completely the methodology of the subject, and case studies also are absent. The contributions, by a multidisciplinary team, summarise the existing state of knowledge in an effort to fuse the approach of the social sciences, principally economics and sociology, and that of geography into a conceptual structure for regional planning. An even wider conceptual framework is envisaged by Walter Isard in his most recent work (in association with others) *General theory: social, political, economic and regional* (Cambridge, Mass, MIT Press, 1969), a framework which would include also political science, anthropology, planning and psychology. The book, which is difficult reading, is an attempt to formulate a common language, in terms of mathematics, through which these various disciplines could communicate their theories, and a common framework into which they could all fit.

The predominance of North American material in this section is clear. In this connection, a warning has been given by J N H Britton: ' although a large and growing international body of theoretical literature is available on possible aims and methods of regional analysis much of this has been produced and published in the United States and reflects the influence of American regional problems, American urban and other distribution patterns, and differences in the geographic scale at which regions tend to be defined in the two trans-Atlantic areas. The North American research literature tends either to utilise data not available in Britain, or to elaborate on theoretical concepts and analytical methods for which no data exists either in Britain or North America—at least at the regional level. It also suggests techniques of analysis that have never been seriously evaluated for practical application in British situations.'[51] Britton offers one of the few case studies in which techniques of description and analysis are adapted and rigorously used in a British region, using British data from a variety of sources, in *Regional analysis and economic geography: a case study of manufacturing in the Bristol region* (G Bell, 1967).

398

Most of the books and journal articles mentioned in connection with regional science are fully (though not always meticulously) documented. To quote Needleman again, ' the fecundity and heterogeneity of the subject has always encouraged the production of survey articles ', and literature surveys are to be found in some of the standard texts. *Regional development and planning* includes a guide to the literature, annotated and sectionalised, and the first chapter of Alonso's *Location and land use* reviews some documentary sources of relevant information. Haggett appends an annotated review of basic sources to his already full list of references for *Locational analysis in human geography*. *Regional analysis* edited by Needleman has, as its first contribution, J R Meyer's survey ' Regional economics ', an excellent review of the whole subject with 130 references. The most substantial separate review in the field focuses on economic analysis: T A Broadbent's *Some techniques for regional economic analysis* (Centre for Environmental Studies, 1969, CES-WP-23). The paper reviews the theory of non-spatial economic models as a preliminary to the main treatment of analytical techniques. There are also case studies of economic models in practice. The treatment is complex and highly mathematical but it reviews in its course a large quantity of literature on these subjects and is therefore (in addition to its basic exposition of techniques) an extremely valuable documentary source. A more specialised review, also by T A Broadbent, concentrating in detail on only one technique is *An introduction to factor analysis and its application in regional science* (Centre for Environmental Studies, 1968, CES-WP-13) which follows the same pattern of treatment as WP 23, including a review of the literature.

SUB-REGIONAL PLANNING AND THE CITY REGION

We take the sub-region and the city region together in this one section because the theoretical literature devoted to each one is slender (the relevant development plan literature is discussed in chapter 9). But this is not to assert that the two concepts are synonymous. The city region is a concept formulated by Patrick Geddes before World War I and postulated in his book *Cities in evolution* (see the section on urban planning). Geddes referred to the aggregate of closely spaced and functionally related towns as a city region, referring to Greater London and Lancashire as examples, and proposed the term conurbations for such regions. Outside London he identified six such existing or potential conurbations : Lancashire; the West Riding ' dark galaxy of towns '; the city region of Midlandton around Birmingham; Swansea and Cardiff with their valleys forming South Waleston; Tyne-Wear-Tees; and in Scotland the merging of Greater Glasgow and Greater Edinburgh to form a bi-polar city region tentatively called Clyde-Forth. In Geddes' language, these six city regions, or conurbations, together with Greater London, formed the country's ' new heptarchy '. Geddes' ideas have become reinforced in more recent years by the growing conviction that the city region, and larger units generally, would form more meaningful units of local government administration, and this trend is reinforced in the plans for reorganisation of local government put forward in the White Papers of February 1971 (see chapter 3). The larger administrative unit is important for planning purposes, and it has already been observed that proper implementation of the structure plan system under the 1968 Act will await full local government reorganisation. But it has been central government policy to promote, in advance of such full implementation, cooperation where possible between local planning authorities in the towns and their surrounding authorities, and to set up in selected areas *ad hoc* teams to devise ' broad brush ' plans for land use and transportation over the whole of this area. Thus arose the concept of the ' sub-region ', consisting of a town and its hinterland, that whole area which looks to the town for the major part of its employment, shopping facilities, cultural and recreational provision.

The major modern consideration of the concept of the city region is offered by Robert E Dickinson in *City and region: a geographical interpretation* (Routledge and Kegan Paul, 1964; also available in abridged form in paperback as *The city region in western Europe,* Routledge and Kegan Paul, 1967, omitting chapters on the structure of the city and on the United States). Dickinson analyses the region, then the city, and then views the city as a regional centre and as a self-contained entity; then goes on to a thorough examination of the regional relations of the city and an analysis of the city region in the United States, Western Europe, and Great Britain. The third

400

part of the book looks at regionalism and regional policies in various countries and the place of the city region within this framework. Two papers originally given at the 1963 meeting of the British Association for the Advancement of Science are brought together under the title *The city and the region* by R Grieve and D J Robertson (Edinburgh, Oliver and Boyd, 1964, University of Glasgow Social and Economic Studies, Occasional Papers 2). Robertson's paper on the city moves towards a view of it in a regional context, while Grieve's paper on the region moves towards a view of regional studies based on cities and their areas of influence. Derek Senior has edited the record of a seminar under the title *The regional city: an Anglo-American discussion of metropolitan planning* (Longmans, 1966), which was designed to examine the problems of urban regions and the lessons that are to be learned from comparisons of British and American experience. There are contributions by seventeen authorities, with linking commentaries and notes on discussions. In 1968 the Centre for Environmental Studies and the Social Science Research Council held a joint conference whose papers are published as *The future of the city region* (CES, 1968, CES-WP-5, WP-6).

Several excellent and authoritative studies have been made of urban regions. Perhaps the best-known of these is *Megalopolis* (Cambridge, Mass, MIT Press, 1961) Jean Gottmann's study of the urbanised north eastern seaboard of the United States which now houses one fifth of the population of the United States. This is a very large volume of some eight hundred pages which traces the growth of the region and examines in great detail its land uses, its economics, and its overall planning; despite its size it is eminently readable, and, as a reviewer observed in *JTPI*,[52] ' it should be compulsory reading for every economic and physical planner as many lessons can be learnt from this American experience, which can have a distinct bearing on regional planning in this country [*ie* Great Britain] '. The city of Pittsburgh has been the focus of a searching analysis in three volumes by the Pittsburgh Regional Planning Association in *Economic study of the Pittsburgh region* (Pittsburgh, University of Pittsburgh Press, 1963-64). The first volume, entitled *Region in transition,* is a detailed examination of the economy of the Pittsburgh region consisting of Allegheny,

Armstrong, Beaver, Butler, Washington and Westmoreland counties. The second volume *Portrait of a region* by Ira S Lowry (which has also some reputation as an independent volume) looks at the emerging patterns of land use, local employment and population characteristics, concentrating primarily on the individual counties. The third volume, *Region with a future,* contains plans for the future and alternative methods of development based on the survey of the first two volumes. There is also a fourth summary volume which incorporates the major findings of the economic study as a whole. Detroit has been the subject of a research project, begun in January 1965, directed by Constantinos Doxiadis for the Detroit Edison Company and other interests, the volumes of which are appearing under the title *Emergence and growth of an urban region: the developing Detroit area* (Detroit, Detroit Edison Co, 1966-67). Two volumes have so far been published, the first being an *Analysis* and the second on *Future alternatives.* The purpose of the research project is to study the growth patterns, potential and future require- ments of the Detroit urban area which takes in parts of south east Michigan, northern Ohio and western Ontario (Canada). The first volume is a detailed analysis, copiously illustrated with tables and diagrams of the region itself and its surrounding larger region, and provides an example of the practical application of ekistics; the second volume discusses the alternative solutions selected for pro- jection to the year 2000. The third phase, due for completion in 1970, will interpret the findings of the first two phases to provide a broad basis for planning to meet growth objectives in the Detroit urban area. The Dutch Randstad, the ring of cities north of the Rhine, including Rotterdam, The Hague, Amsterdam and Hilver- sum, which contain more than a third of Holland's population, is the subject of a study by Gerald L Burke in *Greenheart metropolis: planning in the western Netherlands* (Macmillan, 1966). The towns in this region are separate entities but the danger is that they will all expand and merge to submerge the agricultural green heart of the region. Discussion of the problems involved in this city region forms the main part of the book, but Burke also looks at western Holland's two other major planning projects, the reclamation of the Zuider Zee, and the Delta Plan to link all the islands between the Hook and the Scheldt with flood barriers.

On sub-regional planning, there is little to which to refer the enquirer, other than the plans themselves. The main source is a volume of papers given at a symposium on sub-regional studies at Nottingham University in September 1968 organised by the East Midlands Group of the Regional Studies Association (Nottingham, East Midlands Group of RSA, 1969). The proceedings open with a general background paper by Maurice Ash, progress through contributions on the respective roles of the local authority standing conference and the private consultant, and then turn to discussions of some current sub-regional studies; the final sessions on land use are concerned with land use studies, the evaluation of alternatives in land use planning, and land use models. Also of interest are the papers from another meeting, *Papers from the seminar on the process of the Notts/Derbys sub-regional study* by A Thorburn and others (Centre for Environmental Studies, 1970, CES-IP-11). The report consists of five papers presented by members of the Notts/Derbys sub-regional planning unit all describing aspects of the process of the study: the decision-orientated framework, the evaluation process and the criteria to be used in it, analysis by the potential surface method, analysis by the Garin-Lowry method, and finally a comparison of these two methods of analysis. These papers are a valuable contribution to the methodology of the sub-regional study.

URBAN PLANNING

In this section we are concerned with the planning, layout and design of towns and cities in general terms. This comes under various labels, principally permutations and combinations of urban, city or town planning or design, although variants such as civic design are sometimes used. Some elaboration of this statement of content is required. We are discussing under this heading firstly, individual statements of how cities or towns should be conceived and created, whether these statements are based on theory or on practice; secondly, texts which set out guidelines or principles for practical urban design and planning, and these may be applicable to the town as a whole or to particular parts of it such as central areas or residential areas; thirdly, case studies of how planning is being carried on in individual towns; fourthly, overspill, town expansion, and new towns. The criterion of inclusion common to all these is that they are concerned either with something which is going on or with laying down principles for doing it. What we are not discussing are firstly, the actual development plans for towns or parts thereof, these being considered with others of the same genre in chapter 9; and secondly, studies and analyses of existing cities or towns from various social, economic or other viewpoints, which are included in the section on urban studies.

Throughout history, men (and a few women) have been fascinated by the idea of the city and have propounded principles for its creation. As long ago as the fourth century BC, Plato had his vision of *The republic;* followed by Aristotle, who criticised Plato's ideas (as did Lewis Mumford some time later) and produced his own ideas on the ideal city state. 'A state, then, comes into existence only when the population has grown large enough to live well as a political association. Should it exceed this limit, it may indeed be a greater state; but, as I was saying, there must be some point at which it stops increasing. What that point should be, it is not difficult to gather from experience.'[53] But the ideal city states of Plato and Aristotle, while they were conceived with practical roots (Plato's concern was the reformation of Athens), were presented in mythical dress, and their direct descendants, the utopias of the Renaissance period, were equally products of the imagination and destined to remain so.

Not until the nineteenth century did statements of the ideal city appear which were actually translated into practical terms on the ground, or which at least had that capability. Robert Owen established and ran a community at New Lanark as well as publicising his idea in *A new view of society, and other writings* (Dent, 1927, Everyman's Library, first published 1813-14). In the middle of the century James Silk Buckingham put forward his plan for a model town, Victoria, in *National evils and practical remedies, with the plan of a model town* (Peter Jackson, 1849), which merits inclusion despite its non-implementation, for his ideas influenced others after him (including Ebenezer Howard) and some of them were subsequently adopted by other pioneers. The literature of utopias, ideal cities and model cities, some of it based on factual experiments in community building but much of it never progressing beyond paper

404

and print, is extensive: it is discussed summarily in chapter 1 of Gordon E Cherry's *Town planning in its social context* (Leonard Hill, 1970) and fully in W H G Armytage's *Heavens below: utopian experiments in England 1560-1960* (Routledge and Kegan Paul, 1961, Studies in Social History).

At the end of the nineteenth century, there appeared two important and seminal statements of town planning. In Germany in 1889 Camillo Sitte published *Der Städtebau*, translated into English as *The art of building cities* (New York, Reinhold, 1945) subsequently, and more completely, as *City planning according to artistic principles* by George R Collins and Christiane Crasemann Collins (Phaidon Press, 1965). Sitte had made a careful study of the plans of medieval European cities and analysed their special features, and on the basis of this analysis he formulated a set of principles for the artistic design of cities; he considered that the irregularity found in these old towns was consciously introduced and that, if it could be reintroduced into modern town design, then the beauty of towns would be re-established. ' Impressed by the picturesque and beautiful results which sprang from devious lines and varying widths of streets, and from irregular *places* planned with roads entering them at odd angles, the Germans are now seeking to reproduce these, and to consciously design along the same irregular lines.'[54] Sitte's principles are discussed by G R and C C Collins in *Camillo Sitte and the birth of modern city planning* (Phaidon Press, 1965). In Britain in 1898 appeared the vision of Ebenezer Howard as propounded in *Tomorrow: a peaceful path to real reform*, subsequently revised and reissued as *Garden cities of tomorrow* (1902; new edition with introduction by Sir Frederic Osborn, Faber, 1946). Howard, growing up against a background of widespread migration of population from the country into the towns and the resultant urban overcrowding, acknowledged the attractions of country and of town life—the town and country ' magnets '—but recognised also the disadvantages of each, and postulated as a third alternative a town-country magnet in which ' all the advantages of the most energetic and active town life, with all the beauty and delight of the country may be secured in perfect combination '. Howard's plan was for a satellite community, limited in size to around thirty thousand population, and limited in physical growth by a surround-

405

ing green belt, with employment and services sufficient to make it independent and self-supporting, together with public ownership of land. Howard envisaged several of those communities eventually forming a cluster of garden cities. The town itself was to be laid out for maximum light and air, of circular form and with a central garden space: 'six magnificent boulevards—each 120 ft wide—traverse the city from centre to circumference . . .' Howard was not content with seeing his plan in print, he wanted it in reality too, and following the formation in 1899 of the Garden City Association a company was formed in 1903 to undertake the creation of the first garden city at Letchworth. Despite difficulties the project prospered, and was eventually followed by the initiation of the second garden city at Welwyn in 1920. Howard and his garden city movement have not been lacking in chroniclers. *The garden city movement* by G Montagu Harris (Hitchin, Garden City Press, 1905) which carries a preface by Howard himself, is propagandist and aims to put over Howard's ideas and the urgency of implementing them, and includes a progress report on Letchworth, then at a very early stage of development. Nearly twenty years later came Dugald MacFadyen's *Sir Ebenezer Howard and the town planning movement* (Manchester, Manchester UP, 1933). For a better perspective on the movement we must turn to C B Purdom's *The building of satellite towns: a contribution to the study of town development and regional planning* (Dent, revised edition 1949), which describes at some length the establishment and physical plans of Letchworth and Welwyn, their organisation, finance, shops, industries and other aspects. Ruth Glass[55] deems it disappointing for its lack of social and economic information, and for its failure to indicate guidelines for future new towns on the basis of experience of these two. A lack of socio-economic information is also evident in Frederic J Osborn's *Green-belt cities: the British contribution* (Faber, 1946), a much shorter account than Purdom's of the foundation and development of Letchworth and Welwyn, with a strongly practical bias towards discussion of tangible factors. Osborn was a disciple and companion of Howard, who appointed him to set about the formation of a development company for the Welwyn project; Osborn subsequently became the development company's first estate manager, and his success is reflected in his own booklet *Genesis of Welwyn Garden*

406

City (TCPA, 1970) issued to mark the garden city's golden jubilee. It often happens that a transatlantic view of British achievements lends an added dimension to our own view of them, and frequently also an objectivity which may be absent from partisan accounts. Such a prospect is provided by Walter L Creese in *The search for environment: the garden city, before and after* (New Haven, Yale UP, 1966) which takes the first model villages of the West Riding of Yorkshire as a starting point and progresses through 'the bad example of Leeds' to Bedford Park (London), Port Sunlight and Bournville, to Howard, Parker and Unwin and their practical realisations, and thence to the post-war new towns.

An advocate of the garden city principle was Raymond Unwin, an architect who translated Howard's ideals of open layout into the low-density Hampstead garden suburb, along with his partner Barry Parker. Unwin's kind of town planning—'to the architect town planning specially appeals as an opportunity for finding a beautiful form of expression for the life of the community'—was not without its critics: C B Purdom, for one, asserted that 'I see very little that is good in the garden suburb, or "town planning on garden city lines" . . . I always regretted the day that the Garden City Association weakened its good wine with the water of town planning';[56] but it had enormous influence in practical terms. Unwin's conception of town planning is embodied in his massive treatise *Town planning in practice: an introduction to the art of designing cities and suburbs* (Fisher Unwin, second edition 1911). Walter L Creese has edited *The legacy of Raymond Unwin: a human pattern for planning* (Cambridge, Mass, MIT Press, 1967), the main part of which is composed of extracts from Unwin's writings.

As an antidote to the architectural manifestations of town planning, there was Patrick Geddes, a biologist and sociologist who became one of the seminal figures of town planning. Geddes, working in his 'Outlook Tower' in Edinburgh, applied the principles of his own disciplines to the study of civics, or the effective arrangement of towns, and developed empirically his system of survey, followed by analysis, followed by plan—a principle which still holds good. Geddes' Edinburgh survey was first publicly displayed at the exhibition organised in conjunction with the 1910

407

Town Planning Conference in London; and his comprehensive view of town planning was contained in the book *Cities in evolution: an introduction to the town planning movement and to the study of civics* (Benn, new edition with introduction by Percy Johnson-Marshall, 1968; first published 1915). According to Lewis Mumford, the foremost Geddesian proponent, ' none of Geddes' thinking about cities was ever adequately embodied in a monograph or a book '. *Cities in evolution* is his most lasting testament in book form; but the most complete statement of his methods (between 1914 and 1924 he made or revised plans for about fifty cities in India and Palestine) is to be found in *Town planning towards city development: a report to the Durbar of Indore* (Indore, 1918) in two volumes. Jacqueline Tyrwhitt has edited extracts from his writings between 1915 and 1919, reports on eighteen Indian cities, in *Patrick Geddes in India* (Lund Humphries, 1947). Books notwithstanding, there can be no doubt of Geddes' importance to town planning and, as Sir Patrick Abercrombie has commented, ' it is safe to say that the modern practice of planning in this country would have been a more elementary thing if it had not been for the Edinburgh room and all that this implied '.[57] All the more regrettable, therefore, that a definitive biography has not appeared. Philip Boardman's *Patrick Geddes: maker of the future* (Oxford UP, 1957; first published 1944) was the first biography to be published after Geddes' death in 1932. The author knew his subject personally and provides much biographical and anecdotal detail, in a rather flamboyant style. Shorter, but more authentic, is Philip Mairet's *Pioneer of sociology: the life and letters of Patrick Geddes* (Lund Humphries, 1957) which includes a number of previously unpublished letters. The complete collection of Geddes' notes and papers is now located in the Department of Urban and Regional Planning of the University of Strathclyde, Glasgow, and a new biography based on these is in course of preparation by Peter Green.

The chief urban prophet of the century has surely been Le Corbusier, a power-house of ideas through the whole range of architecture and town planning. His theories of urban design began with *La ville contemporaine* in 1922 and ended with the realisation of India's capital city of Chandigarh. His most complete documentary statement is his book *La ville radieuse,* first published in

1933 and reissued in 1964 with his own additional comments; the work achieved English translation three years later, as *The radiant city: elements of a doctrine of urbanism to be used as the basis of our machine-age civilization* translated by P Knight and others (Faber, 1967). Le Corbusier has to be read, rather than written about; even in translation, his text, freely interspersed with diagrams, plans and sketches, communicates very directly to the reader his exuberant ideas for his radiant city whose inhabitants' will all be able freely to see and feel the sun. Another giant of the century has been Frank Lloyd Wright, who rejected the contemporary city and postulated his own solution, Broadacre City, in which each and every individual was to be allocated one acre of living space. Wright's testament is contained in his book *The living city* (New York, Horizon Press, 1958). Time and the perspective of history will judge whether Constantinos Doxiadis joins the ranks of planning giants. His ' science ' of human settlements, known as ' ekistics ', has been developed in Greece and is expounded in his book *Ekistics* (Hutchinson, 1968) an expensive ' coffee-table ' production whose value lies in its ideas rather than in its possibilities for practical application. His theory of city-building is contained in a short book *Between dystopia and utopia* (Faber, 1968), which is the text of three lectures delivered in 1966 in his capacity as Lecturer-in-Residence at Trinity College, Hartford, Connecticut. ' Our mistake is in building bad places or dystopias, while dreaming of an escape to utopia for which there is no-place. Instead we should be seeking out the good place, entopia, a product of reason and dream ... Entopia differs from utopia in its reliance on a systematic knowledge of the present. In its physical manifestation, entopia is " ecumenopolis ", the world-city or cosmopolis.'

It is a moot point whether Jane Jacobs' unique statement, *The death and life of great American cities* (Cape, 1962) should be classified as an individual statement of how cities should be created or as a text setting out principles for practical urban planning, and so we shall compromise (and what is classification but a compromise, anyway, in many cases?) by including it at the end of the first category and the beginning of the second, thereby effecting a bridge between the two. Mrs Jacobs is an uncompromising writer. ' This book is an attack on current city planning and rebuilding ' runs her opening sentence. But it is also constructive. 'It is also, and mostly, an attempt to introduce new principles of city planning and rebuilding, different and even opposite from those now taught in everything from schools of architecture and planning to the Sunday supplements and woman's magazines.' Mrs Jacobs' principles are based on personal observation and her experience is drawn from a limited number of city sectors (mainly Greenwich Village), but her book is vigorous and stimulating and in its progress takes a push at a goodly number of idols.

Idols are well known to have feet of clay, and the titles which follow are well-rooted in a ground of fact, being serious expositions or discussions of the principles of urban planning and design. Starting from an architectural viewpoint—for 'town planning is but a prelude to town design '—with Frederick Gibberd's *Town design* (Architectural Press, sixth revised and metricated edition, 1970). This is a practical book about designing towns. 'Town design embraces architecture, landscape and road design, and these arts being so embraced lose their individual identity to become a new thing, " the urban scene ". It is with the making of this scene that this book is primarily concerned, and in particular with its visual qualities.' The book is in four parts, dealing in turn with the complete town, central areas, industry, and housing, each part ending with analyses of examples of the form discussed within that part. There are copious photographs and plans. Sir Frederick 'had hoped to include a bibliography but the subject is so vast it was impracticable.' Fortunately, other authors are not so easily deterred! Gibberd was also one of the authors of the Ministry of Housing and Local Government's *Design in town and village* (HMSO, 1953) now out of print but available in many libraries. His section on 'Residential design' was preceded by William Holford's on 'Town centres' and followed by Thomas Sharp's on 'Villages'.

An American treatise which has become a standard in Britain also is F Stuart Chapin's *Urban land use planning* (Urbana, Illinois UP, second edition 1965). Chapin is concerned with the theory and methods of urban land use planning, paying special attention to the techniques of analysing land use, measuring trends, and estimating present and future requirements. The emphasis is on small to

410

medium-sized North American urban centres of population range 100,000 to 500,000; the absence of detailed treatment of the legal and administrative framework means that the principles expounded are applicable to similarly-sized urban centres everywhere. A more general treatment, but specifically related to American problems, is *City planning in the sixties: a restatement of principles and techniques* by William I Goodman and Jerome L Kaufman (Urbana, Illinois UP, 1965), which is basically a concise summary of the problems encountered in practical planning in North America. *Cities and space: the future use of urban land* edited by Lowdon Wingo (Baltimore, Johns Hopkins Press, 1963) contains essays from the fourth Resources for the Future forum in 1962 on the future use of urban space. The contributors include city and regional planners, economists, a lawyer, and a psychiatrist. The purpose of the papers is to postulate policies for use as guidelines for the growth and organisation of cities—or, as Wingo expresses it in his own paper ' Urban space in a policy perspective ', ' can cities be planned so that this metropolitan future will be a progression towards higher levels of material, aesthetic, social, and even spiritual satisfaction for the urban citizen?' Herbert Gans is an American sociologist-planner with practical experience of city planning but now primarily an academic and a researcher into patterns of human behaviour in American cities. His collection of essays *People and plans: essays on urban problems and solutions* (New York, Basic Books, 1968) has at least one foot in the urban sociology camp but seems more relevant in this context as representative of the sociological aspect of practical urban planning; the essays are based in American experience but contain much of relevance and more of interest to British planners, and constitute a significant contribution to the effort of bridging the gulf between sociology and planning. They are divided into six sections: environment and behaviour; city planning and goal oriented planning; planning for the suburbs and new towns; planning against urban poverty and segregations; the racial crisis; and sociological analysis and planning.

Turning from the planning of the city as a whole, to the planning of distinct parts of it, there are two sectors which carry the burden of advice and instruction: central areas, and residential areas. The planning and replanning of the central areas of towns and cities,

411

which frequently necessitates comprehensive redevelopment resulting from sub-standard and inadequate buildings and out of date road systems, has been the subject of a regular succession of handbooks from the Ministry of Housing and Local Government. The earliest, the *Advisory handbook on the redevelopment of central areas* (HMSO, 1947, now out of print), was produced against the background of the urgent need to rebuild after the end of World War II, and introduced the plot ratio control system (or floor space index). Three current MOHLG Planning Bulletins deal with the problems of city centre planning. Planning Bulletin 1 *Town centres: approach to renewal* (HMSO, 1962) gives guidance to local planning authorities in the preparation of a non-statutory town centre map, showing in broad outline proposals for the future development of the town centre. The bulletin underlines the importance of the survey-analysis-plan procedure in the preparation of a land-use framework allied to a firm road and traffic pattern. Subsequently, Planning Bulletin 3 discusses *Town centres: cost and control of redevelopment* (HMSO, 1963) and Planning Bulletin 4 (HMSO, 1963) outlines *Town centres: current practice*. A demonstration of how the guidelines of Planning Bulletin 1 are put into practice by a planning authority is given in a booklet prepared by Kent County Planning Department *Town centre maps: a guide to their preparation in Kent* (Maidstone, 1964), which consists of a series of check lists of the various stages to be carried out in this type of planning work.

A method of redevelopment, not necessarily confined in its application to city centres, is the comprehensive development area (CDA), superseded in the new legislation by action area plans, but still in practical operation in some towns and cities. ' The present development plan system [*ie* that operating under the Town and Country Planning Act 1947] makes provision for large scale maps for areas of comprehensive development (CDA maps) . . . But in practice these have not proved an adequate basis for detailed planning.'[58] In *The comprehensive development area* (Edinburgh, Oliver and Boyd, 1968, University of Glasgow Social and Economic Studies Occasional Papers 9) T Hart investigates the lack of progress, and the reasons therefor, in redevelopment using the CDA method. He firstly outlines the historic background to planning legislation, from Barlow to the

Planning Advisory Group, and then moves on to a detailed study of the CDA in operation in Glasgow, a city which has considerable experience with twenty nine CDA's outlined and eight in progress, paying particular attention to the scheme at Anderston. On the basis of his conclusions from this study, Hart looks at future problems, improvements in legislation and considers the place of redevelopment in the regional context. Redevelopment is also the theme of Percy Johnson-Marshall's large, well-produced volume *Rebuilding cities* (Edinburgh, Edinburgh UP, 1966), a comparative study of city redevelopment since World War II concentrating mainly on Britain with London and Coventry as the main examples, but looking also at other countries and in particular the experience of Rotterdam. Australian experience of redevelopment is discussed in two sets of papers: *Urban redevelopment in Australia: papers presented to a joint urban seminar held at the Australian National University, October and December 1966* edited by P N Troy (Canberra, Australian National University, 1967) gives a broad view, most of the discussion centring on Sydney and Melbourne; *Urban redevelopment in inner city areas: ways and means of achievement* edited by John Roseth (Collaroy, NSW, James Bennett, 1966) is a report of proceedings at the discussion series on urban redevelopment in inner city areas held by the Planning Research Centre of Sydney University in August and September 1965. There are five papers discussing the need for urban redevelopment and its politico-legal, administrative, financial, and design problems.

A more total approach to the replanning of towns and cities is indicated by the term urban renewal, a phrase imported from America. ' It is increasingly realised that the improvement of urban living conditions requires . . . an approach which is aimed at improving the whole physical fabric of urban life—not merely replacing the threadbare patches. Urban renewal is a convenient shorthand description of this approach. It implies not only redevelopment but also rehabilitation and conservation.'[59] J B Cullingworth, the writer of these words, was the author also of one of the first British statements on the subject, *New towns for old: the problem of urban renewal* (Fabian Society, 1962); followed closely by Wilfred Burns in *New towns for old* (Leonard Hill, 1963). An analysis of areas in need of renewal forms the main part of *Urban decay: an*

413

analysis and policy by F Medhurst and J Parry Lewis (Macmillan, 1969), the analysis being based on sample studies of housing in Manchester, Salford and Stratford and of commercial property in Manchester. The results so obtained are used as the basis for the second part of the book in which the authors propose a policy for dealing with such areas. There are nine appendices dealing with various aspects of methodology for urban renewal and redevelopment. A record of the history and effectiveness of the urban renewal programme in the United States is provided in *Urban renewal: the record and the controversy* edited by James Q Wilson (Cambridge, Mass, MIT Press, 1967). The volume takes the form of separate contributions, dating from between 1959 and 1965, by American academics and administrators; it is large and inevitably diffuse, but authoritative and well-documented. A practical plan for urban renewal is proposed in detail in *The Springburn study: urban renewal in a regional context* (Glasgow, City Planning Department, 1966) prepared by the City Planning Department and Glasgow University Department of Social and Economic Research. The object of the study was 'to establish the redevelopment potential of some 1,200 acres in the north east quarter of the city and to advise on the best ways of realising this potential '.

Urban renewal is concerned with housing as one of the principal components, and while housing in its policy, management and social aspects is considered in another section of this chapter, the planning and layout of residential areas does come within the scope of this present section. Broadly speaking, in the planning of such areas there are two main aspects: the density of the development, and the layout, which is primarily a question of separation or otherwise of traffic from the residential area. Standards for density were laid down in a publication of the Ministry of Housing and Local Government, *The density of residential areas* (HMSO, 1952, now out of print); and following these, in Planning Bulletin 2, *Residential areas: higher densities* (HMSO, 1963). More recently, the Ministry's Urban Planning Directorate produced their Technical Study 1 on *Land use and densities in traffic-separated housing layouts* (MOHLG, 1968). The study describes an examination of twelve examples of local authority and new town housing and the application to them of a new method of land use analysis. Resulting from this, a new density measurement—local residential density, where density values are expressed in bedspaces per acre—is introduced which is claimed to be more accurate than that of the original 1952 publication *Density of residential areas*.

The earliest proponent of proper residential area layout was Ebenezer Howard; followed by Raymond Unwin, whose *Town planning in practice* (see above) contains detailed instructions for the planning and arrangement of residential sites. In the United States, Clarence Perry introduced the concept of the neighbourhood unit in the *Regional survey of New York and its environs, v7, The neighbourhood unit: a scheme of arrangement for the family life community* (New York, Regional Plan of New York, 1929), of which Wythenshawe, Manchester, is the most complete British example. A development of the neighbourhood unit was the plan prepared by Clarence Stein and Henry Wright for Radburn, New Jersey, which also aimed at solving the traffic problem, and which, although never fully built (it was a victim of the American depression) nevertheless gave its name to a well-recognised concept, Radburn planning. There is an exposition of the principles of Radburn in Stein's own book *Towards new towns for America* (see below); and quite recently, it has been the subject of a Current Paper of the Building Research Station by Andrew Miller *Radburn planning: an examination of its validity today* (Garston, Herts, BRS, 1969). Stevenage new town has been the locus for examination of the merits and demerits of traffic separated and non-separated layouts by a team from the Architecture Research Unit of Edinburgh University. Their study, *Aspects of traffic-separated housing layouts* (Stevenage, Stevenage Development Corporation, 1970), compares three traffic-separated housing estates and one non-separated layout. The main conclusions reached are that separation does have advantages, especially for children's safety, and does cope adequately with high levels of car ownership. The report contains practical recommendations in the form of a check list for planning traffic-separated layouts. ' Ironically ', as a reviewer pointed out in *New Society* ' most of the items on this check list seem to have been admirably met in the world's first separated layout—Clarence Stein's Radburn, nearly forty years ago '!

Case studies of urban planning in individual towns and cities, in narrative form as distinct from embodied in development plans and reports, are not as common as might be expected. Naturally, London has received the major share of attention, but most frequently in the form of analyses of particular aspects, such as industry or office location. The most comprehensive account of planning in progress in the metropolis is Peter Hall's *London 2000* (Faber, second edition 1969). Hall's object is ' to look at the lessons of these fifteen years [*ie* 1945-early 1960's] planning and to use them for the next forty years, to see how we can most effectively remake our London for the year AD 2000 '. He re-examines the principles of the Barlow Report (see chapter 2) in terms of London's growth and trends in employment, and then considers population and its location, transport and a traffic plan, new and expanded towns, urban renewal, land values and comprehensive development, finally attempting a projection into 2000 AD through the eyes of an ordinary family. In the second edition, the text has not been altered, but each chapter has been given a postscript summarising progress in the years since the first edition. In the same year as the first edition of *London 2000* appeared Donald L Foley's *Controlling London's growth: planning the great wen 1940-1960* (Berkeley, University of California Press, 1963), another of the objective transatlantic studies of British planning which form such a valuable part of the literature. Foley examines the plans for London's post-war development and the ideas contained in them; he then looks at the machinery and policies through which the plans were put into action and the ways in which they were modified; and finally at the implications and future of the policies involved. One of the policies involved, that of the green belt around London to contain its growth, is examined in detail in *London's green belt* by David Thomas (Faber, 1970), which traces the steps by which the green belt came into being and proceeds to a detailed analysis of how it is working and of the uses which are actually made of green belt land, from which arises a speculation on the possible land use pattern had the green belt not been created. A great quantity of print has been expended on the subject of the Greater London Development Plan and of London's planning priorities and policies. In May 1970 the Town and Country Planning Association held a conference ' Whither London?', and the papers from this event (subsequently revised in

416

the light of the Burns report on south east England issued in July 1970—see chapter 9) are collected in *London under stress: a study of the planning policies proposed for London and its region* (TCPA, 1970). The topics covered include open space for leisure, conservation, administration, employment and transportation, and the speakers included Maurice Ash, Derek Senior, W F Luttrell and Peter Hall. In 1969 the Greater London Council issued a slim volume *Tomorrow's London* (GLC, 1969) as a background for the layman to the policies of the Greater London Development Plan. Judy Hillman has edited *Planning for London* (Harmondsworth, Penguin Books, 1971) with several notable contributors.

One of the chief figures in the planning of London and the south east region is Dr Wilfred Burns, Chief Planner at the Department of the Environment, who heads the south east region planning team. Previously, Dr Burns was City Planning Officer of Newcastle upon Tyne, and from his work in that city he drew the material for a book, *Newcastle: a study in replanning at Newcastle upon Tyne* (Leonard Hill, 1967), one of the best and clearest studies available of a city development plan (conceived within the PAG structure), the philosophy behind it, and the ways in which it is being put into practice in a complex city.

Across the Atlantic, the city of Boston has much the same planning problems as many major cities in Britain, and these are outlined in *Boston: the job ahead* by Martin Meyerson and Edward C Banfield (Cambridge, Mass, Harvard UP, 1966). Twelve quite short chapters each deal with a ' planning problem ' of Boston and its region—the range is wide, from youth to freight. The theme of public participation in the planning process runs through all the chapters, and in fact the book is aimed not at professional planners but at the educated layman—and for this reason, as a reviewer once remarked, it should be read by planners! A diagnosis of urban ills, and a solution to them, are offered by Victor Gruen in *The heart of our cities* (Thames and Hudson, 1965). After a dissertation on the city as it is and as it should be, the ills are examined: the destructive effects of traffic, urban sprawl, central area decay, *inter alia*. In the second half of the book, the solutions are put forward, as Gruen discusses the theories behind his own practical planning schemes in the US, and then postulates a new urban pattern (out of

417

Howard by way of Stein) based on groupings of cellular units, from neighbourhoods up to metrocentres of a quarter of a million. The problems of Australian cities are examined in a series of papers read at the 32nd summer school of the Australian Institute of Political Science at Canberra in 1966 and collected under the title *Australian cities: chaos or planned growth?* edited by John Wilkes (Sydney, Angus and Robertson, 1966). Together these form a view of Australia's cities from ecological, administrative, financial, and political bases. *Urban planning in the developing countries* edited by John D Herbert and Alfred P Van Huyck (New York, Praeger, 1968, Praeger Special Studies in International Economics and Development) is made up of material from a seminar held in Washington in 1967 sponsored by the Planning and Development Collaborative International (PADCO Inc), and the major contributions are on Japan and India.

New urban patterns have always been preferred as solutions to old urban ills. New communities, new towns have always been proposed as a result of existing poor conditions, being simply a manifestation of the normal human urge to start afresh. The first British new towns, properly so called, were designated after the war as a solution to the increasing problems of London, in the universal spirit of optimism and enthusiasm which pervaded the country and the planning movement at the end of World War II. There are now thirty new towns in Britain. 'Few people now dispute that new towns represent the one really solid and successful achievement of the voluminous planning legislation of the last twenty five years. Visitors come from afar to look at and learn from the British new towns, and frequently to admire them. Nothing else that we have done excites this interest, understandably enough. Most town planning has a restrictive image; new towns are positive achievements, the unique flowering of public initiative and enterprise. With all their faults and limitations, the new towns point a finger towards a better environment and society.'[60]

As one of the major achievements of British planning the new towns are reasonably well documented. Continuing data and information are contained in the annual *Report of the Commission for the New Towns* (HMSO), the annual *Reports of the . . . Development*

Corporations (HMSO), separate volumes covering the English and the Scottish new towns, and in the January issue each year of the journal *Town and country planning*, which is devoted to British new towns including those of Scotland and Northern Ireland.

There are now several comprehensive accounts of the British new towns, although the earlier of them have been overtaken by events. One of the earliest in the field, and still the most penetrating critical analysis available, came from the United States: Lloyd Rodwin's *The British new towns policy* (Cambridge, Mass, Harvard UP, 1956). The first overall British view was A C Duff's *Britain's new towns* (Pall Mall Press, 1961). Neither of these books has been revised in the light of more recent developments. Not so *The new towns: the answer to megalopolis* by F J Osborn and A Whittick, now in a second edition (Leonard Hill, 1969). This is a less than total view, for it reviews only the first twenty three of the thirty towns authorised at the time of the second edition. Osborn is responsible for the general sections with which the book begins, relating the story of the new towns, their birth, growth, finance and ownership, legislation, and other pertinent matters; Whittick is the compiler of the second section, which contains concise dossiers on the selected towns. The most comprehensive and up to date account now available is Frank Schaffer's *The new town story* (MacGibbon and Kee, 1970). The author is the Secretary of the Commission for the New Towns; he traces their origins in ancient and medieval times, and discusses their history and development in Britain from post-war to the present with a look to the future. Schaffer is clearly an enthusiast for new towns, and the enthusiasm comes over strongly in his book: but the reader will find no evaluation, and no criticism in it; indeed the only thing he can find wrong with the British new towns is that there are not enough of them. There is a useful appendix which lists all the new towns up to and including Milton Keynes, with the essential facts about each one and the publications relating to it.

More selective in their coverage, but more evaluative in their approach, are two Broadsheets published by Political and Economic Planning, written by Ray Thomas: *London's new towns: a study of self-contained and balanced communities*, v35 Broadsheet 510, and

Aycliffe to Cumbernauld: a study of seven new towns in their regions, v35 Broadsheet 516 (PEP, 1969). These small volumes are both reports of research forming a part of PEP's study of urban growth, financed by the Leverhulme Trust and Resources for the Future Inc. The theme of the first is ' to compare the aims of the new town planners with the outcome some twenty years later '. The aims are rehearsed in a summary of the strategy of Abercrombie's *Greater London plan 1944* and the *Final report of the New Towns Committee* (Cmnd 6876). Then there is a comparative assessment of the eight towns in terms of migration, travel to work, relation of resident population to employment, socio-economic and social structure, based on data from the 1951 and 1961 censuses and the 1966 sample census; followed by a detailed case study of Basildon, in its sub-regional context of south-east Essex. There is a final chapter on the necessity to decentralise office employment from London. The second, more substantial volume looks at seven of the older new towns outside London : Corby, Cwmbran, Newton Aycliffe, Peterlee, East Kilbride, Cumbernauld, and Glenrothes. Although on the face of it these seven towns have little in common, yet there are similarities, and an analysis of these in terms of employment, housing, and the notion of the ' self-contained community ' forms the first section of the report. This is followed by case studies of the seven towns, their successes and failures in terms of their regional context, and the findings of these lead to a final chapter stressing the importance of coordinating new town and regional planning. The bulk of the information on individual new towns is contained in their development plans and, in some cases, the successive studies which have preceded the development plan; and these plans and studies are discussed in chapter 9. There are also a small number of books and booklets which look at aspects of a new town, many of them published by the town's development corporation. The majority of these are listed in Schaffer's book (see above).

There is no comparable experience overseas to British new town planning, therefore no comparable literature. Some information on foreign achievements is provided in chapter 13 and appendix 1 of Osborn and Whittick's *The new towns* (see above). Detailed analyses of American schemes, experiments in ' community building ' rather than new towns in the British sense, are provided in *Towards new towns for America* by Clarence Stein, the joint planner of Radburn, New Jersey (Liverpool, Liverpool UP, second edition 1958).

New towns are in the main created for the purpose of receiving overspill population from a large and overcrowded urban centre. Another method of accommodating overspill population is provided under the Town Development Act of 1952, which encourages local authorities to solve overspill problems themselves by making mutual arrangements for surplus population from the large authority to be accommodated in a smaller one, by expansion of the latter. Progress under the Act has been slow in the provinces, although rather better in the London and south east region. An account of work undertaken is provided by Ivor H Seeley in *Planned expansion of country towns* (George Godwin, 1968), in which the author moves from a statement of the basic concept of dispersal of population and employment from large units to small ones and a description of the procedures involved, to a consideration of various aspects of town expansion and finally to a view of progress and the future. The fifty two town expansion schemes in operation at the time of the book's writing are listed, but the text is concerned principally with those which receive overspill from London, and of these Haverhill and Bletchley provide most of the material. A practical demonstration of the procedures and problems of accommodating overspill is given in *Birmingham overspill study* produced by the Worcestershire County Planning Department (Worcester, County Planning Department, 1967). The volume contains the results of a 'rapid planning study' of three months duration carried out by county technical staff in consultation with traffic engineers from Birmingham, Worcestershire and the Conurbation Land use Transportation Study to find sites for 15,000 public sector houses in an area to the south-west of the city. The study is in four parts: firstly, a survey of the possibilities of the area for development and the practical limitations of sewerage and water supply; secondly, a study of the likely overspill, its composition and the effects of this; thirdly, an analysis of demographic, economic and financial characteristics and their implications for development; fourthly, an examination of four types of development in four different locations, the feasibility of implementing them, and a tentative choice of one as being the most suitable.

This section is about the city, and about all things urban, as they exist at present and have existed in the past. If we agree, with Robert Park, that ' the city is . . . a state of mind, a body of customs and traditions, and of the organised attitudes and sentiments that inhere in these customs and are transmitted with this tradition ',[61] then clearly the potential scope of this section is very wide. For convenience it is viewed in two parts: the first looks at the city and the process of urban growth and urbanisation generally, and includes studies of cities, individually or collectively, first from the aesthetic or architectural point of view, and then from a comprehensive point of view embracing all aspects of urban life. The second part considers urban studies generally, and looks at urban history, at urban sociology, and then at urban geography, in all cases both generally and applied to individual cities or groups of cities.

There are plenty of books, some of them consisting primarily of photographs, which purport to capture the ' essence ' of this or that town, or of towns generally. Many of these can be disregarded in the context of this book; but there remain some which have a serious purpose in this direction, and which set out to examine urban aesthetics in a constructive manner, either over the whole range of the urban landscape or with regard to selected features of it. Gordon Cullen's *Townscape* (Architectural Press, 1961), for example, is an analysis and demonstration of the elements which make up the urban environment generally, followed by eight studies of individual towns with proposals for infusing life into ten individual urban areas, the whole illustrated with excellent photographs and thumbnail sketches. Gordon Logie's *The urban scene* (Faber, 1954) is another example of a thoughtful approach to the appearance of cities. ' This is a book about towns, and in it they are looked at from one particular point of view, their success or failure as pieces of scenery . . . our subject is the beauty and visual character of towns, how it has been achieved in the past and what new forms of beauty we may achieve in the future '. Logie considers first the broad pattern of towns, then the various devices of urbanism—framing, linear perspective, contrast, and so on—and then in turn, urban furnishings, planting, enclosure of space, streets, open space around

422

buildings, and towers, and illustrates his subject matter with photographs from all parts of the world. Another well-illustrated book which demonstrates the visual character of cities is Fran P Hosken's *The language of cities* (New York, Macmillan, 1968) which looks at the texture of grass and stone, the way light and fog affect the look of things, shadows and water and buildings, in other words, the elements as well as the whole pattern of urban form. More predominantly concerned with the built expression of the urban environment are Ewart Johns' *British townscapes* (Edward Arnold, 1965) and Steen Eiler Rasmussen's *Town and buildings* (Liverpool, Liverpool UP, 1951); while Geoffrey Martin's *The town* (Vista Books, 1961) goes rather wider in that it embraces the human as well as the physical features of British towns since the Middle Ages. Even a casual observer must notice that the character and the shape of the British urban landscape is undergoing some change, frequently radical change: writers who concentrate primarily on such changes usually do so from the point of view of their deleterious effect on the urban aesthetic. This is certainly true of Thomas Sharp, whose *Town and townscape* (John Murray, 1968) is a look back rather than a look forward, and in examining towns such as Oxford, Durham, Cambridge and others of similar type, he bewails the effects of ' architectural gangsterism ' and ' sad corruption into triviality ' on these towns. In a comparable vein, Ian Nairn's *Britain's changing towns* (BBC, 1967) gives personal impressions of sixteen towns ranging in size from Birmingham to Derry. Rather more sanguine in its hopes for the future is Theo Crosby's *Architecture: city sense* (Studio Vista, 1965), a kind of latter-day Sitte, which ' attempts to synthesise ideas from many sources into a coherent approach to city planning, with the basic assumption that city life is desirable and exciting '. Crosby's hopes for tomorrow are interspersed with photographs and drawings from around the world. Finally, two well-conceived and well-produced books which focus more selectively on specific features of towns. *Man-made America: chaos or control* by Christopher Tunnard and Boris Pushkarev (New Haven, Yale UP, 1963) is concerned with urban aesthetics in general and with, in particular, the problems of low density residential developments, freeways, industry and commerce in the landscape, open space, preservation and conservation. Paul Zucker in *Town and square: from the agora to the village green* (New York, Columbia UP, 1959) is concerned not with the buildings—the volume—but with the void, or the open spaces which the buildings surround, and he traces its development and examines its aesthetics from the acropolis and the agora of ancient Greece to the modern square. These last two books have good bibliographies.

The growth of cities and the progress of urbanisation have been a topic for discussion since the nineteenth century, when Adna Ferrin Weber produced his monumental classic of statistical compilation *The growth of cities in the nineteenth century* (New York, 1899; Ithaca, Cornell Reprints in Urban Studies, 1963) proving conclusively the relationship between industrial growth and the growth of cities, and demonstrating that urbanisation had been one of the most characteristic and universal features of the nineteenth century. The growth of urbanisation is well demonstrated in the example of the United States. Blake McKelvey has chronicled the process in two volumes, *The urbanisation of America (1860-1915)* (New York, Rutgers UP, 1963) and *The emergence of metropolitan America (1915-66)* (New York, Rutgers UP, 1969), probably the best introduction available to the organisation of America's cities; the major themes of both volumes are synthesised in a shorter volume by the same author, *The city in American history* (Allen and Unwin, 1969), the second half of which consists of a series of book extracts, government reports, and articles which illustrate these themes. Lewis Mumford is one American writer who sees continued urban growth as almost unrelieved gloom : ' the continued expansion of the metropolis into the formless megalopolitan conurbation, and the multiplication and extension of these conurbations reveal the depth of the plight every society now faces . . . .'[62] Mumford's *City development: studies in disintegration and renewal* (Secker and Warburg, 1946) is a collection of essays named after Patrick Geddes' *City development,* being, according to the author, ' the most representative selections of my work in the field of urbanism during the last quarter century '. The essays range from his youthful analysis of ' The city ' (1922) to his essay criticising the London plan of Abercrombie and Forshaw, first printed in *Architectural review* in 1943. In 1961, Jean Gottmann published his classic study *Megalopolis* of the urbanised north-eastern seaboard of the United States (see the sec-

424

tion on the sub-region and city region) an area which comes close to fulfilling Mumford's gloomy prophecies. Resulting from this study, a conference was held in 1964 at the University of Southern Illinois in honour of Jean Gottmann, the objective of which was to expand on the theme of urban sprawl, the spread of urban development beyond the limits of city boundaries. The proceedings of this conference were published as *Metropolis on the move: geographers look at urban sprawl* edited by Jean Gottmann and R A Harper (New York, John Wiley, 1967). A well-known British statement on urban growth is Peter Self's *Cities in flood* (Faber, second edition 1961), a clear exposition of the problems of the growth of the major conurbations and a solution to them. Self examines the scale of congestion in the big cities, warning against high-density redevelopment as a short-term solution, and describes in detail the experience of dispersal to new towns and expanded towns. Employment is discussed in relation to urban growth and dispersal, and the problem of compensation and betterment is lucidly reviewed. Finally, the planning machinery of central and local government comes under fire. Self is free to criticise, but always supports his arguments well.

In 1967 the Centre for Environmental Studies set up a working group to consider the developing pattern of urbanisation in Britain and to essay a broad brush forecast of what urban Britain will look like around the year 2000. The first fruits of this project are a set of papers by a series of experts such as Peter Willmott, Peter Hall, and Peter Cowan, first published as a complete issue of the journal *Urban studies* 6(3) November 1969 and subsequently issued in book form with the addition of two papers on technology and learning as *Developing patterns of urbanisation* edited by Peter Cowan (Edinburgh, Oliver and Boyd, 1970). The papers are largely exploratory, raising issues of policy and indicating questions for research but setting no goals. The papers themselves, and the issues they raise, were in turn the subject of a small select conference held at the Centre for Environmental Studies in 1969 at which they were discussed by the members of the working group and six invited experts. The verbatim record of the proceedings is available as *Developing patterns of urbanisation* (ces, 1969, ces-ip-10). A comparable American volume is *The future metropolis* edited by Lloyd

425

Rodwin (Constable, 1962), made up of essays first published as a special issue of *Daedalus* in 1961. This is a collection of speculative descriptions of the form and character of the huge urban complexes with populations of twenty million and more, in which most of the world's population may be living in fifty years time, and ways of controlling their growth. Urbanisation, of course, is not a phenomenon confined to Britain or the United States—it is one which is endemic the world over; and during the last decade or so the United Nations has become increasingly concerned with questions and problems raised by urban growth, especially in the developing countries of the world. Papers contributed to a United Nations seminar in Pittsburgh in 1966 on the theme ' Development policies and planning in relation to urbanisation ' form the basis of *International social development review no 1*,[63] issued by the United Nations' Department of Economic and Social Affairs under the title *Urbanisation: development policies and planning* (New York, UN, 1968). Two papers on demographic aspects of urban growth and population distribution provide the demographic background and statistical data relevant to the subject; four papers then outline the particular urbanisation problems of the developing regions of the world; then follow five papers on economic, social and physical aspects of urbanisation policies and planning, including a comparison of the approach to urban programmes in the US and the USSR. A final paper deals with slums and shanty towns.

British towns and cities collectively form the focus of two notable studies. The earlier, *The conurbations of Great Britain* by T W Freeman (Manchester, Manchester UP, second edition 1966) is a comprehensive and readable account of the urban areas of Britain: lack of definition of the term conurbation leads to the inclusion of most of the urban areas of the country. In fact, the book is a descriptive review of the larger towns in many of their aspects—site and situation, growth, communication patterns, population, administrative divisions, and land use patterns. The second edition is brought up to date with material from the 1961 census and census of distribution. The second study is by C A Moser and Wolf Scott, *British towns: a statistical study of their social and economic differences* (Edinburgh, Oliver and Boyd, 1961, Centre for Urban Studies Report 2). This contains the results of a Centre for Urban Studies study called 'Urban typology' aimed at identifying and relating urban characteristics in such a way that towns, and perhaps regions, could be 'typed' into fairly distinct groups. An examination of all British towns with populations in 1951 of over 50,000, in terms of demographic, economic and social features—a total of sixty variables in all—results in a classification of towns and a methodology for tracing the interdependence of the characteristics of various towns. On a world scale, Peter Hall has made a study of *The world cities* (Weidenfeld and Nicolson, 1966, World University Library). 'There are certain great cities, in which a quite disproportionate part of the world's most important business is conducted. In 1915 the pioneer thinker and writer on city and regional planning, Patrick Geddes, christened them the world cities. This book is about their growth and problems'. In the early 1960's, there were twenty four metropolitan centres in the world each with a population of over three million: Hall's book takes seven of them—London, Paris, the Dutch Randstad, the Rhine-Ruhr complex, Moscow, New York, and Tokyo—and analyses their growth, their problems and their respective solutions to the problems. There is a good annotated bibliography. Rather different urban problems are encountered in a developing continent like Africa. Some of these are discussed in *The city in modern Africa* edited by Horace Miner (Pall Mall Press, 1967), papers given to a conference on methods and objectives of urban research in Africa in Virginia, April 1965, which collectively form a group of multi-disciplinary studies of African cities.

For studies of individual towns and cities in Britain, the handbooks published for the annual meetings of the British Association for the Advancement of Science form a notable library of urban analyses. The meetings usually take place in a provincial city with a university, and the handbooks are concerned with the description and analysis of the city and of its surrounding region, often by subject specialists from the university concerned. The most recent volume is that for the 1970 meeting held in Durham; previous meetings have been held in, for example, Exeter, Southampton and Nottingham. An independent study of a small provincial town is Margaret Stacey's *Tradition and change: a study of Banbury* (Oxford UP, second edition 1970).

London has inevitably been the focus of a good deal of attention, from experts from many disciplines. Two comprehensive studies are outstanding. *London: aspects of change* (Macgibbon and Kee, 1964) emanates from the Centre for Urban Studies, and is a symposium covering the full spectrum of urban life deriving from a seminar on social studies relating to London which met regularly from March 1956 to January 1959. The seminar was convened—as Ruth Glass explains in her introduction—'for the purpose of bringing together specialists from different disciplines of the social sciences and allied fields who had a common interest in research into the growth, habitat and society of London'. The volume is in four parts. In the first, three papers examine features of metropolitan growth; in the second, the contemporary scene is examined in two papers by John Westergaard and William Holford; the third is concerned with new communities, and includes the well-known study by Westergaard and Ruth Glass of Lansbury, a neighbourhood in Poplar, 'the first outstanding example of comprehensive reconstruction in the metropolis'; finally, in a section on segments of London, the Irish and Polish settlements are discussed. *Greater London* edited by J T Coppock and Hugh C Prince (Faber, 1964) is a well-documented and well-illustrated volume, the theme of which is 'the growth and character of contemporary London, as seen through the eyes of a group of geographers'. The various chapters consider the physical environment, the growth of London since the beginning of the railway age, the principal aspects of London's economy, and the surrounding countryside, with a final chapter by Coppock on the future of the city. In the United States, New York was the subject of one of the most comprehensive city studies ever, conducted between 1956 and 1961 by the Graduate School of Public Administration at Harvard University and published under the collective title *New York metropolitan region study* (Cambridge, Mass, Harvard UP, 1959-61). There are nine volumes, as follows. *Anatomy of a metropolis* by Edgar Hoover and Raymond Vernon (1959); *Made in New York* by Roy B Helfgott and others (1959); *The newcomers* by Oscar Handlin (1959); *Wages in the metropolis* by Martin Segal (1960); *Money metropolis* by Sidney M Robbins and Nestor E Terleckyj (1960); *Freight and the metropolis* by Benjamin Chinitz (1960); *One-tenth of a nation* by Robert M Lichtenberg (1960); *1,400 governments* by Robert C Wood (1961);

and *Metropolis 1985 by* Raymond Vernon (1960). There is also a technical supplement containing the economic projection to 1985: *Projection of a metropolis* by Barbara R Berman and others (1960).

We turn now to urban studies proper, and firstly to urban history. 'The literature of town planning is becoming more sociological' claims H J Dyos, 'and it is not surprising that the history no less than the present problems of urban society should be recognised more and more as one of the major pre-occupations of the social sciences.'[64] The main wellspring of urban history in Britain is the University of Leicester, where, in 1966, an international round-table conference of the Urban History Group was held: the proceedings of this conference, *The study of urban history* edited by H J Dyos (Edward Arnold, 1968) constitute an authoritative report on work in progress in urban research (a report which is kept up to date in the University's *Urban history newsletter*).

There are basically two themes in the volume: the materials and methods of urban history, and the comparative study of British cities. The volume begins with two very useful state of the art surveys of urban research activity, in Britain and in France: the first of these, by H J Dyos, entitled 'Agenda for urban historians' is an extended bibliographical review of the methods and scope of urban historical studies. The second group of papers concentrates on methods and sources of data—census sources, computerising census data, the use of town plans, sources and methods used for the survey of London; the third group is made up of macro- and microstudies. Finally, the conference looked towards a definition of urban history: almost as difficult to define as other things urban. As Dyos observes, 'though we would probably all agree that urban history does not comprise everything that happened in towns in the past, we would not agree so easily about what to leave out, nor how to interpret what is put in '.[65]

The Victorian age was contemporaneously considered to be the age of great cities. Certainly the period saw the rapid and mostly unplanned expansion of many urban areas. These are ' the cities of the railway and the tramway age, of the age of steam and of gas, of a society sometimes restless, sometimes complacent, moving, often fumblingly and falteringly, towards greater democracy. The building of the cities was a characteristic Victorian achievement, impressive in scale but limited in vision, creating new opportunities but also providing massive new problems.'[66] H J Dyos has reviewed some of the writing on the cities of this period in an article ' The growth of cities in the nineteenth century: a review of some recent writing ' in *Victorian studies* 9(3) March 1966 225-237. An authoritative and very readable account of the period is given in *Victorian cities* by Asa Briggs (Odhams Press, 1963; Harmondsworth, Penguin Books, revised edition 1968). Briggs sets the background to the growth of urbanisation and examines the general climate of opinion and the styles of life engendered by this growth before embarking on a detailed study of Manchester, Leeds, Birmingham, Middlesbrough, London, and, from overseas, Melbourne in Australia. Briggs refers to the lack of a good general history of London in the nineteenth century despite the obvious importance of the subject. The English provinces, on the other hand, have had some attention: S G Checkland, for example, discussed questions of provincialism in the context of a review of the *History of Birmingham* in ' English provincial cities ' in *Economic history review* second series 6(2) August 1953 195-203; and in *The English provinces c. 1760-1960: a study in influence* (Edward Arnold, 1964) Donald Read provides a detailed study of the origin of the provinces as an entity of ' England outside London ' in the Industrial Revolution, their development and influence through the nineteenth century, and their declining influence and role in the twentieth. A study of suburban development is given by H J Dyos in *Victorian suburb: a study of the growth of Camberwell* (Leicester, Leicester UP, 1961). One of the major factors in Victorian urbanisation was the railway. As Asa Briggs points out, ' the automobile age separates our own urban experience from the Victorian urban experience just as surely as the coming of the railway separated the Victorian age from earlier ages . . . Railway building led to drastic changes, usually in the poorer parts of the cities . . . If railways were symbols of progress, all too often the railway embankment became a symbol of the ruthless terror of the mid-Victorian city . . .'[67] In *The impact of railways on Victorian cities* (Routledge and Kegan Paul, 1969) J R Kellett investigates this whole railway influence; firstly, he examines how the railways came and encroached on the cities, then he provides case studies of Birmingham, Manchester, Liverpool, Glasgow, and London, and finally he looks at the effects of the railway on different sectors of the city—city centre, inner districts, and suburbs.

The best introduction to urban history in the United States is Charles N Glaab's 'The historian and the city: a bibliographic survey' in *The study of urbanisation* edited by Philip M Hauser and Leo F Schnore (see below), an American parallel to Dyos' 'Agenda for urban historians' in *The study of urban history*. Professor Glaab is the present editor of the American Urban History Group *Newsletter* which has been a stimulus to the subject since it was started within the ranks of the American Historical Association in 1954. Other sources are Eric Lampard's 'American historians and the study of urbanisation' in *American historical review* 67(1) October 1961 49-61; and the proceedings of a conference held in 1961 to consider the city in history and published as *The historian and the city* edited by Oscar Handlin and John Burchard (Cambridge, Mass, MIT Press, 1963), one of a series published under the auspices of the Joint Center for Urban Studies of MIT and Harvard University.

The beginning of the study of cities from a scientific point of view occurred in Germany in the nineteenth and early twentieth centuries, where pioneers from Von Thünen to Christaller laid down the basis of a theory of location and studied the patterns of urban settlements within a region (see the section on regional planning). Germany was also the home of a pioneer work of urban sociology, Max Weber's *The city,* translated and edited by Don Martindale and Gertrude Neuwirth (Heinemann, 1958), first published in 1921. But it was in Chicago in the 1920's that Robert Park and Ernest Burgess began their studies of the internal structure of the city and the patterns of human life therein which later flowered as the great Chicago school of urban sociology before and during World War II. Park, Burgess, and Roderick McKenzie were the 'founding fathers' of urban sociology: not only did they study the workings of the city, they mounted a live project, based on the Department of Sociology at the University of Chicago, in the 1930's —the Chicago area project—which aimed to bring community development to the city's north side slums. Their collected theoretical statements were published in the classic volume *The city*

431

(Chicago, Chicago UP, 1925; new edition with introduction by Morris Janowitz, 1968). Janowitz, commenting on the place of Park, Burgess and McKenzie in urban sociology, observes that 'these men were fascinated with the complexities of the urban community and the prospect of discovering patterns of regularity in its apparent confusion . . . They did not produce definitive answers, but they posed crucial questions which still dominate the thinking of urban sociologists.' The next decade saw two further important statements from American sociologists. One was Lewis Mumford's vast work *The culture of cities* (Secker and Warburg, 1938) in which the development of cities is traced from the Dark Ages through the 'insensate industrial town', 'the rise and fall of megalopolis', an investigation of the 'regional framework of civilisation' and 'the politics of regional development' to an analysis of the 'social basis of the new urban order'. Mumford's ideas inspired a whole generation of British planners; indeed, Ruth Glass observes that 'when British planners speak of " sociology " they refer usually to this book . . . So far their thoughts on the " social aspects " of urbanism have been conditioned primarily by Ebenezer Howard and Lewis Mumford.'[68] Though it is as well to note that Mumford's ideas had progressed and in some respects altered by the time he wrote *The city in history* (see the section on planning: history). The second notable statement was that of Louis Wirth, a distinguished Chicago sociologist, which was contained in 'Urbanism as a way of life' in *American journal of sociology* 44(1) July 1938 1-24. 'In Wirth's theory, three concepts—size, density, and heterogeneity—were taken to be the key features of the city. These key features were then related to each other by a set of propositions, setting out the conditions under which a large, dense, heterogeneous aggregate of people might be expected to cooperate enough to maintain the complex organisation of the city.'[69] This classic paper, together with others of Wirth's output are collected together and edited with an introduction by A J Reiss as *On cities and social life* (Chicago, Chicago UP, 1964). Wirth's essay is also the subject of a detailed analysis by R N Morris in *Urban sociology* (Allen and Unwin, 1968), in which the theory is examined in the context of pre-industrial cities, industrial cities, and bureaucracies.

There has been no strong tradition of urban sociology in Britain comparable to that of the United States. Ruth Glass wrote in 1955 about the British tradition of 'anti-urbanism' and remarked that 'the absence of any general British texts on urbanism . . . is undoubtedly in keeping with the native dislike of towns'.[70] Ten years later, her view was corroborated by Peter Mann, in whose view 'British urban sociology, itself a comparatively neglected field, tends to be greatly tied up with social policy, town planning and various aspects of social work. If urban sociology is worthy of the name sociology it should be more than any of these, even though it may well include such details within its purview';[71] and most recently by R E Pahl who asserts that 'Britain is physically as urbanised as any nation in the world, yet as a society we seem to be extraordinarily reluctant to accept this fact. How else can the dearth of books on urbanism and urbanisation in Britain be explained . . . Students of the subject in this country learn more about Chicago than Glasgow or Birmingham.'[72] Ruth Glass, herself one of the foremost British sociologists and director of the Centre for Urban Studies in London, was the author of 'Urban sociology in Great Britain: a trend report' which appeared in *Current sociology* 4(4) June 1955 5-76, consisting of a state of the art survey followed by a classified and annotated bibliography; the survey is reprinted without the bibliography in *Readings in urban sociology* edited by R E Pahl (see below). This is an excellent summary of urban studies as at 1955 (a revision is said to be in progress). Glass refers to the difficulty of defining the city and therefore urban sociology: 'Urbanism as a whole, like each large city, is an entity of which we are acutely aware, though we cannot unanimously trace its boundaries, nor transfix its individuality'. After discussing the scope of urban studies, she traces the development of sociological studies concerned with urbanism from the mid-nineteenth century to the time of writing; she is critical of the current lack of policy-orientation in social investigation—'six social workers in search of a theme'—and of the desire to 're-investigate the ABC of social knowledge or the trivial trimmings of social institutions'. She is critical also of the contribution of town planners to the study of urbanism—'town planning has thus been mainly the field of the amateurs in sociology'. The bibliography, which forms the major part of the survey, indicates the documented background of British

433

urban social studies, and has the additional aim of channelling future research in two directions, firstly into patterns of urban growth and patterns of life in contemporary towns, secondly into the growth of British thinking, individual and collective, on urbanism. Since this survey was written, two writers have in some measure redeemed the situation. The first of these was Peter H Mann, whose *An approach to urban sociology* (Routledge and Kegan Paul, 1965) is the only available comprehensive British text on the subject, and was written with the aim of introducing 'an element of theoretical consideration into the study of urbanism in contemporary Britain'. Mann examines in detail, both descriptively and quantitatively, the different concepts of urban and rural life, and then moves to an analysis of urbanism and urban society using the criteria of ecology, social organisation, and the ethos of the community. Detailed chapters on the control of urban growth and the neighbourhood unit within the city lead up to an attempt to establish a theoretical concept of urban sociology, based on the works of well-known sociologists. More recently, Dr Ray Pahl has produced a short work *Patterns of urban life* (Longmans, 1970, The Social Structure of Modern Britain 9), a concise and cogent discussion of a diffuse subject. It has been described as a 'mini-textbook' but in fact is a selective rather than a systematic treatment which provides a stimulating introduction to a wide field of interest. It considers preindustrial urbanism and the emergence of industrial urbanism, both with case studies, before embarking on the main subject which is the relationships between social and spatial structure in Britain today. There are many case studies throughout, and a useful guide to further reading.

In his penultimate chapter, Pahl looks at the ideology of town planning in the context of social engineering and examines the possible contribution of sociology to planning. This theme is followed in three University Working Papers issued by the Centre for Environmental Studies in 1970 under the collective title *Urban sociology and planning*. uwp-5 *Urban social theory and research* is by Pahl himself. uwp-6 is by J Musil, and considers *Examples of sociological research relevant to planning problems in some European countries*. uwp-7 is on *Sociology of planning and urban growth* and is by Harry Gracey.

Writings on many and various aspects of urbanism, urban sociology, and urban studies generally have proliferated in the last few decades, and there has been as a result a corresponding burgeoning of readers in the field, originating principally in the United States. Of special merit is *Cities and society: the revised reader in urban sociology,* edited by Paul K Hatt and Albert J Reiss (New York, Free Press, 1964), which is a collection of papers by a wide range of authoritative writers—Wirth, Hauser, Chauncy Harris, R E Dickinson, for example—comprising a thorough coverage of the sociology of the city; the volume is well-documented throughout and has also an extensive bibliography. Of equal stature, and a seminal source of study, is *Contributions to urban sociology* edited by E W Burgess and D J Bogue (Chicago, Chicago UP, 1964) which brings together the main results of a selection of doctoral dissertations produced in the Chicago school over the years. Another seminal volume emanating from the Chicago mainspring is *The study of urbanisation* edited by Philip M Hauser and Leo F Schnore (New York, Wiley, 1965), which has already been mentioned as containing a bibliographic survey of American urban history. This volume is not a reader but a collection of papers having their origins in an interdisciplinary conference held in 1958 by the American Social Science Research Council, and embracing representatives of economics, geography, history, political science, social anthropology, and sociology. It falls into three parts. The first is concerned with the study of urbanisation in the social sciences, and reviews the literature and identifies the basic problems of urbanisation as considered by the various disciplines; the second focuses on current research into urban situations; while the third picks out some areas for future research. The contents are fragmented and specialised, but the whole is a stimulating and provocative volume. It is the subject of a detailed review by Asa Briggs in *Urban Studies* 4(2) June 1967 165-169. More recently, a British reader has joined the ranks: *Readings in urban sociology* edited by R E Pahl (Oxford, Pergamon Press, 1968), the purpose of the volume being to bring together important papers covering a wide range of topics, from many countries, which are not easily accessible in their original form: some of the contributions are by no means new, for example, Ruth Glass's review of 1955, discussed above. Pahl is also the author of all but two of the papers collected in *Whose city? and other essays on sociology and planning* (Longman, 1970), previously published papers on a variety of subjects, collectively forming a view of Pahl's contribution to urban sociology so far, expressed in a concern for real, practical problems. A reader which is totally the work of one writer is *The urban scene: human ecology and demography* by Leo F Schnore (New York, Free Press, 1965), which is made up of papers reprinted from various journals over a period of ten years. Schnore, one of the major researchers and writers on the subject in the United States, defines the scope and limits of human ecology and demography, arguing that human ecology 'represents one effort to deal with *the central problem of sociological analysis*' (author's italics) and that demography 'must be regarded as an approach that is broader than the simple analysis of fertility, mortality, and migration'. In the light of this, Schnore goes on to examine metropolitan growth and decentralisation, suburbs, socioeconomic status of cities and suburbs, racial composition of metropolitan areas, and finally urban transportation.

'It is interesting to note that, while literature in Britain on urbanism *per se* is difficult to find, writings on the neighbourhood are by no means scarce . . . These studies are in essence studies of social reform and amelioration. The emphasis on the slum and the council estate has left the literature practically bare of studies of middle class privately owned housing areas, or upper class housing areas.'[73] Some of these studies have already been mentioned in the section on housing. Others which can perhaps claim to have a wider sociological content are T Young's *Becontree and Dagenham: the story of the growth of a housing estate* (Samuel Sidders, 1934) and its sequel, *The evolution of a community: a study of Dagenham after forty years* by Peter Willmott (Routledge and Kegan Paul, 1963, Institute of Community Studies Report 8). A classic of its kind is *Family and kinship in East London* by Michael Young and Peter Willmott (Routledge and Kegan Paul, 1957, Institute of Community Studies Report 1). Obviously, as Mann points out, 'from the viewpoint of sociological analysis of village, neighbourhood and city, the concept of *community* is the key one'[74] (author's italics). Gordon Cherry, in his chapter on social issues for the town planner in *Town planning in its social context* (see the section on planning in practice) stresses the vital importance of community studies to the concept of planning as an adaptive process concerned with the city as a social system in action. 'Up till now planning has been obsessed with the idea of place: instead, it is argued that the essence of the city and city life is interaction. Urban communities are not merely places but processual systems in which people interact with each other. This assumption gives planning a radically different starting point from previous concepts, and involves the practising planner in a much more fundamental concern for community studies than has so far been recognised.'[75] In this context, studies of communities and of community life and structure from all points of view, social, economic, and political, are clearly of some importance to the planner: macrostudies such as *Dilemmas of social reform: poverty and community action in the United States* by Peter Marris and Martin Rein (Routledge and Kegan Paul, 1967, Institute of Community Studies Report 15) which covers the whole gamut of social ills and their causes in the context of the American programme of community action projects; and microstudies such as the classic studies of Sparkbrook, Birmingham, contained in *Race, community and conflict* by John Rex and R Moore (Oxford UP, 1967), and S Patterson's *Dark strangers: a sociological study of the absorption of a recent West Indian migrant group in Brixton, South London* (Tavistock Publications, 1963), which analyse the problems of the immigrant community and although concentrated on a particular locality nevertheless have wider implications for any urban community with an immigrant population.

The relationship between environment and social disorders has by now been fairly decisively established, and studies such as *Mental health and environment* by Lord Taylor and Sidney Chave (Longmans, 1964) and J B Mays' *Growing up in the city: a study of juvenile delinquency in an urban neighbourhood* (Liverpool, Liverpool UP, 1956) are of value in understanding the implications of such interactions. Sociological studies have been made of different types of locality, for instance new towns, which form the context of Harold Orlans' *Stevenage: a sociological study of a new town* (Routledge and Kegan Paul, 1952). One feature of cities, in which commuting to work plays an increasingly significant part in the determination of urban patterns, is the blurring of division between urban and rural, the lack of a clear line where urban ends and rural begins, and this has resulted in rural-urban fringe zones in which rural and urban land uses and social characteristics are mixed. This type of fringe was the subject of an early American study, *The rural-urban fringe: a study of adjustment to residence location* by Walter T Martin (Eugene, Oregon, University of Oregon Press, 1953) which is a study of personal reactions to urban-rural life carried out in 1949 in the fringe area shared by Eugene and Springfield, in Oregon. In Britain, Ray Pahl studied the effects of urbanisation on a rural area of Hertfordshire in *Urbs in rure: the metropolitan fringe in Hertfordshire* (London School of Economics, 1965, Geographical Papers 2) based on his PHD thesis to the University of London, a thoroughly documented essay with a separate bibliography.

The suburb has also been a focus of much attention, mainly in the United States, though, as Herbert Gans has pointed out, less than responsible reports and a flood of popular fiction relating to the American suburb have created the ' myth of suburbia ' in which the suburb is seen as the destroyer of community life and the seat of urban spiritual poverty.[76] Serious studies, such as Willmott and Young's *Family and class in a London suburb* (Routledge and Kegan Paul, 1960, Institute of Community Studies Report 4) have proved that in reality suburban communities do exist in an organised form and that suburbia does not dissolve family ties. Such findings are corroborated by Herbert Gans' well-known study *The Levittowners: ways of life and politics in a new suburban community* (Allen Lane, The Penguin Press, 1967), a meticulously detailed sociological analysis based on a study of a single new commuter suburb, Levittown, New Jersey, the prototype of post-war suburban development in the United States. Gans examines the origin of the community, the quality of life within it, its politics, and the effects of suburbia on its inhabitants; and concludes from the evidence that basic life-styles are not changed by a move to the suburbs, and that the changes which do occur are those that were expected or desired as a result of moving from the city centre outwards. *Crestwood Heights: a study of the culture of suburban life* by J R Seeley and others (New York, Wiley, 1956) is a study of an inner suburban area of Toronto which was mounted as a

438

mental health project, its emphasis being on children, education, and socialisation. Other serious studies of suburbia are *The suburban community* edited by William M Dobriner (New York, Putnam, 1958), a collection of papers providing analyses of the suburbs by demographers, economists, social commentators, and a wide spectrum of sociologists; Bennett M Berger's *Working class suburb* (Berkeley, University of California Press, 1960) a study of a suburb inhabited principally by industrial workers; and Suzanne Keller's *The urban neighbourhood: a sociological perspective* (New York, Random House, 1968) an analysis of urban neighbourhood community life drawing extensively on British and American studies.

It has already been mentioned that a positive relationship exists between man and his environment, that his environment exerts an influence, whether for good or ill, upon him. Environment in this sense is not confined to the physical, built environment but embraces a much wider concept of social, political and economic as well as physical. The scientific study of human beings in relation to this environment is known as human ecology. Ecology has become one of the overworked words of 1970, with consequent loss of clarity of definition. Roderick McKenzie, the founder, with Park and Burgess, of the Chicago school of urban sociology, defined the subject thus in his essay ' The ecological approach to the study of the human community ' in *The city* (see above): ' Human ecology is fundamentally interested in the effect of position in both time and space upon human institutions and human behaviour ', where position is defined as ' the place relation of a given community to other communities, also the location of the individual or institution within the community itself '. A collection of McKenzie's writings on ecology dating from between 1921 and 1936 has been published under the title *On human ecology* (Chicago, Chicago UP, 1968). The contents are amazingly valid considering their age : the re-issue of the papers demonstrates not only the continuing authority of McKenzie but also how slowly the science has developed since he conducted his pioneering studies. Other volumes which cover much the same ground as McKenzie's essays are *Human ecology: a theory of community structure* by Amos H Hawley (New York, Ronald Press, 1950); D J Bogue's *Structure of the metropolitan community: a study of dominance and sub-dominance* (Ann Arbor, Michigan UP,

1949); and two collections of papers by various authorities, *Human communities* edited by Robert E Park (Glencoe, Illinois, Free Press, 1952) and *Studies in human ecology* edited by G A Theodorson (Evanston, Illinois, Harper and Row, 1961).

Environment is not the sole preserve of ecologists and sociologists: Griffith Taylor points out that, in addition, 'the peculiar province of the geographer is to interpret the relation between man and his environment ',[77] and in the context of towns and cities this is the province of urban geography. There is indeed some degree of overlap between urban geography and human ecology in that both are interested in the structure and the pattern of land uses within an urban settlement: this aspect of urban geography could be said to be coincident with the spatial aspects of ecological analysis. On the central theme of urban geography there are two British texts which give a full coverage, although their approaches are different. The earliest of these is Griffith Taylor's *Urban geography: a study of site, evolution, pattern and classification in villages, towns and cities* (Methuen, second revised edition 1951). Taylor starts by examining general features such as the effect of latitude on settlements; then traces the historical evolution of urban settlement from primitive and asiatic towns to the modern city typified by London and New York; finally analysing types of town classified by topographic and other controls, such as river towns, mountain towns, mining towns, and religious centres. James H Johnson adopts a different approach in *Urban geography: an introductory analysis* (Oxford, Pergamon Press, 1967) which covers a broad field from the historic growth of urban settlements to theories of urban form. Between these poles, there are concise accounts of different functional areas of the western city and of the size and location of cities within regions. The whole is a well-written, well-presented outline, backed with useful reading lists. A long and detailed study of the physical structure of towns in western Europe, excluding Great Britain, forms the substance of R E Dickinson's *The west European city: a geographical interpretation* (Routledge and Kegan Paul, second edition 1961, International Library of Sociology and Social Reconstruction). The first part deals with individual towns, from the small historic towns of France to modern capitals such as Paris and Berlin, and the second part reviews the morphology of the urban habitat in general from medieval towns up to World War II, ending with the components of modern urbanism and urbanisation.

The British gap is partially filled by Harold Carter with *The towns of Wales* (Cardiff, University of Wales Press, 1965) which describes, in three sections, the development of the urban network in Wales, the contemporary functions of Welsh towns, and the morphology of the towns. Also useful is *The geography of towns* by Arthur E Smailes (Hutchinson, fifth revised edition 1966) which, like Johnson's book, starts from the origin of towns and the bases of urban development, going on to towns in their physical setting, characteristics of towns, the morphology of urban regions, the development of the town structure, and the town in its regional setting. Emrys Jones' *Towns and cities* (Oxford UP, 1966) is a slighter book which follows yet another pattern, first attempting a definition of the town, and then studying the progress of urbanisation through pre-industrial cities and the modern western city with some discussion of the size and classification of cities, going on to the city in its regional setting and concluding with a consideration of the human society which inhabits the city. An excellent collection of papers by forty eight authorities, mainly geographers, from various countries is brought together in *Readings in urban geography* edited by Harold M Mayer and Clyde F Kohn (Chicago, Chicago UP, 1959), which largely reflects American work in this field up to the mid-1950's. The second contribution to the volume is a bibliographical study by Robert E Dickinson, ' The scope and status of urban geography: an assessment ', which ' attempts to sum up the general trend in concepts and techniques in urban geography as revealed in a very considerable literature over the last fifty years, and especially in the interwar period '.

Urban sociology and urban geography have been much concerned to establish common characteristics by which typologies of cities can be distinguished. The study of *British towns* by Moser and Scott (see above) is essentially an attempt to identify groups of towns with common or similar features. The pre-industrial city was the subject of a similar attempt by Gideon Sjoberg in *The pre-industrial city past and present* (Glencoe, Illinois, Free Press, 1960), the thesis being that the pre-industrial city forms a ' distinct form which is

441

repeated in a wide range of cultures, areas and times '.[78] Sjoberg's book has been the subject of a good deal of controversy, and his theories are criticised by, among others, R E Pahl in *Patterns of urban life* (see above). The internal structure of the city has also been a subject of concern, and of repeated efforts to establish the patterns of specialised land uses within the city. As Johnson indicates, 'it can also be sensed that there is repetition in the geographical arrangement of these different areas, reflecting such factors as land values, accessibility and the history of urban growth. As a result a number of theories have been devised which attempt to generalise about the management of land use regions within a typical city.'[79]

The first such theory was Ernest Burgess' concentric theory, first put forward in 1924 and reprinted in *The city* (see above) as ' The growth of the city ' in 1925, thus achieving much wider circulation. Burgess' theory of concentric zones was based on his analysis of Chicago and rests on the premise that the development of a city takes place in an outward direction from its central business area in a series of concentric zones. Burgess' theory was followed by the sector theory of Homer Hoyt, who advanced his ideas in *The structure and growth of residential neighbourhoods in American cities* (Washington, 1939; reprinted Washington, Homer Hoyt Associates, 1968). This is a classic study of the American suburb. On the basis of data relating to a wide range of cities, Hoyt develops generalisations firstly about the structures of cities, then about their growth and the movement of the high rent sector, from which he develops his sector theory of residential urban structure which, while based on a circular concept, sees the growth of a city as being wedge shaped rather than in concentric rings. Peter Mann in *An approach to urban sociology* (see above) combines the sector and the concentric theories in a ' model ' for application to British towns. An elaboration of previous structural theories was presented by Chauncy D Harris and Edward L Ullman in a paper ' The nature of cities ' in *Annals of the American Academy of Political and Social Science* 242 November 1945 7-17, reprinted in *Readings in urban geography* edited by Mayer and Kohn (see above). Harris and Ullman propose the multiple nuclei theory which sees urban growth as cellular, with distinctive types of land use developing around growth points, or nuclei, within the urban area. Two years later,

442

Walter Firey published the results of his studies of a district of Boston, *Land use in central Boston* (Cambridge, Mass, Harvard UP, 1947) which propounded no new theory but emphasised the importance of the role of social forces in shaping the pattern of land use. More recently, the advent of computers has made the handling of large quantities of data about the city feasible, and extremely complex analyses can be carried out using advanced statistical techniques. Brian Robson's *Urban analysis: a study of city structure with special reference to Sunderland* (Cambridge, Cambridge UP, 1969) is a major contribution to the factor analytic study of urban spatial structure and ecology, focusing on the social ecology of Sunderland (population about 200,000). Robson reviews the literature of urban spatial structure—the familiar parade from Burgess onwards—and then embarks upon his highly technical factor analysis of thirty variables covering social composition, age structure, household tenure, and so on, over, in the case of the whole city, 263 enumeration districts. A comparable study to Robson's emanating from North America is Robert Murdie's *Factorial ecology of metropolitan Toronto 1951-1961: an essay in the social geography of a city* (Chicago, Chicago University Department of Geography, 1969, Research Papers 116). Murdie's opening literature review covers much the same ground as Robson's. His subject, however, is larger; metropolitan Toronto has a population of about 1,600,000, and the data cover up to 109 variables for two periods, 1951 and 1961, for between 235 and 277 census tracts. Again, the value of the work lies in its descriptive analysis of the ecology of a single city. An earlier survey of the literature can be found in Elizabeth Gittus' paper 'The structure of urban areas; a new approach' in *Town planning review* 35(1) April 1964 5-20, which also embodies suggestions for a new approach to the subject. A general reader is Melvin M Webber's *Explorations into urban structure* (Philadelphia, University of Pennsylvania Press, 1964), with contributions by Donald Foley, Webber, William Wheaton, Albert Guttenberg, and John Dyckman.

VILLAGE AND RURAL PLANNING, AND STUDIES

Village planning and rural planning are by no means synonymous. The village is a small urban settlement, no less, and village planning

443

as we are concerned with it here is methods of practical planning which are specifically related to such small urban settlements. Rural planning is something much wider, being frequently referred to now as rural resource planning, and is concerned with planning the resources of land which are not in use for urban purposes : it therefore involves the planning of the countryside for leisure and recreation, for forestry, for agriculture, and for many other purposes. These wider issues are dealt with in subsequent sections of this chapter; what we are concerned with here is the older and narrower concept of country planning, as opposed to town planning, as an identified single entity. Also included are the rural equivalent of urban studies, studies of villages and of the characteristics of village life, and the wider issues of rural sociology.

The first step towards a national policy for comprehensive planning of rural areas was the establishment of a Committee on Land Utilisation in Rural Areas by the government in the early 1940's which in 1942 produced the well-known Scott Report (HMSO, 1942, Cmnd 6378). The terms of reference of the committee were ' to consider the conditions which should govern building and other constructional development in country areas consistently with the maintenance of agriculture, and in particular the factors affecting the location of industry, having regard to economic operation, part-time and seasonal employment, the well-being of rural communities and the preservation of rural amenities '. The committee was, as Peter Mann points out, ' by its terms of reference, preservative rather than initiatory ',[80] but its recommendations laid the foundation for a national policy of planning and preserving the countryside including the setting up of national parks and nature reserves, and ensuring that all people had access to the amenities of the countryside. The Scott Report, and its relevance to present conditions and requirements, is discussed by G P Wibberley in a paper called ' The changing rural economy of Britain ' in *Report of the Town and Country Planning Summer School, Exeter, 1964* (TPI, 1964). The most comprehensive recent text on the subject of rural planning is *Modern agriculture and rural planning* by John Weller (Architectural Press, 1967), a well-illustrated book with a useful (though not exhaustive) bibliography, which argues for a thorough planning policy for rural land use in the light of current developments in agriculture, an industry which occupies a large portion of Britain's rural land (see the section on land use). The first part of the book contains a summary of the development of agriculture and of rural planning; the second part deals with the use and economics of rural land; and the third part discusses some significant trends in modern agriculture which have a clear implication for the industry's requirement and use of land.

Rural planning is concerned not only with the use of the land but with the pattern and functional size of rural or village settlements. In this connection rural depopulation has had severe effects, leaving villages in some cases deprived of virtually an entire population or at least of its younger stratum. This being the case, as Cherry stresses, ' except where a distinct hierarchy of rural settlements can be established and larger focal points enhanced as service centres, local authority investment tends to be very thinly spread, with consequent effects on health, education and welfare services '.[81] This is much the same argument as that of R J Green in a paper ' The remote countryside: a plan for contraction ' in *Planning outlook* new series 1 December 1966 17-37, in which he examines the problems of the countryside and rural communities, particularly in Norfolk, and proposes progressive redistribution of rural settlements into more viable units, and the establishment of an executive committee to carry out the plans of the local planning authority in these areas. The Ministry of Housing and Local Government has also proffered advice on this problem in Planning Bulletin 8 *Settlement in the countryside* (HMSO, 1967) which ' outlines a staged process of formulating policy and preparing settlement plans in the light of information currently available '. The bulletin is the subject of criticism in the ' current practice and research ' section of *JTPI* 53(10) December 1967 474-475, where it is suggested that the more progressive authorities have advanced beyond the Ministry's recommended practice and that the publications of rural authorities such as Cambridgeshire and Huntingdonshire are more useful as practical guides.

Rural problems and planning are not confined to any one country, and some comparative information is to be found in a publication of the National Council of Social Service entitled *People in the countryside: studies in rural social development* (NCSS, 1966), which is a report based on the work of the United Nations European Study Group held at Beaumont Hall, University of Leicester, in 1963. This is not a verbatim report of the proceedings, but a discussion of the most important problems supplemented by case studies from various countries. Problems discussed are urbanisation and the countryside, development problems in rural areas, rural policies in northern Europe and in southern Europe; the case studies are from France, West Germany, Eire, Israel, Italy, the Netherlands, Sweden, and Yugoslavia.

On the practical problems of planning as applied to villages, there is little guidance. The Ministry of Housing and Local Government's *Design in town and village* (HMSO, 1953, out of print) contains three separate sections one of which, by Thomas Sharp, deals with ' Villages '. Quite recently, the Civic Trust for the North West has produced a pilot manual of townscape design, *Cheshire villages: an environmental vocabulary* (Manchester, Civic Trust for the North West, 1969) which gives guidance on such aspects as street furniture, shop fronts, garages, fences and highway surfaces.

Rural areas require thorough survey before planning in just the same way as more populous areas do. At about the same time as the Scott Committee was compiling its report, the Agricultural Economics Research Institute at Oxford was carrying out an investigation into a methodology for such a rural survey. *Country planning: a study of rural problems* edited by C S Orwin (Oxford UP, 1944) embodies the findings of their experimental survey designed to test the method and the scope of an inquiry which would provide a basis for country planning, the survey having been done in 1943 in an area of about 15,000 acres of a south midland county. This was an economic and social survey ' planned to establish the facts of the countryman's life, to point out their consequences, to compare them with conditions, as established, in the lives of other sections of the community . . . '. To fulfil these requirements ' the life of the countryman, as exemplified by conditions in the survey area, has been followed from the prenatal clinic to the old-age pension—his education, his adolescence and employment, his housing, health, citizenship, social life, and recreations '.

Many writers have studied the English village in most of its aspects, the pioneer in this respect being Thomas Sharp whose *The*

446

anatomy of the village (Harmondsworth, Penguin Books, 1944) has become a minor classic of its kind. Other writers on the same topic are W P Baker, whose *The English village* (Oxford UP, 1953, Home University Library) analyses village life, its work, community structure and institutions, church and chapel, education, and government; and E W Martin, author of *The secret people: English village life after 1750* (Phoenix House, 1954) ' being an account of English village people, their lives, work and development through a period of two hundred years '. Most recently, a different approach has been adopted by Paul Jennings, whose *The living village: a report on rural life in England and Wales* (Hodder and Stoughton, 1968) presents a composite picture of contemporary rural life drawn from scrapbooks compiled in villages throughout the country by the villagers themselves. More sociological in nature is *English rural life: village activities, organisations and institutions* by H E Bracey (Routledge and Kegan Paul, 1959, International Library of Sociology and Social Reconstruction) which is primarily a textbook on rural social institutions. It expounds the development of rural social organisation, various types of farms, occupations and crafts, rural migration, village leadership, preservation of the countryside, local government in rural areas, town and country planning as applied to rural counties, and services and institutions such as church, pubs and clubs, and education. Bracey is also the author of *People and the countryside* (Routledge and Kegan Paul, 1970) which is discussed more fully in the section on the countryside, but which must be included at this point for its discussion of topics such as rural depopulation, rural industries, local government and rural communities. Specific aspects of rural life are discussed in *The country craftsman: a study of some rural crafts and the rural industries organisation in England* (Routledge and Kegan Paul, 1963) by W M Williams; and in *Rural depopulation in England and Wales, 1851-1951* by J Saville (Routledge and Kegan Paul, 1957).

The texts detailed above all refer to matters specifically British. But the United States has also in recent years had considerable rural problems, and indeed in that country rural sociology has been a subject of academic study for several decades. There is no lack of writing on the subject, but little need in this context to discuss it fully. Two titles are worthy of investigation. David E Linstrom's

American rural life: a textbook in sociology (New York, Ronald Press, 1948) is a discussion of a wide range of topics pertaining to rural life. T Lynn Smith's *The sociology of rural life* (New York, Harper, revised edition 1947) is rather narrower in focus and is mainly a detailed discussion of population, social organisation, and social processes.

There are several excellent sociological studies of rural life in regions of Britain or in individual villages. John M Mogey's exposition of *Rural life in Northern Ireland* (Oxford UP, 1947), for example, is based on five regional studies carried out for the Northern Ireland Council of Social Service, and describes the way of life of country people in the province. Chapters on the country as a whole and the rural area in general precede the five studies, of County Fermanagh; Hilltown, County Down; the Braid Valley, County Antrim; North Down; and North Antrim. Wales is the subject of *Welsh rural communities* edited by Elwyn Davies and Alwyn D Rees (Cardiff, University of Wales Press, 1960), which is the result of four studies carried out between 1945 and 1950 from the University of Wales at Aberystwyth, collectively forming a picture of the pattern of Welsh rural community life and structure. The studies are of a coastal village in South Cardiganshire, a market town in central Cardiganshire, a small region in the Llyn Peninsula, and chapel and community in Glan-Llyn, Merioneth. There is no comparable composite portrait of Scottish rural life, but Frank Fraser Darling's *West Highland survey: an essay in human ecology* (Oxford UP, 1950) can be mentioned as a detailed portrait of one of the country's most rural areas. One of the best-known studies of an individual village is that by W M Williams, *The sociology of an English village: Gosforth* (Routledge and Kegan Paul, 1956, International Library of Sociology and Social Reconstruction), based on first-hand study of the West Cumberland village between 1950 and 1953. Williams examines the economic context, and detailed aspects of the community—family, life cycles, kinship, social classes, neighbours, institutions, religion, and relationships with the outside world. W M Williams is also the author of a similar study of *A West Country village, Ashworthy: family, kinship and land* (Routledge and Kegan Paul, 1963).

448

LAND AND LAND USE

Land is basic to the planning process. However the plan is conceived and whatever its objectives, in the end it has to be committed to the land and decisions have to be made regarding the allocation of the available land resources to the various uses which must be accommodated. In this section we are concerned not with the land itself (geology, soil structure, and other matters are beyond the scope of this book) but with the way in which it is used.

Contrary to much popular supposition, the major part of Britain's land is not given to urban use, although in the densely built-up regions of the south east and the west midlands it is easy to gain this impression. Agriculture still accounts for about eighty percent of the land surface, and the rate of conversion to urban use is much slower than might be supposed, although it is faster in some regions than others. The other major uses of land in Britain are woodland, urban development, and other uses not within these three major categories which include mineral workings, and military sites. There are also about 99,000 acres (at 1964) of derelict land throughout the country, the bulk of it north of a line between the Wash and the Severn, with particularly high incidence in regions such as the Black Country and industrial Lancashire.

The first major survey of the land use of Britain was that carried out by the first Land Utilisation Survey of Britain, under the direction of L Dudley Stamp, mainly in the years 1931 to 1933. The maps associated with this survey were discussed in chapter 7. The written *Report* was issued in ninety two parts under the title *The land of Britain* between 1936 and 1946. Each part deals with one administrative county of England, Wales, and Scotland, and is by an expert with local knowledge of that county. The parts vary in length from forty to two hundred pages. Each has a historical introduction, an account of the physical background, an analysis of the distribution of each type of land use, and a detailed treatment of land use regions. In addition to these ninety two volumes, a summary volume was prepared by L Dudley Stamp under the title *The land of Britain and how it is used* (Longmans Green, 1948) which had the dual purpose of summarising the entire findings of the Survey and also of ' analysing those findings, and so of evaluating the factors which had determined the complex and intricate

449

pattern of rural Britain '.[82] A third edition of this book subtitled ' its use and misuse ' was published in 1962, which leaves the body of the text substantially as it was, but adds a final chapter of thirty nine pages on ' Fourteen years of national planning 1947-1960 '. The first official move towards a national policy to govern the use of land was made during World War II, with the setting up of the committee under the chairmanship of Lord Justice Scott on Land Utilisation in Rural Areas (see preceding section on rural planning). The Scott Report stressed the vital need to maintain good agricultural land for, in the inter-war period, as Stamp points out,[83] ' over a million acres passed out of agricultural into other uses in Britain. This is a large total when it is remembered that the total area of the country is only fifty six million acres, at least one third of which is mountain and moorland. The losses of agricultural land were taking place at an ever-increasing rate . . . [and] the loss was not merely of agricultural land but of the best types of agricultural land.' The data and information available about the detailed use of land in Britain as described in the publications of the first Land Utilisation Survey are now out of date; the results of the second Land Utilisation Survey are not yet available in written form (the maps emanating from it are described in chapter 7). As an interim measure, and before the second survey had begun, Robin H Best carried out an examination and an evaluation of the then existing land use records—those of the Ministry of Agriculture and Fisheries, the first Land Utilisation Survey, the Ordnance Survey, and development plan documents prepared under the 1947 Town and Country Planning Act—in an attempt to build up a more reliable estimate of the pattern of land use. These results are presented in *The major land uses of Great Britain* (Ashford, Kent, Wye College Department of Agricultural Economics, 1959, Studies in Rural Land Use, Report 4).

In a more recent publication with J T Coppock, *The changing use of land in Britain* (Faber, 1962), Best draws attention to the lack of reliable quantitative data on land uses. ' The emotional attitudes and vagueness which enter into many current discussions of land-use topics stem, in no small part, from the inadequacy of precise, quantitative studies of the important problems involved.

450

Much of the blame for this lies at a government level. The collection of land-use data is the special responsibility of no single government department, and official policy has been little concerned with other than national acreages of a few of the more important land uses.'[84] The book is a compilation of a number of studies in land use statistics and in the mapping and measurement of changes in land use which originally appeared in journals, some of them by Best and some by Coppock, all of them revised since original publication. The studies range through two essays based on papers by Coppock on agricultural statistics, and their accuracy and comparability, and then focus on specific types of land use such as arable land, forestry, and urban development; there is a summary of the loss of farmland to other uses, and the final study is an evaluation of British land use statistics. The book is well illustrated with maps, diagrams, and tables, and is well and accurately documented.

The competition between agricultural land and the encroachment of urban growth is examined in G P Wibberley's *Agriculture and urban growth: a study of the competition for rural land* (Michael Joseph, 1959). The book is based on the research into land use problems which has been going on for many years at the Department of Agricultural Economics at Wye College (University of London), and attempts to present a factual account of how Britain's land is actually being used and the effects of the encroachment of towns into agricultural land. A method is proposed for assessing the value of alternative sites of differing agricultural values in relation to differences in the cost of urban development, and the concept of food replacement is examined. The author pleads for a more systematic procedure for balancing competing claims for rural land, and claims that current rural and urban land use policies do not make economic sense. Most recently, Robin Best and A G Champion have studied and analysed new data from the census branch of the Ministry of Agriculture, Fisheries and Food in *Regional conversions of agricultural land to urban use in England and Wales 1945-1967* (Centre for Environmental Studies, 1970, CES-UWP-3; also published in *Transactions of the Institute of British Geographers* 49 March 1970 15-32). The results indicate that there are major regional variations in the scale of conversion of agricultural

451

land to urban use, and that some of the rates of transfer have altered significantly since 1945. The most prominent areas of urban growth are now the northern and midland conurbations. The dissimilarities between the distribution patterns of urban growth and population trends emphasises that no direct relationship necessarily exists between the extension of urban land and population growth. A forecast for the next thirty years is given by Angela Edwards in ' Land requirements for United Kingdom agriculture by the year 2000—a preliminary statement ' *Town and country planning* 37(3) March 1969 108-115, in which she asserts that ' it seems a reasonable assumption that serious conflict between agriculture and urban growth should not occur in the period up to 2000, in terms of land competition '.

All non-urban land is not used for agricultural purposes. ' The economic and social problems of hill and upland areas have long been the subject of earnest debate. Important questions arise concerning the long term viability of agricultural production in such areas, and it is often asserted that forestry might provide a more fruitful activity. A potential area of conflict thus emerges.'[85] There have been two major studies which have attempted a comparison of the economic returns from the two competing land uses. These two studies were undertaken by the Land Use Study Group set up by the Committee on Agriculture of the Natural Resources (Technical) Committee, and appeared in 1957 and 1966. The first, known as the Zuckerman Report after its chairman comes from the Natural Resources (Technical) Committee, under the title *Forestry, agriculture and marginal land: a report* (HMSO, 1957); the second, known as the Ellison Report, comes from the Department of Education and Science as *Report of the Land Use Study Group: forestry, agriculture and the multiple use of rural land* (HMSO, 1966). Further information on the two land uses in contradistinction comes from Gwyn James in 'An economic appraisal of the use of hills and uplands for agriculture and forestry respectively ' *The farm economist* 10(12) 1965 497-506, which relates to mid-Wales; and from K R Walker in ' The Forestry Commission and the use of hill land ' *Scottish journal of political economy* 7(1) February 1960 14-35, which relates to Scotland. Among land use studies which have been carried out over limited geographical areas, the report on *Land use in the Highlands and Islands* by the Advisory Panel on the High-lands and Islands of the Department of Agriculture and Fisheries for Scotland (Edinburgh, HMSO, 1964) is well worth attention. Forest lands alone have been surveyed by the Forestry Commission and the results are summarised by G M L Locke in *Census of woodlands 1965-67: a report on Britain's forest resources* (HMSO, 1970).

A major part of the uncommitted land of Britain is taken up by the common lands and village greens which cover about one and a half million acres of England and Wales. They include woodlands and scrub, marsh and moorland, grass, pasture and arable land, and they sustain a wide variety of activities from grazing cattle to human recreation. Between 1955 and 1958 a Royal Commission on Common Land made an exhaustive survey of commons and their *Report* (HMSO, 1958, Cmnd 462) is a mine of information on the extent of common land in England and Wales, the use made of it, and the general lack of management of such land which prevailed. Among their recommendations was one that all common lands should be registered; and this was implemented in the Commons Registra-tion Act 1965 under which registration of the common land and vil-lage greens in England and Wales was to be completed by the end of 1969. Bryan Harris and Gerald Ryan are the authors of *An outline of the law relating to common land and public access to the country-side* (Sweet and Maxwell, 1967), which constitutes a comprehensive statement of the legal position of common land after the passing of the 1965 Act. There are two parts: firstly, the various aspects of the law of common land, secondly, the legal basis of public access to privately owned land. Appendices explain the Commons Registra-tion Act and the Commons Registration (General) Regulations 1966. Between 1961 and 1966 a major study into the management of common land was sponsored by the Nuffield Foundation and Cam-bridge University, and the results of this were published as *Com-mons and village greens: a study in land use, conservation and management* by D R Denman and others (Leonard Hill, 1967). The first half of the text describes the physical features of the various kinds of commons and their economic and social organisation and considers their future use and management problems; this is fol-lowed by a section of codes of practice covering various activities such as grazing, and problems such as litter. There is a detailed discussion of the administration of common lands, and proposals for voluntary local management schemes. Further survey information is presented by Jonathan Wager in ' Outdoor recreation on common land ' *JTPI* 53(9) November 1967 398-403, based on an unpublished thesis from the Department of Land Economy at Cambridge; some of the results from a survey carried out in 1962 and 1963 of the public use of thirty commons in various parts of England are described. A descriptive survey of commons is included in *The common lands of England and Wales* by W G Hoskins and Sir L Dudley Stamp (Collins, 1963, New Naturalist Series). The new towns are the focus of a study by Robin Best, *Land for new towns* (Town and Country Planning Association, 1964) which provides a concise summary, based on statistics of existing (at 1960-61) and proposed development, of the densities of the major land use categories for the overall urban areas of the new towns (as opposed to their designated areas); these densities are then compared with those in existing towns, and conclusions drawn as to the effect of new town growth on Britain's land resources. A single new town is the subject of a research project based on the Department of Agricultural Economics at the University of Reading into the use of agricultural land in the Milton Keynes area. The report, *Milton Keynes, 1967: an agricultural inventory* (Reading University, 1968) contains the results of a survey of farmers and farm-workers carried out as a first stage; future work will involve inventories of agricultural land, ownership and working, to be followed by studies to demonstrate how the agricultural pattern is affected by the development of the new town.

Two collective items are of particular note. The first is the collection of essays in tribute to Sir L Dudley Stamp, the father of British land use studies, forming Institute of British Geographers Special Publication no 1 November 1968 under the title *Land use and resources: studies in applied geography*. The essays fall into three groups : four of them make up a philosophical background to land use and conservation, following which four more discuss aspects of land use in Britain (including Best on the competition between urban and rural land uses, and Coppock on rural land use); the third section focuses on developing countries. The second item is by a single author but takes the form of a review of studies in land use and their associated literature. G H Peters' 'Land use studies in Britain: a review of the literature with special reference to applications of cost benefit analysis' *Journal of agricultural economics* 21(2) May 1970 171-214 is the first of a series of review articles commissioned by the Agricultural Economics Society's sub-committee on research, a series which is intended to review the state of knowledge and available data on specific subjects, to indicate the methodological and theoretical problems involved and to consider the needs for further, more detailed, research. Peters' article describes very briefly the framework of British planning; then reviews the general studies which have been made of land use in Britain from Stamp through Wye College to the work of Ruth Gasson and Angela Edwards; then to recent developments in cost benefit analysis and the application of this technique to land use planning, in sections on agriculture versus urban growth, agriculture and forestry, and recreational economics.

The definition of derelict land, as put forward by the Ministry of Housing and Local Government, is essentially 'land so damaged by industrial or other development that it is incapable of beneficial use without treatment'.[86] As early as 1956, the Ministry of Housing and Local Government issued Technical Memorandum 7, *Derelict land and its reclamation* (HMSO, 1956). But it has only been in the last decade, or perhaps a little more, that public interest has been awakened to the problem of derelict land, and that efforts have begun to be made by the authorities responsible for it to ameliorate the situation referred to at the beginning of this section. Two major reports paved the way for this activity: that of the Ministry, *New life for dead lands: derelict acres reclaimed* (HMSO, 1963); followed by that of the Civic Trust in the following year, *Derelict land: a study of industrial dereliction and how it may be redeemed* (Civic Trust, 1964), both of which offered practical solutions for action. J R Oxenham's *Reclaiming derelict land* (Faber, 1966) examines major types and causes of dereliction, and outlines the methods of reclamation that are available. Plans for action are usually more inspiring than texts on how to do it, and one project in Wales can be said to have fired the imagination (and perhaps the conscience) of many: this was the *Lower Swansea Valley project* edited by K J Hilton (Longmans, 1967) the report of a project involving six departments of the University of Swansea to carry out a basic study of an area of industrial dereliction at Landore. The text is based on twelve study reports, and discusses in detail the site problems in re-development, methods of revegetation, and a regional road and trans-portation network, together with sociological and economic studies of the region. On the basis of the studies, a plan is formulated for the renewal of the valley, and an economic assessment of it is made. A description of the Swansea Valley project forms the central part of John Barr's paperback book *Derelict Britain* (Harmondsworth, Penguin Books, 1969, Pelican Original), a 'national study of indus-trial wastelands and how to redeem them'. Barr not only becomes angry at the existence of dereliction, he bestows praise on projects such as that at Swansea and cites examples of work done elsewhere in the country, smaller schemes which have actually been put into practice. Inevitably, he concludes with an eye to the future, 'We need a radical change in attitudes about dereliction. The Lower Swansea Valley project has shown how people can be brought together in the attack on one city's shame—*if* the will is there. The will behind the Swansea project should be repeated on a thou-sand other ravaged landscapes.'

THE COUNTRYSIDE

In the short description of the emergence of countryside planning in chapter 2 it was noted that there is increasing difficulty in separ-ating the functions of countryside planning generally and planning for outdoor recreation. One of the major features of countryside planning is the exploitation of rural resources for recreational activ-ities of all kinds, and this is reflected by the dominant interest in recreation planning and research on the part of the Countryside Commission, who issue a monthly news sheet *Recreation news* to provide an information service in this field and also maintain a Countryside Recreation Research Advisory Group to coordinate research activities into outdoor recreation.[87] In this section we shall restrict the scope of the discussion to the countryside generally and distinct parts of it, such as the coast, in which the primary concern is the nature of the countryside, its ecology, and its planning, rather than its exploitation for recreational purposes. The next section will deal with information which is primarily concerned with recreational and leisure planning and the resources which are available for it.

There are two major sources of information about the countryside in all its aspects. The first is the proceedings of the ' Countryside in 1970 ' conferences, held in 1963, 1965, and 1970. From these conferences a set of study group reports have accumulated (at the time of writing the reports of the 1970 conference are not yet to hand) published by the Royal Society of Arts; further information is contained in unpublished papers prepared for the study groups, which may be available through libraries, for example, in the extensive collection on leisure and land use in the Department of Town and Country Planning at the University of Newcastle upon Tyne.[88] These reports cover all aspects of the countryside, including its exploitation for outdoor recreation, and are a fruitful source of information. The second comprehensive source is a single volume work, *People and the countryside* by H E Bracey (Routledge and Kegan Paul, 1970) which, in addition to being a readable text on the countryside, its way of life, and its management, is also a source book on all aspects of the countryside which gathers together and provides guidance to the extensive but scattered literature on these subjects. Included in its wide scope are rural depopulation, rural industries, local government, rural communities, and all aspects of recreation and amenity, including reference to legislation and voluntary and official bodies working in these fields.

A dominant question in consideration of the countryside is that of access to it. A special committee studied this matter in 1947 at the instigation of the Ministry of Town and Country Planning, and their report *Footpaths and access to the countryside: report of the special committee (England and Wales)* (HMSO, 1947, Cmnd 7207) called for a complete survey of rights of way and for a procedure for resolving disputes over the legal status of rights of way. These recommendations were incorporated into the National Parks and Access to the Countryside Act 1949, under which the National Parks Commission had the right to designate Long Distance Footpaths with the aim of developing a national system of public rights of way through some of the country's best scenery. Implementation was the responsibility of local authorities, and this has fallen short of

457

intent: the 250 mile long Pennine Way, opened in 1965, is the outstanding example of the concept, but of the other approved schemes, several are still held up because of lack of agreement over rights of way. The national survey of footpaths has also fallen short of intent, for the principal reason that much of the work devolved upon local voluntary associations and parish councils and was therefore slow. In 1967 a Footpaths Committee was appointed under Sir Arthur Gosling to ‘ consider how far the present system of footpaths, bridleways, and other comparable rights of way in England and Wales and the arrangements for the recording, closure, diversion, creation and maintenance of such routes are suitable for present and potential needs in the countryside and to make recommendations ’. In its *Report of the Footpaths Committee* (HMSO, 1968) various recommendations were made, such as placing a duty on landowners to maintain stiles and gates and providing for pedal cyclists to use bridleways, and the majority of these were incorporated into the Countryside Act 1968 and the Town and Country Planning Act 1968. *A practical guide to the law of footpaths* by Ian Campbell was published by the Commons, Open Spaces and Footpaths Preservation Society in 1969. Some more fundamental thinking about footpaths is crystallised in *Footpaths in the countryside* by T Huxley (Perth, Countryside Commission for Scotland, 1970) which the author states may be read as a follow up to the Gosling Report. Huxley is concerned with aspects of biological and physical construction and maintenance, but not with the legal and administrative aspects. He postulates a distinction between ‘ natural ’ and ‘ constructed ’ footpaths, classified according to the way in which they traverse the land form of the ground; and reviews their purposes under five heads—route, safety, human comfort, resource conservation, and type of user. *The Pennine Way* (HMSO, 1969) is the subject of a Countryside Commission guide by Tom Stephenson, the rambler who first suggested the route in 1935; the content is mainly descriptive.

Designation of national parks was the principal function of the original National Parks Commission, and these are now a normal feature of the British countryside. They are described collectively in *Britain's national parks* edited by Harold M Abrahams (Country Life, 1959) and individually in the series of national park guides

458

produced by the Countryside Commission and published by HMSO. A valuable summary of the origins and legislative structure of the national parks is provided by Arthur Blenkinsop in ' The national parks of England and Wales ' *Planning outlook* 6(1) 1964, 9-75. Continuing information is contained in the annual reports of the National Parks Commission and now in those of the Countryside Commission, which also contain details of countryside parks designated under the Countryside Act 1968. Short descriptions of the first nine country parks to be approved under the Act are contained in *Recreation news supplement no 1* June 1970, issued by the Countryside Commission, which also carries a fuller description of the first country park to be opened, at Easter 1970, at Elvaston Castle in Derbyshire. The Forestry Commission provide information about forest parks (their own special responsibility under the terms of the Countryside Act 1968) in *Forest parks* by H L Edlin (HMSO, 1961), which is a collective description, and in their series of individual park guides. Further descriptive accounts are produced by the Forestry Commission in *Forestry in the British scene* by R F Wood and I A Anderson (HMSO, 1968) and in *Forestry in Wales* (HMSO, 1967); and in the annual reports of the commission.

Inland water is fulfilling an increasingly important role in the countryside, particularly for recreational purposes but the multiple use of water resources such as reservoirs is being investigated. As early as 1963 the Institution of Water Engineers held a conference and published its proceedings as *The recreational use of waterworks* (IWE, 1963). Conflict between various potential uses is inevitable, and such conflict is illustrated in the comprehensive study carried out by Birmingham University Department of Physical Education *Inland waters and recreation: a survey of the recreational use of inland waters in the west midlands* (Central Council of Physical Recreation, 1964). The British Waterways Board is primarily concerned with canals, and in particular with the maintenance of those which are no longer commercially viable as transport routes. Their concern is expressed in three factual publications, *The future of the waterways* (HMSO, 1964), *The facts about the waterways* (HMSO, 1966), and *Leisure and the waterways* (HMSO, 1967). The Ministry of Transport were responsible for the White Paper *British waterways: recreation and amenity* (HMSO, 1967, Cmnd 3401) whose recommendations concerning the development of canals and inland waterways for the purposes stated were incorporated into the Transport Act 1968. ' If the countryside in general is assuming an increasingly important role in the field of outdoor recreation, the rural-urban fringe is likely to be a key element since it is the most easily accessible area from large centres of population. In Great Britain most major rural-urban fringe areas are either defined or proposed as green belts . . . and they offer considerable scope for open space planning.'[89] Notwithstanding, the primary function of green belts is regulatory and not recreational, a point which is emphasised in the descriptive booklet issued by the Ministry of Housing and Local Government on *The green belts* (HMSO, 1962). Despite the constant nibbling which goes on into the green belts, they remain the nearest countryside for many urban dwellers, and contain commons or other open space as well as a variety of other land uses. The most penetrating analysis of the green belt concept and how it works in practice is in David Thomas's *London's green belt* (Faber, 1970).

The element of the countryside which has attracted most attention as regards its conservation and proper development is the coast and its immediate hinterland, and a substantial quantity of information is now available about its use and misuse. ' Indeed,' Professor J B Cullingworth has observed, ' it is a pity that the number of reports which have been published on this issue in recent years is not a reflection of the action which is under way.'[90] This degree of attention has been necessary because of the inordinate pressures which increase yearly on coastal resources. ' In many ways, the coast is Britain's most important resource from a recreational point of view. With no part of England and Wales more than seventy five miles from tidal water, the coast is easy of access and satisfies a very large part of the total demand for outdoor recreation . . . one fifth of half-day trips, one third of day trips and three quarters of all holidays have the seaside as their destination.'[91] In 1966, at the request of the Ministry of Housing and Local Government, the National Parks Commission embarked upon a comprehensive study of the coastline of England and Wales. The main elements of the study were a series of nine regional conferences with the maritime local planning authorities; these were held between May 1966 and March 1967. MOHLG Circular 7/66 *The coast* (HMSO, 1966) explained

460

the purpose of the conferences as being ' to provide a firm foundation for long term policies for safeguarding the natural beauty of the coast as a whole and promoting its enjoyment by the public '. For the conferences each local planning authority was asked to prepare a report, accompanied by maps, showing the development, protection and recreational use of the coast within its area. The nine *Regional coastal reports* (HMSO, 1967-1968) are as follows:

1 The coasts of Kent and Sussex
2 The coasts of Hampshire and the Isle of Wight
3 The coasts of south west England
4 The coasts of south Wales and the Severn estuary
5 The coasts of north Wales
6 The coasts of north west England
7 The coasts of north east England
8 The coasts of Yorkshire and Lincolnshire
9 The coasts of East Anglia.

The commission also prepared a separate booklet *The coasts of England and Wales: measurements of use, protection and development* compiled . . . from data supplied by local planning authorities (HMSO, 1968) showing, mainly in tabular form, the overall picture of the coast, and the extent of protection and development both existing and proposed along the entire coastline. The culmination of the exercise is in two reports from the commission, *The planning of the coastline* (HMSO, 1970) and *The coastal heritage* (HMSO, 1970). The first of these presents the evidence about existing land use culled from the regional conferences, and uses this as a basis for proposals for a coordinated land use policy for the whole coast by means of which the remaining unspoiled stretches will be safeguarded and the rest exploited in an appropriate manner. The second volume elaborates one recommendation from the first report: that thirty four areas, covering over a quarter of the coastline, should by virtue of their outstanding scenic quality be designated by the commission as ' heritage coasts ' and should be subject to strict development control. The report contains detailed proposals for the conservation and management of these areas. A further volume from the Countryside Commission represents the contribution of the Nature Conservancy to the general discussion of coastal

461

preservation and development in England and Wales: *Nature conservation at the coast* (Coastal Preservation and Development Special Study Report volume two) (HMSO, 1969). After some general discussion, the main part of this report presents a classification of the coast into four categories of conservation worthiness and lists 371 sites or stretches of coast in England and Wales classified by these categories. The National Trust exercise 'Enterprise Neptune', aimed at acquiring for the trust and thus bringing under its protection as much of the remaining unspoiled coastline as possible, is described in the trust's booklet *Enterprise Neptune: the National Trust campaign to save the coast* (National Trust, 1967). No discussion of the coast can be complete without a reference to J A Steers' monumental work *The coastline of England and Wales* (Cambridge, Cambridge UP, second edition 1964), primarily concerned with the physiography and ecology of the coastline, and a most important source of information.

RECREATION AND LEISURE PLANNING

Recreation and leisure are sometimes used interchangeably although in fact the two are not synonymous. Palmer offers a convenient definition and distinction: 'Leisure is essentially the time one has free from income-earning responsibilities and from personal and family housekeeping activities such as eating, sleeping, keeping house, shopping and similar activities that are necessary for day to day existence. Recreation, in any socially accepted sense, involves constructive activities for the individual and the community. Sport is essentially recreation involving physical effort. The more leisure time available, the more recreation is demanded, and the greater are the pressures on land use for recreational purposes.'[92]

Planning is concerned primarily with outdoor recreation, for the fairly obvious reason that indoor recreation and non-recreational leisure are not generally susceptible to external regulation, with the exception of organised indoor facilities such as sports halls. A few general statements on leisure, as distinct from recreation, are available. One of the seminal sources, and one of the first to realise the coming revolution, is Michael Dower's *Fourth wave, the challenge of leisure: a Civic Trust survey* (Civic Trust, 1965) originally printed

462

in the *Architects' journal* 141(3) January 20 1965 122-190. Dower's view is apocalyptic. ' Three great waves have broken across the face of Britain since 1800. First, the sudden growth of dark industrial towns. Second, the thrusting movement along far-flung railways. Third, the sprawl of car-based suburbs. Now we see, under the guise of a modest word, the surge of a fourth wave which could be more powerful than all the others. The modest word is *leisure.*' A photograph of Bank Holiday crowds by the Thames at Runnymede shows what is in store. Dower discusses leisure and its requirements in urban, regional, and national contexts, and appends a bibliography. Leisure in its sociological aspects is the theme of Kenneth Roberts' *Leisure* (Longman, 1970, The Social Structure of Modern Britain), which ' endeavours to clarify the role that leisure plays in contemporary society '. Topics considered are the relationships of leisure to work, the family and community life, and the growth of the leisure industry. The two final chapters pose questions of whether present day society is a society of leisure, and the ways in which leisure is now a social problem.

The general area of recreation and recreation planning is well documented. ' Recreational planning—a bibliographic review ' by J E Palmer in *Planning outlook* new series 2 Spring 1967 19-69 is a very efficient concise review of all aspects of the subject referring to a classified bibliography of over four hundred items. This is a very useful base of information, although much has been published since it appeared which would merit inclusion. Another well documented source is *Land and leisure in England and Wales* by J Allan Patmore (Newton Abbot, David and Charles, 1970), which is concerned primarily with outdoor recreation. This is a valuable synthesis of existing knowledge on all aspects of demand for recreation and the pressures of those demands on existing and future resources of land and water, much of it presented in the form of line maps, bar graphs and other graphic forms. The 1960's have witnessed an upsurge of interest in recreation research, and two publications, one British and one American, summarise much of the progress in this field. In *Economics of outdoor recreation* (Baltimore, Johns Hopkins Press, 1966) Marion Clawson and Jack L Knetsch cover outdoor recreation comprehensively, both in its resource, or supply aspects, and in its user, or demand aspects. Discussion ranges from

463

general characteristics of leisure activity to current research gaps. The book is not aimed at the specialist, and the theoretical framework is established from first principles. Much of the illustrative material is from the United States, and some sections are relevant only in an American context; the principle value of the book, therefore, is as a general methodological survey giving a useful perspective on outdoor recreation theory, and supplemented by a full bibliography. The British survey, *Recreation research methods: a review of recent studies* by T L Burton and P A Noad (Birmingham University, Centre for Urban and Regional Studies, 1968) relates in larger measure to British studies, and is intended for the specialist. It reviews the whole field of data collection, analysis and projection, evaluating the merits of alternative methods and raising some important issues such as comparability—or lack of it—between user surveys. There is a short section on proposals for experimental studies, and a bibliography of over one hundred items. This is in fact only an interim report, as part of a project based on the Centre for Urban and Regional Studies concerned with ' research techniques in the assessment, measurement and projection of supply and demand for sport and recreation '.

Burton is also the editor of *Recreation research and planning: a symposium* (Allen and Unwin, 1970, University of Birmingham Urban and Regional Studies 1). This is a collection of twelve essays which is intended as a general introduction to the subject of recreational planning, to be followed by a volume in the same series which will present a detailed account of the CURS studies between 1967 and 1969. The proceedings of a seminar held by the Planning and Transport Research and Computation Co are published under the title *Recreation land use, planning and forecasting* (PTRC, 1969); they include papers on planning and research in local authorities, the Countryside Commission, research organisations and universities.

Turning to the practical aspects of planning for recreation, Elizabeth Beazley's *Designed for recreation* (Faber, 1969) is a systematic review of the requirements of informal recreation in the countryside, and how to provide for them. The vast range of recreation components, from small items such as picnic tables through camping and caravan sites to large features such as man made lakes, are discussed and standards proposed. Foreign experience is included, both in text and illustration. This is a well-documented text which brings together within one pair of covers a very wide range of information. One of the notable publications of recent years is the Specimen Development Plan Manual 2-3 *Planning for amenity and tourism* issued by An Foras Forbartha (Dublin, AFF, 1966), a practical manual designed mainly for use by local planning authorities. The Countryside Commission's booklet on *Picnic sites* (HMSO, 1969) is a practical text, with good illustrations and bibliography, containing basic information on all aspects of picnic sites from location, siting and landscaping to litter and signs. *Land for play* by M Ommanney and J Clark (National Playing Fields Association and National Association of Parish Councils, 1967) is a small pamphlet packed with practical information about the acquisition, laying out, and management of land for playing fields, including advice on the legal and administrative problems involved. A Sports Council booklet *Planning for sport: report of a working party on scales of provision* (Central Council of Physical Recreation, 1968) is an exemplary assembly of data providing a base for estimating the amount of land required for all forms of outdoor sports in both town and country (superseding the old standards of the National Playing Fields Association) and the demand for provision of indoor facilities such as swimming pools. There is a considerable lack of coordination between the various organisations concerned with planning the provision of recreational facilities: ' providing for recreation . . . in many respects and in many geographic areas . . . is an industry, and as such, it must rank as one of the most inefficiently organized industries in the country. Much individual effort by both private and public interests is being misused or duplicated by the lack of cooperation and the absence of collective policy decisions.'[93] P T Kivell outlines a scheme of responsibility to overcome these deficiencies in ' The roles of public authorities and private interests in providing for recreation in the countryside ' *Planning outlook* new series 7 Autumn 1969 54-64.

There have been a number of surveys and studies of recreation patterns in Britain and in the United States, in the main concentrating on existing use of resources rather than on establishing the demand for them. The most thorough and comprehensive study

465

ever carried out in the field of outdoor recreation was that by the US Outdoor Recreation Resources Review Commission (ORRRC) whose report fills twenty seven volumes (Washington DC, US Government Printing Office, 1962), summarised in one volume as *Outdoor recreation for America* (Washington DC, USGPO, 1962). There is nothing comparable to this basic source of information in the British literature: but two national surveys supplement each other to provide a comprehensive source of data on British leisure activities. The first was carried out by the British Travel Association and the University of Keele and published as *Pilot national recreation survey* (BTA, 1967) covering the whole country; a breakdown by regions was provided in a second report *Regional analysis* (BTA, 1969). The second survey was carried out by the Government Social Survey on behalf of the Ministry of Housing and Local Government and the Sports Council and is published as *Planning for leisure* by K K Sillitoe (HMSO, 1969), subtitled ' an enquiry into the present pattern of participation in outdoor and physical recreation and the frequency and manner of use of public open spaces, among people living in the urban areas of England and Wales '. The BTA survey made extensive inquiry into life styles and the use of leisure time and also investigated participation in sport, day trip excursions and future aspirations. The Social Survey project examined roughly the same range of variables but made a deeper study of patterns of participation in sport and outdoor recreation generally and of the use of public open spaces in urban areas. An earlier study of a more descriptive nature is *Outdoor recreation in the British countryside* by Thomas L Burton and G P Wibberley (Ashford, Wye College Department of Economics, 1965, Studies in Rural Land Use, Report 5), a short text which outlines the recent development of recreation in Britain, estimates the amount of land in recreational use and its distribution, the role of the coast and its holiday resorts, holiday patterns and weekend recreation, future demands for recreation and their effect. Comparisons are drawn with practice and trends in the United States.

Other studies have been made which concentrate either on a defined region or locality, or on a specific element of the countryside as a recreational resource. In the former category come the regional appraisals carried out by the regional sports councils, bodies set

466

up, with their parent the Sports Council, in 1965 to coordinate surveys of facilities for sport and physical recreation within their respective areas. These surveys, or ' initial appraisals ', ' were not exclusively urban or outdoor in emphasis, though they were directed particularly towards such capital intensive facilities as swimming pools, indoor sports centres, athletics stadia and golf courses which by their very nature are located most often within or adjacent to towns. The material collected permits useful comparisons to be made within each region, but it is unfortunate that no attempt was made to standardise the terms of reference between the regions to enable an accurate national picture to emerge. Variations exist both in topics covered and in basic definitions.'[94] The appraisals are as follows:

Cheshire County Council *Recreation in Cheshire: survey of existing facilities for sport and physical recreation—preliminary report* (1967).

Eastern Sports Council *First appraisal of major facilities and field games* (1967).

East Midlands Sports Council and Technical Panel *Recreation in the east midlands, an initial appraisal of major facilities* (1967).

Greater London and South East Sports Council *Sports facilities initial appraisal vol 1* (1968).

County of Lancashire *Survey of existing facilities for sport and physical recreation, an appraisal* (1967):

Volume 1 *The county*

Volume 2 Parts 1-8 *Sub-regional reports*

Volume 3 *Swimming baths.*

North East Advisory Council for Sport and Recreation *Provision for sport and recreation in the north east* (1965).

Northern Advisory Council for Sport and Recreation *Public swimming baths in the north east* (North Regional Planning Committee, 1966).

Northern Advisory Council for Sport and Recreation *Water sports in the northern region* (North Regional Planning Committee, 1967).

Northern Advisory Council for Sport and Recreation *Survey of golf facilities* (North Regional Planning Committee, 1967).

467

Southern Sports Council *Major sport and recreation facilities, a first appraisal* (1967).

South Western Sports Council *Initial appraisal of major facilities* (1967).

South Western Sports Council *The use of coastal waters for recreation* (1967).

Sports Council for Wales *Major sports facilities, an initial appraisal* (1967).

West Midlands Sports Council Technical Panel *Regional recreation* (1966).

Yorkshire and Humberside Sports Council *Sports facilities, an initial appraisal* (1967).

Further regional surveys have been produced by the North Regional Planning Committee on *Outdoor leisure activities in the northern region* (Newcastle upon Tyne, 1969) and by the West Midlands Sports Council on *Regional recreation 1970* (Birmingham, 1970). A part of the northern region has been the subject of a research study from the Centre for Urban and Regional Research at Manchester University Department of Town and Country Planning, reported in *The Tyne recreation research study* by D J Thomas and J T Roberts (Manchester, 1970); a synopsis of the main report is also available. Recreational use of outdoor facilities is studied by Thomas L Burton in *Windsor Great Park: a recreation study* (Ashford, Wye College Department of Economics, 1967, report 8) and in the supplementary volume number two to the South Hampshire study, *The New Forest study* (HMSO, 1966). Urban facilities, their provision and use are examined in Pearl Jephcott's *Time of one's own* (Edinburgh, Oliver and Boyd, 1967, University of Glasgow Social and Economic Studies Occasional Paper 7), which is a study of young people's leisure time interests in central Scotland, based on a survey of young people aged between fifteen and nineteen in three urban areas, two in Glasgow and one in West Lothian. The London Borough of Southwark's Department of Architecture and Planning have prepared a survey of *Recreation in Southwark* (1970) in two volumes, the first being a survey of leisure and the second containing tables based on data from 2,500 questionnaires. The report takes in the home, meeting places, open space, sports facilities and commercial

468

entertainment. Like Pearl Jephcott's study, it identifies gaps in provision and suggests remedies.

In the second category of specific elements of the countryside used for recreational purposes, come studies such as that by the Countryside Commission of *Coastal recreation and holidays* (HMSO, 1969, Special Study Report 1). The Forestry Commission have surveyed the use made of their own parks in *Public recreation in national forests: a factual study* by W E S Mutch (HMSO, 1968), based on surveys carried out in the New Forest in 1963 and in Cannock Forest, Allerston Forest (Yorkshire), Glenmore and Queen Elizabeth Forest Parks in Scotland all in 1964. R W Douglass has also studied the subject over a wider field in *Forest recreation* (Oxford, Pergamon Press, 1969). Urban open space is examined in the Greater London Council Planning Department's *Surveys of the use of open spaces* (GLC, 1968, Research Paper 2), which reports an extensive and detailed set of surveys by the (then) London County Council and the Centre for Urban Studies in 1964 to determine the patterns of use of open spaces in London. The present volume discusses the results, tests two hypotheses in an attempt to clarify some of the elements in the pattern of demand, and offers the conclusions. A second volume will contain the complete data tabulations. Surveys of the recreational use of commons in England and Wales in 1962 and 1963 are reported by Jonathan Wager in ' Outdoor recreation on common land ' *JTPI* 53(9) November 1967 398-403.

Various practical plans for provision of outdoor recreational facilities have been drawn up for various parts of the country. One for regional organisation of leisure resources is that prepared by a team from the Heriot-Watt University in Edinburgh for the Countryside Commission for Scotland, *Recreation planning for the Clyde: Firth of Clyde study phase two* (Edinburgh, Scottish Tourist Board, 1970), developed from an earlier study by Miles-Kelcey Limited *A study of tourism, Firth of Clyde region* (Edinburgh, Scottish Tourist Board, 1968). The objective of the phase two study was to evolve a strategy for the leisure use of land and water in the study region which comprises the sub-region west of Glasgow including the Firth of Clyde and the Ayrshire coast. The study develops a Clyde Recreation Resource Classification, based on that of the US Outdoor

Recreation Resources Review Commission, and applies it in a theoretical model of the city region; three alternative strategies are tested against a check list of design criteria, resulting in one strategy being thrown up as practicable (this exercise is of limited value owing to the uncertainty which existed at the time of the study—and to a large extent still exists at the time of writing—about future large-scale industrial development in the area). Seven model case studies were carried out and are described fully, for a marina development; an indoor recreation centre; a scenic route with full facilities; a heritage site; a resort improvement scheme; outdoor recreation in a national park type area; and for coastal control policies in the environs of a country park. From these studies, 'design templates' are produced, these being defined as 'a method and approach which can be adapted for use elsewhere in the region or the nation, as and when similar types of facility may be required'. Two further regional studies and plans within Scotland have been carried out by Brian S Duffield and M L Owen both under the generic title *Leisure+countryside=*, both edited by Professor J T Coppock, and both based on and published by the Department of Geography at Edinburgh University. The first study, issued in 1970, reports a joint project, by the local authorities within Lanarkshire and the university, to determine present resources and the use made of them, the present pattern of leisure and recreation pursuits, the impact of outdoor recreation on the countryside and its conflict with other land uses, the results of these studies being used as the basis of proposals for exploitation and development of the available resources. The second study, issued in 1971, follows a similar approach in the Edinburgh area and again makes detailed proposals for development. A much smaller report, but one which offers a good example of positive planning on the part of a local planning authority, is *Seaburn and Roker: a policy for coastal recreation* by J E Barlow (Sunderland, County Borough Council, 1970). The physical advantages and disadvantages of the two resort suburbs are analysed and their changing functions examined; in the light of this, the feasibility of Seaburn and Roker's several possible future roles are discussed, and the report concludes that the seafront should be enhanced and developed as a town park for residents and day trip visitors. The practical methods of recreation

470

planning used in East Sussex County Planning Department are described by John Furmidge in ' Planning for recreation in the countryside ' *JTPI* 55(2) February 1969 62-67. A practical scheme which has actually been implemented, and which has been the focus of considerable interest and attention, is that for the Lee Valley regional park. The plan for this scheme was prepared by the Civic Trust in *A Lea Valley regional park: an essay in the use of neglected land for recreation and leisure* (Civic Trust, 1964) containing concrete proposals for developing uncommitted land along twenty miles of the Lea river valley from West Ham to Ware. In 1967 the Lee Valley Regional Park Authority was set up and in 1969 produce the master plan for the park *Lee Valley Regional Park* (Enfield, The Authority, 1969) providing for a wide variety of facilities for recreation and education including twelve major multi-purpose recreation centres, and four regional centres of specific type, one each for youth activity, water sports, motor sports, and industrial archaeology, these facilities to be linked up by river and canal, by continuous parkland in the northern area, and by linear dual carriageway park roads. This exercise is of great significance for recreation planning in Britain, being the first regional recreation park and the first specific authority to be set up to build such a park. An American scheme similar to the Lee Valley undertaking is described in the Tennessee Valley Authority's report *The land between the lakes: a demonstration in recreation resource development (revised concept statement)* (Knoxville, Tennessee, TVA, 1964). This is a demonstration project designed to boost the economy of a whole region, and was based on a report from the US Department of the Interior *A study of the economic effects of a between-the-lakes national recreation area in Kentucky and Tennessee* (Washington, USGPO, 1963). The demonstration is intended to show how the resources of a large area can be developed to provide for a wide range of recreation and conservation programmes. The entire area of land between the lakes is being developed to provide multiple use open-air facilities, designed to attract a large influx of tourists.

The tourist and holiday industry is now one of the major features of recreation planning. Not only this, it forms an increasingly important part of the British national economy as a major source of foreign currency. The importance of the industry was recognised in the Development of Tourism Act 1969, which established a new statutory tourist organisation, the British Tourist Authority, together with Tourist Boards for England, Wales, and Scotland, whose function is ' to encourage the provision and improvement of tourist amenities and facilities in Great Britain ', and which also made provision for financial assistance to hotels. The main institutional source of information and data on holiday patterns has been the British Travel Association, which carried out a British national travel survey annually since 1960. The association and its functions have now been superseded by the British Tourist Authority, which continues the survey. This is a large scale random sample survey, carried out by Gallup Polls until 1970, when the operation was taken over by National Opinion Polls, of holiday-makers within the United Kingdom and of British holiday makers abroad, designed to produce data about holidays of four or more nights. The main results of the survey are produced annually in the form of computer printout, and are confidential, although they are summarised in the press, and information can be obtained on application. A summary of the results of the surveys between 1961 and 1968 was published by the British Travel Association as *Patterns in British holiday-making 1961-1968* (BTA, 1969). The results of the 1970 survey became available at the beginning of 1971, in four volumes of printout, and these results will be published in summary form by the British Tourist Authority. The Government Social Survey were responsible for a survey of *Scottish tourism* (HMSO, 1968, SS 368) carried out in September/October 1964 for the Scottish Devolopment Department to give guidance to the department in the future development of the tourist industry in Scotland. The Welsh Tourist Board carried out its own survey *Tourism in Wales: a research study* (Cardiff, WTB, 1969).

The majority of studies of this type concentrate on the consumers and their patterns of behaviour. A regional study which focuses primarily on the supply side of the industry is *The holiday industry of Devon and Cornwall* (HMSO, 1970), prepared between 1966 and 1969 by members of the Economics Department of Exeter University for the Ministry of Housing and Local Government, which is concerned with the type of industry which has grown up and the impact of holiday makers upon the economy and society of Devon

472

and Cornwall. An interdisciplinary study of south west Scotland is reported in *The Galloway project: a study of south west Scotland with particular reference to its tourist potential* edited by G Davies (Edinburgh, Scottish Tourist Board, 1968), which is made up of independent reports by specialists on various aspects of the region. A detailed study of *The Shannon estuary: report and plan for the development of tourism and recreation* was prepared by Nathaniel Lichfield and Associates as a supplement for their *Advisory outline plan for Limerick 1967,* and published in 1969 by the Mid-Western Regional Tourism Organisation Limited; the report contains detailed proposals for guiding the development of tourism and recreation in the area.

The impact of holiday makers, day-trippers, and recreation generally on the countryside has not been the subject of a great deal of research. One study sponsored by the Countryside Commission for Scotland is reported in *The beaches of Sutherland* by W Ritchie and A Mather of Aberdeen University Department of Geography (Perth, Countryside Commission for Scotland, 1969). The study was designed to assess the ecological and geomorphological impact of recreational use, particularly that of caravans, on selected beaches in Sutherland. A report by R J Lloyd on *Countryside recreation: the ecological implications* (Lincoln, Lindsey County Council, 1970) forms part of the wider Lindsey countryside recreational survey. The main concern of the study was to reconcile human pressures with nature conservation in a county of intensive farming. The first part of the report relates specifically to Lindsey and describes its physical structure and habitats; the second and third parts have wider than local relevance, the second being a review of the effects of recreation on the ecology of a lowland county, and the third constitutes a review of management procedures for avoiding, or redressing, these effects. Appendices summarise the agencies and legislation involved.

The severest recreational pressure on the countryside is that imposed by the motor car. It has been established that 'a trip into the country is the most popular form of outing in Britain today. Indeed, the car has become an instrument of recreation in itself.'[95] The Ramblers' Association carried out an early survey, *Motor vehicles in national parks* (Ramblers' Association, 1963). The adverse effects of traffic were recognised and discussed at the second

473

Countryside in 1970 conference in 1965, reported in the ' Countryside in 1970 ' Second Conference, Study Group 7, *Traffic and its impact on the countryside* (Royal Society of Arts, 1965). The problem has been under serious consideration in the West Riding of Yorkshire, and the County Planning Department produced a report of their findings as *Recreation traffic in the Yorkshire dales* (Wakefield, West Riding County Council, 1969). A supplement to this is the Countryside Commission report by W B Yapp *The weekend motorist in the Lake District* (HMSO, 1969), based on a survey of motorists leaving the Lake District on specified weekends in 1966. Two articles by W Houghton-Evans and J C Miles offer an up to date review of American and British studies of recreational motoring and a review of the concept of environmental capacity. These are ' Week-end recreational motoring in the countryside ' *JTPI* 56(9) November 1970 392-397, and ' Environmental capacity in rural recreation areas ' *JTPI* 56(10) December 1970 423-427.

An important aspect of recreation planning in towns and cities is the provision of facilities for children's play. One of the chief proponents in this field is Lady Allen of Hurtwood, whose accumulated knowledge is contained in *Planning for play* (Thames and Hudson, 1968). ' The purpose of this book is to explore some of the ways of keeping alive, and of sustaining, the innate curiosity and natural gaiety of children . . . The task is to create a sympathetic environment in which they can flourish.' The book is a record, in text and illustration, of how this is being done in many parts of the world, showing creative projects in individual and group play facilities, both as organised purpose-made space and as incidental activity, adventure playgrounds, play parks, neighbourhood playgrounds, and play facilities for handicapped, subnormal and maladjusted children. An early factual study was initiated by the Building Research Station in *Children's play on housing estates* by Vere Hole (HMSO, 1966, National Building Studies, Research Paper 39). Factual analysis, with graphic presentation of data, is provided over a wider field by Anthea Holme and Peter Massie in *Children's play: a study of needs and opportunities* (Michael Joseph, 1970) whose evidence is based on a study of 467 playgrounds in twenty boroughs. There are valuable sections on planning for play and on administration of play provision. Richard Dattner's *Design for*

474

play (New York, Van Nostrand, 1970) starts not from the playground but from the child and examines as background the philosophy and psychology of play before going on to review examples of creative play provision in Europe and the United States. One of the most comprehensive texts on the subject is *Environmental planning for children's play* (Crosby Lockwood, 1970) by Arvid Bengtsson, the Parks Director of Gothenburg in Sweden, which is in the forefront of playground planning and the integration of play facilities into the urban environment. Illustrations are taken from all over the world, both of complete playgrounds of all types and also of the components of the playgrounds, and there is much practical advice.

ENVIRONMENT

Environment must surely be one of the most overworked words of 1970. Efforts to provoke public consciousness of it have resulted in a popular currency in which the word may mean all things to all men. In this section it is taken to mean the physical surroundings in which people live: these may be urban or rural, land or water, tangible or intangible. Implicit in the notion of environment now is the damage which human beings do to it in a variety of ways and equally implicit is the corollary that measures must be taken to conserve it.

There are several quite recent books which discuss the environment in a general way, some of them with optimism, others with pessimism. One of the most unemotive factual accounts is Robert Arvill's *Man and environment* (Harmondsworth, Penguin Books, second edition 1969). Arvill (the pen name of Robert Boote, the chairman of European Conservation Year 1970 Committee) describes the various components of the British environment—the land and the uses made of it, air, water, wild life, for examples—and the pressures on them, and puts forward concrete proposals for the conservation of all these components, together with suggestions for required research and practical measures such as the collection of national data on land uses. Another noted conservationist, E Max Nicholson, has written an equally factual but rather more polemical account of the environment and its problems in *The environmental revolution* (Hodder and Stoughton, 1970).

475

Two catalogues of environmental catastrophes, both pessimistic in tone, are John Barr's *The assaults on our senses* (Methuen, 1970) and Gordon Rattray Taylor's *The doomsday book* (Thames and Hudson, 1970) The first is a compendium of failures without much alleviation; the second is primarily concerned with the effects of the technological measures which are now being used, often in the fight against pollution. The constant battle between resources and the demands made upon them was spotlighted in the BBC Reith lectures for 1969, given by Sir Frank Fraser Darling and published as *Wilderness and plenty* (BBC Publications, 1970).

It was perhaps significant that these lectures were given by an internationally renowned ecologist, for along with environment, ecology has become a popular word in the British vocabulary in recent years. Robert Arvill defines ecology as ' the science which seeks to elucidate the principles governing the interactions of the natural processes of land, water and all living things '.[96] In November 1968 an Ecology Bookshop was opened in London. During 1969, the International Association of Ecology (a section of the International Union of Biological Sciences) was established and began publication of its *Intecol bulletin;* 1970 saw the birth of another title in the field, *The ecologist.* An authoritative text on the subject is *Ecology and resource management* by K E F Watt (New York, McGraw-Hill, 1968) (texts on human ecology dealing principally with the interaction of man and his urban environment are discussed in the section on urban studies within this chapter).

If the environment is to be made, or kept, as good as possible, conservation of what is already good must be an important part of its protection. This again applies equally to both the urban and the rural environment. Sir L Dudley Stamp, having defined ecology rather more concisely than Arvill as ' the study of plants, animals (and man) in relation to the environment ' goes on to affirm that ' nature conservation is essentially applied ecology '.[97] The movement for nature conservation goes further back in time than that for urban conservation: it has its origins in the Scott Report of 1942, of which Section 179 *Nature reservations* stated ' While some of the larger national parks will naturally form or contain " nature reserves " and it may be possible to set aside portions of them specifically for the purpose, it is essential in other cases that prohibition of access shall be a first consideration, and for this reason nature reserves should also be established separately from national parks. We recommend that the central planning authority, in conjunction with the appropriate scientific societies, should prepare details of areas desired as nature reserves (including geological parks) and take the necessary steps for their reservation and control—which must be strict if rare species are to be safeguarded.'

Nature conservation was the subject of further study subsequent to the Scott Report by a special committee under Dr Julian Huxley, which produced the report *Conservation of nature in England and Wales* (HMSO, 1947, Cmnd 7122), which, as embodied in the legislation of 1949, defined the role and sphere of operations of the Nature Conservancy (already established earlier in 1949 as a research council). The first national nature reserve was declared at Beinn Eighe in the Scottish Highlands in 1951; the first in England was Scolt Head on the coast of Norfolk in 1954. The progress of nature conservation is reflected in the publications of the Nature Conservancy (now part of the Natural Environment Research Council): its annual reports; its *Nature Conservancy: the first ten years* (HMSO, 1959); and its *21 years of conservation* (HMSO, 1970) produced to mark the twenty first anniversary and recording conservation policy in Britain up to the present day. The National Trust is also concerned with nature conservation in that it owns and administers some nature reserves but its interests go much wider and embrace the conservation of buildings, gardens, parks and islands in its objective of ensuring the preservation of lands and buildings of historic interest or natural beauty for public access and benefit. The work of the Trust and all it stands for are described by Robin Fedden in *The continuing purpose: a history of the National Trust, its aims and work* (Longmans, 1968). A full and authoritative account of nature conservation in Britain is provided by Sir L Dudley Stamp in *Nature conservation in Britain* (Collins, 1969, New Naturalist Series). Stamp was vice chairman of the Scott committee and was closely identified with nature conservation up to his death in 1968; his text reviews the development of conservation, current thinking and achievements, and proposes a statement of future aims. This is a valuable handbook, full of firsthand information and containing, in appendices, lists of the main bodies con-

477

cerned with conservation and a gazetteer of the national parks, reserves, and areas of outstanding natural beauty in Britain, plus a bibliography.

There is increasing appreciation that a better urban environment does not materialise simply by creating new physical surroundings, by knocking down the old and replacing it or even by rehabilitating the old. Conservation is as relevant to the fabric of towns and cities as to the open country: in the former case it may be concerned with single buildings, or groups of buildings or with whole areas which have special historic, architectural or amenity significance. Since the passing of the Civic Amenities Act in 1967 there has been an up-surge of interest in urban conservation, manifested in many practical ways. Before the passing of this Act, the machinery of preservation had no particular force or relevance. ' Historic areas have, at best, been regarded as aggregates of individual buildings to be preserved for posterity by various means of defence; they have not been planned for as an integral element of urban structure . . . a comprehensive approach linked with local planning has been very rare.'[98] The Civic Amenities Act 1967 introduced the concept of conservation areas, as distinct from individual buildings, and placed an obligation on local planning authorities to adopt positive conservation policies by determining ' which parts of their areas are areas of special architectural or historic interest, the character of which it is desirable to preserve or enhance ' and by designating these as conservation areas. Once an area has been so designated, the authority must pay particular attention ' to the character or appearance of the conservation area ' in the exercise of any planning powers involving the area. Further regulations reinforcing these measures are embodied in the Town and Country Planning Act 1968. The Civic Amenities Act and other relevant measures, and practical action which has resulted from it, are fully discussed by David Smith in ' The Civic Amenities Act: conservation and planning ' *Town planning review* 40(2) July 1969 149-162. Progress in declaring conservation areas since the Act came into force has been steady: the Civic Trust issues a newsletter *Progress in creating conservation areas* eight times a year, each issue including a cumulative list of approved conservation areas, and short reports on new ones.

Most of the significant literature pertaining to conservation dates

478

from 1967 and later. The Ministry of Housing and Local Government issued in that year a 'glamorous book' on *Historic towns: preservation and change* (HMSO, 1967), which contains a statement of the problems, an indication of what should be preserved, a call for conservation policy, and statement of conservation in practice. The Civic Trust, the foremost body associated with the conservation movement, has been active in publication. *Street improvement schemes* (Civic Trust, 1967) focuses on a specific aspect of practical conservation; the comprehensive survey forming the basis for *Conservation areas: preserving the architectural and historic scene* (Civic Trust, 1967) was followed by a conference held at the Guildhall in October 1967 whose results produced the study *The protection of areas of architectural importance* (Civic Trust, 1967). In 1968, the Historic Towns and Cities Conference was held at York and the record of some of the contributions to these proceedings are contained in *Conservation and development in historic towns and cities* edited by Pamela Ward (Newcastle upon Tyne, Oriel Press, 1968). There are seven sections, on economics, traffic, conservation management, research, design, conservation policies in Europe and the United States, and policy in general. Roy Worskett's *The character of towns: an approach to conservation* (Architectural Press, 1969) is a publication which emanates from the Ministry of Housing and Local Government, although it is not one of its official publications. This is an architect's approach, and the philosophy is set out in the first few chapters. Then the principles are expounded, followed by a discussion of the concept of planning for conservation, followed by design, and ending with a section on survey and analysis. It is a practical, how to do it book, with special reference made to the action to be taken in the declaration of conservation areas under the Civic Amenities Act. Worskett's book may be compared with an American publication by Ralph W Miner on *Conservation of historic and cultural resources* (Chicago, American Society of Planning Officials, 1969) which takes the form of a short advisory report written for the ASPO, and which reflects an increasing American interest (as in Britain) in conservation of groups of buildings rather than of individual ones.

Some practical examples of conservation planning are available. As early as 1959 the Civic Trust produced its booklet illustrating

479

the improvement of *Magdalen Street, Norwich* (Civic Trust, 1959) an example of 'face-lifting' applied to a single street which has been followed with success elsewhere. Action by a local planning authority is documented in *Newark: action for conservation* by the Nottinghamshire County Planning Department (West Bridgford, Nottinghamshire County Council, 1968). This is a record, in photograph, drawing, map and written text, of action taken by the county and borough to preserve the character of Newark, and of the recommendations made to this end. ' The character of Newark, like that of many of our historic towns, is slowly being eroded away by the ever increasing pressure for redevelopment and by the voracity of the motor car. In this book the main problems have been examined and solutions suggested which, it is hoped, will enable the town, and perhaps others with similar problems, to develop in a satisfactory manner without endangering its fabric.' In 1966 the Ministry of Housing and Local Government commissioned four studies of historic towns all of which reported in 1968. The four volumes— *Bath: a study in conservation, Chester: a study in conservation, Chichester: a study in conservation,* and *York: a study in conservation* (all HMSO, 1968)—together make up a valuable set of studies and should ideally be considered together: to this end, each volume carries a four page insert giving cross references between the volumes to selected topics. The studies are notable for the depth and detail of their visual appraisal and their land use analysis, also for their attention to the financial and legal implications of conservation. Proposals are put forward in each volume for practical conservation of the areas of study. James Craig's new town of Edinburgh has been the subject of a detailed social survey by the city authorities, reported in *Conservation report: zone 1 of the new town* (Edinburgh, City Council, 1968), which incorporates many recommendations for preserving the character of the area. A rather different problem arose in Glamorgan where the old hill town of Llantrisant was in danger of losing its identity in the face of large scale urban development close by, unless a conservation policy was formulated and implemented for the original town. Gordon Cullen was appointed as townscape consultant in 1966 to define a conservation area and to suggest methods for enhancing the natural character and amenities of the town and area. His report

480

Llantrisant, a Welsh hill town: an environmental study (Cardiff, Glamorgan County Council, 1968) is a fine recreation, with the aid of photographs, of the atmosphere of the place, and constitutes a thorough analysis of the townscape, followed by proposals, illustrated with many sketches, for treatment of the various facets of the town.

Control of the visual quantity of the environment is enforced by legislation on intrusive factors such as advertisements and caravan sites. The first governmental measure on caravans was the Caravan Sites and Control of Development Act 1960 and the accompanying MOHLG Circular 42/60 (HMSO, 1960) which followed the Arton Wilson Report *Caravans as homes* (HMSO, 1959, Cmnd 872). Further legislation followed with the Caravan Sites Act 1968 and accompanying MOHLG Circular 49/68 (HMSO, 1968). Regulations concerning advertising were formulated in a joint publication of the Ministry of Housing and Local Government and the Welsh Office *Planning control of signs and posters* (HMSO, 1966). All previous regulations were consolidated and superseded by the Town and Country Planning (Control of Advertisement) Regulations 1969 (HMSO, 1969, SI 1969 no 1532) and the accompanying MOHLG Circular 96/69 (HMSO, 1969), which became operational at the beginning of 1970.

Perhaps predominantly, the environment to the majority of people is represented by the fight against pollution of all the elements which affect human life. Certainly this is the aspect which principally concerns the government and the international organisations. *Controlling our environment* by Lord Kennet (Fabian Society, 1970, Fabian Research Series 283) is a concise rundown on the British governmental and extra-governmental system of controlling the various forms of pollution, and the steps being taken to improve the controls both nationally and internationally. 1970 saw the production of a White Paper *The protection of the environment: the fight against pollution* (HMSO, 1970, Cmnd 4373) and the setting up of a Royal Commission on Environmental Pollution. The commission's first *Report* was published in February 1971 (HMSO, 1971, Cmnd 4585), and provides a broad review of the state of the British environment together with a statement of the social implications of remedying what is wrong. Air pollution is a matter of international concern, for obvious reasons. Two publications of the Council of

481

Europe are worth noting: *Regional planning and air pollution* (Strasbourg, Council of Europe, 1964, CPL (5)15) emanating from the fifth session of the European Conference of Local Authorities: and *Effects of air pollution on animals and plants: general report* by M Tendron (Strasbourg, Council of Europe, 1964, CPA/RG 2) emanating from the major European Conference on Air Pollution held at Strasbourg, and including a bibliography to further sources of information. In 1966 the council began its 'Clean Air Charter' to give guidance to governments on how to deal with major sources of pollution. In Britain official thinking has been mainly directed at control of chimneys and smoke and a policy of smokeless zones has been operated: the relevant legislation is the Clean Air Act 1968. *Pesticides and pollution* are the subject of a book by Kenneth Mellanby (Collins, 1968, New Naturalist Series) in which these topics are dealt with in a broad framework of history, present knowledge and future prospects. There is an excellent bibliography.

The Council of Europe has also been active in the documentation of water pollution: the *Report on fresh water pollution in Europe* (Strasbourg, Council of Europe, 1965, Doc 1965) is a product of its Consultative Assembly and lays down general principles for the conservation, supply and use of water for adoption by all member countries. Subsequently the council produced its 'Water Charter' in 1966 to disseminate its ideas. *Urban planning aspects of water pollution* by S Grava (New York, Columbia UP, 1969) contains the results of a study on water pollution sponsored by Columbia University's Institute of Urban Environment. The author discusses the various techniques and methods currently available in water pollution control and considers the way in which they affect the policy choices open to the urban planner. He deals in detail with regional and local planning, with technological, administrative and financial aspects, and with the specific problems of developing countries. There is a bias towards American practice, and the comments on administration and finance are relevant only to that country, but the general guidelines are universally applicable. A manual issued jointly by the Ministries of Technology, and Housing and Local Government on *Water pollution control engineering* (HMSO, 1970) describes the problems of effluent control, and the knowledge and specialised plant available to deal with them. British legislation on water pollution is contained in the Water Resources Acts of 1963 and 1968 and in the Rivers (Prevention of Pollution) Act 1961. A S Wisdom produced a guide to this legislation in *The law on the pollution of waters* (Shaw and Sons, second edition 1966) first published in 1956 and completely revised for the second edition to incorporate major legislative changes; this is an exhaustive treatment of all aspects of water pollution, well documented with case law and footnotes, although now out of date. In 1969 the Ministry of Housing and Local Government and the Welsh Office set up a working party under Mrs Lena Jeger to 'consider and report on the public health, amenity and economic aspects of the various methods of sewage disposal'. The working definition of sewage was taken as 'the liquid waste of the community' and this was considered from domestic, industrial, agricultural and transport sources. The report *Taken for granted: report of the working party on sewage disposal* (HMSO, 1970) considers the current use and management of water and methods of sewage treatment in general, followed by sections on disposal to rivers and canals, to estuaries and tidal rivers, to the sea, and to the land; effluent disposal problems in industry and agriculture are discussed, as are education and research in water pollution control, and future administration to cope with the problems. Recommendations are made at all sections.

The Jeger Report states that 'the volume of water used is rising at the rate of about three per cent per year'. There is therefore a need to conserve the water resources which are available and to create new sources wherever feasible. As early as 1962, the Institution of Civil Engineers held a symposium on this subject, the proceedings of which are published as *Conservation of water resources in the United Kingdom* (ICE, 1963). The Council of Europe is also concerned with the problems involved: its Committee of Experts for the Conservation of Nature and Landscape prepared a statement on *Water conservation: ecological consequences of the management of catchment areas and influence of forests on river basins* by Z Salverda (Strasbourg, Council of Europe, 1966, EXP/Nat (66)7). In Britain the main agent of water resource and conservation is the Water Resources Board. In 1966 the board published a major report on the future water supplies of south east England, *Water supplies in south east England* (HMSO, 1966), stressing the need to consider these on a regional basis. A further report surveys the problem of the north: *Water resources in the north* (HMSO, 1970). The board has further sponsored desk studies (primarily theoretical studies as opposed to full engineering and scientific surveys which involve field and laboratory work) of barrages across the Wash, the Solway, and Morecambe Bay which are reported in *The Wash: estuary storage* (HMSO, 1967); *Solway barrage desk study: report of consultants* (HMSO, 1967); *Morecambe Bay and Solway barrages: report on desk studies* (HMSO, 1967).

A major factor in environmental quality is noise, from whatever source it comes. The first major investigation into the problem in Britain was that of the Wilson committee, whose report *Noise: final report of the committee on the problem of noise* (HMSO, 1963, Cmnd 2056) postulated a standard of dissatisfaction with noise and formulated proposals for acceptable noise levels based on this. More recently further standards have been produced. The Traffic Noise Index (TNI) of F J Langdon and W E Scholes was presented in *Architects' journal* 147(16) April 17 1968 813-820. Subsequently, a new unit of Noise Pollution Level (NPL) was proposed which takes into account all types of urban noise nuisance, not only that of traffic: this is explained by D W Robinson in *The concept of noise pollution level* (HMSO, 1968, National Physical Laboratory Aero Report Ac38) and in *An outline guide to criteria for the limitation of urban noise* (HMSO, 1969, NPL Aero Report Ac39). Several surveys of noise and its effects have been carried out, mainly in London. The major exercise was the *London noise survey* (HMSO, 1968) which demonstrated that in central London traffic noise is the most frequently experienced source of disturbance. London's noise problem has been examined fairly extensively, for example in ' Environmental noise in London ' by R J Stephenson *Quarterly bulletin of the Research and Intelligence Unit of the Greater London Council* 4 October 1968 3-8, and in the Greater London Council's *Urban design bulletin 1: traffic noise, major urban roads* (GLC, 1970), which lays down standards for new routes and gives guidance on upgrading existing roads. 'A review of research on noise, with particular reference to schools ' by Priscilla Wrightson is in *Quarterly bulletin of the Research and Intelligence Unit of the Greater London Council* 8 September 1969 20-27. In ' Noise: economic aspects of choice '

Urban studies 7(2) June 1970 123-135, C D Foster and P J Mackie discuss the measures which can be used to alleviate noise nuisance and give directions for costing these measures so that decisions may be taken on a cost effectiveness basis.

Can the environment be quantified and costed? An attempt is made to define a methodology for such an exercise by R A Waller in ' Environmental quality: its measurement and control' *Regional studies* 4(2) August 1970 177-191, a paper which summarises techniques of evaluation and puts forward a method by means of which the various aspects of the environment can be related to a common scale which in turn can have a monetary value attached to it. The authors demonstrate an example of cost benefit analysis applied to environmental matters, and explore the philosophy of the technique and its implications.

LANDSCAPE AND LANDSCAPE DESIGN
Landscape can be defined as ' the whole of the outdoor environment in both town and countryside ',[99] and landscape planning (or landscape design, or landscape architecture) is concerned with the design of the environment so defined and with the conscious arrangement of objects within open spaces.

Brenda Colvin's *Land and landscape* (John Murray, 1969) is a rewritten version of her book of the same title published in 1947 and long out of print. It covers a very wide range, and is aimed principally at a student audience. The volume is an indispensable introduction to landscape architecture and the influence that land and landscape should be having on contemporary policies and attitudes. G E Jellicoe's *Studies in landscape design* (Oxford UP, 1960-1970, three volumes) comprise essays based on lectures and addresses given to varying types of audiences. Each volume is self-contained, but the set forms a coherent pattern leading from the Italian garden of the Renaissance period to more modern problems of landscaping. A wide range is covered in Sylvia Crowe's *Tomorrow's landscape* (Architectural Press, 1956) from the evolution of landscape and the forces which shape it to its consideration in four different forms—open country, the farmlands, the townsman's country or land subject to influence by the city and its dwellers, and urban landscape. A similar coverage is contained in one of the most stimulating books published in this field in 1970, Nan Fairbrother's *New lives, new landscapes* (Architectural Press, 1970). The author traces the evolution of the landscape and the effects on it of external factors such as changes in farming methods and the requirements of industry, and in the light of her conclusions that modern society is trying abortively to fit new uses into an old landscape she goes on to propose that we should consciously create a new landscape to suit modern and future needs. This new landscape she envisages in terms of city regions, the built-up urban landscape, the green-urban landscape (the city fringes), the new farming landscape, the man made wild, and finally roads as a new environment. A four point plan is then expounded for putting these ideas into practice. Miss Fairbrother's book is well written and well produced with excellent photographs, and it is full of ideas—' for a new form of car park for instance? At present we either leave our cars on a patch of ground or house them in human-style buildings. Why not new structures, half landscape half engineering, where cars are the natural inhabitants instead of being, as they now are, a large and prosperous form of landscape litter?'

The foremost textbook of landscape is *Techniques of landscape architecture* edited for the Institute of Landscape Architects by Arnold Weddle (Heinemann, 1967).[100] Weddle views the components of the landscape function as ranging from paving and fencing to coastal management and countryside conservation. His text considers only the urban and suburban aspects, but within this limitation are brought together contributions on the whole range of landscaping by twelve authoritative experts including Brenda Colvin on trees, Sylvia Crowe on site planting, and Frederick Gibberd on enclosure. The book is full of information of practical use, well illustrated with photographs, line drawings, tables, diagrams and other visual aids, and includes lists of documentary and institutional sources of further information.

On urban landscape, Garrett Eckbo has written a handsomely-produced book *Urban landscape design* (New York, McGraw-Hill, 1964). 'The central concern of this book is the quality of the physical landscape in which we all live. By quality we mean the relationship between an individual, a group of people, or a community and the landscape which surrounds each of them. By landscape we mean the total complex of physical elements within a given area of movement zone.' The main part of the book is given over to examples of various aspects of urban landscape: room and patio, building and site, buildings in groups, parks and playgrounds, streets and squares, neighbourhood, community, and region. There are many fine photographs and well executed sketches. More specific in its focus is Elizabeth Beazley's *Design and detail of space between buildings* (Architectural Press, 1960), a standard work which contains full and authoritative guidance on the treatment of urban spaces of all sizes. The Ministry of Housing and Local Government Design Bulletin 5 *Landscaping for flats: the treatment of ground space on high density housing estates* (HMSO, 1963) contains detailed advice, supported by graphic and tabulated material, on the 'detailed treatment of ground spaces around buildings . . . surfacings of all kinds, planting of grass, trees and shrubs, and different forms of barriers and screens'. It includes general and technical bibliographies and a list of relevant British Standard Specifications and Codes of Practice. A feature of urban landscape are the parks which distinguish many towns and cities. George Chadwick has written about them in *The park and the town: public landscape in the 19th and 20th centuries* (Architectural Press, 1966). He deals at length with the English civic parks of the nineteenth century including the more important park designers, then goes on to Paris, the American park movement, and the continental contribution up to date. He concludes with a chapter on the future of the park in the urban structure. His book is attractively produced, lavishly illustrated, and has a full bibliography.

Trees are demonstrably a most important factor in the landscape both of the town and the countryside. Guidance on the right types of trees to suit various situations and the correct method of growing and transplanting are contained in *Trees in town and city* from the Ministry of Housing and Local Government (HMSO, 1958); in *Trees for town and country: a selection of sixty trees suitable for general cultivation in England* prepared by the Association for Planning and Regional Reconstruction (Lund Humphries, third edition 1961) and in *Trees for the farmer* (Lincoln, Council for the Protection of Rural England, Lincolnshire Branch, 1967) which is full of practical information on treeplanting and encompasses spinneys, shelterbelts, choice of trees, preservation and wild life, economics, amenity, and professional help. It specifically refers to Lincolnshire, but applies equally to other counties in eastern England, and its policy is universal. Trees *en masse* are discussed by Sylvia Crowe in *Forestry in the landscape* (HMSO, 1966, Forestry Commission Booklet 18). Miss Crowe is landscape consultant to the Forestry Commission, and this illustrated booklet summarises her views on all aspects of forest landscape, including scale of development, choice of trees, and techniques of felling.

Nan Fairbrother and other writers have stressed the need to realise that this is an industrial age, and that with careful planning industry can be in tune with the landscape instead of in conflict with it. The place of industry in the landscape and the methods of creating good industrial landscape are elaborated by Sylvia Crowe in *The landscape of power* (Architectural Press, 1958). An account of a practical project in creating good industrial landscape is given by J St Bodfan Gruffydd in *Esso refinery, Fawley: landscape report and development plan* (the Author, 1970). The refinery was established before World War II on the shore of Southampton Water below Fawley village, since when it has developed and expanded inland, and will expand further, with consequent demand for adequate land resources for future development: a consultant was therefore commissioned to consider the landscape requirements of the site and to draw up a development plan based on these which will meet Esso's needs without impairing the visual quality of the area. Farm buildings, although in most cases smaller, can be just as obtrusive in the landscape as industrial buildings. In *Farm buildings and the countryside* (HMSO, 1970) a consortium of government departments headed by the Ministry of Housing and Local Government offers guidelines on various aspects of designing and siting farm buildings to fit in with the landscape while achieving maximum efficiency.

Landscape, like planning generally, has its own specific techniques, its methods of survey and analysis, its classifications and quantifications. Some of these are discussed in a set of papers given at the 1967 annual conference of the Institute of Landscape Architects at Durham, which collectively form a complete issue of *Plan-*

ning outlook new series 4 Spring 1968: four papers on survey and appreciation are followed by four on more general topics of landscape and landscape planning. The Landscape Research Group was formed in 1966 with the object of promoting 'broadly based studies of the landscape that cross and recross the arbitrary boundaries that at present separate disciplines'. *Methods of landscape analysis* (LRG, 1967) contains nine papers presented at its symposium held in May 1967 'in order to survey the means available to acquire information about the landscape, and to see what problems and possible solutions might exist in the collection, handling, storage and analysis of the data'. There is a contribution by P E Colinese on 'Information handling techniques'; Clifford Tandy and Derek Rigby Childs discuss their own respective proposals for recording and storing information; and the other papers range over various landscape techniques from the use of air photographs to the siting of power stations. One aspect of landscape on which some attention has been focused and which is the subject of a paper by J A C Higgins in the Landscape Research Group symposium is the formulation of a method for quantifying its value. A project to establish an evaluation system is described by K D Fines in 'Landscape evaluation: a research project in East Sussex' *Regional studies* 2(1) September 1968 41-55; and a 'Critique' by D M Brancher was printed in *Regional studies* 3(1) April 1969 91-92.

TRAFFIC AND TRANPORTATION PLANNING

Traffic and transportation planning are inseparable, and jointly they cannot be divorced from the planning and design of the communications infrastructure. Further than that, the whole range of transport planning is now seen as an integral part of the urban and regional planning process, and indeed has been a decisive factor in the broadening of the concepts of planning, both spatially and methodologically. This section takes into its purview, the forward planning and the design of the various parts of the communications network; the components of traffic planning and traffic management, including the measurement and forecasting of traffic and the devising of schemes which make the most efficient use of present resources for future traffic; and finally the integrated process of transportation planning as a function of land use and in conjunction with land use planning, including individual transportation systems. Inevitably, since roads form the major part of the communications network, and since road traffic is the primary agent of transportation, the emphasis on these subjects in the literature is apparent.

The national programme of road-building is set out in the Ministry of Transport White Paper *Roads for the future: the new inter-urban plan for England* (HMSO, 1969, Cmnd 4369) embodying proposals for a ' primary strategic national network ' and trunk road improvements; and for Scotland in the Scottish Development Department White Paper *Scottish roads in the 1970s* (Edinburgh, HMSO, 1969, Cmnd 3953). Progress on road building in the respective countries is reported in the Ministry of Transport annual *Roads in England* (HMSO) and the *Scottish roads report* issued annually with the *Report* of the Scottish Development Department.

The main carriers of road traffic are the motorways, both inter-urban and intra-urban. *Motorways* by James Drake and others (Faber, 1969) is concerned almost exclusively with the former, urban motorways being mentioned only in a short concluding chapter. The treatment of inter-urban motorways is comprehensive: their characteristics are described, their advantages over other types of road, and their pre- and post-war development in Europe, North America, Africa, and Asia. The legal, administrative, and financial procedures involved in motorway building are considered, and the remainder of the text is a full exposition of the principles of construction, landscaping, bridge design, interchanges, contract procedures, maintenance, and servicing. The route which a new motorway follows has clear implications in the context of overall planning and must be preceded by extensive research and survey not only in physical but also in human terms, for ' the chance of any motorway route being implemented is slight unless it is accepted by the community '.[101] A detailed discussion of how one firm of engineers approaches the problems involved is described by A Goldstein in ' Motorway route location studies ' in *Report of the Town and Country Planning Summer School, Keele, 1966* (TPI, 1966). The techniques described have application to both urban and inter-urban motorways, although most of the author's references are to urban motorways, ' for this is the problem of the next decade '.

490

Even those with no interest in planning must be aware that London has its motorway problems: public opposition to the road network plans of the Greater London Council and reactions to the *fait accompli* have frequently figured in national headlines. *Motorways in London* by J Michael Thompson and others (Duckworth, 1969) is the report of a working party set up by the London Amenity and Transport Association, which represents a uniquely well-organised effort of public participation in the planning process, in this case of opposition to the GLC proposals for London's road network. For a balance on this subject, a critical article on the report by Paul Kirby appeared in *JTPI* 55(10) December 1969 422-427.

On the more general topic of roads, C A O'Flaherty has written a major British text on the subject in *Highways* (Edward Arnold, 1967), which is an excellent general reference book on highway design and construction (though taking no account of the wider issues of transportation planning or of such associated topics as landscaping and environmental effects). The Ministry of Transport prepared a manual *Roads in urban areas* (HMSO, 1966) setting out recommended standards of urban road design and layout, replacing the old Blue Book of 1946 prepared by the Ministry of War Transport, *Design and layout of roads in built-up areas*. The new manual is well laid out and sub-headed throughout the text, data are presented mostly in tabular form, and there are explanatory diagrams and photographs. The companion manual for rural areas, by the Ministry of Transport in conjunction with the Scottish Development Department and the Welsh Office, is *The layout of roads in rural areas* (HMSO, 1968) which, together with the *Advisory manual on traffic prediction for rural areas* (HMSO, 1968), replaces the former pronouncement on the subject *Memorandum on the design of roads in rural areas* (HMSO, 1961, Memorandum 780). An integral feature of roads are the various types of signs which must be exhibited for the direction and control of traffic. In 1963 the Worboys Committee on Traffic Signs for All-purpose Roads presented its report *Traffic signs* (HMSO, 1963) recommending the introduction of entirely new traffic signs, and proposing that an illustrated manual should be published dealing with the use of these signs. Subsequently the Ministry of Transport with the Scottish Development Department issued *Informatory signs for use on all-purpose roads* (HMSO, 1964) and the Statutory Instrument SI 1964 no 1857 *The traffic signs regulations and general directions* (HMSO, 1964) in which the new signs were prescribed. The booklet on informatory signs will eventually be re-issued as chapter 2 in the Ministry of Transport loose-leaf *Traffic signs manual* (HMSO, 1965-), where it will join chapters 1, 3 and 4, an introduction, and chapters on regulatory signs, and warning signs. Further chapters of the manual will be issued in due course.

Photographs of new roads and motorways scarring the countryside successfully stress the importance of proper landscaping for all new communication routes. Sylvia Crowe's *The landscape of roads* (Architectural Press, 1960) stresses the importance of designing roads in relation to their surroundings—'constructions conceived as self-contained problems of design have been the bane of the landscape for the past century '—and brings together in the text ' all the factors which affect the appearance of roads '. This is a practical manual, which draws heavily on American and West German experience for illustration. Papers given at a conference organised by the British Road Federation and held at the Institution of Civil Engineers in London in 1962 are collected under the title *Landscaping of motorways* (BRF, 1963). There are three papers : ' the landscape architect as the collaborator on motorway alignment and design '; ' landscape engineering '; and ' the design of the motorway ', with discussions and introductions to each paper. The first British planning authority to think seriously and constructively about motorway landscaping within its area of responsibility—beyond the motorway boundary—was Durham County Planning Department, who issued in 1965 a report *Landscape and the Durham motorway*. This was a pioneering effort to assess the impact of the motorway, then under construction, on the countryside and to formulate a policy for the treatment of those parts of the countryside visible from the motorway, as a result of which a comprehensive ten year plan has been put in hand. A concise statement of the problems of blending urban motorways into the existing environment is contained in O A Kerensky's Rees Jeffreys Triennial Lecture of 1968 *Urban motorways and their environment* (Town Planning Institute, 1968). The Ministry of Transport has issued a small booklet, written by Clough Williams-Ellis, entitled *Roads in the landscape* (HMSO, 1967), which gives a brief history of road development and an outline of the aims and functions of the Ministry's Landscape Advisory Committee, together with a short discussion of the problem of land acquisition and amenity and practical considerations of landscaping. Although it is not confined to roads, mention can usefully be made here of the Ministry of Transport publication *The appearance of bridges* (HMSO, 1964) which gives guidance on the design and structure of bridges of all types and sizes from small footbridges to the large structures associated with new motorways, including advice on the problems of historic bridges, the whole fully illustrated with photographs.

While roads are the main part of the communications network, the other components of the network—railways, waterways, ports, airports—are an integral part of the total transport system and integrally involved also in urban and regional planning. A source of general information on air traffic and transport is *The geography of air transport* by Kenneth R Sealy (Hutchinson University Library, 1962) which discusses the pattern and distribution of air transport throughout the world, and includes a chapter on airport location. Sealy is also the author of an article ' The siting and development of British airports' *Geographical journal* 133(2) June 1967 148-171 which contains a thorough analysis of all aspects of air travel and airport location. Continuing information and data are provided in the annual reports of the British Airports Authority, published by HMSO. A major source of information on the siting of airports in Britain is the *Report* of the Roskill Commission on the Third London Airport (HMSO, 1971) together with the published evidence emanating from the lengthy inquiry proceedings. R C Fordham has set out to ' explain the economic context of a major airport planning problem and . . . some of the requirements for solving such problems ' in 'Airport planning in the context of the third London airport' *Economic journal* 80(318) June 1970 307-322. Both the method of approach and the final conclusions of the Roskill Commission have been the subject of some criticism; the bias towards economic analysis and in particular the use of cost benefit analysis were criticised by Professor Peter Self in ' Nonsense on stilts: the futility of Roskill ' in *New society* 16(405) July 2 1970 8-11, and in *Political quarterly* 41(3) July/September 1970 249-260. The evidence as presented in the report was re-examined by Professor Peter

493

Hall in ' The Roskill argument: an analysis ' in *New society* 17(435) January 28 1971 145-148, under the main heads of planning, noise, and method. One of the criticisms levelled at the Roskill recommendation of a new airport at Cublington has been that only potential sites in the south east region were considered (under the terms of reference), and these in relation to London. In fact, experts point out, London may not need a third airport, and the south east region may not be the best location for it: an international airport centred on the midlands may be a more viable solution, and the evidence to support this proposal is presented by Raymond Spurrier in 'Airport location: define the catchment area ' *Official architecture and planning* 32(12) December 1969 1477-1479. Another technical possibility in the light of VTOL and STOL aircraft is the urban vertiport, as discussed by Ian Fulton in ' City-centre vertiports: growth points for renewal ' *Official architecture and planning* 32(12) December 1969 1474-1476.

If the problem with roads is to build more of them, the problem with the railways is frequently to decide whether to keep them open, and what to do with them once closed. The whole system of rail transport, as was indicated in chapter 2, has to be viewed in the context of transport as a whole, as it is in the Transport Act of 1968; and in pursuance of the Act, the British Railways Board presented to Parliament its *Report on organisation* (HC50, 1969). At the same time as rail transport as a whole looks forward to new developments, it is also true that many lines have been closed and others struggle for their continued existence. This situation has resulted in the publication of such reports as the Countryside Commission's *Disused railways in the countryside of England and Wales* (HMSO, 1970), prompted by the volume of redundant land now existing; and *Cambrian coast line: a cost/benefit analysis of the retention of railway services on the Cambrian coastline* (*Machynlleth-Pwllheli*) (HMSO, 1970). The future of canals is equally in the balance, though in this case their non-use for transport is likely to be succeeded by their increasing use for recreation (see the section on recreation within this chapter). The principal source of information for inland waterways as part of the transport system is the British Waterways Board, whose annual reports are published by HMSO; now out of print are their earlier publications, *The future of the waterways* (HMSO, 1964) and *The facts about the waterways* (HMSO, 1966). On ports the principal source is the National Ports Council, whose annual reports are likewise published by HMSO; and ports collectively are the subject of a statement of government policy, *The reorganisation of the ports* (HMSO, 1969, Cmnd 3903) in which proposals for nationalisation are put forward: proposals which have since been rejected by the Conservative government.

One of the earliest statements on traffic planning was that by Sir H Alker Tripp, *Town planning and road traffic* (Edward Arnold, 1942). Tripp's book was produced in the wartime atmosphere of enthusiasm for planning and rebuilding of devastated towns and cities, and embodied some significant and forward-looking ideas. The principal one was his concept of precincts, which foreshadow Buchanan's environmental areas. Tripp proposed a road system having three levels of roads: the national network of arterial roads, connected to towns by sub-arterial roads, and local roads which would give access to sub-arterial but not to arterial roads. Such a system would create precincts serviced by a system of local roads carrying essential services and giving access to necessary functions; public transport services being carried on sub-arterial or arterial roads within easy distance of each precinct. Tripp's precincts were, as Tetlow and Goss point out, 'no more than an English version of the Radburn superblock, evolved by a traffic expert looking at problems produced by the motor vehicle from his own specialised point of view [Tripp was Assistant Commissioner of the Metropolitan Police]. But it was a most important contribution; it is remarkable that the differing functions of roads are only now beginning to be studied seriously.'[102] The total number of motor vehicles on Britain's roads had roughly quadrupled before another important statement on traffic problems appeared: Colin Buchanan's *Mixed blessing: the motor in Britain* (Leonard Hill, 1958) which embodied the ideas which were later to be crystallised as a major statement of practice in the government-sponsored report *Traffic in towns* (see below). Two further books on the general problems of increasing traffic and how to cope with and plan for it are Paul Ritter's *Planning for man and motor* (Oxford, Pergamon Press, 1964) and *Homes, towns and traffic* by John Tetlow and Anthony Goss (Faber, second edition 1968). The former of these is a big international picture book recording the various methods of reconciling man and the motor vehicle. It includes glossaries and extensive bibliographies, and a comprehensive collection of photographs and plans demonstrates examples from seventeen new towns, thirty three urban renewal schemes, and forty six residential areas, from twenty different countries. *Homes, towns and traffic* is concerned with the effect of traffic on town planning and in particular with its effect on residential areas of towns. The authors trace the development of the motor age, the early attempts to deal with it—for example, Radburn, Corbusier, the linear city—the blinkered attitude towards its increasing impact, and the practical ways in which it has been accommodated (or not accommodated) in the new towns, in redevelopment schemes, and in town centres. Examples are drawn from experience abroad as well as in Britain, and there are many plans and photographs for illustration. In the second edition of the book, new developments, new ideas and new opinions which have emerged since the first edition in 1965, particularly in the field of regional planning, have been incorporated in the largely rewritten second half.

The major statement on traffic planning in the decade just passed was the Buchanan Report *Traffic in towns* (HMSO, 1963; shortened version, Harmondsworth, Penguin Books, 1964), commissioned by a Conservative Minister of Transport and promoted by a Labour administration, which was to become responsible for the comprehensive Transport Act of 1968 discussed in chapter 2. Buchanan acknowledges the debt to Alker Tripp, but develops much further: what is embodied in the report is not a national road or traffic plan, nor specific proposals for any one place, but the ' broad outline of a comprehensive approach to the problems raised by traffic in towns '. The basic principle of the report is ' the canalisation of longer movements on to properly designed networks serving areas within which, by appropriate measures, environments suitable for civilised urban life can be developed '. The importance of coordination between the various forms of private and public transport, and between transport and land use planning, is pointed up clearly, and to this coordinating end the report recommends that the statutory development plan should incorporate a transportation plan. The recommendation became the letter of the law in the Town and Country Planning Act 1968, and the Transport Act of 1968 further strengthens the link between transport and town planning. Since this major statement of traffic and transport planning, and its acceptance by central government, there has been a steady flow of publications from the Ministry of Transport giving guidance to local authorities and making known the results of studies of various aspects of the problem.

In the *Advisory memorandum on urban traffic engineering techniques* issued jointly by the Ministry of Transport and the Scottish Development Department (HMSO, 1965) it is recognised that the land use/transportation surveys recommended in the Buchanan Report and in the MOHLG and MOT Joint Circular 1/64 cannot be implemented immediately and that in many areas action is urgently required. The memorandum therefore gives guidance on short to medium term solutions to traffic problems, from the importance of data to the conduct of surveys. In a later Circular 1/68 from the Ministry of Transport on *Traffic and transport plans* (HMSO, 1968) guidance is given to local authorities in the preparation of the traffic and transport plans for which the Minister had called, which would show how they intend to relate their traffic and parking policies to their available road capacities and to their immediate and longer term policy objectives. The first part of the Circular is ' to indicate the desirable range of subject material and degree of detail, and to suggest one method of presentation '. The second part details the scope of the plan and the information it should contain, together with an illustration of a plan for an imaginary county borough of 125,000 population. *Better use of town roads: the report of a study of the means of restraint of traffic on urban roads* (HMSO, 1967) also emanates from the Ministry of Transport, and considers various methods of limiting the volume of traffic in towns ' in order to bring about a better relationship between the amount of road space available and the vehicles that want to use it '. Methods considered include road pricing, parking controls, loading restrictions, and direct charges for road use; methods of enforcement and the effects of implementation in terms of costs, manpower and so on, are also discussed. The Ministry of Transport and the Welsh Office jointly produce a big loose-leaf manual *Traffic management and parking* (HMSO, 1968-) to give guidance to local authorities with traffic and parking responsibilities under the Transport Act 1968. It is not intended as a comprehensive textbook on traffic management and law but to give practical information and advice on day to day matters; it is intended that the manual should be up-dated. A report of a practical experiment in traffic and transport planning is issued jointly by Leeds City Council, the Ministry of Transport and the Ministry of Housing and Local Government under the title *Planning and transport: the Leeds approach* (HMSO, 1969). This is the record of a ' joint study to consider the application of integrated parking, traffic management and public transport policies within the framework of land use planning, and to consider the design and improvement of environmental areas from which extraneous traffic could be excluded as a result of these policies ', and includes an outline plan of action based on the study. Transport control generally, applied to all modes of transport, is described by Paul M Danforth in *Transport control* (Aldus Books, 1970) an illustrated text on methods of controlling road, sea, rail, and air traffic and the technical problems involved.

On traffic engineering and management generally, an introductory text is provided by F D Hobbs and B D Richardson in *Traffic engineering* (Oxford, Pergamon Press, 1967, two volumes) aimed not only at engineers but also at other professionals who may require a knowledge of traffic techniques. The first volume outlines the development of road legislation, and goes on to characteristics of vehicles and human road users, traffic studies in general and origin and destination studies in particular, traffic signals, and road accidents. The second volume begins with an introduction on traffic and planning, and then proceeds to matters of capacity and intersections, street lighting, signs and road markings, road alignment, and parking. Two fruitful sources of detailed information are the volumes *Research on road safety* (HMSO, 1963) and *Research on road traffic* (HMSO, 1965) both compiled by the Road Research Laboratory. More technical, and written for the traffic engineer rather than the planner, is *The theory of road traffic flow* by Winifred D Ashton (Methuen, 1966) which draws together all the mathematical work of relevance to traffic engineering concerned with the fundamentals of road traffic flow and its theories.

Two particular problems of traffic planning are the acceptance of cars in residential areas, and the perennial question of parking. In respect of the former, guidance has been given by the Ministry of Housing and Local Government in Design Bulletin 10, *Cars in housing 1. Some medium density layouts* (HMSO, 1966) and the Design Bulletin 12, *Cars in housing 2. Dimensions; and multi-storey parking garages* (HMSO, 1967). Parking alone is the topic of the same ministry's Planning Bulletin 7, *Parking in town centres* (HMSO, 1965) issued jointly with the Ministry of Transport and the Scottish Development Department. The Institution of Municipal Engineers had already by then produced their statement on *Provision of car parks in shopping and commercial centres* (IME, 1961). The design of car parks and garages is not our province here; but some general texts on parking are worth noting, all of them American in origin. *Parking* by Geoffrey Baker and Bruno Funaro (New York, Reinhold, 1958) is a well-illustrated volume demonstrating solutions to parking problems throughout the world. The Eno Foundation for Transportation, of Saugatuck in Connecticut, has compiled many volumes of great value to traffic in general and in particular two titles on parking, *Traffic design of parking garages* (Saugatuck, Eno Foundation, 1957) and *Parking* (Saugatuck, Eno Foundation, 1957). Among the many publications of the Highway Research Board of Washington are Special Report 11 *Parking as a factor in business* (Washington DC, HRB, 1953) and Special Report 11B *Shopping habits and travel patterns* (Washington DC, HRB, 1955), both of these summarised in Special Report 11D *Parking and its relationships to business* (1956).

Mention has been made in passing of methods of controlling or deliberately restricting traffic in its use of existing facilities. One of the most promising of such restrictive measures is road pricing, and on this subject the Ministry of Transport issued *Road pricing: the economic and technical possibilities* (HMSO, 1964) known as the Smeed Report, after the chairman of the study group which investigated the problem. The report examines various methods of pricing, for example, differential fuel taxes and parking charges, and puts forward the conclusion that the best method would be to charge for the actual use made of congested roads, using some form of meter. Further contributions to the subject are made by J M W Stewart in *A pricing system for roads* (Edinburgh, Oliver and Boyd, 1965, University of Glasgow Social and Economic Studies, Occasional Paper 4), and by G J Roth in a series of papers, *Paying for parking* (Institute of Economic Affairs, 1965, Hobart Paper 33), *A self-financing road system* (Institute of Economic Affairs, 1966, Research Monograph 33), and *Paying for roads: the economics of traffic congestion* (Harmondsworth, Penguin Books, 1967). Road pricing, and making the private motorist pay for his privileged facilities, is only one aspect of the general economics of transport. Another aspect is the pricing of public transport in relation to private transport. Penelope M Williams discusses this in respect of a study based on central London in ' Low fares and the urban transport problem ' in *Urban studies* 6(1) February 1969 83-92 which examines the effects of reducing public transport fares on rush hour congestion. The economics of the total transport system in Britain are thoroughly analysed by K M Gwilliam in *Transport and public policy* (Allen and Unwin, 1965). The author concentrates primarily on inter-urban transport, in general and in separate chapters dealing with the individual transport agencies, and examines various schemes for coordination between different transport modes.

Attacking the problem of traffic congestion from the other end, as it were, the Ministry of Transport has also considered the modification of the vehicles themselves in *Cars for cities: a study of trends in the design of vehicles with particular reference to their use in towns* (HMSO, 1967). This embodies reports of a steering group and a working group set up in 1964 arising out of the Buchanan Report proposals to consider the changes in the design of vehicles which could contribute towards the solution of traffic problems. The study took in personal transport, with two, three or four wheels, taxis, buses and coaches, and goods vehicles, and examined also the related problems of safety, noise, and air pollution.

Of crucial importance to any system of traffic management is the number of vehicles which will have to be accommodated in the future. As J B Cullingworth points out, the ' enormous increase in traffic and the resultant urban thrombosis to which it has given rise is too striking and obvious to require detailed documentation. What is less apparent is the even greater rate of increase which may be anticipated in the future.'[103] In planning for the future, estimates have to be obtained from reliable sources on which to base calculations. The traffic forecasts used in the Buchanan Report were those by J C Tanner in ' Forecasts of future numbers of vehicles in Great Britain ' in *Roads and road construction* 40(477) September 1962 263-274. These forecasts are criticised, in the context of a full discussion of the issues involved in the forecasting of car ownership with special reference to the case of Leeds, by J F Kain and M E Beesley in ' Forecasting car ownership and use ' in *Urban studies* 2(2) November 1965 163-185. Tanner replied to the criticisms in ' Comments on " Forecasting car ownership and use " ' in *Urban studies* 3(2) June 1966 143-146, rejecting Kain and Beesley's argument and criticising their own method of forecasting car ownership in Leeds. Tanner's 1962 estimates have been superseded by a paper in which earlier methods and forecasts have been reconsidered, ' Forecasts of vehicle ownership in Great Britain ' in *Roads and road construction* 43(515) November 1965 341-347 and 43(516) December 1965 371-376. Further estimates were produced by Tanner in *Revised forecasts of vehicles and traffic in Great Britain* (Crowthorne, Berks, Road Research Laboratory, 1967) and these have been further supplemented by *Forecasts of vehicle ownership in counties and county boroughs in Great Britain* by P G Herrmann (Crowthorne, Road Research Laboratory, 1968) and by *Forecasts of vehicles and traffic in Great Britain: 1969* by A H Tulpule (Crowthorne, Road Research Laboratory, 1969, Report LR 288). An indication of how the vehicles on the roads are distributed is given in *The distribution of traffic in Great Britain through the twenty four hours of the day in 1968* by J B Dunn and I J Hutchings (Crowthorne, Road Research Laboratory, 1969, Report LR 295).

Transportation planning is a wider field of study than traffic planning or traffic engineering or the Buchanan concept of traffic architecture, and considerably wider than traffic management. Clearly a study of existing traffic—its origin and destination, flow patterns, and so on—is basic to transportation planning, but this latter goes further in that it is concerned with predicting demand for movement as represented by different land uses, and planning the distribution of that demand between various forms of transport; and the basis of such forward planning is the transportation study, which Buchanan defines as ' a comprehensive study of all the demands for movement in a locality (including the use of origin and destination surveys, home interview surveys, and other investigations) to provide a basis for a coordinated planning of transport systems '.[104] The classic seminal study which established the thesis that different types of land use generate different and variable traffic flows is *Urban traffic: a function of land use* by Robert B Mitchell and Chester Rapkin, of the University of Pennsylvania (New York, Columbia UP, 1954). Their thesis was based on an analysis of movement and land use data relating to Philadelphia, and represented a significant breakthrough in that it switched the emphasis from the analysis and extrapolation of existing traffic flows to the study of the land uses that generate the traffic flows. Their approach has dominated land use/transportation studies in the United States since the early 1950's, and came later to Britain in the Buchanan Report, though the theory was not put into practice fully until the later 1960's. Transportation techniques have thus been earlier and more fully developed in the United States than in Britain, and for this reason the most notable texts on the subject are American in origin. Lowdon Wingo's *Transportation and urban land* (Baltimore, Johns Hopkins Press, 1961) is a fairly technical discussion of the requirements of urban transportation within the framework of urban decision- and policy-making, and incorporates the development of a model for predicting requirements, together with discussion of its application. *The urban transportation problem* by J R Meyer, J F Kain, and M Wohl (Cambridge, Mass, Harvard UP, 1965) is a product of a Rand Corporation study of urban transportation problems, started in 1960, and financed mainly by a grant from the Ford Foundation. It concentrates on basic issues rather than the particular problems of specific areas, and studies most closely changes in the technology of urban transportation, the changing pattern of land use within American metropolitan areas, trip-making behaviour, including choice of mode, and governmental policy affecting land use and transportation requirements. *Readings in urban transportation* edited by G M Smerk (Bloomington, Indiana UP, 1968) is a collection of papers by fourteen contributors, three of them British, each one having an editorial synopsis. The first group deals with urban traffic congestion and its amelioration; the second, more specifically relating to the United States, discusses the federal role in urban transportation. The federal role was discussed

502

also in an earlier book by Smerk, *Urban transportation: the federal role* (Bloomington, Indiana UP, 1965), in which he diagnoses the problems in the United States and argues the case for more federal assistance and control. The first British comprehensive treatment is *Introduction to transportation planning* by M J Bruton (Hutchinson, 1970) which conveniently gathers together and reviews existing experience. Bruton limits himself to the techniques of estimating future demands for movement and his book is a sound introduction to traffic estimation procedures in particular and the transportation planning process in general. He outlines the history of transportation planning and describes the overall land use/transportation planning process as it currently operates; and goes on to discuss in detail the various stages involved—data collection, trip generation, trip distribution, traffic assignment, and modal split. His final two chapters deal concisely with computers in transportation planning, and techniques of economic evaluation of proposals. Also now available in English translation is a classic German-Swiss work, *Transportation and town planning* by Kurt Leibbrand (Leonard Hill, 1970) which is a development in depth of the relationships between urban structure and urban transportation systems, supported with a wealth of quantified data (though now some years old).

In a contribution on ' Economics and methodology in urban transport planning ' to *Regional and urban studies* edited by J B Cullingworth and S C Orr (see above) Richard Kirwan argues that transport planning is ' the most developed part of urban planning at the present time (in terms of technique and methodology, rather than of results or administrative machinery) . . . the development of new techniques has focused attention on to the relationship between transport planning and the rest of the urban planning process and on to the methodology in general '. There is now a substantial documentation on the techniques and the methodology of transportation planning and the transportation study in particular. One study which stresses the relationship of transport and the planning process is ' Transportation studies and British planning practice ' by William Solesbury and Alan Townsend in *Town planning review* 41(1) January 1970 63-79, a review of the development and impact of transportation studies with emphasis on the role they have come

503

to play in British planning practice, both in its methodology and its administration. *Metropolitan plan making: an analysis of experience with the preparation and evaluation of alternative land use and transportation plans* by David E Boyce and others (Philadelphia, Regional Science Research Institute, 1970, Monograph Series 4) contains a comparative analysis of thirteen major metropolitan land use and transportation planning programmes. A substantial comprehensive review of transportation methods currently in use or being developed is provided by Alan G Wilson and others in *New directions in strategic transportation planning* (Centre for Environmental Studies, 1969, CES-WP-36) which is also a literature review. The study was undertaken as a report to OECD, and contains much interesting material, with the technical details relegated to seven appendices. Another substantial report on progress in this field is embodied in the proceedings of the *Transportation engineering conference* held by the Institution of Civil Engineers in London in 1968 (ICE, 1968). There are two major sections within the proceedings: the first is concerned with transportation studies and reviews results to date from typical areas, with critical assessment of London, the west midlands conurbation, and Belfast; the second examines technological and operational advances in public transport in the United States, Germany, and the United Kingdom. *The conurbations: a study* by Colin Buchanan and Partners (British Road Federation, 1969) is a comparative study of progress in road and transportation planning in each of the seven conurbations—Greater London, west midlands, south east Lancashire, Merseyside, west Yorkshire, Tyneside, and central Clydeside, with a summary and conclusions. A comparable compilation relating to Canadian experience is *Urban transportation developments in eleven Canadian metropolitan areas* prepared by N D Lea Associates for the Transportation Planning Committee of the Canadian Good Roads Association (Ottawa, CGRA, 1966), which is a summary of transportation facilities related to urban structure and population characteristics in a representative group of Canadian cities. World coverage is available in the proceedings of the *Symposium on transportation studies in very big cities* held in London in 1969 by the Planning and Transport Research and Computation Co Ltd (PTRC, 1969) which covers the studies carried out in London, Paris, Rotterdam, Copenhagen, Montreal, the SELNEC region (SE Lancs-NE Cheshire) and the US Tri-state region.

Individual transportation studies, with or without a land use element, are also well documented. The prototype of the large-scale North American computerised transportation studies, which first applied the approach of Mitchell and Rapkin, was the *Detroit metropolitan area traffic study* (1953), followed by the *Chicago area transportation study* (1956) and the continuing large-scale exercises of the *Penn-Jersey transportation study* and the *Tri-state New York metropolitan transportation study* which refine and extend the basic techniques to a considerable degree of sophistication. These studies, and other subsequent large urban transportation studies, are supported by the Bureau of Public Roads of the US Department of Commerce in Washington DC.

In Great Britain, the early studies of the 1960's were still based on the traffic survey concept. The first phase of the London traffic survey, initiated in 1960, was designed within this framework, and the results of it are published in *The London traffic survey v1* (London County Council, 1964). A similar type of study is reported in *SELNEC: a highway plan 1962* (Manchester, William Morris Press, 1962), and in *Merseyside conurbation traffic survey 1962* (Liverpool, Steering Committee on Merseyside Traffic and Transport, 1965). A good example of a more modest study is the *Leicester traffic plan* by W K Smigielski, the City Planning Officer (Leicester, City Council, 1964).

The first impact of American concepts and methods was felt in the second phase of the London traffic survey, and its amended objectives and report are contained in *The London traffic survey v2* (Greater London Council, 1966); and the introduction of the land use factor as promoted in the Buchanan Report, was reinforced by Joint Circular 1/64 of the Ministry of Transport and the Ministry of Housing and Local Government, *Buchanan Report, traffic in towns* (HMSO, 1964). The first land use/transportation study commissioned by the government was that for the west midlands conurbation, carried out by Freeman, Fox, Wilbur Smith and Associates and published by them in three volumes as *West midlands transportation study* (1968). With the start of the Tyneside study in 1967/68 all the country's major conurbations are being, or have

505

been covered. Studies are also in progress, or have been completed for many other smaller urban groupings and for several independent towns. Results are available from some of these studies, for example, the *Greater Glasgow transportation study* by Scott Wilson Kirkpatrick and Partners (v1 1967, v2 1968); the final report of the *City of Worcester transportation study* by Transportation Planning Associates (1967); the *Hitchin, Letchworth, Baldock transportation study* (1968) and the *Hertford, Ware, Hoddesdon transportation study* (1968) both by Hertfordshire County Council; the *Harlow transportation study* by W S Atkins and Partners (v1 1968); and the *Belfast transportation plan* by R Travers Morgan and Partners (1969). This is in no way a comprehensive list of the study reports arising out of transportation studies: many are in any case not yet completed or published. Figure 14 shows the location of the studies completed or in progress in England and Wales.

With regard to these studies, Solesbury and Townsend write ' the coordination of transportation studies with land-use planning has by no means been straightforward. All the studies have collected information related to present and future land use as part of their input data, and for that reason are commonly called land use/transport studies. Land use is, however, only one of the exogenous inputs and the studies, as they have been mostly conducted to date, are more accurately described simply as transportation studies for they have only slowly and unevenly been opened to the influence of wider urban planning.[105] Later, they comment ' its [*ie* the study's] interaction with other forms of urban activity has generally been through only a one-way relationship, that is of receiving the best available set of estimates for exogenous variables, and of building the traffic forecasts upon them. Thus the procedure involves the consideration of alternative transportation solutions, but is normally based on only one set of zonal land use data, which controls the final outcome.'[106] In the context of these remarks, the study of Teesside, completed in 1968, is of considerable significance, being ' the first major study in Britain that can be described as a land use/transportation study ',[107] its aim being to produce an urban strategy plan for 1991. Carried out jointly by Scott Wilson and Kirkpatrick, and Wilson and Womersley, the first volume has been published as *Teesside survey and plan* (HMSO, 1969) a joint production of MOHLG

FIGURE 14: Transportation studies completed and in progress at 1970 in England and Wales. Courtesy of *Town planning review*.

and MOT (see also chapter 9). The study is notable in that it develops alternative transport plans against seven alternative strategies of development, by means of a two stage process, 'a first stage for exploring alternative urban strategies at a coarse level of aggregation, and a second stage for refining a preferred strategy into a final land use and transport plan at a fine level. The evaluation of the latter was against criteria of travel volume and cost.'[108] Similar objectives have been adopted in the studies of west Yorkshire and Merseyside, both by Traffic Research Corporation.

It has become evident in general terms that the traffic generation of the various land uses is a vital factor in planning transport systems. Clearly, different types of land use generate different types and volumes of traffic and it is important to recognise what these are. In 'Transportation and land use structures' in *Urban studies* 4(3) November 1967 201-217, G B Jameson, W K Mackay and J C R Latchford describe a research programme to demonstrate in quantitative terms the transportation implications arising from alternative distributions of the three primary urban land uses—residential, commercial, and industrial. Industry alone was the subject of a Ministry of Transport enquiry, reported in full as *Industrial demand for transport* by B T Bayliss and S L Edwards (HMSO, 1970) and in summary form as *Transport for industry* (HMSO, 1970). This was a study of the determinants of demand for transport, of transport facilities and the different characteristics of consignments in manufacturing industry. A study carried out in the Medway towns of the relationship between commercial road traffic and the characteristics of the firms that generate the traffic is reported by D M Starkie in *Traffic and industry: a study in traffic generation and spatial interaction* (London School of Economics, 1967, Geographical Paper 3), which shows in particular how differing local industrial structures can have enormous effects on traffic flows. One of the principal elements of traffic is the journey to work, particularly in the larger urban areas and the conurbations where there is a heavy incidence of commuting. Ray Thomas' *Journeys to work* (Political and Economic Planning, 1968) concentrates mainly on central London, and his analysis is based on the mass of data resulting from recent investigations into London work journeys and from the 1966 sample census. The study takes as its starting point the how and why of the Victoria underground line and then examines the economics and form of public transport systems. Its main value is that it draws together a quantity of relevant material from a diverse range of sources. Although it has virtually the same title, F R Wilson's *Journey to work* (Croydon, MacLaren, 1967) is quite different from the PEP study in that it is concerned with modal split in the journey to work. It describes a piece of applied research—the devising of a mathematical model capable of evaluating choices between work journey modes. The author is American, the prose is mid-Atlantic, and the work is based to some extent on similar models already developed in the United States, but an enormous exercise in fact-finding—32,000 questionnaires distributed in Coventry and Greater London—gives the study solid British roots. It is natural that the commuting patterns in London and its surrounding region should attract much interest, since they are on a more intensive scale than those of any other region. One of the earliest papers on the subject was ' Journey to work in the London region ' by John Westergaard in *Town planning review* 28(1) April 1957 37-62. Subsequent examinations have been reported by J S Wabe in ' Commuter travel in Central London ' in *Journal of transport economics and policy* 3(1) January 1969 48-68; by D A Quarmby in ' Travel mode for journey to work ' in *Journal of transport economics and policy* 1(3) September 1967 297-300; by David Jordan, who examines the data from which journey to work analyses can be made in ' Commuting into London: a commentary on the 1966 census workplace tables ' in *JTPI* 55(2) February 1969 72-73; and by the Greater London Council Planning Department in *Generation of business traffic in Central London* (GLC, 1968, Research Paper 3). Some more general observations are contained in ' The journey to work in Britain: some trends and problems ' by R Lawton in *Regional studies* 2(1) September 1968 27-40; in ' Traffic induced by central area facilities ' by Franklin Medhurst in *Town planning review* 34(1) April 1963 50-60; and in *White collar commuters: a second survey* carried out by National Opinion Polls (Location of Offices Bureau, 1967, Research Paper 1).

Finally we come to consider the transport systems themselves. ' Every transportation system is designed to fulfil a primary task in the movement of people. These functional roles of transportation relate directly to trip distances. Some systems are designed to move people over short distances, such as moving sidewalks; others are designed for trips of thousands of miles, such as jet aircraft.'[109] The most popular transportation system for the individual is of course the motor car, and the private motorist is the main generator of traffic on the roads. The characteristics of private motorists were examined and analysed thoroughly in a survey carried out for the Government Social Survey and reported in *Private motoring in England and Wales* by P G Gray (HMSO, 1969). Surveys have also been done of specialised sections of the motoring community, for example the Countryside Commission report *The weekend motorist in the Lake District* by W B Yapp (HMSO, 1969) based on a survey of motorists leaving the Lake District on specified weekends in 1966 (see also the section on recreation). Private motorists are obviously causing much of the congestion which now prevails in most urban areas, and therefore, as Buchanan emphasised, the role of public transport in combating this congestion is important. *Urban mass transit planning* edited by W S Homburger (Berkeley, University of California Institute of Transportation and Traffic Engineering, 1967) is a very full textbook on the theory and practice of public transport in the United States, which is relevant for British planners as a reference book, with good references and bibliography. New systems are being evolved to provide satisfactory alternatives to the convenience of the private car. Some developments in the United States are described by Allan M Voorhees as ' Tomorrow's transportation ' in *Planning outlook* new series 7 Autumn 1969 19-34.

In *New movement in cities* (Studio Vista, 1966) Brian Richards examines a wide range of movement systems for people in towns; the book is profusely illustrated and the accompanying text is entertaining and thought-provoking. Some reports are also available of practical experiments and feasibility studies in individual towns and cities. *The Manchester rapid transit study* (Manchester, City Transport Department, 1968) is a three-volume report, of which the second volume is a ' Study of rapid transit systems and concepts ' by DeLeuw Cather and Partners and Hennesey Chadwick OhEocha and Partners, and the third volume contains the results of a preliminary study to identify the first constructional priorities and prepare

510

a plan of action which would allow the earliest possible starting date for services. The study of systems arose out of a Ministry of Transport request for a feasibility study for a monorail from city centre to Manchester airport, which was widened to a study of the characteristics and suitability of various types of rapid transit systems for a sixteen mile route through the centre of the city; four systems are intensively examined: the Alweg monorail, the duorail steel wheeled (railway), the Safége monorail and the Westinghouse transit skybus. The report finds in favour of the railway. The findings of the study are summarised by John Millar and John Dean in ' Practical considerations of rapid transit ' in *JTPI* 54(4) April 1968 158-171. Experience from abroad is summarised by H P White in ' The rapid transit revival: a comparative review of overseas practice ' *Urban studies* 4(2) June 1967 137-148.

Specific studies of bus services of various kinds are described in *One-man bus operation* by N Morton (Newcastle upon Tyne, Oriel Press, 1969) which describes experience in Sunderland; in the *City of Chichester mini-bus feasibility study* (Chichester, West Sussex County Council, 1967); in ' Passengers per mile ' by L H Smith in *Municipal journal* 78(28) July 10 1970 1546-1549, which describes the present use and future potential of bus services in Leicester; and in ' Dial-a-ride demand actuated public transport ' by P R Oxley in *Traffic engineering and control* 12(3) July 1970 146-148 which describes British and American projects in buses on demand. These studies all relate to the transport of humans, whether publicly or privately.

Freight is an equally important factor in the transport system and the need for an overview of all methods of carrying it is clear, so that overloading of one part of the network—roads, for example —can be relieved by making other parts—canals or railways— more efficient. Government policy on freight was outlined in the White Paper *The transport of freight* (HMSO, 1967, Cmnd 3470) and subsequently incorporated into the Transport Act 1968. The National Freight Corporation was set up as a result, and submitted to Parliament its *Report on organisation* (HC 72, 1970). New techniques in freight transport are also important, for example developments in containerisation have effects on both terminal facilities at ports and on the road network. ' Containerisation refers to the transport of goods in special standard freight containers generally with a cross section of eight feet by eight feet and available in various standard lengths between ten and forty feet . . . and made so that they may be lifted by special devices for transfer to and from one mode of transport to another or to the ground . . . the primary advantage of this system is the cheap and rapid transfer of goods from one mode of transport to another.'[110] The effects of containerisation on inland transport networks have been examined in a joint research project by the Universities of Strathclyde and Glasgow, the findings of which are contained in the *Final report on containerisation: implications for distribution and transportation in west central Scotland* (Glasgow, University of Strathclyde, 1970); and the implications for ports are examined in *Containerisation in the North Atlantic: a port-to-port analysis, and the 1970 outlook for deep sea container services,* a report prepared by Arthur D Little Ltd for the National Ports Council (NPC, 1967), which is a study of UK container berth requirements. Nor can transportation be considered any longer in an isolated national context, and as Britain moves towards Europe, W Frain's *Transportation and distribution for European markets* (Butterworths, 1970, Marketing in Europe Series), is a timely indication of the implications of the wider scene.

REFERENCES

1 Aristotle's *Politics* and *Athenian constitution* edited and translated by John Warrington (Dent, 1959, Everyman's library) 46n.

2 Brenda White *Planners and information* (Library Association, 1970, Research Publications 3) 101-103.

3 Gordon E Cherry *Town planning in its social context* (Leonard Hill, 1970) in particular chapter 2 ' Social objectives of planning '.

4 J Brian McLoughlin *Urban and regional planning: a systems approach* (Faber, 1969) 94 (author's italics).

5 Raymond Unwin *Town planning in practice* (Fisher Unwin, fifth impression 1917) 289.

6 J B Cullingworth and S C Orr (*eds*) *Regional and urban studies: a social science approach* (Allen and Unwin, 1969) 12.

7 R E Pahl *Patterns of urban life* (Longmans, 1970) 130.

8 J B Cullingworth *Town and country planning in England and Wales* (Allen and Unwin, third edition 1970) 319.

9 J B Cullingworth *op cit* 320.

10 J B Cullingworth *op cit* 321.

11 Britton Harris ' How to succeed with computers without really trying ' *Journal of the American Institute of Planners* 33(1) January 1967 11.

12 C Lee ' Models in planning: some observations and reservations ' *Planning outlook* new series 8 Spring 1970 14.

13 Margaret M Camina ' Plan-design models: a review ' *Town planning review* 40(2) July 1969 127-128.

14 Peter Hall in *New society* 16(426) November 26 1970.

15 Leo F Schnore ' Problems in the quantitative study of urban history ' in *The study of urban history* edited by H J Dyos (Edward Arnold, 1968) 190.

16 Gordon E Cherry *op cit* chapter 3 ' Social issues for the town planner '.

17 Peter Cox *Demography* (Cambridge, Cambridge UP, fourth edition 1970) 1.

18 T H Hollingsworth *Historical demography* (Hodder and Stoughton, 1969) 37.

19 Peter Cox *op cit* 21.

20 R K Kelsall *Population* (Longmans, 1967) 89.

21 William Lean *Economics and land use planning: urban and regional* (Estates Gazette, 1969) 45.

22 William Alonso *Location and land use: toward a general theory of land rent* (Cambridge, Mass, Harvard UP, 1964) 2.

23 J B Cullingworth *op cit* 150.

24 *The Land Commission* (HMSO, 1965, Cmnd 2771).

25 Desmond Heap *Introducing the Land Commission Act 1967* (Sweet and Maxwell, 1967) 14.

26 William Lean *op cit* vi.

27 D V Donnison *The government of housing* (Harmondsworth, Penguin Books, 1967) 9.

28 See, for example, Lionel Needleman's article ' The comparative economics of improvement and new building ' in *Urban studies* 6(2) June 1969 196-209, in which the author offers formulae to aid local authorities in deciding between rebuilding and modernising areas of sub-standard housing, a choice which is examined first in the case of an individual dwelling and then for groups of dwellings.

513

29 J B Cullingworth *op cit* 264.

30 Ministry of Health: Central Housing Advisory Committee *Standards of fitness for habitation: report by a sub-committee,* chairman, Sir Miles E Mitchell (HMSO, 1946).

31 J B Cullingworth 'Housing analysis' in *Urban and regional studies* edited by J B Cullingworth and S C Orr (Allen and Unwin, 1969) 152.

32 D V Donnison *op cit* 176.

33 Editor's note by R E Pahl to *Readings in urban sociology* (Oxford, Pergamon Press, 1968) 159.

34 B Mottershaw 'Estimating shopping potential' *Planning outlook* new series 5 Autumn 1968 41-42.

35 John Goddard 'Changing office location patterns within central London' *Urban studies* 4(3) November 1967 276.

36 Maurice Wright 'Provincial office development' *Urban studies* 4(3) November 1967 218.

37 Peter Hall *Theory and practice of regional planning* (Pemberton Books, 1970) 21.

38 Peter Hall *Theory and practice of regional planning op cit* 22.

39 P M Smith 'What kind of regional planning?' *Urban studies* 3(3) November 1966 254-255.

40 Peter Hall *Theory and practice of regional planning op cit* 74.

41 Derek Lee *Regional planning and location of industry* (Heinemann Educational, 1969) 43-46, for discussion of the Regional Employment Premium.

42 J N H Britton *Regional analysis and economic geography* (G Bell, 1967) 2.

43 John Friedmann and William Alonso (*eds*) *Regional development and planning* (Cambridge, Mass, MIT Press, 1964) 75.

44 John Friedmann and William Alonso *op cit* 704.

45 Michael Chisholm *Rural settlement and land use* (Hutchinson University Library, 1962) 21.

46 William Alonso *op cit* 2.

47 Peter Haggett *Locational analysis in human geography* (Edward Arnold, 1965) 327.

48 J Brian McLoughlin in *JTPI* 56(8) September/October 1970 368.

49 Peter Haggett *op cit* 13.

50 Service centres are defined as 'centres where shopping, entertainment, cultural, professional and similar services are sought by people from the surrounding areas' by Ian Carruthers in 'A classification of service centres in England and Wales' *Geographical journal* 123(3) September 1957 371-385.

51 J N H Britton *op cit* 5.

52 G C R Wheeler in *JTPI* 54(4) April 1968 188-189.

53 Aristotle *op cit* 198.

54 Raymond Unwin *op cit* 98.

55 Ruth Glass 'Urban sociology in Britain: a trend report' *Current sociology* 4(4) June 1955 5-76.

56 C B Purdom 'A criticism' in *Garden cities and town planning* new series IV 124-125. Quoted in William Ashworth *The genesis of modern British town planning* (Routledge and Kegan Paul, 1954) 196.

57 Sir Patrick Abercrombie *Town and country planning* (Oxford UP, third edition 1959) 128.

58 Planning Advisory Group (of MOHLG, MOT, and SDD) *The future of development plans* (HMSO, 1965) 27.

59 J B Cullingworth *Town and country planning* (Allen and Unwin, third edition 1970) 262.

60 Peter Self 'A new vision for new towns' *Town and country planning* 38(1) January 1970 4.

61 Robert Park *and others* *The city* (Chicago, Chicago UP, new edition 1968) 1.

62 Lewis Mumford *The city in history* (Harmondsworth, Penguin Books, 1966) 630.

63 The *International social development review* takes the place of three earlier United Nations publications—*International social service review, Housing, building and planning,* and *Population bulletin.* The Social Commission recommended that these journals be discontinued and replaced by a single review that would focus attention on the ways in which social policy and planning, housing, population, community development and social welfare were related. (Stated in the preface to *International social development review* no 1.)

64 H J Dyos 'Agenda for urban historians' in *The study of urban history* edited by H J Dyos (Edward Arnold, 1968) 4.

65 H J Dyos *op cit* 2.

66 Asa Briggs *Victorian cities* (Harmondsworth, Penguin Books, new edition 1968) 16.

67 Asa Briggs *op cit* 14-15.

68 Ruth Glass *op cit.*

69 R N Morris *Urban sociology* (Allen and Unwin, 1968) 15.

70 Ruth Glass *op cit.*

71 Peter H Mann *An approach to urban sociology* (Routledge and Kegan Paul, 1970, Routledge Paperbacks) 1.

72 R E Pahl in the foreword to *Patterns of urban life op cit.*

73 Peter H Mann *op cit* 149.

74 Peter H Mann *op cit* 182.

75 Gordon E Cherry *op cit* 61-62.

76 Some of the focuses of attack are examined and analysed by Scott Donaldson in *The suburban myth* (New York, Columbia UP, 1969) a journalistic attempt to explode the myth which, however, contributes little to the planning argument.

77 Griffith Taylor *Urban geography* (Methuen, second revised edition, 1951 reprinted 1968) 3.

78 James H Johnson *Urban geography: an introductory analysis* (Oxford, Pergamon Press, 1967) 175.

79 James H Johnson *op cit* 163.

80 Peter H Mann *op cit* 134.

81 Gordon E Cherry *op cit* 104.

82 Preface to the third edition.

83 L Dudley Stamp *The land of Britain* (Longmans, third edition 1962) 439.

84 Robin H Best and J T Coppock *The changing use of land in Britain* (Faber, 1962) 26.

85 G H Peters ' Land use studies in Britain ' *Journal of agricultural economics* 21(2) May 1970 171-214.

86 Robert Arvill *Man and environment* (Harmondsworth, Penguin Books, 1967) 86.

87 Seven bodies have permanent representation on the Group : the Countryside Commission itself, the British Tourist Authority, British Waterways Board, Forestry Commission, Nature Conservancy, Sports Council, Water Resources Board.

516

88 Described by J E Palmer in ' Recreational planning: a bibliographic review ' *Planning outlook* new series 2 Spring 1967 19-69.

89 J E Palmer *op cit.*

90 J B Cullingworth *op cit* 217.

91 J Allan Patmore *Land and leisure in England and Wales* (Newton Abbot, David and Charles, 1970) 210-211.

92 J E Palmer *op cit.*

93 P T Kivell ' The roles of public authorities and private interests in providing for recreation in the countryside ' *Planning outlook* new series 7 Autumn 1969 54-64.

94 J Allan Patmore *op cit* 78.

95 W Houghton-Evans and J C Miles ' Week-end recreational motoring in the countryside ' *JTPI* 56(9) November 1970 392-397.

96 Robert Arvill *op cit* 9.

97 L Dudley Stamp *Nature conservation in Britain* (Collins, 1969, New Naturalist Series) 191.

98 David Smith ' The Civic Amenities Act: conservation and planning ' *Town planning review* 40(2) July 1969 149-162.

99 Arnold Weddle *Techniques of landscape architecture* (Heinemann, 1967) vii.

100 At the time of writing a further text by Professor Brian Hackett is announced for early publication.

101 A Goldstein ' Motorway route location studies ' *Report of the Town and Country Planning Summer School,* Keele, 1966 (TPI, 1966) 25.

102 John Tetlow and Anthony Goss *Homes, towns and traffic* (Faber, second edition 1968) 55.

103 J B Cullingworth *op cit* 274.

104 Definition taken from the Buchanan Report *Traffic in towns* (Harmondsworth, Penguin Books, short edition 1964) glossary of terms.

105 William Solesbury and Alan Townsend ' Transportation studies and British planning practice ' *Town planning review* 41(1) January 1970 63-79.

106 William Solesbury and Alan Townsend *op cit.*

107 Michael Bruton *Introduction to transportation planning* (Hutchinson, 1970) 17.

108 William Solesbury and Alan Townsend *op cit.*

109 Allan M Voorhees ' Tomorrow's transportation ' *Planning outlook* new series 7 Autumn 1969 19-34.

110 Universities of Strathclyde and Glasgow *Final report on containerisation* (Glasgow, University of Strathclyde, 1970) S 1.

12

JOURNALS

THE JOURNAL LITERATURE represents one of the as yet unsolved mysteries in planning information. It has been established that the 'average planner' regularly sees six journals: and it is not difficult to list six journals whose titles include the word 'planning'. If the words 'urban', 'regional', and 'environment' are added, the list expands, particularly if overseas journal literature is brought in. And to drop a few other related words into the pool of journal literature—such as transport, economic, and geographical—is to spread the ripples in ever-widening circles. It has not yet been ascertained just how far these ripples can spread into the constantly increasing pool of journal literature on all subjects, nor has the circumference of the pool been accurately described. If, in theory, the ripples can spread very wide, which seems likely, is this necessarily synonymous with the necessity for them to do so? It is possible to make an intelligent guess that there is a lot of information relevant to planning scattered throughout a very wide range of journals—the fact that the Library of the former Ministry of Housing and Local Government take over one thousand journal titles demonstrates that the net has to be cast widely—but the extent of the scatter is a matter for conjecture. Research is now under way to attempt to establish the extent and the structure of the journal literature relevant to planning, and if concrete results can be obtained from this work, then the information pool can be more clearly delineated.

It is quite impossible within the confines of this chapter to do more than offer a signpost to some of the more interesting of the journals in related or unrelated subjects, in addition to describing those titles which are more obviously of interest to planning. Most of the titles included are British, with a few international and some American, but these latter are limited to the titles which seem to be really important and relevant in the context of British planning, and which contain something which cannot be obtained equally satisfactorily in the British literature. The method of signposting has been to cite a few of the more interesting articles from each journal title whose relevance may not be immediately apparent, in the hope that the planner may obtain from these an indication of the flavour of the journal and its degree of relevance to his own particular work.

For the planner who wants to know the range of titles which are in existence (and this does not necessarily mean readily accessible) there are several guides to journals, which can be consulted in most university or public libraries.

The *British union catalogue of periodicals* is not strictly a listing of existing journals, it is a catalogue of those journals which are held in libraries throughout the United Kingdom, which in effect amounts to almost the same thing, since the basic four-volume catalogue (Butterworths, 1955-8) lists some 140,000 titles held in 441 libraries. A single volume supplement was issued in 1962 covering additional titles added to contributing libraries up to 1960. The contents are now up-dated by *New periodical titles* edited by C J Koster for the National Central Library and published quarterly, with an annual cumulation, by Butterworths, the issues being prepared from the punched card records held at the National Central Library. The annual volumes average about 3,500 entries. A cumulative volume containing the updated material issued in the annual volumes 1964 to 1968 and covering the period 1960 to 1967 and most of 1968 has been published as *New periodical titles 1960-1968* (Butterworths, 1970). In all volumes and parts, the journals are listed alphabetically by title, the main purpose of the catalogue being to list the libraries in which a particular journal is available. A subject arrangement by broad subject groupings is adopted in *Ulrich's international periodicals directory* (New York, R R Bowker, thirteenth edition 1969-70) in two volumes, with a title index in the second. Sub-titled ' a classified guide to current periodicals, foreign and domestic ', this directory enables the user to select a subject grouping and to see what titles are available within it. Both of these titles are international in scope, both give full bibliographical details of the journals and serial publications which are included, and neither of them supplies any descriptive notes about them. The *Guide to current British journals* edited by David Woodworth (Library Association, 1971) is a guide to over three thousand British journals giving details of publishers, contents and readership level, among other details. The Department of the Environment Library Bibliography 75 lists the journals taken in the library and thus constitutes a basic, though unannotated, list of planning and related journals.

PLANNING JOURNALS

The majority of planners express themselves satisfied with the journal literature of their subject as a medium for disseminating current thought and developments. The small proportion who are not satisfied that it is performing this function adequately are by no means unanimous in their criticisms, which in fact are frequently contradictory. The current trend in journals appears to be towards the reportage of research and discussion of sophisticated methodologies: this may well conflict with the requirements of planners, the majority of whom are in practice and engaged on practical problems to which advanced mathematical techniques have no application. From an objective viewpoint, the principal gap in the journal literature of planning is the lack of a vehicle for concise, up to the minute reportage of current events in planning practice throughout the country. Of necessity, this has to be a weekly production. Weekly publications such as the *Architects' journal, New society* and *The economist* carry news items and sometimes more substantial items on matters of topical planning interest, but inevitably, since planning is not their primary sphere of interest, the matters reported are those of near-universal interest—the third London airport, the census, the controversial planning decisions, the major new town plans. The Town and Country Planning Association compile a weekly *Planning bulletin* which comes nearest to fulfilling the requirement for current reportage devoted exclusively to planning: it is a digest of news items, taken mainly from *The times* and *The guardian,* together with a note of recent publications and forthcoming events, and although it performs a useful function and is quite widely used, its scope is obviously very limited.

521

The shortest frequency for planning journals, therefore, is monthly, and of the three general planning titles which appear on this schedule, the major one, the *Journal of the Town Planning Institute*[1] (1914-) is not strictly a monthly in that only ten issues are published each year, July/August and September/October being bi-monthly issues. Articles cover a wide range of topics from British and overseas planning, with an increasing methodological content. Regular features include the Association of Student Planners news page, reports of institute meetings throughout the country, book reviews, correspondence, and—one of the most useful and most widely-read sections—a digest of current practice and research, compiled at Lanchester Polytechnic Department of Town Planning, based on published or unpublished research reports and development studies, and including a monthly bibliography of books and articles from a wide range of current journals. *Town and country planning* (1932-) is published each month by the Town and Country Planning Association, edited by Colin Amery. The January issue of each year is an enlarged one devoted to new towns, and is the most up to date source of facts and statistics on new town development. The appeal of *Town and country planning* is more popular than that of the other British planning journals: articles generally are shorter, often undocumented, and frequently polemical. Regional planning is frequently a subject for discussion, and for criticism. Coverage of recent development plans is fairly thorough, mainly in the form of review articles. Book reviews are also included, usually short and always unhelpfully omitting the date of publication of the book in question. Space is also provided for correspondence and for news items, including regular features on events in Wales and Scotland. The other monthly is *Official architecture and planning* (1937-) published by Architecture and Planning Publications Ltd. Sub-titled 'journal for the built environment', its emphasis is on architecture rather than on planning, and it is subject to the usual type of architectural advertising. This is not a heavyweight journal: articles are normally short, and lightly-documented, with a wide range of contributors from a variety of contexts. Frequently a theme is adopted, and several articles devoted to different aspects of it: the themes are chosen with catholicity and cover both architectural and planning topics. The journal also runs series of articles over a period of time, for example, the issues of 1970 and 1971 have carried contributions to a series on planning techniques. Correspondence, reviews, and current events feature regularly. Also on a monthly frequency is the *Journal of planning and property law* edited by John Burke and published by Sweet and Maxwell Ltd. Each issue conforms to a standard format: articles on legal matters, summaries of new Statutory Instruments, parliamentary intelligence, ministerial information and circulars, notes of cases, Lands Tribunal decisions, enforcement notice appeal decisions, and notes of planning decisions. Articles often give 'state of the law' reviews on topics such as trees, advertisements, and planning permission. This is an invaluable source of continuing current information about the practical and administrative aspects of planning as it is carried on throughout Britain. There is an annual consolidated table of contents, and a very detailed cumulative index.

A group of three university-based titles together provide a very substantial contribution to British planning information. *Planning outlook* (1948-) published twice yearly by Oriel Press Ltd for the Department of Town and Country Planning at the University of Newcastle upon Tyne, each issue constituting a separate volume, is a slight volume containing between two and six articles and a selection of reviews. The articles are weighty and authoritative, and have included in the past some notable bibliographical reviews and state of the art surveys: emphasis is on the practical aspects of land-use planning, including recreation and resource planning, and landscape, and on techniques for practical application. *Town planning review* (1910-) is edited at the Department of Civic Design in the University of Liverpool and is published quarterly by Liverpool University Press, the issues now (from January 1970) numbering from January through to October. An average of six articles in each issue is supplemented by a section of signed reviews. The articles cover a range of urban and regional studies, planning techniques and planning practice in all parts of the world, fully-documented and illustrated. This is the only British planning journal to incorporate half-tone plates. *Urban studies* (1964-) edited at Glasgow University mainly from the Department of Social and Economic Research, and published three times a year in February, June and October by the Longman Group Ltd, is a scholarly multi-disciplinary journal dealing with all aspects of the urban scene, and taking in regional studies also from time to time. Authoritative, fully-documented articles cover urban planning practice and techniques, urban studies from all angles, housing, studies of industry and office structure, and regional planning and policies throughout the world. Full and properly-documented book reviews are followed by shorter book notes. A folded card insert carries abstracts of the major articles, which can be cut out and filed.

Regional studies (1967-) is the journal of the Regional Studies Association, and is published quarterly by Pergamon Press Ltd. This is a glossy international journal in the best scholarly tradition, impeccably documented in every way, and with abstracts of each article in English, German, French, and Russian. Each issue contains up to ten lengthy articles, predominantly on the theoretical and methodological aspects of regional planning and development, although from time to time material of a more general nature is included. The articles are fully illustrated with line diagrams, graphs, maps, and other forms of presentation, and are frequently highly technical in nature. The review section is also impeccably documented. The issue of December 1970 included for the first time the contents lists of forthcoming issues of the *Journal of the American Institute of Planners*. Another international and multi-disciplinary journal is *Environment and planning* (1969-) edited by Alan G Wilson and published quarterly by Pion Ltd (the first volume, 1969, had only two issues). From 1971, the journal is to accept papers for inclusion in French and German, although English will continue to be the main language. Each issue contains some six or seven papers reporting the results of original research in all parts of the world relating to urban and regional planning studies, many of them highly technical, all of them well-documented and preceded by abstracts. A selective review section is included. *The new Atlantis* (1969-) is another newcomer to the literature, and has yet to prove its worth. Subtitled ' an international journal of urban and regional studies ' it is edited in Italy and published twice a year by Marsilio Editori of Padua. The first volume comprised two issues, dated summer 1969 and winter 1970; the first number of the second volume is dated simply 1970. The three issues so far have each concentrated on single themes: problems of theory and method of regional planning, comparative research on community decision-making, and minorities in European cities. The aim of the journal is to present a thoroughly international and multi-disciplinary view of each selected topic. Notes on relevant research throughout the world are included at the end of the issue.

Ekistics (1955-) sub-titled 'reviews on the problems and science of human settlements' is published monthly by the Athens Center of Ekistics and is unique in the field in that it consists essentially of long summaries of major articles from the world press on planning and the environment generally. The journal coverage is wide, embracing the scientific and technical fields in addition to those of the human and social sciences. Some issues concentrate on a single theme—that of April 1971, for example, is devoted to 'man and nature'—others range widely among a variety of topics.

A very useful publication, also unique in its way, is the *Quarterly bulletin of the Research and Intelligence Unit of the Greater London Council* (1967-). This is a very professional production containing up to ten articles per issue, plus a section of 'London research abstracts' covering a wide range of journals. The articles, which are predominantly by members, or former members, of the GLC staff, deal with a wide range of practical planning problems encountered in the course of British local planning, and also report surveys and studies carried out in London, either by the GLC itself or by the various boroughs. In the main, the contributions are based on London practice and data, but their application is countrywide.

It was once observed (though the observation is now out of date) that only one American journal included a form of the word 'planning': this is the *Journal of the American Institute of Planners* (1917-) now published bi-monthly by the institute. The contents of the journal are in sections: first come articles on a wide range of planning and related topics in the United States and other parts of the world, authoritative and often heavily documented, and headed with short abstracts; research reports present the results and conclusions of a catholic representation of research studies and surveys; a section headed 'interpretation' offers comment on current problems; the technical review section brings together current practice and reading on the more technical aspects of planning, for example, tree-planting; finally the review section includes extensive signed reviews of important books and, sometimes, development plans. Contents of a world coverage of current journals are detailed, some in full and some selectively, and publications received at the institute are listed. Special issues from time to time deal with diverse themes, from citizen participation to planning models. Also published by the institute is the *AIP newsletter,* a monthly paper which carries news items about the planning profession in the United States, about planning events and publications, and institute news.

The comparable publication in Australia is the *Royal Australian Planning Institute Journal* (1964-) published quarterly for the institute by West Publishing Corporation Pty Ltd. Its contents are mainly articles, on techniques and on planning developments usually in Australia, the emphasis being practical. There is a short review section, and an equally short correspondence column. *PLAN Canada* (1959-) is the journal of the Town Planning Institute of Canada, and is published by the institute three times a year until vol 10, whose three component issues have appeared in April 1969, August 1969, and June 1970. Articles, on a variety of practical and methodological planning issues in a world wide context, form the main part of the journal; most of them are in English, but some are in French. Each article is followed by a summary of its contents, in the other language. Sometimes, though not always, the issue ends with a book review, or a comment on a current planning topic. More ephemeral material and notes on current events, are contained in the institute's *Newsletter.*

JOURNALS IN RELATED SUBJECTS

ARCHITECTURE AND HOUSING

Architectural journals are not necessarily a profitable area of investigation, since the majority of them are preoccupied with the built environment. *The architects' journal* (1895-) is published weekly by the Architectural Press Ltd. Its planning content varies in quantity from week to week, but in general it consists of comments on current planning events, planning inquiries, and development plans. The news items include topical matters such as local government reorganisation and the third London airport. Housing and conservation are regularly reported. The major features sometimes focus on topics such as urban landscape which are relevant to planning.

The monthly *RIBA journal* (1893-), the official mouthpiece of the Royal Institute of British Architects, is concerned with the practical aspects of architecture, in both public and private practice, and in its built manifestations, and with building science in its most basic form, rather than with disseminating scholarly articles for permanent reference. Correspondence, news, and reviews, and the articles themselves, only lightly and occasionally touch on planning. The *Architectural Association quarterly* (1969-) is published quarterly for the association by Pergamon Press. Its content is articles and book reviews, and its range of subject coverage is much wider, its taste more catholic, than that of many architectural journals. Its issues usually contain something of interest to planners. The issue 2(2) April 1970 56-61, for example, contained a discussion by Nigel Moor on ' Planning and information '.

A new journal *Architectural research and teaching* (1970-) is sponsored by the RIBA Board of Education Research Committee: two issues appeared in 1970, but it is intended to produce it three or four times a year. Its purpose is to review and report on research work in schools of architecture and other research, and of education in the field of environment generally. Although it is yet too early to offer a concrete opinion on the extent of its continuing interest for planners, it will—if it fulfills its stated objectives—surely contain something relevant in most of its issues.

Journals on housing are likewise frequently preoccupied with built houses and physical design standards. One which has a broader outlook is the *Housing review* (1951-), the journal of the Housing Centre Trust. Its bi-monthly issues contain articles, news items, and details of recent official and unofficial publications on all aspects of public and private housing both in plan and in built form. The emphasis is on British practice, but overseas developments are included as relevant. A useful series of reference sheets give state of the art reviews of specific housing topics, for example, housing old people, and house improvement, with bibliographies.

SURVEYING AND LOCAL GOVERNMENT FUNCTIONS
The Royal Institution of Chartered Surveyors publish their journal monthly under the title *Chartered surveyor* (1921-). The numbering of issues within the volume runs from July to June. In addition to

527

articles on a wide range of topics relevant to all branches of surveying, there are a number of regular features including legal notes, agricultural law and practice, rural notes, land survey notes and planning notes. The book review section is comprehensive.

The surveyor (1892-), subtitled ' local government technology ', is a weekly journal published by IPC Building and Contract Journals Ltd, which covers the entire range of local government functions including planning, roads, traffic engineering, parks and recreation. Articles on these subjects are interspersed among a substantial job advertisement section, notes on plant and equipment, notes on publications, reports of conferences, and news items. The companion journal to *The surveyor* is the *Local government chronicle* (1855-), and in the same field, though narrower in scope, is the monthly *Journal of the Institution of Municipal Engineers* (1909-) which carries articles and news items on all aspects of municipal engineering.

LANDSCAPE

Landscape design (1941-) the quarterly journal of the Institute of Landscape Architects is concerned with the practical aspects of landscape. It contains short articles and papers reprinted from institute meetings demonstrating landscape in action or discussing specific topics, such as industry or the countryside, in relation to landscape. Full reports of relevant conferences and meetings are included, and tear-out information sheets are incorporated giving technical advice on landscape topics. A series on techniques is also running. There is a book review section and a bibliography of salient articles from other journals.

Landscape architecture (1910-) is the quarterly journal of the American Society of Landscape Architects, published in January, April, July, and October, the October issue being the first in the volume. Subtitled ' the international magazine of regional and land planning, design, and construction ' it casts its net widely among these interests and disseminates the results in articles and reports of landscape projects supplemented with book reviews and news items.

Landskap (1923-) formerly called *Havekunst,* is a Scandinavian review covering garden and landscape planning, appearing eight times a year from Arkitektens Forlag of Copenhagen. It is a Danish language journal on all aspects of urban and country landscape including countryside planning and recreation, with English summaries of the main articles, and an English language subject index in the last issue of each year.

COUNTRYSIDE AND RECREATION PLANNING

The principal continuing source of information on recreation planning and associated countryside topics in Britain is the monthly news sheet *Recreation news* (1968-) issued by the Countryside Commission. It provides regular reports of interesting events, new reading, and research in progress in the field of outdoor recreation planning. Since 1970, it has been joined by the quarterly *Recreation news supplement,* whose emphasis is on rural planning at home and abroad. It includes reviews of current plans and studies and articles on management and design topics, illustrated as appropriate with maps, diagrams and photographs, and takes in also the landscape and conservation aspects of rural planning and management.

These two bulletins together do a worthwhile job, within their limits, of providing regular information on this increasingly important area of planning; but there is room for a weightier journal covering the whole field in more detail and carrying articles as well as current news. The gap has not been filled adequately by the American *Journal of leisure research* (1969-), published quarterly by the National Recreation and Park Association in Washington, which leans heavily towards methodology.

Rather narrower in scope is *Sport and recreation* (1960-), formerly *Physical recreation,* the quarterly journal of the Central Council of Physical Recreation, which is supplemented by the *Sports development bulletin* which carries the more technical information on physical recreation, both oudoor and indoor.

ENVIRONMENT

The wider aspects of the environment generally are the subject of some recent journals, popular in tone, and reflecting the aroused public interest in this undefinable subject. First in the field was *Your environment* (1969-) a privately published quarterly edited by a natural history writer, a sovietologist, and a poet, containing articles, reviews, and news of current events including legislation, on an all-embracing list of subjects including derelict land and its reclamation, all forms of pollution and their effects, pesticides and chemicals, and the built environment.

Environment Scotland (1969-) is the journal of the Scottish Civic Trust, a slim magazine containing short articles, notes on civic societies, and details of new publications. Two undated issues have appeared so far, the second of which includes the remark (p 4) that ' each issue of *Environment Scotland* carries a number, but not a date, since the reference value of the publication is not affected by weeks or months '.

The most recent addition to the field is *The ecologist,* published monthly since July 1970 by Ecosystems Ltd, of London, and containing articles at a popular level and news on all aspects of environment, conservation, population and related subjects. It has hardly had time yet to settle down into a recognisable pattern, but at present it seems a little thin in pages for such an all-encompassing subject.

PLANNING CONTENT OF JOURNALS IN OTHER SUBJECTS

TRAFFIC AND TRANSPORT

There are many journals which deal with various aspects of traffic, transportation and roads, but some of them, such as *Transport engineer* and *Transport journal,* are concerned with the technical and engineering side of transport and have no general application to planning and the planning aspects of traffic and transport, while others, such as *Roads and road construction,* are primarily concerned with road engineering and have only occasional items on aspects of roads which are pertinent in a planning context. One of the most generally useful journals in this field is *Traffic engineering and control* (1959-) edited by Ernest Davies and published monthly by Printerhall Ltd. The volume runs from May to April. Each issue contains articles, with abstracts in English and French, reviews, news items and regular features on road lighting and on parking. The coverage is of all aspects of transport and traffic management and planning, roads, transport users and the effects of traffic, including methods such as traffic prediction, trip generation studies, data collection, and case studies of traffic and transport in practice. The focus is mainly on British practice, but this is by no means to say that overseas developments are ignored. There is no need to cite articles from this journal: its contents are almost entirely pertinent to planning, and it is the most practically-based journal in the field.

The *Institute of Transport journal* (1920-) is published bi-monthly by the institute, one volume constituting two years' issues and the volumes starting in November. In addition to an average of three articles per issue on all forms of transportation and transport planning, the journal contains institute notes and comments, book reviews, and a list of additions to the library. Like the preceding title, the journal is entirely relevant, as is *Traffic quarterly* (1946-) published by the Eno Foundation for Transportation in Saugatuck, Connecticut. The issues contain only articles, on all forms of transportation and transport and traffic planning, with a balance between theory and practice, and a good coverage of ongoing research. The coverage is world wide, and although there is an American bias in the practical studies, the many methodological articles are relevant to British practice.

Two relatively recent titles add further information to transportation. The first is the *Journal of transport economics and policy* (1967-) edited by D L Munby and J M Thomson and published three times a year in January, May and September by the London School of Economics. The articles, many of which emanate from the United States, deal with all forms of transport and communications from the economic point of view and include many of interest to planners, for example, N W Mansfield 'Recreational trip generation' 3(2) May 1969 152-163; C Joort 'The evaluation of travelling time' 3(3) September 1969 279-286; Michael A Goldberg and Trevor D Heaver 'Evaluating transport corridors: an economic model' 4(3) September 1970 255-264; and H Newberger 'User benefit in the evaluation of transport and land use plans' 5(1) January 1971 52-75. The second is *Transportation research* (1967-), an international journal published quarterly by Pergamon Press and edited by Frank A Haight. It is designed 'to meet the need for rapid publication of the most significant scientific results in the field of transportation systems, on the comparison (including economic comparison) of these

systems with one another and on results which tend to unify transportation theory'. In addition to articles, which are abstracted in
English, German, French, and Russian, each issue carries a lengthy
bibliographic section containing notes of publications from all parts
of the world, and details of forthcoming events. The articles in
general tend to be technical in content and mathematical in presentation, but some which are of interest to British planners have included Britton Harris 'Goals for urban transportation' 2(3) September 1968 249-252; John B Lansing 'The effects of migration
and personal effectiveness on long-distance travel' 2(4) December
1968; and Leslie Fishman and J S Wabe 'Restructuring the form of
car ownership: a proposed solution to the problem of the motor
car in the United Kingdom' 3(4) December 1969 429-442.

GEOGRAPHY
Journals with a geographical base have much to offer to planners,
and a range of titles can profitably be investigated on a regular
basis. *Geographical review* (1916-) is published quarterly by the
American Geographical Society, the issues appearing in January,
April, July and October. The editor is Wilma B Fairchild. It comprises scholarly articles, each of which is abstracted at the end of
the issue, with supporting illustrations and diagrams; American
Geographical Society notes; a regular geographical record, which
contains international news; and a section of signed reviews. The
articles cover all aspects of geographical study in all parts of the
world, those with a country-orientation outnumbering those on
general geographical topics. Despite the wide range of coverage,
there is not a great deal of direct interest to planners. Relevant
articles have included: W R Derrick Sewel *et al* 'Human response
to weather and climate: geographical contributions' 58(2) April
1968 262-280; James W Simmons 'Changing residence in the city: a
review of intraurban mobility' 58(4) October 1968 622-651; Bruce
E Newling 'The spatial variation of urban population densities'
59(2) April 1969 242-252.

The British equivalent to this journal is the *Geographical journal*
(1893-) published quarterly in March, June, September, and December, by the Royal Geographical Society. It is edited by L P Kirwan.
It aims to cover 'accounts of recent exploration and travel, original

contributions to geographical research, papers read at the meetings of the society and articles on every aspect of geography as well as on the geographical aspects of other sciences '. In addition to articles, there is a comprehensive review section supplemented sometimes by lengthier review articles in the body of the journal, a section on cartographical survey and notes, including notification of new and revised maps and atlases, society, university, and general news items. There are not all that many articles of major interest to planners. The volume for 1969, for example, contained three: Kenneth Warren ' Recent changes in the geographical location of the British steel industry ' 135(3) September 1969 343-361; Peter Haggett ' On geographical research in a computer environment ' 135(4) December 1969 497-507; R N E Blake ' The impact of airfields on the British landscape ' 135(4) December 1969 508-528.

Geography (1901-) is the journal of the Geographical Association, and is published quarterly in January, April, July and November. The honorary editor is Professor N Pye. The Geographical Association ' exists to further the knowledge of geography and the teaching of geography in all categories of educational institutions from preparatory school to university, in the United Kingdom and abroad ', and the journal reflects these aims. It is made up of scholarly, well documented articles; notes on international developments in a regular section entitled ' this changing world '; association notes, courses, conferences, and library news and additions, and a comprehensive section of signed reviews. There is much of interest to planners in most issues of the journal. For example : Derek Thompson 'A selective bibliography on quantitative methods of geography ' 54(1) January 1969 74-83; Michael Dower ' Leisure —its impact on man and the land ' 55(3) July 1970 253-260; D C Mercer ' The geography of leisure—a contemporary growth point ' 55(3) July 1970 261-273.

The professional geographer (1946-) edited by H F Raup is the mouthpiece of the Association of American Geographers, and is published bi-monthly from January to November. It consists of short scholarly articles, association and general geographical news, correspondence, cartographic news items, and a review section. Articles such as Frank E Horton and Robert I Whittick 'A spatial model for examining the journey to work in the planning context '

21(4) July 1969 223-226, and D C Mercer 'Urban recreational hinterlands: a review and an example' 22(2) March 1970 74-78, have been of interest, but in general there is not much of interest to the British planner.

Geographical magazine (1935-) edited by Derek Weber is published monthly by New Science Publications Ltd, the volume running from October to September. The journal has no professional affiliations, as the preceding four titles have, and is aimed at a more popular level altogether, the articles generally short and fully illustrated, often in colour. This is popular geography and travel, in the main, and the articles of interest to planners are frequently concerned with maps or atlases, for example, Emrys Jones 'London life in maps' 41(1) October 1968 62-66, which describes his *London atlas;* David P Bickmore 'Maps for the computer age' 41(3) December 1968 221-227; J Allan Patmore 'New directions for transport' 41(10) July 1969 769-776; Hugh D Clout 'Auvergne: a challenge for country planners' 41(12) September 1969 918-926.

The *Scottish geographical magazine* (1885-) edited by Alfred Jefferies is the journal of the Royal Scottish Geographical Society, and is published three times a year, in April, September, and December. The issues are composed of articles and reviews. Articles are not exclusively Scottish in focus, although their main emphasis is on that country, but there is much of wider interest based on the Scottish example, for instance, D C D Pocock 'Economic renewal : the example of Fife' 86(2) September 1970 123-133, and Richard V Welch 'Immigrant manufacturing industry established in Scotland between 1945 and 1968: some structural and locational characteristics' 86(2) September 1970 134-147.

The east midland geographer (1954-) is a semi-annual journal produced from the Department of Geography of Nottingham University in June and December. Its production is supervised by an editorial committee. It contains articles, notes and news in a regular feature, the east midland record, and sometimes short reviews. Articles focus primarily on all aspects of the east midlands region, the objective being to ' provide information on geographical aspects of the east midlands and to stimulate further interest in the geography of an area not to be precisely defined, but broadly taken to mean the eastern counties of midland England which form the natural sphere of interest of the University of Nottingham'. Contributions are frequently of interest to planners. The special issue 5(33-34) June-December 1970 in honour of Professor K C Edwards, for example, contained J M Smith ' The Erewash valley intermediate area ' 80-88; D M Smith ' The location of the British hosiery industry since the middle of the nineteenth century ' 71-79; and D C D Pocock ' Land ownership and urban growth in Scunthorpe ' 52-61.

The Institute of British Geographers publish in two series. Their *Transactions* (1935-) are scholarly productions, each issue being taken up almost entirely with fully referenced articles with English abstracts at the head and abstracts in French and German at the end, and published at irregular intervals. They contain articles of much relevance to planning, for example Isobel M L Robertson ' The census and research: ideals and realities ' 48 December 1969 173-187; Robin H Best and A G Champion ' Regional conversions of agricultural land to urban use in England and Wales 1945-67 ' 49 March 1970 15-32; J B Goddard ' Functional regions within the city centre: a study by factor analysis of taxi flows in central London ' 49 March 1970 161-182. The institute have more recently introduced a new medium *Area* (1969-) for the publication of shorter, though still scholarly, articles, and also of news items and reports of the activities of the institute and its various specialist groups. Production is semi-annual, but the month of issue is not indicated. As with the *Transactions,* planners will find *Area* a profitable journal to scan. Articles of interest have included R J Colenutt ' Modelling travel patterns of day visitors to the countryside ' 1969(2) 43-47; Ewart Johns ' Symmetry and asymmetry in the urban scene ' 1969(2) 48-57; A Perry ' Spatial variations of income in southern Hampshire in 1961 ' 1970(1) 12-14.

Annals of the American Association of American Geographers (1911-) is edited by John Fraser Hart and published quarterly by the association in March, June, September and December. The *Annals* were instituted ' to stimulate scholarship and to provide for publication of significant contributions to knowledge in geography '. The contents of each issue are mainly lengthy articles, each one with an abstract. The focus is world-wide. There are occasional articles of interest to British planners, for example, C F J Whebell ' Corridors: a theory of urban systems ' 59(1) March 1969 1-26;

535

John C Hudson 'A location theory for rural settlement' 59(2) June 1969 365-381; and M E Eliot Hurst 'An approach to the study of nonresidential land use traffic generation' 60(1) March 1970 153-173.

An American university product is *Economic geography* (1925-), a quarterly edited by Gerald J Karaska and published in January, April, July and October by Clark University in Worcester, Massachusetts. Its coverage takes in the fields of economic geography and urban geography, and its contents are articles, some of them lengthy, and reviews. The focus is world-wide, and there is much material relevant to planning. Recent articles have included Allen Pred and Barry M Kibel 'An application of gaming simulation to a general model of economic locational processes' 46(2) April 1970 136-156; W A V Clark and Gerard Rushton 'Models of intra-urban consumer behavior and their implications for central place theory' 46(3) July 1970 486-497; Anthony V Williams and Wilbur Zelinsky 'On some patterns in international tourist flows' 46(4) October 1970 549-567.

The Canadian geographer (1951-) edited by J H Galloway is the journal of the Canadian Association of Geographers, and appears quarterly in spring, summer, fall, and winter. Some of the articles are in French, although the majority are in English; the content is mainly articles, with a review section, and there is a Canadian bias in the subject matter but much of wider application. Abstracts in English and French are supplied at the end of each issue. Pertinent articles for planning are mainly methodological in character, like so many in the geographical journals, and have included, in recent issues, G B Norcliffe 'On the use and limitations of trend surface models' 13(4) winter 1969 338-348; and Guy P F Steed 'Changing linkages and internal multiplier of an industrial complex' 14(3) fall 1970 229-242.

The Department of Geography of the Royal University of Lund, in Sweden, is responsible for the series of *Lund studies in geography*, each one of them a monograph on a specific subject. Series A is devoted to physical geography (1950-); series B covers human geography (1949-); series C deals with general and mathematical geography (1962-). The second and third of these are primarily of interest to planners. In series B, numbers 27 and 28 1967 and 1969 contain Allen Pred's 'Behavior and location: foundations for a geographic and dynamic location theory', and number 30 is Gunnar Tornqvist's 'Flows of information and the location of economic activities '. In series C, number 9 is devoted to ' Computer-cartography: shortest route programs (for use with traffic distribution models) ' by Stig Nordbeck and Bengt Rystedt.

From Holland comes the *Tijdschrift voor economische en sociale geografie* (1910-) the Netherlands journal of economic and social geography, published bi-monthly by the Royal Dutch Geographic Society, and containing mostly articles with a few reviews. The articles are in the main quite short, the majority being in English with some in Dutch, and all of them with English language abstracts. There is a great deal of interest to planners in this source. Recent articles have included W A Sentance ' The graphic representation of computer output ' 60(3) May/June 1969 180-186; J E Martin ' Size of plant and location of industry in Greater London ' 60(6) November/December 1969 369-374; and F Dacey 'Alternative formulations of central place population ' 61(1) January/February 1970 10-15.

One of the most recent contenders in the geographical field is the American *Geographical analysis*: an international journal of theoretical geography (1969-) issued quarterly by the Ohio State University Press, and edited by Professor L J King. Its objective is the encouragement of ' significant research aimed at the formulation and verification of geographical theory through model development and mathematical and statistical analysis ', and it fulfils this in scholarly articles, book reviews, the occasional listing of source material, and through a section of research notes and comments ' designed to report work in progress in the development of innovative theoretical concepts, solutions to particular technical problems, and computer algorithms of special interest to geographical analysis '. Contributions are therefore quantitative and technical, and of interest perhaps not so much to the planner in practice as to the research worker. Contributors to the first issue 1(1) January 1969 included Brian J L Berry and Paul J Schwind ' Information and entropy in migrant flows ' and M F Dacey ' Some spacing measures of areal point distributions having the circular normal form '.

Closely allied to economic geography and to statistical techniques in geography generally is the *Journal of regional science* (1958-)

published by the Regional Science Research Institute and edited by Walter Isard and Benjamin H Stevens. There are three issues each year, in April, August, and December. Articles and book reviews comprise the major part of the contents. The contents are entirely relevant to that part of planning which is based on, or concerned with, regional science, the techniques of economic analysis and locational analysis. Examples from recent issues are Daniel H Garnick 'Differential regional multiplier models' 10(1) April 1970 35-47; R H Day and P E Kennedy 'On a dynamic location model of production' 10(2) August 1970 191-197; and Wesley H Long 'The economics of air travel gravity models' 10(3) December 1970 353-363.

Closely related to geography in a different way are the journals which are concerned with maps and map-making and associated techniques. Some of these are very technical, and clearly intended for a highly specialist audience, but there are two titles which from time to time carry articles which are of value to planners in connection with their use of maps and air photographs. The *Cartographic journal* (1964-) is the journal of the British Cartographic Society; edited by A Jones, it is published by the society twice a year in June and December. It consists of articles, society news, cartographic news generally, reviews, and notes of recent maps and recent literature. The articles, which are fully referenced and well illustrated, are on all aspects of cartography in all parts of the world, including discussion of new atlases and maps, automatic cartography and historical cartography. Recent pertinent items have included G M Gaits 'Thematic mapping by computer' 6(1) June 1969 50-68; L Scott 'Early experience in the photo mapping technique' 6(2) December 1969 108-113; and R P Kirby 'A survey of map user practices and requirements' 7(1) June 1970 31-39. The Photogrammetric Society journal *Photogrammetric record* (1953-) is issued twice a year in April and October and consists of articles (usually reprints of papers read at Society meetings, with discussions), book reviews, international abstracts from a range of foreign and home journals, and news notes. The journal is not liberally endowed with articles relevant to planning, but occasionally there is one of background interest, such as V A Williams 'Thoughts on mapping by photogrammetry' 6(31) April 1968 18-23, and D A

Tait 'Photo-interpretation and topographic mapping' 6(35) April 1970 466-479.

ECONOMICS

In the field of economic journals, there are several titles which would profitably bear investigation by planners. *The economic journal* (1891-) is the official mouthpiece of the Royal Economic Society, and is published quarterly in March, June, September, and December by Macmillan (Journals) Ltd. It is edited by C F Carter and others. This is a fruitful source of information. Each issue comprises, in addition to articles, a very extensive review section, notes of news and research, contents lists of a wide range of journals, notes on new books, all of these having world coverage. The articles are thoroughly documented, and from time to time take the form of review articles with lengthy bibliographies. Two representative articles which have appeared recently are R C Fordham 'Airport planning in the context of the third London airport' 80(318) June 1970 307-322; and A J Brown ' Surveys of applied economics : regional economics, with special reference to the United Kingdom' 79(316) December 1969 759-796, which constitutes the first of a series of surveys of applied economics to be published jointly for the Social Science Research Council and the Royal Economic Society.

The American economic review (1911-) is an approximate American equivalent to *The economic journal*. It is the journal of the American Economic Association, and is published quarterly by the association. Its editor is George H Borts. Each issue contains long articles, and a section of shorter articles headed ' Communications '. Relevant items which have appeared in the past year are Donald A Nichols ' Land and economic growth ' 60(3) June 1970 332-340; and Alan Carlin and R E Park ' Marginal cost pricing of airport runway capacity ' 60(3) June 1970 310-319.

The *Journal of economic studies* (1965-) is edited by David M Kelly and David Forsyth and published by Pergamon Press. Its article content is supplemented by short notes on research in progress. The contents are useful to planners, for example, T L Burton and M N Fulcher ' Measurement of recreation benefits: a survey ' 3(2) July 1968 35-48, and Douglas Mair and Donald J Mackay

'Regional policy and labour reserves in Scotland' 3(1) March 1968
55-72.

SOCIOLOGY

The content of sociological journals in general bears out the assertion quoted in chapter 11 that, within the social sciences, the minor
contribution has been from sociology, as opposed to the much
greater one from economics. There are many sociological journals
with interesting and promising titles, such as *Sociological review,*
the *British journal of sociology,* and *Sociology* from the British
output, which contain few articles of relevance to planning and its
problems for the reason that their content is mainly theoretical.
The occasional article on methodology might be relevant to the
work of a planning authority research section, though even here
there is little added over and above the basic requirements which
can be supplied from the texts mentioned in chapter 11 in the section
on planning techniques. The bi-lingual *Current sociology* is discussed in chapter 13 in the context of bibliographies, since many
of the issues take the form of a trend report and bibliography on a
specific topic often related to planning. The journal is published
by Mouton and Co of The Hague and Paris, with financial support
from Unesco, and it is prepared for the International Sociological
Association under the auspices of the International Committee for
Social Sciences Documentation. The *American behavioral scientist*
(1957-) published bi-monthly by Sage Publications Inc of Beverly
Hills, California, is primarily theoretical in content and its bias is
obviously behavioural and psychological but it is marginally worth
noting for its issue 13(1) September/October 1969 devoted to migration and adaptation, edited by Eugene B Brody, and including a
general introductory article by Brody, 'Differential experience paths
of rural migrants to the city' by Robert C Hanson and Ozzie G
Simmons, 'The economic absorption and cultural integration of
immigrant workers' by Lyle W Shannon, and 'Preventive planning
and strategies of intervention: an overview' by Brody. The issue
is stated to be 'concerned with the human consequences, the socio-
behavioral corollaries of migration'.

The *International social science journal* (1949-) is published
quarterly by Unesco in Paris, in English, and also in French as the

540

Revue internationale des sciences sociales. It is international in scope, as its title might suggest, and its contributors come from a variety of disciplines. Its issues concentrate on themes many of them relevant to planning: 22(2) 1970 'Towards a policy for social research' and 22(4) 1970 'Controlling the human environment' are two of recent interest, while a forthcoming issue in 1971 will focus on 'Documentation in the social sciences'. Each issue has a section of 'professional and documentary services' which includes information about forthcoming international conferences, details of documents and publications of the United Nations and its specialised agencies, and a list of books received. The issue 22(4) 1970 also included, as a special service, a 'World index of social science institutions: research, advanced training, documentation and professional bodies' compiled from a card index maintained in the Unesco Social Science Documentation Centre.

Another international multi-disciplinary journal is *Socio-economic planning sciences* (1967-) published by Pergamon Press, and appearing bi-monthly from 1971. The editor is Sumner N Levine. The journal is of considerable interest to planners, for its approach is to the scientific bases of planning for community services and public welfare and the application of quantitative methods to them, with a strong methodological bias apparent in the contents. The whole issue 4(1) March 1970 was devoted to the 'Application of computers to the problems of urban society', including Britton Harris' well-known paper 'Computation is not enough' 1-9, and George C Hemmens 'Analysis and simulation of urban activity patterns' 53-66. Other examples which demonstrate its relevance to planning are Martin H Krieger 'Modelling urban change' 5(1) February 1971 41-55, and Michael Batty 'Design and construction of a subregional land use model' 5(2) April 1971 97-124. In general, the articles report the results, or progress, of original research. There are also occasional review articles.

Human relations (1947-) is subtitled 'a journal of studies towards the integration of the social sciences' and is published six times a year by the Plenum Publishing Co Ltd. It consists entirely of articles, which have an interest to planning in their treatment of concepts and methodologies which are pervasive to the social sciences generally. Examples from recent issues are A C Bebbington

' The effect of non-response in the sample survey with an example '
23(3) 1970 169-180; Albert Cherns ' Social research and its diffusion '
22(3) 1969 210-218; and Robert N Rapoport ' Three dilemmas in
action research ' 23(6) 1970 499-513. A second, more recent title
which adopts a similar approach in its catchment of the underlying
philosophies and scientific methods of the various social sciences
is *Theory and decision* (1970-) published in Holland by D Reidel
Publishing Co of Dordrecht, and scheduled to appear five or six
times a year. The first issue 1(1) October 1970 reported papers from
a symposium on decision theory. The third issue 1(3) March 1971
concentrates on economics. Further issues are announced dealing
with the analysis of human behaviour, with decision theory again,
and with sociology and economics in conjunction.

POLITICS

Politics, like sociology and economics, is reckoned to be a major
component of the social sciences, and the bridge between social and
political science in the journal literature is conveniently formed
here by the *Annals of the American Academy of Political and Social
Science* (1890-) edited by Richard D Lambert and published bi-
monthly by the academy, each issue constituting a separate volume
for numbering purposes. Each volume is devoted to a special theme
and has its own author and subject index, together with a lengthy
review section. The subject coverage is the whole broad social
science field. From time to time, a volume contains articles on a
theme of interest to planning, for example, that of May 1970, vol
389, on ' Society and its physical environment ' which contains
sections on the nature of environmental threat; society, personality,
and environmental usufruct; the economics of common environmental property; emerging environmental law; and organising for
environmental planning.

Two journals concerned with the practicalities of politics rather
than with its scientific bases are sources worth investigating by
planners. *The political quarterly* (1930-) edited by William A
Robson and Bernard Crick, is published quarterly by its own publishing company the Political Quarterly Co Ltd, and takes into its
view the discussion of social policy, public administration, and
questions of industrial and political organisation mainly as they

542

affect Great Britain. Recent articles having a bearing on planning include Peter Self 'Nonsense on stilts: cost benefit analysis and the futility of the Roskill Commission' 41(3) July/September 1970 249-260; John Page 'A protest at urban environment' 40(4) October/December 1969 436-446; and John Greve 'Housing policies and prospects' 40(1) January/March 1969 23-34. Also published quarterly is *Political studies* (1953-) the official journal of the Political Studies Association of the United Kingdom, edited by F F Ridley and published by the Clarendon Press at Oxford. Each issue contains, in addition to articles, review articles, and short reviews, a substantial section of research notes. Articles which have been published recently and which make a contribution to the administrative aspect of planning include L J Sharpe 'Theories and values of local government' 18(2) June 1970 153-174, and Noel Boaden 'Central departments and local authorities: the relationship examined' 18(2) June 1970 175-186.

POPULATION

Population studies (1947-) is a journal of demography edited by David V Glass and E Grebenik, published three times a year by the Population Investigation Committee of the London School of Economics. It has world wide coverage of all aspects of population and demography, including fertility, migration, and birth control policies, and while much of its content has little practical application to planning work in Britain there are nevertheless items of interest from time to time. Some recent examples are Peter Laslett 'Size and structure of the household in England over three centuries' 23(2) July 1969 199-223; Peter J Lloyd 'A growth model with population as an endogenous variable' 23(3) November 1969 463-478; Dov Friedlander 'The spread of urbanisation in England and Wales 1851-1951' 24(3) November 1970 423-443.

Of much more limited appeal is *Local population studies* (1968-) a small magazine and newsletter emanating from the Cambridge Group for the History of Population and Social Structure. Issued twice a year, its subject is historical demography, and it aims to provide a forum for those working in the fields of parish register analysis and the study of populations and social structure on a local scale. It consists of news items from CAMPOP, articles, letters, notes of recent publications, and local research in progress.

The *Journal of the Royal Statistical Society* is in three series. Series A general (1838-), series B methodical (1934-), and series C applied statistics (1952-) are all published by the society, and appear three times a year. Series A and C are the most fruitful sources of information for planners, series B being principally for statisticians. Series A consists of articles, reviews, the contents lists of recent journal issues covering some thirty journals, current notes, and library accessions. The articles are on general statistical topics, and their relevance to planning may be gauged by the following examples: ' Statistics in town planning ' by Bernard Benjamin 132(1) 1969 1-15; 'Aggregate models of consumer purchases' by James R Emshoff and Alan Mercer 133(1) 1970 14-28; ' The 1971 population census and after ' by Bernard Benjamin 133(2) 1970 240-256; ' Problems in the bibliography of statistics ' by H O Lancaster 133(3) 1970 409-441. The contents of series C is made up principally of articles, with some book reviews and a regular section of ' statistical algorithms '. The relevant items here are more scattered: for example, W E Cox ' The estimation of incomes and expenditures in British towns ' 17(3) 1968 252-259; J S Wabe ' Congestion and the speed of traffic on trunk roads ' 19(1) 1970 42-49.

The American equivalent is the *Journal of the American Statistical Association* (1888/9-) edited by Robert Ferber and published quarterly by the association. The contents of each issue are divided into two sections, the first on applications, the other on theory and methods, and made up mainly of articles, plus a review section. Each article carries an abstract at its head. The items on methods are relevant to British planners; recent examples have been Larry H Long ' On measuring geographic mobility ' 65(331) September 1970 1195-1203; David F Andrews ' Calibration and statistical inference ' 65(331) September 1970 1233-1242; John F Kain and John M Quigley ' Measuring the value of housing quality ' 65(330) June 1970 532-548. The American Statistical Association also publish *The American statistician* (1947-) which is edited by Morris Hamburg and appears five times each year in February, April, June,

October, and December. The contents are short articles, supported by items of news on statistical topics in general, and association information. The articles are fairly theoretical, and American-biased. Again, it is the methodological content which is the most relevant, for example, David Rosenblatt and others ' Principles of design and appraisal of statistical information systems ' 24(4) October 1970 10-15.

The *Operational research quarterly* (1950-) is published for the Operational Research Society Ltd by Pergamon Press, and appears in March, June, September, and December. Its emphasis is on practical case studies, and on state of the art reviews and reviews of development, and it is aimed at the practitioner; though this is not to state that theory and methodology are excluded altogether. The content is mainly articles, which carry abstracts at the head, and book reviews. There is plenty here to interest planners, both in the applications discussed, and in the procedural background subjects such as decision-making. Recent pertinent articles include ' Monitoring an exponential smoothing forecasting system ' by Michael Batty 20(3) September 1969 319-325; ' Operational research as revelation ' by Stafford Beer 21(1) March 1970 9-21; ' The use of the concept of entropy in system modelling ' by Alan G Wilson 21(2) June 1970 247-265; and ' Some new techniques in transportation planning ' by Alan K Halder 21(2) June 1970 267-278. The contributions are in general well-documented. The American equivalent is *Operations research* (1952-) the bi-monthly journal of the Operations Research Society of America, containing articles, letters, and reviews. The level is very technical, and contributions are devoted to all aspects of operations research, including programming and statistical theory. Sometimes a part of the issue is devoted to the application of operations research to a specific area, such as health. This is not nearly such a profitable field of exploration as the British journal.

ADMINISTRATION

Public administration (1923-) edited by Nevil Johnson is the journal of the Royal Institute of Public Administration, and is published quarterly by the institute, in spring, summer, autumn, and winter. It consists of articles and book reviews. The articles disseminate much useful background information on local and central government administration in the United Kingdom, including the techniques and procedures involved. The review section is also valuable for its authoritative reviews of books which provide background to planning in both central and local government contexts. Some relevant articles which have appeared within the last year are 'The decision process in local government: a case study of fluoridation in Hull' by Alan P Brier 48(2) Summer 1970 153-168, and 'The regional decentralisation of British government departments' by J A Cross 48(4) Winter 1970 423-441. Each issue ends with a listing of recent British government publications.

The American Society for Public Administration publish a bimonthly journal *Public administration review* (1940-) edited by Dwight Waldo, consisting of articles, reviews, and news notes, and covering much the same ground as the British *Public administration* in an American context. The contents in general, therefore, are not applicable to British circumstances and practice, but some items on methods are relevant, such as 'Four years of PPBS: an appraisal' by Stanley B Botner 30(4) July/August 1970 423-431, and the issue of March/April 1969 devoted entirely to 'PPBS reexamined: development, analysis, and criticism'.

The *Journal of management studies* (1964-) edited by T Lupton and published by Basil Blackwell at Oxford, comes out three times each year, in February, May, and October, and is a useful source of information on a background field similar to that of the operations research and public administration journals. The emphasis in this title is on the practice of management, taking in areas such as organisation structure, decision-making, and communication theory. An indication of the type of article which may prove useful to the planner is given by the following selection of 'Organisation theory and the public sector' by R J S Baker 6(1) February 1969 15-32; 'Prescription in management decisions' by Samuel Eilon 6(2) May 1969 181-197; and 'The goal formation process in complex organisations' by Walter Hill 6(2) May 1969 198-208. The American *Management science* (1959-) is the journal of the Institute of Management Sciences and is published monthly by that institute. Its content is much more theoretical than its British counterpart, and in most parts highly technical.

546

More specific in its focus is *Long range planning* (1968-) the journal of the Society for Long Range Planning, edited by Bernard Taylor and published quarterly by Pergamon Press. This is an international journal devoted to the 'concepts and techniques involved in the development of strategy and the generation of long range plans' and is aimed at an audience of senior managers, administrators, and academics. Long range planning itself is defined as 'dealing with the future implications of present decisions in terms of: 1, setting goals and developing strategies to achieve them, 2, translating strategy into detailed operational programmes and ensuring that plans are carried out'. The content of the journal is entirely articles, each one with a short abstract. The issue of December 1970 3(2) contained articles by J Brian McLoughlin on 'Controlling the urban system' 61-64, and by R S Scorer on 'Air pollution: its implications for industrial planning' 46-54.

Similar in some respects to the journal just cited is *Futures* (1969-) an international quarterly published by IPC Science and Technology Press Ltd in cooperation with the Institute for the Future. There are contributions on the future state of society and its environment which should be of interest to planners, for example, Gordon Rattray Taylor 'Trends in pollution' 2(2) 1970 105-113; J K Page 'Possible developments in the urban environment' 2(3) 1970 215-221; and Jack Tizard 'On planning research training in the social sciences' 3(1) 1971 62-67.

REFERENCE

1 From the issue of June 1971, this became the *Journal of the Royal Town Planning Institute*.

13

GUIDES TO SOURCES OF INFORMATION

PLANNING IS SHORT of basic quick reference material of the type which abounds in some other subject fields—up to date and comprehensive encyclopedias and dictionaries, for instance, are lacking in English, and other types of reference sources, such as research registers and guides to thesis material, are not necessarily aimed at a planning audience, although their contents may be of incidental interest. This chapter, therefore, contains a large quantity of references to material which is not directly connected with urban and regional planning as such, but which may provide pointers to sources which the planner could profitably know about.

It is worth mentioning, for the sake of completeness, that although there is no English-language encyclopedia of planning, there is a German volume, of over one thousand pages, under the title *Handwoerterbuch fur Raumforschung und Raumordnung* edited by Professor Konrad Meyer for the Akademie fur Raumforschung und Landesplanung (Hanover, 1968). The scope of the volume is physical planning and related subjects, with the main emphasis on Germany, although other countries are included. The articles, in German, cover about three hundred topics. The coverage is fairly comprehensive so far as Germany is concerned, but much of significance relating to other countries is missing.

DICTIONARIES, GLOSSARIES

There is no dictionary of planning in the sense of an alphabetical listing of planning terms with their meanings against them. Two reasons can be advanced for this lack. First, that a large number of words and phrases used by planners do not have a nationally-accepted standard meaning—open space, for example, can mean different things to different planning authorities—and the production of a dictionary would, if it were to be in any degree authoritative, have to wait on the ideal of national standardisation of terms. Secondly, that the vocabulary of planning is being continually enlarged by the importation of jargon from other disciplines and techniques. Two volumes, however, lay claim to attention here. One is E A Powdrill's *Vocabulary of land planning* (Estates Gazette, 1961) which is not a glossary in the normal sense of the word but is written in continuous prose; as the author explains in his introduction, it is an attempt ' to try and exhibit the logic, where it exists, of certain words and expressions that occur in the everyday working of the administration and technique of planning, and . . . to show the true application of the principles they demonstrate '. It is, as the title indicates, a land-based view of planning. The terms included are those used in administration, in the process of control, in industry and employment, and in settlement relationships and patterns. The second volume is altogether different. It is the *International glossary of technical terms used in housing and town planning*, issued by the International Federation for Housing and Town Planning (Amsterdam, second revised and enlarged edition, 1951). The languages included are English, French, German, Italian, and Spanish (the last added only in the second edition). Terms in all languages are incorporated into a single alphabetical sequence, and against each one are given its equivalents in the other languages, where these exist. The volume makes no claim to be a dictionary, and it does not include terms which can readily be found in an ordinary non-specialist bi-lingual dictionary. A further edition of the glossary is being prepared, but no date for publication has been announced.

DIRECTORIES AND GUIDES TO SOURCES

The *Year book* formerly issued by the Town Planning Institute has now been split into two parts, the one a *Handbook of practice* and the other a *List of members*. The latter is a listing of members in all categories of membership, with degrees and addresses supplied. The fullest planning directory now available is the annual *Directory of official architects and planners* (Architecture and Planning Publications Ltd) which is a guide to architects and planners occupying official positions throughout the country. The directory is divided into sections, progressing systematically through central departments and local authorities of England and Wales, listing officials and addresses of departments, including the national park planning boards, followed by similar information for Scotland and Northern Ireland, and local officials of the Isle of Man and the Channel Islands. Following sections list architects and planning officers to statutory undertakings including the New Towns Commission, new town development corporations, hospital boards, universities, and nationalised industries; staff architects of commercial and industrial firms and non-statutory organisations; institutions and associations of direct or indirect interest to architects and town planners; and other categories of information of more or less relevance to planning. In the related field of architecture there is the annual *RIBA directory* published by the Royal Institute of British Architects, which contains a quantity of preliminary matter about the institute and about architects and architectural practice generally, including an index to private practices by names and one by geographical locations, followed by the full membership list of the institute.

There is a wide range of directories and yearbooks issued by professional associations and organisations in subject fields related to planning, for example, the Royal Institution of Chartered Surveyors and the Association of Consulting Engineers, which are too numerous to be detailed here, but which are available for consultation in most university and large public libraries. Directory information over the whole range of local government functions covering England, Wales, Scotland, Ireland and the Isle of Man is contained in the annual *Municipal year book* (Municipal Journal Ltd). It has an introductory section setting out information and data on a range of subjects which come within the local government province, followed by the main directory covering county councils, London government, municipal corporations, urban and rural district councils throughout England and Wales, with separate sections for Scotland, Ireland and the Isle of Man, and concluded with a classified list of officers. There is an index.

The construction industry is covered in the annual *Redland guide to the recommendations, regulations and statutory and advisory bodies of the construction industry* (Reigate, Redland Ltd, 1971-), which is the new version of *House's guide to the building industry*.

550

The guide is, as its predecessor was, in three parts. The first is a directory of government departments, professional and specialist associations and societies, unions, research bodies, information services, and other corporate bodies. The second is an extensive digest of major reports on the industry, legislation, education and training. Thirdly, there is a simplified guide to the Building Regulations. The 1971 edition is up to date on most of the major changes of 1970. In the same field, the Construction Industry Research and Information Association (CIRIA) publish a *Guide to sources of information* (1970) which gives details of 550 organisations which provide information on all aspects of the construction industry, supplemented by a subject index.

The most comprehensive guidance to both institutional and reference sources in planning will be a directory to be published during 1971 by the Centre for Environmental Studies under the title *A guide to sources of information in planning* (CES, CES-IP-12) which has been prepared with the cooperation of the Department of the Environment Library. The aim of the paper is to gather together details of the main sources of information available to those interested in planning, whether as professionals or as interested laymen. There will be four sections, on specialised library and information services provided by organisations concerned with all aspects of planning; a listing of directories and reference books; indexes of research; and bibliographies and abstracting services. The first two sections will list only British sources, but the third and fourth sections will include the major overseas sources. It is intended that the paper should be revised at regular intervals.

Over the general field of institutional sources, comprehensive guidance is provided by the Aslib (Association of Special Libraries and Information Bureaux) *Directory* (Aslib, third edition 1970). In two volumes, the second covers information sources in medicine, the social sciences and the humanities and takes in planning along with many of its related subjects (the first covers science, technology, and commerce). The second volume contains 2,338 entries giving details of organisations, not all of them having large, well-organised libraries or information services, which are able and willing to provide information on their specialised subjects. The arrangement is by place, with the organisations listed alphabetically within each place; there is a detailed subject index, and also an index to organisations included. The subject index includes entries under town planning, town and country planning, regional planning, regional studies, several beginning with ' urban ', and many under related interest headings. The details supplied for each organisation include its subject specialisation, the scope of the information available and its accessibility, and publications emanating from the organisation. On a much smaller scale, the Ministry of Defence issue a *Guide to government department and other libraries and information bureaux* (MOD, nineteenth edition 1969) arranged in subject sections, and including libraries in all types of organisation. The details given are similar to those in the Aslib *Directory*. The Library Association has published a series of regional guides to library resources, regions covered so far being Yorkshire, Merseyside, Wales and Monmouthshire, Greater Manchester, south west England and the Channel Islands, the west midlands, and London and the south east. The Scottish Library Association has published its own directory *Library resources in Scotland 1968* (Glasgow, SLA, 1968) as part of this series, and this is currently in process of revision. All the volumes follow a similar presentation, an alphabetical listing of libraries throughout the region, giving details about each one similar to those included in the Aslib *Directory*, and supported by topographic and subject/name indexes.

There are, of course, many directories covering broad fields or very specialised fields which are potentially useful to planners for guidance to sources of information on matters relevant to planning. As only two random examples, there are the *Register of local amenity societies* (Civic Trust, third edition 1970) which lists more than seven hundred societies with their dates of formation and the identification details of their secretaries; and the series of publications compiled by the Council of Europe under the generic title *Long term forecasting in Europe,* the eighth volume of which covers the United Kingdom, which are to be published as a single volume constituting an inventory of forecasting studies throughout Europe, including details under each country of experts, institutions, academics, associations and projects in the field of long term forecasting and future research. The inventory will also contain a list of the international non-governmental organisations which are active in this field. Guidance to relevant organisations, and to relevant directories also, will be found in the forthcoming CES information paper. There are also available several directories which list a comprehensive representation of institutions, organisations and corporate bodies, generally with brief details supplied for each, for example, *Trade associations and professional bodies of the United Kingdom* compiled by Patricia Millard (Library Association, fifth edition 1971), and the *Directory of British associations* (Beckenham, CBD Research Ltd, third edition 1970); and some directories of directories, which list directory type material in a wide range of subject fields, such as *Current British directories* (Beckenham, CBD Research Ltd, sixth edition 1970). Rather more specialised, but a useful source of information, is *Councils, committees, and boards: a handbook of advisory, consultative, executive and similar bodies in British public life* (Beckenham, CBD Research Ltd, 1970) which gives all relevant information, including publications, for a wide range of bodies including, for example, Passenger Transport Authorities, the Sports Council, and the Royal Commission on Environmental Pollution. There is a subject index, and also indexes of abbreviations (*eg* SELNEC) and of chairmen of bodies.

RESEARCH REGISTERS
The major source of information about research central and related to the field of planning is the register published by the Town Planning Institute under the title *Planning research* (TPI, third edition 1968). This most recent edition records work commenced or completed between 1964 and 1967. The two problems of the scope of planning and the definition of research have been countered by casting the subject net widely to take in related subjects as well as those central to planning, and by including research activities at all levels. The register is arranged in accordance with a specially devised classification scheme which provides a fairly detailed subject breakdown, and within each subject group the arrangement is alphabetically by institution. The information set out about the 1,502 research projects included in the third edition is derived from questionnaire responses; details given include the researcher(s), relevant dates, an abstract (where it has been supplied) of the research, and details of publications or sources of further informa-

553

tion. There is a subject index and indexes of research workers and of contributing organisations; a directory of research institutions gives outline descriptions of the organisation of research and relevant publications of a selection of relevant institutions. The register begins with a series of trend reports by subject experts on defined subject areas, each one reviewing the current state of research and development within its field. Since publication of the third edition, a further questionnaire survey has been carried out to up date the information in the published volume, and the information from this survey is being maintained on cards at the Town Planning Institute. The cards are supplemented by a subject index, an index of contributing bodies and an index of research workers. This up to date information can be made available to enquirers, either in person or by telephone. The continuing maintenance of the card register is supported by a small grant from the Centre for Environmental Studies, but funds are not adequate to allow publication of a new full edition of the register; the institute, however, is preparing a duplicated supplement listing the 1968-70 research projects in the form of title entries, and this is expected to be available for purchase during 1971.

Planning is included in the annual publication *Scientific research in British universities and colleges* compiled by the Department of Education and Science and the British Council (HMSO, 1969-1970 publ 1970) in three volumes. The first covers the physical sciences, the second covers biological sciences, and the third volume is devoted to the social sciences. It is the third volume which is of particular interest to planning, and the scope of this volume is broader than that of the other two in that it includes research in government departments and other institutions and also the projects of PhD students. The aim is to give brief details of active research topics in British institutions in the current academic year. The volume is divided into broad subject groups, and within each of these the arrangement is by institutions. A list of all institutions represented is provided, together with subject and name indexes. Only the briefest details are given about each project: the researcher(s), a short description of the research subject, and the dates of commencement and conclusion where relevant. These volumes replace the former *Register of research in the human sciences* compiled by the Warren Spring Laboratory of the former Department of Scientific and Industrial Research.

The *Directory of national bodies concerned with urban and regional research* compiled and published by the United Nations (New York, UN, 1968) covers almost all the countries of the UN Economic Commission for Europe, including the United Kingdom and the United States. The directory attempts to identify and to some extent describe and assess the main national bodies, as well as other bodies of major public importance, concerned with urban and regional research mainly as it refers to physical planning. The contents are organised by countries. Each section has an introduction outlining the organisation and structure of research in that country, and then proceeding to a listing of organisations giving pertinent details for each and outlining the nature of its work. The information is based upon questionnaires completed within the respective countries: the amount of detail varies according to the significance and quantity of research.

A register which provides comprehensive coverage within its circumscribed field of countryside recreation and landscape conservation is the *Research register* compiled and published by the Countryside Commission, and revised annually (third edition 1970). The three editions so far published in 1968, 1969, and 1970 represent research undertaken and completed since 1962: the most recent edition includes 198 projects either completed since January 1 1969 or currently on-going. Coverage takes in all types of organisation, including post-graduate work in universities (but not undergraduate). Only studies relating to the United Kingdom are included. Like most other registers of this type, the information is based on questionnaire responses. The arrangement of the register is geographical, commencing with national and general studies and continuing through a regional breakdown. Within each section, arrangement is alphabetical by short titles of the projects. Information about each project is full, including the names of the researchers and their organisation, the funding body, and an abstract of the research under the headings aims, methods, and results, together with relevant dates and publication details. There are indexes by subjects and by names of organisations.

Some journals regularly provide notes on research in progress, although the planning journals are not among them. The American quarterly *Geographical analysis*, for example, contains a section of research notes and comments ' designed to report work in progress in the development of innovative theoretical concepts, solutions to particular technical problems, and computer algorithms of special interest to geographical analysis '. The British quarterly *Political studies* includes a substantial section of research notes over a wide area of study, while the economic field is covered in the quarterly journal of the Royal Economic Society, *The economic journal*. *Local population studies*, the magazine and newsletter of the Cambridge Group for the History of Population and Social Structure, includes notes on research into local studies; while the *Urban history newsletter* from Leicester University does the same for urban history. In the United States, the Bureau of Community Planning of the University of Illinois produced a *Quarterly digest of urban and regional research*, which ceased publication in 1971.

TRANSLATION INDEXES

In view of the apparent lack of linguistic ability on the part of planners, brought to light in the OSTI survey of information use,[1] and the equal lack of translation facilities available to them, it is unfortunate that neither of the two standard indexes to translated material serves planning adequately. *Chartotheca translationum alphabetica* is a monthly card service with annual cumulations in book form, published by Hans W Bentz Verlag in Frankfurt am Main. The annual volume is a single sequence by authors, without indexes to subjects. *Index translationum: international bibliography of translations* is published in an annual volume by Unesco in Paris, arranged by countries and by broad subject headings within each country, with an index of authors. Both these services have international coverage, but in each the planning content is minimal.

INDEXES TO THESES

Thesis material generally is little used by planners. This may be to some extent because they are not aware of its existence, of its location or of its availability. Two services, one British and one American, give assistance in this respect. The annual *Index to theses accepted for higher degrees by the universities of Great Britain and*

Ireland and the Council for National Academic Awards is compiled and published by Aslib. The eighteenth volume covering 1967-1968 (Aslib, 1970) records 6,712 theses, much the largest proportion of these emanating from London University, with substantial representation also of Wales, Oxford, Cambridge, Manchester and Birmingham. Theses indexed are arranged in broad subject order: details supplied are brief, consisting only of the author, title, type of degree, and the institution. There are author and subject indexes, and an editorial note indicates the extent of availability of thesis material in the various universities. Town planning is included under the group art and architecture; and related headings, such as regional geography, regional studies, and economic geography, are also of interest.

The American service is *Dissertation abstracts international* published by University Microfilms Inc of Ann Arbor, Michigan. The service is subtitled 'abstracts of dissertations available on microfilm or as xerographic reproductions' and it is in fact a monthly compilation of abstracts of doctoral dissertations submitted to University Microfilms by more than 250 co-operating institutions in the United States and Canada. The word 'international' was incorporated into the title at vol 39 (1969) to reflect the anticipated inclusion of material from European universities. There are two series: series A covers humanities and social sciences and series B covers the sciences and engineering. The monthly parts in each series are arranged by subjects: regional and city planning are included under the general heading of sociology in series A. Keyword title and author indexes produced monthly are cumulated annually, separately for each series. The dissertations themselves can be purchased from University Microfilms, either on microfilm or as xerox copies. University Microfilms also operate the DATRIX service (Direct Access to Reference Information: a Xerox Service), a computer-based service whose data base is the complete store of microfilmed dissertations. The data base is classified into three broad subject groups: chemistry/life sciences, engineering/physical sciences, and humanities/social sciences, each one having its own list of keywords. Order forms specifying the keywords required are mailed to University Microfilms, and the service returns a bibliography in accordance with these giving brief details of each disserta-

557

tion listed and reference to its abstract in *Dissertation abstracts international*.

Information about higher degree thesis projects is selectively included also in *Planning research* (see above).

NEWSPAPER INDEXES

Newspapers do not rank highly as sources of information for planners but, in particular in practice, coverage of planning topics and reportage of the results of plans or reactions to proposals in the more responsible sections of the press is worth following. *The guardian* is particularly good for reliable coverage of planning. It could therefore be advantageous to be able to locate items of value in retrospect, and this can be done through indexes to newspapers. There are only two such indexes. The *Index to The times* (Times Newspapers Ltd, 1906-) has appeared bi-monthly since 1957; there is a three to four months time lag in publication. The *Index* is compiled from the final edition of the paper, although items appearing only in earlier editions are also included: the references give the date of issue, page and column numbers, and are listed in a straight through alphabetical sequence of subjects, personal names, place names, and other headings. The *Index to the Glasgow herald* (Glasgow, Outram, 1907-) is an annual production, and the time lag is correspondingly longer. It is similar in content and presentation to the *Index to The times,* with an alphabetical listing of all references. These indexes are useful not only for their specific guidance to their own newspapers but also because they give an indication of the date on which the same topic would have been included in other English and Scottish newspapers.

INDEXES TO COMPUTER PROGRAMMES

A new type of guide is that which lists computer programmes which have been used already, and which are available for re-use under similar circumstances. *Computers in geography* compiled by J R Tarrant (Norwich, University of East Anglia, 1970) lists about six hundred programmes currently in use by some two hundred geographers throughout the world. The entry for each programme gives the name and address of its user, the type of computer used and its core size and peripherals required, the programme language and required core size, the author of the programme and his address, and a description of the programme and details of its application. The entries are arranged alphabetically by name of user, and there is a subject index. It is proposed that this becomes an annual publication, and that the edition for 1971 should be re-titled *Computers in the environmental sciences* reflecting its expansion to include entries on geology, urban and regional planning, transportation, and other related fields. An announcement in *JTPI* 56(8) September/October 1970 362 stated that ' the Computer Research Group of the Institute, in collaboration with the National Computing Centre and the Local Authorities Management Services and Computer Committee, is shortly to undertake a survey of computer programmes which can be used in the planning field . . . Questionnaires are to be circulated to all local planning authorities and to other agencies and research bodies engaged in work closely related to planning. It will cover computer programmes currently in use, work in hand on programme development, and projected future work, and it is hoped to go on to make some evaluation of the utility of these programmes. It is hoped that the Index will be maintained by the National Computing Centre and the Local Authorities Management Services and Computer Committee.'

GOVERNMENT PUBLICATIONS
The principal source of continuing information about British government publications is the government publisher, Her Majesty's Stationery Office (HMSO). The *Daily list,* which can be posted daily to subscribers or in weekly batches, covers the day's output of all priced publications sold or published by the London Stationery Office, including reprints where their prices are revised. The *List* is in five sections: statutory instruments; parliamentary papers; non-parliamentary publications, by departments; reprints; publications of international organisations. A card service giving the information in the form of cards for incorporation into catalogues or filing systems, is also available. The *Monthly list* cumulates the contents of that month's *Daily lists* with the exception of statutory instruments, which are cumulated into separate monthly lists. There are three sections: parliamentary papers; non-parliamentary publications emanating from British departments and from international

organisations; and journals. An author, title, and catchword subject index is incorporated. The *Monthly lists* are in turn cumulated to form the annual *Catalogue of government publications,* with its own cumulated index. The annual indexes are cumulated five-yearly into one alphabetical sequence of personal names, titles, and subject catchwords. The *Consolidated index to government publications 1961-1965* was published in 1967; previous quinquennial indexes were compiled from 1936 to 1960, but all of them are now out of print except for the one covering the years 1955-1960. The annual *Catalogue* contains all items published by HMSO during the year, excepting statutory instruments. Parliamentary papers are listed numerically in their various series, followed by non-parliamentary publications arranged by their originating departments; the third section is a list of officially published journals. Supplementary to the annual *Catalogue* is the *International organisations and overseas agencies publications* also published by HMSO, with its own index. Sectional lists are also issued for most, though not all government departments; some have grouped titles, and there is also a miscellaneous list (no 50) which includes a variety of departments with small publishing output. The contents of the lists are normally confined to priced items: all current non-parliamentary publications are included (some lists also include selected out of print material) and also a selection of parliamentary publications. The Library of the Department of the Environment have prepared a bibliography (no 142 in their series of Library Bibliographies) listing the publications of the Ministries of Town and Country Planning, Local Government and Planning, and Housing and Local Government from 1943 to 1966.

Three narrative guides to government publications and information are useful sources of information. *Government information and the research worker* edited by Ronald Staveley and Mary Piggott (Library Association, second revised edition 1965) consists of chapters on the functions and sources of information of twenty three government departments or agencies, some of them contributed by their librarians. Although now out of date, it yet remains a valuable source of reference for publications up to the date of writing. A short text which does no more than provide an outline of the output of the various departments and agencies, but which also includes discussion of the problems associated with the acquisition and organisation of British government publications is *An introduction to British government publications* by James G Ollé (Association of Assistant Librarians, 1965) now also out of date, but a new edition is in preparation and is due to be published during 1971. John E Pemberton's *British official publications* (Oxford, Pergamon Press, 1971) is a comprehensive guide to the many categories of official publications, described against a contextual background of the parliamentary and governmental processes which give rise to them. The book is also helpful about the methods of obtaining official publications, and of organising them.

BIBLIOGRAPHIES, LIBRARY CATALOGUES, GUIDES TO DOCUMENTARY SOURCES

Over a general field, one of the most comprehensive guides to published sources of information is the *Guide to reference material* edited by A J Walford (Library Association, second edition 1966-70) in three volumes. The first of these covers science and technology, the second covers philosophy and psychology, religion, social sciences, geography, biography and history, and the third takes in generalities, languages, the arts and literature. The second volume is therefore of interest to planners for its coverage of the standard reference works in all formats in subject areas, such as sociology and economics, which are of relevance to planning, and the third volume covers planning itself under the general subject heading of the arts. The scope of the *Guide* is international, though the main emphasis is on British material, and does not claim to be comprehensive—rather it is intended as a ' signpost '. Each volume is arranged in subject order, and within each subject all types of reference works are discussed, including bibliographies, quick reference guides, dictionaries, textbooks, and abstracting and indexing services, giving full bibliographical details of each; an index of authors, titles and subjects is included. The coverage of planning within the arts is sketchy, some notable signposts being conspicuous by their absence, and it is disappointing that in the section on recreation, no guidance is given to works on the subject in general as well as to the specific components of it. The main interest of the *Guide* for planners, therefore, lies in the second volume, with its intro-

561

ductory guidance to a number of related subjects. Much the same comment applies to the American counterpart of Walford's work, the *Guide to reference books* by Constance M Winchell (Chicago, American Library Association, eighth edition 1967) which contains in one volume about 7,500 entries referring to reference works in English and other languages published up to and including 1964. The entries are arranged into subject sections: those covering the humanities, social sciences, and history and area studies, are all relevant in part to planning.

Over the field of the social sciences there is also a source of major importance, the *London bibliography of the social sciences,* which is the subject catalogue of the British Library of Political and Economic Science and the Edward Fry Library of International Law at the London School of Economics. The basic volumes, dating from 1931-1932, incorporate the holdings of these two libraries plus a number of others which are now no longer specified, up to 1931; the most recent printed supplement brings the record up to 1962. This is the largest subject bibliography of its kind, and it is supplemented by the British Library's *Monthly list of additions.*

Over the combined fields of architecture and planning, there are some major American sources. The principal one is the *Catalogue* of the Harvard University Graduate School of Design Library (Boston, G K Hall, 1968) in forty four volumes. This is a photo-lithographic reproduction of 611,000 author and subject entry cards, covering books, pamphlets, journals, theses, and journal articles. The library is internationally known as a source of research in architecture, landscape architecture, and urban planning, and its catalogue is the main reference source in these subjects. Two important sources derive from the Avery Architectural Library of Columbia University. The *Catalogue* of the library was first published in 1895, subsequently in six volumes in 1958, and most recently in 1968 in an enlarged edition in nineteen volumes (Boston, G K Hall, 1968). This is a photolithographic edition, reproducing 335,000 cards representing subject/author entries for around 75,000 books and journals. There is emphasis on the literature of urban renewal and on the social aspects of urban design. Supplements are projected. The other source, the *Avery index to architectural periodicals* is described below in the section on indexing and abstracting services.

562

Continuing records of the holdings of a library are publicised in the form of accessions lists, providing, where the library is comprehensive and the bibliographical detail is adequate, a useful source of recent planning information. The *Classified accessions list* (1949-) issued bi-monthly by the Library of the Department of the Environment[2] fulfills both these criteria, and is a useful guide to books, reports, development plans, government publications, first issues of new journals, and other relevant material on the same wide range of subjects as are covered in other DOE publications. Each issue contains some two hundred entries, arranged in classified subject order, with cross references between related items inserted where necessary. The former Ministry of Public Building and Works, now also part of the Department of the Environment, prepares *Consolidated accessions lists* (1945-) which are a catalogue of the library's[2] books and pamphlets compiled every six months, and arranged in classified order by UDC with author and subject indexes. The fortnightly *Library bulletin* is in three parts, of which the second is an annotated list of selected additions to the library. The Library of the GLC Department of Planning and Transportation is now also producing a duplicated list of new publications, arranged in UDC classified order. The former Ministry of Technology (now the Department of Trade and Industry) is another source of continuing information.

Rather different, but a continuing record nevertheless, of additions to a large library is the monthly *British research and development reports* issued by the National Lending Library for Science and Technology which lists, in subject groups, published and unpublished reports deposited at the NLL by organisations of all types. From January 1971 this has expanded into the monthly *Announcement bulletin,* and now includes not only reports but also translations produced by government organisations, industry, universities and learned institutions, as well as a selection of doctoral theses. Material can be borrowed from the NLL by organisations (not by individuals) through the library's normal loan service, or photocopies obtained through the photocopy service.

A number of organisations and libraries prepare comprehensive series of bibliographies or bibliographical reviews. Foremost, again, in Great Britain, is the Library of the Department of the Environment[2] which has to its credit a long series of duplicated bibliographies based on its own resources and covering a wide range of subjects in accordance with departmental interests. Notable among these bibliographies are no 65, plus substantial supplements, on new towns; no 70, which is a general list on town and country planning forming an excellent basic guide to the subject; no 140 on settlement in the countryside; and no 144 on land use. One of the department's functions is to service the various royal commissions which are set up at its instigation, and this concentration on a specific area often results in a bibliography: service to the Royal Commission on Environmental Pollution, for example, has resulted in Bibliography no 149 on environmental pollution (March 1971). A list of bibliographies available can be obtained from the Chief Librarian of the department. All of them are dated, and most are revised from time to time in accordance with demand; they vary in length from under one hundred items to several hundreds of references. The American counterpart is the series of bibliographies produced by the US Department of Housing and Urban Development. These are, in general, substantial productions, printed by the US Government Printing Office and intended for a wider circulation than are the British lists. An indication of the range of coverage may be gained from the examples of a few titles: *Bibliography on building, housing and planning prepared for program use in developing countries* (four hundred items); *Citizen and business participation in urban affairs* (six hundred items); *Operation breakthrough: mass produced and industrialized housing* (four hundred items); and *New communities* (six hundred items). There is no standardised format or presentation for these bibliographies, but they normally include an index to the arrangement, and frequently lists of relevant journals, addresses of organisations included, and other helpful information. Some of them are annotated. Also in the United States is the Council of Planning Librarians, a nationally organised group of librarians, planners and organisations interested in the organisation and dissemination of information about city and regional planning. The council have produced, over a period of nearly fifteen years, a long list of Exchange Bibliographies, varying in size from a few pages to over one hundred, and covering a very wide range of general and specialist subjects, from the history of city planning, and planning theory, to mass transit and 'current trends in planning and their effect on planning literature'. A complete list of bibliographies in print is available from the council.

Two British libraries are further sources of bibliographical guidance. The Library of the Building Research Station serves, and reflects the interests of, the entire station and the bibliographies which it produces are only in small part relevant to planning; but the titles, for example no 237 on 'Modernising old dwellings' are valuable sources of information, containing annotated references to books, reports, and journal articles. The Library of the GLC Department of Planning and Transportation has also begun to prepare duplicated lists of annotated references on subjects which are close to the council's interests, for example, no 3 on 'V/STOL: economic and environmental aspects'. The lists are very short at present, but there is clearly potential for growth. Details of these services will be supplied by the librarians of the respective organisations. The bibliographical services detailed above are all based on the resources of libraries; the major non-library source of bibliographies in Britain is the Centre for Environmental Studies, whose papers frequently take the form of bibliographical reviews, or state of the art surveys with substantial references. One of the best-known of these reviews is Alan G Wilson's 'Models in urban planning: a synoptic review of recent literature' reprinted in *Urban studies* 5(3) November 1968 249-276. But Wilson's references, like those in some of the centre's other papers, are open to criticism on bibliographical grounds: in the main they are sufficiently full, but sometimes are totally inadequate—'mimeo, 1967' just will not do in a review which claims to be authoritative. Details of the centre's publications are available from its secretary; many of them have been mentioned in the course of chapter 11 of this book.

The report of the OSTI survey of the information requirements of planners incorporated two recommendations made with the object of improving the physical availability of sources of information to planners.[3] The first of these was for the compilation of an authoritative list of selected published documentary information sources which 'should form the nucleus of a representative collection on planning within a general library'. The second recommendation was for the compilation of an authoritative list of basic information sources which would provide a minimum of necessary information within planning organisations, in particular those in local authorities. It was suggested that the then Ministry of Housing and Local Government would be an appropriate body to compile these lists, in view of its substantial library resources, perhaps in collaboration with the Town Planning Institute. The first of these lists is under active consideration, drafts having been prepared for comment, and it is probable that the final list will be published by the Library Association.

In the meantime, pending the appearance of these lists, and of the CES list (see above), the fullest basic guide to sources of information on planning is the DOE Library Bibliography 70 mentioned above. Apart from this, information has to be derived from publications which treat the combined fields of architecture and planning, or architecture and building alone. There is a fairly full listing of information relevant to planning in *Planning information: a catalogue of available sources in Oxford* (Oxford, Polytechnic School of Town Planning, 1970) which records the resources of the libraries of the Polytechnic and the University. While this may be a useful locational tool for planners working in Oxford, as a reference source it falls well below required standard by reason of its sketchy bibliographical detail. A narrative text giving guidance to sources over a wide field, mainly in architecture and building but taking in planning also, is *How to find out in architecture and building* by D L Smith (Oxford, Pergamon Press, 1967). Introductory chapters provide the professional contextual background, and sources discussed include books, journals, indexing and abstracting services, reference books, and institutional sources. The information, as in all books of this type, has gone quickly out of date, and no revision is projected. Narrowing the field further, the Royal Institute of British Architects compile and publish a periodically revised list *Keys to published sources of information* (formerly *Keys to published technical and management information*), which is intended as a list of basic sources for inclusion in architectural office libraries. It covers quick reference sources, such as directories and dictionaries, journal guides, bibliographies, official publications, and information on the organisation of architectural libraries. The Construction Industry Research and Information Association publish

566

an *Index of technical publications* (second edition 1970), which is a subject guide to 3,700 'definitive publications' for the construction industry, covering technical, professional and managerial fields, and including wide coverage of British Standards and Building Research Station publications.

There are a number of bibliographies emanating from various countries in various published and semi-published formats on the central theme of town and country planning and its American variant of city and regional planning, compiled from a variety of viewpoints and varying in out of dateness. Starting with the oldest, there is the *References on city and regional planning* compiled by Caroline Shillaber (Cambridge, Mass, MIT Press, 1959), intended as a guide to libraries in developing their city planning and architectural departments. The references are mainly to books, journal articles being included only when they are significant contributions to a subject not adequately represented by books, and the emphasis is strongly on American material. Lists of journals and bibliographies are included. *City planning: a basic bibliography of sources and trends* by George C Bestor and Holway R Jones was published by the California Council of Civil Engineers and Land Surveyors in Sacramento in 1956, and went into a third edition in 1962. The main bibliography of around 1,200 annotated references to mainly English-language publications relating predominantly to American theory and practice, is supplemented by lists of professional organisations, journals, publishers' addresses, author/title and subject indexes, references to other bibliographies, major city planning collections in the United States, and a 'basic library' of under fifty books for Planning Commissions.

The *International bibliography and reference guide on urban affairs* compiled by Rosemary H Wallace (Ramsey, NJ, Ramsey-Wallace Corporation, 1966) contains some five hundred references to literature from 1823 through May 1966, comprising books, journal articles and reports on urban affairs generally, lightly annotated and achieving world wide coverage although the emphasis is on American material. Bibliographical details are sometimes sketchy. A large number of references appear from the *New York times* and the *Record* of Hackensack, New Jersey. There is a combined author and subject index. *Metropolis: a selected bibliography on adminis-*

567

trative and other problems of metropolitan areas throughout the world compiled by D Halasz for the International Union of Local Authorities (The Hague, Nijhoff, second edition 1967) covers a similar wide field but more comprehensively, the entries being arranged by countries, Great Britain being represented on pages 95-129. The fourth edition of *Principles and practice of urban planning* by William I Goodman and Eric C Freund (Washington, DC, International City Managers' Association, 1968) contains an extensive bibliography on pages 585-604. *A bibliography of city and regional planning* compiled by Katharine McNamara (Cambridge, Mass, Harvard UP, 1969) lists abut 20,000 books and journal articles from early literature to the end of 1968. Most recently, Melville C Branch has compiled *Comprehensive urban planning: a selective annotated bibliography with related materials* (Beverly Hills, California, Sage Publications, 1970) in which ' the focus is almost entirely on experience, problems, and the future of cities in the United States '. The bibliography contains around 1,500 references arranged in broad subject sections, each one consisting of articles from journals and books, reports and pamphlets. Bibliographical details are full for all types of material; annotations take the form mainly of lists of contents, sometimes descriptive comments, or quotations from other sources. A section on general urban planning bibliographies includes those incorporated in books and journal articles. The emphasis is heavily on American material: the list of journals shows 117 citations for the *Journal of the American Institute of Planners* followed by forty seven for *Scientific American*. Subject, author and title indexes are provided to contents as well as to independent items. The bibliography is supplemented by notes on municipal and metropolitan planning agencies in the US and Canada, colleges and universities in the US and Canada offering planning courses, and lists of publishers and sources with addresses. The closing date for inclusion of material is not stated, but items published in 1969 are included. Planning bibliographies were reviewed by Caroline Shillaber in 'A review of planning bibliographies ' in *Journal of the American Institute of Planners* 31(4) November 1965 352-360.

'A select bibliography on aspects of regional planning' by Ken Bradbury in *Town and country planning* 36(6) June 1968 301-304 is the single guide to information on British regional planning in the round. It consists of eighty one references, arranged by authors, to books, reports, journal articles, and some unpublished material. Bradbury is preparing a comprehensive bibliography on regional planning as a submission for the fellowship of the Library Association, and it is possible that in the fullness of time, this may be published by the association or by another agency. The DOE Library Bibliography 65 on new towns has been mentioned above, with its supplements bringing the record up to June 1967, covering British and overseas new towns as reported in books, government reports and selected journal articles, arranged in a chronological sequence. *New towns: a selected annotated bibliography* compiled by Jean Viet (Paris, Unesco, 1960, Reports and Papers on the Social Sciences 12) draws heavily on the Ministry lists, and includes 865 items covering around two hundred new towns in ten countries, mainly post-1940, with an index of the towns referred to. A specialised aspect of planning is represented in *A selected bibliography of land use and built form studies* (1969) compiled as Working Paper 16 of the Centre for Land Use and Built Form Studies in the University of Cambridge, in conjunction with the programme of research in progress at the centre. The studies are concerned with the use of land in physical and spatial terms, and with the built form as an abstraction of building rather than the building itself. The bibliography lists nearly five hundred references to books, reports and journal articles of British and American origin, up to and including December 1968. The entries, which are unannotated, are arranged into five sections, each one characterised by a scale of interest, from the building up to national scale, with a sixth section listing other relevant bibliographies, and a seventh containing a random selection of the literature on models and quantitative analysis. Entries are printed on one side of the page only, in the form of cards which can be cut out and filed. There are no indexes, and bibliographical detail is minimal: journal articles do not give volume, part or page numbers.

The economic aspect of regional planning is dominant in *Regional economic analysis in Britain and the Commonwealth: a bibliographic guide* by F E Ian Hamilton (Weidenfeld and Nicolson, 1969) prepared for the Commission on Methods of Economic Regionalisation of the International Geographical Union. Roughly one third of the text relates to the British Isles, and this consists of a textual introduction on regionalism and the development of regional planning and the economic planning regions, followed by the bibliography itself which is divided into sections according to broad aspects of the total subject. A total of 1,148 references cover books and journal articles, giving full cover of 1967 and partial cover of 1968. OECD Special Annotated Bibliographies 8 and 9 on *Regional economic policies* between them cover, in sections, the industrialised countries and the developing countries, with lengthy abstracts, some in French and some in English, covering mainly the period 1961 to 1965, and taking in books, reports, and journal articles. A J Brown is the compiler of ' Surveys of applied economics: regional economics, with special reference to the United Kingdom ' *The economic journal* 79(316) December 1969 759-796, which is the first of a series of surveys of applied economics to be published jointly for the Social Science Research Council and the Royal Economic Society. The survey is concerned primarily with the work relating to regional economic problems and their analysis in the UK, with some comparative reference to other countries. There are 152 references, to books, papers and journals, unannotated, and with some bibliographical detail missing, such as publishers of books and page numbers of journal articles.

P M Townroe's *Industrial location and regional economic policy: a selected bibliography* (Birmingham, Centre for Urban and Regional Studies, 1968, CURS Occasional Paper 2) is not intended to be comprehensive: rather, ' attention has been centred on papers, articles and books published during the last eight years, particularly in the UK '. Material published before 1960 is included only if of historical importance. A total of 349 entries are arranged in six broad categories, with cross references between, and supported by an author index.

Industrial location alone is the focus of *Industrial location: a review and annotated bibliography of theoretical, empirical and case studies,* by Benjamin Stevens and Carolyn A Brackett (Philadelphia, Regional Science Research Institute, 1967, Bibliography Series 3), for the purposes of which it is defined as ' the geographic distribution of industrial establishments '. Only references in which industrial location forms the main theme of discussion are included: others on, for example, regional economics, are excluded. There are 854 entries referring to English language material only, published between the end of World War II and the end of 1965. The bibliography is arranged by authors or titles, and each entry is coded in accordance with a classification code to indicate the subjects covered. A subject index is arranged by the same code. Entries refer to books, parts of books, journals, and a limited amount of unpublished material such as dissertations, mainly American in origin, with annotations of varying length supplied where the title is not self-explanatory. The bibliography is preceded by a review of the subject based on the literature.

The Regional Science Research Institute are responsible also for other bibliographies on regional science in their bibliography series. The first of the series, and a classic in its field, is *Central place studies: a bibliography of theory and applications, including supplement through 1964* by Brian J L Berry and Allen Pred (Philadelphia, Regional Science Research Institute, 1965, Bibliography Series 1). The introduction on the theory of central places is followed by a long abstract of Christaller's theories (see chapter 11, section on regional planning) and then comes the bibliography which is arranged into sixteen sections each one covering a different aspect of the subject. The coverage is mainly of books and journal articles, but takes in some other formats also, mainly in the English language with a small proportion of foreign material. The main bibliography comes up to 1960, and the supplement which follows it brings the record up through 1964. The subject coverage takes in sociology, public health, marketing, ecology, planning, business theory, and land economics. The main bibliography and the supplement each have an author index, and the major serial publications in which relevant studies appear, are listed. There are nearly one thousand entries in the main bibliography, with decent bibliographical details and abstracts of varying lengths. The supplement not only updates the main list, it also contains an extensive listing of Japanese language literature, and an extension of the coverage of the section on fairs and markets. *Distance and human interaction: a review and bibliography* by Gunnar Olsson (Philadelphia, Regional Science Research Institute, 1965, Bibliography Series 2) is roughly two thirds review and one third bibliography. The review falls into three parts, discussing in turn the distance factor in location theory, the distance factor in economic migration theory and in diffusion models, and gravity and potential models. The bibliography is a straight through listing by authors of nearly four hundred references to books, journal articles and other material, mainly in English with some foreign language entries principally Scandinavian, covering the literature up to 1964. The entries are unannotated. The diffusion aspects of location are separately treated by Lawrence A Brown in *Diffusion processes and location: a conceptual framework and bibliography* (Philadelphia, Regional Science Research Institute, 1968, Bibliography Series 4). Office location is documented in the Location of Offices Bureau's *Offices: a bibliography* (LOB, 1970) which contains 145 references divided into eight sections, on general aspects, human aspects, office development, office location, decentralisation, office planning policy, commuting, and current research. Coverage is of books, journals, reports, conference proceedings, and some unpublished material such as theses, all in the English language, and mainly British. The period covered is 1957 to 1969. Bibliographical details in some cases could be fuller—no page numbers are given for journal articles, for example—and the entries are not annotated.

The seventh research bibliography from the GLC Department of Planning and Transportation Library is devoted to *Statistical techniques: a bibliography of books in the research library* (1970) and takes the form of a duplicated list of eighty six references to English language books, divided into eight sections, on bibliographical sources; general statistical techniques; tables, models and graphs; statistical analysis; forecasting, planning and operational research; demography; economics and trade; and traffic and transport. The coverage is confined in the main to the 1960's, and the entries are unannotated. Techniques used in planning, in particular mathematical models, are documented in the papers produced by the Centre for Environmental Studies (see above, and throughout chapter 11, section on planning techniques). 'A selective bibliography on quantitative methods in geography ' by Derek Thompson in *Geography* 54(1) January 1969 74-83, is in two main sections : first, general accounts of statistical and other procedures and methods, with a rating system to indicate the level of difficulty; second, applications of these methods in geography. Books and journal articles are included, both British and American, dating mainly from the 1950's and 1960's. Simulation in education is documented in *Social science instructional simulation systems: a selected bibliography* by John L Taylor (Sheffield, Sheffield University, 1969, SURISS Project Papers 4). A total of 492 references to books, pamphlets and journal articles up to October 1969 are listed in an alphabetical sequence by authors. Coverage is primarily of British and American material. Key references to other instructional simulation bibliographies, and four broad subject areas, are identified at the beginning. There are no annotations.

The wider subject of planning education generally is covered in *A bibliography on planning education* (Centre for Environmental Studies, 1970, CES-IP-13) which is stated to be provisional as it is certainly incomplete—a comment which could in honesty be applied to most bibliographies. This one is made up of references to articles, papers and books that are known to mention, or to discuss, subjects closely relevant to the education of planners, mainly in the British literature, though North American items are listed where they have come to light, and also a few from other countries.

Urban sociology, and the social aspects of planning generally, have been well documented, although not recently. The seminal source on the subject is the bibliographic review by Ruth Glass ' Urban sociology in Great Britain ' in *Current sociology* 4(4) June 1955 5-76 which consists of a state of the art survey followed by a classified and annotated bibliography. The survey part of the review is discussed in the section on urban studies within chapter 11. The bibliography, which forms the major part of the review, contains 432 items divided into sections on the background in Britain; social surveys and studies, mainly local and regional; the structure of urbanism, studies and source materials; and town planning. It is particularly useful for historical material, and for its listing of the social surveys which preceded planning proposals, the surveys of planned areas and towns, and for special aspects such as poverty. The annotations are generally brief, and very much to the point.

Now of historical interest is Louis Wirth's 'A bibliography of the urban community ' in *The city* by Park, Burgess and McKenzie (see chapter 11, the section on urban studies) pages 161-228. It contains references to work published up to and including 1924, arranged within the framework of a specially devised scheme of classification for many aspects of the city, such as the city and its hinterland, the ecological organisation of the city, and eugenics of the city. This is actually more of a literature review than a straight bibliography, each section and subsection being introduced with notes on its content. Wirth seems doubtful about his bibliographic ability, inserting the compiler's usual comment about including much of small value and omitting much of importance, and he goes on to say (page 162) that ' the list of books and articles includes many works which were inaccessible at the time the bibliography was compiled, and whose contents could therefore not be examined. They are included because either the titles were suggestive or else the reputation of the authors merited attention.'

The bibliography on *Urban sociology* compiled by Robert Gutman from the Urban Studies Center at Rutgers State University (New Brunswick, NJ, Rutgers State University, 1963) was initially prepared to meet the needs of graduate students in urban sociology at that university. It contains about 450 references to English language books and journal articles, mainly American but including some British material, published between 1945 and the end of 1962, although some significant older sources are included. The contents are arranged in subject sections, with an index of authors. The entries are not annotated. The major British source in the field is *Land use planning and the social sciences: a selected bibliography of literature on town and country planning and related social studies in Great Britain, 1930-1963* (London, Centre for Urban Studies, 1964). The bibliography, which is largely the work of John Westergaard, contains 564 references to books, reports, journal articles, conference proceedings, and some unpublished material, all in the English language, and most of it British. The coverage is confined mainly to the dates stated, but some older material is included if it provides a background to subsequent development. The list is by no means comprehensive, but it is nevertheless a fairly full coverage of literature on land use planning and the social context within which it operates. Arrangement is in accordance with a fairly detailed classification scheme, with cross references between sections; there is an author index. There are no annotations, but the work is notable for the systematically full bibliographic details. There are also sections listing guides to official statistics, and statistical sources both local and national; bibliographies and guides to surveys and registers of research; and a selected list of journals. It has been intended to keep the bibliography up to date through the issue of supplements, but none have so far been issued (as at March 1971).

The journal *Current sociology*, in which Ruth Glass's trend report appeared in 1955, is worthy of mention in this context as a continuing source of such bibliographic reviews on sociological subjects, some of them very relevant to the planning field. Each issue of the journal is devoted to a topic, and as relevant examples we can cite 15(2) 1967 ' Community research ' by Robert J Havighurst and Anton Jansen, a trend report on urban and rural community studies which erects a conceptual framework for the ensuing bibliography of 410 items, annotated references to books and journal articles in all languages up to and including 1967. The bibliographical details, though not always complete, are yet sufficient for identification. 15(3) 1967 ' The sociology of sport ' by Günther Lüschen is a similar treatment of its subject, with a bibliography of 892 items referring to books, journal articles, mimeo and unpublished reports and dissertations produced up to 1967, in all languages, with short annotations at some entries. 16(1) 1968 ' La sociologie du loisir : tendances actuelles de la recherche et bibliographie (1945-1965) ' by Joffre Dumazedier and Claire Guinchat, is a trend report in French with an English summary, followed by a bibliography of 487 items, some of them with annotations in English and some in French, of international coverage between 1945 and 1965.

On urban history, a very good bibliographic review is provided by H J Dyos in his contribution 'Agenda for urban historians ' in *The study of urban history* which he edited for Leicester University (see chapter 11, the section on urban studies). The review incorporates some parts of Dyos' earlier article ' The growth of cities in the nineteenth century: a review of some recent writing ' *Victorian studies* 9(3) March 1966 225-237. References are sometimes in the text, but more often in the form of footnotes, and are to books and journal articles. The review itself tries to state the scope of urban

575

history, the directions in which it should be moving, the most suitable areas for research, and the methods which should be employed. The references are to the source material and the descriptive literature on all these aspects of urban history, and include several to review articles and bibliographies which, if followed up, will cumulate the bibliography. There are a total of 141 footnotes, but many of these contain a number of references. Bibliographical details are not always of the fullest, some books, for example, lacking details of publisher and place of publication. Dyos cites the ' most instructive but patchy bibliography ' in Lewis Mumford's *The city in history* (pages 579 to 634), and the ' more catholic but better organised ' list of references compiled by Philip Dawson and Sam B Warner in 'A selection of works relating to the history of cities ' in *The historian and the city* edited by Handlin and Burchard (both of these titles discussed in the section on urban studies in chapter 11) as further sources of information on urban history. But the major source in the field is *A bibliography of British municipal history* by Charles Gross (New York, 1897: reprinted with an introductory preface by G H Martin, Leicester, Leicester UP, 1966), and this is being supplemented by *A bibliography of British and Irish municipal history,* compiled by G H Martin and Sylvia MacIntyre, covering the printed sources and literature of the four countries of the United Kingdom from earliest times through 1966, excluding all those titles cited by Gross. The first volume of the new bibliography, containing some six thousand entries, is due in 1971 from Leicester UP.

Landscape is documented in a selective bibliography ' Landscape survey and appreciation ' in *Planning outlook* new series 4 Spring 1968 54-59, a reading list compiled from the resources of the Department of the Environment Library to accompany a paper by S B K Clark ' Landscape survey and analysis on a national basis ' in the same issue of the journal. Its total of over seventy references provide a comprehensive coverage of landscape classification and appreciation in books, journal articles, reports, and corporate volume, both British and foreign, published between 1927 and 1968. They are arranged into five sections, on general background, landscape in qualitative terms, landscape use and misuse, landscape in quantitative terms, and landscape mapping. There are no annotations, and bibliographical details are not always adequate, for example, a few entries bear no indication of their date of publication. On the environment generally, the Civic Trust have produced a short bibliography of thirty nine annotated entries on *Conservation areas* (1969) covering the period 1961 to 1969, and referring to British books, pamphlets, reports, and journal articles. The Ministry of Technology (as it then was) produced a bibliography on *Environmental pollution: a list of periodical references* (MoTechnology, 1969, L266 1969-10) which covers all forms of atmospheric and water pollution as represented in the British and American journal literature mainly in 1968 and 1969. Annotations are given where the title is not explicit. From the same source comes a bibliography on *Air pollution: a list of periodical references* (MoTechnology, 1969, L252 1969-10) which is a list of about sixty references to British and American journal articles arranged in chronological order from Spring 1967 through August 1969. DoE Library Bibliography 149 on *Environmental pollution* (1971) has been mentioned above.

The major sources of guidance to the literature of recreation are American. *Outdoor recreation literature: a survey* prepared by the Library of Congress in 1959 was commissioned by the Outdoor Recreation Resources Review Commission to assess the extent and quality of materials available on outdoor recreation, indicating areas of strength and weakness, and identifying basic sources and useful studies on significant problems in outdoor recreation in the United States. It was published in 1962 as the ORRRC Study Report 27 (see chapter 11, section on recreation and leisure planning). This basic source has been updated and extended by James R and Marjorie J Pinkerton in *Outdoor recreation and leisure: a reference guide and selected bibliography* (Columbia, Missouri, Research Center of the School of Business and Public Administration, University of Missouri, 1969), which concentrates basically on the years 1960 to 1966, though incorporating some material from 1959 and taking in also up to 1968. The survey of bibliographic sources goes back to 1953. There are 1,096 entries arranged into ten sections, with cross references listed at the end of each section, and supplemented by author and title indexes. References are to all types of monographs, including books, pamphlets, mimeographed studies and reports, dissertations and theses, and to chapters and sections of books, journal

577

articles, and serial publications of various types, most of them North American in origin. Annotations are included only in the first two sections of the bibliography, discussing general reference sources, and serials. Contemporary with the end coverage of the Pinkertons' guide is the *Index of selected outdoor recreation literature* published by the Bureau of Outdoor Recreation of the Department of the Interior. The first volume, covering the calendar year 1966, appeared in 1967; the second volume, covering Winter 1966 through June 1967, appeared in 1968, both of them based on material received in the Library of the Department of the Interior. References, with abstracts, are to journal articles and selected books, reports and other material, much of it originating in Canada and the United Kingdom. Arrangement is in very broad subject sections, with indexes to authors, subjects, and places. The main British source is a bibliographic review by J E Palmer on ' Recreational planning ' in *Planning outlook* new series 2 Spring 1967 19-69. The bibliography is based on a collection of literature compiled in the Department of Town and Country Planning at the University of Newcastle upon Tyne. A total of 368 references cover books, reports, government publications, journal articles, and some unpublished material, principally of British and American origin with a few from other countries, and issued in the 1950's and, mainly, the 1960's. A supplementary list of forty six references covers literature identified between June 1966 and Spring 1967. The entries, which are unannotated, are arranged in accordance with a specially devised broad classification. Bibliographical details are neither full nor systematically identified: journal articles, in particular, are wanting in this respect, lacking not only page numbers but also volume and part numbers in some cases. Compilers of bibliographies should be made aware of the intricacies of obtaining books and journals through the machinery of the British inter-library lending system, which would surely impress upon them the necessity for better documentation.

INDEXING AND ABSTRACTING SERVICES
There is no abstracting or indexing service designed specifically for planners which comprehensively covers all the subject areas in which they are likely to be interested. Perhaps this is an unattainable ideal.

There are, however, a number of services which provide systematic coverage of the main areas of planning; and a much greater number of services in related subject fields which include planning topics within their coverage, whether consciously or accidentally. There is, in short, no lack of guidance, if the planner is aware of its existence, and if he has the stamina and the time to explore it. It seems reasonably certain that the minimal use made by planners of abstracting and indexing services is due in large measure to their ignorance of existing sources.

The most comprehensive British service, and certainly the one best known to planners, is the monthly *Index to periodical articles* (1949-) compiled and produced by the Library of the Department of the Environment,[2] the entries being based on the stock of around one thousand journals taken in the library of the former Ministry of Housing and Local Government and the subject coverage being in accordance with the functions of that Ministry. Planning in all its aspects is thus fully covered, as are related functions such as housing, pollution, sewerage, roads and transport. The journal coverage is world-wide, though the abstracts are all in English; each issue is arranged in a classified subject order which corresponds to that used in the library itself, and a list of subjects covered prefaces the abstracts. Annual author and subject indexes are produced. There is no annual cumulation of abstracts, however; another omission which could be usefully rectified is a listing of the journals on which the abstracts are based. The *Index to periodical articles* is not commercially published and is not advertised: in common with the other most valuable services of this excellent library, it must be requested from the Chief Librarian of the department.

Another library which is establishing itself as a potentially valuable source of information on planning and transport in particular is that within the Department of Planning and Transportation of the Greater London Council. Since 1969, the library has compiled and issued a monthly abstract bulletin under the title *Planning and transportation abstracts,* based on its own journal stock and covering a range of topics very similar to that covered by the DOE *Index.* The abstracts are arranged by subject headings, a list of which is announced on the front sheet: each issue contains upwards of one hundred abstracts. The journal coverage includes titles such as

Autocar, Engineer, Flight and *Modern railways,* which provide the technical angle on the various aspects of transportation which form the dominant part of the bulletin. Abstracts are also included of separate publications, for example, the GLC's own research reports and papers produced by the Centre for Environmental Studies, and of parts of corporate texts. The *Quarterly bulletin of the Research and Intelligence Unit* now also carries a selection of abstracts prepared by the library.

Two institutional sources in related subject fields are well worth investigating. The Royal Institute of British Architects issue a quarterly *Library bulletin* (1946-) which records the accessions of new material in book form to the institute's library, and also (its major part) the contents of that quarter's intake of journals. The journal coverage is world-wide, taking in the major subject areas of architecture, building, and planning, and the titles scanned number well over two hundred. The index to journals—there are no abstracts —is arranged in subject classified order according to the UDC classification used in the library itself. Each year, since 1967, an annual volume is produced, the *Annual review of periodical articles,* which cumulates into a single classified sequence the journal articles indexed in the preceding year's four quarterly *Bulletins,* a total of around three thousand articles, together with an alphabetical subject index. The text is printed only in the right-hand half of each page, so that entries can be cut out and filed if necessary.

The Royal Institution of Chartered Surveyors produce a comprehensive *Technical information service,* aimed primarily at surveyors but containing a good deal of interest to planners. The service comprises several parts. *The weekly briefing* is a digest of news of interest to surveyors which appeared in the press during the preceding week, and which is posted weekly to subscribers. *RICS abstracts and reviews* is the major part of the service: this is a monthly bulletin containing up to two hundred references to journal articles, books, and reports, with English language abstracts, arranged in accordance with a subject arrangement displayed on the title page. The references are based on the institution library's regular accessions, and over 250 journals are scanned for articles. There is a specific section on planning and development, but the whole issue contains relevant material. The bulletin also incorporates a section of reviews, each review devoted to a specific topic, for example, conservation areas, or timber, and brings together sources of information on that topic, in the form of bibliographies or short articles. Each monthly issue includes a digest of statistical information. The third part of the service is the *Monthly briefing and cumulative index*, which lists all new government circulars and statutory instruments, gives news of proceedings in Parliament and the courts, and also incorporates a cumulative subject index to *Abstracts and reviews*. An annual cumulated subject index is also issued separately. In addition to these three regular services, the Information Service collaborates with the *Municipal journal* to produce digests of new legislation, written in non-legal language, whenever relevant new Acts are passed.

These four British services described above, based on the resources of three long-established and eminent specialist libraries and a fourth, rapidly-expanding collection, together present a fair conspectus of published planning information, each one having a different slant on the subject as reflected in the interests of the respective parent institutions and their users. To supplement their coverage, some overseas services concerned with planning may be mentioned briefly. The most substantial is the *Avery index to architectural periodicals* from Columbia University (Boston, G K Hall, 1963) in twelve volumes, with supplements 1965-. The basic twelve-volume index has 265,000 photolithographically reproduced entries, covering architecture in its widest sense, and including much material on city planning and housing. Indexing began in 1954, and over two hundred titles are currently scanned. Supplements are issued periodically in volumes of around ten thousand entries each. From the United States Department of Housing and Urban Development comes the bi-monthly *Housing and planning references,* based on the regular accessions to the department's library. Books, reports, and journal articles are included, and each issue includes up to one thousand items arranged in an alphabetical subject sequence. Abstracts of varying lengths are appended to most of the references. Each issue bears a list of subjects included, and indexes of authors and places referred to. There are no cumulations; but the individual parts constitute a valuable record of current American information over a range of subjects similar to that of the DOE *Index to periodi-*

cal articles. From the Athens Center of Ekistics, in Greece, comes the monthly *Ekistic index*, which is in fact the nearest approach to a service compiled specifically for planners. But its computer type-face is unattractive and the long lines of the entries are inhospitable to the eye, making it awkward to use, and the contents add little to the service provided by the four British sources. Finally, for situations where German translation is available, there is the quarterly abstract journal *Referateblatt zur Raumordnung* published by Carl Heymanns Verlag of Cologne (1969-), and prepared in the Institut für Raumordnung. Each issue contains around three hundred abstracts, from books, journals and reports; coverage is world-wide, and over seven hundred journals are scanned. The abstracts are all in German. The issues are in the form of tear-out sheets, so that abstracts can be filed. The subject range is comprehensive, taking in all aspects of national, regional, and urban planning together with such contributory studies as regional economic planning, regional science and migration.

Planning, it has been noted, is also included in a wide range of abstracting and indexing services whose primary subject focus lies elsewhere, either in a broad field which includes planning, or in a specialised one which impinges upon it. Clearly, the value of such services to the planner varies enormously. While it is difficult to categorise, there are three identifiable groups: those services, mainly the broader-based ones, which re-abstract planning journals already abstracted in one of the four main services described at the beginning of this section, along with a wide subject range of material of potential interest; services which focus on a subject area such as sociology or economics, which abstract the planning content from a wide range of specialist journals; services which focus on a subject which has nothing specifically to do with planning, such as applied statistics or operations research, but which abstract information on methods which may be adapted for planning purposes. Some services, of course, combine these characteristics to a greater or a lesser degree; and within each category, usefulness varies according to individual editorial policies. Below, are briefly described some of the abstracting and indexing services which are most relevant to planning, with an indication wherever possible of the nature and extent of their usefulness.

582

In the first, general category of broader-based services, fall the two indexes published by the Library Association, the *British technology index* (1962-) and the *British humanities index* (1962-) which together cover a large proportion of human knowledge. The monthly *BTI* is a guide (there are no abstracts) to the subject content of the major articles in nearly four hundred British technical journals. The subject coverage takes in all branches of engineering and chemical technology, together with the manufacturing processes based on them; and within this purview, several architectural journals are indexed, together with a range of titles concerned with roads, traffic and the various forms of transport. A list of the journals indexed is included in each monthly issue, and also in the annual cumulated volume. There is in fact a good coverage of articles on roads and traffic; and there are also headings for town planning, and town and country planning. Entries are arranged alphabetically by subject headings, and cross references are incorporated to link related entries. The rather complicated structure of headings and subheadings is explained in a detailed prefatory note. There is no author index.

British humanities index appears quarterly, also with an annual cumulation, and is a guide to the contents of around 350 British journals in the broad field of the humanities, whose titles are listed in each issue and in the annual volume. The list includes titles in architecture, planning, geography, economics, and particularly in local history. There is some duplication between *BTI* and *BHI* in the journals indexed. In the quarterly issues, one alphabetical sequence includes subject headings and authors; in the annual volume, authors are contained in an independently arranged section. The subject headings incorporate a system of cross-references, as does *BTI*, but there is no explanatory note to guide the user. The main advantage of these broad-based services is their coverage of a wide range of subjects (though none of them in depth) within one pair of covers.

These two indexes are exclusively British in their coverage of journals. An American service which covers, of necessity selectively, world output of books, reports, government publications, and journal articles in the English language, is the *Bulletin* of the Public Affairs Information Service Inc (1915-). Its subject coverage is economic and social conditions, public administration, and international relations, and takes in a substantial proportion of material relevant to planning within this broad context; the emphasis throughout is on factual and statistical information. The *Bulletin* is published weekly from September through July, fortnightly through August, and misses one issue in December. It cumulates five times a year, the fifth and final cumulation being a bound volume for permanent reference. Alphabetical subject order prevails throughout. This is not primarily a journal index, although over one thousand journals are scanned and their articles selected to contribute to the total of some thirty thousand entries per year, making it the major indexing service in the field.

Within the second category of services in related subject areas, there are many candidates for inclusion. Geography is an area which has much in common with planning, not least in the number of geographers who now work in the planning field, and the major service here is *Geographical abstracts,* published six times a year from the University of East Anglia since 1966. There are four separate series: A on ' geomorphology ', B on ' biogeography and climatology, C on ' economic geography ' and D on ' social geography and cartography '. Series A preceded the other three, and was independently produced from 1960 to 1965 as *Geomorphological abstracts.* Each issue of each series contains around three hundred English-language abstracts of journal articles and some books and development reports, from most countries of the world. Arrangement is by subject, and an indication of the order is given at the front of each issue. Author and regional indexes for each series appear in the last issue of each year. In addition, comprehensive author and subject indexes to all series for 1966 and 1967 have been produced by computer, with those for 1968 and 1969 due soon. Most relevant to planners are series C and D. The first of these includes sections on agriculture, forestry, land use, resource utilisation and conservation, tourism, urban studies, and statistics; the second is almost wholly of interest, and includes sections on photogrammetry, cartography, maps and atlases, and bibliography and source material.

The social sciences, particularly the field of economics and sociology, are well served by guides to information. An annual publication covering a wide field in four separate volumes, is the *International bibliography of the social sciences* prepared by the International Committee for Social Sciences Documentation (Tavistock Publications/Chicago, Aldine, 1952-). The four volumes deal with sociology, economics, political science, and social and cultural anthropology, of which the first three are of interest to planners. Each of the four annual volumes is presented in standard format: a list of the journals consulted and a layout of the classification scheme used precede the bibliographical section, which is followed by an author index and subject indexes in English and French. There are no abstracts; foreign titles are given also in English translation. Each volume covers all countries of origin and all languages, and all documentary formats except unpublished material and ephemera are included. There is some intentional duplication between volumes for the sake of completeness. The *International bibliography of sociology,* containing upwards of five thousand entries, includes sections on sociological survey and research techniques; demographic and population studies; a wide range of social factors such as migration, rural studies, housing and town planning, community studies; and social problems such as poverty and delinquency. The comprehensive list of nearly two thousand journal titles consulted includes only a very few specifically planning-oriented journals. The *International bibliography of economics* is the largest of the four volumes, containing around eight thousand entries including articles from some two thousand journals, and includes an extensive section on methodology including mathematical and statistical methods, models, and linear programming; decision and game theory; regional planning; labour and employment; transportation and communication; income; social economics including standard of living; and public economy and economic planning. The *International bibliography of political science* contains roughly five thousand entries culled from sources including some two thousand journals; the extensive sections referring to central and local government structure and functions, arranged by countries, are relevant to the work of planners. The principal disadvantage of these volumes is the long delay in their publication, of two to three years.

585

In the field of sociology, the *International bibliography* is updated by the major abstracting service *Sociological abstracts* (New York, Sociological Abstracts Inc, 1952-). Published eight times each year, with a cumulative index issue, the year's coverage is of about five thousand lengthy signed abstracts of books and journal articles. Each issue is divided into sections dealing with broad topics, with an index of authors; each section ends with a list of the journals from which abstracts are taken. Sections of particular interest in a planning context include those on methodology and research technology; community development and rural sociology; urban structure and ecology: demography and human biology; and social problems and social welfare.

Economics is well covered by three separate services. The quarterly *Journal of economic abstracts* (Cambridge, Mass, Harvard University, Journal of economic abstracts, 1963-) is a cooperative publishing venture under the auspices of the American Economic Association. It offers world coverage of pure and applied economics in the journal literature. Each issue is prefaced with a listing of the journal issues examined and details the articles in each issue with an indication of those which are abstracted. The abstracts are long, frequently incorporating the documentary references of the original, and are arranged under subject headings with an author index which is cumulated annually. Planning interest lies in the sections on consumer economics, land economics, housing, industrial organisation, statistical methods, and income and employment. Walford (see above) points out that the appeal of this service is academic, in contrast to the ' commercial-world appeal ' of *Economic abstracts* (The Hague, Nijhoff, 1953-) a ' semi-monthly review of abstracts on economics, finance, trade and industry, management and labour '. The service is prepared principally by the Library of the Economic Information Service of the Ministry of Economic Affairs at The Hague. It aims at world coverage of reports and about four hundred journals, and abstracts are given in the language of the original, with English language summaries if the language is other than French or German. The abstracts are arranged by the UDC classification; there are annual author and subject indexes. The areas of interest to planners are broadly similar to those mentioned above in connection with the *Journal of economic abstracts,* bearing in mind

586

Walford's proviso. An annual volume which indexes both journals and collective works including festschriften, conference proceedings, collected essays and readers, and translations into English of foreign articles and essays, is the *Index of economic articles in journals and collective volumes* previously the *Index of economic journals* (Homewood, Ill, Richard D Irwin Inc, vol I 1886-1924, 1961-) prepared under the auspices of the American Economic Association. World coverage is provided. Each volume includes a list of the collective works indexed and of journals indexed, and is laid out in accordance with a specially devised classification scheme which is presented in the preliminary pages; an author index is provided. There is a substantial section on regional planning and development and housing, and also sections on methodologies, economic statistics, agriculture, natural resources, land economics, population, consumer economics, and a polyglot section comprising health, education, welfare, and poverty. The first seven volumes of the *Index* covered the years 1886-1965, while the eighth and successive volumes each cover only one year.

Four other services which fall within the social science range (although definitions of the constitution of the social sciences vary widely) are deserving of inclusion for their potential relevance to planning. *International political science abstracts* (Oxford, Blackwell, 1951-) is a quarterly bi-lingual (English and French) service prepared by the International Political Science Association in Paris, and offering world coverage of some 150 journals. English-language articles are abstracted in English, all other languages in French. Nearly six hundred abstracts are in each issue, which are arranged under broad subject headings with a subject index; annual cumulated subject and author indexes are produced. Planners may find relevant information in the sections on central and local government and administration. The major abstracting service in the field of psychology is *Psychological abstracts* (Washington DC, American Psychological Association, 1927-), which offers a monthly coverage of the world output of psychological and related literature. Each monthly issue is arranged into broad subject groups, with an author index; there are also annual cumulated author and very full subject indexes. Some twenty thousand entries appear in the year. Headings which are potentially useful to planning are those focusing on urban environment, rural environment, the community, decision-making, and social structure.

Population index is a quarterly guide to information on all aspects of demography and population (Princeton, NJ, Office of Population Research of Princeton University, 1935-), published for the Population Association of America, Inc. The issues contain items on current developments in population studies, followed by the index arranged in classified subject order. Journal coverage is world-wide (a list of titles appears with the annual cumulative index) but translated titles are given and abstracts are in English. Not all entries have abstracts. Each issue carries a geographical and an author index. Planners should find relevant information in the majority of the index's subject headings. The *Index to legal periodicals* (New York, H W Wilson Co, 1909-) is a monthly index to around three hundred legal journals published in common law countries, with a strong bias towards American material. Planning and related law is included, but the usefulness of the index to British planners is obviously reduced by the American bias.

In the technical field, one of the main related subject services is *Building science abstracts* (HMSO, 1925-) prepared by the Building Research Station. From 1969, the journal underwent a complete physical transformation, enlarging to A4 size, each page being printed on one side only and laid out in the form of four cards, intended for cutting out. A wide range of British and foreign journals are abstracted: the complete list is produced annually and includes many titles of planning interest. The monthly issues are arranged in subject order, to which a key is provided, with serial numbering of abstracts throughout the year; author and KWIC subject indexes are produced annually by computer. There are four main subject groups, of which the fourth, design and environment, is of primary interest to planners; the sub-headings are urban planning, design process, spatial studies, environmental studies, thermal factors, acoustics, lighting, and service systems. The Library of the former Ministry of Public Building and Works[2] compile *Consolidated building references* (1946-), which is an annual list of references to articles selected from the six hundred journals taken in the library, arranged in classified UDC order with annotations and full cross references, and author and subject indexes. The entries are cumulated from the fortnightly *Library bulletin* which contains journal references in its third part. *Water pollution abstracts* (HMSO, 1928-) is a monthly service from the Ministry of Technology, now within the Department of Trade and Industry. It provides world coverage of journals, arranged in broad subject groups, with abstracts in English and annual author and subject indexes. The subjects covered are conservation of water resources; analysis and examination of water and wastes; sewage; trade waste waters; effects of pollution. *Road abstracts* (HMSO, 1934-) is a monthly service from the Road Research Laboratory, indicating well over one thousand items in a year, the English-language abstracts arranged in subject sections, with full cross-referencing and annual author and subject indexes. Nearly two hundred journals, as well as books and reports, are covered. The subject coverage takes in all aspects of road construction, traffic engineering, planning and economics, road layout, direction and control of traffic, traffic studies and parking, methods and apparatus for traffic studies, road user characteristics, and other topics less relevant to planning.

In the third category of services which cover techniques which may be relevant to planning administration, processes, or methodologies, there are at least four worth investigating. *Statistical theory and method abstracts* (Edinburgh, Oliver and Boyd, 1959-) is produced quarterly by the International Statistical Institute, its object being to cover published papers concerned with statistical theory, including relevant aspects of probability and mathematical methods, and new contributions to statistical methods. Some 150 journals from all over the world are listed, also research reports and papers from collective works. The abstracts are arranged in subject order in twelve main sections, each one printed on different coloured paper, with an author index in each issue and cumulated annually. There is a listing of 'bibliographic papers', those which cite more than twenty references. *International abstracts in operations research* (Baltimore, Operations Research Society of America, 1962-) is a bi-monthly journal listing some 1,200 abstracts per year, many of them reprinted from *US Government research reports*. *Management abstracts* (Manchester Publications Ltd, 1948-) is a quarterly journal produced by the British Institute of Management covering about three hundred abstracts each year. The fullest source on computer science and methods is *Computer abstracts* (London Information Co, 1960-), a monthly journal comprising about three thousand abstracts in a year and covering journals, books, patents, US government research reports, and papers. An additional source in the field is the *Computing reviews* (1960-) issued bi-monthly by the Association for Computing Machinery of New York, which records up to two thousand abstracts per year from around one hundred journals, on computers and information theory in general.

REFERENCES
1 Brenda White *Planners and information* (Library Association 1970) 97.
2 With the merging of the Ministries of Housing and Local Government, Public Building and Works, and Transport into the Department of the Environment, and a forthcoming move into new premises, it seems clear that eventually there will be some merging of the substantial library resources of the three departments. What form this merger will take, and when it will come about, is as yet undecided. In the meantime, although the various publications are now issued under the style of Department of the Environment, they do continue to represent their own former Ministry's interests and are based on the individual Library resources.
3 Brenda White *op cit* 118.

APPENDIX

THE FOLLOWING IS A LIST of the principal organisations mentioned in the text of this book together with the addresses to which requests for data or information should be directed. The address given is not necessarily that of the central part of the organisation, but is that relevant to the context in which the organisation is mentioned in the text. Two main categories are omitted: commercial publishers, whose productions are retailed through bookshops; and local authority planning departments and new town development corporations, whose addresses are listed in the *Directory of official architects and planners*. Private practices are included only if they are the publishers and sole retailers of their reports and plans. The purpose of this list is not as a comprehensive directory of organisations concerned with planning, but as a location tool for following up sources of information mentioned in the body of the book. The addresses are as up to date and complete as possible at the date of compilation, but users will appreciate that it is not without the bounds of possibility that some of them may change while the book is in press.

Acton Society Trust, 30 Craven Street, London WC2

Advisory Centre for Education, 32 Trumpington Street, Cambridge

Aerofilms Limited, 4 Albemarle Street, London W1

American Academy of Political and Social Science, Prince and Lemons Streets, Lancaster, Pennsylvania 17604, USA

American Economic Association, 629 Noyes Street, Evanston, Illinois 60201, USA

American Geographical Society, Broadway at 156th Street, New York, NY 10032, USA

American Institute of Planners, 917 Fifteenth Street NW, Washington DC 20005, USA

591

American Library Association, 50 East Huron Street, Chicago, Illinois 60611, USA

American Psychological Association Inc, 1200 Seventeenth Street NW, Washington DC 20036, USA

American Society of Landscape Architects, Schuster Building, 1500 Bardstown Road, Louisville, Kentucky 40205, USA

American Society of Photogrammetry, 105 North Virginia Avenue, Falls Church, Virginia 22046, USA

American Society of Planning Officials, 1313 East Sixtieth Street, Chicago, Illinois 60637, USA

American Society for Public Administration, 1225 Connecticut Avenue NW, Washington DC 20036, USA

American Statistical Association, 806 Fifteenth Street NW, Washington DC 20005, USA

Aslib (Association of Special Libraries and Information Bureaux), 3 Belgrave Square, London SW1

Association of American Geographers, 1146 Sixteenth Street NW, Washington DC 20036, USA

Association of Assistant Librarians, Hon Sales Officer (Publications), J S Davey, 49 Halstead Gardens, London N21

Association for Computing Machinery, 1133 Avenue of the Americas, New York, NY 10036, USA

Athens Center of Ekistics, Division of Documentation, 24 Stratiotikou Syndesmon, Athens 136, Greece

BKS Surveys Ltd, Cleeve Road, Leatherhead, Surrey

Bank of England, Economic Intelligence Department, London EC2R 8AH

Bath University of Technology, Library, Claverton Down, Bath BA2 7AY

Birmingham Polytechnic, Corporation Street, Birmingham B4 7DX

Board of Inland Revenue, Statistics and Intelligence Division, Somerset House, London WC2

Bodleian Library, Oxford

British Association for the Advancement of Science, 3 Sanctuary Buildings, 20 Great Smith Street, London SW1

British Bureau of Television Advertising, 52-66 Mortimer Street, London W1N 7DG

British Cartographic Society, 2 Calder Court, Gringer Hill, Maidenhead, Berkshire

British Committee of Historic Towns, Hon Secretary, Mrs M D Lobel, 16 Merton Street, Oxford

British Railways Board, 222 Marylebone Road, London NW1

British Road Federation, 26 Manchester Square, London W1M 5RF

British Tourist Authority, 64 St James's Street, London SW1

British Waterways Board, Melbury House, Melbury Terrace, London NW1

Brixton School of Building *see* Polytechnic of the South Bank

Building Design Partnership, Chamber of Commerce House, Great Victoria Street, Belfast BT2 7DQ

Building Research Station, Bucknalls Lane, Garston, Watford, Hertfordshire WD2 7JR

Canadian Association of Geographers, Morrice Hall, McGill University, Montreal 2, PQ, Canada

Capital and Counties Property Company Limited, 40 Broadway, London SW1

Careers Research and Advisory Centre, Bateman Street, Cambridge

Cartographic Laboratory, 37a St Giles, Oxford

Central Council of Physical Recreation, 26 Park Crescent, London W1N 4AJ

Central Electricity Generating Board, Information Services, Sudbury House, 15 Newgate Street, London EC1

Central Statistical Office, Great George Street, London SW1

Center for Community Affairs, NTL Institute for Applied Behavioral Science, 1201 Sixteenth Street NW, Washington DC 20036, USA

Centre for Environmental Studies, 5 Cambridge Terrace, London NW1 4JL (moving to new premises in 1971)

Centre for Land Use and Built Form Studies, University of Cambridge School of Architecture, 16 Brooklands Avenue, Cambridge

Centre for Urban and Regional Research, University of Manchester Department of Town and Country Planning, University of Manchester, Manchester M13 9PL

Centre for Urban and Regional Studies, University of Birmingham, Selly Wick House, Selly Wick Road, Birmingham 29

Publications retailed through Research Publications Services Ltd, 11 Nelson Road, Greenwich, London SE10

Center for Urban Studies, University of Chicago, 5852 University Avenue, Chicago, Illinois 60637, USA

Centre for Urban Studies, University College London, 87 Gower Street, London WC1

Chamber of Shipping of the United Kingdom, 30/32 St Mary Axe, London EC3

Civic Trust, 18 Carlton House Terrace, London SW1

Civic Trust for the North West, Oxford Road, Manchester

Clark University, 950 Main Street, Worcester, Massachusetts, USA

Colin Buchanan and Partners, 47 Princes Gate, London SW7

College of Estate Management, St Albans Grove, Kensington, London W8 5PW

Commission for the New Towns, Glen House, Stag Place, London SW1

Commons, Open Spaces and Footpaths Preservation Society, Suite 4, 166 Shaftesbury Avenue, London WC2

Construction Industry Research and Information Association, 6 Storey's Gate, Westminster, London SW1

Council of Planning Librarians, PO Box 229, Monticello, Illinois 61856, USA

Council for the Protection of Rural England, 4 Hobart Place, London SW1

Countryside Commission, 1 Cambridge Gate, London NW1

Countryside Commission for Scotland, Branklyn House, 116 Dundee Road, Perth

Coventry, Solihull and Warwickshire Sub-regional Planning Study, Council House, Coventry CV1 5RT

Department of Education and Science, Curzon Street, London W1Y 8AA

Department of Employment, Statistics Division C5, Orphanage Road, Watford, Hertfordshire

Department of the Environment, Whitehall, London SW1 (formerly Ministry of Housing and Local Government); St Christopher House, Southwark Street, London SE1 (formerly Ministry of Transport); Lambeth Bridge House, London SE1 (formerly Ministry of Public Building and Works)

Department of Health and Social Security, Alexander Fleming House, Elephant and Castle, London SE1

Department of Trade and Industry, Business Statistics Office, Lime Grove, Ruislip, Middlesex HA4 8RS

Ditchley Foundation, Ditchley Park, Enstone, Oxfordshire

Duncan of Jordanstone College of Art, Perth Road, Dundee

Ealing Technical College, St Mary's Road, London W5

East Anglia Regional Studies Association, Centre of East Anglian Studies, University of East Anglia, Norwich NOR 88C

Ecology Bookshop, 45 Lower Belgrave Street, London SW1

Economic Development Committees ('little neddies') *see* National Economic Development Office

Economic Planning Councils: East Anglia EPC, 2 Queen Anne's Gate Buildings, Dartmouth Street, London SW1; East Midlands EPC, Cranbrook House, Cranbrook Street, Nottingham NG1 1FB; North West EPC, Sunley Building, Piccadilly Plaza, Manchester M1 4BE; Northern EPC, Wellbar House, Gallowgate, Newcastle upon Tyne NE1 4TD; South East EPC, 2 Queen Anne's Gate Buildings, Dartmouth Street, London SW1; South West EPC, The Pithay, Bristol BS1 2NG; West Midlands EPC, Five Ways House, Islington Row, Birmingham 15; Yorkshire and Humberside EPC, City House, Leeds LS1 4PS; Scottish EPC, c/o Regional Development Division, Scottish Development Department, St Andrew's House, Edinburgh EH1 3DD; Welsh Council, c/o Welsh Office, Cathays Park, Cardiff CF1 3NQ; Northern Ireland Economic Council, c/o Ministry of Commerce, Linenhall Street, Belfast BT2 8BY

Ecosystems Limited, 11 Mansfield Street, Portland Place, London W1M 0AH

Edward Stanford Limited, 12-14 Long Acre, London WC2; replaced as main Ordnance Survey agent, from April 1 1971 by Cook, Hammond and Kell Limited, 22-24 Caxton Street, London SW1

Electricity Council, 30 Millbank, London SW1 (requests for unpublished data to Commercial Department)

Eno Foundation for Transportation (formerly for Highway Traffic Control), Saugatuck, Connecticut 06882, USA

Experimental Cartography Unit, Royal College of Art, 6A Cromwell Place, London SW7

Fabian Society, 11 Dartmouth Street, London SW1

Fairey Surveys Limited, Reform Road, Maidenhead, Berkshire SL6 8BU

Field Studies Council, 9 Devereux Court, Strand, London WC2

An Foras Forbartha (National Institute for Physical Planning and Construction Research), St Martin's House, Waterloo Road, Dublin 4

Forestry Commission, 25 Savile Row, London W1X 2AY

Freeman, Fox, Wilbur Smith and Associates, 28 Grosvenor Gardens, London SW1

Gas Council, 59 Bryanston Street, London W1A 2AZ

General Register Office, Northern Ireland, Fermanagh House, Ormeau Avenue, Belfast BT2 8HX

Geographical Association, 343 Fulwood Road, Sheffield S1O 3BP; Edinburgh branch: Hon Secretary, Miss G P Mowat, 40 Craigmount Hill, Edinburgh 4

Geological Survey of Northern Ireland, 20 College Gardens, Belfast BT9 6BS

Geologists' Association, Secretary, F H Moore, 278 Fir Tree Road, Epsom Downs, Surrey; publications from Benham and Co Limited, Sheepen Road, Colchester, Essex

Glasgow School of Art, Department of Planning, 197 Bath Street, Glasgow C2

Heriot-Watt University, Department of Town and Country Planning, 48 Manor Place, Edinburgh 3

Highlands and Islands Development Board, 6 Castle Wynd, Inverness

Highway Research Board, 2101 Constitution Avenue NW, Washington DC 20418, USA

Housing Centre, 13 Suffolk Street, Pall Mall East, London SW1

Housing Research Foundation, 58 Portland Place, London W1N 4BU

Hunting Surveys and Consultants Limited, 6 Elstree Way, Borehamwood, Hertfordshire

Incorporated Association of Architects and Surveyors, 29 Belgrave Square, London SW1

Inland Revenue *see* Board of Inland Revenue

Inland Waterways Association, 114 Regents Park Road, London NW1

Institute of British Geographers, 1 Kensington Gore, London SW7

Institute of Community Studies, 18 Victoria Park Square, London E2

Institute for Economic Affairs Limited, 2 Lord North Street, London SW1

Institute for the Future, Riverview Center, Middletown, Connecticut 06457, USA

Institute of Geological Sciences, Exhibition Road, South Kensington, London SW7

Institute of Landscape Architects, 12 Carlton House Terrace, London SW1

Institute of Management Sciences, 321 South Main Street, Providence, Rhode Island 02904, USA

Institute of Municipal Treasurers and Accountants, Secretary, M F Stonefrost, 1 Buckingham Place, London SW7

Institute of Transport, 80 Portland Place, London W1N 4DP

Institution of Civil Engineers, Great George Street, London SW1

Institution of Municipal Engineers, 25 Eccleston Square, London SW1

Institution of Water Engineers, 6-8 Sackville Street, London W1X 1DD

International Association of Ecology (International Union of Biological Sciences): journal and membership from Dr F H Whitehead, Intecol, c/o Institute of Biology, 41 Queens Gate, London SW7

International Federation for Housing and Town Planning, 43 Wassenaarseweg, The Hague, Netherlands

Jack Holmes Planning Group, 62 Kelvingrove Street, Glasgow C3

John Madin Design Group, 123 Hagley Road, Edgbaston, Birmingham 16

Lanchester Polytechnic, Priory Street, Coventry CV1 5FB

Landscape Research Group, Hon Secretary, A C Murray, Walden House (Room 1005), 24 Cathedral Place, London EC4

Lee Valley Regional Park Authority, Myddleton House, Bulls Cross, Enfield, Middlesex

Leeds Polytechnic, School of Town Planning, 14 St Paul's Street, Leeds 1

Library Association, 7 Ridgmount Street, Store Street, London WC1E 7AE

Llewelyn-Davies Weeks Forestier-Walker and Bor, 4 Fitzroy Square, London W1P 6JA

Location of Offices Bureau, 27 Chancery Lane, London WC2

London School of Economics and Political Science, Houghton Street, Aldwych, London WC2A 2AE

London Transport Executive, 33 Broadway, London SW1

Macaulay Institute for Soil Research, Craigiebuckler, Aberdeen

Map Collectors' Circle, Durrant House, Chiswell Street, London EC1

Meridian Airmaps Limited, Marlborough Road, Lancing, Sussex

Meteorological Office, London Road, Bracknell, Berkshire RG12 2SZ

Midlands New Towns Society, 36 Cannon Street, Birmingham 2

Ministry of Agriculture, Fisheries and Food, Publications Division, Tolcarne Drive, Pinner, Middlesex HA5 2DT

Multiple Shops Federation, 1-19 New Oxford Street, London WC1A 1PA

National Bus Company, 25 New Street Square, London EC4

National Coal Board, Hobart House, Grosvenor Place, London SW1

National Computing Centre, Quay House, Quay Street, Manchester 3

National Council of Social Service, 26 Bedford Square, London WC1B 3HN

National Economic Development Office, Millbank Tower, 21/41 Millbank, London SW1

National Food Survey, Ministry of Agriculture, Fisheries and Food, Tolcarne Drive, Pinner, Middlesex HA5 2DT

National Institute for Economic and Social Research, 2 Dean Trench Street, Smith Square, London SW1

National Lending Library for Science and Technology, Boston Spa, Yorkshire

National Library of Scotland, George IV Bridge, Edinburgh 1

National Playing Fields Association, Playfield House, 57B Catherine Place, London SW1

National Ports Council, 17 North Audley Street, London W1Y 1WE

National Recreation and Park Association, 1700 Pennsylvania Avenue NW, Washington DC 20006, USA

National Trust for Places of Historic Interest and Natural Beauty, 42 Queen Anne's Gate, London SW1

National Trust for Scotland, 5 Charlotte Square, Edinburgh EH2 4DU

Nature Conservancy, 19 Belgrave Square, London SW1

Northern Ireland Government Offices, Stormont, Belfast BT4 3SS

Nottinghamshire/Derbyshire Sub-regional Planning Unit, Cressy Road, Alfreton, Derbyshire DE5 7BR

Office of Population Censuses and Surveys, Titchfield, Fareham, Hampshire

Office for Scientific and Technical Information, Elizabeth House, 39 York Road, London SE1

Ohio State University, 2070 Neil Avenue, Columbus, Ohio, USA

Operational Research Society Limited, 62-64 Cannon Street, London EC4

Operations Research Society of America, 428 East Preston Street, Baltimore, Maryland 21202, USA

Ordnance Survey, Romsey Road, Maybush, Southampton SO9 4DH

Ordnance Survey of Northern Ireland, 83 Ladas Drive, Belfast BT6 9FJ

Oxford Polytechnic, Headington, Oxford OX3 OBD

Passenger Transport Authorities: Merseyside PTA, 24 Hatton Garden, Liverpool L3 2AN; South East Lancashire and North East Cheshire PTA, Peter House, Oxford Street, Manchester M1 5AW; Tyneside PTA, 3rd Floor, Erick House, Princess Square, Newcastle upon Tyne NE1 8EY; West Midlands PTA, Council House, Birmingham

Photogrammetric Society, 47 Tothill Street, London SW1

Planning and Transport Research and Computation Co Limited, 40 Grosvenor Gardens, London SW1

Political and Economic Planning, 12 Upper Belgrave Street, London SW1

Political Studies Association of the UK, London School of Economics and Political Science, Houghton Street, Aldwych, London WC2A 2AE

Polytechnic of Central London, 309 Regent Street, London W1R 8AL

Polytechnic of the South Bank, Brixton School of Building, Ferndale Road, London SW4

Public Affairs Information Service Inc, 11 West Fortieth Street, New York, NY 10018, USA

Public Record Office, Chancery Lane, London WC2A 1LR

Public Record Office of Northern Ireland, Law Courts Building, May Street, Belfast BT1 3JJ

Queen's University of Belfast, Belfast BT7 1NN

R Travers Morgan and Partners, 125-130 Strand, London WC2

Ramblers' Association, 124 Finchley Road, London NW3

Rand Corporation, 1700 Main Street, Santa Monica, California 95001, USA

Rating and Valuation Association, 29 Belgrave Square, London SW1

Regent Street Polytechnic *see* Polytechnic of Central London

Regional Plan Association Inc, 230 West 41st Street, New York, NY 10036, USA

Regional Science Research Institute, PO Box 8776, Philadelphia, Pennsylvania 19101, USA

Regional Studies Association, Newcombe House, 45 Notting Hill Gate, London W11

Registrar General, Scotland, Census Branch, 35 Station Road, Edinburgh 12

Research Institute for Consumer Affairs, 43 Villiers Street, London WC2N 6NE

Road Research Laboratory, Crowthorne, Berkshire RG11 6AU

Royal Dutch Geographic Society, 1 Banierstraat, Rotterdam 1, Netherlands

Royal Economic Society, The Marshall Library, Sidgwick Avenue, Cambridge

Royal Geographical Society, Kensington Gore, London SW7

Royal Institute of British Architects, 66 Portland Place, London W1N 4AD

Royal Institute of Public Administration, 24 Park Crescent, London W1N 4BP

Royal Institution of Chartered Surveyors, 12 Great George Street, London SW1

Royal Scottish Geographical Society, 10 Randolph Crescent, Edinburgh 3

Royal Society of Arts, 6 John Adam Street, Adelphi, London WC2

Royal Statistical Society, 21 Bentinck Street, London W1M 6AR

Royal Town Planning Institute, 26 Portland Place, London W1N 4BE

Royal University of Lund, Sölvegatan 13, Lund, Sweden

Scott Wilson Kirkpatrick and Partners, 5 Winsley Street, London W1N 7AQ

Scottish Civic Trust, 24 George Square, Glasgow C2

Scottish Council (Development and Industry), 1 Castle Street, Edinburgh 2

Scottish Library Association, Publications Officer, Public Library, Hope Street, Falkirk

Scottish Office, St Andrew's House, Edinburgh 1

Scottish Record Office, Register House, Edinburgh 1

Scottish Tourist Board, 2 Rutland Place, Edinburgh 1

Second Land Utilisation Survey of Great Britain, Department of Geography, King's College (University of London), Strand, London WC2

Shankland Cox and Associates, 16 Bedford Square, London WC1

Social and Community Planning Research, 16 Duncan Terrace, London N1 8BZ

Social Science Research Council, State House, High Holborn, London WC1

Society of County Treasurers, Hon Secretary, W Hollinrake, County Hall, Taunton, Somerset

Society for Long Range Planning, Terminal House, Grosvenor Gardens, London SW1

Society of Motor Manufacturers and Traders Limited, Statistical Department, Fifth Floor, 21-24 Grosvenor Place, London SW1

Soil Survey of England and Wales, Rothamsted Experimental Station, Harpenden, Hertfordshire

Soil Survey of Scotland *see* Macaulay Institute

Solicitors' Law Stationery Society Limited, Oyez House, Breams Buildings, London EC4P 4BU

South Hampshire Plan Technical Unit, The Castle, Winchester

Sports Councils: Sports Council, 26 Park Crescent, London W1N 4AJ; East Midlands Sports Council, 26 Musters Road, West Bridgford, Nottingham NG2 7PL; Eastern Sports Council, 5A Harpur Street, Bedford; Greater London and South East Sports Council, Portland Court, 160 Great Portland Street, London W1N 5TB; North West Sports Council, Ralli Building, Stanley Street, Salford M3 5JF; Northern Advisory Council for Sport and Recreation, 40 Saddler Street, Durham City; South Western Sports Council, 17 The Square, Crewkerne, Somerset; Southern Sports Council, Watlington House, Watlington Street, Reading, Berkshire; West Midlands Sports Council, 52 Frederick Road, Edgbaston, Birmingham 15; Yorkshire and Humberside Sports Council, CCPR Offices, 2 Park Square East, Leeds LS1 2NQ; Sports Council for Scotland, 4 Queensferry Street, Edinburgh EH2 4PB; Sports Council for Wales, 47 Cathedral Road, Cardiff CF1 9UH

Standing Conference on London and South East Regional Planning, 26 Old Queen Street, London SW1

Tennessee Valley Authority, New Sprankle Building, 508 Union Avenue, Knoxville, Tennessee 37902, USA

Thoresby Society, 22 Clarendon Road, Leeds 2

Town and Country Planning Association, 17 Carlton House Terrace, London SW1Y 5AS

Town Planning Institute *see* Royal Town Planning Institute

Town Planning Institute of Canada, Suite 1507, 80 King Street West, Toronto 1, Ontario, Canada

Trent Polytechnic, Dryden Street, Nottingham

Trinity College, Dublin 2

United States Department of Housing and Urban Development, 451 7th Street SW, Washington DC 20410, USA

University College London, Department of Town Planning, Flaxman House, Flaxman Terrace, London WC1

University College of Swansea, Singleton Park, Swansea

University College of Wales, Department of Geography, Llandinam Building, Penglais, Aberystwyth

University Grants Committee, 14 Park Crescent, London W1

University of Aberdeen, Department of Geography, St Mary's, High Street, Old Aberdeen AB9 2UF

University of Cambridge, Committee for Aerial Photography, 11 West Road, Cambridge CB3 9DP

University of Durham, Department of Geography, South Road, Durham City

University of East Anglia, School of Environmental Sciences, University Village, Norwich NOR 88C

University of Edinburgh, Department of Urban Design and Regional Planning, 60 George Square, Edinburgh 8; Planning Research Unit, 57 George Square, Edinburgh 8; Recreation Survey, Department of Geography, High School Yards, Edinburgh 1

University of Exeter, Department of Geology, North Park Road, Exeter

University of Glasgow, Department of Town and Regional Planning, Adam Smith Building, Glasgow W2. Department of Social and Economic Research, Adam Smith Building, Glasgow W2

University of Hull, Hull

University of Illinois, Bureau of Community Planning, Urbana, Illinois, USA

University of Leeds, Air Photo Unit, Department of Civil Engineering, Leeds LS2 9JT

University of Leicester, University Road, Leicester

University of Liverpool, Department of Civic Design, PO Box 147, Liverpool L69 3BX

University of London, Senate House, London WC1E 7HU

University of Manchester, Manchester M13 9PL

University of Newcastle upon Tyne, Newcastle upon Tyne NE1 7RU

University of Nottingham, University Park, Nottingham NG7 2RD

University of Reading, Whiteknights, Reading, Berkshire RG6 2AF

University of Sheffield, Sheffield S10 2TN

University of Strathclyde, Department of Urban and Regional Planning, Livingstone Tower, Richmond Street, Glasgow C1

University of Wales Institute of Science and Technology, Cathays Park, Cardiff CF1 3NU

W S Atkins and Partners, Ashley Road, Epsom, Surrey

Water Resources Board, Reading Bridge House, Reading, Berkshire

Wates Limited, 1260 London Road, London SW16

Welsh Office, Cathays Park, Cardiff CF1 3NQ

Welsh Tourist Board, 7 Park Place, Cardiff

Wisconsin Bureau of State Planning, State Office Building, Madison, Wisconsin 53702, USA

Wye College (University of London), Wye, Ashford, Kent.

AUTHOR INDEX

This part of the index is a guide to personal authors solely or jointly responsiblie for works cited in the body of the text. Page references in italic refer to journal articles; those in roman refer to all other types of source, principally books. Where a single work is cited more than once in the text, the page reference refers to that place where it is discussed most fully.

608

609

20

611

612

GENERAL INDEX

This contains references to subjects, places, serial titles, White Papers and Acts, individuals and firms, and organisations. It has not been possible, for reasons of space, to include a complete title index of all publications cited in the text; but titles of serial publications, mainly statistical series and journals, and of government White Papers and the principal Acts referred to in the text, have been incorporated since they can be difficult to trace. Organisations are included as they are discussed in general terms in the text and also as corporate authors, though not as publishers of items which are the responsibility of individual authors (these latter are listed in the author index). Page references in italic at organisation entries refer to publications; those in roman refer to general discussion of the organisation. Page references at place entries without sub-headings refer to development plans or similar information relating to that place; otherwise as indicated in the sub-headings. The following abbreviations are used:

BC   Borough Council
CC   County Council or City Council
CPD   County Planning Department
DC   Development Corporation
EPC   Economic Planning Council.

Air transport maps 92
Air transport planning 493-4
Alnwick
Plan analysis 149
American Academy of Political and Social Science *542*
American behavioral scientist 540
American Economic Association *539*
American economic review 539
American Geographical Society *532*
American Institute of Planners *525-6*
American Psychological Association *587*
American Society for Public Administration *546*
American Society of Landscape Architects *528*
American Society of Photogrammetry *158-9*
American Society of Planning Officials *326, 343*
American Statistical Association *544*
American statistician 544-5
Analysis of Interconnected Decision Areas (AIDA) 341-2
Annals of the American Academy of Political and Social Science 542
Annals of the Association of American Geographers 535-6
Announcement bulletin 563
Annual abstract of Greater London statistics 248
Annual abstract of statistics 244-6, 256
Annual estimates of the population of Scotland 256
Annual report of the Registrar General for Scotland 256
Annual review of periodical articles (RIBA) 580
Annual statement of the trade of the UK 270-1
Antrim/Ballymena 233-5
Architects' journal 521, 526
Architectural Association quarterly 527
Architectural bibliography 566-7
Architectural directories 550
Architectural journals 526-7
Architectural research and teaching 527

Area 535
Areas of outstanding natural beauty 36
Arton Wilson Report 481
Ashford 193-4
Aslib *551, 557*
Association for Computing Machinery, 324-5, *590*
Association for Planning and Regional Reconstruction *299, 487*
Association of American Geographers *533, 535*
Association of Planning Teachers 61-2
Association of Student Planners 62-3
Athens Center of Ekistics *525, 582*
Atkins, W S & Ptnrs 506
Austin-Smith/Lord Partnership 54, 199-200
Australia
Planning practice 302
Urban planning 418

Banbury
Urban studies 427
Bank of England *260-1*
Barlow Report 18-9, 23-4, 176, 373, 387
Baroque cities 13
Base maps 87, 90, 101-2
Basic road statistics 280
Basildon DC *204-5*
Basildon new town 204-5
Bath
Conservation 480
Belfast sub-region 231-2
Belfast urban area 237-8
Transportation studies 506
Berinsfield
Rehousing 371
Bibliographies 561-78
Maps 137-9
Binnie & Ptnrs 214
Birmingham
Community studies 437
Historical maps 132
History 430-1
Overspill 421
Redevelopment 371
BKS Surveys Ltd 161-2

616

Central Statistical Office 243, *244-6, 258, 260, 264, 273, 283*
Central Unit for Environmental Planning 210-1
Centre for Environmental Studies *59, 64-5, 66-7,* 71, 75, *285-6, 329-30, 333-4, 336,* 340, *342, 347, 399, 401, 403, 425, 434, 451, 504, 551, 565, 573*
Centre for Urban Studies 367, 368, 426, 428, 433
Chamber of Shipping of the UK *281*
Channel Islands
Maps 104
Chartered surveyor 527
Chartotheca translationum alphabetica 556
Cheshire
Recreational facilities 467
Chester
Conservation 480
Chicago, USA
Transportation studies 505
Chichester
Bus services 511
Conservation 480
Children services statistics 275
Children's play facilities 474-5
Citizen participation
See Public participation
City regions 399-403
Civic Amenities Act 1967 38, 478
Civic Trust *455, 471, 478, 479, 552, 577*
Civic Trust for the North West *365, 446*
Civil Service **Department** *273*
Civil service statistics 273
Clark University, USA *536*
Classified accessions list (DOE) 135, 563
Clean Air Act 1968 482
Climatological maps 92, 116-7, 148
Clyde Valley 217, 219-20
Recreation planning 469-70
Coasts 460-2, 469, 473
Maps 118
Coleraine sub-region 236
Collins, W Gordon 157, 158, 163-6, 168

COLMAP 152
Columbia University: Avery Architectural Library *562, 581*
Commission for the New Towns 51, *418*
Common lands 453-4
Commons, Open Spaces and Footpaths Preservation Society *148-9*
Commons Registration Act 1965 453
Community Land Use Game 337-8
Community studies
Rural 448
Urban 436-40
Commuting
See Journey to work
Compensation and betterment 353-5
Composite aerial photographs 157
Comprehensive development areas 28, 412-3
Compulsory purchase 316
Computer abstracts 590
Computer programme indexes 558-9
Computers 324-5
Cartographic techniques 151-3
Computing reviews 590
Concentric theory of urban structure 442
Conservation (urban) 478-81
Bibliographies 577
See also Nature conservation
Consolidated building references 588
Construction industry bibliographies 566-7
Construction industry directories 550-1
Construction Industry Research and Information Association *551, 566*
Construction industry statistics 268, 283
Containerisation 511-2
Control of immigration statistics 257
Control of Office and Industrial Development Act 1965 380
Corby new town 205-6
Cost benefit analysis 356
Council for the Protection of Rural England *487*
Council of Europe *385, 482, 483, 552*
Council of Planning Librarians *564-5*
Country Parks 37, 459
Countryside Act 1968 37

617

Dower Report 35-6
Dudley Report 359
Durham
  Maps 94
  Motorway landscaping 492
Durham CPD *492*

Ealing Technical College *135*
Earth Resource Technical Satellites
  166-7
East Anglia EPC *175*
East Anglia region 175, 391
East Kilbride new town 223
East midland geographer 534-5
East Midlands EPC *174-5*
East midlands region 174-5, 391
  Population maps 127
  Recreation facilities 467
East Sussex CPD *321*, 326, 471
Ecologist 530
Ecology 476
  See also Human ecology
Economic abstracts 586
Economic Associates Ltd 212
Economic Commission for Europe
  357
Economic geography 536
Economic journal 539, 556
Economic journals 539-40
Economic planning 351
  See also Regional planning; Re-
    gional science
Economic planning councils 25-6,
  174-5
  See also under individual EPC's
Economic planning regions 25-6
Economic statistics 258-73, 284
Economic trends 258
Economics in planning 307-9
Economics of housing 363-5
Economics of planning 350-6
Economist 521
Edinburgh
  Conservation 480
  Maps 94, 138
  Planning history 295
Edinburgh/Lothians sub-region 217-
  8, 220-1
  Recreation planning 470
Education statistics 277

Education statistics for the UK 277
Eire
  Tourism planning 473
Ekistic index 582
Ekistics 525
Electricity Council *268*
Electronics industry statistics 284
Ellison Report 452
Employment models 334
Employment statistics 271-3, 283, 286
Enforcement 315
Eno Foundation for Transportation
  499, 531
Enterprise Neptune 118, 462
Entropy 336-7
Environment 475-85
Environment and planning 524
Environment journals 529-30
Environment Scotland 530
Esk Valley 228
Essex
  Maps 140
Essex CPD *316*
Estate management 355-6
Experimental Cartography Unit 152-3

Factor analysis 399, 443
Fairey Surveys Ltd 161-2
Family expenditure survey (NI) 263
Family expenditure survey report
  262
Farm buildings 488
Farm incomes in England and Wales
  263
Field studies 110, 115
Finance accounts 261
*Financial and general statistics of
  county councils* 261
Financial statistics 260-4
Financial statistics 260
Food statistics 283
Footpaths in the countryside 457-8
Forecasting 339-41
Forest land 452-3, 469
  Maps 116
Forest parks 459, 469
Forestry Commission *116, 452, 453,
  459*
France
  Planning history 297
  Regional planning 385

619

Italy
  Regional planning 385-6
Japan
  Regional planning 386
Jeger Report 483
Joint Unit for Planning Research 380-1
Jones Report 258
Journal of economic abstracts 586
Journal of economic studies 539
Journal of leisure research 529
Journal of management studies 546
Journal of planning and property law 523
Journal of regional science 537-8
Journal of the American Institute of Planners 525
Journal of the American Statistical Association 544
Journal of the Institution of Municipal Engineers 528
Journal of the Royal Statistical Society 544
Journal of the Royal Town Planning Institute 522
Journal of transport economics and policy 531
Journey to work 508-9

Kent CC *194*
Kent CPD *412*

Lake District
  Recreational traffic 474
Lanarkshire
  Recreation planning 470
Lancashire
  Recreational facilities 467
Lancaster
  Housing 367
Land Commission 353-4
Land Commission Act 1967 38
Land economics 350-6
Land use 449-56
Land use maps 88, 90, 110-4, 146-7, 163-4
Land use statistics 284
Land use transportation studies
  See Transportation studies
Land Utilisation Survey of Great Britain (1st) 110-1, 449-50

Land Utilisation Survey of Great Britain (2nd) 111-2, 114, 146-7
Landscape architecture 528
Landscape design 528
Landscape journals 528-9
Landscape planning 485-9
  Bibliographies 576-7
  Roads 492-3
Landscape Research Group *161, 489*
Landskap 528-9
Lee Valley Regional Park 471
Leeds
  History 430
  Maps 139
  Office location 382
  Traffic planning 498
Leeds CC *498*
Leicester
  Bus services 511
  Traffic planning 505
Leicester CC *207*
Leicester/Leics sub-region 207-8
Leisure 462-3
Letchworth Garden City 406
Levittown, USA
  Urban studies 438
Leyland-Chorley new town 200-1, 331
Library accessions lists 134, 135, 563
Library and information directories 551-2
Library Association *284, 552, 583*
Library bulletin (RIBA) 580
Library catalogues 562
  Maps 139-40
Library provision 79
Lichfield, Nathaniel & Associates 473
Lindsey (Lincs)
  Recreation survey 473
Linear programming 336
Ling, Arthur 198-9
LINMAP 152
Liverpool
  History 431
  Housing 372
  Redevelopment 371-2
Livingston DC *221*
Livingston new town 220-1
  Planning administration 52

622

New York, USA
  Transportation studies 505
  Urban studies 428-9
New Zealand
  Planning practice 306
Newark
  Conservation 480
Newcastle upon Tyne
  Planning history 295
  Urban planning 417
Newspaper indexes 558
Newtown new town 212-3
Noise 484-5
Noise Pollution Level 484
North east Scotland 226-7
  Maps 93
North Gloucestershire sub-region 209
North West EPC *174-5*
North west region 174-5, 197-201
  See also individual towns etc within
  the region
Northampton DC *193*
Northampton new town 192-3
Northern EPC *174-5*
Northern Ireland 231-8
  Maps 102-4, 105-6, 107, 113, 119-20,
  137
  Rural studies 448
  Statistical sources 247-8, 252, 256,
  261, 263, 266, 267, 270, 276-7
Northern Ireland: Ministry of Agri-
  culture *267*
Northern Ireland: Ministry of Com-
  merce
  Statistics *266*
Northern Ireland: Ministry of De-
  velopment 44, *231, 233, 236, 276*
Northern Ireland: Ministry of Edu-
  cation *277*
Northern Ireland: Ministry of Fin-
  ance
  Statistics *247, 263*
Northern Ireland: Ministry of Health
  and Local Government *261*
Northern Ireland: Ordnance Survey
  102, *103-4, 119-20, 133-4*
Northern Ireland: Public Record
  Office 162
Northern Ireland education statistics
  277

Northern Ireland Information Ser-
  vice *248*
Northern region 25, 172-3, 174-5,
  201-3, 391
  Population maps 128-9
  Recreational facilities 467
  Water resources 484
  See also individual towns etc within
  the region
Norwich
  Conservation 480
Nottinghamshire CC *207*
Nottinghamshire CPD *210, 480*
Notts/Derbys sub-region 207, 208-9,
  403

Oblique aerial photographs 157
Office development 380-3
  Bibliographies 572
Office for Scientific and Technical
  Information
  Survey of information provision in
  planning 38, 66, 77-82
Office of Population Censuses and
  Surveys 244
Official architecture and planning
  522-3
Operational research quarterly 545
Operational Research Society Ltd *545*
Operations research 545
Operations Research Society of
  America *545, 589*
Optimisation method 339
Ordnance Survey 84-5, *86-90, 95-102,
  104-5, 118-9, 129-30, 131-2, 133-4,
  136,* 141, 150-1, 160, 161
  See also Northern Ireland: Ord-
  nance Survey
Organisation for Economic Coopera-
  tion and Development *384*
Orthophotos 158, 160
Outdoor Recreation Resources Re-
  view Commission 466, *577*
*Output and utilisation of farm pro-
  duce in the UK* 267
Overseas trade statistics of the UK
  270
Overspill 31, 421
Oxford
  Housing 373
Oxford Polytechnic *566*

627

Royal Institute of Public Administration 545
Royal Institution of Chartered Surveyors 527, 580
Royal Scottish Geographical Society 138, 534
Royal Society: Cartography Sub-committee 146
Royal Society of Arts 457, 474
Royal Statistical Society 282, 284, 544
Royal Town Planning Institute 16, 47, 55-7, 59, 60, 61, 64, 69, 72, 318, 325, 333, 522, 549, 553, 559, 566
Royal University of Lund, Sweden 536
Runcorn DC 198-9
Runcorn new town 198-9
Rural planning 444-6
Rural studies 446-8
Rural-urban fringe 437-8
Russia
  Planning practice 306

Sand and gravel production 268
Schuster Report 55-6
Scientific research in British universities . . . 554
Scotland 173-4, 217-31
  Housing 361-3, 367
  Land uses 452-3
  Leisure surveys 468
  Maps 93, 94, 106, 107, 119, 120, 127, 138, 139-40
  Regional planning 390
  Roads 490
  Rural studies 448
  Statistical sources 247, 252-3, 256, 261, 267, 274, 275, 276, 277
  Tourism planning 472-3
Scotland : Department of Agriculture and Fisheries 267, 453
Scotland : Department of Health 18, 34
  now Scottish Home and Health Department
Scotland : Scottish Development Department 34, 44, 68, 139, 162, 220, 224, 225, 229, 318, 362, 367, 490, 491, 497, 499
  Statistics 261, 276, 280

Scotland : Scottish Education Department 277
Scotland : Scottish Home and Health Department 274
Scotland : Scottish Home Department 34
  Now Scottish Home and Health Department
Scotland : Scottish Office
  Economics and Statistics Unit 247
Scotland : Scottish Record Office 139-40
Scott Report 19, 35, 444, 450, 476-7
Scott Wilson Kirkpatrick & Ptnrs 506
Scottish borders 217-8, 225-6
Scottish Civic Trust 530
Scottish Council (Development and Industry) 25, 219, 349
Scottish educational statistics 277
Scottish geographical magazine 534
Scottish health statistics 275
Scottish hospital in-patient statistics 275
Scottish Housing Advisory Committee 361-3
Scottish Library Association 552
Sector theory of urban structure 442
SELNEC region (SE Lancs-NE Cheshire)
  Housing 368
  Transportation studies 505
Service centres 378
Severnside sub-region 216
Sewage disposal 483
Shankland, Cox & Associates 190-1, 214-6
Sheffield
  Housing 372
  Shopping 377-80
  Models 333-4
Shopping centres 378-80, 499
Simulation studies 336
Site planning 302
Skeffington Report 318
Skelmersdale
  Rehabilitation 365-6
Skelmersdale DC 197-8
Skelmersdale new town 197-8
Skylab 167
Slum clearance
  See Rehousing

628

Smeed Report 499
Social science information 77-8
Social Science Research Council 72
Social statistics 273-8, 283
Social Survey *366-7, 466, 472, 510*
Social trends 273
Society for Long Range Planning *547*
Society of County Treasurers *261,
275, 277, 278*
Society of Motor Manufacturers and
Traders Ltd *280*
Socio-economic planning sciences 541
Sociological abstracts 586
Sociological journals 540-2
Sociology in planning 307-9
Soil maps 92, 109-10
Soil Survey of England and Wales
109-10
See also Macaulay Institute
South America
Regional development 386
South East EPC *174-5, 180-1*
South east region 173-94
Sports facilities 467
See also individual towns etc within
the region
South Hampshire Plan Technical
Unit *184-5*
South Hampshire sub-region 183-5
South West EPC *174-5*
South west region 174-5, 391
Recreational facilities 468
Tourism planning 472
See also individual towns etc within
the region
South west Scotland 227-8
Tourism planning 473
Spain
Planning practice 306
Sport and recreation 529
Sports Council *465, 467-8*
Standing Conference on London and
South East Regional Planning 50,
179, *181*
Statistical journals 544-5
Statistical mapping 145-6, 151-3
Statistical news 283
*Statistical theory and method ab-
stracts* 589
*Statistics for town and country plan-
ning* 257, 277-8

Statistics of education 277
*Statistics of foreigners entering and
leaving the UK* 257
Statistics of science and technology
273
*Statistics on incomes, prices, employ-
ment and production* 272
Stevenage DC *205*
Stevenage new town 205
Residential area planning 415
Social studies 437
Structure plan system 28-30, 35
Students 62-3
Sub-regional planning 22, 29, 206-9,
238-9, 399-403
See also individual sub-regions
Suburbs 438-9, 442
Sunderland
Bus service 511
Coastal recreation 470
Housing 372
Urban structure 443
Survey of manufacturing industry 123
Survey techniques 320-1, 366
Surveying journals 527-8
Surveyor 528
Sutherland
Coastal recreation 473
Swansea Valley
Rehabilitation 455-6
Sweden
Planning practice 306
Swindon 188-9
Swindon BC *188-9*
Switzerland
Regional planning 386
SYMAP 151
Systemic planning 309-11

Tayside sub-region 217-9, 229-31
Teaching methods 61
Technical information service (RICS)
580-1
Technicians 60-1
Teesside sub-region 202-3, 506-8
Telford new town 195-6
See also Dawley new town
Tennessee Valley Authority *471*
Theory and decision 542
Theses indexes 556-8
Thorburn, Andrew 208

629

University of Chicago: Department of Sociology 431, 435
University of Durham *94*
University of Durham: Rowntree Research Unit *246*
University of Edinburgh: Department of Geography 470
University of Edinburgh: Planning Research Unit 338-9
University of Glasgow: Department of Social and Economic Research *523*
University of Hull 127-8
University of Illinois: Bureau of Community Planning *556*
University of Leeds: Air Photo Unit 163-6
University of Leicester: Urban History Group 429
University of Liverpool: Department of Civic Design *523*
University of Manchester: Department of Town and Country Planning *333, 379*
University of Newcastle upon Tyne *128-9*
University of Newcastle upon Tyne: Department of Town and Country Planning *523*
University of Nottingham *127, 534*
University of Reading: Urban Systems Research Unit *243, 285,* 323-4, 332
University of Strathclyde *512*
Unpublished information 86
Urban aesthetics 422-4
Urban development models 330-2
Urban geography 440-3
Urban history 429-31
  Bibliographies 575-6
Urban open space 469
  See also Parks
Urban planning 403-21
  Industry 373-4
Urban renewal 413-4
Urban sociology 411, 431-40
  Bibliographies 573-5
Urban studies 422-43
Urban studies 523-4
Urbanisation 424-6, 451-2

User surveys
  Housing 369-70
  Information 77-82
Uthwatt Report 19, 353

Vegetation maps 89, 92, 115-6, 137-8, 147
Vehicle design 500
Vertical aerial photographs 157
Victoria model town 404
Village greens 453-4
Village planning 446
Village studies 446-8
Vincent and Gorbing 190

Wales 173, 175, 211-7
  Land uses 452
  Maps 92-3, 112-3, 115, 137
  Recreation facilities 468
  Regional planning 390
  Rural studies 448
  Statistical sources 246-7
  Tourism planning 472
  Urban geography 441
Warrington DC *199*
Warrington new town 199-200
Warwickshire
  Maps 139
Warwickshire CC *139*
Washington DC *202*
Washington new town 201-2
Washington, USA
  Planning history 297
Water conservation 483-4
Water pollution 482-3
Water pollution abstracts 589
Water Resources Acts 1963, 1968 483
Water Resources Board *117, 483-4*
Waterways maps 92, 121-2
Welfare services statistics 275
Welsh Office 44, *318, 363, 481, 483, 491, 497*
  Statistics *246-7, 261, 276, 280*
Welsh Tourist Board *472*
Welwyn Garden City 406-7
West Germany
  Planning practice 306
  Regional planning 386
West Midlands EPC *174*
West midlands region 174, 194-7, 391
  Housing 368

West midland region (*contd*)
Industry 375, 390-1
Recreational facilities 468
Transportation studies 505
See also individual towns etc within
the region
West Sussex CC *204, 511*
White Papers
Belfast regional survey and plan
(Cmnd 451) 232
Central Scotland (Cmnd 2188) 25,
172-3, 219-20
*Development areas: regional em-
ployment premium* (Cmnd 3310)
387
*Economic development in Northern
Ireland* (Cmnd 479) 232
Investment incentives (Cmnd 2874)
387
Investment incentives (Cmnd 4516)
388
Leisure in the countryside (Cmnd
2928) 37
Local government in England
(Cmnd 4584) 46
*London — employment: housing:
land* (Cmnd 1952) 25, 179
New policies for public spending
(Cmnd 4515) 388
North east (Cmnd 2206) 25, 172-3,
201
*Northern Ireland development pro-
gramme 1970-75* (Cmnd 547)
233
Old houses into new homes (Cmnd
3602) 361
Older houses in Scotland (Cmnd
3598) 362
Protection of the environment
(Cmnd 4373) 481
Public transport and traffic (Cmnd
3481) 33
*Reform of local government in
Scotland* (Cmnd 4583) 46
Reorganisation of the ports (Cmnd
3903) 495

White Papers (*contd*)
Roads for the future (Cmnd 4369)
490
Scottish economy 1965 to 1970
(Cmnd 2864) 174, 224-5
Scottish roads in the 1970s (Cmnd
3953) 490
Town and country planning (Cmnd
3333) 28
Transport in London (Cmnd 3686)
34
Transport of freight (Cmnd 3470)
511
Transport policy (Cmnd 3057) 33
Wales: the way ahead (Cmnd 3334)
175, 211-2
Wilson, Hugh 197-8
Wilson, Thomas 232
Wilson and Womersley 185-6, 192-3,
196-7, 202-3, 224, 506
Wilson Report 484
Windsor Great Park
Recreation studies 468
Worboys Report 491
Worcester
Transportation studies 506
Worcestershire CPD *421*
Wye College: Department of Agri-
cultural Economics 450, 451

Yearbook of labour statistics 272
York
Conservation 480
Yorkshire
Housing 368
Maps 142
Recreation traffic 474
Yorkshire and Humberside EPC *174-5*
Yorkshire and Humberside region
174-5, 210-1
Population maps 127-8
Recreational facilities 468
Your environment 529-30

Zoning 317
Zuckerman Report 452